Handbook of Psychosocial Interventions for Chronic Pain

Handbook of Psychosocial Interventions for Chronic Pain provides a cutting-edge and comprehensive review of interventions for chronic pain grounded in biopsychosocial frameworks.

Each chapter gives readers the opportunity to solidify their knowledge of major approaches to chronic pain in an accessible format. Reflecting national efforts to reduce prescriptions for pain medications and increase access to interdisciplinary treatment approaches, the book also considers a wide range of person-level variables such as age, cultural factors, and comorbid mental health conditions.

In this book, mental health and allied health professionals will find the tools they need to understand the real-world delivery of chronic pain treatments in a wide variety of settings.

Andrea Kohn Maikovich-Fong, PhD, ABPP, is a board-certified clinical health psychologist with significant experience working with chronic pain populations.

Clinical Topics in Psychology and Psychiatry

Series Editor: Bret A. Moore, PsyD, Boulder Crest Retreat, Virginia, USA

Much of the available information relevant to mental health clinicians is buried in large and disjointed academic textbooks and expensive and obscure scientific journals. Consequently, it can be challenging for the clinician and student to access the most useful information related to practice. **Clinical Topics in Psychology and Psychiatry** includes authored and edited books that identify and distill the most relevant information for practitioners and presents the material in an easily accessible format that appeals to the psychology and psychiatry student, intern or resident, early career psychologist or psychiatrist, and the busy clinician.

NEURODEVELOPMENTAL DISORDERS IN CHILDREN
AND ADOLESCENTS
A Guide to Evaluation and Treatment
Christopher J. Nicholls

COGNITIVE BEHAVIORAL THERAPY FOR BEGINNERS
An Experiential Learning Approach
Amy Wenzel

HANDBOOK OF PSYCHOSOCIAL INTERVENTIONS
FOR CHRONIC PAIN
An Evidence-Based Guide
Edited by Andrea Kohn Maikovich-Fong

For more information about this series, please visit: www.routledge.com/Clinical-Topics-in-Psychology-and-Psychiatry/book-series/TFSE00310

Handbook of Psychosocial Interventions for Chronic Pain

An Evidence-Based Guide

Edited by Andrea Kohn Maikovich-Fong

Routledge
Taylor & Francis Group

NEW YORK AND LONDON

First published 2019
by Routledge
52 Vanderbilt Avenue, New York, NY 10017

and by Routledge
2 Park Square, Milton Park, Abingdon, Oxon, OX14 4RN

Routledge is an imprint of the Taylor & Francis Group, an informa business

Library of Congress Cataloging-in-Publication Data
A catalog record for this title has been requested

ISBN: 978-0-8153-7082-6 (hbk)
ISBN: 978-0-8153-7083-3 (pbk)
ISBN: 978-1-351-16404-7 (ebk)

Typeset in Bembo
by Apex CoVantage, LLC

Contents

Contents

Contributors

Abbie O. Beacham, PhD, Associate Professor, Departments of Psychiatry and Family Medicine, University of Colorado Anschutz Medical Campus, Aurora, CO

Eleanor S. Brammer, RN, MSN, FNP, Kaiser Permanente Colorado

Darcy E. Burgers, PhD, Predoctoral Psychology Intern, Children's Hospital Colorado

Amanda L. Bye, PsyD, Clinical Psychologist and Behavioral Medicine Specialist, Kaiser Permanente Colorado Integrated Pain Service Department

Jennifer M. Caspari, PhD, Clinical Psychologist, VA Portland Health Care System

Jeffrey E. Cassisi, PhD, Department of Psychology, University of Central Florida

David K. Choi, PharmD, Clinical Pharmacist, University of Illinois at Chicago College of Pharmacy

Colleen Conry, MD, Professor and Senior Vice Chair of Quality and Clinical Affairs, Department of Family Medicine, University of Colorado School of Medicine, Aurora, CO

Emily Cox-Martin, PhD, Assistant Professor, University of Colorado Anschutz Medical Campus, Division of Medical Oncology

Natasha S. DePesa, PhD, Psychologist, Durham VA Health Care System, NC

Catherine G. Derington, PharmD, Clinical Pharmacist, University of Colorado Skaggs School of Pharmacy and Pharmaceutical Sciences and Kaiser Permanente Colorado

Stephanie Parazak Eberle, MA, Practice Manager, School Based and Integrated Behavioral Health, Mercy Health Physicians, Cincinnati, OH

Allison Gray, MD, Neurologist and Brain Injury Specialist

Anya Griffin, PhD, Department of Anesthesiology, Perioperative and Pain Medicine, Stanford University School of Medicine

Hunter Hansen, PsyD, Psychology Postdoctoral Fellow, Department of Psychiatry, University of Texas Health Science Center San Antonio

Christina Hardway, PhD, Developmental Psychologist, Merrimack College

James M. Hawkins, DDS, MS, Department of Orofacial Pain, Naval Postgraduate Dental School, Navy Medicine Professional Development Center, Walter Reed National Military Medical Center; Associate Professor, Uniformed Services University of the Health Sciences Postgraduate Dental College

Melissa Hunt, PhD, ACT, Diplomate—Academy of Cognitive Therapy; Associate Director of Clinical Training, Department of Psychology, University of Pennsylvania

Nuwan Jayawickreme, PhD, Associate Professor, Department of Psychology, Manhattan College, Bronx, NY

Jessica Ketterer, PhD, Clinical Psychologist, Memorial Cancer Institute

Ian Kodish, MD, PhD, Associate Professor, University of Washington Department of Psychiatry and Behavioral Sciences

Jinsoon Lee, PsyD, Clinical Psychologist, Rocky Mountain Pediatric OrthoONE, Center for Concussion

RuthAnn R. Lester, PsyD, Clinical Psychologist, Kaiser Permanente Colorado

Kenneth R. Lofland, PhD, Northshore Integrative Healthcare and Department of Anesthesiology, Northwestern University, Chicago, IL

Andrea Kohn Maikovich-Fong, PhD, ABPP, Clinical Health Psychologist and Behavioral Medicine Specialist, Kaiser Permaente Colorado

Don McGeary, PhD, ABPP, Associate Professor, Department of Psychiatry, and Clinical Assistant Professor, Department of Family and Community Medicine, University of Texas Health Science Center San Antonio

Valentina Mihajlovic, BSc, Department of Psychology, Queen's University, Canada

Contributors

Emily F. Muther, PhD, Assistant Professor, University of Colorado School of Medicine Anschutz Medical Campus, Departments of Psychiatry and Pediatrics and Children's Hospital Colorado

J. Curtis Nickel, MD, FRCSC, Department of Urology, Queen's University and Kingston General Hospital, Canada

Melannie D. Nienaber, LCSW, Licensed Clinical Social Worker and Behavioral Medicine Specialist, Kaiser Permanente Colorado Integrated Pain Service Department

Diane M. Novy, PhD, Professor, University of Texas MD Anderson Cancer Center

John D. Otis, PhD, Clinical Psychologist, Boston University, VA Boston Healthcare System

Jessica Payne-Murphy, PhD, Clinical Health Psychologist and Director of the Insomnia and Behavioral Sleep Medicine Clinic, Department of Clinical and Health Psychology, University of Florida Health Sciences, Gainesville, FL

Howard B. Pikoff, PhD, Pain Management Psychologist, Lockwood Library SUNY/Buffalo

Eva Pugliese, Department of Psychology, Manhattan College, Bronx, NY

Luis Richter, PsyD, ABPP, Clinical Health Psychologist, VA Puget Sound

Emily J. Ross, MA, Department of Psychology, University of Central Florida

John E. Schmidt, PhD, Department of Psychology, Naval Postgraduate Dental School, Navy Medicine Professional Development Center, Walter Reed National Military Medical Center; Associate Professor, Uniformed Services University of the Health Sciences Postgraduate Dental College

Shruti Shah, PhD, Clinical Geropsychologist, VA Puget Sound

Beverly S. Shieh, PsyD, Pediatric Psychologist, Pepperdine University, Graduate School of Education and Psychology

Adrianne Sloan, PhD, Clinical Health Psychologist, Rocky Mountain Regional VA Medical Center, Aurora, CO

Michael Tees, MD, MPH, Oncologist, Hematology, Hematopoietic Cell Transplantation and Cellular Therapy, Colorado Blood Cancer Institute

Jody Thomas, PhD, Department of Psychiatry and Behavioral Sciences, Stanford University School of Medicine

Lisa H. Trahan, PhD, Clinical Psychologist, Trahan Counseling, PLLC

Katy E. Trinkley, PharmD, Clinical Pharmacist, University of Colorado Skaggs School of Pharmacy and Pharmaceutical Sciences

Dean A. Tripp, PhD, Departments of Psychology, Anesthesiology, and Urology, Queen's University, Canada

Amy Wachholtz, PhD, MDiv, MS-PsyPharm, ABPP, FACHP, Assistant Professor, Psychology University of Colorado Denver, Adjunct Assistant Professor, Psychiatry University of Massachusetts Medical School

Stephanie Wheeler, MD, MPH, Physician, VA Puget Sound

Chelsea Wiener, MS, Doctoral Student, Department of Psychology, University of Central Florida

Series Editor's Foreword

Handbook of Psychosocial Interventions for Chronic Pain is the latest volume in one of Routledge's most popular series, Clinical Topics in Psychology and Psychiatry (CTPP). The overarching goal of CTPP is to provide mental health practitioners with practical information on psychological and psychopharmacological topics. Each volume is comprehensive but easy to digest and integrate into day-to-day clinical practice. It is multidisciplinary, covering topics relevant to the fields of psychology and psychiatry, and appeals to the student, novice, and senior clinician. Books chosen for the series are authored or edited by national and international experts in their respective areas, and contributors are also highly respected clinicians. The current volume exemplifies the intent, scope, and aims of the CTPP series.

The psychological, social, and economic impact of chronic pain has garnered considerable attention over the past decade. Directly, tens of millions of Americans are affected by chronic pain, and hundreds of millions more are impacted at the global level. Billions of dollars are spent each year addressing the biopsychosocial effects of chronic pain, and billions more are lost to reduced work productivity and disability compensation. To posit that chronic pain is a public health concern is both reasonable and important for addressing the totality of its impact.

Considering the global psychological, social, and economic effects of chronic pain, it is imperative that effective and practical evidence-based interventions are readily available to mental health clinicians. It is unlikely that any mental health-care provider will not encounter comorbid psychiatric and pain conditions in their practice. In fact, it's likely that most clinicians have a significant portion of patients with chronic pain and comorbid psychiatric conditions like depression, anxiety, and insomnia. For these patients, treating "one or the other" is not an option. Integrated treatment that considers the myriad effects of pain is key if the clinician is to help patients reduce symptoms and improve quality of life. The current volume helps the mental health clinician do exactly that.

In *Handbook of Psychosocial Interventions for Chronic Pain*, Dr. Andrea Kohn Maikovich-Fong provides a superb review of the most important aspects of effective psychosocial treatment of chronic pain. She brings together some of the country's top experts in chronic pain assessment and management and draws upon her own wealth of knowledge and experience to create one the field's most comprehensive and practical texts on the topic. This impressive volume includes a thorough review of effective pain assessment, two key theoretical orientations to chronic pain management (CBT and mindfulness), the most effective treatment modalities, and the most current updates on pharmacological interventions. In addition, Dr. Maikovich-Fong addresses common mental health comorbidities associated with chronic pain and reviews special topics such as the impact of culture on effective care and how to effectively work with children and older adults.

I am convinced that *Handbook of Psychosocial Interventions for Chronic Pain* will become one of the lead textbooks in training future psychotherapists in the effective psychosocial treatment of chronic pain. It will also function as an excellent review for experienced practitioners looking for an easily digestible presentation of basic but crucial components of effective delivery of evidence-based treatments for the myriad chronic pain conditions.

Bret A. Moore, PsyD, ABPP
Series Editor
Clinical Topics in Psychology and Psychiatry

1

Introduction

Andrea Kohn Maikovich-Fong

Chronic pain (i.e., pain that lasts beyond normal healing time or more than three to six months) is a public health concern of great significance in the United States, and indeed throughout the world. According to the Centers for Disease Control National Health and Nutrition Examination Survey, nearly one-quarter of Americans are limited by pain at least one day per month, and over 25 million Americans are disabled because of a pain condition (CDC, 2014).

Of patients in the United States seeking medical care, nearly 50% endorse pain as a primary presenting concern (Abbott & Fraser, 1998; Turk & Burwinkle, 2005). Approximately 20% of the population worldwide is estimated to be impacted directly by chronic pain conditions (Gatchel, Peng, Peters, Fuchs, & Turk, 2007; Treede et al., 2015). These estimates do not account for the indirect (and often significant) impact of the pain conditions on family members, work colleagues/employers, and friends. Estimated annual costs of chronic pain in the United States range from $550 to $625 billion (Dansie & Turk, 2013), inclusive of direct healthcare costs and indirect costs such as lost productivity, lost tax revenue, legal services, and disability compensation (Stewart, Ricci, Chee, Morganstein, & Lipton, 2003).

Biomedical models that conceptualize chronic pain as the direct result of tissue damage largely have been replaced by biopsychosocial models that recognize the complex ways in which biological, psychological, and social factors interact to produce and shape the subjective experience of pain (e.g., Gatchel et al., 2007; Novy & Aigner, 2014). Biological components of the biopsychosocial model typically encompass genetic factors, physiological disease states, sleep patterns and disruptions, physical impairments, and other facets of the neuroscience of pain. Psychological factors typically include behaviors, emotions, thought patterns/ cognitions, and perceptions that contribute to and are influenced by pain. Finally,

1

social factors encompass cultural variables, family dynamics (especially around pain and pain behaviors), and interpersonal relationships (including within the school or workplace).

As biopsychosocial models evolved away from purely biomedical models, so too did interdisciplinary treatment approaches evolve away from exclusively medical interventions. Today, collaborative care intervention models are frequently recognized as preferable to purely pharmacological or surgical treatment approaches (Becker, Sjogren, Bech, Olsen, & Eriksen, 2000; Dobscha et al., 2009). Depending upon resource limitations, comprehensive pain management teams may include a primary care physician, occupational therapist, physical therapist, pharmacist, medical specialists appropriate for the pain condition (e.g., neurologist for headache conditions; gynecologist for chronic pelvic pain conditions), and psychologist.

Psychologists provide non-pharmacological treatments that may include cognitive-behavioral therapy, mindfulness-based interventions, and group therapy. These treatments target many aspects of the chronic pain experience, including but not necessarily limited to pain intensity, pain interference, comorbid mental health conditions, adherence to and tolerance of medical treatments, and interpersonal effectiveness. Psychologists often also assist with conducting pre-treatment assessments of chronic pain patients, aiming to identify maladaptive behavioral, emotional, coping, and relationship patterns that may be contributing to (and/ or emerging from) the chronic pain experience. These psychosocial interventions and approaches are covered extensively throughout this handbook.

A number of factors coalesced to create a need for this handbook: 1) the ascension of the biopsychosocial model to its current accepted status; 2) the increasing emphasis in pain medicine on interdisciplinary treatment approaches; and 3) the current large-scale societal focus on reducing prescription pain medications during the "opioid crisis." Herein you will find a comprehensive source of information on the biopsychosocial model as applied to various pain conditions. This need was the impetus for creating this handbook, which provides readers with a thorough and timely review of the literature on evidence-based psychosocial approaches to treating chronic pain.

The handbook is organized as follows: chronic pain assessment (Chapter 2); historical context of psychological approaches to pain (Chapter 3); reviews of two important current theoretical orientations, CBT and mindfulness (Chapters 4–5); modalities of treatment delivery, including group settings and primary care (Chapters 6–7); pharmacology overview (Chapter 8); review of several common chronic pain conditions (Chapters 9–16); discussion of common behavioral health comorbidities (Chapters 17–19); and topics for special consideration, including pediatrics, geriatrics, and culture (Chapters 20–23).

References

Abbott, F. V., & Fraser, M. I. (1998). Use and abuse of over-the-counter analgesic agents. *Journal of Psychiatry and Neuroscience, 23*, 13–34.

Becker, N., Sjogren, P., Bech, P., Olsen, A. K., & Eriksen, J. (2000). Treatment outcome of chronic non-malignant pain patients managed in a Danish multidisciplinary pain centre compared to general practice: A randomised controlled trial. *Pain, 84*(2–3), 203–211. doi:10.1016/s0304-3959(99)00209-2.

Centers for Disease Control and Prevention (CDC). (2014). *National Center for Health Statistics (NCHS). National health and nutrition examination survey data.* Hyattsville, MD: U.S. Department of Health and Human Services, Centers for Disease Control and Prevention.

Dansie, E. J., & Turk, D. C. (2013). Assessment of patients with chronic pain. *British Journal of Anesthesia, 111*(1), 19–25.

Dobscha, S. K., Corson, K., Perrin, N. A., Hanson, G. C., Leibowitz, R. Q., Doak, M. N., . . . Gerrity, M. S. (2009). Collaborative care for chronic pain in primary care. *JAMA, 301*(12), 1242–1252. doi:10.1001/jama.2009.377.

Gatchel, R. J., Peng, Y. B., Peters, M. L., Fuchs, P. N., & Turk, D. C. (2007). The biopsychosocial approach to chronic pain: Scientific advances and future directions. *Psychological Bulletin, 133*(4), 581.

Novy, D. M., & Aigner, C. J. (2014). The biopsychosocial model in cancer pain. *Current Opinion in Supportive and Palliative Care, 8*(2), 117–123.

Stewart, W. F., Ricci, J. A., Chee, E., Morganstein, D., & Lipton, R. (2003). Lost productive time and cost due to common pain conditions in the US workforce. *Journal of the American Medical Association, 290*, 2443–2454.

Treede, R.-D., Rief, W., Barke, A., Aziz, Q., Bennett, M. I., Benoliel, R., . . . First, M. B. (2015). A classification of chronic pain for ICD-11. *Pain, 156*(6), 1003.

Turk, D. C., & Burwinkle, T. M. (2005). Clinical outcomes, cost-effectiveness, and the role of psychology in treatments for chronic pain sufferers. *Professional Psychology: Research and Practice, 36*, 602–610.

2

Assessment of Chronic Pain Patients

Adrianne Sloan

Introduction

Chronic pain affects approximately 20–30% of the population in developed countries, making it a major public health concern (Dansie & Turk, 2013). Pain is one of the most common reasons patients seek care in the United States, with nearly one-half reporting pain as a primary presenting concern (Abbott & Fraser, 1998; Turk & Burwinkle, 2005b). Chronic pain impacts not only the patient but also his or her significant others, family, and society at large. Estimates of annual incremental healthcare costs resulting from pain range from $261 to $300 billion (Bianchini et al., 2017). In addition, there are indirect costs, such as lost productivity, lost tax revenue, legal services, and disability compensation (Stewart, Ricci, Chee, Morganstein, & Lipton, 2003). Although difficult to assess precisely, estimated costs of chronic pain (including indirect costs) in the United States range from $550 billion to $625 billion annually (Dansie & Turk, 2013).

The lack of a one-to-one relationship between physical damage and the experience of pain makes managing chronic pain difficult. As stated by Dansie and Turk (2013), "patient reports of pain severity often demonstrate modest associations with objective physical and laboratory findings: there is no direct linear relationship between the amount of detectable physical pathology and the reported pain intensity" (p. 13). Multiple sources note that many common pain conditions (both acute and chronic) like headache, fibromyalgia, and back pain have largely unknown causes (Robbins & Lipton, 2010; Shuer, 2003; Abeles, Solitar, Pillinger, & Abeles, 2008), whereas asymptomatic patients may show significant findings on imaging, such as herniated discs, that clearly would explain pain if it were present (Borenstein et al., 2001; Jensen et al., 1994).

Furthermore, agreement among providers regarding diagnoses and etiologies of pain in the routine clinical assessment of chronic pain patients is surprisingly low (Gladman et al., 2004; de Winter et al., 2004), and the treatment of chronic pain often remains challenging due to its multifactorial nature. However, research over the past four decades has begun to uncover a multi-layered answer to the question of why some patients seem to suffer more than others from potentially debilitating chronic pain symptoms, making it essential to thoroughly assess the contributing factors to each patient's individual pain experience so as to inform the most effective intervention approaches.

The biopsychosocial model provides an effective framework for understanding what contributes to, and stems from, chronic pain. This model purports that the pain experience is a product of multiple cognitive, emotional, and behavioral constructs and processes, in addition to physical, biological, and medical factors that interact in complex ways (Turk, Fillingim, Ohrback, & Patel, 2016). The interaction of the physical domain with psychosocial factors contributes to variation in disability and responses to treatment over time (Edwards, Dworkin, Sullivan, Turk, & Wasan, 2016). This model shifts focus from exclusive pathophysiology to the involvement of the patient's cognitions, emotional state, and past pain history, which influence his/her pain experiences and subsequent behavior. Therefore, diagnosing and treating chronic pain requires consideration of multiple factors, including but not limited to the following: a history and physical examination; pain intensity, quality, and location; functional abilities and quality of life; beliefs, appraisals, and expectations; emotional functioning; overt expressions of pain/pain behaviors; and sleep quality.

Additionally, due to the escalation in opioid-related deaths and overdoses stemming in part from increased prescribing of these medications for the management of chronic pain, the topics of assessing aberrant behaviors and potential malingering also are important. This chapter examines the common variables that have been identified as relevant and significant for assessing, understanding, and treating chronic pain.

Medical Assessment Overview

Dansie and Turk (2013) describe the primary goals of medical history taking and evaluation as follows: 1) determine the necessity of additional diagnostic testing; 2) determine if the medical data can explain the patient's symptoms, symptom severity, and functional limitations; 3) make a medical diagnosis; 4) evaluate the availability of appropriate treatment; 5) establish the treatment's objectives; and 6) determine the appropriate course for symptom management if a complete cure is not possible. Please see Chapters 9–16 of this handbook for discussion of relevant aspects of medical assessment specific to common pain conditions.

Beyond the medical exam, it can be helpful to consider the psychosocial and behavioral aspects that can influence a patient's pain experience. As described by Dansie and Turk (2013), the acronym ACT-UP (activity, coping, think, upset, people's responses) can remind providers performing a medical exam to ask about other aspects contributing to, or stemming from, pain.

---

1. *Activities*: How is your pain affecting your life (i.e., sleep, appetite, physical activities, and relationships)?
2. *Coping*: How do you deal/cope with your pain (what makes it better/worse)?
3. *Think*: Do you think your pain will ever get better?
4. *Upset*: Have you been feeling worried (anxious)/depressed (down, blue)?
5. *People*: How do people respond when you have pain?

Depending upon the patient's answers to these questions, the provider may opt for a more in-depth psychological interview or assessment. Keep in mind that the expectations of patients and their significant others can play a role in eventual treatment adherence. A patient's patterns of thoughts and beliefs about pain and treatment can interfere in a multitude of ways, including fear of activity, medication seeking or avoidance, etc. Treatment especially can be challenging when patients believe pain must be, or can be, completely removed. Thus, assessing the patient's and his/her caregivers' expectations and beliefs about pain and pain treatment is important early on in the physician–patient relationship.

Pain Intensity, Quality, and Location

Pain Intensity

Measures of pain intensity are often single-item measures that ask patients to quantify their pain intensity by providing a single, general, categorical, and/or numerical rating. The most common scales used are numerical rating scales (NRS; Price, Bush, Long, & Harkins, 1994), verbal rating scales (VRS; Jensen & Karoly, 2011), and visual analog scales (VAS; Jensen & Karoly, 2011). Each of these scales can detect improvements associated with treatment; however, there are important differences among these measures with respect to lost data from patients failing to complete the measure correctly, patient preferences, ease of data recording, and ability to administer the measure by telephone or with electronic diaries (Dworkin et al., 2005; Dansie & Turk, 2013; Turk & Burwinkle, 2005a). Patients tend to prefer VRS and NRS measures over VAS measures (Turk & Burwinkle, 2005a). VAS measures have good test-retest reliability (Fischer et al., 1999). However, there are drawbacks: they require more motor ability, which may be difficult for some patients; and they are more difficult to understand than NRS or VRS measures, which is relevant especially for patients with cognitive difficulties or head injuries (Jensen & Karoly, 2011). Increased age and opioid intake are associated with greater difficulty completing VAS measures (Jensen & Karoly, 2011).

Measures with a large number of response levels (like the VRS or NRS) allow for detection of smaller changes and therefore may be more sensitive to changes in pain intensity following treatment than the VAS (Jensen & Karoly, 2011).

NRS measures have demonstrated validity (Owen, Klapow, & Casebeer, 2000) and good test-retest reliability (Bergh, Sjorstrom, Oden, & Steen, 2000). As the NRS can be administered orally, it may be easier for patients with motor difficulties (Turk & Burwinkle, 2005a). However, cognitive impairment is associated with difficulty completing an NRS rating of pain intensity (Jensen & Karoly, 2011). Patients unable to complete an NRS rating may prefer VRS ratings (Dworkin et al., 2005).

VRS measures have been shown to be somewhat problematic as test-retest reliability coefficients are in the low to moderate range (Ellershaw, Peat, & Boys, 1995). Additionally, adjectives used in the VRS may not mean the same thing to different respondents, and patients appear to prefer NRS measures to VRS measures (Herr, Spratt, Mobily, & Richardson, 2004). Furthermore, older patients may have difficulty using VRS measures due to cognitive and psychomotor impairment (Herr et al., 2004).

A number of scales have been developed for patients who have challenges completing common pain intensity measures. For example, the Faces Scale of Pain Intensity (e.g., Wong & Baker, 1988), which presents drawings of facial expressions imitating various levels of pain, has been used extensively with children (Turk & Burwinkle, 2005a). While other mechanisms of measurement (e.g., observations of behavior, surrogate ratings) have demonstrated similar measurement properties as VAS scales and can be considered as additional methods of measuring pain intensity (Turk & Melzack, 2011), the most common and preferred method is the Faces Scale.

Although scales measuring pain intensity generally have well-documented validity and reliability, additional studies are needed exploring generalizability of these properties to multiple races, ethnicities, and cultures (see Chapter 23). In addition, sex differences in norms and preferences for each scale need additional study.

Pain Quality and Pain Location

Pain has different sensory and affective qualities in addition to intensity, and measures of these qualities can be used to assess more fully the patient's pain experience (Price, Harkins, & Baker, 1987). Independent of intensity, understanding the *quality* of a patient's pain through assessment can inform treatments that may be appropriate or effective for certain types of pain (Dansie & Turk, 2013).

One way to describe the quality of a patient's pain experience is "pain affect," which can be defined as the emotional arousal and disruption created by the pain experience (Jensen & Karoly, 2011). There is evidence that the affective component of pain is empirically distinct from pain intensity and may be differentially responsive to treatments (Dworkin et al., 2005; Price, 1999). As with pain intensity, pain affect can be assessed using VAS, NRS, and VRS items having different anchors (e.g., "not unpleasant," "most unpleasant feeling possible") (Dworkin et al., 2005).

In addition to pain affect, there are a number of additional qualities one may assess (e.g., "constant," "aching," "sharp"). Pain can be caused by different sources of stimuli, such as nerve pain, soft tissue pain, or bone pain, all of which may have different qualities (e.g., "burning," "stabbing," or "throbbing"). There is widespread agreement that *the Short-Form McGill Pain Questionnaire revised* (SF-MPQ-2; Ware & Sherbourne, 1992) can be used to assess for pain quality (Dworkin et al., 2009; Piotrowski, 1998). The SF-MPQ-2, which assesses three categories of word descriptors of pain qualities (sensory, affective, and evaluative), can be enhanced by including a body diagram for patients to identify the area(s) of their pain (Dansie & Turk, 2013). This questionnaire, which is reliable and well-validated (Dworkin et al., 2005), was recommended for use in clinical trials at the Initiative on Methods, Measurement, and Pain Assessment in Clinical Trials (IMMPACT) meeting held in April 2003.

For the reader's reference, a comprehensive table (Table 2.1) has been provided here, which lists all questionnaires discussed, outside of the intensity scales (NRS, VRS, VAS, and Faces Scale) mentioned above.

Measures of the temporal aspects of pain—variability in intensity; time to onset of meaningful pain relief; durability of pain relief; breakthrough pain; and frequency, duration, and intensity of pain episodes—assess another important dimension of pain (Jensen & Karoly, 2011). Patients can be asked to rate their pain over a specific time period (e.g., past week, past 24 hours, past month) or several times per day (e.g., when walking, at meals, at bedtime) for several days or weeks using daily diaries. This allows for an in-depth understanding of pain patterns and variables that can predict pain increases and/or decreases. However, there are drawbacks to using self-report diaries (e.g., they are time-consuming; the diaries may be filled in ahead of time or after the fact). Thus, some clinicians and researchers utilize electronic devices to attenuate these limitations. For a further review of self-report diaries and the use of electronic devices as components of chronic pain assessment, see Turk and Burwinkle (2005a).

Functional Abilities and Quality of Life

Chronic pain often interferes with multiple domains of functioning, from activities of daily living to overall quality of life. It has been assumed that a reduction in pain allows for an increase in activity and function; however, studies indicate that pain intensity and physical functioning are only modestly associated (Turk, 2002). Furthermore, the ability to perform certain functions of daily life can impact a person's quality of life. Thus, it is important to assess the ways that pain may be interfering with daily functioning and overall quality of life.

There are two types of measures of physical functioning and, more generally, health-related quality of life (HRQOL). Generic measures of physical functioning ask respondents to report their ability to engage in a range of functional

Table 2.1 Recommended Measures in Pain Assessment for Adults

Area of Measurement	Pain Questionnaire	Domains Assessed	Number of Items
Pain Quality and Location	SF-MPQ-2 (Ware & Sherbourne, 1992)	Measures pain quality and affect. Assesses three categories of word descriptors of pain qualities (sensory, affective, and evaluative) and includes a body diagram. Contains two subscales (sensory and affective).	36
Functional Abilities: Specific	WOMAC (Bellamy, Buchanan, Goldsmith, Campbell, & Stitt, 1988)	Assesses lower-extremity pain and functional symptoms in osteoarthritis (three dimensions: pain, stiffness, physical activity). Items rated on a 5-point scale ranging from none to extreme.	24
	RMDQ (Roland & Morris, 1983)	Assesses pain and disability in patients with back pain.	24
	Disability of Arm, Shoulder, and Hand Quick Form Outcome Measure: QuickDASH (Beaton, Wright, & Katz, 2005)	Measures ability to perform personal, home, work, and community tasks, pain severity, interference, and sleep interruption related to the shoulder. Questions presented on a 5-point scale. Scoring is offered on the test itself with directions for how to plug the patient's score into an equation to get a final outcome: 0 = no disability, 100 = most severe disability.	11
	Neck Disability Index (Vernon & Mior, 1991)	Addresses functional activities such as personal care, lifting, reading, work, sleeping, and recreational calculated by totaling the responses for each activity as well as pain intensity, concentration, and headache. Six potential responses to each item range from no disability (0) to total disability (5).	10

(Continued)

Table 2.1 (Continued)

Area of Measurement	Pain Questionnaire	Domains Assessed	Number of Items
Functional Abilities: General	MPI—Interference Scale (Kerns, Turk, & Rudy, 1985)	Measures the degree to which pain interferes with performance and satisfaction with social, occupational, and family activities.	11
	BPI, Short Form (Cleeland & Ryan, 1994)	Measures pain severity, impact of pain on daily functions, pain location, and pain medications.	15
Health-Related Quality of Life (HRQOL)	SF-36 (Ware & Sherbourne, 1992)	Measures physical health and mental health. Provides scores on eight domains (limitations in physical/social/ role activities, pain, mental health, vitality, and health perceptions).	36
Beliefs and Expectations	Catastrophizing PCS (Sullivan, Bishop, & Pivik, 1995)	Measures catastrophic thoughts related to pain. Three subscales include rumination, magnification, and helplessness.	13
	Helplessness Pain Locus of Control (Toomey, Mann, Abashian, Barnrike, & Hernandez, 1993)	Measures three dimensions – internality, powerful others, and chance – which help to parse out external versus internal locus of control.	36
	Self-Efficacy Pain Self-Efficacy Scale (Nicholas, 2015)	Assesses strength of respondents' confidence in their ability to accomplish their daily activities despite their pain.	10
	Chronic Pain Self-Efficacy Scale (Anderson, Dowds, Pellets, Edwards, & Peeters-Asdourian, 1995)	Assesses perceived self-efficacy to cope with the consequences of chronic pain.	22
Emotional Functioning	Depression BDI (Beck, Ward, Mendelson, Mock, & Erbaugh, 1961)	Measures depressed mood.	21

	POMS (McNair, Lorr, & Droppleman, 1971)	Multidimensional measure of emotional functioning that assesses six mood states: tension-anxiety, depression-dejection, anger-hostility, vigor-activity, fatigue-inertia, and confusion-bewilderment.	65
Anxiety	STAI (Spielberger, Gorsuch, & Lushene, 1970)	Assesses current symptoms of anxiety and generalized propensity to be anxious. Two subscales: state (right now) and trait anxiety (in general).	40/20
	PASS (McCracken, Zayfert, & Gross, 1992)	Assesses fear of pain across cognitive, emotional, and behavioral domains. Four subscales: fear of pain, cognitive anxiety, somatic anxiety, and fear and avoidance.	53
Pain Behaviors	Pain Behavior Checklist (Richards, Nepomuceno, Riles, & Suer, 1982)	Assesses patient's pain behaviors via observation (measures vocalizations, facial grimaces, bracing, rubbing, restlessness, and verbal complaints).	10 categories
Sleep	Polysomnography and Actigraphy	Polysomnography is a technique that measures various physiologic parameters of sleep, including electroencephalography (EEG), eye movements, muscle activity, heart rate, and respiratory function. Actigraphy measures movement from a device that is strapped to a patient's wrist. Actigraphy can overestimate sleep and underestimate wake time as immobility is often what marks the beginning of a sleep period. Polysomnography takes into account brain waves and other physiologic patterns more consistent with actual sleep versus just simply immobility. Both have their pros and cons; the investigator would need to take these into account prior to deciding which is best to use.	

(*Continued*)

Table 2.1 (Continued)

Area of Measurement	Pain Questionnaire	Domains Assessed	Number of Items
	PSQI (Buysse, Reynolds, Monk, Berman, & Kupfer, 1989)	Assesses sleep quality and disturbance over a one-month time period. Nineteen individual items generate seven "component" scores: subjective sleep quality, sleep latency, sleep duration, habitual sleep efficiency, sleep disturbances, use of sleeping medication, and daytime dysfunction.	19
	ISI (Morin, Belleville, Belanger, & Ivers, 2011)	Assesses severity of insomnia with seven questions about sleep quality.	7
Aberrant Behaviors	SOAPP (Butler, Budman, Fernandez, & Jamison, 2004)	Assesses eight concepts: substance abuse history, medication-related behaviors, antisocial behaviors/history, psychosocial problems, psychiatric history, doctor-patient relationship factors, emotional attachment to pain meds, and personal care and lifestyle issues.	24
	COMM (Butler et al., 2007)	Measures whether a patient (currently on long-term opioid therapy) may be exhibiting aberrant behaviors associated with the misuse of opioid medications. Behaviors measured include: signs and symptoms of intoxication, emotional volatility, evidence of poor response to medications, addiction, healthcare use patterns, and problematic medication behavior.	17
	PMQ (Adams et al., 2004)	Assesses aberrant use of opioid medication. Items reflect a range of potentially dysfunctional attitudes and behaviors.	26

Measure	Description	Number of items
PDUQ (Miotto, Compton, Ling, & Conolly, 1996)	Assesses patterns of prescription drug compliance in chronic pain patients. Evaluates the pain condition, opioid use patterns, social and family factors, family history of pain and substance abuse syndromes, patient history of substance abuse, and psychiatric history.	42
STAR (Friedman et al., 2003)	Assesses addiction risk in chronic pain patients. The questions cover: cigarette, alcohol, and drug use; family or household members with drug or alcohol abuse; visits to pain clinics and emergency rooms; and feelings of depression, anxiety, and altered mood. Questions are in a yes/no format and the test is self-administered.	14
ORT (Webster & Webster, 2005)	Addresses age, personal and family history of substance abuse, history of preadolescent sexual abuse, and presence of certain psychological conditions.	10
ABQ (Passik et al., 2000)	Addresses issues such as medication use, present and past drug abuse, patient's beliefs about the risk of addiction in the context of pain treatment, and aberrant drug-taking attitudes and behaviors.	72
PADT (Passik, Kirsch, Whitcomb, Portenoy, & Schein, 2004; Passik et al., 2005)	Charting device that assists with documenting compliance and progress in pain management therapy over a period of time.	41
Substance Use Questionnaire (Cowan, Allan, & Griffiths, 2002)	Assesses withdrawal and general drug use; questionnaire is divided into two sets of questions for these two domains.	15 questions for withdrawal and 11 for opioid use

(Continued)

Table 2.1 (Continued)

Area of Measurement	Pain Questionnaire	Domains Assessed	Number of Items
	CAGE (Etter & Etter, 2004)	Screens for problem drinking and potential alcohol problems. Questions can be easily modified for pain medications. It is comprised of four questions using the acronym CAGE (cut, annoy, guilty, eye).	4
	Prescription Opiate Abuse Checklist (Chabal, Erjavec, Jacobson, Mariano, & Chaney, 1997)	Measures potential abuse or misuse of opioids using five criteria: an overwhelming focus on drug-related issues that persists beyond three treatment sessions, pattern of early refills, multiple telephone calls, lost or stolen meds, and obtaining opiates from multiple providers.	5
Malingering or Response Bias	TOMM (Tombaugh, 1996)	Distinguishes between malingered and true memory impairments via a visual response test.	50
	WMT (Green, Allen, & Astner, 1996)	Measures verbal and nonverbal memory; computerized memory tests with multiple subtests. Contains hidden measures, which serve to check the validity of the patient's test scores.	20 word pairs
	CARB (Allen, Conder, Green, & Cox, 1997)	Detects malingered memory deficits via a computerized forced-choice symptom validity test.	3 blocks of 37 trials
	PDRT (Binder & Willis, 1991)	Employs visual recognition of orally presented 5-digit number strings; forced-choice symptom validity test.	2 sets of 36 trials
	RDS (Greiffenstein, Baker, & Gola, 1994)	Measures symptom validity. Embedded in the digit span subtest of the WAIS-IV. Scoring consists of summing the longest string of digits repeated without error over two trials under both forward and backward conditions.	Sum of longest string of digits
	MMPI-2 or MMPI-2-RF (Ben-Porath & Sherwood, 1993; Ben-Porath & Tellegen, 2008)	Measures personality; administered by computer or in paper/pencil format. Please see text, specifically the section on malingering and response bias, for more details on how to use the MMPI for measuring malingering.	338

activities (e.g., ability to climb stairs, sit for specified periods of time, lift specific weights, perform activities of daily living, chew certain types of food). Generic measures provide information that can be compared across different conditions and studies. The *SF-36* health measure (Medical Outcomes Study Short-Form Health Survey; Ware & Sherbourne, 1992) is the most commonly used generic measure of HRQOL. It has been used in studies of diverse medical and psychiatric conditions and in numerous clinical trials; large amounts of available data allow for comparisons among different disorders and treatments (Dworkin et al., 2005).

Disease-specific measures, on the other hand, assess for functional limitations associated with specific conditions and may be more appropriate when assessing for the functional interference of pain from a particular disorder. For example, a patient with carpel tunnel syndrome may not be limited when walking up and down a set of stairs, whereas a patient with knee pain may not be limited when typing on a keypad but may endorse significant pain with stair climbing (Turk, Fillingim, Ohrback, & Patel, 2016). Therefore, disease-specific measures may capture clinically relevant information that a general measure may not (Turk et al., 2016).

The Initiative on Methods, Measurement, and Pain Assessment in Clinical Trials (IMMPACT) group recommends using disease-specific measures whenever possible, or a combination of disease-specific and general measures, when evaluating chronic pain (Dworkin et al., 2005). Examples of well-validated, disease-specific measures include the **Western Ontario** *McMaster Universities Osteoarthritis Index* (WOMAC; Bellamy et al., 1988) and the *Roland and Morris Back Pain Disability Scale* (RDQ; Roland & Morris, 1983). Please see Table 2.1 for a more comprehensive list of other disease-specific measures.

In situations where disease-specific measures are not available, using either the *Multidimensional Pain Inventory* (MPI; Kerns et al., 1985) Interference Scale or the *Brief Pain Inventory* (BPI; Cleeland & Ryan, 1994) pain interference items (i.e., general activity, mood, walking ability, work, relations with other people, sleep, enjoyment of life) is recommended (Dworkin et al., 2005). The MPI and BPI, which are both valid and reliable measures of pain interference on physical functioning, have been studied with diverse chronic pain conditions in multiple countries (Dworkin et al., 2005). While both measures are used widely and assess similar areas of functioning, a benefit of the BPI is that it includes an item about the impact of pain on sleep (whereas the MPI does not).

Beliefs and Expectations

The influence of beliefs and cognitions on pain is profound. Pain is subjective, influenced by a person's learning history and background. Each individual learns the application of the word "pain" through experiences related to injury in early life. Pain is unquestionably a sensation in a part or parts of the body. However, it also is inherently an emotional experience in that pain is unpleasant. An individual's maladaptive beliefs about his/her pain predict changes in pain, response to treatment, and disability (Jensen, Turner, & Romano, 2007; Nieto, Raichle, Jensen, & Miro, 2012), and therefore are necessary to assess.

Catastrophizing

A large body of evidence suggests that catastrophizing plays a significant role in the pain experience. Catastrophizing is a cognitive process in which a person assumes the worst possible outcome, perseverates on this, and interprets minor problems as major disasters (Turk et al., 2016). This pattern of thinking can lead to the development of more passive styles of coping, such as rumination and help-lessness, and thereby exacerbate the pain. This pattern has been associated with greater emotional distress and disability. One imaging study of patients with fibro-myalgia showed that catastrophizing (independent of depression) was associated with pain-related activation in the brain areas that reflect attentional, anticipatory, and emotional responses to pain (Gracely et al., 2004). Another study reported that catastrophizing, when compared with baseline physical measures, was more predictive of onset of back pain and disability (Jarvik et al., 2005). Catastrophiz-ing also has been identified as a significant predictor of pain-related disability in chronic pain patients (Arnow et al., 2011).

One measure with good psychometric properties is the *Pain Catastrophizing Scale* (PCS; Sullivan et al., 1995), which measures three areas of concern: rumina-tion, magnification, and helplessness. The PCS is a 13-item scale that is quick to administer and score and can easily be added to a test battery. Examples of items on this questionnaire include "I worry all the time about whether the pain will end" and "I keep thinking about how much it hurts."

Helplessness

The perception that one has a sense of control, or an ability to manage pain, is related to greater functionality and coping in chronic pain patients (Turner, Jensen, & Romano, 2000). Further, an increase in control beliefs following treat-ment result in reduced pain and disability (Jensen et al., 2007). In contrast, helpless-ness (or the lack of feeling in control) has been associated with poorer outcomes in physical and psychological well-being, as well as increased pain (Keefe, Rumble, Scipio, Giordano, & Perri, 2004).

The *Pain Locus of Control* instrument (Toomey et al., 1993) is an example of a measure that can assess for helplessness in pain patients. This measure's 36 items explore a patient's sense of perceived control over pain and health-related out-comes. The scale is composed of three dimensions—internality, powerful others, and chance—that help parse out external from internal locus of control. Examples of items on this scale include "no matter what I do, if my pain is going to get worse, it will get worse" and "the main thing that affects relief of my pain is what I myself do." The PCS also has a subscale that measures helplessness; however, it is not used regularly as a single measure for this construct in the literature.

Self-Efficacy

Self-efficacy, or the personal conviction that one can succeed in accomplishing a task or succeed in specific situations, is related to a greater sense of ability to manage chronic pain. Self-efficacy beliefs within the context of chronic pain include the perception that one can perform a particular activity, confidence that one can accomplish activities despite pain, and a belief that one has the ability to manage pain. Patients with low self-efficacy commonly rate their pain as worse (Chong, Cogan, Randolph, & Racz, 2001) and exhibit greater disability (Benyon, Hill, Zadurian, & Mallen, 2010). Further, longitudinal studies suggest that low self-efficacy beliefs are a risk factor for people with chronic pain developing functional disability and work absenteeism (Busch, Goransson, & Melin, 2007). Please see Table 2.1 for examples of questionnaires that assess for self-efficacy.

Emotional Functioning

Depression

Chronic pain often is comorbid with symptoms of emotional distress and psychiatric disorders such as depression, anxiety, and anger (Fernandez, 2002). Depending on the study and under what conditions measures of emotional distress were administered (e.g., acute pain episode versus a good pain day), rates of depression in people with chronic pain range from 5% to 100% (Turk et al., 2016). The overlap of symptoms constitutes a challenge that providers or researchers may face when assessing for mood in pain patients. Specifically, many symptoms of depression—memory and concentration deficits, low libido, fatigue, sleep disturbance, weight and appetite changes—also are common consequences of chronic pain and the medications used to treat pain (Gallagher & Verma, 2004). Untangling what may be depression from symptoms secondary to a pain syndrome can be challenging.

The IMMPACT group (Dworkin et al., 2005) recommends using the *Beck Depression Inventory* (BDI; Beck et al., 1961) and the Profile of Mood States (POMS; McNair et al., 1971) for assessing emotional functioning. Both the BDI and the POMS have well-established reliability and validity in the assessment of depression and emotional distress, and both have been used in numerous studies, including several chronic pain clinical trials (Kerns, 2003).

Anxiety

Anxiety disorder prevalence in chronic pain patients may be twice as high as in the general public (i.e., 35% versus 18%) (Turk et al., 2016). Diagnoses of panic disorder and posttraumatic stress disorder are three times more common in patients with chronic pain (McWilliams, Cox, & Enns, 2003). Anxiety and fear contribute to the cycle of disability and the maintenance of pain. Specifically, patients can develop multiple avoidance behaviors out of fear that they will experience pain, increased pain, increased disability, or rejection by others and the medical field. Unfortunately, these avoidance behaviors often contribute to maintaining and increasing pain via numerous pathways. Patients experiencing anxiety also may experience muscle tension and physiological arousal that can contribute to pain. Additionally, they may remain inactive and sedentary, adding to weight loss or gain and to muscle atrophy, which in turn can increase pain and disability.

Turk et al. (2016) recommend the *State-Trait Anxiety Inventory* (STAI; Spielberger et al., 1970) and the *Pain Anxiety Symptoms Scale* (PASS; McCracken et al., 1992) to assess anxiety in chronic pain patients.

Expressions of Pain and Pain Behaviors

Patients express pain in multiple ways, including nonverbal expressions (controllable and uncontrollable actions; facial expressions conveying pain, distress, and suffering) and verbal expressions (Fordyce, 1976). These behaviors are relevant to assess, as they can elicit both solicitous and negative responses from significant others and from medical providers. The assistance of others following (or cueing) these behaviors can be helpful, but also can contribute to enabling and maintaining maladaptive coping (e.g., taking medications, avoiding activity, increasing anxiety and depression).

For example, a number of studies have shown that significant others unintentionally can reinforce the patient's pain and related disability through actions such as taking over the patient's job, roles, or duties (Block, Ben-Porath, & Marek, 2012). Significant others may give the patient medications that are not needed; encourage the patient to rest while discouraging physical activity; and/or pay attention when the patient appears to be in pain, while ignoring him or her at other times. Block, Kremer, and Gaylor (1980) found that when in the presence of a spouse, patients were more likely to report greater pain levels when that spouse was solicitous rather than non-solicitous.

Standardized observational procedures such as the *Pain Behavior Checklist* (PBC; Richards et al., 1982) have been developed to quantify pain behaviors, but are most often used in clinical research settings (Dansie & Turk, 2013). Observations of pain behaviors can be noted while patients are in the waiting room, or during the interview process, and these behaviors can change depending on who is present or the situation at hand (e.g., compensation and pension review, disability claim, requesting medications, in the presence of a significant other). Additionally, examining a patient's healthcare use and medication use patterns can be used to assess pain behaviors. Specifically, patients can complete diaries to track the frequency and amount of medications used, and events preceding and following the use of medication (e.g., stress and activity) that may be associated with factors other than pain (Dansie & Turk, 2013).

Sleep Quality

Optimizing sleep is essential when managing chronic pain and regulating emotions. Sleep, much like emotional distress, appears to be reciprocally related to pain; while acute and chronic pain can disrupt sleep, difficulty with sleep impacts pain as well (Finan, Goodin, & Smith, 2013). Experimental and clinical data indicate that sleep deprivation lowers the pain threshold, lowers cognitive ability to cope with pain, and increases ratings of pain intensity (Okifuji & Hare, 2011; Onen, Alloui, Gross, Eschallier, & Dubray, 2001). The relationship between sleep disruptions and pain appears to be mediated by a number of factors, especially psychological distress. For example, people with comorbid chronic pain and sleep problems are more likely to have symptoms of depression and anxiety than chronic pain patients who do not have sleep problems (McCracken & Iverson, 2002; Nicassio, Moxham, Schuman, & Gevirtz, 2002).

Objective ways of measuring sleep include polysomnography and actigraphy, with polysomnography being the "gold standard" for measuring sleep disturbance (Menefee et al., 2000). Sleep diaries and questionnaires such as the *Pittsburgh Sleep Quality Index* (PSQI; Buysse et al., 1989) and the *Insomnia Severity Index* (ISI; Morin et al., 2011) also are used to assess symptoms of insomnia and sleep problems.

Sleep can be impacted by a number of factors, including psychological distress, particularly anxiety and depressive symptoms such as ruminative cognitive processes. Further, in an effort to manage sleep or pain, many patients inadvertently develop poor sleep habits that then further contribute to insomnia. Therefore, assessing the specific factors contributing to sleep problems is helpful; it may not be enough to simply assess for insomnia severity alone.

Aberrant Behaviors

Using opioid medications to manage chronic pain is common but fraught with a multitude of problems, including the potential for misuse of (and dependence upon) this drug class. As prescribing rates have increased over the past few decades, the escalation of opioid-related deaths and overdoses has been well documented. It has become increasingly important for providers to identify which specific patients are at increased risk of misusing this medication class; these patients require more intense monitoring and/or should avoid opioids altogether. The difficulty is finding easy and convenient ways for providers to assess which patients may be at increased risk for misuse.

The consensus in the literature is that providers should review multiple sources of data (PDMPs, urine drug screens, assessment instruments, etc.), as no single fool-proof instrument exists to identify at-risk individuals. Turk, Swanson, and Gatchel (2008) found that across a range of studies, the strongest predictor of opioid misuse was a personal history of alcohol abuse or illicit drug use, particularly a history of polysubstance abuse. Moderate predictors of misuse included younger age, history of legal problems, and a positive urine toxicology screen for drugs other than opiates (Turk et al., 2008). Multiple other studies note that heavy smoking also is predictive of abuse (Manchikanti, Atluri, Trescot, & Giordano, 2008; Akbik et al., 2006).

It is highly recommended that providers initiate an opioid agreement that explicitly spells out what is expected of both the patient and provider in terms of treatment. This is a good time to review risks and benefits of using opioids for the treatment of chronic pain. A convenient way to speak with patients about opioid use is to discuss the four As, developed by Passik and Weinreb (2000): 1) analgesia (pain relief); 2) activities of daily living (psychosocial functioning); 3) adverse side effects; and 4) aberrant drug-taking behaviors (addiction-related outcomes). Patients can be re-assessed using these four areas of questioning during each return visit.

Aberrant behaviors can be difficult for providers not only to manage but also to measure and understand. Portenoy (1996) and Manchikanti (2008) spelled out some of the differences between behaviors that may be indicative of true addiction rather than undertreated pain (Figure 2.1).

In addition to the opioid agreement, it is highly recommended that providers regularly check their state's prescription drug monitoring programs (PDMP) and order random urine drug screens (at least two per year). Use of the PDMP is a straightforward way for providers to see if patients are being prescribed pain medications either from other providers or at emergency room visits, and how frequently they have been prescribed different classes of drugs. Urine drug screens enable a provider to manage compliance and/or to determine whether the patient is using illicit substances. These steps can be helpful (in conjunction with patient self-report and physician observations) in determining which patients are best suited to use, or continue using, opioid medications. For more information, please see the *CDC Guidelines for Prescribing Opioids for Chronic Pain* (2017).

As noted previously, no one instrument can reliably predict which patients may have problems with opioid use. Therefore, instruments are used most appropriately in conjunction with other tools and clinical judgment when making these determinations. Manchikanti et al. (2008) described the utility of multiple brief screening instruments, including the *Screener and Opioid Assessment for Pain Patients* (SOAPP; Butler et al., 2004) and the *Current Opioid Misuse Measure* (COMM; Butler et al., 2007).

The SOAPP is a 24-item questionnaire that can be answered using a 5-point scale. The questions address eight concepts: substance abuse history, medication-related behaviors, antisocial behaviors/history, psychosocial problems, psychiatric history, doctor–patient relationship factors, emotional attachment to pain medications, and personal care and lifestyle issues. A score greater than 18 indicates a high risk of aberrant drug-related behavior. The 17-item COMM is shorter and

---

Behaviors more likely to be associated with medication abuse/addiction:

- Selling medications (diversion) or obtaining them from non-medical sources
- Falsification of prescription—forgery or alteration
- Injecting medications meant for oral use; oral or IV use of transdermal patches
- Resistance to changing medications despite deterioration in function or significant negative effects
- Loss of control over alcohol use
- Use of illegal drugs or controlled substances that are not prescribed for the patient
- Recurrent episodes of
    o Prescription loss or theft
    o Obtaining opioids from other providers in violation of treatment agreement
    o Increases in dosing without provider's instruction
    o Running short with medication supply and requests for early refills

Behaviors that look aberrant, but may be more a part of stabilizing a patient's pain condition, and less predictive of medication abuse/ addiction

- Asking for, or even demanding, more medications
- Asking for specific medications
- Stockpiling medications during times when pain is less severe
- Use of the pain medications during times when pain is less severe
- Use of the pain medications to treat other symptoms
- Reluctance to decrease opioid dosing once stable
- And, in the earlier stages of treatment:
    o Increasing medication dosing without instruction to do so from the provider
    o Obtaining prescriptions from sources other than the primary pain provider
    o Sharing or borrowing similar medications from friends/family

---

Figure 2.1   Aberrant Behaviors Providers May Encounter, and Ones That Are More Indicative of Abuse/Addiction

Adapted from www.drugabuse.gov/nidamed-medical-health-professionals

less cumbersome. Scores higher than the clinical cutoff of 9 indicate potential risk of aberrant drug-use behavior. While this test has good internal consistency and test-retest reliability, its utility has not been replicated with more diverse patients in a variety of clinical settings (Manchikanti et al., 2008). The COMM can be quite sensitive and higher scores do not necessarily indicate a true problem. Accordingly, it should be used in concert with other data when making a clinical judgment.

Other screening tools recommended by Manchikanti et al. (2008) are the *Pain Medicine Questionnaire* (PMQ; Adams et al., 2004), the *Prescription Drug Use Questionnaire* (PDUQ; Miotto et al., 1996), the *Screening Tool for Addiction Risk* (STAR; Friedman, Li, & Mehrotra, 2003), the *Opioid Risk Tool* (ORT; Webster & Webster, 2005), and the *Attitude and Behavior Questionnaire* (ABQ; Passik et al., 2000).

The PMQ may be of limited use in a clinical setting, as it is moderately lengthy with 26 items reflecting a range of potentially dysfunctional attitudes and behaviors. The PDUQ, which is quite lengthy (42 items), takes approximately 20 minutes to administer. The PDUQ's key criteria have not been completely established or validated to be wholly predictive of addictive problems or tendencies (Manchikanti et al., 2008). Both the STAR and the ORT are shorter instruments, with 14 items and 10 items respectively. Both tools, however, have limits in terms of their universal applicability. The ABQ, which is a much longer survey, was piloted with cancer and HIV/AIDS patients. Results of the study were presented as percentages of attitudes and behaviors occurring in these populations; however, no attempt was made to validate whether these percentages actually were reflective or predictive of drug use (Manchikanti et al., 2008).

Other potential tools available to providers include the *Pain Assessment and Documentation Tool* (PADT; Passik et al., 2004; Passik et al., 2005) and the *Substance Use Questionnaire* (Cowan et al., 2002). Although 41 items in length, the PADT can be administered in about 10 minutes. It is a simple charting device that focuses on key outcomes (e.g., analgesia, activities of daily living, adverse effects of medications, and potential aberrant drug-taking behavior). The PADT provides a consistent approach to documenting compliance and progress in pain management treatment over a period of time. The chart, which can be incorporated easily into a patient's medical record, is adaptable in various clinical situations (Manchikanti et al., 2008; Smith & Kirsh, 2007). The Substance Use Questionnaire was evaluated with 168 chronic pain patients and 39 street heroin users. The instrument has been shown to reliably differentiate pain patients from addicted patients; however, this tool may be valid in substance abuse settings and less applicable in a chronic pain care setting (Manchikanti et al., 2008).

Finally, two other tools that may be helpful and convenient when assessing substance use risk are the *CAGE Questionnaire* (Etter & Etter, 2004) and the *Prescription Opioid Abuse Checklist* (Chabal et al., 1997). The former asks questions about alcohol use but can easily be modified for pain medications. The latter attempts to identify people who may be abusing or misusing opioids via five criteria: an overwhelming focus on drug-related issues that persists beyond three treatment sessions; a pattern of early refills; multiple telephone calls; lost or stolen meds; and obtaining opiates from multiple providers.

Malingering and Response Bias

Measuring or assessing malingering can be complicated and challenging. A persistent myth is that chronic pain patients regularly attempt to exaggerate symptoms. In fact, chronic pain patients rarely attempt to deliberately exaggerate or fake their symptoms; when they do, it is usually for monetary gain (e.g., disability payments, compensated time off from work) (Doleys & Olson, 1997).

Malingering involves patients intentionally attempting to present themselves in a negative fashion for secondary gain. Examples include exaggerating or fabricating pain for monetary gain, to receive prescription medication for recreational or illicit resale, to escape responsibilities (e.g., seeking military discharge), or to escape consequences (e.g., criminal penalties) (Slick, Sherman, & Iverson, 1999; Bianchini, Greve, & Glynn, 2005; Etherton, 2014). Providers may find it difficult to discern intentionality, as many patients with somatization can appear to be fabricating or exaggerating pain. However, individuals who somaticize lack awareness of the relationship between their psychological distress and physical complaints and are not deliberately exaggerating physical complaints (Gatchel, 2004).

"Secondary gain" is a term frequently used in conjunction with persistent complaints of pain or impairment when referring to the influence of factors such as sympathy, avoidance of duties, or financial payments (Etherton, 2014). If there is an incentive to appear disabled, a significant proportion of people will do so (e.g., Gervais, Green, Allen, & Iverson, 2001). One meta-analysis demonstrated that the presence of disability compensation was associated with pain ratings of greater severity and reduced treatment efficacy relative to pain patients who had no incentive to appear impaired (Rohling, Binder, & Langhinrichsen-Rohling, 1996). The most common forms of financial incentive associated with pain-related malingering include worker compensation claims, personal injury litigation, and Social Security Disability claims (Chafetz & Underhill, 2013). While the majority of individuals reporting chronic pain are not malingering, it has been estimated that malingering is involved in approximately 20% to 50% of these types of claims (Greve, Ord, Bianchini, & Curtis, 2009).

The diagnosis of malingering asserts that the individual has engaged in intentional misrepresentation. As a result, the individual may face social consequences, financial consequences, and even legal consequences if insurance fraud charges are filed (Etherton, 2014). Thus, the diagnosis of malingering must be based on careful methodology, empirical evidence, and sound reasoning, as well as taking into account alternative explanations for seeming inconsistencies or non-credible performance (Etherton, 2014). The diagnosis of malingering should not be based upon a single test result; rather, it is a clinical decision based upon consideration of the full range of data, including interview data, data from testing, and information from medical records and, if available, from relevant collaterals.

The following system was proposed by Bianchini et al. (2005), and also described in Etherton (2014), as a diagnostic framework for assessing whether someone is malingering. The system, called the Framework for Malingered Pain-Related Disability (MPRD), aides in determining whether the person is possibly malingering, probably malingering, or definitely malingering. For full details regarding the diagnostic framework, please refer to Bianchini et al. (2005).

Criterion A: Evidence of External Incentive. This may include benefits arising from worker's compensation, avoiding military duty or criminal responsibility, or accessing prescription medications.

Criterion B: Evidence From Physical Evaluation. This refers to evidence of intentional exaggeration or feigning of physical disability (e.g., discrepancy between behaviors during physical examination and time when patient is unaware of being observed).

Criterion C: Evidence From Cognitive/Perceptual Testing. This refers to evidence of lacking effort or intentionally exaggerating or feigning cognitive impairment as demonstrated during cognitive testing. Examples include failing a cognitive validity test such as the *Test of Memory Malingering* (TOMM; Tombaugh, 1996) or the *Word Memory Test* (WMT; Green et al., 1996). The *Computerized Assessment of Response Bias* (CARB; Allen et al., 1997), a computerized forced-choice symptom validity test designed to detect malingered memory deficits (Bianchini et al., 2005), also can be used. Other tests include embedded clinical indicators of malingering in the *Portland Digit Recognition Test* (PDRT; Binder & Willis, 1991) and *Reliable Digit Span* (RDS; Greiffenstein et al., 1994). Additional evidence could include discrepancies between test data and observed behavior (e.g., the individual demonstrates intact verbal expression and comprehension during a clinical interview, yet impaired performance on standard measures of verbal ability.)

Criterion D: Evidence From Self-Report. This refers to self-report during the clinical interview and self-report on measures such as the *MMPI-2*, or *MMPI-2-RF.* An example would be evidence of exaggeration from a well-validated validity measure of physical or psychological complaints (e.g., MMPI-2 FBS, RBS, F, Fp).

Criterion E: Behavior Meeting the Above Criteria Cannot Be Fully Accounted for by Psychiatric, Neurologic, or Developmental Factors. This requires evidence from factors B, C, and D that "are not fully accounted for by psychiatric, neurologic, or developmental factors. The behaviors meeting the above criteria represent a likely volitional act aimed at achieving some secondary gain and cannot be fully accounted for by other disorders that result in significantly diminished capacity to appreciate laws or mores against malingering or inability to conform behavior to such standards" (Bianchini et al., 2005, p. 412).

When attempting to discern whether a patient is malingering, examine for evidence of somatization. The MMPI-2 and the MMPI-2-RF are both helpful in distinguishing between somatization and malingering. In general, somatization includes the presence of excessive concern with physical functioning and pain, but with little or no failure of validity measures. The FBS scale on the MMPI-2 is helpful in detecting those with evidence of malingering (Bianchini et al., 2005). It was reported that 69% of those in a definite MPRD group scored at or above 28 (raw score), whereas only 5% of the non-malingering chronic pain group scored as high as 28. Etherton (2014) reported that elevations above a T score of

65 on scales 1 (hypochondriasis) and 3 (hysteria) on the MMPI-2, and elevations on RC1 (Som), but absence of an elevation on RC3 (Cyn) on the MMPI-2-RF, indicate the presence of somatization. For a conclusion of somatization rather than malingering, FBS (MMPI-2) or Symptom Validity Scale (for MMPI-2-RF) should remain below cutoffs. Conversely, elevations on measures of somatic pre-occupation accompanied by validity measure elevations and/or performance validity test failure would warrant consideration of the diagnosis of malingering (Etherton, 2014).

Assessment of Pain in Children

Chronic pain in children is less frequent than in adults. Though estimates vary, some estimate that around 8% of otherwise healthy children and adolescents experience severe chronic pain, most commonly in the head, limbs, and abdomen (Perquin et al., 2000). Other chronic or recurrent conditions reported in children include chronic regional pain syndrome and episodic sickle cell pain (McGrath et al., 2008).

When assessing chronic or recurrent pain in children, the recommended assessment domains are similar to those in adults. The Ped-IMMPACT group (McGrath et al., 2008) recommends assessing the areas of pain intensity; global judgment of satisfaction with treatment; symptoms and adverse events; physical functioning; emotional functioning; role functioning; sleep; and economic factors. Only the areas pertaining to clinical care will be discussed here: pain intensity, physical functioning, emotional functioning, role functioning, and sleep. Additionally, many of the domains recommended as outcome measures for use in research have not been well-studied or documented in the literature, and thus, the Ped-IMMPACT group (McGrath et al., 2008) was unable to provide any guidelines or recommendations in these areas of measurement: global judgment of satisfaction with treatment, symptoms and adverse events, economic factors. For a list of instruments that can be used for the assessment of pain and relevant domains of functioning in children, please see Table 2.2.

Pain Intensity

The *Poker Chip Tool* (Hester et al., 1990), used for children ages 3 to 4 years old, asks the child to choose "how many pieces of hurt" he/she has in the moment. Each chip indicates a different level of hurt. This tool has undergone extensive psychometric testing in numerous studies (Gharaibeh & Abu-Saad, 2002; Good-enough et al., 1997; Suraseranivongse et al., 2005). For children 4 to 12 years old, the *Faces Pain Scale—Revised* (FSP-R; Hicks et al., 2001) is recommended. For children 8 years and older, an NRS or VAS is most commonly used. Note that the NRS (most commonly the 0–10 scale) has been used extensively in clinical practice, but the literature reveals a lack of research on its use with children (McGrath

25

Table 2.2 Recommended Measures in Pain Assessment for Children

Area of Measurement	Pain Questionnaire	Domains Assessed	Number of Items	Scoring
Pain Intensity	Poker Chip Tool (Hester, Foster, & Kristensen, 1990)	3–4 years old. Assesses procedure-related and postoperative pain.		Consists of a set of four red plastic poker chips, each used to denote a "piece of hurt." Score is 0 to 4 with higher score = greater level of pain.
	FSP-R (Hicks, von Baeyer, Spafford, van Korlaar, & Goodenough, 2001)	4–12 years old. Assesses procedure-related, postoperative, and disease-related pain.		Consists of six gender-neutral line drawings of faces that are scored from 0–10.
	NRS or VAS	8 years of age and older. Respondents rate their pain usually on a 0–10 scale with 0 being "no pain" and 10 being "worst pain."		Most commonly used is the 0–10 scale.
Physical Functioning	FDI (Walker & Greene, 1991)	8–17 years old. Measures pain interference with daily activities.	15 items for both parent and child ratings	Total scores are computed by summing the ratings for each of the 15 items. Alternatively, an average score may be computed by dividing the total score by the number of item ratings completed. Higher scores = greater perceived functional disability.
	PedsQL (Varni, Seid, & Rode, 1999)	2–18 years old. Assesses physical, emotional, and social functioning, including school functioning.	23 items for both parent and child ratings	Higher scores = better HRQOL

Emotional Functioning	CDI (Kovacs, 1981)	27	Assesses for depressive symptoms in children and adolescents (ages 7–17). Patients rate themselves based on how they feel and think, with each statement being identified with a rating from 0 to 2.	The total score can range from 0 to 54 with higher scores = greater levels of depression.
	CBCL (Achenbach, 1991)	118	Caregiver report form identifying problem behavior in children. There are two versions: one for pre-school (1½ — 5 y/o) and one for school-age children (6–18 y/o). Eight syndrome scales include aggressive behavior, anxious/depressed, attention problems, rule-breaking behavior, somatic complaints, social problems, thought problems, withdrawn/depressed.	Higher scores = greater problems.
	RCADS (Chorpita, Yim, Moffitt, Umemoto, & Francis, 2000)	47	This measure can be completed by young people from ages 8–18. This is a self-report questionnaire with subscales including: separation anxiety disorder, social phobia, generalized anxiety disorder, panic disorder, obsessive-compulsive disorder, and major depressive disorder. There is also a parent version that can be completed by the child's parent.	Yields a Total Anxiety Scale (sum of the five anxiety subscales) and a Total Internalizing Scale (sum of all six subscales). Items are rated on a 4-point Likert scale from 0 ("never") to 3 ("always").

(Continued)

Table 2.2 (Continued)

Area of Measurement	Pain Questionnaire	Domains Assessed	Number of Items	Scoring
Role Functioning	PedsQL (see above) School Attendance			
	PedsQL (see above) PedMIDAS (Hershey, Powers, Vockell, LeCates, & Kabbouche, 2001)	6–18 years old. Assesses migraine disability in pediatric and adolescent patients. Parent and child forms.	6	Total the items. Scores range from 0–50+ with higher scores = greater severity.
Sleep	CSHQ (Owens, Spirito, & McGuinn, 2000)	4–12 years old. Completed by parents, although there is a child version for those ages 7+. Evaluates the child's sleep based on behavior within eight different subscales: bedtime resistance, sleep-onset delay, sleep duration, sleep anxiety, night wakings, parasomnias, sleep-disordered breathing, and daytime sleepiness.	33	Scoring involves assigning responses values from 1 to 3. Higher scores = greater level of sleep disturbance.

et al., 2008). Additionally, self-report measures of pain intensity with children under the age of 3–4 years have not been well validated due to the inability of many of these young children to accurately self-report their pain (McGrath et al., 2008). Observational methods are recommended in these cases.

Physical Functioning

Assessment of physical functioning in children and adolescents tends to focus on areas such as school functioning, social and relationship functioning, physical activity, and family responsibilities. Many studies, and clinical providers, mention the use of the *Functional Disability Inventory* (FDI; Walker & Greene, 1991), which measures physical functioning in school-age children and adolescents. The psychometric properties of the FDI are well established with different populations (Claar & Walker, 2006). For children under the age of 7 years, the *Pediatric Quality of Life Inventory* (PedsQL; Varni et al., 1999) is recommended. The PedsQL is multidimensional, with both parent and child report versions. Areas measured include physical functioning, emotional functioning, social functioning, and school functioning. It also can be used with children ages 2–18 years old, if desired.

Emotional Functioning

The emotional functioning domain for children with chronic or recurrent pain typically refers to depression and anxiety, which are often related. Both depression and anxiety symptoms are found to be elevated in children with chronic or recurrent pain, but often do not reach clinical levels (Larsson, 1991; McGrath et al., 2008). There are a number of well-established measures for child and adolescent depression and anxiety, including the *Children's Depression Inventory* (CDI; Kovacs, 1981) (used with children ages 7–17 years) and the *Child Behavior Checklist* (CBCL; Achenbach, 1991). Additionally, the Ped-IMMPACT group (McGrath et al., 2008) recommends the *Revised Child Anxiety and Depression Scale* (RCADS; Chorpita et al., 2000), which can be used to measure depression and anxiety as separate dimensions, or combined to measure negative affect. As noted above, use of the PedsQL (Varni et al., 1999) can be used to assess emotional functioning in younger children.

Role Functioning

The Ped-IMMPACT group (McGrath et al., 2008) recommends using school attendance as a measure of the impact of chronic pain on role functioning in school-age children, as attendance is mandatory and easily measured. Once again the PedsQL (Varni et al., 1999) can be used for all ages to assess for role functioning in children, along with the *PedMIDAS* (Hershey et al., 2001; Hershey et al., 2004), which has been well-validated for measurement of role functioning in children ages 6–18 years with persistent headache.

Sleep

As in adult populations, sleep appears to be disrupted due to chronic or recurrent pain in children and adolescents (Palermo & Kiska, 2005). Walters and Williamson (1999) reported that more than half of children with pain-related conditions also report difficulties with sleep. Depressed mood also is predictive of sleep problems in adolescents with headache pain, juvenile idiopathic arthritis, or sickle cell disease (Palermo & Kiska, 2005). The Ped-IMMPACT group (McGrath et al., 2008) recommends that sleep be considered a core outcome domain for chronic and recurrent pain clinical trials, but does not make specific recommendations on how to measure this domain because it has not been explicitly studied in clinical research.

The gold standard for measuring sleep is the polysomnography, but this is not always feasible or realistic (McGrath et al., 2008). Other measures mentioned by the Ped-IMMPACT group are actigraphy and sleep diaries completed by the parent, the child, or both. Actigraphy is a small, watch-like device that measures movement via a sensor. The *Children's Sleep Habits Questionnaire* (CSHQ; Owens et al., 2000), which surveys school-age children regarding their sleep, also could be useful (McGrath et al., 2008).

Conclusions

Chronic pain in both adults and children is multifactorial in nature, requiring an in-depth assessment of the myriad of factors that play a role in a given individual's experience of pain. This chapter reviewed multiple ways providers can assess a patient's pain intensity, as well as his/her emotional and physical functioning, quality of life, beliefs and expectations, sleep disturbance, pain behaviors, etc. This is by no means an exhaustive list of factors that can contribute to and/or stem from chronic pain. Many of the domains selected were derived from multiple recommendations based upon the literature and from the IMMPACT group for both adults and children. A history and physical exam is always a good starting point when assessing for chronic pain, but it is also often beneficial to assess for other areas of functioning. This all depends, of course, on the level of resources and available disciplines to administer, interpret, and treat patients with chronic pain. Other notable areas for consideration, particularly in the current culture of opioid misuse and increased rates of death from overdose, include examining the potential risk for opioid misuse.

References

Abbott, F. V., & Fraser, M. I. (1998). Use and abuse of over-the-counter analgesic agents. *Journal of Psychiatry and Neuroscience, 23*, 13–34.

Abeles, M., Solitar, B. M., Pillinger, M. H., & Abeles, A. M. (2008). Update on fibromyalgia therapy. *American Journal of Medicine, 121*, 555–561.

Achenbach, T. M. (1991). *Manual for the child behavior checklist/4–18 and 1991 profile*. Burlington, VT: Department of Psychiatry, University of Vermont.

Adams, L. L., Gatchel, R. J., Robinson, R. C., Polatin, P., Gajraj, N., Deschner, M., & Noe, C. (2004). Development of a self-report screening instrument for assessing potential opioid medication misuse in chronic pain patients. *Journal of Pain Symptom Management, 27*, 440–459.

Akbik, H., Butler, S. F., Budman, S. H., Fernandez, K., Katz, N. P., & Jamison, R. N. (2006). Validation and clinical application of the screener and opioid assessment for patients with pain. *Journal of Pain Symptom Management, 32*, 287–293.

Allen, L., Conder, R. L., Green, P., & Cox, D. R. (1997). *CARB '97 manual for the computerized assessment of response bias*. Durham, NC: CogniSyst.

Anderson, K. O., Dowds, B. N., Pellets, R. E., Edwards, W. T., & Peeters-Asdourian, C. (1995). Development and initial validation of a scale to measure self-efficacy beliefs in patients with chronic pain. *Pain, 63*, 77–84.

Arnow, B. A., Blasey, C. M., Constantino, M. J., Robinson, R., Hunkeler, E., Fireman, L. J., . . . Haywayd, C. (2011). Catastrophizing, depression, and pain-related disability. *General Hospital Psychiatry, 33*, 150–156.

Beaton, D. E., Wright, J. G., & Katz, J. N. (2005). Development of the quickdash: Comparison of three item-reduction approaches. *Journal of Bone and Joint Surgery, American Volume, 87*, 1038–1046.

Beck, A. T., Ward, C. H., Mendelson, M., Mock, J., & Erbaugh, J. (1961). An inventory for measuring depression. *Archives of General Psychiatry, 4*, 561–571.

Bellamy, N., Buchanan, W. W., Goldsmith, C. H., Campbell, J., & Stitt, L. W. (1988). Validation study of WOMAC: A health status instrument for measuring clinically important patient relevant outcomes to antirheumatic drug therapy in patients with osteoarthritis of the hip or knee. *Journal of Rheumatology, 15*, 1833–1840.

Ben-Porath, Y. S., & Sherwood, N. E. (1993). *The MMPI-2 content scales: Development, psychometric characteristics, and clinical application*. Minneapolis, MN: University of Minnesota Press.

Ben-Porath, Y. S., & Tellegen, A. (2008). *MMPI-2: Restructured for (MMPI-2-RF) manual for administration*. Minneapolis, MN: Universtiy of Minnesota Press.

Benyon, K., Hill, S., Zadurian, N., & Mallen, C. (2010). Coping strategies and self-efficacy as predictors of outcome in osteoarthritis: A systematic review. *Musculoskeletal Care, 8*, 224–236.

Bergh, I., Sjostrom, B., Oden, A., & Steen, B. (2000). An application of pain rating scales in geriatric patients. *Aging, 12*, 380–387.

Bianchini, K. J., Aguerrevere, L. E., Curtis, K. L., Roebuck-Spencer, T. M., Frey, F. C., Greve, K. W., & Calamia, M. (2017). Classification accuracy of the Minnesota multiphasic personality inventory-2 (MMPI-2)-restructured form validity scales in detecting malingered pain-related disability. *Psychological Assessment, 15*, 435–449.

Bianchini, K. J., Greve, K. W., & Glynn, G. (2005). On the diagnosis of malingered pain-related disability: Lessons from the cognitive malingering research. *The Spine Journal, 5*, 404–417.

Binder, L. M., & Willis, S. C. (1991). Assessment of motivation after financially compensable minor head trauma. *Psychological Assessment: A Journal of Consulting and Clinical Psychology, 3*, 175–181.

Block, A. R., Ben-Porath, Y. S., & Marek, R. J. (2012). Psychological risk factors for poor outcome of spine surgery and spinal cord stimulator implant: A review of the literature and their assessment with the MMPI-2-RF. *The Clinical Neuropsychologist*, 1–27.

Block, A. R., Kremer, E. F., & Gaylor, M. (1980). Behavioral treatment of chronic pain: The spouse as a discriminative cur for pain behavior. *The Journal of Pain, 9*, 243–252.

Borenstein, D. G., O'Mara, J. W., Boden, S. D., Lauerman, W. C., Jacobson, A., Platenberg, C., . . . Wiesel, S. W. (2001). The value of magnetic resonance imaging of the lumbar spine to predict low-back pain in asymptomatic subjects: A seven-year follow-up study. *American Journal of Bone and Joint Surgery, 83*(A), 1306–1311.

Busch, H., Goransson, S., & Melin, B. (2007). Self-efficacy beliefs sustained long-term sick absenteeism in individuals with chronic musculoskeletal pain. *Pain Practice, 7*, 234–240.

Butler, S. F., Budman, S. H., Fernandez, K., Houle, B., Benoit, C., Katz, N., & Jamison, R. N. (2007). Development and validation of the current opioid misuse measure. *Pain, 130*, 144–156.

Butler, S. F., Budman, S. H., Fernandez, K., & Jamison, R. N. (2004). Validation of a screener and opioid assessment measure for patient with chronic pain. *Pain, 112*, 65–75.

Buysse, D. J., Reynolds, C. F., Monk, T. H., Berman, S. R., & Kupfer, D. J. (1989). The Pittsburgh sleep quality index: A new instrument for psychiatric practice and research. *Psychiatry Research, 28*, 193–213.

Centers for Disease Control and Prevention. (2017). *CDC guidelines for prescribing opioids in chronic pain.* Retrieved from www.cdc.gov/drugoverdose/prescribing/guideline. html

Chabal, C., Erjavec, M. K., Jacobson, L., Mariano, A., & Chaney, E. (1997). Prescription opiate abuse in chronic pain patients: Clinical criteria, incidence, and predictors. *Clinical Journal of Pain, 13*, 150–155.

Chafetz, M., & Underhill, J. (2013). Estimated costs of malingered disability. *Archives of Clinical Neuropsychology, 28*, 633–639.

Chong, G. S., Cogan, D., Randolph, P., & Racz, G. (2001). Chronic pain and self-efficacy: The effects of age, sex, and chronicity. *Pain Practice, 1*, 338–343.

Chorpita, B. F., Yim, L., Moffitt, C. E., Umemoto, L. A., & Francis, S. E. (2000). Assessment of symptoms of DSM IV anxiety and depression in children: A revised child anxiety and depression scale. *Behavior Research and Therapy, 38*, 835–855.

Claar, R. L., & Walker, L. S. (2006). Functional assessment of pediatric pain patients: Psychometric properties of the functional disability inventory. *Pain, 121*, 77–84.

Cleeland, C. S., & Ryan, K. M. (1994). Pain assessment: Global use of the brief pain inventory. *Annals of the Academy of Medicine Singapore, 23*, 129–138.

Cowan, D. T., Allan, L., & Griffiths, P. (2002). A pilot study into the problematic use of opioid analgesics in chronic non-cancer pain patients. *International Journal of Nursing Studies, 39*, 59–69.

Dansie, E. J., & Turk, D. C. (2013). Assessment of patients with chronic pain. *British Journal of Anesthesia, 111*(1), 19–25.

de Winter, A. F., Heemskerk, M. A., Terwee, C. B., Jans, M. P., Deville, W., van Schaardenburg, D. J., . . . Bouter, L. M. (2004). Inter-observer reproducibility of measurements of range of motion in patients with shoulder pain using a digital inclinometer. *BMC Musculoskeletal Disorders, 5*, 18.

Doleys, D. M., & Olson, K. (Eds.). (1997). *Psychological assessment and intervention in implantable pain therapies.* Minneapolis, MN: Medtronic.

Dworkin, R. H., Turk, D. C., Farrar, J. T., Haythornthwaite, J. A., Jensen, M. P., Katz, N. P., . . . Witter, J. (2005). Core outcome measures for chronic pain clinical trials: IMMPACT recommendations. *Pain, 113*, 9–19.

Dworkin, R. H., Turk, D. C., Revicki, D. A., Harding, G., Coyne, K. S., Pierce-Sandner, S., . . . Melzack, R. (2009). Development and initial validation of an expanded and revised version of the short-form McGill pain questionnaire (SF-MPQ-2). *Pain, 144*, 35–42.

Edwards, R. R., Dworkin, R. H., Sullivan, M. D., Turk, D. C., & Wasan, A. D. (2016). The role of psychosocial processes in the development and maintenance of chronic pain. *Journal of Pain, 17*, T70–T92.

Ellershaw, J. E., Peat, S. J., & Boys, L. C. (1995). Assessing the effectiveness of a hospital palliative care team. *Palliative Medicine, 9*, 145–152.

Etherton, J. L. (2014). Diagnosing malingering in chronic pain. *Psychological Injury and Law, 7*, 362–369.

Etter, M., & Etter, J. F. (2004). Alcohol consumption and the CAGE test in outpatients with schizophrenia or schizoaffective disorder and in the general population. *Schizophrenia Bulletin, 30*, 947–956.

Fernandez, E. (2002). *Anxiety, depression, and anger in pain: Research findings and clinical options.* Dallas, TX: Advanced Psychological Resources.

Finan, P. H., Goodin, B. R., & Smith, M. T. (2013). The association of sleep and pain: An update and a path forward. *Journal of Pain, 14*, 1539–1552.

Fischer, D., Stewart, A. L., Blich, D. A., Lorig, K., Laurent., D., & Holman, H. (1999). Capturing the patient's view of change as a clinical outcome measure. *Journal of the American Medical Association, 282*, 1157–1162.

Fordyce, W. E. (1976). *Behavioral methods for chronic pain and illness.* St. Louis, MO: CV Mosby.

Friedman, R., Li, V., & Mehrotra, D. (2003). Treating pain patients at risk: Evaluation of a screening tool in opioid treated pain patients with and without addiction. *Pain Medicine, 4*, 181–184.

Gallagher, R. M., & Verma, S. (2004). Mood and anxiety disorders in chronic pain. In R. H. Dworkin & W. S. Breitbart (Eds.), *Psychosocial aspects of pain: A handbook for health care providers* (pp. 589–606). Seattle: IASP Press.

Gatchel, R. J. (2004). Psychosocial factors that can influence the self-assessment of function. *Journal of Occupational Rehabilitation, 14*, 197–206.

Gervais, R. O., Green, P., Allen, L. M., & Iverson, G. L. (2001). Effects of coaching on symptom validity testing in chronic pain patients presenting for disability assessment. *Journal of Forensic Neuropsychology, 2*, 1–19.

Gharaibeh, M., & Abu-Saad, H. (2002). Cultural validation of pediatric pain assessment tools: Jorhanian perspective. *Journal of Transcultural Nursing, 13*, 12–18.

Gladman, D. D., Cook, R. J., Schentag, C., Feleter, M., Inman, R. I., Hitchon, C., . . . Karsh, J. (2004). The clinical assessment of patients with psoriatic arthritis: Results of a reliability study of the spondyloarthritis research consortium of Canada. *Journal of Rheumatology, 31*, 1126–1131.

Goodenough, B., Addicoat, L., Champion, G. D., McInerney, M., Young, B., Juniper, K., & Ziegler, J. B. (1997). Pain in 4-to-6-year-old children receiving intramuscular injections: A comparison of the faces pain scale with other self-report and behavioral measures. *Pain, 13*, 60–73.

Gracely, R. H., Geisser, M. E., Giesecke, T., Grant, M. A., Petzke, F., Williams, D. A., & Clauw, D. J. (2004). Pain catastrophizing and neural responses to pain among persons with fibromyalgia. *Brain, 127*, 835–843.

Green, P., Allen, L. M., & Astner, K. (1996). *The word memory test: A user's guide to the oral and computer-administered forms, US version.* Durham, NC: CogniSyst.

Greiffenstein, M. F., Baker, W. J., & Gola, T. (1994). Validation of malingered amnesia measures with a large clinical sample. *Psychological Assessment, 6*, 218–224.

Greve, K. W., Ord, J. S., Bianchini, K. J., & Curtis, K. L. (2009). Prevalence of malingering in patients with chronic pain referred for psychological evaluation in a medico-legal context. *Archives of Physical Medicine and Rehabilitation, 90*, 1117–1126.

Herr, K. A., Spratt, K., Mobily, P. R., & Richardson, G. (2004). Pain intensity assessment in older adults: Use of experimental pain to compare psychometric properties and usability of selected pain scales with younger adults. *Clinical Journal of Pain, 20*, 207–219.

Hershey, A. D., Powers, S. W., Vockell, A. L. B., LeCates, S. L., Kabbouche, M. A., & Maynard M. K. (2001). PedMIDAS: Development of a questionnaire to assess disability of migraines in children. *Neurology, 57*, 2034-2039.

33

Hershey, A. D., Powers, S. W., Vockell, A. L., LeCates, S. L., Segers, A., & Kabbouche, M. A. (2004). Development of a patient-based grading scale for PedMIDAS. *Cephalagia*, *24*, 844–849.

Hester, N., Foster, R., & Kristensen, K. (1990). Measurement of pain in children: Generalizability and validity of the pain ladder and poker chip tool. *Advances in Pain Research and Therapy*, *15*, 79–84.

Hicks, C. L., von Baeyer, C. L., Spafford, P. A., van Korlaar, I., & Goodenough, B. (2001). The faces pain scale-revised: Toward a common metric in pediatric pain measurement. *Pain*, *93*, 173–183.

Jarvik, J. G., Hollingworth, W., Heagerty, P. J., Haynor, D. R., Boyko, E. J., & Deyo, R. A. (2005). Three-year incidence of low back pain in an initially asymptomatic cohort: Clinical and imaging risk factors. *Spine*, *30*, 1541–1548.

Jensen, M. C., Brant-Zawadzki, M. N., Obuchowski, N., Modic, M. T., Malkasian, D., & Ross, J. S. (1994). Magnetic resonance imaging of the lumbar spine in people without back pain. *New England Journal of Medicine*, *331*, 69–73.

Jensen, M. P., & Karoly, P. (2011). Self-report scales and procedures for assessing pain in adults. In I. D. C. Turk & R. Melzak (Eds.), *Handbook of pain assessment*. New York, NY: The Guilford Press.

Jensen, M. P., Turner, J. A., & Romano, J. M. (2007). Changes after multidisciplinary pain treatment in patient pain beliefs and coping are associated with concurrent changes in patient functioning. *Pain*, *131*, 38–47.

Keefe, F. J., Rumble, M. E., Scipio, C. D., Giordano, L. A., & Perri, L. M. (2004). Psychological aspects of persistent pain: Current state of the science. *Journal of Pain*, *5*, 195–211.

Kerns, R. D. (2003). *Assessment of emotional functioning in pain treatment outcome research*. Presented at the second meeting of the initiative on methods, measurement, and pain assessment in clinical trials (IMMPACT-II), Washington, DC.

Kerns, R. D., Turk, D. C., & Rudy, T. E. (1985). The West-Haven Yale multidimensional pain inventory (WHYMPI). *Pain*, *23*, 345–356.

Kovacs, M. (1981). Ratings scales to assess depression in school-aged children. *Acta Paedopsychiatry*, *46*, 305–315.

Larsson, B. S. (1991). Somatic complaints and their relationship to depressive symptoms in Swedish adolescents. *Journal of Child Psychology and Psychiatry*, *32*, 821–832.

Manchikanti, L., Atluri, S., Trescot, A. M., & Giordano, J. (2008). Monitoring opioid adherence in chronic pain patients: Tools, techniques, and utility. *Pain Physician*, *11*, 155–180.

Manchikanti, L., & Singh, A. (2008). Therapeutic opioids: A ten year perspective on the complexities and complications of the escalating use, abuse, and non- medical use of opioids and other psychotherapeutics. *Pain Physician*, *11*, 63–88.

McCracken, L. M., & Iverson, G. L. (2002). Disrupted sleep patterns and daily functioning in patients with chronic pain. *Pain Research and Management*, *7*, 75–79.

McCracken, L. M., Zayfert, C., & Gross, R. T. (1992). The pain anxiety symptoms scale: Development and validation of a scale to measure for fear of pain. *Pain*, *50*, 67–73.

McGrath, P. J., Walco, G. A., Turk, D. C., Dworkin, M. T., Davidson, K., . . . Zeltzer, L. (2008–2009). Core outcome domains and measures for pediatric acute and chronic/recurrent pain clinical trials: PedIMMPACT recommendations. *Journal of Pain*, *9*, 771–783.

McNair, D. M., Lorr, M., & Droppleman, L. F. (1971). *Profile of mood states*. San Diego, CA: Educational and Industrial Testing Service.

McWilliams, I. A., Cox, B. J., & Enns, M. W. (2003). Mood and anxiety disorders associated with chronic pain: An examination in a nationally representative sample. *Pain*, *106*, 127–133.

Menefee, L. A., Cohen, M. J., Anderson, W. R., Doghramji, K., Frank, E. D., & Lee, H. (2000). Sleep disturbance and nonmalignant chronic pain: A comprehensive review of the literature. *Pain Medicine*, *1*, 156–172.

Miotto, K., Compton, P., Ling, W., & Conolly, M. (1996). Diagnosing addictive disease in chronic pain patients. *Psychosomatics*, *37*, 223–235.

Morin, C. M., Belleville, G., Belanger, L., & Ivers, H. (2011). The insomnia severity index: Psychometric indicators to detect insomnia cases and evaluate treatment response. *Sleep*, *34*, 601–608.

Nicassio, P. M., Moxham, E. G., Schuman, C. E., & Gevirtz, R. N. (2002). The contribution of pain, reported sleep quality, and depressive symptoms to fatigue in fibromyalgia. *Pain*, *100*, 271–279.

Nicholas, M. K. (2015). A 2-item short form of the pain self-efficacy questionnaire: Development and psychometric evaluation of PSEQ-2. *Pain*, *16*, 153–163.

Nieto, R., Raichle, K. A., Jensen, M. P., & Miro, J. (2012). Changes in pain-related beliefs, coping, and catastrophizing predict changes in pain intensity, pain interference, and psychological functioning in individuals with myotonic muscular dystrophy and facioscapulohumeral dystrophy. *Clinical Journal of Pain*, *28*, 47–54.

Okifuji, A., & Hare, B. D. (2011). Do sleep disorders contribute to pain sensitivity? *Current Rheumatology Reports*, *13*, 528–534.

Onen, S. H., Alloui, A., Gross, A., Eschallier, A., & Dubray, C. (2001). The effects of total sleep deprivation, selective sleep interruption, and sleep recovery on pain tolerance thresholds in healthy subjects. *Journal of Sleep Research*, *10*, 35–42.

Owen, J. E., Klapow, J. C., & Casebeer, L. (2000). Evaluating the relationship between pain presentation and health-related quality of life in outpatients with metastatic or recurrent neoplastic disease. *Quality of Life Research*, *9*, 855–863.

Owens, J. A., Spirito, A., & McGuinn, M. (2000). The children's sleep habits questionnaire (CSHQ): Psychometric properties of a survey instrument for school-aged children. *Sleep*, *15*, 1043–1051.

Palermo, T. M., & Kiska, R. (2005). Subjective sleep disturbances in adolescents with chronic pain: Relationship to daily functioning and quality of life. *Journal of Pain*, *6*, 201–207.

Passik, S. D., Kirsch, K. L., McDonald, M. V., Ahn, S., Russak, S. M., Martin, L., . . . Portenoy, R. K. (2000). A pilot survey of aberrant drug-taking attitudes and behaviors in samples of cancer and AIDS patients. *Journal of Pain Symptom Management*, *19*, 274–286.

Passik, S. D., Kirsch, K. L., Whitcomb, L. A., Portenoy, R. K., & Schein, J. (2004). A new tool to assess and document pain outcomes in chronic pain patients receiving opioid therapy. *Clinical Therapy*, *26*, 552–561.

Passik, S. D., Kirsch, K. L., Whitcomb, L. A., Schein, J. R., Kaplan, M., Dodd, S., . . . Portenoy, R. K. (2005). Monitoring outcomes during long-term opioid therapy for non-cancer pain: Results with the pain assessment and documentation tool. *Journal of Opioid Management*, *1*, 257–266.

Passik, S. D., & Weinreb, H. J. (2000). Managing chronic nonmalignant pain: Overcoming obstacles to the use of opioids. *Advanced Therapy*, *17*, 70–80.

Perquin, C. W., Hazebroek-Kampschreur, A. A., Hunfeld, J. A., Joke, A. M., Bohnen, A. M., van Suijlekom-Smit, W. A., . . . Johannes, C. (2000). Pain in children and adolescents: A common experience. *Pain*, *87*, 51–58.

Piotrowski, C. (1998). Assessment of pain: A survey of practicing clinicians. *Perceptual and Motor Skills*, *86*, 181–182.

Portenoy, R. K. (1996). Opioid therapy for chronic nonmalignant pain: A review of the critical issues. *Journal of Pain Symptom Management*, *11*, 203–217.

Price, D. D. (1999). *Psychological mechanisms of pain and analgesia*. Seattle: IASP.

Price, D. D., Bush, F. M., Long, S., & Harkins, S. W. (1994). A comparison of pain measurement characteristics of mechanical visual analogue and simple numerical rating scales. *Pain*, *56*, 217–226.

Price, D. D., Harkins, S. W., & Baker, C. (1987). Sensory-affective relationship among different types of clinical and experimental pain. *Pain*, *28*, 297–307.

Richards, J. S., Nepomuceno, C., Riles, M., & Suer, Z. (1982). Assessing pain behavior: The UAB pain behavior scale. *Pain, 14*, 393–398.

Robbins, M. S., & Lipton, R. B. (2010). The epidemiology of primary headache disorders. *Seminars in Neurology, 30*, 107–119.

Rohling, M. L., Binder, L. M., & Langhinrichsen-Rohling, J. (1996). Money matters: A meta-analytic review of the association between financial compensation and the experience and treatment of chronic pain. *Health Psychology, 14*, 537–547.

Roland, M., & Morris, R. (1983). The study of the natural history of back pain, part I: Development of a reliable and sensitive measure of disability in low back pain. *Spine, 8*, 141–144.

Shuer, M. L. (2003). Fibromyalgia: Symptoms constellation and potential therapeutic options. *Endocrine, 22*, 67–76.

Slick, D. J., Sherman, E. M. S., & Iverson, G. L. (1999). Diagnostic criteria for malingering cognitive dysfunction: Proposal standards for clinical practice and research. *The Clinical Neuropsychologist, 13*, 545–561.

Smith, H. S., & Kirsh, K. L. (2007). Documentation and potential tools in long-term opioid therapy for pain. *Anesthesiology Clinics, 25*, 809–823.

Spielberger, C. S., Gorsuch, R. L., & Lushene, R. E. (1970). *Manual for the state-trait anxiety inventory*. Palo Alto, CA: Consulting Psychologists Press.

Stewart, W. F., Ricci, J. A., Chee, E., Morganstein, D., & Lipton, R. (2003). Lost productive time and cost due to common pain conditions in the US workforce. *Journal of the American Medical Association, 290*, 2443–2454.

Sullivan, M. J., Bishop, S., & Pivik, J. (1995). The pain catastrophizing scale: Development and validation. *Psychological Assessment, 7*, 524–532.

Suraseranivongse, S., Montapaneewat, T., Manon, J., Chainchop, P., Petcharatana, S., & Kraiprasit, K. (2005). Cross-validation of a self-report scale for postoperative pain in school-aged children. *Journal of the Medical Association of Thailand, 88*, 412–418.

Tombaugh, T. (1996). *Test of Memory Malingering (TOMM)*. North Tonawanda, NY: Multi Health Systems.

Toomey, T. C., Mann, J. D., Abashian, S. W., Barnrike, C. L., & Hernandez, J. T. (1993). Pain locus of control scores in chronic pain patients and medical clinic patients with and without pain. *Clinical Journal of Pain, 9*, 242–247.

Turk, D. C. (2002). Clinical effectiveness and cost-effectiveness of treatments for patients with chronic pain. *The Clinical Journal of Pain, 18*, 355–365.

Turk, D. C., & Burwinkle, T. M. (2005a). Assessment of chronic pain in rehabilitation: Outcomes measures in clinical trials and clinical practice. *Rehabilitation Psychology, 50*, 56–64.

Turk, D. C., & Burwinkle, T. M. (2005b). Clinical outcomes, cost-effectiveness, and the role of psychology in treatments for chronic pain sufferers. *Professional Psychology: Research and Practice, 36*(6), 602–610.

Turk, D. C., Fillingim, R. B., Ohrback, R., & Patel, K. (2016). Assessment of psychosocial and functional impact of chronic pain. *Journal of Pain, 17*(9), T21–T49.

Turk, D. C., & Melzack, R. (2011). *Handbook of pain assessment*. New York, NY: The Guilford Press.

Turk, D. C., Swanson, K. S., & Gatchel, R. J. (2008). Predicting opioid misuse by chronic pain patients: A systematic review and literature synthesis. *Clinical Journal of Pain, 24*, 497–508.

Turner, J. A., Jensen, M. P., & Romano, J. M. (2000). Do beliefs, coping, and catastrophizing independently predict functioning in patients with chronic pain? *Pain, 85*, 115–125.

Varni, J. W., Seid, M., & Rode, C. A. (1999). The PedsQL: Measurement model for the pediatric quality of life inventory. *Medical Care, 37*, 126–139.

Vernon, H., & Mior, S. (1991). The neck disability index: A study of reliability and validity. *Journal of Manipulative and Physiological Therapeutics, 14*, 409–415.

Walker, L. S., & Greene, J. W. (1991). The functional disability inventory: Measuring a neglected dimension of child health-status. *Journal of Pediatric Psychology, 16*, 39–58.

Walters, A. S., & Williamson, G. M. (1999). The role of activity restriction in the association between pain and depression: A study of pediatric patients with chronic pain. *Child Health Care, 28*, 33–50.

Ware, J. E., Jr., & Sherbourne, C. D. (1992). The MOS 36-item short-form health survey (SF-36): I. Conceptual framework and item selection. *Medical Care, 30*, 473–483.

Webster, L. R., & Webster, R. M. (2005). Predicting aberrant behaviors in opioid-treated patients: Preliminary validation of the opioid risk tool. *Pain Medicine, 6*, 432–442.

Wong, D. L., & Baker, C. M. (1988). Pain in children: Comparison of assessment scales. *Pediatric Nursing, 14*, 9–17.

3

Historical Context

Psychological Mislabeling and the Emergence of the Biopsychosocial Model

Howard B. Pikoff

Since the end of the last century, we have approached chronic pain through the assumptions of the biopsychosocial model. George Engel, an academic psychiatrist, championed this model in a 1977 *Science* article (Engel, 1977). Engel challenged psychiatry and medicine to move beyond the myopia of biological reductionism. Not without its critics (e.g., McLaren, 1998), Engel's model still stands—bruised but unbowed. In the clinic and the classroom, it continues to provide useful scaffolding for the multiple determinants of human illness. The same cannot be said of the psychogenic model. Grounded in nineteenth-century psychoanalysis, the psychogenic model understood headache, fibromyalgia, and many other pain disorders as psychological problems in disguise (Weiss & English, 1943). Understanding the history, assumptions, and shortcomings of these two models is crucial to understanding the psychosocial treatment of chronic pain.

The concept of psychogenesis started in earnest with Freud and held sway until the 1950s. Only gradually has this concept relaxed its grip on medicine. To this day, although pain specialists recognize that stress and emotional factors can affect but do not cause chronic pain, psychogenic misconceptions persist. For example, the migraine personality (as well as the arthritic personality, the respiratory personality, and the like) no longer attracts research interest, but the suggestion that perfectionism plays more of a role in migraine than in other medical disorders still makes an occasional appearance (Meckling, Becker, Rose, & Dalby, 2001). Such suggestions are a vestige of the psychogenic era. They are undermined by the poor track record of the psychogenic model across medicine and by data on psychiatric comorbidity in chronic pain.

In one large-scale community study ($N > 100,000$), for example, 78% of fibromyalgia sufferers ($N > 1600$) did not report significant levels of depression (Fuller-Thomson, Nimigon-Young, & Brennenstuhl, 2012). The overemphasis on psychological causation may also be attributable, in part, to the effectiveness of cognitive-behavioral therapy (CBT), a psychologically oriented therapy for chronic pain. CBT, however, is not a traditional psychological treatment, certainly not in the sense of psychoanalysis and other insight-oriented therapies. CBT for pain is more often thought of as a psychobehavioral or psychoeducational treatment. Moreover, while CBT practitioners acknowledge that anxiety, depression, or stress may affect certain patients, they do not presume a psychological etiology for chronic pain. In fact, for many pain patients, CBT focuses on behavior— muscle relaxation, medication misuse, suboptimal activity levels—rather than psychology.

In this chapter, I focus on the biopsychobehavioral model, a clinically oriented variant of the biopsychosocial model that highlights the three systems most frequently targeted in chronic pain therapy. I trace the origin and demise of the psychogenic model and its replacement by the biopsychosocial model; I contrast psychoanalytic and psychobehavioral case studies in order to underline the distinction between psychogenically based treatment and contemporary pain management training; and I discuss the risk of psychological mislabeling that is inherent in an overtly psychological medical model.

Origin of the Psychogenic Model

The misdiagnosis of chronic pain is hardly the first example of psychological mislabeling in medicine (Pikoff, 2010). At the middle of the last century, a leading psychosomatic text described more than two dozen fully or largely "psychogenic" conditions, including migraine, asthma, peptic ulcer, arthritis, hypertension, colitis, thyroid disorders, diabetes, menstrual problems, and tuberculosis (Weiss & English, 1943). Antecedents of this kind of psychological thinking in medicine can be found in ancient times (Schneck, 1977). Hippocrates and Galen pondered the effects of phobias and mood on the body. Fifth-century Jerusalem laid claim to a hospital devoted to mental disorders. But it was Freud who produced the first comprehensive analysis of the link between emotion and physical illness (Breuer & Freud, 1957).

Through his seminal writings of the 1890s and a visit to the United States for the Clark University lectures of 1909, Freud propelled psychoanalysis onto the intellectual landscape of America. Extending the work of Janet and Charcot, he mapped a kaleidoscopic mental universe of half-hidden conflicts, desires, and anxieties. Freud's system attracted the attention of physicians from the start because it was built on the physical complaints of people in emotional distress, and the concept of psychogenesis gained a foothold in American medicine that was maintained for almost a century.

Freud's first major publication, *Studies on Hysteria* (1893–1895), became scripture for the emerging field of psychosomatic medicine (Breuer & Freud, 1957). The book is especially significant because in five richly drawn case reports, including Breuer's well-known study of Anna O., Freud fleshed out his ideas about conversion, the linchpin of psychosomatic theory. Freud described a kind of psychological gatekeeper at the center of the conversion process. The job of this gatekeeper was to deny conscious expression to thoughts associated with highly negative emotional experiences. Freud believed such thoughts, which often involved taboo sexual activities that could be real or imagined, remained split off from consciousness. Because they did not enter awareness, these "incompatible ideas" could not undergo the normal "wearing away" process that occurred with new experiences. Sometimes, however, under constant pressure for expression, highly charged thoughts would break into consciousness in the guise of physical symptoms. This was conversion. And over the next 100 years, the assumption that psychological phenomena can metamorphose into physical signs and symptoms—Freud's "mysterious leap"—burrowed deep into medicine and popular thought.

In *Studies on Hysteria*, Freud mused over the role of psychological factors in chronic pain (Breuer & Freud, 1957). Addressing the issue of psychogenesis in a possible instance of fibromyalgia, Freud was open-minded and temperate:

> There were numerous hard fibres in the muscular substance, and these seemed to be especially sensitive. Thus it was probable that an organic change in the muscles of the kind indicated was present and that the neurosis attached itself to this and made it seem of exaggerated importance.
>
> (pp. 137–138)

Freud clearly stated his belief in the organic basis of pain symptoms:

> The circumstances indicate that this somatic pain was not *created* by the neurosis but merely used, increased and maintained by it. I may add at once that I have found a similar state of things in almost all the instances of hysterical pains into which I have been able to obtain an insight. There had always been a genuine, organically-founded pain present at the start.
>
> (p. 174, Freud's italics)

Freud's disciples, on the other hand, could be strident. For example, James Halliday, a disability examiner for the Scottish health department in the 1930s, argued with great zeal for unidimensional psychological determinism in fibromyalgia. To Halliday, a fibromyalgia patient's difficulty bending was a symbolic protest that "I am an upright man and do not stoop to low pursuits" (Halliday, 1937a, p. 216). He could find "no basis for the opinion sometimes expressed that psychoneurosis is nearly always a superstructure on a real organic illness" (Halliday, 1937b, p. 265). In essence, Halliday dismissed fibromyalgia and other chronic pain conditions as neurosis at best, outright malingering at worst.

The influence of psychoanalysis in American medicine peaked in the 1950s with the publication of Franz Alexander's text, *Psychosomatic Medicine* (Alexander, 1950). Alexander was a leader of the Chicago Psychoanalytic Institute and the founder, in 1939, of the journal *Psychosomatic Medicine*. Through these publications, Alexander spread the umbrella of psychoanalysis over a swath of diverse disorders, including hay fever, arthritis, and tuberculosis. At its zenith, however, in the work of Alexander and his predecessors, the psychoanalytic model of chronic pain contained a serious weakness. It was based on anecdote and case report. I could not find a controlled trial of either psychoanalysis proper or a psychodynamically based therapy for chronic pain among the hundreds of studies cited in standard psychosomatic bibliographies through the 1940s (Alexander & French, 1948; Dunbar, 1935).

Psychoanalytic Case Study

Helen Weber's headache study (Weber, 1932) captures the psychogenic approach that came to dominate medicine in the first half of the twentieth century. Her patient, called "Q," was a 56-year-old married woman who had suffered from migraines since childhood. Nervous and self-conscious, the woman dreaded strangers and strange places and feared leaving home even for short trips. As a child she was troubled by night terrors, nocturnal enuresis, and other "definite neurotic symptoms." Her father was overindulgent, her mother cruel and rejecting. The author believed this left Q with a legacy of wounded pride and a chronic longing for motherly affection. Weber pointed to the timing of attacks as evidence of their emotional origin. Q's headaches often would occur within an hour or two of a disappointment or an interpersonal conflict. To Weber, this temporal pattern confirmed that headaches were an outlet for an underlying hostility that belied the patient's outward submissiveness. As such, headaches served practical and intrapsychic ends. They allowed the patient to avoid confrontations with her mother and overt expressions of hostility.

Broadly speaking, the goal of psychoanalytic headache therapy was to help patients uncover the purpose of their headaches. Interpretation and insight were the primary means of discovery. Throughout the analysis, Weber called attention to the symbolic significance of headache triggers and consequences. For example, Weber reasoned that an inordinate love of home explained her patient's relief upon returning to bed during a headache and her general reluctance to travel. Home appeared to represent both mother and womb to Q, a safe haven where she could have "all her needs supplied without effort on her own part." More fundamentally, Weber sensed a pervasive narcissism in her patient. To Weber, this narcissism, and the unconscious sense of omnipotence it engendered psychologically, fueled Q's headaches. In the service of her narcissism, headaches became a "strategy" for compelling compassion from her mother as a child and from her husband later in life.

As the analysis proceeded, Q increasingly recognized the role of narcissism in her basic character, in her "blind urge to dominate," and in her headaches. She became aware of the "infantile methods" she used to control others, both as a child and an adult. Gradually, this growing awareness of unconscious needs and motivations enabled Q to take on more adult responsibilities. She abandoned her "attention-coercing" headaches and other immature means of obtaining gratification. By the end of treatment, she was headache-free for significant periods of time.

Origin of the Biopsychobehavioral Model

A challenge to psychoanalysis began to unfold in the 1930s and 1940s. The challenge came from behaviorism, an approach rooted in the laboratories of Watson, Pavlov, and Skinner. Behaviorism rejected Freud's innate drives and unconscious motivations as the main drivers of psychological development in favor of conditioning (Dobson & Dozois, 2010). Like psychoanalysis, behaviorism encompassed both a worldview and a treatment. The clinical application of behaviorism was behavior modification. Psychologists initially used behavior modification for childhood habit disorders such as tics and bedwetting. As procedures for relaxation and mental imagery were perfected, practitioners took on a more ambitious clinical agenda for both children and adults. They reconceptualized phobias, for example, as problems of conditioning rather than repression. Treatment now focused on substitution of more effective responses to an aversive situation—for example, muscle relaxation in place of tension, and approach instead of avoidance. Success might be measured by completion of an airplane trip rather than the decoding of the symbolism of a fear of flying.

The Real Significance of Biofeedback

The advent of two new treatments—biofeedback and cognitive-behavioral therapy—turned the attention of behavior therapists to chronic pain and other medical disorders. Psychologists initially used biofeedback as a laboratory tool for studying the conditionability of physiological responses that were not normally under voluntary control. By providing immediate feedback and rewards following slight random fluctuations, researchers discovered that cats and monkeys could learn to reduce heart rate, blood pressure, and even intestinal activity.

Although some results could not be replicated, a serendipitous discovery shifted the focus from animal research to humans. During a blood flow biofeedback study at the Menninger Foundation in the 1960s, one of the participants developed a migraine (Sargent, Solbach, Coyne, Spohn, & Segerson, 1986). The attack ended at precisely the moment her hand temperature rose 10°F due to an increase in blood flow. Others who volunteered for blood flow training had similar experiences. Soon "hand warming" became a watchword in the treatment of migraine. Encouraged by these results, behaviorally minded psychologists began to explore ways of applying the most robust of the conditionable responses, skeletal muscle tension, in the psychological clinic.

Two of their earliest targets were musculoskeletal pain and headache. True to its roots in conditioning research, this therapy was viewed as a learning process. Like progressive muscle relaxation, biofeedback would be taught rather than administered, and the therapeutic use of biofeedback would come to be known as "biofeedback training." The goal of therapy was to teach the patient to recognize and reduce muscle tension at will. Using biofeedback equipment in the psychologist's office and relaxation exercises at home, patients learned to decrease muscle tension and overall physiological arousal during daily activities.

A handful of biofeedback trials for headache and other disorders supported the efficacy of this innovative behavioral therapy (Ferraccioli et al., 1987). These early trials, however, with their small samples and modest improvement rates, are of only limited importance for their outcomes. Clinical research and experience over the next 30 years established biofeedback as a useful, if relatively minor, tool in the multimodal treatment of chronic pain. The real significance of the early biofeedback trials was that they brought behavioral psychologists into the treatment of chronic pain. In so doing, biofeedback laid the foundation for a biopsychobehavioral approach to chronic pain that was not predicated on a psychological etiology. Chronic pain would be treated like other organic disorders with a behavioral component. As the diabetic could be taught new eating habits, people with chronic headache or back pain could be taught to relax the muscles.

The melding of cognitive therapy and behavior therapy gave the second big push to the biopsychobehavioral approach to chronic pain that was emerging in the 1970s (Dobson & Dozois, 2010). With a richer set of clinical tools, cognitive-behavioral therapy could offer richer therapeutic possibilities. In addition to a reduction in muscle tension, it was now reasonable for a treatment plan to list significant changes in lifestyle. The new treatment borrowed from cognitive therapy, a form of psychotherapy developed by Albert Ellis, a psychologist, and Aaron Beck, a psychiatrist. Working independently, Ellis and Beck devised similar therapies. Both rested squarely on the interdependence of thought, feeling, and behavior. Over the next two decades, this perspective fused with the behavior therapist's appreciation of observable habits and actions to form a comprehensive psychobehavioral treatment. Today, cognitive-behavioral therapy is widely practiced throughout the world. It is the psychobehavioral treatment of choice for chronic pain and a growing list of medical conditions (Arnberg, Alaie, Parling, & Jonsson, 2013).

In cognitive-behavioral terms, the issues and thoughts in chronic pain are those of any chronic illness or disabling condition: identity ("I'm unable to take care of my children"); depression and anxiety ("Nothing can help me"); and physical limitations ("I can't even make my bed"). Behavioral assignments abound. For example, patients may be asked to schedule a daily productive task, or practice goal setting to reduce overactivity or medication use. If emotional difficulties surface, they usually are addressed as the consequence of chronic pain or as comorbid conditions that may at times intensify the pain experience.

Cognitive-Behavioral Case Study

Martin's prototypical headache study (Martin, 1993) illustrates many of the basic premises and procedures of CBT in pain management. It contrasts sharply with Weber's psychoanalytic report described earlier. Where Weber inferred and interpreted (her patient's unconscious motivations, symbolism, and strategies), Martin taught and encouraged (the practice of physiological self-control, the challenging of inaccurate beliefs, and the testing of new behaviors). Clare was a 32-year-old former teacher who had been married for seven years. She had three young sons. Her migraines began in childhood and remained episodic into early adulthood. Several years prior to treatment, they transformed into near daily tension-type headaches. In Clare's words, these headaches now "dominated my life." She could barely keep up with household responsibilities, had difficulty managing her children, and took part in few social or leisure activities. During headaches, Clare would "verbally abuse" the children, often screaming and shouting through the house. Headaches also were taking a toll on her marriage. She frequently would ask her husband to leave work in order to care for the children. Her husband, Jim, would oblige but was usually "lousy about it," expressing his resentment by "going out of his way to create a mess in the house." Clare described herself as nervous, touchy, and thin-skinned. On standardized psychological testing, she registered a high level of anxiety and mild depression.

Clare's treatment began with the recording of headaches and medication use for two weeks. Self-monitoring continued throughout treatment, with the daily logging of stressful events, triggers, headache-related emotions, and maladaptive thoughts prior to, during, and following attacks. The initial stage of treatment focused on training in physiological self-control techniques such as muscle relaxation, attention diversion, and the use of imagery. The purpose was to provide tools for managing pain, anxiety, and physical tension daily, as well as during headaches. Clare's self-monitoring logs helped set the agenda for the cognitive and behavioral components of treatment. They pinpointed four treatment targets: reducing counterproductive thinking immediately prior to and during headaches; increasing leisure activities; improving parenting skills; and teaching Clare's husband to promote wellness behavior in place of illness behavior.

Martin drew from the standard cognitive-behavioral repertoire for each problem area. He used cognitive reframing tools to help Clare learn to identify, challenge, and alter unrealistic expectations about her children, her ability to cope with severe headaches, and her guilt over being chronically ill. These techniques produced significant changes in dysfunctional thinking. For example, Clare was able to identify and temper a pervasive thought—"Simon [her son] always wants to be the center of attention"—and underlying belief—"children should always be well behaved"—that were at the root of much child-rearing frustration. Behavior modification procedures also were highly effective, especially with family concerns. Through contingency management, role playing, and homework assignments, Jim became less overtly critical of his wife's irritability during headaches, while Clare learned to substitute coping skills for Jim's help during attacks. Midway through treatment, Clare began to explore a variety of leisure activities. Eventually she became actively involved in a community musical, her son's T-ball team, and a course in computer programming. Over five months of therapy, her headaches steadily declined, and by her last session (#15), frequency and intensity were down more than 95%, and medication use had decreased from four pills/day to none.

Retreat of the Psychogenic, Rise of the Biopsychosocial

The treatment described by Martin is a good example of the psychobehavioral approach that gradually replaced the psychogenic model in the final decades of the last century. The impetus for this transition came as much from biomedical research as from psychology. In near lockstep, the psychogenic model retreated in condition after condition as developments in disease mechanisms and medical therapies advanced. The rethinking of asthma and peptic ulcer are especially instructive.

In the 1940s, the psychodynamic explanation of asthma centered on a fear of abandonment (Gerard, 1948). Burdened by guilt associated with forbidden sexual and aggressive impulses, especially toward a sibling, the child developed a lifelong fear of parental abandonment. Guilt and fear would periodically push through the blinders of repression in the form of an asthma attack. At whatever age, this symbolic reenactment of separation from mother would reduce the asthma sufferer to a "shrieking, helplessly sprawling newborn child with blood-red, swollen face" (Gerard, 1948, p. 245). Treatment consisted of identifying and expressing sexual and aggressive desires to a therapist who acted as an accepting mother substitute. On another track, researchers pursued the pathophysiology of asthma (Diamant, Boot, & Virchow, 2007). Basic research began to conceive of the condition as a possible hereditary inflammatory disorder as early as the 1940s. As research progressed in neurotrophins, genetics, and immunological technologies, asthma came to be understood as a chronic inflammatory disorder related to a combination of genetic and environmental factors.

The disintegration of the psychogenic model in peptic ulcer was even more dramatic. At the height of psychoanalytic influence in medicine, Weiss and English (1943) made the psychogenic case for peptic ulcer that was to become a paradigm for psychologically based disorders. There was a mechanism—unconscious dependency needs were believed to cause autonomically induced stomach changes. There was research—pilocarpine injections increased hypersecretion, hypermotility, and hypertonicity in animal models. There was a treatment—psychoanalysis with ulcer patients as reported by Franz Alexander.

45

And then in the 1980s, with the discovery of *H. pylori*, the paradigm swiftly collapsed (Yamada et al., 1994).

Important Dates

1895 Freud and Breuer complete *Studies on Hysteria*. The book remains a core medical text for the next 50 years.

1950 Alexander's *Psychosomatic Medicine* extends the concept of psychogenesis to diverse medical disorders, including arthritis, hay fever, and tuberculosis.

1920s–1950s Behaviorism emerges from the laboratories of Pavlov, Watson, and Skinner.

1970s The psychogenic model recedes as behaviorism gives rise to behavior therapy and other psychobehavioral methods.

1977 George Engel proposes the biopsychosocial model.

1980s CBT and biofeedback become standard methods in the multidisciplinary treatment of chronic pain.

By the second half of the twentieth century, research advances such as these, and a revolution in pharmaceuticals, pushed a biomedical paradigm to ascendancy in medicine. Psychogenesis was yielding to science. In the same period, psychologists brought their cognitive-behavioral toolkit to bear on an array of medical disorders. They also brought an orientation that gave psychological factors a contributory rather than causal role in physical illness and highlighted the importance of lifestyle and behavioral variables. This new behavioral approach was field-tested in the pain management centers that flourished in the 1980s. In these hospital-based multidisciplinary clinics, psychologists, physical therapists, anesthesiologists, and others fused biology with psychology and behavior.

Against this backdrop, with psychogenesis in retreat and biomedicine and behavioral medicine on the rise, Engel issued his call for a new medical model (Engel, 1977). In place of a biomedical model that assumed all disease could be fully accounted for in biological terms, Engel envisioned a model that was sensitive to the psychological and social dimensions of illness. Such a model would promote a better understanding of both the disease process and the therapeutic alliance. It would "reverse the dehumanization of medicine and disempowerment of patients [by] fostering dialogue, not just the mechanical application of protocol" (Borrell-Carrio, Suchman, & Epstein, 2004, p. 576). To do this, the new model would turn a spotlight on the relationship between clinician and patient.

In his call for a more holistic perspective in medicine, Engel zeroed in on the interpersonal. He forcefully argued that "the relationship between patient and physician powerfully influences therapeutic outcome for better or for worse"

(Engel, 1977, p. 132). Twenty-five years later, proponents of the biopsychosocial model continued to stress the importance of a true therapeutic alliance, as distinguished from a mere "set of linguistic tricks to get the patient to comply with treatment" (Borrell-Carrio et al., 2004, p. 579). Engel's successors pressed the point that a therapeutic relationship based on genuineness would prevent "negation of the patient's perspective, as so frequently occurs, for example, when patients complain of symptoms that physicians cannot explain" (Borrell-Carrio et al., 2004, p. 578).

Engel's goals were laudable, but they came with a downside: An overtly psychological model could re-open the door to psychological mislabeling that would undermine the therapeutic alliance it sought to strengthen. Several authors have suggested that this has, indeed, been the case. One group (Shakespeare, Watson, & Alghaib, 2017) accused a conservative British government of using the biopsychosocial model to reduce disability benefits by "blaming the victim." In a compelling argument, these authors charged officials with misapplying the biopsychosocial model to show that "it is the negative attitudes of many recipients [of disability benefits] that prevent them from working, rather than their impairment or health condition" (Shakespeare et al., 2017, p. 23).

Another group (Epstein, Quill, & McWhinney, 1999) called attention to a subtler problem with the biopsychosocial model. These critics raised the possibility that clinicians may invoke the model (or, more precisely, the psychological component) only when they encounter difficult patients or unexplained disorders. This tendency to draw upon the biopsychosocial model selectively, to think biopsychosocially only in the most challenging cases, is an incubator for psychological mislabeling. It runs completely counter to Engel's effort to promote multidimensional thinking about illness in general.

A third paper (Hancock, Maher, Laslett, Hay, & Koes, 2011) put the question directly: "What happened to the 'bio' in the bio–psycho-social model of low back pain?" These papers highlight the risk of psychological mislabeling that is inherent in a psychologically informed medical model.

Clinical Consideration

Clinicians can reduce the risk of real or perceived psychological mislabeling by making the underlying assumptions of behavioral pain management explicit. For example, clinicians can make clear that a referral for CBT is a referral for pain management training and not for psychotherapy. It is also useful to make patients aware that behavioral pain management treats chronic pain as a biologically based disorder. It is not caused by depression, anxiety, emotional trauma, or stress, although any of these factors can influence chronic pain as they can any other medical disorder. Moreover, behavioral practitioners do not view a nonresponse to medication, physical therapy, or surgery as an indicator of psychological involvement. These reassurances can be therapeutic for patients who have been demoralized by the suggestion from friends, family, or previous healthcare providers—explicitly or implicitly—of an underlying psychological problem. Reaffirming the biological side of chronic pain can be useful for clinicians as well. It can serve as a reminder that a nonresponse to medical therapy likely has more to do with our limited understanding of the pathophysiology of pain than with psychopathology, and it can remind the clinician to not reach too quickly for a psychological explanation.

Review of the underlying assumptions of pain management training should also include a brief discussion of treatment goals and procedures. This discussion will further clarify that although typically carried out by psychologists, behavioral pain management is not psychotherapy. The primary goal of treatment is not the alleviation of emotional distress. It is the improvement of function. Procedures focus primarily on pain management, for example the avoidance of triggers and flares, rather than emotional regulation or the development of insight, as is typical in psychotherapy. At the same time, patients should know that the pain management psychologist may recommend direct treatment of mental health symptoms that may be intensifying or emerging from the pain experience.

The shift from a psychogenic to a biopsychosocial model highlights the provisional nature of our insights. At the beginning of the twentieth century, the psychogenic model appeared to offer a psychological inroad into the cause and cure of a host of medical disorders. Within decades, the model was swamped by advances in basic research and pharmacotherapy. Today, the psychosomatic handbook of record does not endorse a psychological etiology for any of the "psychogenic" disorders described in its 1940s counterpart (Levenson, 2011). Instead, we are guided by a biopsychosocial model. It is "bio" because many illnesses have yielded to biological solutions. It is "psychosocial" because many have not. But we expect they will in the future. Alternatively, a truly unitary model may emerge in which the biological, psychological, social, and behavioral lose their separate identities. For now, however, the biopsychosocial model provides a workable balance across differing perspectives. It remains a template for the multidisciplinary understanding and treatment of chronic illness, and our (provisional) medical model of choice.

References

Alexander, F. (1950). *Psychosomatic medicine: Its principles and applications.* New York, NY: Norton.

Alexander, F., & French, T. M. (Eds.). (1948). *Studies in psychosomatic medicine: An approach to the cause and treatment of vegetative disturbances*. New York, NY: The Ronald Press.

Arnberg, F. K., Alaie, I., Parling, T., & Jonsson, U. (2013). Recent randomized controlled trials of psychological interventions in healthcare: A review of their quantity, scope, and characteristics. *Journal of Psychosomatic Research, 75*, 401–408. doi:10.1016/j.jpsychores.2013.08.019

Borrell-Carrio, F., Suchman, A. L., & Epstein, R. M. (2004). The biopsychosocial model 25 years later: Principles, practice, and scientific inquiry. *Annals of Family Medicine, 2*, 576–582. doi:10.1370/afm.245

Breuer, J., & Freud, S. (1957). *Studies on hysteria*. New York, NY: Basic Books.

Diamant, Z., Boot, J. D., & Virchow, J. C. (2007). Summing up 100 years of asthma. *Respiratory Medicine, 101*, 378–388.

Dobson, K. S., & Dozois, D. J. A. (2010). Historical and philosophical bases of the cognitive-behavioral therapies. In K. Dobson (Ed.), *Handbook of cognitive-behavioral therapies* (3rd ed., pp. 3–38). New York, NY: The Guilford Press.

Dunbar, H. F. (1935). *Emotions and bodily changes: A survey of literature on psychosomatic inter-relationships, 1910–1933*. New York, NY: Columbia University Press.

Engel, G. (1977). The need for a new medical model: A challenge for biomedicine. *Science, 196*, 129–136. doi:10.1126/science.847460

Epstein, R. M., Quill, T. E., & McWhinney, I. R. (1999). Somatization reconsidered: Incorporating the patient's experience of illness. *Archives of Internal Medicine, 159*, 215–222. doi:10.1001/archinte.159.3.215

Ferraccioli, G., Ghirelli, L., Scita, F., Nolli, M., Mozzani, M., Fontana, S., . . . DeRisio, C. (1987). EMG-biofeedback training in fibromyalgia syndrome. *The Journal of Rheumatology, 14*, 820–825.

Fuller-Thomson, E., Nimigon-Young, J., & Brennenstuhl, S. (2012). Individuals with fibromyalgia and depression: Findings from a nationally representative Canadian survey. *Rheumatology International, 32*, 853–862. doi:10.1007/s00296-010-1713-x

Gerard, M. W. (1948). Bronchial asthma in children. In F. Alexander & T. M. French (Eds.), *Studies in psychosomatic medicine: An approach to the cause and treatment of vegetative disturbances* (pp. 243–258). New York, NY: The Ronald Press.

Halliday, J. L. (1937a). Psychological factors in rheumatism: A preliminary study part 1. *The British Medical Journal, 1*, 213–217.

Halliday, J. L. (1937b). Psychological factors in rheumatism: A preliminary study part 2. *The British Medical Journal, 1*, 264–269.

Hancock, M. J., Maher, C. G., Laslett, M., Hay, E., & Koes, B. (2011). Discussion paper: What happened to the 'bio' in the bio-psycho-social model of low back pain? *European Spine Journal, 20*, 2105–2110. doi:10.1007/s00586-011-1886-3

Levenson, J. L. (Ed.). (2011). *The American Psychiatric Publishing textbook of psychosomatic medicine: Psychiatric care of the medically ill* (2nd ed.). Washington, DC: American Psychiatric Publishing.

Martin, P. R. (1993). *Psychological management of chronic headaches*. New York, NY: The Guilford Press.

McLaren, N. (1998). A critical review of the biopsychosocial model. *The Australian and New Zealand Journal of Psychiatry, 32*, 86–92.

Meckling, S. K., Becker, W. J., Rose, M. S., & Dalby, J. T. (2001). Sumatriptan responsiveness and clinical, psychiatric and psychological features in migraine patients. *Canadian Journal of Neurological Sciences, 28*, 313–318.

Pikoff, H. (2010). A study in psychological mislabelling: The rise and (protracted) fall of psychogenic fibromyalgia. *International Journal of Musculoskeletal Medicine, 32*, 129–132. doi:10.1179/175361410X12798116924336

Sargent, J., Solbach, P., Coyne, L., Spohn, H., & Segerson, J. (1986). Results of a controlled, experimental, outcome study of nondrug treatments for the control of migraine headaches. *Journal of Behavioral Medicine, 9,* 291–323. doi:10.1007/BF00844775

Schneck, J. M. (1977). History of psychiatry. In B. Wolman (Ed.), *International encyclopedia of psychiatry, psychology, psychoanalysis, & neurology* (Vol. 8, pp. 356–364). New York, NY: Van Nostrand Reinhold Company.

Shakespeare, T., Watson, N., & Alghaib, O. A. (2017). Blaming the victim, all over again: Waddell and Aylward's biopsychosocial (BPS) model of disability. *Critical Social Policy, 37,* 22–41. doi:10.1177/0261018316649120

Weber, H. (1932). The psychological factor in migraine. *British Journal of Medical Psychology, 12,* 151–173.

Weiss, E., & English, O. S. (1943). *Psychosomatic medicine: The clinical application of psychopathology to general medical problems.* Philadelphia: W. B. Saunders Company.

Yamada, T., Ahnen, D., Aipers, D. H., Greenberg, H. B., Gray, M., Joscelyn, K. B., . . . Walsh, J. (1994). Helicobacter pylori in peptic ulcer disease. *JAMA: The Journal of the American Medical Association, 272,* 65–69. doi:10.1001/jama.1994.03520010077036

4

Cognitive-Behavioral Interventions for Chronic Pain

Emily Cox-Martin, Lisa H. Trahan, and Diane M. Novy

Background

Chronic pain, specifically pain that lasts beyond normal healing time or past three to six months, is estimated to directly affect approximately 20% of the population worldwide (Gatchel, Peng, Peters, Fuchs, & Turk, 2007; Treede et al., 2015). "Chronic pain" is a broad term, encompassing a variety of diagnoses that often are classified by etiology (e.g., post-surgical, cancer-related), location (e.g., headache, lower back), or pain type (e.g., neuropathic, musculoskeletal) (Fillingim et al., 2014; Treede et al., 2015). The prevalence of chronic pain in the United States may be even higher, estimated at 19–55% of the population (Gatchel et al., 2007; Kennedy, Roll, Schraudner, Murphy, & McPherson, 2014; Nahin, 2015). This estimate does not account for the additional family members and friends indirectly impacted by a loved one's pain condition (West, Usher, Foster, & Stewart, 2012). Chronic pain also carries a heavy economic burden, affecting healthcare costs and work productivity, and results in estimated costs as high as $635 billion annually (Gaskin & Richard, 2012).

The biopsychosocial model of pain has been widely accepted as one of the most prominent and comprehensive models for understanding and treating various pain conditions (Gatchel et al., 2007; Novy & Aigner, 2014). This model recognizes the complex relations among biological, psychological, and social factors that result in the subjective experience of pain. The model's biological portion encompasses various processes included under the neuroscience of pain, such as physiological disease states or genetic predispositions, as well as physical impairments and sleep disturbance. Emotions, cognitions, perceptions, and behaviors comprise the psychological contribution to the model. Social context can include factors such as culture, family system/environment, general social support, and occupation. Within the framework of this model, the psychological makeup and social relationships of the patient are as important in understanding his/her chronic pain experience as are the biological/physical aspects of the pain. This model informs both the modern conceptualization of the subjective experience of pain and the interdisciplinary nature of its treatment.

The wide recognition of this model has led to the inclusion of behavioral and psychological interventions in various clinical guidelines for pain management. For example, the American Pain Society (APS) recommends interdisciplinary rehabilitation programs that emphasize cognitive and behavioral factors for non-radicular low back pain, particularly if the patient has not responded to more common, non-interdisciplinary treatments (Chou et al., 2009). Similarly, the American Society of Anesthesiologists and the American Society of Regional Anesthesia and Pain Medicine jointly have included psychological treatments in their practice guidelines for chronic pain management (Management, 2010). They endorse several psychological intervention approaches in their treatment recommendations, including CBT, biofeedback, and relaxation training. Treatment guidelines for the management of various osteoarthritis diagnoses, including hand, hip, and knee, also include psychosocial interventions (Hochberg et al., 2012).

Introduction to Cognitive-Behavioral Therapy

The term cognitive-behavioral therapy (CBT) refers to a group of evidence-based psychological treatments used for a multitude of conditions (e.g., depression, anxiety, eating disorders, insomnia). This type of therapy, which is considered post-Freudian, was developed in the mid- to late 1900s. CBT combines theoretical and applied elements of behaviorism (popular in the mid-twentieth century) and cognitive therapy (pioneered by Aaron Beck in the 1960s). Behaviorism is based upon observable and measurable behaviors, whereas internal processes such as thoughts and emotions were the focus of Beck's original cognitive theories. CBT was established with the coalescence of these two theoretical arms.

In the field of pain management, Wilbert Fordyce (1977) pioneered the behavioral arm of treatment, applying learning theory and the concepts of operant conditioning to pain behaviors. Dennis Turk later expanded this approach (Turk, Meichenbaum, & Genest, 1983), including concepts of Beck's cognitive therapy and Fordyce's behavioral work to help develop the foundation of today's CBT for chronic pain (CBT-CP). Researchers in the field of pain psychology have since continuously expanded upon the early work of Fordyce and Turk, building the evidence base for using CBT with this complex and challenging patient population.

Today, CBT operates on the general tenet that a person's thoughts, emotions, and behaviors have a complex and dynamic relationship through which they influence and shape one another. Although the relations among these three factors make up the cornerstone of CBT practice, CBT therapists also recognize the influence that biological (e.g., genetics, neurological functioning, physical impairments) and social (e.g., poverty, education, social support system) variables have on human psychological functioning. In this way, CBT is reflective of the biopsychosocial model discussed previously in the chapter.

Although far from an exhaustive list, the broad reach of CBTs includes therapies such as schema-focused therapy, rational-emotive behavior therapy, prolonged exposure therapy, and cognitive processing therapy. Specific behavioral skills taught through CBTs include, but are not limited to, relaxation skills (e.g., deep breathing), activity planning, and using effective methods of reinforcement. Cognitive strategies may include problem-solving, identifying cognitive distortions, and cognitive restructuring. Recently, constructs such as acceptance, mindfulness, meaningfulness, and self-compassion have been incorporated into more traditional CBTs. Examples of these "third-wave CBTs" include acceptance and commitment therapy, dialectical behavior therapy, compassion-focused therapy, and mindfulness-based cognitive therapy, among others.

Efficacy for CBT for Chronic Pain

Cognitive-behavioral therapy is supported by countless randomized controlled trials (RCTs) and over 250 meta-analytic reviews (e.g., Hofmann, Asnaani, Vonk, Sawyer, & Fang, 2012; McMain, Newman, Segal, & DeRubeis, 2015). Efficacy for CBT for chronic pain is strong generally but varies somewhat based upon the actual pain condition (e.g., lower back pain, headache), the intervention used (e.g., coping skills, relaxation strategies), and the targeted outcome (e.g., pain severity, pain catastrophizing). A comprehensive review of psychological therapies for managing chronic pain included 35 RCTs involving more than 4,000 patients (Williams, Eccleston, & Morley, 2012). This review found CBT interventions have small/moderate effects on pain, catastrophizing, disability, and mood as compared to usual treatment (i.e., not an active, protocol-based treatment) or waitlist control groups. These effects were primarily at post-treatment, with only the effect on mood found at follow-up as well. When compared to active treatment control groups, CBTs were found to have smaller, but still significant, positive effects on disability and catastrophizing. However, this review included only RCTs, focused on a variety of chronic pain conditions, and included all adult subgroups.

Designing studies to examine the efficacy of CBTs for chronic pain that target specific conditions, patient populations, and outcome variables is important, given the heterogeneity of chronic pain patients and conditions. For example, the American Psychological Association's Division for a Society of Clinical Psychology (Division 12) reports strong research support for CBTs in the treatment of chronic lower back pain (CLBP) and rheumatologic pain. Hoffman and colleagues conducted a meta-analytic investigation of psychological interventions for CLBP, finding strong evidence for the efficacy of psychological interventions when used alone or in a multidisciplinary treatment setting (Hoffman, Papas,

Chatkoff, & Kerns, 2007). In particular, CBTs had moderate/large effects on pain intensity when compared to waitlist controls.

A recent systematic review and meta-analysis focused on CBT RCTs for fibromyalgia, a syndrome characterized by widespread musculoskeletal pain, as well as a constellation of other symptoms including fatigue, sleep, and mood issues. This study found that CBTs had a significant impact on the patients' self-efficacy for coping with pain and mood but did not improve pain, fatigue, sleep, or health-related quality of life (Bernardy, Füber, Köllner, & Häuser, 2010).

CBT Interventions for Chronic Pain

Various cognitive and behavioral skills and strategies have been used in CBTs, both generally and specifically for chronic pain. Some of the more common interventions include activity planning, cognitive restructuring, and relaxation training. Other interventions, including stress management or communication skills, indirectly might help a chronic pain patient by affecting other domains such as interpersonal relationships (thereby improving overall quality of life). It should be noted that CBTs can comprise any combination of strategies and rarely consist of a single skill/intervention. Further, CBTs can be offered via individual or group intervention modalities.

Activity Planning

Chronic pain can impact a patient's activity levels, and by proxy his/her social interactions and physical abilities (Dueñas, Ojeda, Salazar, Mico, & Failde, 2016; Spenkelink, Hutten, Hermens, & Greitemann, 2002). Therefore, activity planning should include setting goals for engaging in actual physical activity or exercise to mitigate disability; however, it also may focus on scheduling pleasant events in order to improve mood and social interactions (Carpenter, Stoner, Mundt, & Stoelb, 2012; Otis, 2007).

Regardless of whether it relates to physical activity or pleasant events, activity planning should be done in a way that is compatible with the patient's current functional ability and medical parameters. The patient may need to modify activities that he/she engaged in prior to his/her pain condition. However, similar but smaller-scale versions of those activities may provide similar enjoyment (e.g., putting together planting pots for the porch rather than landscaping the entire yard).

In addition to being feasible physically, the activity must be feasible logistically. Schedule and discuss the activity in detail with the patient so that any potential barriers can be addressed. Select a workable time and place for the activity, as well as deciding whom to do it with—these are important elements of the planning process and can increase the likelihood that the activity will be successful for the patient.

Activity pacing is another strategy often applied to the clinical management of chronic pain and discussed in relation to activity planning. The term, which is unclear within the literature, has been used in reference to both an approach for energy conservation in people with chronic disease and an operant approach in which behaviors become goal-contingent rather than pain-contingent (Gill & Brown, 2009; Nielson, Jensen, Karsdorp, & Vlaeyen, 2013). Evidence for the effectiveness of activity pacing in chronic pain management is mixed, resulting in a debate regarding its utility as a behavioral strategy (Andrews, Strong, & Meredith, 2012; Gill & Brown, 2009; Nielson et al., 2013). Activity pacing commonly has been included in multicomponent CBT programs, such as those discussed below; research regarding its potential effectiveness as a stand-alone strategy is lacking (Nielson et al., 2013). Recommendations regarding future directions for better understanding of activity pacing in chronic pain management include improved clarity of the definition; better measurement of the actual behavior; and better understanding of the role that individual differences and cognitive factors might have on effectiveness for a given patient (Nielson et al., 2013).

Cognitive Restructuring

Implicit in the biopsychosocial model of chronic pain is the role that cognitions, or thoughts, play in one's experience of pain. Pain catastrophizing is a specific type of maladaptive pain cognition that often is characterized as negative or unrealistic/exaggerated (e.g., "This pain is horrible and will never go away"). Pain catastrophizing has been associated with a number of negative pain outcomes, including pain severity, pain sensitivity, disability, and depression (Quartana, Campbell, & Edwards, 2009). Cognitive restructuring targets pain catastrophizing cognitions through 1) identification of maladaptive thinking; 2) implementation of specific cognitive restructuring techniques; and 3) use of adaptive self-statements (Ehde & Jensen, 2004). Restructuring techniques specific to the pain experience may include cognitive evaluations of the thought based on the frequency, intensity, and direct impact of the pain. They also may involve seeking out evidence for and against a particular thought. Due to the relationship between thoughts, emotions, and behaviors, changing a person's thoughts regarding pain can decrease the emotional distress and pain-related behaviors experienced.

Relaxation Training

Chronic pain can lead to both physical and psychological stress. One way this stress manifests is through muscle tension and an activation of the "fight or flight" response. Relaxation training for chronic pain may consist of progressive muscle relaxation (PMR), diaphragmatic/deep breathing, and/or guided imagery. Increased muscle tension can exacerbate the physical pain experience. The goal of PMR is to help the patient become more aware of muscular tension as it begins to occur and then respond by physically relaxing the tense area (McCallie, Blum, & Hood, 2006). Although typically a clinician guides patients through a PMR activity the first time, patients can learn to do this on their own or with a guided recording in order to better self-manage their pain. PMR intervention may include a range of muscle groups, typically starting with 16 major groups including the hands, arms, areas of the face, neck, upper torso, legs, and feet. This can be modified into briefer instructions that include only eight or four muscle groups. The patient is instructed to systematically tense and then relax various areas of the body while focusing on the differences between the sensations of tension and relaxation.

Similar to PMR, deep breathing and guided imagery are used to reduce physical and psychological stress. Deep breathing has been found to have analgesic effects, experimentally impacting pain threshold, pain tolerance, and perception of pain (Busch et al., 2012; Chalaye, Goffaux, Lafrenaye, & Marchand, 2009). Sometimes referred to as "diaphragmatic breathing," deep breathing instructs patients to breathe using the muscles in their diaphragm. This results in deeper breaths, rather than short, shallow breaths that may limit oxygen intake into the body.

Guided imagery, another common pain intervention, not only incorporates relaxation but often utilizes distraction as well. Used either alone, or in combination with another relaxation technique, guided imagery has been shown to have a positive impact on perceived pain, mobility difficulties, and self-efficacy for managing pain (Baird & Sands, 2004; Fors, Sexton, & Götestam, 2002; Menzies, Taylor, & Bourguignon, 2006). Guided imagery typically focuses on pleasant stimuli, including as many sensory details as possible, and can be tailored to the individual patient.

Psychoeducation

While not a behavioral or cognitive intervention per se, education often is an important component of many CBT interventions for chronic pain (Ehde, Dillworth, & Turner, 2014; Williams et al., 2012). Key aspects of psychoeducation in the context of chronic pain can include specific information regarding the etiology or pathophysiology of a particular pain syndrome, the complex nature of pain as conceptualized within the biopsychosocial model, and the role of medications for pain management. Education also can be provided regarding CBT, including conceptual models as they apply to chronic pain and support for the efficacy of the treatments. Psychoeducation may be provided to patients and caregivers (such as spouses).

Manualized CBT-CP Programs

This chapter has provided an overview of specific behavioral and cognitive skills/strategies often employed in CBT for chronic pain. As previously indicated, these individual elements (as well as others) are frequently combined to create a CBT-CP program for providers and patients to follow. These programs often are manualized and offered in a time-limited fashion. Examples of such programs include

Murphy and colleagues' CBT program for chronic pain, developed initially for a veteran population (Murphy et al., 2014); and John Otis's manual, which also presents a CBT approach for management of chronic pain (2007). Both of these programs/manuals include more detailed accounts regarding how to deliver the techniques described above and also offer resources (e.g., worksheets) to help patients engage in these therapeutic processes.

For Whom Does CBT Work? Treatment Moderators

Although the evidence shows that CBT is effective for the management of chronic pain, it is important to examine whether there are certain patients for whom it might be more or less effective. Treatment moderators are the variables that modulate the effectiveness of an intervention on the target issue. Understanding what patient-based (e.g., sex, ethnicity, age) and/or intervention delivery characteristics (e.g., group versus individual delivery) moderate the efficacy and effectiveness of an intervention can enable a clinician to better match a patient with a specific intervention or tailor it to the setting in which it is being delivered. For example, in an RCT comparing standard treatment (ST) to standard treatment with CBT (ST + CBT) for patients with temporomandibular dysfunction-related pain (TMD), investigators found somatization, self-efficacy, and readiness for treatment to be significant moderators of treatment outcomes (Litt, Shafer, & Kreutzer, 2010). Specifically, those with higher readiness for change and higher self-efficacy showed greater benefit from treatment in the ST + CBT group when compared to those in the ST alone group. Additionally, patients with low somatization showed the most gain in the ST + CBT group.

Another CBT trial for the same pain condition (TMD) showed that patients who reported more pain sites, depressive symptoms, nonspecific physical symptoms, rumination, catastrophizing, and stress prior to treatment demonstrated more activity interference one year following treatment (Turner, Holtzman, & Mancl, 2007). Based on these findings, it was recommended that chronic pain patients also presenting with mental health symptoms, such as depression, may require more intensive CBT treatment or treatment specifically focused on the mental health symptoms either prior to or in conjunction with chronic pain treatment (Turner et al., 2007).

In a study of a CBT coping skills intervention for hip and knee osteoarthritis, treatment response was moderated by pain-coping style, patient expectations for treatment response, disease severity, age, and education (Broderick et al., 2016). Specifically, participants with high expectations, moderate to high osteoarthritis disease severity, older age, and more education benefited the most from the treatment. These findings highlight the fact that not every patient may experience the same level of improvement or benefit from CBT interventions. More research on patient moderators is needed in order to better understand which groups may benefit from which specific interventions.

Why Does CBT Work? Treatment Mediators

Evidence supports the efficacy of CBT to improve chronic pain management through various targeted outcomes. Based on the biopsychosocial model of chronic pain, common targets for CBT interventions include pain severity, pain cognitions, quality of life, depression, and/or diagnosis-specific physical functioning/disability. As discussed previously, CBT is a treatment approach that can include a multitude of different intervention strategies, both behavioral (e.g., activity planning) and cognitive (e.g., cognitive restructuring). Pinpointing the treatment mechanisms, or mediators, of CBT on any of the above-mentioned patient-reported outcomes is important for optimizing both the efficacy and the effectiveness of the treatment.

A wide range of potential mediators has been statistically investigated in RCTs for various chronic pain conditions. One study, comparing CBT to an attention control for TMD, investigated self-efficacy, pain beliefs, pain catastrophizing, and coping as potential mediators (Turner et al., 2007). When all mediators were analyzed as a group, self-efficacy was found to be a significant mediator for both one-year activity interference and jaw-use limitations. In a study investigating the use of CBT for lower back pain, catastrophizing was found to significantly mediate the effect of the intervention on depression levels and pain behaviors (Spinhoven et al., 2004). Pain-related acceptance also has been shown to be a significant mediator of "third-wave" CBT treatments that focus on acceptance and mindfulness as therapeutic constructs (Åkerblom, Perrin, Fischer, & McCracken, 2015).

CBT in Interdisciplinary Treatment Programs

Interdisciplinary treatment programs for chronic pain involve a concerted effort at coordination and communication among healthcare professionals from different specialties (Gatchel, McGeary, McGeary, & Lippe, 2014). These types of programs, which are built around a common goal of patient rehabilitation, strongly reflect the biopsychosocial model of pain discussed above. Table 4.1 explicates the overlapping goals of the biopsychosocial model and interdisciplinary treatment programs for chronic pain.

Interdisciplinary treatment programs often include medical staff (e.g., physicians, nurses) as well as occupational and physical therapists and mental health staff (e.g., psychologists) (Turk, Okifuji, Sinclair, & Starz, 1998). A focus of the medical team is optimization of medications, which often means tapering off opioid medications and encouraging proactive behaviors that directly impact health and pain (e.g., weight management, substance abuse treatment, appropriate exercise). A focus of the physical therapy team is to optimize function and pacing of activities. Pain psychologists offer CBT as a key component of these types of treatment programs, addressing the maladaptive cognitions, behaviors, and emotions often associated with the patient's pain condition (Gatchel et al., 2014). In these programs, the CBT element not only improves skills around coping with the affective

Table 4.1 Mutual Goals of the Biopsychosocial Model and Interdisciplinary Treatment Programs

Biological/Physical Goals	Psychological Goals	Social Goals
Reduction of pain	Reduction of negative emotion reactivity	Return to productivity
Improved physical functioning/decreased disability	Improved coping and self-management	Decreased reliance on medical system
Optimization of medications	Acceptance of pain and physical limitations	Improved interpersonal relationships (e.g., family, friends)
Improved sleep quality	Commitment to identified behavioral goals	

issues that stem from a chronic pain condition but also helps motivate the patient to engage in self-management behaviors that may be taught through occupational or physical therapy and safe medication practices that are stressed through patients' medical management.

Aspects of acceptance and commitment therapy, a newer CBT that joins constructs such as acceptance and mindfulness to traditional CBT practices, are beginning to be incorporated into interdisciplinary treatment programs (McCracken & Gutiérrez-Martínez, 2011). Acceptance of living with a chronic pain condition and commitment to values-driven life goals are relevant to the motivation required to engage in proactive and healthful self-management strategies. In this way, the various aspects of interdisciplinary treatment programs are complementary and synergistic.

Interdisciplinary treatment programs have demonstrated reductions in pain equivalent to other medical treatments (e.g., spinal cord simulators, implantable drug delivery systems) (Turk, 2002). Greater effectiveness of interdisciplinary treatment programs has been demonstrated for reduction in medication use, reduction in healthcare utilization, improved functional status, rates of return to work, and rates of closure of disability claims. Finally, interdisciplinary treatment programs are more cost-effective than implantation of spinal cord stimulators, conservative care, and surgery.

Internet-Delivered Cognitive-Behavioral Therapy (iCBT) for Pain

Rationale for iCBT

Internet-delivered cognitive-behavioral therapy (iCBT) for pain is appealing due to its propensity to increase access to effective psychological treatment for pain.

59

It removes commonly cited barriers to treatment, including difficulty accessing qualified mental health professionals and time and cost expenditures (by both clinics and patients) (Buhrman et al., 2013, 2015; Cuijpers, Van Straten, & Andersson, 2008; Dear et al., 2013, 2015; Eccleston et al., 2012; Ehde et al., 2014; Heapy et al., 2015; Lalloo, Jibb, Rivera, Agarwal, & Stinson, 2015; Marks, Cavanagh, & Gega, 2007; Rini, Williams, Broderick, & Keefe, 2012). Access to iCBT may reduce the stigma associated with seeking psychological treatment. It may be especially attractive to patients with pain due to its flexibility; iCBT enables a patient to complete treatment at his/her own pace and at the time and place of his/her choosing (Buhrman et al., 2013; Cuijpers et al., 2008; Dear et al., 2015; Ehde et al., 2014; Heapy et al., 2015; Lalloo et al., 2015; Rini et al., 2012).

This approach also enables patients to access materials in times of need, including after conclusion of treatment (Ehde et al., 2014; Heapy et al., 2015; Lalloo et al., 2015; Rini et al., 2012). Cognitive-behavioral therapy (CBT) is an established treatment for pain, the concepts and structure (e.g., psychoeducation, exercises, homework) of which easily convert to text-based webpages, a format that better ensures treatment fidelity (Heapy et al., 2015; Ritterband, Andersson, Christensen, Carlbring, & Cuijpers, 2006).

ICBT may be offered in several formats (Rini et al., 2012). First, therapists can offer instruction, assist with problem-solving, and provide encouragement and feedback via iCBT. These therapists can maximize their time and reach, while reducing overhead costs. One research group reported that an eight-week iCBT with therapist involvement resulted in 68–82 minutes spent per patient, and as few as 13 minutes when contact was made optional for patients (Dear et al., 2013, 2015). Second, iCBT can be offered in the absence of a therapist, with all contact automated. The ubiquity of cell phone use is a key benefit of the third format, wherein mobile applications (apps) introduce users to a limited menu of self-management tools. A benefit shared among internet-delivered treatments is the ease and consistency with which progress can be monitored and presented to the participant (Heapy et al., 2015; Marks et al., 2007).

Research Support for iCBT

Several recent studies from two research groups offer a depiction of current research questions and methods in the field of iCBT. Buhrman et al. (2013) described an eight-week iCBT intervention with electronic therapist feedback offered to patients who reported residual problems after having completed a multidisciplinary pain program. Relative to a facilitated discussion group, iCBT demonstrated a moderate effect on the primary outcome of pain catastrophizing. This effect persisted at six-month follow-up. Improvements in secondary outcomes included anxiety and depression (small effects that persisted), and thoughts, attitudes, and opinions about pain (moderate to large effects that persisted). There were no between-group effects on psychosocial and behavioral consequences of chronic pain, life satisfaction, or acceptance in relationship to chronic pain.

Buhrman et al. (2015) also conducted a study of a tailored six-module iCBT for anxiety and depression in patients with chronic pain. Relative to an online discussion forum, iCBT demonstrated a moderate effect on depressive symptoms and small effects on anxiety and pain disability, all of which were maintained at one-year follow-up. Improvements in secondary outcomes included large effects on catastrophizing and coping strategies and a small effect on activity engagement, all of which were maintained at follow-up. There was no effect on anxiety sensitivity, consequences of pain, or life satisfaction.

Dear et al. (2013) tested an RCT of clinician-guided iCBT for chronic pain to reduce disability, depression, and anxiety. The Pain Course was comprised of five online lessons, summaries, and homework assignments in conjunction with nine written resources pertaining to a diversity of topics, including sleep hygiene and core beliefs. Contact with patients was via both automated and personalized e-mails, as well as weekly 10–15-minute telephone calls with a clinical psychologist. Relative to a waitlist control group, the intervention group demonstrated a large effect on disability and a moderate effect on depression, both of which were maintained at three-month follow-up. There was no effect of the intervention on anxiety. Improvements in secondary outcomes included a large effect on pain self-efficacy and moderate effects on fears of movement and re-injury, catastrophizing, and average pain, all of which were maintained at three-month follow-up.

Dear et al. (2015) replicated their study of the Pain Course with a new objective: test regular (weekly 10–15-minute telephone or e-mail contact), optional, and no contact from a therapist. Relative to a waitlist control group, the treatments demonstrated a large effect on depression, moderate effects on anxiety and disability, and a small-to-moderate effect on average pain level, with no differences among the treatment groups. There was greater improvement in average pain in the treatment groups, with no difference among the treatment groups at either post-treatment or follow-up. Regular therapist contact was associated with minor increases in depression and anxiety at three-month follow-up, whereas optional therapist contact was associated with a minor reduction in anxiety at three-month follow-up. All treatment groups extended reductions in disability during the follow-up period.

Improvements in secondary outcomes included pain self-efficacy and fear of movement, with the only difference among the treatment groups being somewhat lower pain self-efficacy in patients with no therapist contact compared to patients with regular contact. There was no global effect on pain acceptance, with regular contact only superior to the control group. Patients with regular contact reported improvement across all secondary outcomes at follow-up relative to the control group.

Several meta-analyses and systematic reviews have surveyed RCTs of iCBT for pain and reported on its effectiveness. A recent meta-analysis (Eccleston et al., 2012) of the effect of internet-delivered psychotherapy emphasizing cognitive skill building (e.g., problem-solving skills training) and applied components (e.g., relaxation training) on pain, disability, depression, and anxiety produced improvement at post-treatment in all areas for participants with non-headache pain, including persistent improvement in disability at follow-up (ranging from 3 to 12 months). Improvements in participants with headache pain were limited to pain and disability at post-treatment only. Improved pain resulting from iCBT is consistent with earlier meta-analyses demonstrating this effect in participants with back, headache, non-headache, and osteoarthritic pain (Cuijpers et al., 2008).

A systematic review of randomized controlled trials of internet-delivered psychological treatment for pain conditions, including chronic headache, low back pain, and chronic musculoskeletal pain, demonstrated improvements in pain, activity limitations, and costs associated with iCBT; however, improvements in depression and anxiety were inconsistent (Bender, Radhakrishnan, Diorio, Englesakis, & Jadad, 2011). In a systematic review of 19 internet-delivered chronic pain self-management techniques, more than half demonstrated, at minimum, small effects in pain intensity, and more than two-thirds demonstrated, at minimum, small effects on physical functioning and/or pain interference (Heapy et al., 2015).

Inconsistent results in meta-analytic studies and systematic reviews to date highlight the subtle differences among iCBTs pertaining to module content, treatment protocol, and comparison group (Fox, 2008). The timing of follow-up is important, too, as one meta-analytic study demonstrated greater improvement at long-term than short-term follow-up in secondary outcomes like work capability (Macea, Gajos, Calil, & Fregni, 2010).

Contributors to Early Termination of iCBT

Participants who terminated treatment early cite reasons that include health-related concerns, limited ease or comfort using a computer, personal problems, length and novelty of program content, and lack of time (Buhrman et al., 2013; Eccleston et al., 2012; Heapy et al., 2015). Participants who reported longer-lasting pain and less intense pain, were younger, reported health distress and activity limitations, and who identified as male were more likely to terminate treatment early (Macea et al., 2010). Attrition has been shown to be less evident in iCBT offering web-based live sessions with therapists (Cuijpers et al., 2008). In general, internet-delivered self-management programs for chronic pain demonstrate greater participant engagement than telephone interventions, but this may be due to the ease and consistency with which online assessment measures can be administered and interpreted (Heapy et al., 2015). Although treatment completion is an important marker, a related question is whether patients who complete treatment sustain skill use and maintain gains from treatment (Heapy et al., 2015).

Other Technology-Facilitated CBT for Pain

Although the focus of this section is iCBT, it is important to note that technology may facilitate delivery of CBT over the telephone (McBeth et al., 2012), with the use of interactive voice response (IVR) technology (Lieberman & Naylor, 2012), and via videoconferencing (Gardner-Nix, Backman, Barbati, & Grummitt, 2008). These uses of technology have their own challenges with regard to providing treatment across state lines (Ehde et al., 2014).

Cognitive-behavioral therapy delivered exclusively or in part over the telephone has demonstrated improvement in at least one pain variable (e.g., pain intensity, physical functioning) relative to a control group in nearly half of studies surveyed in a recent review (Heapy et al., 2015). Interactive voice response technology was an effective means of maintaining, and in some cases extending, gains in pain intensity and physical and emotional functioning following completion of an 11-week in-person group CBT by prompting patient report of pain intensity and skill use and by providing pre-recorded skill review and therapist feedback based on patient assessment (Naylor, Helzer, Naud, & Keefe, 2002; Naylor, Keefe, Brigidi, Naud, & Helzer, 2008; Naylor, Naud, Keefe, & Helzer, 2010).

Mobile apps provide easy access to services that otherwise might be cost- or distance-prohibitive (Lalloo et al., 2015). Mobile apps may be highly appealing to younger patients, for whom time spent on smartphones exceeds time spent on most other daily activities (de la Vega & Miró, 2014). At present, it is hard to deduce user perception of pain apps; despite mean ratings exceeding 3/5, 44% of pain apps are unrated (Lalloo et al., 2015). Content currently offered within pain apps, in order of frequency, includes self-care skills (e.g., muscle stretching), education and self-monitoring, assistance with engagement in social support (e.g., via social media), and goal setting (Lalloo et al., 2015). The majority of pain apps offer one (58.5%) or two (38%) self-management functionalities; three or more functionalities are offered by only 3% of available apps (Lalloo et al., 2015).

The availability of empirically supported apps for pain is scarce. One study reported that none of the 34 apps reported in research articles are available commercially; in other words, none of the 283 pain apps available at the time of publication has research support (de la Vega & Miró, 2014). In fact, nearly 92% of pain apps were developed in the absence of guidance from a healthcare professional, and none identified a theoretical or clinical basis (Lalloo et al., 2015). Potential benefits of mobile apps include patient empowerment to manage his/ her condition (Lalloo et al., 2015) and integration of date-stamped assessments that may be shared with a healthcare provider. However, many issues (including confidentiality) need to be addressed before mobile applications can be a viable form of psychological treatment.

Future Directions for iCBT

In time, the number of clinical trials available for meta-analysis will increase and strengthen confidence in conclusions drawn (Eccleston et al., 2012); standardization of assessment and reporting practices will facilitate synthesis of meta-analytic results (Bender et al., 2011; Heapy et al., 2015); and dismantling studies will reveal necessary components of iCBT (Dear et al., 2015; Heapy et al., 2015; Rini et al., 2012). Current research on internet-delivered self-management for chronic pain reveals women are overrepresented, which may be due to the propensity of women to seek treatment relative to men or may represent a need to design self-management programs that appeal to men (Buhrman et al., 2015; Heapy et al., 2015). White patients also are overrepresented in these types of programs, which is troubling on a number of fronts (e.g., relative to White patients, African American patients report more intense pain, disability from pain, and physical and emotional functioning impairment) (Heapy et al., 2015).

Waitlist control has been the most common comparison group in RCTs of iCBT for pain (Eccleston et al., 2012). Future research would do well to study its effectiveness relative to established psychological treatments for pain, including in-person CBT (Buhrman et al., 2015; Cuijpers et al., 2008; Ehde et al., 2014; Macea et al., 2010). Directly comparing internet-delivered to in-person CBT, understanding mechanisms of change in the two delivery formats, and discerning which patients may prefer and benefit from each format will be important tasks. Cost savings analyses and analyses designed to detect improvements in barriers to care will reveal whether there exist trade-offs of one or the other treatments (Bender et al., 2011; Buhrman et al., 2013; Buhrman et al., 2015; Dear et al., 2013, 2015; Heapy et al., 2015; Rini et al., 2012). Direct comparisons among technology-facilitated CBT for pain also would be useful, as there is a noticeable absence of these types of comparisons in the technology-facilitated self-management literature (Heapy et al., 2015).

Some evidence suggests that patients find internet-delivered chronic pain self-management programs to be useful, helpful, and easy to use (Heapy et al., 2015). Broadening the scope of research from pain-related and psychological variables to satisfaction with and acceptability of iCBT for pain (as research group Dear et al., 2013, 2015 have done) is important, as is understanding the effect of myriad personal characteristics on the usefulness of this modality and subsequently tailoring treatment to the patient's individual needs (Eccleston et al., 2012; Heapy et al., 2015; Rini et al., 2012). Beyond the attention that has been given to the importance of cost savings analyses, attention to use of healthcare services, medication, and other objective outcomes would be beneficial (Heapy et al., 2015). Conceptualization of iCBT, whether as an alternative or an adjunct to in-person CBT, and determining how iCBT is best conceptualized within a stepped-care model, remains to be explored (Cuijpers et al., 2008; Eccleston et al., 2012; Heapy et al., 2015).

Discerning the role of the therapist (e.g., as a support person available via e-mail or telephone, provider of web-based live sessions, or other), if any, is an important task (Cuijpers et al., 2008; Dear et al., 2013; Ehde et al., 2014; Heapy et al., 2015). It has been suggested that the absence of consistent contact with a therapist in iCBT may introduce challenges related to providing feedback to patients, sustaining the motivation of patients for treatment, and personalizing treatment (Macea et al., 2010). Additionally, absent a therapist, patients will not have the opportunity to seek clarification on concepts and may not complete all suggested homework (Marks et al., 2007). One particularly exciting future development is the integration of iCBT and medical platforms accessible by medical providers, who may be able to use an integrated system to monitor patient symptoms (Rini et al., 2012).

Summary

Cognitive-behavioral therapies can be a key component of any treatment plan for chronic pain. When evaluated on their own, CBTs have been found to be efficacious and effective for numerous pain-related outcomes (Williams et al., 2012). They also often comprise an important element of interdisciplinary pain programs, working in concert with other pain management modalities (Gatchel et al., 2014). A treatment plan incorporating CBT may include any number of cognitive or behavioral strategies or interventions, as CBTs can be somewhat heterogeneous. However, common components include activity planning, cognitive restructuring, and relaxation skills. These components should be related to the mechanisms or mediators that are known to affect the targeted outcome of the intervention, whether it is pain severity or physical functioning.

Patient-level characteristics such as demographic variables, or even differences in intervention delivery modality, may moderate the efficacy of the intervention. Knowing what CBT interventions work best for differing chronic pain conditions and patient populations is important in personalizing and tailoring treatments to optimize their impact. The internet, smartphones, and other technological advances are broadening the reach and impact of CBTs for chronic pain management. These platforms enable patients to access treatment in ways that can be convenient and cost-efficient. Understanding the differential impact of in-person as opposed to technology-mediated CBT interventions will be important in advancing the dissemination of CBTs in the future.

References

Åkerblom, S., Perrin, S., Fischer, M. R., & McCracken, L. M. (2015). The mediating role of acceptance in multidisciplinary cognitive-behavioral therapy for chronic pain. *The Journal of Pain, 16*(7), 606–615.

American Society of Anesthesiologists Task Force on Chronic Pain Management. (2010). Practice guidelines for chronic pain management: An updated report by the American Society of Anesthesiologists Task Force on Chronic Pain Management and the American Society of Regional Anesthesia and Pain Medicine. *Anesthesiology, 112*(4), 810.

Andrews, N. E., Strong, J., & Meredith, P. J. (2012). Activity pacing, avoidance, endurance, and associations with patient functioning in chronic pain: A systematic review and meta-analysis. *Archives of Physical Medicine and Rehabilitation, 93*(11), 2109–2121.

Baird, C. L., & Sands, L. (2004). A pilot study of the effectiveness of guided imagery with progressive muscle relaxation to reduce chronic pain and mobility difficulties of osteoarthritis. *Pain Management Nursing, 5*(3), 97–104.

Bender, J. L., Radhakrishnan, A., Diorio, C., Englesakis, M., & Jadad, A. R. (2011). Can pain be managed through the Internet? A systematic review of randomized controlled trials. *PAIN, 152*(8), 1740–1750.

Bernardy, K., Füber, N., Köllner, V., & Häuser, W. (2010). Efficacy of cognitive-behavioral therapies in fibromyalgia syndrome-a systematic review and metaanalysis of randomized controlled trials. *The Journal of Rheumatology, 37*(10), 1991-2005.

Broderick, J. E., Keefe, F. J., Schneider, S., Junghaenel, D. U., Bruckenthal, P., Schwartz, J. E., . . . Gould, E. (2016). Cognitive behavioral therapy for chronic pain is effective, but for whom? *Pain, 157*(9), 2115–2123.

Buhrman, M., Fredriksson, A., Edström, G., Shafiei, D., Tärnqvist, C., Ljótsson, B., . . . Andersson, G. (2013). Guided Internet-delivered cognitive behavioural therapy for chronic pain patients who have residual symptoms after rehabilitation treatment: Randomized controlled trial. *European Journal of Pain, 17*(5), 753–765.

Buhrman, M., Syk, M., Burvall, O., Hartig, T., Gordh, T., & Andersson, G. (2015). Individualized guided Internet-delivered cognitive-behavior therapy for chronic pain patients with comorbid depression and anxiety: A randomized controlled trial. *The Clinical Journal of Pain, 31*(6), 504–516.

Busch, V., Magerl, W., Kern, U., Haas, J., Hajak, G., & Eichhammer, P. (2012). The effect of deep and slow breathing on pain perception, autonomic activity, and mood processing—an experimental study. *Pain Medicine, 13*(2), 215–228.

Carpenter, K. M., Stoner, S. A., Mundt, J. M., & Stoelb, B. (2012). An online self-help CBT intervention for chronic lower back pain. *The Clinical Journal of Pain, 28*(1), 14.

Chalaye, P., Goffaux, P., Lafrenaye, S., & Marchand, S. (2009). Respiratory effects on experimental heat pain and cardiac activity. *Pain Medicine, 10*(8), 1334–1340.

Chou, R., Loeser, J. D., Owens, D. K., Rosenquist, R. W., Atlas, S. J., Baisden, J., . . . Resnick, D. K. (2009). Interventional therapies, surgery, and interdisciplinary rehabilitation for low back pain: An evidence-based clinical practice guideline from the American Pain Society. *Spine, 34*(10), 1066–1077.

Cuijpers, P., Van Straten, A., & Andersson, G. (2008). Internet-administered cognitive behavior therapy for health problems: A systematic review. *Journal of Behavioral Medicine, 31*(2), 169–177.

de la Vega, R., & Miró, J. (2014). mHealth: A strategic field without a solid scientific soul: A systematic review of pain-related apps. *PLoS One, 9*(7), e101312.

Dear, B. F., Gandy, M., Karin, E., Staples, L. G., Johnston, L., Fogliati, V. J., . . . Perry, K. N. (2015). The Pain Course: A randomised controlled trial examining an internet-delivered pain management program when provided with different levels of clinician support. *Pain, 156*(10), 1920.

Dear, B. F., Titov, N., Perry, K. N., Johnston, L., Wootton, B. M., Terides, M. D., . . . Hudson, J. L. (2013). The Pain Course: A randomised controlled trial of a clinician-guided Internet-delivered cognitive behaviour therapy program for managing chronic pain and emotional well-being. *PAIN, 154*(6), 942–950.

Dueñas, M., Ojeda, B., Salazar, A., Mico, J. A., & Failde, I. (2016). A review of chronic pain impact on patients, their social environment and the health care system. *Journal of Pain Research, 9*, 457.

Eccleston, C., Fisher, E., Craig, L., Duggan, G. B., Rosser, B. A., & Keogh, E. (2012). Psychological therapies (Internet-delivered) for the management of chronic pain in adults. *Cochrane Database of Systematic Reviews, 2*.

Ehde, D. M., Dillworth, T. M., & Turner, J. A. (2014). Cognitive-behavioral therapy for individuals with chronic pain: Efficacy, innovations, and directions for research. *American Psychologist, 69*(2), 153.

Ehde, D. M., & Jensen, M. P. (2004). Feasibility of a cognitive restructuring intervention for treatment of chronic pain in persons with disabilities. *Rehabilitation Psychology, 49*(3), 254.

Fillingim, R. B., Bruehl, S., Dworkin, R. H., Dworkin, S. F., Loeser, J. D., Turk, D. C., . . . Edwards, R. R. (2014). The ACTTION-American Pain Society Pain Taxonomy

(AAPT): An evidence-based and multidimensional approach to classifying chronic pain conditions. *The Journal of Pain, 15*(3), 241–249.

Fordyce, W. (1977). *Behavioral methods for chronic pain and illness*. St. Louis: Mosby.

Fors, E. A., Sexton, H., & Götestam, K. G. (2002). The effect of guided imagery and amitriptyline on daily fibromyalgia pain: A prospective, randomized, controlled trial. *Journal of Psychiatric Research, 36*(3), 179–187.

Fox, S. (2008). *The engaged E-patient population*. Washington, DC: Pew Internet and American Life Project.

Gardner-Nix, J., Backman, S., Barbati, J., & Grummitt, J. (2008). Evaluating distance education of a mindfulness-based meditation programme for chronic pain management. *Journal of Telemedicine and Telecare, 14*(2), 88–92.

Gaskin, D. J., & Richard, P. (2012). The economic costs of pain in the United States. *The Journal of Pain, 13*(8), 715–724.

Gatchel, R. J., McGeary, D. D., McGeary, C. A., & Lippe, B. (2014). Interdisciplinary chronic pain management: Past, present, and future. *American Psychologist, 69*(2), 119.

Gatchel, R. J., Peng, Y. B., Peters, M. L., Fuchs, P. N., & Turk, D. C. (2007). The biopsychosocial approach to chronic pain: Scientific advances and future directions. *Psychological Bulletin, 133*(4), 581.

Gill, J. R., & Brown, C. A. (2009). A structured review of the evidence for pacing as a chronic pain intervention. *European Journal of Pain, 13*(2), 214–216.

Heapy, A. A., Higgins, D. M., Cervone, D., Wandner, L., Fenton, B. T., & Kerns, R. D. (2015). A systematic review of technology-assisted self-management interventions for chronic pain. *The Clinical Journal of Pain, 31*(6), 470–492.

Hochberg, M. C., Altman, R. D., April, K. T., Benkhalti, M., Guyatt, G., McGowan, J., . . . Tugwell, P. (2012). American College of Rheumatology 2012 recommendations for the use of nonpharmacologic and pharmacologic therapies in osteoarthritis of the hand, hip, and knee. *Arthritis Care & Research, 64*(4), 465–474.

Hoffman, B. M., Papas, R. K., Chatkoff, D. K., & Kerns, R. D. (2007). Meta-analysis of psychological interventions for chronic low back pain. *Health Psychology, 26*(1), 1–9.

Hofmann, S. G., Asnaani, A., Vonk, I. J., Sawyer, A. T., & Fang, A. (2012). The efficacy of cognitive behavioral therapy: A review of meta-analyses. *Cognitive Therapy and Research, 36*(5), 427–440.

Kennedy, J., Roll, J. M., Schraudner, T., Murphy, S., & McPherson, S. (2014). Prevalence of persistent pain in the US adult population: New data from the 2010 national health interview survey. *The Journal of Pain, 15*(10), 979–984.

Lalloo, C., Jibb, L. A., Rivera, J., Agarwal, A., & Stinson, J. N. (2015). "There's a pain app for that": Review of patient-targeted smartphone applications for pain management. *The Clinical Journal of Pain, 31*(6), 557–563.

Lieberman, G., & Naylor, M. R. (2012). Interactive voice response technology for symptom monitoring and as an adjunct to the treatment of chronic pain. *Translational Behavioral Medicine, 2*(1), 93–101.

Litt, M. D., Shafer, D. M., & Kreutzer, D. L. (2010). Brief cognitive-behavioral treatment for TMD pain: Long-term outcomes and moderators of treatment. *Pain, 151*(1), 110–116.

Macea, D. D., Gajos, K., Calil, Y. A. D., & Fregni, F. (2010). The efficacy of Web-based cognitive behavioral interventions for chronic pain: A systematic review and meta-analysis. *The Journal of Pain, 11*(10), 917–929.

Marks, I. M., Cavanagh, K., & Gega, L. (2007). *Hands-on help: Computer-aided psychotherapy*. London: Psychology Press.

McBeth, J., Prescott, G., Scotland, G., Lovell, K., Keeley, P., Hannaford, P., . . . Gkazinou, C. (2012). Cognitive behavior therapy, exercise, or both for treating chronic widespread pain. *Archives of Internal Medicine, 172*(1), 48–57.

McCallie, M. S., Blum, C. M., & Hood, C. J. (2006). Progressive muscle relaxation. *Journal of Human Behavior in the Social Environment, 13*(3), 51–66.

McCracken, L. M., & Gutiérrez-Martínez, O. (2011). Processes of change in psychological flexibility in an interdisciplinary group-based treatment for chronic pain based on Acceptance and Commitment Therapy. *Behaviour Research and Therapy, 49*(4), 267–274.

McMain, S., Newman, M. G., Segal, Z. V., & DeRubeis, R. J. (2015). Cognitive behavioral therapy: Current status and future research directions. *Psychotherapy Research, 25*(3), 321–329.

Menzies, V., Taylor, A. G., & Bourguignon, C. (2006). Effects of guided imagery on outcomes of pain, functional status, and self-efficacy in persons diagnosed with fibromyalgia. *Journal of Alternative & Complementary Medicine, 12*(1), 23–30.

Murphy, J. L., McKellar, J. D., Raffa, S. D., Clark, M. E., Kerns, R. D., & Karlin, B. E. (2014). *Cognitive behavioral therapy for chronic pain among veterans: Therapist manual.* Washington, DC: U.S. Department of Veterans Affairs.

Nahin, R. L. (2015). Estimates of pain prevalence and severity in adults: United States, 2012. *The Journal of Pain, 16*(8), 769–780.

Naylor, M. R., Helzer, J. E., Naud, S., & Keefe, F. J. (2002). Automated telephone as an adjunct for the treatment of chronic pain: A pilot study. *The Journal of Pain, 3*(6), 429–438.

Naylor, M. R., Keefe, F. J., Brigidi, B., Naud, S., & Helzer, J. E. (2008). Therapeutic interactive voice response for chronic pain reduction and relapse prevention. *Pain, 134*(3), 335–345.

Naylor, M. R., Naud, S., Keefe, F. J., & Helzer, J. E. (2010). Therapeutic Interactive Voice Response (TIVR) to reduce analgesic medication use for chronic pain management. *The Journal of Pain, 11*(12), 1410–1419.

Nielson, W. R., Jensen, M. P., Karsdorp, P. A., & Vlaeyen, J. W. (2013). Activity pacing in chronic pain: Concepts, evidence, and future directions. *The Clinical Journal of Pain, 29*(5), 461–468.

Novy, D. M., & Aigner, C. J. (2014). The biopsychosocial model in cancer pain. *Current Opinion in Supportive and Palliative Care, 8*(2), 117–123.

Otis, J. (2007). *Managing chronic pain: A cognitive-behavioral therapy approach.* Oxford: Oxford University Press.

Quartana, P. J., Campbell, C. M., & Edwards, R. R. (2009). Pain catastrophizing: A critical review. *Expert Review of Neurotherapeutics, 9*(5), 745–758.

Rini, C., Williams, D. A., Broderick, J. E., & Keefe, F. J. (2012). Meeting them where they are: Using the Internet to deliver behavioral medicine interventions for pain. *Translational Behavioral Medicine, 2*(1), 82–92.

Ritterband, L. M., Andersson, G., Christensen, H. M., Carlbring, P., & Cuijpers, P. (2006). Directions for the International Society for Research on Internet Interventions (ISRII). *Journal of Medical Internet Research, 8*(3).

Spenkelink, C., Hutten, M. M., Hermens, H., & Greitemann, B. O. (2002). Assessment of activities of daily living with an ambulatory monitoring system: A comparative study in patients with chronic low back pain and nonsymptomatic controls. *Clinical Rehabilitation, 16*(1), 16–26.

Spinhoven, P., Kuile, M., Kole-Snijders, A. M., Mansfeld, M. H., Ouden, D. J., & Vlaeyen, J. W. (2004). Catastrophizing and internal pain control as mediators of outcome in the multidisciplinary treatment of chronic low back pain. *European Journal of Pain, 8*(3), 211–219.

Treede, R-D., Rief, W., Barke, A., Aziz, Q., Bennett, M. I., Benoliel, R., . . . First, M. B. (2015). A classification of chronic pain for ICD-11. *Pain, 156*(6), 1003.

Turk, D. C. (2002). Clinical effectiveness and cost-effectiveness of treatments for patients with chronic pain. *The Clinical Journal of Pain, 18*(6), 355–365.

Turk, D. C., Meichenbaum, D., & Genest, M. (1983). *Pain and behavioral medicine: A cognitive-behavioral perspective* (Vol. 1). New York, NY: The Guilford Press.

Turk, D. C., Okifuji, A., Sinclair, J. D., & Starz, T. W. (1998). Interdisciplinary treatment for fibromyalgia syndrome: Clinical and statistical significance. *Arthritis & Rheumatology*, *11*(3), 186–195.

Turner, J. A., Holtzman, S., & Mancl, L. (2007). Mediators, moderators, and predictors of therapeutic change in cognitive—behavioral therapy for chronic pain. *Pain*, *127*(3), 276–286.

West, C., Usher, K., Foster, K., & Stewart, L. (2012). Chronic pain and the family: The experience of the partners of people living with chronic pain. *Journal of Clinical Nursing*, *21*(23–24), 3352–3360.

Williams, A. C., Eccleston, C., & Morley, S. (2012). Psychological therapies for the management of chronic pain (excluding headache) in adults. *The Cochrane Library*, *11*, #CD007407.

5

Mindfulness-Based Interventions for Chronic Pain

Darcy E. Burgers and Emily F. Muther

Background

Chronic pain is a common health concern, impacting approximately 20% of the world's adult population (Goldberg & McGee, 2011). Research examining the prevalence of chronic pain in children and adolescents has yielded variable findings, with prevalence rates ranging from 4% to 88% depending on pain location, gender, and age of youth studied (King et al., 2011). The experience of chronic pain can impact psychological functioning, increasing risk for anxiety, depression, and overall emotional distress compared to healthy peers (Burke, Mathias, & Denson, 2015). Additionally, chronic pain has been associated with negative sequelae across a variety of domains, including school and work impairment (Logan, Simons, Stein, & Chastain, 2008; Stewart, Ricci, Chee, Morganstein, & Lipton, 2003), as well as reduced engagement in physical (McBeth, Nicholl, Cordingley, Davis, & Macfarlane, 2010) and social (Forgeron et al., 2010) activities.

Over the past several decades, the biopsychosocial theory has become widely accepted as an effective framework for understanding and treating chronic pain (Gatchel, Peng, Peters, Fuchs, & Turk, 2007). This multidimensional model builds upon Melzack and Wall's (1965) earlier "gate control theory of pain," which posited that nerve impulses ascending up the spinal cord are modulated by "gates" that can be influenced by psychological factors, including emotions, past experiences, and attention. More recently, gate control theory has evolved into the "neuromatrix theory of pain," which considers pain to be "a multidimensional experience produced by characteristic 'neurosignature' patterns of nerve impulses" that are comprised of sensory, affective, and cognitive inputs (Melzack, 2005, p. 85). Though theoretical understandings of pain continue to evolve, the notion that psychological factors can impact the pain experience remains consistent and therefore may serve as potential entry points for intervention.

Introduction to Mindfulness

One such category of interventions that may impact the experience of pain is mindfulness. Jon Kabat-Zinn, a pioneer of the application of mindfulness practices and principles in secular therapeutic interventions and the founder of mindfulness-based stress reduction (MBSR), defines mindfulness as "the awareness that emerges through paying attention on purpose, in the present moment, and nonjudgmentally to the unfolding of experience moment by moment" (2003, p. 145). This definition captures the key facets commonly understood as core to mindfulness practice, including being aware of the present moment, and observing and accepting, in a nonjudgmental manner, whatever perceptions, emotions, cognitions, or sensations may be brought into awareness (Baer, 2003; Marlatt & Kristeller, 1999).

Over the last 40 years, the practice of mindfulness increasingly has become present in Western culture, though its roots are in Buddhist traditions (Kabat-Zinn, 2003). Mindfulness-based interventions can be traced back to ancient Vipassana, Buddhist and Zen mindfulness practices (Schidt, 2004). Mindfulness is considered to be the "heart" of meditation practice within various branches of Buddhism (Kabat-Zinn, 2013). Within Buddhism, mindfulness is thought to develop insight; clear comprehension (i.e., the ability to perceive phenomena clearly without moods or emotions interfering, as well as the ability to monitor attention); heedfulness (i.e., recalling past experiences and thoughts that led to happiness versus suffering); and the "sublime states" of loving kindness, compassion, sympathetic joy, and equanimity (Cullen, 2011).

The psychological construct of mindfulness has gained great popularity in recent years, though at times the process of defining, measuring and studying it remains somewhat nebulous. Shapiro, Carlson, Astin, and Freedman (2006) posit that there are three fundamental axioms of the psychological construct of mindfulness: 1) intention; 2) attention; and 3) attitude. Though traditionally the intention of mindfulness within Buddhist traditions was enlightenment and compassion for all, Kabat-Zinn notes that intentions "set the stage for what is possible. They remind you from moment to moment of why you are practicing in the first place" (1990, p. 32). With regard to intentions for practicing mindfulness, Shapiro (1992) argues that, though intentions of mindfulness are dynamic and evolving, most individuals practice mindfulness as a means of self-regulation, while others may practice as a means of self-exploration or self-liberation.

Indeed, understanding *why* one practices mindfulness is critical to understanding how mindfulness works (Shapiro et al., 2006). The second axiom of mindfulness, attention, refers to attending to the experience of mindfulness practice without interpreting the experience, while the third axiom, attitude, refers to *how* one attends (i.e., with acceptance, compassion, and openness; Shapiro et al., 2006). Taken together, these three axioms of mindfulness are considered to contribute to individuals learning to shift their perspective and obtain positive outcomes, such as improvements in mental health (Shapiro et al., 2006).

Mindfulness interventions have been demonstrated to positively impact both physical and mental health as well as interpersonal outcomes. Though mindfulness-based stress reduction was first used with patients with chronic pain (Kabat-Zinn, 1982), mindfulness interventions, which can help promote relaxation, greater aware-ness of the body, and utilization of coping skills, have, in turn, promoted positive health outcomes across a variety of clinical and nonclinical populations (Creswell, 2017). Indeed, mindfulness interventions have been linked to improved outcomes in medical symptoms, physical impairment, and quality of life (for a meta-analysis, see Grossman, Niemann, Schmidt, & Walach, 2004), as well as in biomarkers of immune system activity (for a review, see Black & Slavich, 2016) and general health behaviors (Creswell, 2017), in clinical and nonclinical populations.

The extant literature also suggests that mindfulness interventions are associ-ated with improved mental health functioning among both clinical and non-clinical samples. Indeed, a meta-analysis examining mental health outcomes of adults with chronic medical diseases found small effect sizes of mindfulness on the reduction of depression, anxiety, and overall psychological distress (Bohlmeijer, Prenger, Taal, & Cuijpers, 2010). There also is a strong body of literature showing that mindfulness interventions, specifically mindfulness-based cognitive therapy, reduces the risk of depressive relapse among individuals with a history of mul-tiple major depressive episodes (Creswell, 2017; Ma & Teasdale, 2004; Teasdale et al., 2000). Though findings regarding the impact of mindfulness, compared to active control treatments, on populations with elevated levels of anxiety are mixed, results generally suggest that mindfulness-based interventions reduce anxiety symptoms (Creswell, 2017; Hofmann, Sawyer, Witt, & Oh, 2010; Strauss, Cavanagh, Oliver, & Pettman, 2014). Among healthy adults, mindfulness interven-tions have been found to reduce stress, anxiety, depression, and distress, as well as improve quality of life (see Chiesa & Serretti, 2009; Khoury, Sharma, Rush, & Fournier, 2015, for meta-analyses).

Though the existing literature broadly suggests that mindfulness is associated with beneficial mental and physical health outcomes, several limitations in the literature should be considered. Many studies examining mindfulness present with various methodological shortcomings, including small sample sizes, non-randomization, use of self-reported scales, and variability in control groups (active treatment control versus waitlist). Additionally, there is a paucity of research exam-ining the impact of mindfulness within samples of children and adolescents, creat-ing a limited developmental perspective on its effectiveness. Though the extant literature is promising and suggests that mindfulness interventions are feasible and acceptable within a younger population (e.g., Burke, 2010), additional research in this area is needed in order to draw stronger conclusions on the efficacy of mind-fulness interventions with children and adolescents.

Mindfulness-Based and Mindfulness-Related Interventions for Chronic Pain

A substantial body of research supports the benefit of mindfulness-based interventions in reducing chronic pain, as well as stress, anxiety, and depression, all of which often accompany chronic pain (Chiesa & Serretti, 2011 Hofmann et al., 2010). Individuals experiencing chronic pain are encouraged to change the way they relate to their pain by suspending judgment toward the thoughts accompanying the perception of pain (Majeed, Ali, & Sudak, 2018). This theoretically uncouples the sensory dimension of pain from the affective alarm reaction, resulting in an attenuation of the experience of suffering through cognitive re-evaluation (Kabat-Zinn, 1982).

In other words, mindfulness practice helps the patient distinguish between the physiological experience of pain and the maladaptive thoughts and emotional responses that typically accompany pain. This allows individuals to become detached from the subjective pain experience and accept the pain without the negative cognitive and emotional impact (Kerns, Sellinger, & Goodin, 2011). The goals of any mindfulness-based intervention for chronic pain are to reduce pain, increase functioning, and improve overall quality of life (Majeed et al., 2018). Indeed, a recent review found that pain intensity decreased following participation in mindfulness-based interventions among clinical populations (Reiner, Tibi, & Lipsitz, 2013), which provides promising evidence that mindfulness-based interventions promote pain-specific improvements. While often it is not possible to entirely remit the experience of pain, an individual can learn to live a productive life even in the presence of discomfort or disability through his or her participation in mindfulness-based interventions.

This section will review the primary clinical interventions with a central tenet in mindfulness training (i.e., mindfulness-based interventions), as well as established interventions that utilize components of mindfulness within a broader treatment context (i.e., mindfulness-related interventions). Additionally, the impact of interventions specifically on chronic pain will be discussed for the treatments reviewed.

Mindfulness-Based Stress Reduction

Most frequently examined in the literature, mindfulness-based stress reduction (MBSR) refers to Kabat-Zinn's standardized meditation program created in 1979, which integrates Buddhist mindfulness with contemporary psychology practice (Kabat-Zinn, 1982; Kabat-Zinn, 1990). Initially developed as a group-based program for individuals with chronic pain, MBSR is thought to help individuals separate the sensory pain experience from the cognitive and emotional aspects of pain, thereby reducing the suffering that pain may cause (Kabat-Zinn, 1982).

Mindfulness-based stress reduction traditionally consists of an eight-week program with weekly 2–2.5-hour group-based classes, a day-long mindfulness retreat, and daily home practice (Kabat-Zinn, 1982; Kabat-Zinn, 1990). Components of MBSR include the body scan to mindfully attend to isolated regions of the body; sitting meditation (e.g., mindful breathing); and mindful movement in the form of Hatha yoga postures (Cullen, 2011; Kabat-Zinn, 1982). Mindfulness-based stress reduction increasingly is utilized as a treatment for a wide range of mental and physical disorders (for a review, see Creswell, 2017). Further, numerous meta-analyses have demonstrated that MBSR is effective in reducing stress, anxiety, mood, and overall distress among healthy individuals (Chiesa & Serretti, 2009; Khoury et al., 2015), as well as among individuals with psychiatric and/or medical conditions (Bohlmeijer et al., 2010; Hofmann et al., 2010).

The various components of MBSR, though applicable across populations, particularly can be helpful within the chronic pain population. For instance, body scans involve directing one's attention, nonjudgmentally, to isolated parts of the body (Kabat-Zinn, 1990). Through the development of this skill, in addition to sitting meditation and mindful movements, older adults with chronic pain have noted being able to shift their attention to other, non-painful parts of their bodies, as well as to develop increased awareness of pain sensations earlier than was typical for them (Morone, Lynch, Greco, Tindle, & Weiner, 2008).

Efficacy of Mindfulness-Based Stress Reduction for Chronic Pain

Given that MBSR initially was developed to treat chronic pain, it is not surprising that MBSR is the most frequently studied mindfulness-based intervention for chronic pain. Early treatment outcome studies demonstrate improvements in pain intensity, medical symptoms, psychological symptoms, ability to cope, and activity level, with evidence of general longer-term maintenance of outcomes for several months up to four years following the intervention (Kabat-Zinn, 1982; Kabat-Zinn, Lipworth, & Burney, 1985; Kabat-Zinn, Lipworth, Burncy, & Sellers, 1986). Meta-analyses examining MBSR among patients with chronic illnesses, including pain, have demonstrated small to moderate effects of MBSR on comorbidities such as anxiety, depression, and distress (Bohlmeijer et al., 2010; Merkes, 2010).

However, in a systematic review of mindfulness-based interventions for chronic pain, Chiesa and Serretti (2011) concluded that additional research is needed to demonstrate that MBSR and other mindfulness-based interventions are more efficacious than nonspecific interventions, such as support and educational control groups. Indeed, their review supported the notion that although MBSR is efficacious in reducing pain (e.g., Morone, Greco, & Weiner, 2008) and depressive symptoms (e.g., Sephton et al., 2007), and improving quality of life (e.g., Grossman, Tiefenthaler-Gilmer, Raysz, & Kesper, 2007), among individuals with chronic pain, MBSR did not demonstrate a significant advantage compared to active control treatments (Chiesa & Serretti, 2011).

Indeed, Cherkin and colleagues (2016) also found that, though MBSR was associated with clinically meaningful improvement in pain and functioning compared to baseline among a sample of adults with chronic low back pain, there were no significant differences in outcomes between MBSR and cognitive-behavioral therapy (CBT). Mixed findings in the literature may be due to several study limitations, such as small sample size, lack of randomization, and use of waitlist control versus active control groups. Additionally, in a longitudinal study examining MBSR among chronic pain patients, Rosenzweig and colleagues (2010) found that treatment effects on pain, quality of life, and psychological well-being varied across chronic pain conditions and compliance with home meditation practice, suggesting that MBSR may have a variable impact within the chronic pain population and that adherence to the effective components is critical.

Mechanisms of Mindfulness-Based Stress Reduction

The psychological and physical mechanisms underlying MBSR's effectiveness do not point to one single factor that accounts for observed outcomes in the literature. As noted, favorable outcomes have been found across domains and symptom presentations. In the psychological literature examining depression and anxiety, MBSR has been shown to modulate blood oxygen level-dependent (BOLD) signal responsivity in frontal lobe regions during task-based fMRI paradigms such as labeling emotional faces (Holzel et al., 2013), sadness provocation (Farb et al., 2010), and self-referential processing of emotional words (Goldin, Ziv, Jazaieri, & Gross, 2012). Furthermore, a review of brain mechanisms associated with mindfulness meditation in pain regulation described findings that support focused attention and open monitoring aspects of meditation lead to alterations in frontal lobe and other brain regions during the anticipation of pain (Zeidan, Gordon, Merchant, & Goolkasian, 2010).

When studying pain reduction with the use of MBSR, it is important to rely on biomarkers as well as patient-reported outcomes. Cortisol is considered to be an acceptable stress-related biomarker because anomalous levels of the hormone are found in pathologies associated with stress-related symptoms (e.g., depression, anxiety), and it is known for causing long-term damaging effects as a result of chronic stress (McEwen & Stellar, 1993). It is hypothesized that the hypothalamic–pituitary–adrenal axis (HPAA) may play a significant role in the association between psychological variables and chronic pain (Aloisi et al., 2011), and further research has shown that stressful experiences can alter pain thresholds by producing either stress-induced analgesia or hyperalgesia (Clark, Yang, & Janal, 1986; Gamaro et al., 1998).

Yet, the relationship of HPAA, cortisol, and pain is complex and conflicting, especially since it has been found to exert a paradoxical effect on pain (Ardito et al., 2017; Vachon-Presseau et al., 2013). The same hormone can promote analgesia as well as hyperalgesia, depending on the site and mode of application (Ardito et al., 2017). In a study of an eight-week MBSR intervention for patients with chronic lower back pain, a significant self-reported amelioration of pain symptoms as well as an increase in evening cortisol was found post-MBSR treatment as compared to those in a waitlist control (Ardito et al., 2017). Lower cortisol levels have been found in patients with chronic pain as well as in patients with some stress-related disorders such as fibromyalgia, chronic fatigue syndrome and chronic pelvic pain (Aloisi et al., 2011; Griep et al., 1998; Papadopoulos & Cleare, 2012; Riva, Mork, Westgaard, Ro, & Lundberg, 2010).

To date, most fMRI studies of pain regulation have focused on tasks that provoke exteroceptive pain in healthy individuals, rather than tasks involving the emotional processing in individuals living with chronic pain (Braden et al., 2016). The core elements of MBSR are designed to help the patient cope with the constant presence of pain, thereby reducing the experiential impact of the pain on his/her emotional state, rather than altering the pain itself. A study by Braden and colleagues (2016) sought to examine the effects of MBSR training on emotional processing, rather than on pain responsivity, in patients who have chronic pain. The researchers found that patients receiving four weeks of weekly MBSR training demonstrated significant improvement in back pain and depressive symptoms as compared to those in the control group, who were provided with stress reduction reading. Further fMRI findings indicated that the MBSR group uniquely showed changes in frontal lobe neural network activity implicated in emotional processing. These increases in regional frontal lobe hemodynamic activity are believed to be associated with gaining awareness to changes in one's emotional state (Braden et al., 2016).

Mindfulness-Based Cognitive Therapy

Mindfulness-based cognitive therapy (MBCT) has been studied extensively as an efficacious mindfulness-based intervention. Initially developed for the prevention of relapse and recurrence of depression, MBCT is an eight-week group-based therapy that teaches mindfulness skills, provides psychoeducation about depression, and uses cognitive-behavioral strategies (Segal, Williams, & Teasdale, 2002, 2013). The theoretical underpinnings of MBCT target cognitive reactivation (i.e., the negative thoughts and feelings that can contribute to relapse of depression) by teaching mindfulness skills in order for individuals to be aware of their distressing thoughts and feelings and, in turn, develop acceptance and self-compassion in order to dissociate from their distress (Segal et al., 2002). Though studies examining MBCT typically investigate efficacy with regard to depression relapse (Fjorback, Arendt, Ørnbøl, Fink, & Walach, 2011), Day (2017) developed a treatment manual adapting MBCT specifically to treat chronic pain within a group therapy setting. This adaptation includes, in addition to mindfulness meditation practices, psychoeducation about gate control theory and the impact of stress on pain, discussion of maladaptive thoughts and the impact of emotions on cognitions, and behavioral activation strategies.

Efficacy of Mindfulness-Based Cognitive Therapy for Chronic Pain

Though there are few studies examining the efficacy of group-based MBCT for the treatment of chronic pain, the extant research is promising. In a pilot study examining MBCT for the treatment of headache pain, findings indicated greater improvements in self-efficacy, pain acceptance, pain interference, and pain catastrophizing compared to a delayed treatment control group (Day et al., 2014). Results from a randomized trial examining MBCT within women diagnosed with fibromyalgia demonstrated significant improvements in depressive symptoms and dysfunction due to fibromyalgia symptoms among individuals receiving MBCT compared to those in a treatment as usual control group, though no differences were found in pain intensity (Parra-Delgado & Latorre-Postigo, 2013).

A pilot study examining the impact of MBCT among patients with comorbid chronic pain and depressive disorders also demonstrated improvements in depressive symptoms compared to a waitlist control group (de Jong et al., 2018). Though newer to the literature, the current research examining the efficacy of MBCT for the treatment of chronic pain suggests that MBCT is associated with improvements in the experience of pain, as well as depressive symptoms. Additional research is needed to replicate these findings and to examine additional outcomes and mechanisms of efficacy.

Acceptance and Commitment Therapy

In addition to mindfulness-based interventions for chronic pain, it also is important to consider treatment modalities that incorporate aspects of mindfulness in the treatment of pain. Acceptance and commitment therapy (ACT), considered a third-wave treatment within the umbrella of CBT, combines the concept of acceptance with mindfulness and incorporates behavior change and activation methods (Hayes, Strosahl, & Wilson, 1999). Core to ACT is the concept of psychological flexibility, which refers to the "capacity to continue with or change behavior, guided by one's goals, in a context of interacting cognitive and direct non-cognitive influences" (McCracken & Vowles, 2014, p. 181). Within the domain of psychological flexibility are multiple subprocesses that are critical to ACT, including acceptance, cognitive defusion, flexible attention to the present, self-as-observer, values-based action, and committed action (Hayes et al., 1999).

With regard to the central tenants of ACT applied to the treatment of chronic pain, acceptance refers to the willingness to experience pain without attempting to control it. Values-based action refers to aligning one's actions with one's values, even when living with significant chronic pain (Hayes et al., 1999; Vowles & McCracken, 2008). ACT also emphasizes that it is the struggle with pain that results in the experience of suffering, rather than the physical experience of pain itself (Dahl & Lundgren, 2006). As a result, the intensity of one's suffering is dependent upon an individual's fusion with his/her pain (i.e., the extent to which one believes his/her thoughts about pain, and how these thoughts impact subsequent actions).

For example, thinking "I can't do anything because of my pain and must get rid of it before I can do anything I value" may result in a person no longer engaging in various aspects of life (Dahl & Lundgren, 2006). Consequently, the ACT tenant of cognitive defusion, or the ability to observe thoughts without evaluating or changing them, can be applied to the chronic pain population. Specifically, individuals are taught to observe and "sit with" their thoughts about their pain, without changing or evaluating them. Taken together, ACT principles help patients develop awareness and acceptance of pain, which in turn facilitates their ability to shift focus from reducing pain and/or thinking about pain to fulfilling goals targeting their behavioral functioning (Day, Thorn, & Burns, 2012).

Efficacy of Acceptance and Commitment Therapy for Chronic Pain

Numerous randomized controlled trials have demonstrated support for ACT in the treatment of chronic pain (e.g., Buhrman et al., 2013; Dahl, Wilson, & Nilsson, 2004; Wetherell et al., 2011; Wicksell et al., 2013). ACT-based interventions have been shown to reduce pain intensity and improve secondary depression and anxiety, as well as disability (Buhrman et al., 2013; Vowles & McCracken, 2008; Wetherell et al., 2011). Indeed, a recent meta-analysis found ACT-based interventions to have a small effect size on pain intensity, depression, anxiety, physical functioning, and quality of life (Veehof, Oskam, Schreurs, & Bohlmeijer, 2011) among controlled studies. Despite ACT's evinced efficacy in treating chronic pain, research also has found outcomes from ACT to be similar to those from CBT (Veehof et al., 2011; Wetherell et al., 2011).

Using Mindfulness-Based Interventions in Clinical Settings for Chronic Pain Patients

The extant research suggests that MBSR, MBCT, and ACT are effective chronic pain interventions. However, it may be unrealistic to fully implement these protocols, particularly in fast-paced medical settings (e.g., primary care, outpatient medical clinics) given their intensive, lengthy, and frequently group-based natures. Additionally, some patients may not have the resources for or interest in engaging in comprehensive mindfulness-based treatments. As such, flexibility in the clinical application of mindfulness-based interventions for chronic pain patients is needed.

Prior to the initiation of any chronic pain treatment, a comprehensive pain assessment is critical to understanding a patient's pain condition, including how it impacts daily functioning, pain onset, patterns of pain, triggers, and previous treatments and their effectiveness (Otis & Pincus, 2008). See Chapter 2 for an in-depth discussion of chronic pain assessment. Following a thorough pain assessment, various components of MBSR, MBCT, and ACT can be utilized depending on the patient's specific needs and impairment. Mindfulness practices can be introduced to patients and practiced together, particularly with the aid of mobile applications (discussed in more detail in the section below).

One such element of mindfulness that may be particularly effective in a brief intervention setting is the body scan. Rather than relieving the pain completely, the main goal of the body scan is to get to know the pain and to learn from it in order to manage it. Similar to other aspects of mindfulness, the body scan can improve the person's attention to and increase awareness of the different regions of the body. Specifically, the person begins by focusing on his/her breathing. His/her attention and focus then shift to a small isolated body part, often the foot, before moving slowly up the body. The individual is encouraged to feel all sensations (including any pain) in each isolated body area. Carefully observing the discomfort without judgment, he/she begins to notice increased relaxation in the body.

In a sample of adults with chronic pain, Ussher and colleagues (2014) found that adults who participated in a ten-minute body scan demonstrated a significant reduction in pain-related distress and impairment in social relations due to pain immediately following their body scan in a clinic setting, compared to a control group. Other components of mindfulness-based interventions also can be woven into brief intervention settings, such as by providing psychoeducation about non-judgmentally observing pain-related thoughts, as well as discussing strategies for living a life in accordance with one's values even when in pain. However, research regarding the implementation of core components of mindfulness-based interventions in fast-paced settings is limited and should be explored in future work.

Self-Guided Applications of Mindfulness Practices and Interventions

Smartphones have become one of the most rapidly growing technologies in modern history, allowing for great advances in communication and access to information (Alexander & Joshi, 2016). It is estimated that there are more than 7.8 billion registered users of mobile phones worldwide (Singh et al., 2016). In 2017, 85% of the world's population was covered by a commercial mobile signal. In the United States, approximately 68% of people own a mobile phone, which is up 35% from 2011 and is expected to continue to rise (Singh et al., 2016; Smith, 2017). Smartphones now account for over 25% of total web usage.

While there is established evidence for the positive effects of face-to-face mindfulness-based training programs and interventions, there is growing interest in examining the potential of technology to deliver similar interventions. The use of applications (aka "apps") within the healthcare industry continues to grow. It is estimated that the market for mobile health apps will grow to over $26 billion in 2018 (Research2guidance, 2013). The use of innovative mobile technology as a tool to deliver health interventions increases the self-management of chronic conditions, including pain.

Studies have shown that mobile phone messaging and app-based interventions can improve healthcare outcomes, including increased patient engagement outside of the clinic/hospital setting and improved self-management of chronic diseases (e.g., hypertension, diabetes, asthma; Alexander & Joshi, 2016; McEvoy et al., 2016). Further evidence suggests that self-management of chronic conditions reduces hospitalizations and emergency department use, as well as overall health-care costs (Sundararaman, Edwards, Ross, & Jamison, 2017). Additionally, the use of mobile health (mHealth) technology as a platform for mindfulness-based inter-ventions for individuals with chronic pain increases parsimony, feasibility, and effi-ciency (Cavanagh, Strauss, Forder, & Jones, 2013).

The use of innovative mobile technology to deliver mindfulness-based inter-ventions holds promise as a chronic pain management tool. This technology allows for increased monitoring, self-management, and access to interventions without the inherent challenges of travel, clinic visit costs, or scheduling (Sundararaman et al., 2017). Methods to increase the availability of mindfulness-based approaches include the dissemination of mindfulness-based self-help (MBSH) interventions (Cavanagh, Strauss, Cicconi, et al., 2013). The increased availability of MBSH provides improved access to interventions for patients experiencing functional or financial limitations that impair access to services. Mindfulness-based self-help interventions are widely available in the public domain and include self-help books/workbooks, audio guides, online programs, and mindfulness smartphone apps. With the ever-expanding numbers of smartphones, tablets, and other devices with internet accessibility, people of all ages, incomes, and communities (i.e., rural and urban) increasingly gain access to sophisticated health-related mindfulness apps (Singh et al., 2016; Vardeh, Edwards, Jamison, & Eccleston, 2013).

A meta-analysis of 15 randomized controlled trials evaluating mindfulness self-help interventions showed significant benefits of MBSH (audio-based self-help interventions) in comparison to control conditions for mindfulness skills such as a moderated online discussion forum about mindfulness, psychoeducation, and an active psychotherapy intervention. Outcomes measured in these studies included self-report measures of mindfulness understanding and skill develop-ment, as well as measures of psychological symptoms of anxiety and depression (Cavanagh, Strauss, Forder, et al., 2013). These findings indicate that mindfulness can be learned by self-help. Technology-based applications to disseminate mind-fulness interventions should be utilized for individuals experiencing functional impairments and/or other barriers to more traditional forms of care.

While there are many different mobile technology platforms that address chronic pain (e.g., electronic pain diaries, electronic pain assessment programs, smartphone pain applications, activity trackers), the majority of mindfulness-based mobile interventions are delivered via smartphone apps and internet web-sites. More than 14,000 health-related apps are available for use with the mobile operating system developed by Apple Inc., iOS (Blumenthal & Somashekar, 2015). A systematic review found that most of those apps focus on monitor-ing and collecting data as opposed to behavioral health interventions (Rosser & Eccleston, 2011). Specifically, Rosser and Eccleston (2011) found that of all the health-related apps developed for pain, only 17% provided mindfulness-based intervention.

A more recent systematic review of mindfulness-based iPhone apps identi-fied an initial 606 apps available for download; however, further review resulted in only 23 meeting the criteria of providing mindfulness training with integrity (Mani, Kavanagh, Hides, & Stoyanov, 2015). Mani and colleagues (2015) evaluated the quality of the reviewed mindfulness-based apps. It was noted that effective mindfulness apps should include mindfulness education and training, exposure to the philosophy and a discussion about common misconceptions, and exercises aimed at the various components of mindfulness to treat chronic pain (e.g., contemplative practices, increased awareness of mind–body connection, withdrawing from habitual experiential avoidance; Mani et al., 2015). The quality of the apps included in this review were evaluated based on an expert rating scale, the Mobile Application Rating Scale, developed by the authors (MARS; Stoyanov et al., 2015). The MARS contains three sections: classification, app quality, and satisfaction. It has demonstrated excellent internal consistency ($\alpha = 0.92$) and interrater reliability (ICC =.85) as a measure to evaluate app quality (Stoyanov et al., 2015). Of the 23 mindfulness-based apps that met inclusion criteria, the median MARS score was 3.2 (out of 5.0), which exceeded the published minimum acceptable score of 3.0 (Mani et al., 2015; Stoyanov et al., 2015). The highest quality ranking apps were Headspace (4.0), Smiling Mind (3.7), iMindfulness (3.5), and Mindfulness Daily (3.5; Mani et al., 2015).

Notwithstanding the efforts to review and evaluate the effectiveness and quality of mobile apps for mindfulness, to date there has been no rigorous evaluation of mindfulness apps specifically for treating chronic pain. The acceptability and feasibility of mindfulness apps are known, and the effectiveness of teaching mindfulness skills and reducing psychological symptoms have been demonstrated, yet there remains a need for additional studies to specifically evaluate the effectiveness of mindfulness apps to address and improve symptoms of pain and comorbid emotional outcomes.

Mindfulness to treat chronic pain is a habit and mind-training skill that requires regular practice and sustained effort in order to be effective (Grossman et al., 2004; Kabat-Zinn, 2003). This is a challenge for both face-to-face and app-based mindfulness interventions when treating chronic pain. However, mindfulness apps provide 24/7 access to skill building and practice (Mani et al., 2015), which has the potential to increase adherence. Apps rated as aesthetically pleasing, well designed, and interactive have been shown to be more effective at increasing usage and addressing symptoms (Maghnati & Ling, 2013). The use of mindfulness through apps and other mHealth platforms creates the opportunity to engage patients in between (or in some cases instead of) traditional outpatient visits, empowering them to take a more active role in managing their symptoms; improving pain relief; facilitating functioning; and returning to daily living (Alexander & Joshi, 2016).

Cultural Implications of Mindfulness-Based Interventions for Chronic Pain

There are evidenced racial and ethnic disparities in pain and access to and receipt of care (Anderson, Green, & Payne, 2009; Green et al., 2003). Indeed, culture can impact how symptoms of pain and suffering are understood, as well as how pain is expressed, beliefs about pain, perceptions of healthcare, and appropriate treatments for pain (Kirmayer, Young, & Robbins, 1994; Lasch, 2000; Otis & Pincus, 2008). Given these cultural discrepancies in the experience of pain, it is important to consider the cultural implications of using mindfulness-based interventions within the chronic pain population.

The underpinnings of therapeutic approaches utilizing mindfulness acknowledge that an individual's experience, and in turn his/her distress experience and expression of distress, is impacted by sociopolitical and historical factors (Hayes, Luoma, Bond, Masuda, & Lillis, 2006). Within these treatments, an emphasis is placed on understanding the context in which individuals experience distress, as well as normalizing and validating the distress, prior to guiding the individual toward behavioral change in accordance with his/her values (Fuchs, Lee, Roemer, & Orsillo, 2013).

This approach may resonate with individuals from marginalized and/or non-dominant cultural backgrounds given their potential mistrust of the mental health system, assumptions that they may be blamed for their circumstances, and beliefs that they lack control over their environments (e.g., their experiences with oppression or discrimination; Fuchs et al., 2013). In a meta-analysis examining the use of acceptance- and mindfulness-based interventions with underserved populations, results indicated small to large effect sizes regarding the efficacy of these interventions, with larger effect sizes found for studies with no-contact or waitlist conditions (Fuchs et al., 2013). These findings may demonstrate similar effect sizes to those found in broader meta-analyses not limited to underserved populations (e.g., Grossman et al., 2004).

Considerations also should be given to how mindfulness is introduced to underserved populations. For example, in a study examining African Americans' perspectives on mindfulness, results suggested that an emphasis should be placed on the health benefits of mindfulness, connections between mindfulness and familiar spirituality or cultural practices, and use of African American instructors and readings written by African Americans (Woods-Giscombé & Gaylord, 2014). Indeed, it is important to consider the cultural context within which mindfulness is presented to patients, and to present mindfulness skills in a culturally sensitive manner.

Summary

Chronic pain is a common condition with significant physical, psychological, social, and economic impacts (Waddell, 1996). Estimates are that every fifth person suffers from pain, with approximately every one in ten adults diagnosed with chronic pain each year (Goldberg & McGee, 2011). As research increasingly has demonstrated the benefits and efficacy of many non-pharmacological treatments, these approaches have become more popular. Within this context, mindfulness-based interventions have been proven to be an effective approach by reducing the perception and intensity of pain and increasing mobility and functioning (Hughes, Clark, Colclough, Dale, & McMillan, 2017; Kabat-Zinn et al., 1985). In addition to alleviating pain, mindfulness-based interventions can decrease disruption in activities of daily living and help address comorbidities such as depression and anxiety. Brain and behavior changes in those living with chronic pain have been well-documented as a result of mindfulness-based interventions. Changes in cortisol levels, increases in frontal lobe hemodynamic activity, and changes in activity within neural networks implicated in emotion processing have all supported the biological, psychological, and social impacts of mindfulness in treating chronic pain (Ardito et al., 2017; Braden et al., 2016).

Mindfulness training provides cognitive and emotional strategies for improving pain management, which has positive outcomes for one's mental and physical health. With the rapidly increasing use of technology and development of mobile health solutions for those living with chronic medical conditions, mindfulness is becoming more accessible and acceptable to individuals of many backgrounds and demographics. There are many effective smartphone apps and other mindfulness-based self-help tools available to reduce barriers to traditional pain management interventions.

Limitations in studying the efficacy of mindfulness-based interventions to treat chronic pain exist. Namely, less rigorous study designs and the impact of the many adaptations of these interventions make it difficult to standardize research, which could be responsible for the variations of results across many studies. Limited data is available about long-term effects of treatment, and studies are needed with longer follow-up periods in order to better understand the potential long-term effects of mindfulness training on pain management, as well as neural networks related to cognitive and emotional regulation. Additionally, there is a paucity of research examining how mindfulness-based interventions are applied in settings more suitable for brief interventions, such as outpatient medical clinics or primary care. Finally, cultural factors should be accounted for when utilizing mindfulness-based interventions to address chronic pain in people of underserved and minority backgrounds.

References

Alexander, J. C., & Joshi, G. P. (2016). Smartphone applications for chronic pain management: A critical appraisal. *Journal of Pain Research, 9*, 731–734.

Aloisi, A. M., Buonocore, M., Merlo, L., Galandra, C., Sotgiu, A., Bacchella, L., . . . Bonezzi, C. (2011). Chronic pain therapy and hypothalamic-pituitary-adrenal axis impairment. *Psychoneuroendocrinology, 36*, 1032–1039.

Anderson, K. O., Green, C. R., & Payne, R. (2009). Racial and ethnic disparities in pain: Causes and consequences of unequal care. *Journal of Pain, 10*, 1187–1204.

Ardito, R. B., Pirro, P. S., Re, T. S., Bonapace, I., Menardo, V., Bruno, E., & Gianotti, L. (2017). Mindfulness-based stress reduction program on chronic low back pain: A study investigating the impact on endocrine, physical, and psychologic functioning. *The Journal of Alternative and Complementary Medicine, 23*, 615–623.

Baer, R. A. (2003). Mindfulness training as a clinical intervention: A conceptual and empirical review. *Clinical Psychology Science and Practice, 10*, 125–143.

Black, D. S., & Slavich, G. M. (2016). Mindfulness meditation and the immune system: A systematic review of randomized controlled trials. *Annals of the New York Academy of Sciences, 1373*, 13–24.

Blumenthal, S., & Somashekar, G. (2015). Advancing health with information technology in the 21st century. *The Huffington Post*. Retrieved from www.huffingtonpost.com/susan blumenthal/advancing-health-with-inf_b_7968190.html

Bohlmeijer, E., Prenger, R., Taal, E., & Cuijpers, P. (2010). The effects of mindfulness-based stress reduction therapy on mental health of adults with a chronic medical disease: A meta-analysis. *Journal of Psychosomatic Research, 68*, 539–544.

Braden, B. B., Pipe, T. B., Smith, R., Glaspy, T. K., Deatherage, B. R., & Baxter, L. C. (2016). Brain and behavior changes associated with an abbreviated 4-week mindfulness-based stress reduction course in back pain patients. *Brain and Behavior, 6*, doi:10.1002/brb3.443

Buhrman, M., Skoglund, A., Husell, J., Bergström, K., Gordh, T., Hursti, T., . . . Andersson, G. (2013). Guided internet-delivered acceptance and commitment therapy for chronic pain patients: A randomized controlled trial. *Behaviour Research and Therapy, 51*, 307–315.

Burke, A. L. J., Mathias, J. L., & Denson, L. A. (2015). Psychological functioning of people living with chronic pain: A meta-analytic review. *British Journal of Clinical Psychology, 54*, 345–360.

Burke, C. A. (2010). Mindfulness-based approaches with children and adolescents: A preliminary review of current research in an emergent field. *Journal of Child and Family Studies, 19*, 133–144.

Cavanagh, K., Strauss, C., Cicconi, F., Griffiths, N., Wyper, A., & Jones, F. (2013). A randomized controlled trial of a brief online mindfulness-based intervention. *Behaviour Research and Therapy, 51*, 573–578.

Cavanagh, K., Strauss, C., Forder, L., & Jones, F. (2013). Can mindfulness and acceptance be learnt by self-help? A systematic review and meta-analysis of mindfulness and acceptance-based self-help interventions. *Clinical Psychology Review, 34*, 118–129.

Cherkin, D. C., Sherman, K. J., Balderson, B. H., Cook, A. J., Anderson, M. L., Hawkes, R. J., . . . Turner, J. A. (2016). Effect of mindfulness-based stress reduction vs cognitive behavioral therapy or usual care on back pain and functional limitations in adults with chronic low back pain: A randomized clinical trial. *JAMA, 315*, 1240–1249.

Chiesa, A., & Serretti, A. (2009). Mindfulness-based stress reduction for stress management in healthy people: A review and meta-analysis. *The Journal of Alternative and Complementary Medicine, 15*, 593–600.

Chiesa, A., & Serretti, A. (2011). Mindfulness-based interventions for chronic pain: A systematic review of the evidence. *The Journal of Alternative and Complementary Medicine, 17*, 83–93.

Clark, W. C., Yang, J. C., & Janal, M. N. (1986). Altered pain and visual sensitivity in humans: The effects of acute and chronic stress. *Annals of the New York Academy of Sciences, 467*, 116–129.

Creswell, J. D. (2017). Mindfulness interventions. *Annual Review of Psychology, 68*, 491–516.

Cullen, M. (2011). Mindfulness-based interventions: An emerging phenomenon. *Mindfulness, 2*, 186–193. doi:10.1007/s12671-011-0058-1

Dahl, J., & Lundgren, T. (2006). Acceptance and commitment therapy (ACT) in the treatment of chronic pain. In R. A. Baer (Ed.), *Mindfulness-based treatment approaches: Clinician's guide to evidence base and applications* (pp. 285–306). San Diego, CA: Elsevier.

Dahl, J., Wilson, K. G., & Nilsson, A. (2004). Acceptance and commitment therapy and the treatment of persons at risk for long-term disability resulting from stress and pain symptoms: A preliminary randomized trial. *Behavior Therapy, 35*, 785–801.

Day, M. A. (2017). *Mindfulness-based cognitive therapy for chronic pain: A clinical manual and guide.* West Sussex, UK: John Wiley & Sons.

Day, M. A., Thorn, B. E., & Burns, J. W. (2012). The continuing evolution of biopsychosocial interventions for chronic pain. *Journal of Cognitive Psychotherapy, 26,* 114–129.

Day, M. A., Thorn, B. E., Ward, L. C., Rubin, N., Hickman, S. D., Scogin, F., & Kilgo, G. R. (2014). Mindfulness-based cognitive therapy for the treatment of headache pain. *Clinical Journal of Pain, 30,* 152–161.

de Jong, M., Peeters, F., Gard, T., Ashih, H., Doorley, J., Walker, R., . . . Mischoulon, D. (2018). A randomized controlled pilot study on mindfulness-based cognitive therapy for unipolar depression in patients with chronic pain. *Journal of Clinical Psychiatry, 79,* 26–34.

Farb, N. A., Anderson, A. K., Mayberg, H., Bean, J., McKeon, D., & Segal, Z. V. (2010). Minding one's emotions: Mindfulness training alters the neural expression of sadness. *Emotion, 10,* 25–33.

Fjorback, L. O., Arendt, M., Ørnbøl, E., Fink, P., & Walach, H. (2011). Mindfulness-based stress reduction and mindfulness-based cognitive therapy—a systematic review of randomized controlled trials. *Acta Psychiatrica Scandinavica, 124,* 102–119.

Forgeron, P. A., King, S., Stinson, J. N., McGrath, P. J., MacDonald, A. J., & Chambers, C. T. (2010). Social functioning and peer relationships in children and adolescents with chronic pain: A systematic review. *Pain Research & Management, 15,* 27–41.

Fuchs, C., Lee, J. K., Roemer, L., & Orsillo, S. M. (2013). Using mindfulness- and acceptance-based treatments with clients from nondominant cultural and/or marginalized backgrounds: Clinical considerations, meta-analysis findings, and introduction to the special series. *Cognitive and Behavioral Practice, 20,* 1–12.

Gamaro, G. D., Xavier, M. H., Denardin, J. D., Pilger, J. A., Ely, D. R., Ferreira, M. B., & Dalmaz, C. (1998). The effects of acute and repeated restraint stress on the nociceptive response in rats. *Physiology & Behavior, 63,* 693–697.

Gatchel, R. J., Peng, Y. B., Peters, M. L., Fuchs, P. N., & Turk, D. C. (2007). The biopsychosocial approach to chronic pain: Scientific advances and future directions. *Psychological Bulletin, 133,* 581–624.

Goldberg, D. S., & McGee, S. J. (2011). Pain as a global public health priority. *BMC Public Health, 11,* 770.

Goldin, P., Ziv, M., Jazaieri, H., & Gross, J. J. (2012). Randomized controlled trial of mindfulness-based stress reduction versus aerobic exercise: Effects on the self-referential brain network in social anxiety disorder. *Frontiers in Human Neuroscience, 6,* 295.

Green, C. R., Anderson, K. O., Baker, T. A., Campbell, L. C., Decker, S., Fillingim, R. B., . . . Vallerand, A. H. (2003). The unequal burden of pain: Confronting racial and ethnic disparities in pain. *Pain Medicine, 4,* 277–294.

Griep, E. N., Boersma, J. W., Lentjes, E. G., Prins, A. P., van der Korst, J. K., & de Kloet, E. R. (1998). Function of the hypothalamic-pituitary-adrenal axis in patients with fibromyalgia and low back pain. *Journal of Rheumatology, 25,* 1374–1381.

Grossman, P., Niemann, L., Schmidt, S., & Walach, H. (2004). Mindfulness-based stress reduction and health benefits: A meta-analysis. *Journal of Psychosomatic Research, 577,* 35–43.

Grossman, P., Tiefenthaler-Gilmer, U., Raysz, A., & Kesper, U. (2007). Mindfulness training as an intervention for fibromyalgia: Evidence of postintervention and 3-year follow-up benefits in well-being. *Psychotherapy and Psychosomatics, 76,* 226–233.

Hayes, S. C., Luoma, J. B., Bond, F. W., Masuda, A., & Lillis, J. (2006). Acceptance and commitment therapy: Model, processes and outcomes. *Behaviour Research and Therapy, 44,* 1–25.

Hayes, S. C., Strosahl, K., & Wilson, K. G. (1999). *Acceptance and commitment therapy: An experiential approach to behavior change.* New York, NY: The Guilford Press.

Hofmann, S. G., Sawyer, A. T., Witt, A. A., & Oh, D. (2010). The effect of mindfulness-based therapy on anxiety and depression: A meta-analytic review. *Journal of Consulting and Clinical Psychology, 78,* 169–183.

Holzel, B. K., Hoge, E. A., Greve, D. N., Gard, T., Creswell, J. D., . . . Brown, K. W. (2013). Neural mechanisms of symptom improvements in generalized anxiety disorder following mindfulness training. *Neuroimage: Clinical, 2,* 448–458.

Hughes, L. S., Clark, J., Colclough, J. A., Dale, E., & McMillan, D. (2017). Acceptance and Commitment Therapy (ACT) for chronic pain. *Clinical Journal of Pain, 33,* 552–568.

Kabat-Zinn, J. (1982). An outpatient program in behavioral medicine for chronic pain patients based on the practice of mindfulness meditation: Theoretical considerations and preliminary results. *General Hospital Psychiatry, 4,* 33–47.

Kabat-Zinn, J. (1990). *Full catastrophe living: Using the wisdom of your body and mind to face stress, pain, and illness.* New York, NY: Delacorte.

Kabat-Zinn, J. (2013). *Full catastrophe living: Using the wisdom of your body and mind to face stress, pain, and illness.* New York, NY: Bantam Books.

Kabat-Zinn, J. (2003). Mindfulness-based interventions in context: Past, present, and future. *Clinical Psychology Science and Practice, 10,* 144–156.

Kabat-Zinn, J., Lipworth, L., & Burney, R. (1985). The clinical use of mindfulness meditation for the self-regulation of chronic pain. *Journal of Behavioral Medicine, 8,* 163–190.

Kabat-Zinn, J., Lipworth, L., Burncy, R., & Sellers, W. (1986). Four-year follow-up of a meditation-based program for the self-regulation of chronic pain: Treatment outcomes and compliance. *Clinical Journal of Pain, 2,* 159–173.

Kerns, R. D., Sellinger, J., & Goodin, B. R. (2011). Psychological treatment of chronic pain. *Annual Review of Clinical Psychology, 7,* 411–434.

Khoury, B., Sharma, M., Rush, S. E., & Fournier, C. (2015). Mindfulness-based stress reduction for healthy individuals: A meta-analysis. *Journal of Psychosomatic Research, 78,* 519–528.

King, S., Chambers, C. T., Huguet, A., MacNevin, R. C., McGrath, P. J., Parker, L., & MacDonald, A. J. (2011). The epidemiology of chronic pain in children and adolescents revisited: A systematic review. *Pain, 152,* 2729–2738.

Kirmayer, L., Young, A., & Robbins, J. (1994). Symptom attribution in cultural perspective. *Canadian Journal of Psychiatry, 39,* 584–595.

Lasch, K. (2000). Culture, pain, and culturally sensitive pain care. *Pain Management Nursing, 1,* 16–22.

Logan, D. E., Simons, L. E., Stein, M. J., & Chastain, L. (2008). School impairment in adolescents with chronic pain. *Journal of Pain, 9,* 407–416.

Ma, S. H., & Teasdale, J. D. (2004). Mindfulness-based cognitive therapy for depression Replication and exploration of differential relapse prevention effects. *Journal of Consulting and Clinical Psychology, 72,* 31–40.

Maghnati, F., & Ling, K. (2013). Exploring the relationship between experiential value and usage attitude towards Mobile apps among the smartphone users. *International Journal of Business and Management, 8,* 1–9.

Majeed, M. H., Ali, A. A., & Sudak, D. M. (2018). Mindfulness-based interventions for chronic pain: Evidence and applications. *Asian Journal of Psychiatry, 32,* 79–83.

Mani, M., Kavanagh, D. J., Hides, L., & Stoyanov, S. (2015). Review and evaluation of mindfulness-based iPhone apps. *Journal of Medical Internet Research MHealth and UHealth, 3,* e82.

Marlatt, G. A., & Kristeller, J. L. (1999). Mindfulness and meditation. In W. R. Miller (Ed.), *Integrating spirituality into treatment* (pp. 67–84). Washington, DC: American Psychological Association.

McBeth, J., Nicholl, B. I., Cordingley, L., Davis, K. A., & Macfarlane, G. J. (2010). Chronic widespread pain predicts physical inactivity: Results from the prospective EPIFUND study. *European Journal of Pain, 14,* 972–979.

McCracken, L. M., & Vowles, K. E. (2014). Acceptance and commitment therapy and mindfulness for chronic pain. *American Psychologist, 69*, 178–187.

McEvoy, M. D., Hand, W. R., Stiegler, M. P., DiLorenzo, A. N., Ehrenfeld, J. M., Moran, K. R., . . . Schell, R. M. (2016). A smartphone-based decision support tool improves test performance concerning application of the guidelines for managing regional anesthesia in the patient receiving antithrombotic or thrombolytic therapy. *Anesthesiology, 124*, 186–198.

McEwen, B. S., & Stellar, E. (1993). Stress and the individual: Mechanisms leading to disease. *Archives of Internal Medicine, 153*, 2093–2101.

Melzack, R. (2005). Evolution of the neuromatrix theory of pain. The Prithvi Raj Lecture: Presented at the third World Congress of World Institute of Pain, Barcelona 2004. *Pain Practice, 5*, 85–94.

Melzack, R., & Wall, P. D. (1965). Pain mechanisms: A new theory. *Science, 150*, 971–979.

Merkes, M. (2010). Mindfulness-based stress reduction for people with chronic diseases. *Australian Journal of Primary Health, 16*, 200–210.

Morone, N. E., Greco, C. M., & Weiner, D. K. (2008). Mindfulness meditation for the treatment of chronic low back pain in older adults: A randomized controlled pilot study. *Pain, 134*, 310–319.

Morone, N. E., Lynch, C. S., Greco, C. M., Tindle, H. A., & Weiner, D. K. (2008). "I felt like a new person." The effects of mindfulness meditation on older adults with chronic pain: Qualitative narrative analysis of diary entries. *Journal of Pain, 9*, 841–848.

Otis, J. D., & Pincus, D. B. (2008). Chronic pain. In B. A. Boyer & M. I. Paharia (Eds.), *Comprehensive handbook of clinical health psychology* (pp. 349–370). Hoboken, NJ: John Wiley & Sons.

Papadopoulos, A. S., & Cleare, A. J. (2012). Hypothalamic-pituitary-adrenal axis dysfunction in chronic fatigue syndrome. *Nature Reviews Endocrinology, 8*, 22–32.

Parra-Delgado, M., & Latorre-Postigo, J. M. (2013). Effectiveness of mindfulness-based cognitive therapy in the treatment of fibromyalgia: A randomized trial. *Cognitive Therapy and Research, 37*, 1015–1026.

Reiner, K., Tibi, L., & Lipsitz, J. D. (2013). Do mindfulness-based interventions reduce pain intensity? A critical review of the literature. *Pain Medicine, 14*, 230–242.

Research2guidance. (2013). *Mobile health market report 2013–2017*. Retrieved from http://research2guidance.com/product/movile-health-market-report-2013-2017/

Riva, R., Mork, P. J., Westgaard, R. H., Ro, M., & Lundberg, U. (2010). Fibromyalgia syndrome is associated with hypocortisolism. *International Journal of Behavioral Medicine, 17*, 223–233.

Rosenzweig, S., Greeson, J. M., Reibel, D. K., Green, J. S., Jasser, S. A., & Beasley, D. (2010). Mindfulness-based stress reduction for chronic pain conditions: Variation in treatment outcomes and role of home meditation practice. *Journal of Psychosomatic Research, 68*, 29–36.

Rosser, B. A., & Eccleston, C. (2011). Mobile technology applications for pain management. *Journal of Telemedicine and Telecare, 17*, 308–312.

Schidt, S. (2004). Mindfulness and healing intention: Concepts, practice, and research evaluation. *Journal of Alternative and Complimentary Medicine, 10*, S7–S14.

Segal, Z. V., Williams, J. M., & Teasdale, J. (2002). *Mindfulness-based cognitive therapy for depression* (2nd ed.). London: The Guilford Press.

Segal, Z. V., Williams, J. M., & Teasdale, J. (2013). *Mindfulness-based cognitive therapy for depression: A new approach to preventing relapse*. London: The Guilford Press.

Sephton, S. E., Salmon, P., Weissbecker, I., Ulmer, C., Floyd, A., Hoover, K., & Studts, J. L. (2007). Mindfulness meditation alleviates depressive symptoms in women with fibromyalgia: Results of a randomized clinical trial. *Arthritis & Rheumatology, 57*, 77–85.

Shapiro, D. H. (1992). A preliminary study of long-term mediators: Goals, effects, religious orientation, cognitions. *The Journal of Transpersonal Psychology, 21*, 23–39.

Shapiro, S. L., Carlson, L. E., Astin, J. A., & Freedman, B. (2006). Mechanisms of mindfulness. *Journal of Clinical Psychology, 62*, 373–386.

Singh, K., Bates, D., Drouin, K., Newmark, L. P., Rozenblum, R., Lee, J., . . . Klinger, E. V. (2016). Developing a framework for evaluating the patient engagement, quality, and safety of mobile health applications. *The Commonwealth Fund*. Retrieved from www.common wealthfund.org/publications/issue-briefs/2016/feb/evaluating-mobile-health-apps

Smith, A. (2017). Record shares of Americans now own smartphones, have home broadband. *Pew Research Center*. Retrieved from https://owl.english.purdue.edu/owl/resource/560/10/

Stewart, W. F., Ricci, J. A., Chee, E., Morganstein, D., & Lipton, R. (2003). Lost productive time and cost due to common pain conditions in the US workforce. *JAMA, 290*, 2443–2454.

Stoyanov, S., Hides, L., Kavanagh, D., Tjondronegoro, D., Zelenko, O., & Mani, M. (2015). Mobile app rating scale: A new tool for assessing the quality of health-related mobile apps. *Journal of Medical Internet Research MHealth and UHealth, 3*, e27.

Strauss, C., Cavanagh, K., Oliver, A., & Pettman, D. (2014). Mindfulness-based interventions for people diagnosed with a current episode of an anxiety or depressive disorder: A meta-analysis of randomized controlled trials. *PLoS One, 9*(4), e96110.

Sundararaman, L. V., Edwards, R. R., Ross, E. L., & Jamison, R. N. (2017). Integration of mobile health technology in the treatment of chronic pain. *Regional Anesthesia and Pain Medicine, 42*, 488–498.

Teasdale, J. D., Segal, Z. V., Mark, J., Ridgeway, V. A., Soulsby, J. M., & Lau, M. A. (2000). Prevention of relapse/recurrence in major depression by mindfulness-based cognitive therapy. *Journal of Consulting and Clinical Psychology, 68*, 615–623.

Ussher, M., Spatz, A., Copland, C., Nicolaou, A., Cargill, A., Amini-Tabrizi, N., & McCracken, L. M. (2014). Immediate effects of a brief mindfulness-based body scan on patients with chronic pain. *Journal of Behavioral Medicine, 37*, 127–134.

Vachon-Presseau, E., Roy, M., Martel, M. O., Caron, E., Marin, M. F., Chen, J., . . . Rainville, P. (2013). The stress model of chronic pain: Evidence from basal cortisol and hippocampal structure and function in humans. *Brain, 136*, 815–827.

Vardeh, D., Edwards, R. R., Jamison, R. N., & Eccleston, C. (2013). There's an app for that: Mobile technology is a new advantage in managing chronic pain. *Pain Clinical Updates, 21*, 1–7.

Veehof, M. M., Oskam, M., Schreurs, K. M. G., & Bohlmeijer, E. T. (2011). Acceptance-based interventions for the treatment of chronic pain: A systematic review and meta-analysis. *Pain, 152*, 533–542.

Vowles, K. E., & McCracken, L. M. (2008). Acceptance and values-based action in chronic pain: A study of treatment effectiveness and process. *Journal of Consulting and Clinical Psychology, 76*, 397–407.

Waddell, G. (1996). Low back pain: A twentieth century health care enigma. *Spine, 21*, 2820–2825.

Wetherell, J. L., Afari, N., Rutledge, T., Sorrell, J. T., Stoddard, J. A., Petkus, A. J., . . . Atkinson, J. H. (2011). A randomized, controlled trial of acceptance and commitment therapy and cognitive-behavioral therapy for chronic pain. *Pain, 152*, 2098–2107.

Wicksell, R. K., Kermani, M., Jensen, K., Kosek, E., Kadetoff, D., Sorjonen, K., . . . Olsson, G. L. (2013). Acceptance and commitment therapy for fibromyalgia: A randomized controlled trial. *European Journal of Pain, 17*, 599–611.

Woods-Giscombé, C., & Gaylord, S. A. (2014). The cultural relevance of mindfulness meditation as a health intervention for African Americans: Implications for reducing stress-related health disparities. *Journal of Holistic Nursing, 32*, 147–160.

Zeidan, F., Gordon, N. S., Merchant, J., & Goolkasian, P. (2010). The effects of brief mindfulness meditation training on experimentally induced pain. *Journal of Pain, 11*, 199–209.

6

Group Interventions for Chronic Pain

Amanda L. Bye and Melannie D. Nienaber

Background

The framework within which chronic pain is understood has transitioned over the past several decades from a purely medical to a biopsychosocial model, as discussed at length throughout this volume. With increased understanding of the multifaceted and complex phenomena of chronic pain has come a multitude of intervention developments. Patients no longer have exclusively medical and pharmacological intervention options for their pain; indeed, the incorporation of evidence-based psychosocial interventions is now considered essential as part of a comprehensive, interdisciplinary pain management approach for many chronic pain conditions. Within this context, group-level interventions for chronic pain serve as an evidence-based, often cost-effective option that also carries the additional benefit of facilitating interpersonal interactions and connections for a patient population especially vulnerable to social isolation. This chapter briefly reviews the historical context of group-level interventions in medical and behavioral health, as well as the literature examining efficacy and feasibility of this intervention modality within the chronic pain population. This chapter also discusses patient-level and other variables impacting group design and implementation in varied clinical settings.

Historical Context: Group-Level Intervention as an Evidence-Based Modality in Behavioral Health and Medicine

Although conducted in various forms for several decades prior, psychosocial group treatment began to gain attention in the 1960s as an alternative to individual therapy that was cost-effective for many populations. Further research in the 1970s concluded that group therapy often performed as well as individual psychotherapy, with both modalities outperforming waitlist control groups, spurring further research into the efficacy of group therapy as a stand-alone treatment approach (Bednar & Kaul, 1978; Luborsky, Singer, & Luborsky, 1975; Meltzoff & Kornreich, 1970). In the 1990s, group treatment protocols were developed further for specific diagnoses, settings, and therapeutic orientations (Burlingame, Strauss, & Joyce, 2013). During this time, health maintenance organizations (HMOs) began to recognize that this type of therapy was both cost-effective for healthcare organizations and effective for patients, which had implications for insurance coverage.

Overall, group therapy has been shown to be more effective than no treatment, with variability in outcomes dependent in part on several variables, such as patient characteristics and treatment approach (Burlingame et al., 2013). For example, homogenous groups outperform mixed symptom groups, outpatient groups are more effective than inpatient groups, and cognitive-behavioral groups are superior to strictly behavioral, psychodynamic, or eclectic groups (Burlingame, Fuhriman, & Mosier, 2003).

Group therapy, particularly when grounded in cognitive-behavioral theory, has been used in medical settings as an effective treatment modality for several chronic conditions. As just a few examples, Tkachuk, Graff, Martin, and Bernstein (2003) compared ten sessions of cognitive-behavioral group therapy (CBGT) to weekly telephone visits for irritable bowel syndrome (IBS) patients. Group therapy patients had increased gastrointestinal (GI) symptom improvement, decreased psychological distress, improved quality of life, and reduced self-reported pain at three-month follow-up. As another example, Tatrow and Montgomery (2006) conducted a meta-analysis of 20 studies using CBT with breast cancer patients and found that pain and emotional distress improved from both group and individual therapy. The individual therapy approach yielded slightly more improvement in distress, whereas pain improvements were statistically equivalent in both the group and individual therapy groups when compared to control groups.

Group-level interventions also have been applied to medical populations using allied health professionals as facilitators, a practice that can improve intervention accessibility in settings that do not have behavioral health providers readily available. For example, Espie and colleagues (2007) trained primary care nurses to administer five sessions of CBT insomnia skills in a small group setting and compared this to a treatment as usual control group. The CBT skills included sleep education, sleep hygiene, relaxation, sleep scheduling, and cognitive approaches to improve sleep. The treatment group showed statistically significant improvements in sleep, general mental health, and energy.

A comprehensive review of the history and current use of group-level interventions across medical populations is outside the scope of this chapter. However, suffice it to say that appreciation is increasing for the benefits that CBT and related psychological/behavioral interventions can have for improving physiological and

emotional components of varied disease processes. With this increasing appreciation comes increasing utilization of behavioral health-led and multidisciplinary
group-level interventions for medical populations.

The Emergence of Group-Level Interventions in Chronic Pain Treatment

The limits of exclusively medical interventions for chronic pain historically have
been well documented, informing the transition from medical to biopsychosocial
models. In turn, this shift in conceptualization of pain led to the emergence of integrated, multidisciplinary treatment approaches. By the late 1950s, anesthesiologist
John Bonica established one of the first multidisciplinary pain clinics after recognizing the limitations of medical interventions and pharmacotherapy when treating
soldiers' pain (Tompkins, Hobelmann, & Compton, 2017). The impetus for starting
this clinic was Bonica's dissatisfaction with his own management of soldiers' pain
during World War II. The clinic, originally started at Tacoma General Hospital and
then later moved to the clinic at the University of Washington in Seattle, focused on
increasing the efficiency of consultative practice and decreasing patient burden by
co-locating all staff members to the same space (Tompkins et al., 2017).

Bonica found that patients were more functional and had better overall pain
management when treated in this setting. Wilbert Fordyce, a psychologist at the
clinic, applied operant conditioning methods to patient care with the goals of
extinguishing or decreasing behaviors that were ineffective in managing pain
(e.g., moaning, gasping, verbalizing pain, inactivity, guarding behaviors, and taking medications as needed versus on a time schedule) and increasing behaviors
effective in improving pain management (e.g., engaging with physical and occupational therapy to increase activity level, walking, work-related activities, and
social engagement).

Guidelines for what constitutes a multidisciplinary pain program emerged,
expanding upon Bonica's work. By the 1970s, the clinic at the University of
Washington had added research scientists to study treatment outcomes (Tompkins et al., 2017). The focus for effective pain management was no longer on one
discipline, but on an understanding of the importance of each discipline working in collaboration to provide the best possible care. The providers who were
trained in managing chronic pain included two physicians, a pain psychologist, a
physical therapist, and additional healthcare providers as needed. The entire pain
team met to discuss the patient's care. Comprehensive care included a physical
exam, medication management, biopsychosocial evaluation, cognitive-behavioral
therapy (CBT) for chronic pain, physical therapy, occupational therapy, and referral to other specialists as needed. This pain team also shared space to facilitate
coordination and continuity of care (Tompkins et al., 2017; Scascighini, Toma,
Dober-Spielmann, & Sprott, 2008).

Analysis of this pain treatment program indicated that it was a multidisciplinary approach that effectively helped patients function and cope with pain,

and that one solitary discipline did not outperform the rest (Schatman, 2010). These programs successfully reduced healthcare costs and increased the patients' functionality and ability to return to employment (Flor, Fydrich, & Turk, 1992; Kamper et al., 2015). Based on the momentum from these outcomes, pain programs (along with accredited pain fellowship programs) began to flourish, and recommendations were made to use opioid medications sparingly as they were known to cause addiction and poor outcomes (Meldrum, 2003).

As interdisciplinary treatment models developed, group-level interventions often were essential components, and today are quite common. For example, a 2008 meta-analysis reviewed the effectiveness of multidisciplinary treatment for chronic pain grounded in CBT modalities, operant-behavioral components, and graduated activity exposure (Scascighini et al., 2008). The minimum standard of multidisciplinary therapy was established as specific individual exercising; regular training in relaxation techniques; group therapy led by a clinical psychologist (1.5 hours per week); patient education sessions once per week; two CBT-based physiotherapy treatments per week for pacing strategies; and medical and neurophysiology education provided by trained physicians. The majority of these interventions were delivered in group sessions, with efficacy of these multidisciplinary chronic pain programs significantly better than both standard medical treatment and other non-multidisciplinary treatments.

As noted previously, Bonica's work established the benefits of various medical, behavioral, and emotionally focused group-level interventions for chronic pain patients. Continued research and meta-analyses in the last two decades consistently have demonstrated positive treatment outcomes from group models of various theoretical orientations with chronic pain patients. For example, a systematic review and meta-analysis of chronic pain psychological interventions for older adults with non-cancer pain included 22 studies, with 2,608 participants, and investigated the association between participant (e.g., age, gender), intervention (treatment delivery mode), and study (e.g., methodological quality) characteristics and outcomes (Niknejad et al., 2018). The researchers concluded that treatment outcomes were strongest when delivered in group-based approaches.

Another meta-analysis reviewed 22 randomized controlled trials (RCTs) that examined the efficacy of outpatient psychological interventions for adults with chronic low back pain (Hoffman, Papas, Chatkoff, & Kerns, 2007). The psychological interventions included CBT, self-regulatory approaches such as biofeedback, relaxation, hypnosis, behavioral therapy, supportive counseling, and education. These identified studies included multidisciplinary approaches, with psychological intervention that included group-level intervention or individual work. When contrasted to the waitlist control groups, psychological interventions had a positive impact on decreasing pain intensity, pain-related interference, depression, and health-related quality of life, with CBT and self-regulatory approaches showing the most robust positive effects (Hoffman et al., 2007). The analyses from this review also highlighted findings that multidisciplinary programs with psychological interventions were superior to other active treatment conditions in terms of work-related outcomes at both short- and long-term follow-up. Although the authors did not compare the efficacy of group versus individual treatment modalities, many of the included studies utilized groups.

Another recent systematic review of 11 studies examined the efficacy of acceptance and commitment therapy (ACT) interventions compared to control conditions and other active treatments for adults with chronic pain (Hughes, Clark, Colclough, Dale, & McMillan, 2017). Significant medium to large effect sizes were found for pain acceptance and psychological flexibility, along with significant small to medium effect sizes for measures of functioning, anxiety, and depression. Subgroup analyses looking at group-level interventions found small to large effects on a range of outcomes favoring ACT over control conditions, with the exception of quality of life outcomes, which had insufficient evidence of effect (possibly due to low statistical power). There also was some evidence of continued effect at follow-up.

In 2016, Cherkin and colleagues randomized 345 chronic low back pain patients to receive usual care, or usual care plus either mindfulness-based stress reduction (MBSR) or cognitive-behavioral therapy (CBT), delivered in two-hour group sessions for eight weeks (Cherkin et al., 2016). The colleagues measured outcomes at baseline, four weeks, eight weeks, and 52 weeks using the modified Roland Disability Questionnaire (RDQ; Roland & Fairbank, 2000) and a self-report back pain bothersomeness scale (which measured back pain discomfort on a scale of 0–10). At 26 weeks post-intervention, both MBSR and CBT groups demonstrated clinically meaningful and statistically significant changes on the RDQ and the back pain bothersomeness scale, compared to the usual care group. At 52 weeks, MBSR patients appeared to maintain statistically significant differences compared to usual care patients.

This type of study suggests promise for group-level intervention as a viable long-term pain management option, when currently there are limited interventions with demonstrated long-term benefit (Goyal & Haythornthwaite, 2016). Of note, in this study only 51% of participants in the MBSR group and 57% of participants in the CBT group attended at least six group sessions, highlighting some of the attrition challenges in group models. Additional research examining whether there are partial effects for patients who attend but do not complete group treatment courses, as well as examining strategies for minimizing patient attrition rates and reducing barriers to treatment completion, would be helpful.

Financial, Feasibility, and Logistical Considerations for Chronic Pain Group Treatment

The healthcare costs of treating chronic pain in the United States, which are estimated to be between $560 to $635 billion annually, are higher than for any other medical condition and are increasing annually (Gaskin & Richard, 2011). Although the cost of chronic pain treatment impacts patients across the economic spectrum, often the burden is greatest on people living in poverty.

In 2016, 27.3 million Americans (8.6%) were uninsured, and 48.3% of adults aged 18–64 years were classified as poor or near poor according to U.S. poverty standards (Cohen, Martinez, & Zammitti, 2016). Patients at the lower end of the socioeconomic spectrum often are unable to afford multiple medical visits and pain medications, potentially contributing to sub-optimally managed pain and subsequent decreased ability to work. Group therapy therefore may be especially beneficial to pain patients with financial challenges who cannot afford more individualized forms of psychosocial intervention, as the cost of a group session can be substantially less than the cost of an individual visit with a behavioral health provider in commercial healthcare plans.

In addition, patients who attend and complete group interventions may benefit financially from being able to sustain employment as a result of improvements in functioning. Linton and Andersson (2000) found that a spinal pain patient's likelihood of applying for disability decreased nine-fold when he/she attended a CBT group compared to education-only control groups. In addition, the CBT group participants decreased their use of physician and physical therapy visits when compared to the two control groups.

On the other hand, while cost may be a benefit of group treatment, there can be several logistical challenges. First, patients may have difficulty committing the time needed for a multi-session group. People still working may struggle to obtain adequate time off from work, especially if they have already missed work due to pain. Second, patients may struggle to access viable and consistent transportation, especially if their pain condition or medication side effects restrict their ability to drive themselves.

In light of these and other logistical challenges, single-session groups may be the most logistically feasible group intervention model for some patients, particularly inasmuch as such sessions show promise as an effective means of delivering psychoeducation and pain management skills (Jones, Lookatch, & Moore, 2013). Specifically, several pilot studies have examined the impact of single-session pain management groups on reducing overall pain catastrophizing, a pattern of negative cognitive-emotional responses to real or anticipated pain that can maintain chronic pain and undermine medical treatments (Darnall, Sturgeon, Ming-Chih, Hah, & Mackey, 2014).

One uncontrolled pilot trial with 70 patients conducted at an outpatient pain clinic (Stanford Pain Management Center) consisted of a free, single-session group targeting pain catastrophizing (Darnall et al., 2014). The Pain Catastrophizing Scale (PCS) was administered anonymously at class check-in (baseline) and at two and four weeks post-treatment. Findings demonstrated reductions in pain catastrophizing that were clinically significant at weeks two and four, with 66.7% of patients achieving either moderately or substantially important reductions (Darnall et al., 2014).

Another pilot study using a single-session group intervention for pain management emphasized psychoeducation regarding five key pain management skills: understanding, accepting, calming, balancing, and coping. Over half of the group members (53%) reported that the group helped a "great deal" in managing their pain (Jones et al., 2013). In addition, overall pain scores on the PCS significantly decreased, specifically in the rumination and helplessness subscales, at three-month follow-up.

Single-session group interventions may provide a unique and effective opportunity to support populations that otherwise may be unable to access longer group formats due to financial, occupational, and transportation constraints. Additional studies are needed regarding the most important elements to emphasize in these groups.

Interpersonal and Social Benefits of Group Intervention

The effects of chronic pain on patients' lives are far-reaching, affecting not only the ability to work and complete daily chores/tasks but also interpersonal communication and relationships. Individuals experiencing chronic pain and illness often describe the isolating effects of their conditions, as they are unable to engage in relationships the way they used to. As described elsewhere in this volume, depression and chronic pain frequently co-occur, best understood within the context of the biopsychosocial model, and many patients experience a vicious cycle of pain and negative emotions that further contributes to isolation. Within this context, group treatment is a viable modality not only as a mechanism to disseminate pain management skills but also to facilitate interpersonal interaction and the development of supportive relationships among group members.

Yalom and Leszcz (2005) indicated that most change occurs within the social context of group therapy. Participating in a group allows patients to practice social skills, experience cohesion, and help others while learning from them. Ideally, chronic pain group norms and dynamics are established that facilitate positive patient interactions and provide positive interpersonal feedback for self-efficacy and motivation. Sharing experiences within a group also can contribute to shared accountability for learning and utilizing new skills. Steihaug, Ahlsen, and Malterud (2002) conducted a qualitative study of patients who completed chronic pain group treatment and found that being listened to, understood, accepted, tolerated, and affirmed by the therapist(s) and other group members were highly valued perceived benefits of the group approach for pain management. Similarly, Thorn and Kuhajda (2006) noted that the group process itself is therapeutic in that pain patients often report feeling isolated and misunderstood, and thus peer support aids in decreasing these negative emotions through fostering connections.

Patients often tend to feel as though their experiences are unique to them and that other people (especially health professionals) cannot understand what they are going through. Yalom and Leszcz (2005) use the term *universality* to describe the group benefit of patients realizing that others share their experiences. Relatedly, another advantage of group treatment is that patients gain the opportunity to receive feedback or advice from others with perceived shared pain status, feedback that is often better received than from the facilitator. Group members may be more likely to engage and follow-up with recommendations when other group members advocate that the skills being taught do indeed help.

Many patients with chronic pain have been through extensive medical work-ups and have found that few of the subsequent procedure or treatment recommendations provided relief. They often feel defeated and hopeless about the future as they come into the group. However, group treatment offers a unique experience during which the patient can witness first hand as other group members improve and celebrate their successes. This in turn may instill hope that they too can function better notwithstanding their pain.

Approaches to Chronic Pain Group Intervention

There are many different approaches to group intervention for chronic pain. Though common modalities are described below, providers typically combine elements from each into packaged, cohesive intervention programs.

Psychoeducation

Psychoeducation is often a very important component of group-level interventions. (Pure psychoeducation groups typically serve as control or comparison groups in research studying the efficacy of group intervention packages for chronic pain). Psychoeducation often includes information about the physiology of chronic pain (e.g., models such as "gate control theory," concepts such as pain sensitivity, and theories such as the biopsychosocial model of chronic pain), as well as information about concepts such as self-efficacy, self-management of chronic pain, and coping strategies (e.g., problem-solving, activity pacing, increasing social support). These coping and self-management strategies often derive from cognitive-behavioral and mindfulness-based intervention approaches (see below).

Studies examining groups with primarily a psychoeducation focus most commonly discuss the benefit of disseminating care to populations with logistical limitations (e.g., geographical and resource-based). For example, LeFort, Gray-Donald, Rowat, and Jeans (1998) compared a 12-hour low-cost, community-based psychoeducation group, which they called the Chronic Pain Self-Management Program (CPSMP), to a three-month waitlist comparison group. The CPSMP focused on education about medication, nutrition, depression, communication, and problem-solving. Patients who completed the CPSMP reported significant decreases in pain and improvements in vitality, life satisfaction, resourcefulness, and self-efficacy. The authors discussed how this group, administered by a nurse following a clear protocol, provided a mechanism for disseminating psychoeducation to more rural communities and to clinics without a specialty pain program.

Salvetti et al. (2012) adapted psychoeducation models from more developed countries into an eight-week, nurse-led psychoeducational program for patients in Brazil. The education focused on acute versus chronic pain, physiological responses to pain, exercise, stretching, emotional responses to pain, thoughts about pain, problem-solving, relaxation, diet, sleep, medication, physical therapy, and strategies for increasing functioning. Despite a significant number of patients (36%) being labeled as "low treatment adherent" (withdrawing from the program or attending less than 60% of sessions), patients who were adherent experienced significant decreases in pain intensity, disability, and depression.

Cognitive-Behavioral Therapy

Cognitive-behavioral therapy (CBT) applications to chronic pain populations have been studied at length (e.g., Thorn & Kuhajda, 2006; Williams, Eccleston, & Morley, 2012; Day, Thorn, & Burns, 2012). CBT does not dictate a specific protocol, and therefore group intervention details such as the specific skills taught and the number and length of sessions may vary. Most CBT interventions for chronic pain include psychoeducation (e.g., Ehde, Dillworth, & Turner, 2014; Williams et al., 2012), and common additional intervention components include cognitive restructuring, relaxation training, stress management, activity planning, behavioral activation, scheduling of pleasant activities, and communication skills. Assigning specific homework between sessions is common.

While CBT models address several categories of maladaptive or distorted thinking that can increase the subjective experience of pain, *catastrophizing* about pain in particular has been linked to poorer emotional and social functioning (e.g., Hamilton, Zautra, & Reich, 2005) and poorer medical response to interventions (Mankovsky, Lynch, Clark, Sawynok, & Sullivan, 2012), as well as worse pain coping and functioning (Sturgeon, 2014). Therefore, CBT group interventions typically include content specific to building the skillset for identifying and restructuring catastrophizing thoughts (Thorn & Kuhajda, 2006).

Williams et al. (2012) performed meta-analyses of CBT group treatment and found small to medium effect sizes for pain, disability, mood, and catastrophizing as compared to either treatment as usual (TAU) or waitlist control immediately post-treatment. However, these effects were not found at follow-up, with the exception of mood. Notably, this review included only randomized controlled trials and included all adult subgroups regardless of pain condition. It is important to look at treatment effects for subgroups of patients matched on pain condition as well, given that any intervention for chronic pain may have stronger or weaker efficacy for certain subpopulations. See Murphy et al. (2014) for an example of a comprehensive, manualized group-level CBT-based intervention. In addition, Chapter 4 of this volume reviews cognitive-behavioral interventions for chronic pain in depth.

Acceptance and Commitment Therapy

ACT is a "third-wave" CBT intervention approach that focuses primarily on acceptance, values-based living, commitment to making behavioral changes that align with values, and adopting an "observer" mentality toward the patient's thoughts and experiences (Hayes, Strosahl, & Wilson, 2012). A core concept of ACT is psychological flexibility, which incorporates mindfulness, recognizing values, making a commitment to shifting behaviors, recognizing the observing self, cognitive defusion (recognizing a thought without trying to change it), and acceptance (Harris, 2009).

ACT has begun to be applied to group intervention models for chronic pain. For example, McCracken, Sato, and Taylor (2013) designed an ACT-based chronic pain group consisting of four sessions administered over two weeks in a primary care setting. The researchers administered this to a mixed diagnosis chronic pain group, with 40.3% of the participants having comorbid depression. The treatment manual taught psychological flexibility, acceptance, cognitive defusion, determining values, and making a commitment to action. Experience-based interventions were emphasized over psychoeducation. The ACT treatment group, compared to the TAU group, improved in several areas, including pain, depression, and disability.

Wicksell et al. (2013) compared a 12-week ACT group to a waitlist control for patients with fibromyalgia. Intervention patients experienced improvements in pain-related functioning, impact of fibromyalgia on daily life, quality of life, self-efficacy, depression, anxiety, and psychological flexibility. Wetherell et al. (2011) also designed an eight-session, 90-minute ACT group and compared this to a CBT group, both administered in a primary care setting to a mixed chronic, nonmalignant pain population. Both groups showed improvements in pain interference, depression, and pain-related anxiety, but the ACT group rated higher in treatment satisfaction. ACT skills in this group included body scans, recognizing values, cognitive defusion, mindfulness, and committed action. Please see Chapter 5 for additional information about mindfulness-based interventions, including ACT, for chronic pain.

Mindfulness-Based Stress Reduction

Mindfulness-based stress reduction (MBSR) is a didactic and experiential approach to intervention during which patients learn to be present "in the moment" in a nonjudgmental way (Kabat-Zinn, 1985). In its full form, this manualized program is typically six to eight weeks and includes two-hour weekly group sessions, as well as in-home skills practice for 15–30 minutes per day. This type of group therapy has been found to be effective in helping patients manage their chronic pain (Kabat-Zinn, Lipworth, & Burney, 1985), depression, and anxiety (Serpa, Taylor, & Tillisch, 2014; Hofmann, Sawyer, Witt, & Oh, 2010). Patients with arthritis and chronic low back pain have shown improvements in pain intensity and functional quality of life after completing an eight-week MBSR intervention, with effect sizes increasing in relation to the amount of home practice completed by the individual patient (Rosenzweig et al., 2010).

Components of MBSR also have been effective when integrated into other treatment programs in experimental designs. For example, Sharon et al. (2016) had participants practice mindfulness meditation in a group setting for at least one hour per day for a minimum of three days per week for one year. The study design introduced pain to the participants to obtain their baseline pain thresholds. The participants then were given naloxone, an opioid antagonist. After receiving this medication, the analgesic effects of mindfulness wore off and their pain response to the same stimulus increased, showing that mindfulness practices influence the endogenous opioid system to induce pain relief. In general, research has indicated reductions in pain intensity from 40% to 50% and reductions in pain unpleasantness up to 57% when participants regularly use mindfulness practices (Zeidan et al., 2011; Kabat-Zinn, 1982).

Group Intervention Packages

There are now several manualized chronic pain group interventions that are evidence-based. Though reviewing all of these in depth is outside the scope of this chapter, please refer to Table 6.1 for examples.

Other Group Intervention Components

Group-level interventions for chronic pain frequently will be multidisciplinary or interdisciplinary in content and scope. For example, content may be included from the following disciplines.

Physical Therapy

Physical therapists are often an important part of the chronic pain patient's treatment team, and psychoeducation and interventions drawn from physical therapy have utility when included in group interventions. Physical therapy as a treatment modality for managing chronic pain and increasing functioning has been well-documented (e.g., Tompkins et al., 2017). Psychoeducation content may include body mechanics, the impact of movement on pain, theories on how pain becomes chronic, lifestyle changes, and strategies for moving without the fear of causing more pain. Mannerkorpi, Nyberg, Ahlmén, and Ekdahl (2000) compared a six-month psychoeducation only group to a psychoeducation plus pool-based therapy group for fibromyalgia patients. The psychoeducation plus pool therapy group increased physical functioning, grip strength, social functioning, and quality of life scores immediately following the six-month program. There were no clinically significant improvements within the psychoeducation only group. Notably, the improvements in pain, fatigue, walking, and social functioning remained higher in comparison to the participants' baseline scores two years later (Mannerkorpi, Ahlmén, & Ekdahl, 2009).

Nutrition

The relationship between weight and chronic pain has been documented. For example, Hitt, McMillen, Thornton-Neaves, Koch, and Cosby (2007) found that

Table 6.1 Examples of Established Group Interventions for Chronic Pain

Program	Length of Treatment	Multidisciplinary Team	Program Includes	Outcome Measures
Veterans Administration CBT-CP (Murphy, McKellar, Raffa, Clark, Kerns & Karlin, 2014)	12 sessions	Psychologist, social worker, physical therapist and primary care physician	Psychoeducation, physical activity, relaxation, and CBT skills (e.g., goal setting, pleasant activities, cognitive restructuring, sleep, maintaining gains)	Pain Numeric Rating Scale (NRS), West-Haven Yale Multidimensional Pain Inventory-Interference Subscale (WHYMPI-MPI/INT), Patient Health Questionnaire (PHQ-9), World Health Organization Quality of Life-Brief Version (WHOQOL-BREF), Working Alliance Inventory-Short Revised (WAI-SR), Subjective Units of Distress Scale (SUDS)
Comprehensive Pain Rehabilitation Center (Mayo Clinic, 2006)	3-week outpatient program	Psychologist, biofeedback counselor, chemical dependency counselor as needed, physical therapist, occupational therapist, pharmacist, nurse, physician and family or support person	Psychoeducation, biofeedback, meditation, relaxation through CAM, CBT skills (such as sleep, lifestyle management, pleasant activities)	Center for Epidemiology Study-Depression Scale (CES-D), Patient Satisfaction, Multidimensional Pain Inventory (MPI), Pain Catastrophizing Scale (PCS), SF-36 Health Survey
Chronic Pain Rehabilitation Program (Cleveland Clinic, 2018)	5 days per week for 3–4 weeks	Mental health therapists, chemical dependency counselor if needed, physical therapist, occupational therapist, vocational rehabilitation counselor, nurse, physician and family	Biofeedback, relaxation, CBT skills, yoga, and aquatic therapy	Pain Intensity Scale, Depression Anxiety Stress Scale (DASS-21), Pain Disability Index

morbidly obese people were four times as likely to have a chronic pain complaint as people who were underweight or at a normal body mass index. Decreasing weight and changing diet can positively impact a patient's ability to manage his/her pain. Additionally, anti-inflammatory diets have been found to increase physical functioning in patients with rheumatoid arthritis and osteoarthritis (Clinton, O'Brien, Law, Renier, & Wendt, 2015; Skoldstram, Hagfors, & Johansson, 2003). Skoldstram et al. (2003) found that patients with rheumatoid arthritis who ate a Mediterranean diet experienced a decrease in inflammation, an increase in physical functioning, and an increase in vitality when compared to patients who ate a traditional Western diet. Clinton et al. (2015) found that participants who ate a whole-food, plant-based diet had increased energy, improvements in physical functioning, and decreases in pain compared to patients who continued their current diet. In general, dietary changes come with minimal risk and show promise in helping patients to manage chronic pain. Moreover, groups easily can incorporate healthy eating and weight management strategies into curricula.

Sleep Medicine

The relationship between sleep deprivation and chronic pain has been well-studied. Currie, Wilson, Pontefract, and de Laplante (2000) conducted a randomized controlled trial of 60 participants who were assigned either to a seven-week CBT group focused on sleep habits or to a waitlist control group. The participants had been diagnosed with both insomnia and chronic pain. Results indicated patients in the CBT group reported improved sleep on self-report questionnaires and exhibited fewer motor activities during a sleep study. This effect was still measurable at the three-month follow-up. There also was a trend toward greater decreases in pain severity for those participants in the CBT group, although pain was not a focus of the intervention.

Another study by Vitiello, Rybarczyk, von Korff, and Stepanski (2009) specifically compared Cognitive Behavioral Therapy for Insomnia (CBT-I) interventions to attention control stress management classes in a group setting. These participants were 55 years or older and had osteoarthritic pain. Both groups were eight weeks in duration for two hours per week. CBT-I group patients showed improvements in sleep and decreases in pain. Again, this study provided skills targeting sleep improvement only; no skills targeted the improvement of pain. Incorporating psychoeducation about the relationship between sleep and pain, as well as teaching evidence-based strategies for improving sleep quantity and quality, therefore may have value added for chronic pain group-level interventions.

Complementary and Alternative Medicine (CAM)

CAM has gained a great deal of attention in the past decade given the low risks associated with this type of care. CAM encompasses acupuncture, massage, chiropractic, MBSR (discussed above), yoga, and tai chi. For example, tai chi has been found to help with osteoarthritis; yoga has been found to be effective in managing low back pain (Nahin, Boineau, Khalsa, Stussman, & Weber, 2016). Content from these modalities can be incorporated into group interventions, though further research into their efficacy is needed.

Technology Considerations

Geographical, financial, transportation, and related limitations make some sub-populations of patients particularly vulnerable to increases in risk of morbidity and mortality from multiple medical conditions, with implications relevant to chronic pain patients. For example, the Centers for Disease Control and Prevention (2017) reports that individuals living in rural areas are 50% more likely to die from unintentional injury deaths, including opioid overdoses (which is the leading cause of death in this population). Within this context, the possible benefits of applying videoconferencing technology to these populations are being explored. For example, Gardner-Nix, Backman, Barbati, and Grummitt (2008) had participants complete a two hour per week, ten-week mindfulness-based group intervention that was delivered either in-person or via videoconferencing. When compared to the waitlist control group, the in-person and videoconferencing group members improved in their overall mental health and decreased catastrophizing thoughts. However, the in-person group scored higher on the quality of life scale and had a lower usual pain score than the videoconferencing group.

We recommend reserving videoconference-administered group interventions for situations in which direct services are unattainable, given that social isolation is a common concern for chronic pain patients and therefore interpersonal interaction and in-person social support may be especially appealing components of group treatment for this population, as discussed above. Limitations to videoconference-administered group interventions may include skepticism by both the patient and clinician (Andersson & Titov, 2014), confidentiality and privacy factors (Moock, 2014), and the patient's lack of access to the internet or lack of adequate technological knowledge (van Straten, Cuijpers, & Smits, 2008).

Variables Impacting Treatment Effectiveness

As with any other group intervention in behavioral health, patient-level variables may impact treatment appropriateness and outcomes. In brief, patients should be excluded from group therapy if they cannot engage in the group's primary activities—interpersonal engagement, interpersonal learning, and acquiring insight—for logistical, intellectual, psychological, or interpersonal reasons (Yalom & Leszcz, 2005). Although further exploring and understanding the mediator and moderator variables most relevant to this population and treatment modality should be the focus of future research, we review some key domains for consideration here.

Psychiatric Comorbidities: Many patients in any chronic pain treatment group inevitably will have comorbid mental health conditions (see Chapters 17–19).

However, severe mental health symptoms either may need to be treated prior to group intervention or may be contraindications for group treatment entirely if they will interfere with the patient's ability to benefit from group intervention and/or negatively impact the experiences of the other group members. Mental health conditions that may fall into this category include severe PTSD, panic disorder, and severe mental illness such as schizophrenia. Additionally, patients with underlying personality disorders, or with cluster A, B, and/or C symptoms, may be better suited to gain chronic pain management tools in an individual setting given the interpersonal disturbances fundamental to these conditions.

It is estimated that up to 50% of patients in addictions treatment report chronic pain, and up to 19% of patients seeking treatment for pain report a current substance use disorder (Rosenblum et al., 2003). Patients with a substance addiction may require individual therapy or a referral to chemical dependency treatment as a first step, as they are unlikely to benefit from chronic pain treatment (either individually or group-administered). In extreme situations, a group member with active addiction may pose a risk of diverting or selling medications within the group.

Treatment Expectations: Psychotherapy research shows that a patient's pre-treatment beliefs about the success of the treatment are among the strongest predictors of the actual treatment outcome (Goossens, Vlaeyen, Hidding, Kole-Snijders, & Evers, 2005). Patients often report that they have tried diverse types of treatments, include counseling, with little relief or change. These situations present opportunities to explore expectations with respect to chronic pain management interventions, including any past experiences with group treatment and psychotherapy specific to pain management, and to utilize motivational interviewing or psychoeducation to instill hope and bolster treatment expectancy and self-efficacy.

Cognitive Status

Significant cognitive deficits (e.g., low IQ, dementia, or traumatic brain injury) may be contraindications for group treatment if the patient cannot comprehend the material and participate. Research also shows some relationship between non-adherence to treatment recommendations and cognitive impairment (Moriarty et al., 2017). At times, having a support person (e.g., spouse, friend, adult child) participate in group with the patient may make participation more feasible and appropriate. Other benefits of including caregivers in group interventions when patients are cognitively impaired include exposing caregivers to educational material about risk and safety of controlled medications for pain, and ways to increase safety with these medications.

Sex

A meta-analysis of group-based therapy performed by Burlingame and colleagues (2003) indicated that men tend to benefit more from mixed gender therapy groups than from male-only groups. However, the findings for women were inconclusive. Women may benefit especially from a relational approach that emphasizes interpersonal connections and utilizes their natural support system (Poleshuck et al., 2010). More research is needed to understand what, if any, role sex plays in moderating group treatment outcomes for chronic pain patients specifically. However, therapists should be aware of societal sex and gender expectations and ensure that these are not negatively affecting the therapeutic process in group.

Ethnicity and Culture

As discussed at length in Chapter 23, ethnic and cultural variables are especially important to consider when working with chronic pain patients. Johnson, Saha, Arbelaez, Beach, and Cooper (2004) found that racial and ethnic minorities felt judged by healthcare providers based on their race in comparison to non-Hispanic White patients, and conscious or unconscious biases can impact how chronic pain is managed in different ethnic populations. Many Black adults 65 years and older, born prior to 1951 during times of racial tension and government-mandated segregation, have experienced significant disparities in healthcare, disparities that have contributed to poor health outcomes (Mays, Cochran, & Barnes, 2007). Within the context of pain management groups, these experiences may affect the ability or willingness of older African Americans to self-report pain.

Culturally based responses to pain by patients may be divided into two categories: stoic or emotive (Carteret, 2011). Patients from Asian cultures often exemplify stoicism in response to pain, stoic responses that correlate strongly with cultural values about self-conduct (Carteret, 2011). In traditional Asian cultures, preserving harmony in interactions is critically important, and individuals avoid drawing attention to themselves, especially in negative ways. Not showing sadness or pain is customary. Social status, impacted by variables such as sex, age, education, and occupation, also is emphasized. This may influence the group member–facilitator relationship, as the patient may perceive the facilitator as "high status" and subsequently seek to avoid "burdening" the facilitator with complaints about discomfort (Carteret, 2011).

A 2013 review of relevant research looking at the influence of cultural experiences on pain management identified several relevant provider-level factors: 1) stereotyping or inherent biases based on patients' cultural identities; 2) cultural experiences of the provider that influences communication with patient; 3) an inadequate cultural knowledge base from which to treat a diverse patient population; and 4) culturally insensitive practices that negatively influence the provider–patient relationship (Pillay, Adriaan van Zyl, & Blackbeard, 2013). Within any medical or behavioral health setting, the culturally sensitive clinician presents with an openness and desire to learn about other ethnicities and cultures. This openness, when modeled by a group facilitator, can help establish a group norm that is accommodating and respectful of differences in values, opinions, and attitudes of group members from diverse backgrounds.

Constant self-awareness and understanding of implicit bias may further foster culturally sensitive practice. Identifying and addressing one's implicit and explicit biases is core to professional competence and ethical practice as a group facilitator. Reflecting on one's own beliefs about pain and pain perception, and about "normal" responses to pain, is essential for providers. Culturally sensitive practices can be integrated into all aspects of the group therapy process, from initial contact to the final group session. Intentionally establishing group norms that promote acceptance and respect toward varying viewpoints regarding pain can result in a group process built upon trust and mutual respect. Accommodation and use of interpreters should be considered, as well as development of group materials and handouts that are translated into patients' preferred languages.

Conclusions and Directions for Further Research

Many chronic pain conditions are treated most effectively by utilizing a multidisciplinary team approach, as opposed to solely a medically based model of care. Within this context, group interventions show promise as often cost- and time-effective approaches with well-documented benefits ranging from decreased pain intensity to improved mental health and overall functioning. Group interventions also provide peer modeling, social interactions, and connections to other people with similar pain experiences and challenges. These social benefits especially are important for a population particularly vulnerable to social isolation. Additional research exploring mediator and moderator variables for group therapy in this population, as well as research examining the most feasible and efficient strategies for delivering group care to patients with geographical and financial limitations, would be helpful.

References

Andersson, G., & Titov, N. (2014). Advantages and limitations of Internet-based interventions for common mental disorders. *World Psychiatry, 13*(1), 4–11. http://doi.org/10.1002/wps.20083

Bednar, R., & Kaul, T. (1978). Experiential group research: Current perspectives. In S. Garfield & A. Bergin (Eds.), *Handbook of psychotherapy and behavior change* (2nd ed., pp. 769–815). New York, NY: Wiley.

Burlingame, G. M., Fuhriman, A., & Mosier, J. (2003). The differential effectiveness of group psychotherapy: A meta-analytic perspective. *Group Dynamics: Theory, Research, and Practice, 7*(1), 3–12.

Burlingame, G., Strauss, B., & Joyce, A. (2013). Change mechanisms and effectiveness of small group treatments. In Michael J. Lambert (Ed.), *Bergin and Garfield's handbook of psychotherapy and behavior change* (pp. 640–689). Hoboken, NJ: John Wiley & Sons, Inc.

Carteret, M. (2011). *Cultural aspects of pain management.* Retrieved from http://dimensionsofculture.com/2010/11/culturalaspects-of-pain-management/

Centers for Disease Control and Prevention. (2017). *Rural Americans at higher risk of death from five leading causes.* Retrieved from www.cdc.gov/media/releases/2017/p0112-rural- death-risk.html

Cherkin, D., Sherman, K., Balderson, B., Cook, A., Hawkes, R., Hansen, K., & Turner, J. (2016). Effects of Mindfulness Based Stress Reduction vs Cognitive Behavioral Therapy or usual care on back pain and functional limitations in adults with chronic low back pain. *JAMA*, *315*(12), 1240–1249.

Cleveland Clinic. (2018). *Pain management*. Retrieved from http://my.clevelandclinic.org/departments/anesthesiology/depts/pain-management and personal communication with the department

Clinton, C. M., O'Brien, S., Law, J., Renier, C. M., & Wendt, M. R. (2015). Whole-foods, plant- based diet alleviates the symptoms of osteoarthritis. *Arthritis*, *2015*, 1–9. doi:10.1155/2015/708152

Cohen, R. A., Martinez, M. E., & Zammitti, E. P. (2016, January–March). *Health insurance coverage: Early release of estimates from the National Health Interview Survey*. Retrieved September 25, 2017, from Centers for Disease Control and Prevention, Division of Health Interview Statistics, National Center for Health Statistics. Retrieved from www.cdc.gov/nchs/data/nhis/earlyrelease/insur201609.pdf

Currie, S. R., Wilson, K. G., Pontefract, A. J., & de Laplante, L. (2000). Cognitive-behavioral treatment of insomnia secondary to chronic pain. *Journal of Consulting and Clinical Psychology*, *68*, 407–416.

Darnall, B. D., Sturgeon, J. A., Ming-Chih, K., Hah, J. M., & Mackey, S. C. (2014). From catastrophizing to recovery: A pilot study of single-session treatment for pain catastrophizing. *Journal of Pain Research*, *7*, 219–226.

Day, M., Thorn, B., & Burns, J. (2012). The continuing evolution of biopsychosocial interventions for chronic pain. *Journal of Cognitive Psychotherapy*, *23*(2), 114–129.

Ehde, D. M., Dillworth, T. M., & Turner, J. A. (2014). Cognitive-behavioral therapy for individuals with chronic pain: Efficacy, innovations, and directions for research. *American Psychologist*, *69*(2), 153.

Espie, C. A., MacMahon, K. M. A., Kelly, H. L., Broomfield, N. M., Douglas, N. J., Engleman, H. M., . . . Wilson, P. (2007). Randomized clinical effectiveness trial of nurse-administered small-group cognitive behavioral therapy for persistent insomnia in general practice. *Sleep*, *30*(5), 574–584.

Flor, H., Fydrich, T., & Turk, D. C. (1992). Efficacy of multidisciplinary pain treatment centers: A meta-analytic review. *Pain*, *49*, 221–230.

Gardner-Nix, J., Backman, S., Barbati, J., & Grummitt, J. (2008). Evaluating distance education of a mindfulness-based meditation programme for chronic pain management. *Journal of Telemedicine and Telecare*, *14*(2), 88–92.

Gaskin, D. J., & Patrick, R. (2011). *Relieving pain in America: A blueprint for transforming prevention, care, education, and research*. Institute of Medicine, US Committee on Advancing Pain Research, Care, and Education. National Academic Press.

Goossens, M. E., Vlaeyen, J. W., Hidding, A., Kole-Snijders, A., & Evers, S. M. (2005). Treatment expectancy affects the outcome of cognitive-behavioral interventions in chronic pain. *Clinical Journal of Pain*, *21*(1), 18–26.

Goyal, M., & Haythornthwaite, J. A. (2016). Is it time to make mind–body approaches available for chronic low back pain? *JAMA*, *315*(12), 1236–1237.

Hamilton, N. A., Zautra, A. J., & Reich, J. W. (2005). Affect and pain in rheumatoid arthritis: Do individual differences in affect regulation and affective intensity predict emotional recovery from pain? *Annals of Behavioral Medicine*, *29*(3), 216–224.

Harris, R. (2009). *ACT made simple: An easy-to-read primer on acceptance and commitment therapy*. Oakland, CA: New Harbinger Publication

Hayes, S. C., Strosahl, K. D., & Wilson, K. G. (2012). *Acceptance and commitment therapy: The process and practice of mindful change* (2nd ed.). New York, NY: The Guilford Press.

Hitt, H. C., McMillen, R. C., Thornton-Neaves, T., Koch, K., & Cosby, A. G. (2007). Comorbidity of obesity and pain in a general population: Results from the Southern Pain Prevalence Study. *Journal of Pain, 8*(5), 430–436.

Hoffman, B. M., Papas, R. K., Chatkoff, D. K., & Kerns, R. D. (2007). Meta-analysis of psychological interventions for chronic low back pain. *Health Psychology, 26*(1), 1–9.

Hofmann, S. G., Sawyer, A. T., Witt, A. A., & Oh, D. (2010). The effect of mindfulness-based therapy on anxiety and depression: A meta-analytic review. *Journal of Consulting and Clinical Psychology, 78*(2), 169–183. http://dx.doi.org/10.1037/a0018555

Hughes, L. S., Clark, J., Colclough, J. A., Dale, E., & McMillan, D. (2017). Acceptance and Commitment Therapy (ACT) for chronic pain: A systemic review and meta-analyses. *Clinical Journal of Pain, 33*(6), 552–568.

Johnson, R. L., Saha, S., Arbelaez, J. J., Beach, M. C., & Cooper, L. A. (2004). Racial and ethnic differences in patient perceptions of bias and cultural competence in health care. *Journal of General Internal Medicine, 19*(2), 101–110.

Jones, T., Lookatch, S., & Moore, T. (2013). Effects of a single session group intervention for pain management in chronic pain patients: A pilot study. *Pain and Therapy, 2*(1), 57–64.

Kabat-Zinn, J. (1982). An outpatient program in behavioral medicine for chronic pain patients based on the practice of mindfulness meditation: Theoretical considerations and preliminary results. *General Hospital Psychiatry, 4*, 33–47.

Kabat-Zinn, J., Lipworth, L., & Burney, R. (1985). The clinical use of mindfulness meditation for the self-regulation of chronic pain. *Journal of Behavioral Medicine, 8*, 163–190.

Kamper, S. J., Apeldoorn, A. T., Chiarotto, A., Smeets, R. J. E. M., Ostelo, R. W. J. G., Guzman, J., & van Tulder, M. W. (2015). Multidisciplinary biopsychosocial rehabilitation for chronic low back pain: Cochrane systematic review and meta-analysis. *BMJ, 350*, h444.

LeFort, S. M., Gray-Donald, K., Rowat, K. M., & Jeans, M. E. (1998). Randomized controlled trial of a community-based psychoeducation program for the self-management of chronic pain. *Pain, 74*(2–3), 297–306.

Linton, S. J., & Andersson, T. (2000). Can chronic disability be prevented? A randomized trial of cognitive-behavior intervention and two forms of information for patients with spinal pain. *Spine, 25*(21), 2825–2831.

Luborsky, L., Singer, B., & Luborsky, L. (1975). Comparative studies of psychotherapy. *Archives of General Psychiatry, 32*, 995–1008.

Mankovsky, T., Lynch, M. E., Clark, A. J., Sawynok, J., & Sullivan, M. J. (2012). Pain catastrophizing predicts poor response to topical analgesics in patients with neuropathic pain. *Pain Research and Management, 17*(1), 10–14.

Mannerkorpi, K., Ahlmén, M., & Ekdahl, C. (2009). Six- and 24-month follow-up of pool exercise therapy and education for patients with fibromyalgia. *Scandinavian Journal of Rheumatology, 31*(5), 306–310.

Mannerkorpi, K., Nyberg, B., Ahlmén, M., & Ekdahl, C. (2000). Pool exercise combined with an education program for patients with fibromyalgia syndrome. A prospective, randomized study. *Journal of Rheumatology, 27*, 2473–2481

Mayo Clinic. (2006). *Comprehensive pain rehabilitation center: Program guide.* Rochester, MN: Mayo Foundation for Medical Education and Research (MFMER).

Mays, V. M., Cochran, S. D., & Barnes, N. W. (2007). Race, race-based discrimination, and health outcomes among African Americans. *Annual Review of Psychology, 58*, 201–205.

McCracken, L. M., Sato, A., & Taylor, G. J. (2013). A trial of a brief group-based form of Acceptance and Commitment Therapy (ACT) for chronic pain in general practice: Pilot outcome and process results. *Journal of Pain, 14*(11), 1398–1406.

Meldrum, M. L. (2003). A capsule history of pain management. *JAMA, 290*(18), 2470–2475.

Meltzoff, J., & Kornreich, R. (1970). *Research in psychotherapy.* New York, NY: Atherton Press.

Moock, J. (2014). Support from the Internet for Individuals with Mental Disorders: Advantages and Disadvantages of e-Mental Health Service Delivery. *Frontiers in Public Health*, *2*, 65. http://doi.org/10.3389/fpubh.2014.00065

Moriarty, O., Ruane, N., O'Gorman, D., Maharaj, C., Mitchell, C., Sarma, K., Finn, D., & McGuire, B. (2017). Cognitive impairment in patients with chronic neuropathic or radicular pain: An interaction of pain and age. *Frontiers in Behavioral Neuroscience*, *11*, 100. https://doi.org/10.3389/fnbeh.2017.00100

Murphy, J. L., McKellar, J. D., Raffa, S. D., Clark, M. E., Kerns, R. D., & Karlin, B. E. (2014). *Cognitive behavioral therapy for chronic pain among veterans: Therapist manual*. Washington, DC: U.S. Department of Veterans Affairs.

Nahin, R., Boineau, R., Khalsa, P., Stussman, B., & Weber, W. (2016). Evidence-based evaluation of complementary health approaches for pain management in the United States. *Mayo Clinic Proceedings*, *91*(9), 1292–1306.

Niknejad, B., Bolier, R., Henderson, C. R., Delgado, D., Kozlov, E., Lockenhoff, C. E., & Reid, C. (2018). Association between psychological interventions and chronic pain outcomes in older adults: A systematic and meta-analysis. *JAMA Internal Medicine*, *178*(6), 830–839.

Pillay, T., Adriaan van Zyl, H., & Blackbeard, D. (2013). Chronic pain perception and cultural experience. *Procedia-Social and Behavioral Sciences*, *113*, 151–160.

Poleshuck, E. L., Gamble, S. A., Cort, N., Hoffman-King, D., Cerrito, B., Rosario-McCabe, L. A., & Giles, D. E. (2010). Interpersonal psychotherapy for co-occurring depression and chronic pain. *Professional Psychology, Research and Practice*, *41*(4), 312–318.

Roland, M., & Fairbank, J. (2000). The Roland-Morris disability questionnaire and the Oswestry disability questionnaire. *Spine*, *25*(24), 3115–3124.

Rosenblum, A., Joseph, H., Fong, C., Kipnis, S., Cleland, C., & Portenoy R. K. (2003). Prevalence and characteristics of chronic pain among chemically dependent patients in methadone maintenance and residential treatment facilities. *JAMA*, *289*(18), 2370–2378.

Rosenzweig, S., Greeson, J., Reibel, D., Green, J., Jasser, S., & Beasley, D. (2010). Mindfulness-based stress reduction for chronic pain conditions: Variation in treatment outcomes and role of home meditation practice. *Journal of Psychosomatic Research*, *68*(1), 29–36.

Salvetti, M., Cobelo, A., Vernalha, P., Vianna, C., Canarezi, L., & Calegare, R. (2012). Effects of a psychoeducational program for chronic pain management. *Revista Latino- Americana de Enfermagem*, *20*(5), 896–902.

Scascighini, L., Toma, V., Dober-Spielmann, S., & Sprott, H. (2008). Multidisciplinary treatment for chronic pain: A systematic review of interventions and outcomes. *Rheumatology*, *47*(5), 670–678.

Schatman, M. E. (2010). Interdisciplinary chronic pain management: Perspectives on history, current status, and future viability. In: S. M. Fishman, J. Ballantyne, J. Rathmell (Eds.), *Bonica's management of pain* (pp. 1523–1532). Baltimore, MD: Lippincott Williams & Wilkins.

Serpa, J., Taylor, S., & Tillisch, K. (2014). Mindfulness-Based Stress Reduction (MBSR) reduces anxiety, depression, and suicidal ideation in veterans. *Medical Care*, *52*, 19–24.

Sharon, H., Maron-Katz, A., Simon, E., Flusser, Y., Hendler, T., Tarrasch, R., & Brill, S. (2016). Mindfulness meditation modulates pain through endogenous opioids. *The American Journal of Medicine*, *129*, 755–758.

Skoldstram, L., Hagfors, L., & Johansson, G. (2003). An experimental study of a Mediterranean diet intervention for patients with rheumatoid arthritis. *Annals of the Rheumatic Disease*, *62*(3), 208–214.

Steihaug, S., Ahlsen, B., & Malterud, K. (2002). "I am allowed to be myself": Women with chronic muscular pain being recognized. *Scandinavian Journal of Public Health*, *30*(4) 281–287.

Sturgeon, J. A. (2014). Psychological therapies for the management of chronic pain. *Psychology Research and Behavior Management, 7*, 115–124.

Tatrow, K., & Montgomery, G. H. (2006). Cognitive behavioral therapy techniques for distress and pain in breast cancer patients: A meta-analysis. *Journal of Behavioral Medicine, 29*, 17. https://doi.org/10.1007/s10865-005-9036-1

Thorn, B. E., & Kuhajda, M. C. (2006). Group cognitive therapy for chronic pain. *Journal of Clinical Psychology, 62*(11), 1355–1366.

Tkachuk, G. A., Graff, L. A., Martin, G. L., & Bernstein, C. N. (2003). Randomized control trial of cognitive-behavioral group therapy for Irritable Bowel Syndrome in a medical setting. *Journal of Clinical Psychology in Medical Settings, 10*(1), 57–69.

Tompkins, D. A., Hobelmann, J. G., & Compton, P. (2017). Providing chronic pain management in the "Fifth Vital Sign" Era: Historical and treatment perspectives on a modern-day medical dilemma. *Drug and Alcohol Dependence, 173*, S11–S21.

van Straten, A., Cuijpers, P., & Smits, N. (2008). Effectiveness of a web-based self-help intervention for symptoms of depression, anxiety, and stress: Randomized controlled trial. *Journal of Medical Internet Research, 10*(1), e7.10.2196/jmir.954.

Vitiello, M. V., Rybarczyk, B., Von Korff, M., & Stepanski, E. J. (2009). Cognitive behavioral therapy for insomnia improves sleep and decreases pain in older adults with co-morbid insomnia and osteoarthritis. *Journal of Clinical Sleep Medicine, 5*(4), 355–362.

Wetherell, J., Afari, N., Rutledge, T., Sorrell, J., Stoddard, J., Petkus, A., . . . Atkinson, H. (2011). A randomized, controlled trial of acceptance and commitment therapy and cognitive-behavioral therapy for chronic pain. *Pain, 152*(9), 2098–2107.

Wicksell, R. K., Kemani, M., Jensen, K., Kosek, E., Kadetoff, D., Sorjonen, K., & Olsson, G. L. (2013). Acceptance and commitment therapy for fibromyalgia: A randomized controlled trial. *European Journal of Pain, 17*(4), 599–611.

Williams, A. C., Eccleston, C., & Morley, S. (2012). Psychological therapies for the management of chronic pain (excluding headache) in adults. *The Cochrane Library, 14*, 11. Doi 10.1002/14651858.CD007407.pub3

Yalom, I. D., & Leszcz, M. (Collaborator). (2005). *The theory and practice of group psychotherapy* (5th ed.). New York, NY: Basic Books.

Zeidan, F., Martucci, K., Kraft, R., Gordon, N., McHaffie, J., & Coghill, R. (2011). Brain mechanisms supporting the modulation of pain by mindfulness meditation. *Journal of Neuroscience, 31*(14), 5540–5548.

7

Brief Treatment Approaches for Addressing Chronic Pain in Primary Care Settings

Don McGeary and Hunter Hansen

Introduction

The granular skills required to effectively manage chronic pain are part and parcel of every psychologist's skillset. Indeed, success managing pain in primary care has less to do with the chosen intervention than with how the intervention is packaged, implemented, and assessed. Thus, this chapter will provide an overview of psychological treatment options for chronic pain in primary care rooted in the biopsychosocial model, including brief psychotherapies (especially cognitive and behavioral interventions), complementary and integrative health strategies (specifically mindfulness), basic relaxation techniques, and the use of assistive technologies for pain management in the primary care office (e.g., biofeedback). The protocols that have been tested for all of these approaches are so multitudinous and varied that it would be difficult to summarize the entire body of work; to be most useful, this chapter will meaningfully discuss the models and mechanisms of behavioral health integration that have shown the most promise for successful treatment uptake and effectiveness. By also exploring factors that contribute to pain management treatment failure in primary care settings, this chapter will establish a rubric for explaining how brief psychotherapeutic interventions can and should be implemented in order to maximize positive outcomes in this unique environment.

The Costs of Pain at the National and State Levels

Chronic pain is one of the most significant healthcare problems facing the United States. The Centers for Disease Control (CDC) National Health and Nutrition Examination Survey (CDC, 2014) shows that approximately one-quarter of Americans (23.8%) are limited by pain at least one day per month, and 43% of Americans who report limitations in activity likely do so because of pain. The CDC also reported that in 2014, over 25 million Americans were likely disabled because of a pain condition (CDC, 2014). Relatedly, the American Productivity Audit (Stewart, Ricci, Chee, & Morganstein, 2003) found that 12.7% of the entire U.S. workforce reported lost work time because of pain in a two-week period, with back pain contributing to an average of five or more hours of lost time per week for individuals with back pain. The Audit also revealed that absenteeism and lost productivity during work days due to pain accounted for $61.2 billion of lost time in 2003, and costs likely have risen significantly in the 15 years since. Chronic pain also is being tracked increasingly at the state level because of the significant impact that pain conditions have on state-level economies and health-care systems.

The National Academies Press report "Relieving Pain in America: A Blueprint for Transforming Prevention, Care Education, and Research" included an appendix detailing the economic costs of pain across different states (Gaskin & Richard, 2011). The authors found that in 2010 the average pain patient in the United States with at least "moderate" levels of pain generated annual healthcare costs of almost $5,000 higher per person than people without pain. A review of incremental costs models revealed that the highest proportion of direct and indirect (disability, lost time from work, and lost productivity) costs were accounted for by metropolitan areas and states in the South and West of the United States in 2010. Some states in more affected areas have started tracking pain locally to more precisely identify how pain impacts healthcare utilization and costs. For example, the Texas Department of State Health Services (DSHS) published diagnostic and healthcare utilization online (Texas Health Data Center for Health Statistics) showing that in 2013 there were 236,144 inpatient stays attributed to musculoskeletal disorders in Texas, with an average inpatient stay of five days generating hospital charges of around $75,000 per patient. Although data on Texas outpatient visits are not yet presented on the DSHS website, Texas Injury Statistics (TxHHS, accessed in 2018) show a steady increase in common causes of musculoskeletal pain conditions from 2008 to 2011, including falls (38% increase), motor vehicle accidents (11% increase), and accidental injury (37% increase).

Primary Care Pain Management Limitations and Weaknesses

Primary care providers (PCPs) are a main gateway to medical care for individuals with chronic pain, and the majority of chronic pain patients will be largely managed in a primary care clinic (Schneiderhan, Clauw, & Schwenk, 2017). Unfortunately, PCP management of chronic pain is problematic because of the complexity of chronic pain as a clinical phenomenon, a limited repertoire of effective pain management interventions available to primary care practitioners, and provider concerns about high levels of scrutiny and professional sanction risk when prescribing pain management medications (especially opioids) (Jamison, Scanlan, Matthews, Jurcik, & Ross, 2016; Lazaridou, Franceschelli, Buliteanu, Cornelius, Edwards, & Jamison, 2017).

PCPs report a high level of stress associated with chronic pain management due to perceptions of their own poor training in managing chronic pain and concerns about the potential for patient dependence on and abuse of pain medication (Jamison, Sheehan, Scanlan, & Ross, 2014). A 2017 review of primary care patient and provider communication about pain revealed that both healthcare providers and their patients report lower satisfaction with a visit when they disagree about treatment options and when the patient is requesting higher levels of medication to address problems with pain, though it is unclear how the investigators accounted for the influence of pain intensity on these findings (Henry, Bell, Fenton, & Kravitz, 2018). After observing video from 86 separate primary care pain management encounters, the investigators found that PCPs were more likely to judge a pain patient as "difficult" when the patient presented with higher levels of pain and asked more questions. The investigators aptly recommended more focus on communication skills for PCPs to help them better hear, understand, and address patient concerns.

Despite growing evidence of the dangers associated with opioid medication use, opioids still represent one of the most commonly implemented treatments for chronic pain in primary care settings. According to the CDC (CDC, 2016), over 33,000 Americans died due to opioid use/misuse in 2013, and prescription data for opioid medications (as well as opioid-related deaths) showed an upward trend in the early part of the 2010 decade (Rudd, Aleshire, Zibbell, & Matthew Gladden, 2016). In data presented to the National Summit on Opioid Safety in 2012, Dr. Michael Von Korff (2012) reported that the rate of opioid prescriptions had been rising over the past 15 years, and that increasing dose and duration of opioid use are associated with higher levels of disability and lower levels of employability among pain patients. The CDC National Vital Statistics System (CDC, 2016) showed that the southern United States accounts for more opioid-related age-adjusted deaths per 100,000 people (4.4) than any other region of the U.S., and opioid deaths in the South far outpace age-adjusted opioid deaths for the U.S. as a whole (3.9). For example, data from the 2012 IMS National Prescription Audit revealed that Texans received 72–82 opioid prescriptions per 100 people in 2011, and the CDC indicated that these prescriptions likely accounted for only one-quarter of problematic opioid use (the other three-quarters of opioids were obtained from friends, family, or street purchase).

High levels of opioid misuse and diversion have resulted in significant health concerns in the United States. A 2014 systematic review published in *Annals of Internal Medicine* revealed significant concerns related to the potential for physical harm with long-term opioid use, which is alarming in light of little to no evidence supporting opioid medication use for the long-term management of chronic pain (Chou et al., 2015). As noted by Compton, Jones, and Baldwin

(2016), the growing problems associated with opioid use (including diversion from prescription opioids to illicit drugs like heroin) have been met with significant public policy and prevention efforts aimed at increasing provider responsibility for prescribing and curtailing opioid "pill mill" practices that have fed the opioid epidemic. For example, in 2012 the Veterans Health Administration (VHA) implemented an "Opioid Safety Initiative" (OSI) designed to decrease unsafe opioid prescribing practices, provide guidance for safe opioid prescribing, and encourage non-pharmacological referral options to meet the need for effective, alternative pain care. A 2017 review of the OSI revealed a 16% reduction in high-dose opioid prescribing between 2012 and 2014 in the Veterans Affairs (VA) system, and a notable drop in the number of veterans receiving concurrent opioid and benzodiazepine prescriptions (Lin, Bohnert, Kerns, Clay, Ganoczy, & Ilgen, 2017).

Unfortunately, weaning patients off of opioid medications and/or reducing initial opioid prescription rates in primary care is only part of the solution to this complex problem. There is still a significant dearth of non-opioid pain management options in primary care, and chronic pain patients who are discharged from opioid prescriptions in primary care are at high risk of drug diversion and recidivism to prescription opioid use if they lack other effective means of managing their pain without medication. As noted above, primary care practitioners report feeling unprepared to treat chronic pain, often relying upon opioid medications because they are unaware of better options or do not have the time to implement other treatments (Upshur, Luckmann, & Savageau, 2006). Many non-pharmacological interventions for pain are a poor fit for primary care settings because of the time required to implement them. The average length of time that a primary care physician spends discussing treatment of chronic pain with patients is 2.3 minutes (Tai-Seale, Bolin, Bao, & Street, 2011), so services delivered at the level of the primary care physician must be simple and extraordinarily brief. Medications are quick to prescribe and implement but rarely promote meaningful change in chronic pain (Radcliff et al., 2013). As a result, complex primary care patients with chronic musculoskeletal pain demonstrate high rates of healthcare utilization to obtain the care that they need and to address problems introduced with their opioid medications (Pransky, Borkan, Young, & Cherkin, 2011). Clearly, a more impactful, long-term, and low-risk pain management strategy is needed in this clinical venue and must rely on interdisciplinary collaboration.

Some suggest that PCPs should begin addressing the comorbid problems of pain and opioid risks through clinical practices that guide better implementation of opioids (i.e., this argument maintains that opioids are simply not being used as well as they should be; Chou et al., 2009; Passik & Weinreb, 2000). Unfortunately, optimizing the benefit of prescription opioids in primary care while minimizing the risks of overdose or misuse is extraordinarily complicated (if possible at all) and the effort and time involved in achieving this balance is incompatible with the pace and volume of chronic pain management in primary care clinics (Von Korff, 2012).

One attempt to develop a decision support tool to encourage the safe use of opioid medications was met with mixed results due to the inherent barriers associated with using opioid medications as a first-line treatment for chronic pain (Trafton et al., 2010). Referred to as ATHENA-OT, Trafton and colleagues established a computer-based practice guidelines "interpreter" that adapted practice guidelines for opioid prescription into a searchable, clinically indexed database that included an index of multiple clinical concepts and care recommendations based on inputted patient health information. Users of ATHENA-OT noted that the amount of information provided was "overwhelming" and ironically made decision-making more difficult. Furthermore, although ATHENA-OT provided solid care recommendations, the provider had to translate, implement, and independently document the care, which was perceived as an obstacle to implementation.

The consensus among researchers and clinicians is that simply improving safety and efficacy of opioid medications is an untenable solution to the problem of pain management in primary care, which requires better support for self-management interventions for providers guided by valid clinical decision-making tools (Bodenheimer, Wagner, & Grumbach, 2002). Non-pharmacological interventions, particularly those steeped in behavioral health and functional restoration concepts (Gatchel, McGeary, McGeary, & Lippe, 2014; Barlow, Wright, Sheasby, Turner, & Hainsworth, 2002), offer a safe alternative to opioid medications, but data supporting their use are limited to referral (Von Korff et al., 2005) and consultation models (Katzman et al., 2014), with few documented attempts at tailoring these approaches to the unique infrastructure of the primary care service.

Obstacles to Non-pharmacological Pain Management in Primary Care

Primary care providers rarely utilize behavioral health referral options due to lack of knowledge about the availability and efficacy of these services or the sheer lack of a trained behavioral health provider to whom they can refer. In 2016, the first author of this chapter partnered with the Center for Research to Advance Community Health (ReACH) at the University of Texas Health Science Center San Antonio (UT Health) to address chronic pain management in UT Health Primary Care services in a large UT Health hospital in downtown San Antonio, Texas. Of particular interest was the adequacy of training in chronic pain management for Family Medicine residents rotating through the hospital for training. To capture these data, the author worked with ReACH to develop a survey that was completed by 12 Family Medicine residents assessing their own confidence with chronic pain management, their knowledge of non-pharmacological approaches to chronic pain management, and their willingness to learn more about non-pharmacological pain management as part of their training.

The surveyed Family Medicine residents reported each seeing an average of three chronic pain patients and two patients with acute pain per clinic half-day.

Of those patients presenting with pain, approximately two-thirds presented with pain management as their primary clinical concern. UT Health residents were asked to rate their knowledge, perception of effectiveness, and awareness of the basis of evidence supporting the use of pharmacological, interventional, and non-pharmacological pain management using a 0 to 10 Likert scale with 0 representing no knowledge/efficacy/evidence base and 10 representing expert knowledge, highest efficacy, or preponderance of research evidence. The results of this brief survey (shown in Figure 7.1) revealed a high level of knowledge about pharmacological pain management interventions resulting in a high perception of evidence supporting their use and a moderate to high level of perceived efficacy. Interestingly, although the residents reported much lower levels of knowledge and evidence supporting behavioral health interventions for chronic pain, they endorsed behavioral health interventions as the most efficacious for their patients. Despite their perceptions that pharmacological interventions are less efficacious than non-pharmacological approaches, Family Medicine residents were more likely to recommend medication for pain control because of better knowledge about how medications might help with pain, as well as more familiarity with the research literature supporting their use.

These findings, combined with the findings of previous studies of primary care practitioners discussed above, emphasize the importance of not only identifying best practices in non-pharmacological pain interventions for primary care but also increasing their utilization through better education of referring PCPs and wider dissemination of non-pharmacological pain management study outcomes

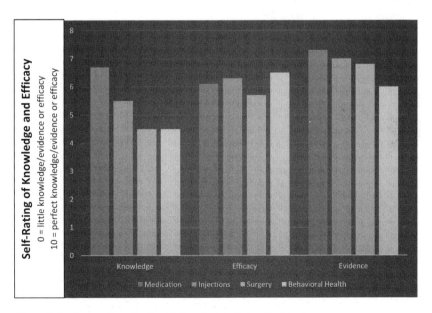

Figure 7.1   Survey Results for 12 Family Medicine Residents

(especially for behavioral health interventions) into venues where PCPs are likely to review them (including training environments). The remainder of this chapter will review models of non-pharmacological pain management (including the rationale for these programs and evidence supporting their efficacy) in primary care and will provide examples of dissemination of these models in a UT Health medical training program.

Brief Interventions for Pain Management in Primary Care

Given the complexity of the problem, there are a multitude of interventions aimed at improving a patient's chronic pain. Extant research on non-pharmacological pain management contains multiple examples of effective, brief interventions. Several theories of chronic pain have informed the development of these interventions, but most brief treatments have arisen from the biopsychosocial model of pain (Waddell, 1987; Gatchel, Peng, Peters, Fuchs, & Turk, 2007). Briefly, the biopsychosocial model describes the multiple dimensions of an individual's life that are affected by pain and how these dimensions interact to create the complex clinical phenomenon of chronic pain. This section of this chapter will describe the different dimensions of the biopsychosocial model of chronic pain and provide a rationale, supporting evidence, and clinical recommendations for select interventions within each dimension. Appendices 1 and 2 contain patient handouts for use when discussing the biopsychosocial model with patients.

Physical Dimension of Chronic Pain

The physical dimension of chronic pain covers a wide array of factors, including stress, physical deconditioning, and neurological pain processes (e.g., central sensitization of pain). The relationship between chronic pain and stress has been widely examined and supported. Chronic stress is a common (if not constant) chronic pain comorbidity likely affecting chronic pain through central mechanisms (e.g., activation of the hypothalamic–pituitary–adrenal axis) and distal mechanisms (e.g., increased muscle tension, changes in mood, distressed social interactions; Blackburn-Munro & Blackburn-Munro, 2001). As stress levels increase, pain and pain-related disability also tend to increase. Therefore, using proven brief methods of stress management are likely to contribute to effective chronic pain management outcomes. Relaxation skills are considered the "aspirin of behavioral medicine," and numerous options/strategies for relaxation skills training are available, allowing the psychologist to tailor interventions to the needs and interests of the patient (Russo, Bird, & Masek, 1980). Brief relaxation strategies are conducive to the brevity of primary care appointments and include diaphragmatic breathing, short progressive muscle relaxation protocols, and guided imagery, all of which show good outcomes for pain (Nahin, Boineau, Khalsa, Stussman, & Weber, 2016).

Physical deconditioning refers to the atrophy and stiffening of muscles, bones, and connective tissue that is likely to result from inactivity due to pain. If the body is viewed as a "kinetic chain" of muscles and bones that all support one another, then maintaining a healthy musculoskeletal system can help support physical "weak links" in the kinetic chain that cause or contribute to pain and disability. To overcome this, the psychologist in primary care can work closely with the PCP to establish an exercise plan using gradual pacing of activity and oriented toward a functional goal of meaningful activity for the patient (e.g., spending more time with family, working longer without needing a break due to pain). Interestingly, exercise programs that emphasize strength may be more effective for pain outcomes than those emphasizing cardiorespiratory health (Searle, Spink, Ho, & Chuter, 2015).

Finally, "central sensitization" refers to changes in central processing of chronic pain (i.e., transmission and processing of pain stimuli within the central nervous system) that occur with repeated exposure to pain. Specifically, central sensitization touts that repeated exposure to pain stimuli that accompany chronic pain can actually sensitize the central nervous system to pain, making the pain patient more responsive to pain signals that previously might have been ignored (Nijs, Goubert, & Ickmans, 2016). Although the primary mechanisms of central sensitization are still subject to some debate, there is some burgeoning evidence suggesting that mindfulness-based stress management may be helpful in taming central sensitization in these patients (Cayoun, Simmons, & Shires, 2018).

Emotional Factors in Chronic Pain

Psychiatric symptoms and conditions frequently co-occur with chronic pain, and the presence of these conditions in the context of pain can alter the pain phenotype and potentially impact response to pain management interventions (McGeary, Moore, Vriend, Peterson, & Gatchel, 2011). Some of the most common and impactful psychiatric comorbidities for chronic pain include depression, posttraumatic stress, and suicidality, all of which should be addressed as part of the primary care visit in order to mitigate their complicating effects on pain.

Depression and clinically significant depressive symptoms are present in approximately 60% of chronic pain patients, almost one-third of whom experience severe depression (Rayner et al., 2016). Studies of depression in chronic pain have shown that depressive symptoms contribute to higher pain intensity, higher levels of disability related to pain, and higher pain-related treatment costs compared to pain patients without depression (Rayner et al., 2016). In some cases (approximately 37%), chronic pain patients with comorbid depression may also experience suicidal ideation, and around 16% of suicide ideating pain patients have reported at least one suicide attempt in the past, often due to low perceptions of efficacy about controlling their pain (Campbell et al., 2016; Bryan, Corsa, Corsa, et al., 2012).

Posttraumatic stress disorder (PTSD) increasingly is being recognized as a frequent and impactful chronic pain comorbidity, especially among military service members and veterans (McGeary et al., 2011). Studies of comorbid pain and PTSD have identified approximately 10% of civilian pain patients and 50% of military pain patients presenting with this comorbidity, resulting in significant impacts on both pain and trauma experience (Fishbain, Pulikal, Lewis, & Gao, 2017). Each of these psychiatric conditions has multiple, evidence-based protocols for management, and it is highly recommended that psychologists practicing in primary care assess for mood on a regular basis and either treat or refer for specialty mental health treatment to ameliorate psychiatric comorbidities in service to better pain treatment. Multiple measures are available in the public domain to assist with psychiatric surveillance, including the PHQ-9 for depression (Kroenke, Spitzer, & Williams, 2001), the GAD-7 for anxiety (Spitzer, Kroenke, Williams, & Löwe, 2006), and the PTSD Checklist for PTSD (PCL-5; Weathers et al., 2013). These measures (especially the PHQ-9 and GAD-7) are already common fixtures for mood assessment in primary care services, and there is good evidence supporting the use of these measures to screen for depression in chronic pain patients despite the potential for artificial score inflation due to pain-related somatic symptoms (Poleshuck et al., 2010).

Interestingly, success with non-pharmacological pain management in the primary care encounter may also result in mood improvement, so primary care practicing psychologists should attempt to manage both pain and comorbid conditions concurrently if they can (McGeary, McGeary, Moreno, & Gatchel, 2016; Bryan, Corsa, Kanzler, et al., 2012; Bryan, Morrow, & Appolonio, 2009). If a patient presents with active suicidal ideation or symptoms scores showing severe or extreme psychiatric symptoms, a referral to psychiatry is recommended.

Cognitive and Behavioral Factors in Chronic Pain

As is true with all aversive stimuli, the ways in which patients think about their pain significantly impact their coping with pain and the contribution of the pain experience to disability. Notable cognitive pain factors include *pain catastrophizing*, *fear avoidance*, and *pain acceptance*. Pain catastrophizing broadly refers to alarming cognitions about pain, often characterized by rumination on pain symptoms, magnified or exaggerated thoughts about the impact of pain on life, and a perceived lack of ability to control or ameliorate pain symptoms (Sullivan, Bishop, & Pivik, 1995). Fear avoidance describes a fundamental confusion between perception of pain as a signal of "hurt" and perception of pain as a signal of "harm." Chronic pain patients struggling with fear-avoidant cognitions may unnecessarily avoid physical activity because of increases in perceived pain during functional activation, and they may become hypervigilant to pain symptoms, resulting in deactivation and physical deconditioning (Vlaeyen & Linton, 2000). Pain acceptance describes the extent to which chronic pain patients find the experience of pain unacceptable and change their behaviors in potentially unhealthy ways in attempts to eliminate the unacceptable stimulus (e.g., avoidance of activity, social isolation, self-medication).

Assessing cognitive pain factors can be burdensome, but excellent measures are readily available for primary care psychologists who wish to assess them, including the Pain Catastrophizing Scale (PCS; Sullivan et al., 1995), the Fear-Avoidance Beliefs Questionnaire (Waddell, Newton, Henderson, Somerville, & Main, 1993), and the Chronic Pain Acceptance Questionnaire (Vowles, McCracken, McLeod & Eccleston, 2008).

Several studies have tested brief psychological interventions focusing on cognitive pain factors in primary care with promising results. Meta-analyses of psychotherapeutic interventions for pain and comorbid psychiatric symptoms have revealed strong evidence for brief and stepped-care psychosocial interventions in this population (Barrett & Chang, 2016). For example, a study of stepped-care for chronic pain management (ESCAPE) in the Veterans Health Administration found that guided medical intervention, coupled with pain self-management training and cognitive-behavioral therapy targeting problem cognitions and behaviors, resulted in reductions in pain-related functional interference (Bair et al., 2015). Interestingly, these brief interventions may be more flexible than just targeted pain management. Systematic review of three integrated behavioral health interventions for chronic pain (including studies of CBT and motivational interviewing) found that psychotherapeutic treatments for pain in primary care can have a general effect on pain-related symptoms, pain-related mood disruption, and substance use disorders (Haibach, Beehler, Dollar, & Finnell, 2014).

There is increasing evidence that problematic pain behaviors (e.g., avoidance of activity, social isolation, decreased engagement in valued activity) can be addressed effectively in the primary care setting using brief third-wave behavioral therapy interventions (e.g., acceptance and commitment therapy) and mindfulness-based interventions. Acceptance and commitment therapy (ACT) has strong potential for improving values-directed behavior and increasing cognitive flexibility and pain acceptance in chronic pain patients (Carnes, Mars, Plunkett, Nanke, & Abbey, 2017; Vowles, Witkiewitz, Sowden, & Ashworth, 2014). Though not yet thoroughly tested in primary care environments, studies of primary care-based ACT are ongoing and offer great promise for effective pain management (Kanzler et al., 2018).

The emergence of non-pharmacological pain management also has given rise to the study of mindfulness-based interventions. Although mindfulness is primarily considered by some to be a stress-management strategy, there is good evidence showing change in pain-related cognitions, mood, and disability in chronic pain patients treated with mindfulness (Turner et al., 2016). Meta-analytic review of mindfulness in primary care has shown significant improvements in mental health comorbidities and quality of life (Demarzo et al., 2015), and focused application of mindfulness to chronic pain in primary care is continuing to grow.

Social Factors in Chronic Pain

Chronic pain is a social phenomenon that impacts multiple relationships in the pain patient's life, including but not limited to the relationships with provider(s), significant others, friends, and coworkers/managers. In recognition of social pain factors, some investigators have begun to examine interventions for pain (using CBT, ACT, and mindfulness concepts) that extend care to both the patient and his/her significant other. For example, Cano and colleagues (2017) highlight the importance of conjoint pain management and treatment goals for improving pain cognitions and cognitive flexibility in both the pain patient and significant other.

McGeary, Blount, et al. (2016) examined data from an intensive outpatient pain management program and found a dynamic relationship between functional improvement in pain treatment and the way in which significant others respond to pain patients. Specifically, partners who responded to pain patients in either punishing (e.g., "I wish you would stop talking about your pain") or solicitous ways (e.g., "I'll take care of the housework, you just rest so you don't hurt your back") contributed to increased levels of disability, catastrophic thoughts about pain, and lower quality of life than those who offered to distract their loved one and encouraged them to be active. Formal studies of conjoint interventions for chronic pain in primary care are sorely lacking, but the available data suggest that including loved ones in the pain care process (and promoting healthier communication styles), ensuring good communication about treatment goals, and exposing significant others to interventions that promote cognitive flexibility (e.g., mindfulness, ACT) are all likely to improve pain outcomes (which subsequently may improve the relationship as well).

Selecting Effective Non-pharmacological Pain Management Options in Primary Care

Primary care pain management options are best viewed across three different dimensions: models, methods, and measures. *Models* refer to the theoretical underpinnings of service delivery that serve as a rationale for how pain management can be delivered in the primary care service environment. These models may include training initiatives for PCPs, referral pathways for services through a chosen pain management champion, or the adoption of a particular theoretical perspective of pain management. *Methods* refer to the specific format, instrumentation, and resource utilization options available for non-pharmacological pain management in primary care. This dimension particularly is important because primary care services widely differ in their capacity for service adoption, from large, well-resourced clinics in metropolitan medical centers equipped with obvious specialty referral options and integrated behavioral health providers, to poorly resourced rural clinics where the closest specialty provider is 90 minutes away (and where a primary care pain management method may be utilizing a telehealth infrastructure to extend services into clinics or regions where they are not otherwise available). Finally, *measures* refer to the options available for tracking service success, ultimately used as a guide for treatment planning. Although the primary tools for assessment in primary care should include direct measures of pain and related symptoms, the predominance of electronic health records now afford opportunities to survey secondary measures that support service use, including frequency of healthcare visits, opioid prescriptions, and high-cost service utilization (specifically Emergency Department visits).

The following sections of this chapter will detail the options available across these three dimensions, culminating in a decision-tree that will guide the practitioner to the best treatment options based on the patient's readiness for change and availability of resources in their primary care service.

Models of Integration in Primary Care Settings

In primary care there are three major models for integrating behavioral healthcare: the Care Management Model (e.g., Witt, Garrison, Gonzalez, Witt, & Angstman, 2017; Dobscha et al., 2009), the Primary Care Behavioral Health Model (PCBH; Hunter, Goodie, Oordt, & Dobmeyer, 2017; Vogel, Kanzler, Aikens, & Goodie, 2017), and the Transdisciplinary (e.g., PCP education) Model (McGeary, McGeary, Nabity, et al., 2016).

Care Management Model

The Care Management Model (Figure 7.2) uses specific clinical protocols to target discrete clinical problems (e.g., depression, chronic pain). The PCP works collaboratively with a trained care manager (often, but not always, a clinical psychologist) and a care management team, who follow a standard method for assessing, planning, and facilitating care. The care manager and management team use assessment data and health records to develop care recommendations that are communicated to the patient's primary care physician. In many cases, the care management team may arrange to refer the patient to more specialized care and may periodically contact the patient to ensure care needs are met.

Dobscha and colleagues (2009) assessed the Care Management Model using a chronic pain protocol in a VHA cluster randomized trial and found promising results. Patients in these programs received an assessment visit with the care manager focused on identifying fear-avoidance beliefs (e.g., fear of movement or other activities) that might exacerbate pain, discussed barriers to pain treatment, were screened for mental health disorders, and developed functional goals. Patients were invited to attend a four-session workshop that used a brief activating approach and primary care group visit models. The primary intervention involved care recommendations developed by a care manager psychologist in partnership with an intervention internist (almost always a physician). Recommendations for treatment then were communicated back to the PCP through medical record alerts and e-mail. Educational materials were also provided. Patients were contacted

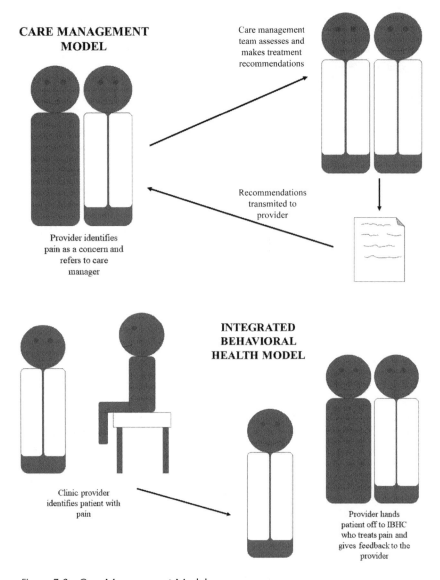

CARE MANAGEMENT MODEL

Care management team assesses and makes treatment recommendations

Recommendations transmited to provider

Provider identifies pain as a concern and refers to care manager

INTEGRATED BEHAVIORAL HEALTH MODEL

Clinic provider identifies patient with pain

Provider hands patient off to IBHC who treats pain and gives feedback to the provider

Figure 7.2 Care Management Model

by telephone every two months for a year to re-administer pain, depression, and substance use disorder screenings, assess goals and activities, and provide support. Compared with a treatment-as-usual group that was more likely to receive care through specialty pain services (including physical, occupational, and recreational therapy and co-located mental health services), patients receiving the primary care protocol reported greater improvements in pain-related disability and pain intensity. A follow-up study indicated that the VA program saved thousands of dollars per patient when compared to pharmacological management based on pain disability free days (Dickinson et al., 2010).

The Care Management Model shows a great deal of promise for pain management in primary care services. Dobscha and colleagues (2009) report modest pain management outcomes compared to more intensive outpatient services, but the primary care environment does not feature the infrastructure necessary for intensive non-pharmacological pain management, making the outcomes of these programs impressive. Furthermore, the Care Management Model functions as a consultation model that is likely to be robust in clinical environments where providers change frequently (e.g., teaching hospitals, military clinics). As long as the care management and intervention internist stay consistent and are able to track when patients are meeting with new providers, then pain management should be able to continue with minimal disruption.

Unfortunately, the use of specialized and targeted pain management consultation may mean that some patients who present with pain as one of many complaints may not receive care management intervention. Care managers do not target patients within the primary care setting who do not meet criteria for specific clinical protocol; therefore, pain complaints that arise as a secondary issue in primary care visits may not trigger a referral to care management. Due to the significant frequency and variability of chronic pain as a presenting problem in primary care, the focused Care Management Model could be overly sensitive and may exclude a large proportion of pain patients who do not fit model parameters (though these inclusion parameters can be adjusted to allow for broader application of the model). Care Management Models of chronic pain management are likely to work very well in highly resourced medical treatment facilities that can hire and train the care manager (psychologist) and internist needed to provide specialty consultation, but may be less effective in small treatment facilities where primary care providers are the only local option for pain management and local specialty consultation may be unavailable.

Primary Care Behavioral Health (PCBH) Model

The PCBH model (Figure 7.3) was pioneered almost 20 years ago in large health systems that experimented with integrating a behavioral health provider (i.e., a psychologist, counselor, or social worker) directly into a primary care service (Hunter et al., 2017). Under PCBH, the behavioral health provider/consultant assists primary care providers with the gamut of behavioral health concerns (e.g., anxiety, chronic pain, depression, insomnia, tobacco cessation), offering real-time consultation and referral options through convenient and local referral mechanisms (e.g., a warm hand-off from the PCP during or immediately after a medical appointment, or co-visits where the PCP and behavioral health consultant meet with the patient together for part of the visit).

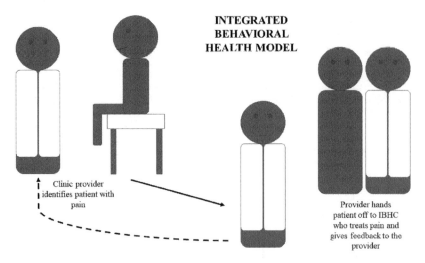

Figure 7.3 Primary Care Behavioral Health Model

Although the PCBH provider lacks the focus and resource breadth of a care manager, this model allows for a broader range of intervention that may suit more complex chronic pain patients (i.e., those presenting with chronic pain and comorbid psychosocial and behavioral health concerns). Whereas care management aims to make the most out of local specialty resources available to the clinic, the PCBH provider serves as a one-stop shop for behavioral health intervention (part of which may include a referral to specialty pain management services if available). As a result, the PCBH model may be the better option for clinical services that lack convenient specialty pain management services or the mental health resources needed to handle psychosocial comorbidities that affect pain.

The embedded PCBH provider typically sees patients for one to four appointments lasting 20 to 30 minutes each (i.e., modeling the typical primary care appointment). A patient may be seen for more than four appointments if the patient has a chronic condition and if it would benefit the primary care team to have a behavioral health consultant periodically see the patient to assist with ongoing biopsychosocial assessment and intervention. Clinical pathways may be developed under the PCBH model, with pathway focus on increasing behavioral health consultant and team efficacy and effectiveness on a given clinical presentation. This way, the PCBH model may resemble care management; however, the impetus for treatment remains with the Integrated Behavioral Health Consultant (IBHC) instead of the primary care practitioner as dictated in the Care Management Model.

Many primary care services may prefer to hire and embed an IBHC because they lack the time or resources for establishing a coordinated care team, and training individual providers on how to better manage chronic pain would be burdensome. An added benefit of PCBH is the potential for the IBHC to address more than pain problems. Indeed, there is ample evidence in the extant research literature showing that the use of IBHCs can lead to significantly improved functioning and fewer symptoms across a host of health conditions (Bryan et al., 2009), including anxiety and depressive symptoms (Angantyr, Rimner, & Norden, 2015; Katon et al., 1996;), PTSD symptoms (Cigrang et al., 2011), sleep symptoms (Goodie, Isler, Hunter, & Peterson, 2009), tobacco use (Sadock, Auerbach, Rybarczyk, & Aggarwal, 2014), and weight management (Sadock et al., 2014).

In some cases, these additional PCBH benefits are both effective and long-lasting. For example, Cigrang et al. (2015) found that PTSD symptom improvements observed in a prior study (Cigrang et al., 2011) were maintained after 6 and 12 months. Ray-Sannerud et al. (2012) found that functional improvements after PCBH intervention for a number of conditions were sustained an average of two years following visits with IBHCs, even when controlling for receipt of other mental healthcare. Unfortunately, there are few formal studies of an IBHC model focused specifically on chronic pain management in primary care, though data supporting brief behavioral interventions for chronic pain are promising (e.g., Gatchel et al., 2014; McCracken & Vowles, 2014; Ehde, Dillworth, & Turner, 2014).

In 2007, the first author of this chapter teamed with investigators in the United States Air Force to conduct a preliminary test of a brief, non-pharmacological intervention for chronic pain management delivered in a primary care setting using the PCBH model (Morrow, Bryan, Kanzler, & McGeary, 2009). We tracked 71 military service members and dependents who were referred to PCBH by their primary care physician and who received a four-session non-pharmacological treatment for chronic pain. PCBH appointments lasted between 25 and 30 minutes and all patients were asked to complete the Behavioral Health Measure-20 (BHM-20; Kopta & Lowry, 2002) to assess for multiple dimensions of response to the treatment. The BHM-20 is a brief assessment of behavioral health interventions, often taking less than two minutes to complete (making it a valid, unobtrusive clinical measure of change in pain coping). Most patients received treatment every two weeks. The sample for this study was primarily female (63%) and patients had a mean age of 35 years. Examination of BHM-20 revealed a significant improvement in general mental health (GMH), well-being (WB), and physical symptoms (SYM) across the four IBHC sessions, with per-session data showing a steady decline across sessions. Of note, analysis revealed statistically significant differences from Session 1 to Sessions 2 through 4 on all three BHM-20 subscales. These findings suggest that statistically significant change occurred in as little as one session (from Session 1 to 2) and that improvements continued with each subsequent session (Figure 7.4).

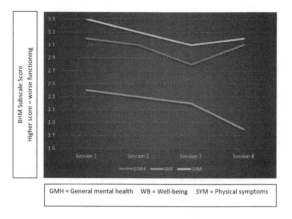

GMH = General mental health   WB = Well-being   SYM = Physical symptoms

Figure 7.4   BHM-20 Subcale Changes in IBHC

Transdisciplinary Model

To maximize the reach of non-pharmacological pain management, the most effective option for many primary care settings may be to directly train the PCPs on brief non-pharmacological pain management strategies that they can implement during their own care appointments, nullifying the need for a specialty-trained care manager or behavioral health consultant. In so doing, the PCP can tailor interventions directly to her or his patients and integrate non-pharmacological recommendations with medication prescriptions and referrals. The transfer of skills across providers of different specialties is gaining increasing attention as researchers and clinicians seek to balance the significant effectiveness of interdisciplinary pain management programs with the availability and lower cost of individual pain management providers (Gatchel et al., 2014). In interdisciplinary pain management, multiple disciplines share information about patient progress during treatment and use feedback to optimize care across professions.

Transdisciplinary pain management (Figure 7.5) represents a next step in interdisciplinary pain management by encouraging different professions to share skills, allowing one provider to represent multiple disciplines (McGeary, McGeary, Nabity, et al., 2016). If effective, a transdisciplinary model would be a good fit for primary care services that lack the space and other resources needed for care management or integrated behavioral health, though the requirement for additional time in already time-strained primary care encounters may make a referral or hand-off option more desirable for clinics with the resources to implement them.

The cornerstone of effective behavioral health interventions for chronic pain management is the notion that patients can be taught basic skills to learn how

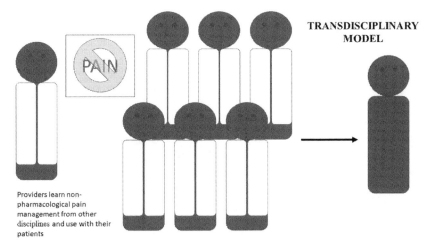

PAIN

TRANSDISCIPLINARY
MODEL

Providers learn non-
pharmacological pain
management from other
disciplines and use with their
patients

Figure 7.5   Transdisciplinary Model

to identify pain-related symptoms and implement self-management strategies to decrease the impact of pain on their lives. Healthcare providers (especially PCPs) play an important role in this process. Medical providers who learn how to provide encouragement and a diverse menu of different pain management options report better outcomes and more confidence in their care (Bair et al., 2009). While unfortunately there are few formal studies of non-pharmacological pain management training for PCPs, the few studies that have been done showed initial promise (e.g., Dorflinger, Fortin, & Foran-Tuller, 2016).

Methods of Primary Care Pain Management

Advances in technology and treatment formats have increased access to effective non-pharmacological pain management interventions in primary care. The three models described above have all been preliminarily tested using in-person care models that require a patient to present individually to the primary care encounter to begin care. In many cases, a single patient, in-person approach may lack either the *breadth* to adequately address the large number of chronic pain patients presenting to the primary care service or the *reach* for those pain patients who have difficulty attending primary pare appointments due to geographic distance, pain-related disability, or both. The following methods of pain management service delivery offer new options that may help address these obstacles. Although numerous care methods have been developed and studied over the years, this chapter will focus on two that are receiving increasing attention: telehealth and group/shared medical appointments.

Telehealth for Chronic Pain Management in Primary Care

In many cases, a patient presenting with chronic pain in primary care is too complex for adequate management without a specialty referral. Cognitive and behavioral therapies (CBT) represent some of the most efficacious non-pharmacological treatments for chronic pain, and "functional restoration" (FR) and other truly interdisciplinary pain services are a very effective option for managing complex patients (Proctor, Mayer, Gatchel, & McGeary, 2004). Unfortunately, primary care physicians may have difficulty referring their patients to CBT programs (like FR), because these programs are not geographically available (Mitchinson, Kerr, & Krein, 2008). Most pain patients must be managed in primary care for up to three years before a specialty referral can be made, resulting in increased disability and depressive symptoms (Schulte et al., 2010). Telehealth programs allow providers to extend specialty pain care options to patients lacking access (McGeary, McGeary, & Gatchel, 2012). A prior meta-analysis revealed that telehealth-based CBT programs for pain management are non-inferior to in-person treatment, and superior to treatment as usual, but poor trial quality in some of the extant research makes it difficult to describe fully the extent of the benefits to be gained through a telehealth program (McGeary, McGeary, Gatchel, Allison, & Hersh, 2013).

Telehealth interventions can be broadly sub-categorized across three different mechanisms. *Store-and-forward* telehealth programs offer an opportunity for patients to connect with pain management specialty providers in a turn-taking format in which the patient submits information and questions to a provider who reviews them later. Once reviewed, the provider can respond in a similar fashion with recommendations for pain management, including supplemental materials like worksheets, education materials, and videos that the patient can use at his or her leisure. One study of an online mind–body intervention for older adults with chronic pain found significant improvement in pain after patients logged on and engaged with the stored website content (Berman, Iris, Bode, & Drengenberg, 2009). Interestingly, these store-and-forward telehealth formats have also shown promise when applied to the PCP as an educational tool (Harris et al., 2008).

Direct care/live treatment telehealth involves delivery of pain management services in real time over a telehealth medium, often using either telephone or video teleconferencing platforms. The ubiquity of broadband internet access and smartphone technologies have vastly broadened the reach of real-time videoconferencing, and live telehealth formats have been used effectively for non-pharmacological pain management (Kroenke, 2014). Despite the explosion of technology facilitating live telemedicine for pain care, surprisingly few studies have tested its efficacy. One study of an eight-session acceptance and commitment therapy (ACT) model of pain management found that ACT delivered by video teleconference was non-inferior to in-person care; however, the investigators noted a higher level of dropout in the telehealth arm despite high levels of reported satisfaction from patients (Herbert et al., 2017). A recent meta-analysis of telehealth-based interventions for chronic low back pain returned some evidence suggesting that telehealth may improve quality of life in pain patients compared to a control condition, but the investigators found little evidence supporting its effectiveness on pain symptoms (Dario et al., 2017). It is possible that the "distance" created between patient and provider through the telehealth format may increase the likelihood that patients will discontinue treatment or discount treatment recommendations compared to in-person care. Further research is likely required to address this concern.

Telehealth consultation for pain management is one of the most impactful uses of telehealth for primary care pain management and includes using a telehealth framework to connect PCPs with a specialist consultant. In so doing, telehealth can be used to train, supervise, and boost PCPs in non-pharmacological pain management skills resulting in a better equipped workforce. To date, several studies have explored this telehealth innovation with strong results. The United States Army has implemented a "Telepain" consultation service in which providers have regular teleconference access to a panel of pain management specialists (including psychologists) with whom they can consult about the management of challenging or complex patients (Flynn et al., 2017). Perhaps most notable among telehealth consultation models for pain is the University of New Mexico Health Sciences Center Project ECHO Pain service. PCPs participating in Project ECHO (especially those working in rural communities) have access to a weekly, teleconference-based interprofessional consultation that includes case examples, skill demonstrations, and formal didactics. Participation in Project ECHO has shown significant improvement in provider knowledge, skill, and practice in pain management (Katzman et al., 2014).

Group Medical Appointments for Pain Management

Over the past few decades there has been increasing attention on the need to expand access to primary care services by supplanting or supplementing individual care appointments with group-based clinic visits. This revolution in care method is best exemplified by shared medical appointments (SMAs), which attempt to structure groups of similar patients into one efficient appointment. This allows patients to receive education, share experiences, develop peer support, and improve access to care (Coates, Gething, & Johnson, 2017). Although promising, SMAs do offer some challenges for implementation, including the need for a strong clinic champion to perpetuate and disseminate the model through the clinic, as well as support from management (McCuistion et al., 2014). Interestingly, direct physician involvement may not be needed for an effective SMA for pain, and the SMA venue need not be limited to the clinic. Turner and colleagues (2017) developed a community-based pain management group intervention in a low-income, rural, mostly Hispanic location. Using a community health worker (a position filled by a wide range of individuals, including local peers and professionals; Perry & Crigler, 2014), non-pharmacological pain management services were offered to individual patients in rural primary care clinics or using a group format at a local library. Both services resulted in a significant improvement in multiple functional domains. These findings are notable because, although chronic pain prevalence is equally distributed across racial and ethnic groups, Hispanic pain patients are significantly less likely to seek treatment for pain (Portenoy, Ugarte, Fuller, & Haas, 2004), and racial/ethnic minorities consistently receive less adequate treatment for acute or chronic pain compared to White, non-Hispanic populations (Mossey, 2011). Mediating factors like socioeconomic status likely play a role in these disparities, but there has been little systematic research exploring racial and ethnic health disparities for pain treatment.

Pain Assessment in Primary Care

Ideally, chronic pain assessment should be multidimensional and include assessment of functional domains, psychosocial factors that affect the pain phenotype, health behaviors that may complicate pain, mechanistic variables of pain coping (e.g., cognitive flexibility), and measures of pain-related interference and subjective disability. The primary care visit is brief and covers a lot of ground, so a comprehensive assessment repertoire is not feasible in these encounters. Instead, the primary care practitioner is challenged with finding brief and impactful assessment tools that are easy to implement and interpret. Numerous options are available for brief primary care assessment, so a review of all options is untenable in this chapter. A few options will be reviewed as exemplars of available assessments for pain in primary care.

Perhaps the most ubiquitous measure of pain in any treatment setting is the visual analog or numeric rating scale. Although much maligned in the extant research due to poor reliability and inconsistent use, some basic guidelines make this measure useful in primary care. First, sporadic use of pain ratings may lead to unreliable results, but increasing the frequency of rating will improve the reliability of pain ratings as treatment outcomes (Heapy et al., 2014). Second, although granular pain rating may prove relatively useless in tracking ongoing care, pain ratings in the higher range of the scale (i.e., from 8 to 10 on a 0–10 numeric scale) consistently seem to indicate a high risk for treatment failure and later complications (McGeary, Mayer, & Gatchel, 2006).

Self-report measures of pain-related disability can provide valuable data about a patient's perception of his or her capacity to complete daily tasks in light of pain. One of the most commonly utilized measures of self-reported disability is the Oswestry Disability Index (ODI), a ten-item self-report measure that produces a percent disability rating (Fairbank & Pynsent, 2000). Although easy to score and interpret, this measure may not be sensitive to change over short periods of time.

Finally, two of the most useful measures for chronic pain assessment in primary care include the 3-item PEG screener and the Brief Pain Inventory (BPI, Tan, Jensen, Thronby, & Shanti, 2004). The PEG was designed to assess pain intensity

(P), interference of pain in life enjoyment (E), and general levels of activity (G). The measure has demonstrated solid construct validity and is sensitive to change within six months of care (Krebs et al., 2009). Like the PEG, the BPI assesses multiple pain domains and includes a brief version consisting of only 12 items. The BPI has been widely used in studies of pain management with solid reliability and validity in chronic non-cancer pain (Cleeland & Ryan, 1994; Tan et al., 2004).

Conclusion

Chronic pain is a growing problem in the United States, and primary care services offer the first line of defense in chronic pain management. Attention to and research regarding non-pharmacological pain management has grown significantly in the past decade due to the rise in chronic pain prevalence and increasing awareness of the dangers associated with pharmacological pain management strategies that used to be a lynchpin of primary care for pain (i.e., opioid medications). Fortunately, contemporary research on pain management in primary care offers a promising array of options for service implementation, including direct care and consultation models. As behavioral health providers continue to work alongside medical providers in primary care, the field is certain to notice significant improvements in overall chronic pain outcomes.

References

Angantyr, K., Rimner, A., & Norden, T. (2015). Primary care behavioral health model: Perspectives of outcome, client satisfaction, and gender. *Social Behavior and Personality*, *43*, 287–302.

Bair, M. J., Ang, D., Wu, J., Outcalt, S. D., Sargent, C., Kempf, C., . . . Davis, L. W. (2015). Evaluation of Stepped Care for Chronic Pain (ESCAPE) in veterans of the Iraq and Afghanistan conflicts: A randomized clinical trial. *JAMA Internal Medicine*, *175*(5), 682–689.

Bair, M. J., Matthias, M. S., Nyland, K. A., Huffman, M. A., Stubbs, D. L., Kroenke, K., & Damush, T. M. (2009). Barriers and facilitators to chronic pain self-management: A qualitative study of primary care patients with comorbid musculoskeletal pain and depression. *Pain Medicine*, *10*(7), 1280–1290.

Barlow, J., Wright, C., Sheasby, J., Turner, A., & Hainsworth, J. (2002, November 30). Self-management approaches for people with chronic conditions: A review. *Patient Education and Counseling*, *48*(2), 177–187.

Barrett, K., & Chang, Y. P. (2016). Behavioral interventions targeting chronic pain, depression, and substance use disorder in primary care. *Journal of Nursing Scholarship*, *48*(4), 345–353.

Berman, R. L., Iris, M. A., Bode, R., & Drengenberg, C. (2009). The effectiveness of an online mind- body intervention for older adults with chronic pain. *The Journal of Pain*, *10*(1), 68–79.

Blackburn-Munro, G., & Blackburn-Munro, R. E. (2001). Chronic pain, chronic stress and depression: Coincidence or consequence? *Journal of Neuroendocrinology*, *13*(12), 1009–1023.

Bodenheimer, T., Wagner, E. H., & Grumbach, K. (2002). Improving primary care for patients with chronic illness. *JAMA*, *288*, 1775–1779.

Bryan, C. J., Corso, K. A., Corso, M. L., Kanzler, K. E., Ray-Sannerud, B., & Morrow, C. E. (2012). Therapeutic alliance and change in suicidal ideation during treatment in integrated primary care settings. *Archives of Suicide Research, 16,* 316–323.

Bryan, C. J., Corso, K. A., Kanzler, K. E., Corso, M. L., Morrow, C. E., Ray-Sannerud, B. (2012). Severity of mental health impairment and trajectories of improvement in and integrated primary care clinic. *Journal of Clinical and Consulting Psychology, 80,* 396–403.

Bryan, C. J., Morrow, C., & Appolonio, K. (2009). Impact of behavioral health consultant interventions on patient symptoms and functioning in an integrated family medicine clinic. *Journal of Clinical Psychology, 65,* 281–293.

Campbell, G., Bruno, R., Darke, S., Shand, F., Hall, W., Farrell, M., & Degenhardt, L. (2016). Prevalence and correlates of suicidal thoughts and suicide attempts in people prescribed pharmaceutical opioids for chronic pain. *The Clinical Journal of Pain, 32*(4), 292–301.

Cano, A., Corley, A. M., Clark, S. M., & Martinez, S. C. (2017). A couple-based psychological treatment for chronic pain and relationship distress. *Cognitive and Behavioral Practice, 25,* 119–134.

Carnes, D., Mars, T., Plunkett, A., Nanke, L., & Abbey, H. (2017). A mixed methods evaluation of a third wave cognitive behavioural therapy and Osteopathic Treatment Programme for Chronic Pain in Primary Care (OsteoMAP). *International Journal of Osteopathic Medicine, 24,* 12–17.

Cayoun, B., Simmons, A., & Shires, A. (2018). Immediate and lasting chronic pain reduction following a brief self-implemented mindfulness-based interoceptive exposure task: A pilot study. *Mindfulness,* 1–13.

Centers for Disease Control and Prevention (CDC). (2014). *National Center for Health Statistics (NCHS). National health and nutrition examination survey data.* Hyattsville, MD: U.S. Department of Health and Human Services, Centers for Disease Control and Prevention.

Centers for Disease Control and Prevention (CDC). (2016). *Wide-ranging online data for epidemiologic research (WONDER).* Atlanta, GA: CDC, National Center for Health Statistics. Retrieved from http://wonder.cdc.gov

Chou, R., Fanciullo, G. J., Fine, P. G., Adler, J. A., Ballantyne, J. C., Davies, P., . . . Gilson, A. M. (2009). Clinical guidelines for the use of chronic opioid therapy in chronic noncancer pain. *The Journal of Pain, 10*(2), 113–130.

Chou, R., Turner, J. A., Devine, E. B., Hansen, R. N., Sullivan, S. D., Blazina, I., . . . Deyo, R. A. (2015). The effectiveness and risks of long-term opioid therapy for chronic pain: A systematic review for a National Institutes of Health Pathways to Prevention Workshop. *Annals of Internal Medicine, 162*(4), 276–286.

Cigrang, J. A., Avila, L. L., Goodie, J. L., Peterson, A. L., Rauch, S. A. M., Bryan, C. J., & Hryshko- Mullen, A. (2011). Treatment of active-duty military with PTSD in primary care: Early findings. *Psychological Services, 8,* 104–113.

Cigrang, J. A., Rauch, S. A. M., Mintz, J., Brundige, A., Avila, L. L., Bryan, C. J., . . . Peterson, A. L. (2015). Treatment of active duty military with PTSD in primary care: A follow-up report. *Journal of Anxiety Disorders, 36,* 110–114.

Cleeland, C. S., & Ryan, K. M. (1994). Pain assessment: Global use of the brief pain inventory. *Annals, Academy of Medicine, Singapore, 23,* 129–138.

Coates, J., Gething, F., & Johnson, M. I. (2017). Shared medical appointments for managing pain in primary care settings? *Pain Management, 7,* 223–227.

Compton, W. M., Jones, C. M., & Baldwin, G. T. (2016). Relationship between nonmedical prescription-opioid use and heroin use. *New England Journal of Medicine, 374*(2), 154–163.

Dario, A. B., Cabral, A. M., Almeida, L., Ferreira, M. L., Refshauge, K., Simic, M., . . . Ferreira, P. H. (2017). Effectiveness of telehealth-based interventions in the management of non-specific low back pain: A systematic review with meta-analysis. *The Spine Journal, 17*(9), 1342–1351.

Demarzo, M. M., Montero-Marin, J., Cuijpers, P., Zabaleta-del-Olmo, E., Mahtani, K. R., Vellinga, A., . . . García-Campayo, J. (2015). The efficacy of mindfulness-based interventions in primary care: A meta-analytic review. *The Annals of Family Medicine, 13*(6), 573–582.

Dickinson, K. C., Sharma, R., Duckart, J. P., Corson, K., Gerrity, M. S., & Dobscha, S. K. (2010). VA healthcare costs of a collaborative intervention for chronic pain in primary care. *Medical Care, 48*(1), 38–44.

Dobscha, S. K., Corson, K., Perrin, N. A., Hanson, G. C., Leibowitz, R. Q., Doak, M. N., . . . Gerrity, M. S. (2009). Collaborative care for chronic pain in primary care: A cluster randomized trial. *JAMA, 301*(12), 1242–1252.

Dorflinger, L. M., Fortin, A. H., & Foran-Tuller, K. A. (2016). Training primary care physicians in cognitive behavioral therapy: A review of the literature. *Patient Education and Counseling, 99*(8), 1285–1292.

Ehde, D. M., Dillworth, T. M., & Turner, J. A. (2014). Cognitive-behavioral therapy for individuals with chronic pain: Efficacy, innovations, and directions for research. *American Psychologist, 69*, 153–166.

Fairbank, J. C., & Pynsent, P. B. (2000). The Oswestry disability index. *Spine, 25*(22), 2940–2953.

Fishbain, D. A., Pulikal, A., Lewis, J. E., & Gao, J. (2017). Chronic pain types differ in their reported prevalence of Post-Traumatic Stress Disorder (PTSD) and there is consistent evidence that chronic pain is associated with PTSD: An evidence-based structured systematic review. *Pain Medicine, 18*(4), 711–735.

Flynn, D. M., Eaton, L. H., McQuinn, H., Alden, A., Meins, A. R., Rue, T., . . . Doorenbos, A. Z. (2017). TelePain: Primary care chronic pain management through weekly didactic and case- based telementoring. *Contemporary Clinical Trials Communications, 8*, 162–166.

Gaskin, D. J., & Richard, P. (2011). Appendix C: The economic costs of pain in the United States. In *Relieving pain in America: A blueprint for transforming prevention, care, education, and research*. Institute of Medicine (US) Committee on Advancing Pain Research, Care, and Education. Washington, DC: National Academies Press.

Gatchel, R. J., McGeary, D. D., McGeary, C. A., & Lippe, B. (2014, February). Interdisciplinary chronic pain management: Past, present, and future. *American Psychologist, 69*(2), 119.

Gatchel, R. J., Peng, Y. B., Peters, M. L., Fuchs, P. N., & Turk, D. C. (2007). The biopsychosocial approach to chronic pain: Scientific advances and future directions. *Psychological Bulletin, 133*(4), 581.

Goodie, J. L., Isler, W. C., Hunter, C., & Peterson, A. L. (2009). Using behavioral health consultants to treat insomnia in primary care: A clinical case series. *Journal of Clinical Psychology, 65*, 294–304.

Haibach, J. P., Beehler, G. P., Dollar, K. M., & Finnell, D. S. (2014). Moving toward integrated behavioral intervention for treating multimorbidity among chronic pain, depression, and substance-use disorders in primary care. *Medical Care, 52*(4), 322–327.

Harris, J. M. Jr., Elliott, T. E., Davis, B. E., Chabal, C., Fulginiti, J. V., & Fine, P. G. (2008). Educating generalist physicians about chronic pain: Live experts and online education can provide durable benefits. *Pain Medicine, 9*(5), 555–563.

Heapy, A., Dziura, J., Buta, E., Goulet, J., Kulas, J. F., & Kerns, R. D. (2014). Using multiple daily pain ratings to improve reliability and assay sensitivity: How many is enough? *The Journal of Pain, 15*(12), 1360–1365.

Henry, S. G., Bell, R. A., Fenton, J. J., & Kravitz, R. L. (2018). Communication about chronic pain and opioids in primary care: Impact on patient and physician visit experience. *Pain, 159*(2), 371–379.

Herbert, M. S., Afari, N., Liu, L., Heppner, P., Rutledge, T., Williams, K., . . . Atkinson, J. H. (2017). Telehealth versus in-person acceptance and commitment therapy for chronic pain: A randomized noninferiority trial. *The Journal of Pain, 18*(2), 200–211.

Hunter, C. L., Goodie, J. L., Oordt, M. S., & Dobmeyer, A. C. (2017). *Integrated behavioral health in primary care: Step-by-step guidance for assessment and intervention.* Washington, D.C.: American Psychological Association.

Jamison, R. N., Kerry Anne Sheehan, B. A., Elizabeth Scanlan, N. P., & Ross, E. L. (2014). Beliefs and attitudes about opioid prescribing and chronic pain management: Survey of primary care providers. *Journal of Opioid Management, 10*(6), 375–382.

Jamison, R. N., Scanlan, E., Matthews, M. L., Jurcik, D. C., & Ross, E. L. (2016). Attitudes of primary care practitioners in managing chronic pain patients prescribed opioids for pain: A prospective longitudinal controlled trial. *Pain Medicine, 17*(1), 99–113.

Kanzler, K. E., Robinson, P. J., McGeary, D. D., Mintz, J., Potter, J. S., Muñante, M., . . . Velligan, D. I. (2018). Rationale and design of a pilot study examining Acceptance and Commitment Therapy for persistent pain in an integrated primary care clinic. *Contemporary Clinical Trials, 66*, 28–35.

Katon, W., Robinson, P., Von Korff, M., Lin, E., Bush, T., Ludman, E., . . . Walker, E. (1996). A multifaceted intervention to improve treatment of depression in primary care. *Archives of General Psychiatry, 53*, 924–932.

Katzman, J. G., Comerci, G., Boyle, J. F., Duhigg, D., Shelley, B., Olivas, C., . . . Kalishman, S. (2014). Innovative telementoring for pain management: Project ECHO pain. *Journal of Continuing Education in the Health Professions, 34*(1), 68–75.

Kopta, S. M., & Lowry, J. L. (2002). Psychometric evaluation of the Behavioral Health Questionnaire- 20: A brief instrument for assessing global mental health and the three phases of psychotherapy outcome. *Psychotherapy Research, 12*(4), 413–426.

Krebs, E. E., Lorenz, K. A., Bair, M. J., Damush, T. M., Wu, J., Sutherland, J. M., . . . Kroenke, K. (2009). Development and initial validation of the PEG, a three-item scale assessing pain intensity and interference. *Journal of General Internal Medicine, 24*(6), 733–738.

Kroenke, K. (2014). Distance therapy to improve symptoms and quality of life: Complementing office- based care with telehealth. *Psychosomatic Medicine, 76*(8), 578–580.

Kroenke, K., Spitzer, R. L., & Williams, J. B. (2001). The PHQ-9. *Journal of General Internal Medicine, 16*(9), 606–613.

Lazaridou, A., Franceschelli, O., Buliteanu, A., Cornelius, M., Edwards, R. R., & Jamison, R. N. (2017). Influence of catastrophizing on pain intensity, disability, side effects, and opioid misuse among pain patients in primary care. *Journal of Applied Behavior Research, 22*, n/a, e12081. doi:10.1111/jabr.12081

Lin, L. A., Bohnert, A. S., Kerns, R. D., Clay, M. A., Ganoczy, D., & Ilgen, M. A. (2017). Impact of the opioid safety initiative on opioid-related prescribing in veterans. *Pain, 158*(5), 833–839.

McCracken, L. M., & Vowles, K. E. (2014). Acceptance and commitment therapy and mindfulness for chronic pain: Model, process, and progress. *American Psychologist, 69*, 178–187.

McCuistion, M. H., Stults, C. D., Dohan, D., Frosch, D. L., Hung, D. Y., & Tai-Seale, M. (2014). Overcoming challenges to adoption of shared medical appointments. *Population Health Management, 17*(2), 100–105.

McGeary, C. A., Blount, T. H., Peterson, A. L., Gatchel, R. J., Hale, W. J., & McGeary, D. D. (2016). Interpersonal responses and pain management within the US military. *Journal of Occupational Rehabilitation, 26*(2), 216–228.

McGeary, C., McGeary, D. Moreno, J., & Gatchel, R. J. (2016). Military chronic musculoskeletal pain and psychiatric comorbidity: Is better pain management the answer? *Healthcare, 4*(3), 38–48.

McGeary, D. D., Mayer, T. G., & Gatchel, R. J. (2006). High pain ratings predict treatment failure in chronic occupational musculoskeletal disorders. *JBJS*, *88*(2), 317–325.

McGeary, D. D., McGeary, C. A., & Gatchel, R. J. (2012). A comprehensive review of telehealth for pain management: Where we are and the way ahead. *Pain Practice*, *12*(7), 570–577.

McGeary, D. D., McGeary, C. A., Gatchel, R. J., Allison, S., & Hersh, A. (2013). Assessment of research quality of telehealth trials in pain management: A meta-analysis. *Pain Practice*, *13*(5), 422–431.

McGeary, D. D., McGeary, C. A., Nabity, P., Villarreal, R., Kivisalu, T., & Gatchel, R. J. (2016). Improving stress reduction and wellness in interdisciplinary chronic pain management: Is transdisciplinary care a better option? *Journal of Applied Biobehavioral Research*, *21*(4), 205–215.

McGeary, D., Moore, M., Vriend, C. A., Peterson, A. L., & Gatchel, R. J. (2011). The evaluation and treatment of comorbid pain and PTSD in a military setting: An overview. *Journal of Clinical Psychology in Medical Settings*, *18*(2), 155.

Mitchinson, A. R., Kerr, E. A., & Krein, S. L. (2008). Management of chronic noncancer pain by VA primary care providers: When is pain control a priority? *The American Journal of Managed Care*, *14*(2), 77–84.

Morrow, C. E., Bryan, C. J., Kanzler, K., & McGeary, D. (2009, April). *Effectiveness of treating chronic pain in an integrated primary care setting*. Poster presented at the 30th Annual Meeting & Scientific Sessions of the Society of Behavioral Medicine, Montreal, Quebec, CA.

Mossey, J. M. (2011). Defining racial and ethnic disparities in pain management. *Clinical Orthopaedics and Related Research®*, *469*(7), 1859–1870.

Nahin, R. L., Boineau, R., Khalsa, P. S., Stussman, B. J., & Weber, W. J. (2016, September). Evidence- based evaluation of complementary health approaches for pain management in the United States. *Mayo Clinic Proceedings*, *91*(9), 1292–1306. Elsevier.

Nijs, J., Goubert, D., & Ickmans, K. (2016). Recognition and treatment of central sensitization in chronic pain patients: Not limited to specialized care. *Journal of Orthopaedic & Sports Physical Therapy*, *46*(12), 1024–1028.

Passik, S. D., & Weinreb, H. J. (2000). Managing chronic nonmalignant pain: Overcoming obstacles to the use of opioids. *Advances in Therapy*, *17*(2), 70–83.

Perry, H., & Crigler, L. (2014). *Developing and strengthening community health worker programs at scale: A reference guide and case studies for program managers and policymakers*. Baltimore: Jhpiego Corporation.

Poleshuck, E. L., Bair, M. J., Kroenke, K., Damush, T. M., Krebs, E. E., & Giles, D. E. (2010). Musculoskeletal pain and measures of depression: Response to comment on the article by Poleshuck et al. *General Hospital Psychiatry*, *32*(1), 114.

Portenoy, R. K., Ugarte, C., Fuller, I., & Haas, G. (2004). Population-based survey of pain in the United States: Differences among white, African American, and Hispanic subjects. *The Journal of Pain*, *5*(6), 317–328.

Pransky, G., Borkan, J. M., Young, A. E., & Cherkin, D. C. (2011, September 1). Are we making progress? The tenth international forum for primary care research on low back pain. *Spine*, *36*(19), 1608–1614.

Proctor, T. J., Mayer, T. G., Gatchel, R. J., & McGeary, D. D. (2004). Unremitting healthcare- utilization outcomes of tertiary rehabilitation of patients with chronic musculoskeletal disorders. *JBJS*, *86*(1), 62–69.

Radcliff, K., Freedman, M., Hilibrand, A., Isaac, R., Lurie, J. D., Zhao, W., . . . Weinstein, J. (2013, June 15). Does opioid pain medication use affect the outcome of patients with lumbar disk herniation? *Spine*, *38*(14), E849.

Ray-Sannerud, B. N., Dolan, D. C., Morrow, C. E., Corso, K. A., Kanzler, K. E., Corso, M. L., & Bryan, C. J. (2012). Longitudinal outcomes after brief behavioral health intervention in an integrated primary care clinic. *Families, Systems & Health*, *30*, 60–71.

Rayner, L., Hotopf, M., Petkova, H., Matcham, F., Simpson, A., & McCracken, L. M. (2016). Depression in patients with chronic pain attending a specialised pain treatment centre: Prevalence and impact on health care costs. *Pain, 157*(7), 1472.

Rudd, R. A., Aleshire, N., Zibbell, J. E., & Matthew Gladden, R. (2016). Increases in drug and opioid overdose deaths—United States, 2000–2014. *American Journal of Transplantation, 16*(4), 1323–1327.

Russo, D. C., Bird, B. L., & Masek, B. J. (1980). Assessment issues in behavioral medicine. *Behavioral Assessment, 2*(1), 1–18.

Sadock, E., Auerbach, S. M., Rybarczyk, B., & Aggarwal, A. (2014). Evaluation of integrated psychological services in a university-based primary care clinic. *Journal of Clinical Psychology in Medical Settings, 21*, 19–32.

Schneiderhan, J., Clauw, D., & Schwenk, T. L. (2017). Primary care of patients with chronic pain. *JAMA, 317*(23), 2367–2368.

Schulte, E., Hermann, K., Berghöfer, A., Hagmeister, H., Schuh-Hofer, S., Schenk, M., . . . Boemke, W. (2010). Referral practices in patients suffering from non-malignant chronic pain. *European Journal of Pain, 14*(3), 308–e1.

Searle, A., Spink, M., Ho, A., & Chuter, V. (2015). Exercise interventions for the treatment of chronic low back pain: A systematic review and meta-analysis of randomised controlled trials. *Clinical Rehabilitation, 29*(12), 1155–1167.

Spitzer, R. L., Kroenke, K., Williams, J. B., & Löwe, B. (2006). A brief measure for assessing generalized anxiety disorder: The GAD-7. *Archives of Internal Medicine, 166*(10), 1092–1097.

Stewart, W. F., Ricci, J. A., Chee, E., & Morganstein, D. (2003). Lost productive work time costs from health conditions in the United States: Results from the American Productivity Audit. *Journal of Occupational and Environmental Medicine, 45*(12), 1234–1246.

Sullivan, M. J., Bishop, S. R., & Pivik, J. (1995). The pain catastrophizing scale: Development and validation. *Psychological Assessment, 7*(4), 524.

Tai-Seale, M., Bolin, J., Bao, X., & Street, R. (2011, November 1). Management of chronic pain among older patients: Inside primary care in the US. *European Journal of Pain, 15*(10), 1087.e1–1087.e8.

Tan, G., Jensen, M. P., Thornby, J. I., & Shanti, B. F. (2004). Validation of the brief pain inventory for chronic nonmalignant pain. *The Journal of Pain, 5*(2), 133–137.

Texas Department of State Health and Human Services (TxDHS). *Texas health data center for health statistics.* Retrieved January 4, 2018, from http://healthdata.dshs.texas.gov/Home

Trafton, J., Martins, S., Michel, M., Lewis, E., Wang, D., Combs, A., . . . Goldstein, M. K. (2010). Evaluation of the acceptability and usability of a decision support system to encourage safe and effective use of opioid therapy for chronic, noncancer pain by primary care providers. *Pain Medicine, 11*, 575–585.

Turner, B., Yin, Z., Bobadilla, R., Rodriguez, N., Liang, Y., Winkler, P., & Simmonds, M. (2017). (351) Randomized trial of multimodality chronic pain care for primary care patients in clinic versus in community: Preliminary results. *The Journal of Pain, 18*(4), S62.

Turner, J. A., Anderson, M. L., Balderson, B. H., Cook, A. J., Sherman, K. J., & Cherkin, D. C. (2016). Mindfulness-based stress reduction and cognitive behavioral therapy for chronic low back pain: Similar effects on mindfulness, catastrophizing, self-efficacy, and acceptance in a randomized controlled trial. *Pain, 157*(11), 2434–2444.

Upshur, C. C., Luckmann, R. S., & Savageau, J. A. (2006, June 1). Primary care provider concerns about management of chronic pain in community clinic populations. *Journal of General Internal Medicine, 21*(6), 652–655.

Vlaeyen, J. W., & Linton, S. J. (2000). Fear-avoidance and its consequences in chronic musculoskeletal pain: A state of the art. *Pain, 85*(3), 317–332.

Vogel, M. E., Kanzler, K. E., Aikens, J. E., & Goodie, J. L. (2017). Integration of behavioral health and primary care: Current knowledge and future directions. *Journal of Behavioral Medicine*, *40*(1), 69–84.

Von Korff, M. R. (2012). Opioids for chronic noncancer pain: As the pendulum swings, who should set prescribing standards for primary care? *The Annals of Family Medicine*, *10*(4), 302–303.

Von Korff, M. R., Balderson, B. H., Saunders, K., Miglioretti, D. L., Lin, E. H., Berry, S., . . . Turner, J. A. (2005). A trial of an activating intervention for chronic back pain in primary care and physical therapy settings. *Pain*, *113*(3), 323–330.

Vowles, K. E., McCracken, L. M., McLeod, C., & Eccleston, C. (2008). The chronic pain acceptance questionnaire: Confirmatory factor analysis and identification of patient subgroups. *Pain*, *140*(2), 284–291.

Vowles, K. E., Witkiewitz, K., Sowden, G., & Ashworth, J. (2014). Acceptance and commitment therapy for chronic pain: Evidence of mediation and clinically significant change following an abbreviated interdisciplinary program of rehabilitation. *The Journal of Pain*, *15*(1), 101–113.

Waddell, G. (1987). 1987 Volvo award in clinical sciences: A new clinical model for the treatment of low-back pain. *Spine*, *12*(7), 632–644.

Waddell, G., Newton, M., Henderson, I., Somerville, D., & Main, C. J. (1993). A Fear-Avoidance Beliefs Questionnaire (FABQ) and the role of fear-avoidance beliefs in chronic low back pain and disability. *Pain*, *52*(2), 157–168.

Weathers, F. W., Litz, B. T., Keane, T. M., Palmieri, P. A., Marx, B. P., & Schnurr, P. P. (2013). The PTSD checklist for DSM-5 (PCL-5). *Scale available from the National Center for PTSD*. Retrieved from www.ptsd.va.gov

Witt, D. R., Garrison, G. M., Gonzalez, C. A., Witt, T. J., & Angstman, K. B. (2017). Six-month outcomes for collaborative care management of depression among smoking and nonsmoking patients. *Health Services Research and Managerial Epidemiology*, *4*, doi:10.1177/2333392817721648

Appendix 1
Patient Handout

The Biopsychosocial Model of Pain

Pain affects you in many ways. Although this makes pain hard to treat, it also gives a lot of chances to change your pain. Use the diagram below to note how your pain affects you and the different ways you can work on it!

Patient Instructions

[*STEP 1*] Using a red pen/pencil, write examples of how your pain affects you in each of the circles (this is your PROBLEM LIST).

[*STEP 2*] Using a green pen/pencil, write one way to work on how pain affects you in each circle (this is your TREATMENT PLAN).

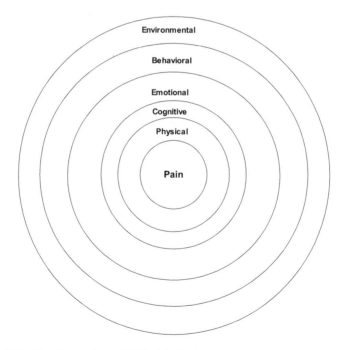

Figure 7.6 The Biopsychosocial Model of Pain

Appendix 2

Overlap in the Biopsychosocial Model of Pain

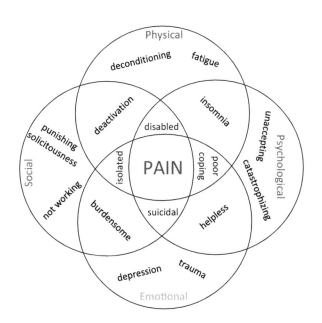

Figure 7.7   How Biopsychosocial Domains Overlap?

8

Pharmacological Treatment Approaches
Strengths, Risks, and the Role for Interdisciplinary Care

Catherine G. Derington, David K. Choi, and Katy E. Trinkley

Introduction and History

In the late twentieth century, healthcare professionals voiced concerns that acute and chronic cancer pain were not being appropriately treated (Acute Pain Management Guideline Panel, 1992; Kamdar, 2010; Marks & Sachar, 1973; Porter & Jick, 1980; Ready, Edwards, & International Association for the Study of Pain. Task Force on Acute Pain, 1992; Savage, 1996). During this time, there was an increased focus on pain as the fifth "vital sign," which called attention to pain management and relief on a national stage (Hanks, 2008; Lanser & Gesell, 2001; Tompkins, Hobelmann, Compton, & Bonica, 2017). As a result, opioid treatment was encouraged and became a mainstream standard of care for acute and chronic, malignant and nonmalignant pain alike (e.g., Foley, 1979; McGivney & Crooks, 1984; Portenoy, 1990).

While the initial intention was to improve pain management, the movement led to the current state of concern surrounding excessive opioid prescribing, overdoses, and deaths (Cochran, Hruschak, DeFosse, & Hohmeier, 2016; Hedegaard, Warner, & Miniño, 2017; Jones, Mack, & Paulozzi, 2013; Shipton, Shipton, Williman, & Shipton, 2017; Volkow & McLellan, 2016). Heavy marketing from pharmaceutical companies and minimization of the associated risks further accelerated the spread of opioids (Cheatle, 2015; Clark & Sees, 1993; Portenoy, 1990; Portenoy & Foley, 1986; Schofferman, 1993; Schug, Merry, & Acland, 1991; Tompkins et al., 2017; Van Zee, 2009). Cities, counties, mental health professionals, states, and other organizations are pursuing litigation against large chain pharmacies and opioid manufacturers for their roles in fueling the rapid increase in opioid prescriptions throughout the late 1990s and early 2000s (Hegyi, 2017; Ingersoll, 2018; Pembroke, 2017; Raymond, 2018; Schweers, 2018; Semuels, 2017; Smith & Davey, 2017).

As the nation continues to develop solutions for what is now known as "the opioid epidemic," individual clinicians face a variety of challenges when treating patients for pain disorders. Pain is a subjective measure that is not as easily assessed, treated, or tracked as other chronic conditions such as hypertension or diabetes. Additionally, in the last ten years, multiple chronic pain management guidelines have been published by national or professional bodies, but with differing recommendations (American Society of Anesthesiologists and the American Society of Regional Anesthesia and Pain Medicine, 2010; Chou et al., 2009; Dowell, Haegerich, & Chou, 2016; Manchikanti et al., 2012; Nuckols et al., 2013; Qaseem, Wilt, McLean, & Forciea, 2017; Utah Department of Health, 2009; Washington State Agency Medical Directors' Group (AMDG), 2010). Insurance providers, including the Centers for Medicare and Medicaid Services, are implementing opioid prescribing restrictions, further complicating pharmacologic management of patients with chronic pain.

Goals and strategies of treatment can vary drastically on inter- and intra-patient levels depending upon the duration, type, and intensity of pain. There also is a wide variety of medications to treat pain, all with varying levels of effectiveness, safety, and evidence for use in specific pain populations. Finally, although opioids have gained widespread use, long-term safety concerns and disappointing clinical trial results have further called into question both the role of opioids and the patient populations appropriate for opioids.

In this complex era of pain management, where there is intense focus on appropriate pain management and where opioids are feared by many clinicians and patients, healthcare professionals must understand and synthesize basic pain pathophysiology principles, clinical experience, and available evidence to institute safe and effective pharmacotherapy and non-pharmacotherapy pain management strategies. This chapter focuses on opioid and non-opioid pharmacologic strategies for outpatient chronic pain management.

Epidemiology

Chronic Pain

Chronic pain affects 100 million people annually in the United States, roughly 30–40% of the nation's adults, according to recent estimates (Gaskin & Richard, 2012; Volkow & McLellan, 2016). The estimated annual economic costs of pain, including direct healthcare expenses and indirect costs such as lost wages, range from $560 to $630 billion annually. This is more than the individual treatment costs of cardiovascular, malignant, respiratory, digestive, endocrine, or metabolic diseases (Gaskin & Richard, 2012; Institute of Medicine Committee on

Advancing Pain Research Care and Education, 2011). While the etiologies, risk factors, and socioeconomic influences vary from patient to patient, studies have shown that women, older patients, persons with lower household incomes, and patients with concurrent mental illness are more likely than other populations to present with chronic pain complaints (Tompkins et al., 2017).

Opioid Use

The United States consumes more than 80% of the world's supply of opioids, despite representing only 5% of the world's total population (International Narcotics Control Board, 2014; Manchikanti, 2007). More than 245 million opioid prescriptions were dispensed in the United States in 2014. Sixty-five percent of these prescriptions were for short-term (less than three weeks) treatment (Jones, 2015; Levy, Paulozzi, Mack, & Jones, 2015; Volkow, McLellan, Cotto, Karithanom, & Weiss, 2011). Primary care providers write nearly half of all opioid prescriptions, which highlights the volume of chronic pain management that occurs in this setting (Dowell et al., 2016; Jamison, Sheehan, Scanlan, Matthews, & Ross, 2014; Levy et al., 2015; Wilson et al., 2013).

Pathophysiology of Pain

Many chemicals and receptors are involved in sensing, transmitting, modulating, and sensitizing pain. The following provides a high-level review of pain mechanisms. This book's subsequent chapters provide more detailed, disease-specific pathophysiologies of specific types of chronic pain where appropriate.

At the site of injury, neurotransmitters and chemicals act on specific receptors (called "nociceptors") to mediate pain, including substance P, calcitonin gene-related peptide, bradykinin, nerve growth factor, prostaglandins, thromboxanes, leukotrienes, endocannabinoids, neurotrophins, cytokines/chemokines (e.g., interleukin-1β, interleukin-6, and tumor necrosis factor α), extracellular proteases, and protons. These chemicals may be released by inflammatory cells, cells that are damaged, or in response to a chemical or mechanical stimulus. The nerves that sense and respond to a pain stimulus express one or more nociceptors that are able to recognize and initiate the transmission of the pain signal to the central nervous system (spinal cord and brain) (Basbaum, Bautista, Scherrer, & Julius, 2009; Julius & Basbaum, 2001). Common nociceptors include TRPV1 (heat and mechanical stimuli), TRPV2 (heat and osmotic stretch), TRPM8 (cold stimuli), and TRPA1 (mechanical, cold, and chemical stimuli), among many others. Different forms and types of voltage-gated sodium and potassium channels transmit pain along nerve fibers to the spinal cord and brain. Voltage-gated calcium channels allow for the release of neurotransmitters at the end of nerves to send pain signals to other nerves.

Once the central nervous system receives a pain signal, several receptors can modulate how the body processes and perceives the signal, including calcium, opioid, glutamate, α-amino-3-hydroxy-5-methyl-4-isoxazolepropionic acid (AMPA), N-methyl-D-aspartate (NMDA), gamma-aminobutyric acid (GABA), sodium, serotonin, and norepinephrine receptors. Calcium channels at the end of nerves stimulate the release of specific neurotransmitters to act on other nerves. The binding of opioids to opioid receptors prevents the nerve from continuing pain transmission by blocking calcium channel action. The binding of glutamate to glutamate, AMPA, and NMDA receptors excites nerves and stimulates the nerve to continue pain processing. Conversely, blocking sodium channels and/ or promoting the action of GABA, serotonin, and norepinephrine inhibit the transmission and processing of pain signals.

The body also can become more sensitive to pain signals by a variety of mechanisms. In response to a pain signal, the body may make more receptors to sense, transmit, and respond to pain as a natural protective mechanism in anticipation of additional pain stimuli. In addition, the chemicals and neurotransmitters released in response to inflammation or trauma promote the generation of more pain receptors and chemicals and change how the receptors respond to painful stimuli. During repeated pain signal transmission, the body may suppress pathways that prevent the perception of pain to allow more pain signals to get through in the future, a process called "disinhibition" (Vardeh, Mannion, & Woolf, 2016). Finally, a growing body of evidence suggests that immune system activation in the brain occurs in response to continued pain signal transmission, which allows the pain signal to persist past the initial injury (Luo, Feng, Liu, Walters, & Hu, 2015; Mantyh, 2014; Vardeh et al., 2016).

When a medication acts on a receptor, it may either agonize (i.e., make the effects greater) or antagonize (i.e., lessen the effects of) the receptor. Many receptors and neurotransmitters that assist in pain signal transmission are also physiologically located in other parts of the body. Thus, when administering a medication for pain that acts on one type of receptor on nerve tissue, there is the potential for the medication to also act on the same receptor on another type of tissue and cause adverse effects. For example, when administering an opioid medication, the opioid will agonize opioid receptors on nerve tissue to prevent a pain signal from being perceived by the brain. However, opioid receptors also are abundant in intestinal tissue, and when an opioid medication binds to these receptors, it will slow down intestinal muscle contractions and cause constipation. The clinician must be wary of the therapeutic benefits and risks of using medications so that they are able to anticipate adverse effects prior to starting therapy, detect adverse effects when they occur, and manage adverse effects after they occur.

Classification of Pain

Pain can be classified, assessed, and treated by investigating its duration, type, and intensity. Medication decisions are influenced by available evidence supporting use, but the underlying pathophysiology also should inform treatment. Therefore, it is pertinent to know how the body chemically and biologically responds to pain so that an appropriate medication can be selected.

Duration of Pain

In general, pain duration can be classified into acute or chronic. Acute pain refers to pain that has been present for less than three to six months. Chronic pain persists beyond three to six months (International Association for the Study of Pain, 1994).

Type of Pain

Acute pain may occur in the post-injury or postoperative setting. Acute pain is a biologic response to a chemical or physical harm and is intended to signal the body to recognize tissue damage. Examples include surgery, acute illness, trauma, medical procedures, and short-term inflammation (such as a bee sting).

Chronic pain may arise from untreated or undertreated acute pain and may exist whether or not true tissue injury occurs. In general, three subtypes of chronic pain are mediated by different pathophysiologic mechanisms: nociceptive pain, neuropathic pain, and mixed pain/central hypersensitivity.

Nociceptive pain is a protective biologic instinct that signals tissue damage in response to chemical, thermal, or mechanical stimuli. These stimuli can represent trauma, inflammation, or another disease process such as ischemia (i.e., lack of oxygen delivery to the tissue). Nociceptive pain can take place in musculoskeletal tissues (skeletal muscle or body surface structures such as connective tissues) or visceral tissues (smooth muscle-covered or other abdominal organs such as the intestines or pancreas). Patients with nociceptive musculoskeletal pain describe their pain using terms such as "sharp," "throbbing," "dull," or "achy," and the pain usually can be identified as originating from one or more areas of the body. Patients may describe nociceptive visceral pain as "deep," "squeezing," or "pressure," and patients may not be able to identify the exact place on their body causing the pain.

Nociceptive pain is largely mediated by substance P, calcitonin gene-related peptide, bradykinin, nerve growth factor, prostaglandins, thromboxanes, leukotrienes, endocannabinoids, neurotrophins, and cytokines/chemokines in response to an injury. Medications used to treat nociceptive pain target enzymes that produce the aforementioned chemicals, reduce inflammation, or act on the mediation of pain signals via the opioid or norepinephrine receptors. Spasm pain may accompany musculoskeletal pain, but the mechanisms behind this type of pain are not well understood and are beyond the scope of this chapter. Examples of somatic nociceptive pain include osteoarthritis and rheumatoid arthritis. Examples of visceral nociceptive pain include pancreatitis and irritable bowel syndrome (IBS).

Neuropathic pain is triggered in response to central or peripheral nerve tissue damage, and is described as "lancing," "burning," "electric," "on fire," or "shooting." In response to an initial nerve injury or disease process, nerves structurally and functionally change the way they conduct electrical signaling and respond to chemical stimuli. Calcium channels are up-regulated, which allows for the release of additional neurotransmitters to continue pain processing and signaling. Sodium channels also are up-regulated at nerve endings, which promote pain sensation and transmission.

Neuropathic injury also induces disinhibition of the pain pathway, making GABA agonism and glutamate antagonism targets for treating neuropathic pain. Finally, biologic targets that are involved in modifying the emotional response to pain (such as serotonin and norepinephrine) are therapeutic targets for neuropathic pain management. Patients with neuropathic pain may experience a phenomenon termed allodynia, which is a pain experience resulting from a non-painful stimulus (such as the wind or a light touch on the skin) (International Association for the Study of Pain, 1994). Examples of peripheral neuropathic pain include diabetic neuropathy and postherpetic neuralgia. Examples of central neuropathic pain include multiple sclerosis, spinal cord injury, and migraine.

Mixed pain may be present in patients with combinations of neuropathic and nociceptive pain in response to tissue damage, or mixed pain may occur in the setting of no true tissue damage. The patient may not have an identifiable noxious stimulus, inflammation, or structural damage. In these cases, the patient experiences sensory hypersensitivity, which is a pain response to dysregulation or dysfunction of normal neuron activity (Phillips & Clauw, 2011). A variety of neurotransmitters mediate mixed pain, including those previously mentioned for nociceptive and neuropathic pain. Patients with mixed pain may experience allodynia in addition to hyperalgesia, a phenomenon whereby a normally painful stimulus elicits a pain response of greater intensity than normally would be expected (Basbaum et al., 2009; International Association for the Study of Pain, 1994). Examples of mixed pain include back pain, cancer pain, or fibromyalgia.

Intensity of Pain

Pain is difficult to treat because of its subjective nature. One individual may perceive a pain stimulus to be more intense than another individual experiencing the same pain stimulus. There have been multiple efforts to standardize pain intensity using pain scales, scores, and questionnaires that seek to objectify pain symptoms so that clinicians can appropriately assess and measure pain treatment. These pain scales, scores, and questionnaires vary significantly in focus, purpose, length, time to administer, ease of use, intended patient population, intended care setting, and validated use in other pain populations. Overall, it is recommended to use one type of pain assessment tool consistently throughout the patient's pain management continuum to track treatment effectiveness.

Goals of Treatment

Chronic pain treatment goals are highly individualized and depend upon the type of pain and the patient's functionality. Complete resolution of pain often is impossible. Pain reduction should be emphasized over pain abolishment, especially when using medications. The medication treatment goal often is not to eliminate pain, but to reduce it by 50% or to a satisfactory level (Manchikanti et al., 2012). Thorough discussions with patients regarding realistic treatment expectations should occur with a focus on improving functionality rather than achieving a specific pain score. The clinician may consider implementing SMART goals, which encourage individuals to set goals in specific, measurable, assignable (or "achievable" in the healthcare setting), realistic, and time-bound ways (Doran, 1981).

Broad goals of treatment may include:

1. Decrease pain perception
2. Maintain or improve level of function
3. Reduce use of and dependence on medications when possible
4. Avoid or reduce medication-related adverse effects
5. Improve quality of life

To work toward these treatment goals, clinical pharmacists often are part of interdisciplinary treatment teams. Clinical pharmacists serve as experts in the appropriate selection, dosing, monitoring, and alteration of medication management plans. Pharmacists also provide clinical expertise in medication taper schedules, interpretation of urine drug screens, drug–drug interactions, drug–disease interactions, recognition and management of drug-related adverse effects, and risk mitigation strategies. Pharmacist involvement may vary from a clinical pharmacist present within the clinic providing on-site consultations, patient education, and patient care (most preferred) to a dispensing pharmacist in an off-site pharmacy dispensing medications in a retail or community setting. Depending upon the state, clinical pharmacists can enter collaborative practice agreements with primary pain management providers and see patients (similar to advanced nurse practitioners and physician assistants).

Strengths of Opioids for Chronic Pain Management

Opioids were avoided for many decades after the passage of the Harrison Narcotic Act in 1914. It was not until clinicians in the 1970s and 1980s started using opioids for pain relief in terminal illness that their benefits became well known. Opioids provide patients with short-term pain relief, which eases suffering. In addition, as a result of the blocked pain transmission, patients taking opioids may be less apt to move or disrupt a site of trauma or surgery, thereby promoting healing. Similarly, opioid use may allow patients to increase their level of functionality by minimizing pain associated with common activities, such as standing and walking. However, all of these strengths also may be achievable with non-opioid medications, which are most often preferred in light of the risks of chronic opioid therapy.

Risks of Opioids for Chronic Pain Management

Opioids are associated with a multitude of side effects (see Table 8.1). The potential risks of abuse or addiction should be differentiated from physical dependence. With continued opioid exposure, the patient will become more tolerant to his or her current dose of the opioid—the body will require more of the opioid in order to achieve the same level of analgesia. Consequently, the patient will find himself/herself unable to go without opioid doses due to symptoms of withdrawal and must maintain a baseline daily opioid burden in order to preserve functionality and pain relief. If a patient takes additional opioid above and beyond that prescribed or uses opioids in routes other than prescribed (e.g., snorting rather than ingesting), he or she is participating in opioid misuse, which could also point to opioid abuse.

In contrast, addiction is characterized as out-of-control use, compulsivity (devoting mental and physical energy to obtaining and using opioids), and continued use despite consequences (American Psychiatric Association, 2013). While the risk of addiction with opioid use initially was thought to be small (Portenoy & Foley, 1986; Porter & Jick, 1980), recent studies indicate that the prevalence of addiction may range from 2% to 14%, and may be as high as 50% in patients who are prescribed chronic opioid therapy (Banta-Green, Merrill, Doyle, Boudreau, & Calsyn, 2009; Boscarino et al., 2011; Højsted & Sjøgren, 2007; Naliboff et al., 2011; Nguyen, Raffa, Taylor, & Pergolizzi, 2015; Sweis, Huffman, Shella, & Scheman, 2012).

Another concern with opioid use is the risk of overdose and respiratory depression, which could result in death. Many studies indicate that as the opioid dose increases (that is, the burden of opioids on the system increases), the risks of overdose, death from overdose, and all-cause mortality increase (Bohnert et al., 2011; Dasgupta et al., 2016; Dunn et al., 2010; Gomes, Mamdani, Dhalla, Paterson, & Juurlink, 2011; Ray et al., 2015; Ray, Chung, Murray, Hall, & Stein, 2016).

Additional risk factors for opioid overdose beyond opioid burden include combinations with sedatives like benzodiazepines, muscle relaxants, or alcohol, long-acting formulation use, previous overdose experience, history of substance use disorder or opioid addiction, impaired organ function, age over 65 years, resuming opioid therapy after a period of abstinence, comorbid respiratory disorders, and switching or reducing opioids (Binswanger et al., 2012; Chou et al., 2015; Larochelle, Liebschutz, Zhang, Ross-Degnan, & Wharam, 2016; Lembke, Humphreys, & Newmark, 2016; Miller et al., 2015; Smith, 2007; Zedler et al., 2014). These studies led to the guideline-endorsed recommendations that opioid doses should be limited to less than 50–90 morphine milligram equivalents (MMEs) daily (see Table 8.2 for opioid conversion ratios) (Dowell et al., 2016; Utah Department of Health, 2009; Washington State Agency Medical Directors' Group, 2010).

Finally, animal and human studies have shown that opioid use results in hyperalgesia by disrupting the body's normal biologic responses to pain sensation,

Table 8.1 Opioid Adverse Effects

Adverse Effect	Tolerance With Continued Use?	Possible Physiologic Mechanism	Management	Other Comments
Immunosuppression[a] (Gudin, Laitman, & Nalamachu, 2015)	No	Inhibition of opioid receptors may lead to decreased activation of the immune system	Reduce or discontinue opioid	Caution long-term use of opioids in patients with baseline immunosuppression (transplant, cancer treatment, etc.)
Endocrine dysfunction[a] (Benyamin et al., 2008; Gudin et al., 2015)	No	Inhibitor of GnRH secretion	Reduce or discontinue opioid; treat underlying conditions	May lead to hypogonadism, sexual dysfunction, fatigue, depression, dysmenorrhea, infertility, hypothyroidism reduced bone mineral density
Major adverse cardiac events[a]	No	QTc interval prolongation	Reduce opioid dose, discontinue other agents that prolong QaTc interval, change to different opioid	Most common with methadone
Osteopenia/fractures[a]	No	Inhibitor of GnRH secretion which leads to decreases in estrogen	Reduce or discontinue opioid; consider use of calcium, vitamin D, and/ or bisphosphonate; stay physically active if possible	
Analgesic tolerance[a] (Benyamin et al., 2008)	Yes	Loss of analgesic benefit due to up-regulation of receptors	Increase dose if needed; change to different opioid	If pain increases with increased dose, may indicate hyperalgesia rather than analgesic tolerance
CNS depression[b] (Benyamin et al., 2008; Young-McCaughan & Miaskowski, 2001)	Yes	Mechanism unknown	Reduce opioid dose, change to different opioid, prescribe naloxone	Can lead to overdose and death

Respiratory depression (Dahan, Aarts, & Smith, 2010)	Yes	Activation of the mu-opioid receptor	Reduce opioid dose, change to different opioid, prescribe naloxone	Can lead to overdose and death
Neurotoxicity (Gallagher, 2007; Mercadante & Portenoy, 2001)	No	Potentially due to active metabolite	Reduce opioid dose, change to different opioid	Common with hydromorphone; may present as acute delirium, tremors, myoclonus, seizures, and hallucinations
Allergic response[c] (Baldo & Pham, 2012)	No	Direct degranulation of mast cells to release histamine and initiate allergic response	May require immediate emergency personnel intervention if airway is affected; epinephrine and diphenhydramine administration; document as allergy and do not re-administer; change to different opioid (preferably more synthetic)	More common with natural opioids versus synthetic
Constipation (Benyamin et al., 2008)	No	Activation of opioid receptors in the gastrointestinal tract causes decrease in gut motility	Use a bowel regimen of a stool softener and stimulant daily (usually docusate and senna); stay hydrated and physically active if possible; avoid constipating foods; reduce dose of opioid; can consider other laxatives if needed	Can result in significant or life-threatening complications; patients should be on stool softener AND bowel stimulant as prophylaxis

(Continued)

Table 8.1 (Continued)

Adverse Effect	Tolerance With Continued Use?	Possible Physiologic Mechanism	Management	Other Comments
Nausea, vomiting (Smith, Smith, & Seidner, 2012)	Yes	Mechanism is not clear (may enhance vestibular sensitivity, direct effect on chemoreceptor trigger zone and delayed gastric emptying)	Take opioid with food; avoid irritating foods (caffeine, spicy, fatty foods); reduce dose of opioid	Not a true allergy

GnRH = gonadotropin-releasing hormone; QTc = corrected QT interval

[a] Effects may present after long-term use of opioid
[b] May present as dizziness, sedation, drowsiness, altered mental status, or coma
[c] May present as itching, rash, redness, shortness of breath or difficulty breathing, or anaphylaxis

References:

Baldo, B. A., & Pham, N. H. (2012). Histamine-releasing and allergenic properties of opioid analgesic drugs: Resolving the two. *Anaesthesia and Intensive Care, 40*(2), 216–235.

Benyamin, R., Trescot, A. M., Datta, S., Buenaventura, R., Adlaka, R., Sehgal, N., . . . Vallejo, R. (2008). Opioid complications and side effects. *Pain Physician, 11*(2 Suppl), S105–120.

Dahan, A., Aarts, L., & Smith, T. W. (2010). Incidence, reversal, and prevention of opioid-induced respiratory depression. *Anesthesiology, 112*(1), 226–238. http://doi.org/10.1097/ALN.0b013e3181c38c25

Gallagher, R. (2007). Opioid-induced neurotoxicity. *Canadian Family Physician, 53*(3), 426–427.

Gudin, J. A., Laitman, A., & Nalamachu, S. (2015). Opioid Related Endocrinopathy. *Pain Medicine, 16*(Suppl 1), S9–S15. http://doi.org/10.1111/pme.12926

Mercadante, S., & Portenoy, R. K. (2001). Opioid poorly responsive cancer pain. Part 1: clinical considerations. *Journal of Pain and Symptom Management, 21*(2), 144–150.

Smith, H., Smith, J., & Seidner, P. (2012). Opioid-induced nausea and vomiting. *Annals of Palliative Medicine, 1*(2), 121–129. http://doi.org/10.3978/j.issn.224-5820.2012.07.08

Young-McCaughan, S., & Miaskowski, C. (2001). Definition of and mechanism for opioid-induced sedation. *Pain Management Nursing, 2*(3), 84–97. http://doi.org/10.1053/jpmn.2001.25012

Table 8.2 Oral Morphine Milligram Equivalent Conversions

Opioid	Equivalent Dose to 30 mg Oral Morphine
codeine	200 mg
oxycodone	20 mg
oxymorphone	10 mg
hydrocodone	20–30 mg
hydromorphone	7.5 mg
methadone	2–20 mg*
tramadol	150–300 mg*
tapentadol	12 mg*
fentanyl (patch)	12.5 mcg/hour*

* Recommend consultation with pharmacist or pain specialist

References:

Dowell, D., Haegerich, T. M., & Chou, R. (2016). CDC guideline for prescribing opioids for chronic pain—United States, 2016. *MMWR. Recommendations and Reports, 65*(1), 1–49. http://doi.org/10.15585/mmwr.rr6501e1er

transmission, perception, and response (Lee, Silverman, Hansen, Patel, & Manchi-kanti, 2011). In effect, while administering an opioid results in short-term pain relief, it can be harmful to the patient to continue and escalate therapy. The only way to relieve a patient of opioid-induced hyperalgesia is to reduce the dose of the opioid or to discontinue it altogether.

Risk Mitigation Strategies and Considerations

There are a variety of ways that the medicolegal risks conferred to clinicians and patients can be mitigated when treating patients with opioids. However, it is important to note that these strategies have yet to be tied to concrete economic benefits or clinical effectiveness data to reduce risk behaviors, addiction, dependence, abuse, or misuse. These risk mitigation strategies often are called "universal precautions" and often are debated in pain and public medicine (Fishman, 2005; Gourlay & Heit, 2006; Gourlay, Heit, & Almahrezi, 2005). Other risk mitigation strategies not discussed at length here include quantity limitations and mandated clinician continuing education on opioid safety.

Electronic Prescribing: All opioid medications are classified as controlled substance class II agents, a Drug Enforcement Administration (DEA) designation for drugs that have a high potential for abuse that may lead to severe psychological or physical dependence. Medications in this class are the most regulated drugs allowed for public consumption. Prior to 2010, class II controlled substances only could be dispensed if the patient was given a hard copy prescription and dropped it off at the pharmacy. This led to the forging of illegal prescriptions and the subsequent dispensing of opioids to patients without valid prescriptions.

Opioid abusers may steal prescriptions or pills from friends or loved ones who are prescribed opioids for a valid medical purpose; this is the most common source of illegally obtained opioids (Cochran et al., 2016; Fishman et al., 2000; Gasior, Bond, & Malamut, 2016; Hahn, 2011; Volkow & McLellan, 2016). E-prescribing allows the prescriber to electronically send opioid prescriptions to the pharmacy if the prescriber's office and the pharmacy have the appropriate computer technology to securely sign, encrypt, and receive the prescription. This technology has been available to use for non-controlled prescriptions in the past, but e-prescribing for class II controlled substances requires more technological encryption and set-up. E-prescribing effectively eliminates the need for, and subsequent risk of, hard copy prescriptions vulnerable to copying, forging, stealing, and illegal dispensing. Unfortunately, adoption is slow. While more than 90% of pharmacies nationwide have technology capable of receiving these prescriptions, it has been implemented and used in less than 25% of prescriber offices (Surescripts, 2018).

Treatment Contracts: Many experts, clinicians, and agencies in the pain medicine field encourage the use of treatment contracts (Chou et al., 2009; Utah Department of Health, 2009; Volkow & McLellan, 2016). The patient and primary pain management provider sign these formal, explicit documents at least annually. These agreements outline the risks of opioid therapy, as well as patient and provider expectations. In general, treatment contracts have three main objectives: 1) to describe treatment parameters; 2) to document bilateral (patient and provider) agreement to comply with the contract; and 3) to document informed consent for treatment with opioids (Fishman, Bandman, Edwards, & Borsook, 1999). There is no standard treatment contract. While significant practice variation exists, common components include how the prescriber will monitor the patient; how many days' supply the patient may receive at one time; inappropriate patient behaviors that will lead to discontinuation of opioid prescribing; a requirement to submit to random urine drug testing; a requirement to use one prescriber and pharmacy for all drug dispenses; and the encouragement of honest communication between patient and clinician.

Urine Drug Screens: Similar to treatment contracts, urine drug screening (UDS) is a widely accepted and recommended opioid monitoring technique (Chou et al., 2009; Dowell et al., 2016; Nuckols et al., 2013; Turner et al., 2014). UDS may be required by the treatment contract signed by patient and clinician, but the frequency of UDS is often institution- and clinician-specific. As with the ordering of any laboratory test, the intent of the UDS and plan for interpretation of results should be known and communicated to the patient. Most clinicians opt to use UDS to ensure adherence to the prescribed regimen, as the medication should appear in the urine if the patient is taking the medication. In addition, clinicians utilize UDS to monitor for use or abuse of other medications, as non-prescribed therapies should not appear in the urine. A clinician well trained in the interpretation of these screening tools should be providing recommendations based upon the results. These results can be impacted by the drug's pharmacodynamics and pharmacokinetics, the patient's organ function and pharmacogenetics, the sample's storage and transportation, and assay used within the laboratory.

The laboratory that processes the UDS strongly impacts the results. Some laboratories only can assess whether there is drug in the urine (called "qualitative" detection), while more advanced laboratories can detect exactly how much drug is in the urine (called "quantitative" detection). The amount of drug in the urine generally correlates with the doses the patient ingested. The clinician should anticipate and be prepared to discuss with the patient the results of the UDS, including the implications for opioid discontinuation if aberrancies are discovered.

Prescription Drug Monitoring Programs: Prescription drug monitoring programs (PDMPs) are implemented by individual states and are a relatively new tool in the monitoring of controlled substance prescribing and dispensing. The PDMP most often is run by the state's board of pharmacy and includes a web-based portal that can be accessed by state-specified clinicians to view any and all controlled substance medications written by any prescriber and dispensed by any pharmacy within the state. A clinician viewing a PDMP record for a given patient in one state may be able to see the PDMP for the same patient in another state, depending upon the technology available to interface between state PDMPs. A clinician must register to access the state's PDMP in which he or she is licensed, and some states mandate that clinicians of certain training credentials register with the PDMP.

While the adoption and recommended or required use of PDMPs varies between states (National Alliance for Model State Drug Laws, 2017a, 2017b, 2018), the use of PDMPs is expert- and guideline-supported (Chou et al., 2009; Dowell et al., 2016; Hahn, 2011; Jones et al., 2013; Lembke et al., 2016; Levy et al., 2015; Manchikanti et al., 2012; Pergolizzi et al., 2018; Schuchat, Houry, & Guy, 2017). In general, it is recommended that clinicians review the PDMP record prior to the patient's appointment in order to identify any aberrancies or violations of the treatment contract. The PDMP record also should be reviewed in the visit with the patient in order to promote open and honest communication.

Abuse-Deterrent Formulations: In recent years, pharmaceutical companies have developed unique formulations that prevent the crushing of a tablet and subsequent snorting or injecting of the medication, which leads to heightened euphoria. These formulations can prevent tampering with the product in a variety of ways: 1) preventing mechanical or chemical manipulations such that when the physical tablet is crushed or dissolved, it will not turn into a fine powder that would facilitate snorting or injecting and will instead turn into a clumpy sludge, thick paste, or viscous gel; 2) formulating with either naloxone, an opioid-reversal agent that will render the opioid inactive only when injected into the blood stream and not when ingested orally (see the next section), or naltrexone, a medication that competes with opioids to bind to the opioid receptor; 3) formulating with an unpleasant substance that discourages injection, like niacin (which induces flushing); or 4) formulating as a pro-drug such that the drug is only activated in the body's intestinal environment (Cicero & Ellis, 2015; Gasior et al., 2016; Hale, Moe, Bond, Gasior, & Malamut, 2016; Lee, Brown, & Chen, 2017; Nguyen et al., 2015; Roland, Setnik, & Brown, 2017).

Research is ongoing to determine new formulations of abuse-deterrent opioid delivery (Maincent & Zhang, 2016; Mastropietro & Omidian, 2015a; Mastropietro & Omidian, 2015b). However, it should be noted that these formulations, while abuse-deterrent, are not abuse-proof. Patients may still abuse the medication orally by taking more medication than needed, by finding ways around the abuse-deterrent technology, by combining the medication with other drugs or substances like alcohol, or by switching to heroin. The abuse-deterrent formulations are expensive, often are not preferred by insurance companies, and have questionable cost- and clinical comparative outcomes for safety and effectiveness when compared to traditional opioid formulations.

Naloxone: As described previously, naloxone is an opioid-reversal agent that, when administered via injection or intranasally, immediately reverses any effect of an opioid present in the body. Naloxone will not have any effect on an individual who does not have opioid in the body, and it has little to no clinically relevant side effects beyond immediate opioid withdrawal symptoms. In recent years, naloxone has become available in naloxone kits or intranasal formulations from pharmacies pursuant to a prescription. Depending upon the state, a pharmacist may be allowed to dispense naloxone to a patient or a third party (someone who would use naloxone on another person) without a prescription (National Alliance for Model State Drug Laws, 2015).

There is much debate as to the most ideal population to receive naloxone kits. In general, it is appropriate to ensure that a patient prescribed opioids or a caregiver has access to naloxone if he or she is at risk for an opioid overdose (as described previously); if the patient stores the opioids in a home with young children or addicts; it the patient expresses a desire to have naloxone in the home; or it the patient lives in a remote area without close access to emergency services. Naloxone co-prescription with chronic opioid use is widely recommended by experts and guidelines (Boscarino et al., 2016; Dowell et al., 2016; Lembke et al., 2016; Volkow & McLellan, 2016). Appropriate patient education should be provided on when to use, how to use, and other overdose care when providing naloxone prescriptions to patients.

Preferred Treatment Approaches

Selecting a Medication

First-line medication selection for chronic pain depends upon many factors, including the type of pain, patient's age, organ function, concurrent medications, and comorbidities (Chou et al., 2009; Manchikanti et al., 2012). Severity and location of the pain also influence medication selection. Selecting the best medication regimen for each patient requires a risk-benefit analysis at multiple steps.

Consideration 1: Select a Medication Based Upon the Pain Type(s)

This is generally the first step in selecting an appropriate medication to treat pain. With the exceptions of pain in the settings of cancer, palliative care, or end-of-life care, opioids are reserved as last-line options when an appropriate trial of adequate dose and duration of other pharmacologic and non-pharmacologic treatments have not been sufficient. (See Table 8.3 for a comparison of opioid products). Cancer-related pain is unique and typically managed with opioids, often at high doses with other pain medications. Because cancer-related pain often is managed by comprehensive oncology care teams with integrated mental health specialists, details of managing cancer-related pain are not discussed here. (See Chapter 10 for a thorough discussion of cancer-related pain). Further, the use of medical or recreational marijuana is not discussed here, as its role in therapy is still evolving.

As discussed previously, nociceptive pain includes musculoskeletal and visceral pain, which may require different treatment strategies. Musculoskeletal pain generally follows the treatment algorithm displayed in Figure 8.1. In contrast, visceral pain treatment is more individualized based upon location and severity of pain. For example, IBS and unspecified abdominal pain are both visceral pain, but IBS is often treated with antidepressants (Trinkley & Nahata, 2014), whereas unspecified abdominal pain likely will be treated with acetaminophen or nonsteroidal anti-inflammatory drugs (NSAIDs). See Table 8.4 for a comparison of the non-opioid analgesic agents.

Treatment approaches to visceral pain are not discussed in detail within this chapter given that treatment is highly individualized to the culprit organ, which may require significant diagnostic and imaging work-up prior to implementing appropriate pharmacologic strategies. In general, pain related to organs that are highly innervated (such as the pancreas, intestines, and uterus) should first be trialed with agents used to treat neuropathic pain. (See Table 8.5.) Other organs can be trialed on non-opioid analgesic agents (see Table 8.4) before moving to other agents, as chronic, nonmalignant visceral pain tends to be non-responsive to opioid agents (Lembke et al., 2016; Stein & Lang, 2009).

Fibromyalgia and neuropathic pain have many similarities in the preferred medication approach to treatment, but there are key differences in the pathophysiology and corresponding treatments. (See Figures 8.2 and 8.3 for fibromyalgia and neuropathic pain treatments, respectively.) Although there are many subtypes of neuropathic pain, such as postherpetic and diabetic neuropathy, the treatment approach is similar. Opioids with mu-receptor agonism alone are not considered appropriate for neuropathic pain (Manchikanti et al., 2012); however, tramadol and tapentadol are two opioid receptor agonists that have demonstrated efficacy for treating neuropathy in randomized controlled trials, likely due to their effects on norepinephrine (Ortho-McNeil-Janssen Pharmaceuticals, 2010; Ortho-McNeil Pharmaceutical, 2008; Stein & Lang, 2009). Although opioids with NMDA receptor activity (such as methadone)

Table 8.3 Opioid Descriptions

Generic Name (Brand Name)[a]	Available Formulations	Mechanism of Action	Role in Pain Management[b]	Specific Risks or Adverse Effects[c]
codeine	Oral solution, immediate release tablet	Agonizes mu-opioid receptors	Mild to moderate musculoskeletal pain	Metabolized into morphine by liver; use with caution in patients with liver dysfunction
morphine (Avinza, MS Contin, MSIR, Roxanol)	Extended release capsule, extended release tablet, immediate release tablet, injection solution, oral solution, rectal suppository	Agonizes mu-opioid receptors	Moderate to severe musculoskeletal pain	Metabolized into an active metabolite that is cleared by kidneys; use with caution in elderly and patients with kidney dysfunction
hydrocodone (Norco, Lortab, Zohydro ER, Vicoprofen)	Extended release capsule, extended release tablet; in combination with acetaminophen in solutions, tablets, capsules, extended release tablet; tablet in combination with ibuprofen	Agonizes mu-opioid receptors	Moderate to severe musculoskeletal pain	Metabolized into hydromorphone by liver; use with caution in patients with liver dysfunction
hydromorphone (Dilaudid, Exalgo)	Immediate release oral solution, injection solution, rectal suppository, immediate release tablet, extended release tablet	Agonizes mu-opioid receptors	Moderate to severe musculoskeletal pain	
oxycodone (Percocet, Oxy IR, Roxicodone, Oxycontin)	Immediate release oral solution, extended release capsule, extended release tablet; in combination with acetaminophen in solutions, tablets, capsules, extended release tablet	Agonizes mu-opioid receptors	Moderate to severe musculoskeletal pain	Metabolized into oxymorphone by liver; use with caution in patients with liver dysfunction

Drug	Formulations	Mechanism of action	Indication	Clinical considerations
oxymorphone (Opana, Numorphan)	Injection solution, immediate release tablet, extended release tablet	Agonizes mu-opioid receptors	Severe musculoskeletal pain	
methadone (Dolophine, Methadose)	Oral solution, injection solution, oral tablet, soluble tablet	Agonizes mu-opioid receptors; antagonizes NMDA receptors	Detoxification and treatment of substance use disorder; management of moderate to severe musculoskeletal pain	Can be used for treatment of substance use disorder (once daily dosing)—requires special DEA number; highly variable half life—requires careful dose adjustment; can cause QTc prolongation; concerns for serotonin syndrome; many drug interactions
fentanyl (Duragesic, Subsys)	Transmucosal lozenge, buccal tablet, buccal film, intranasal, sublingual tablet, sublingual spray, injection solution, transdermal patch	Agonizes mu-opioid receptors	Severe musculoskeletal pain	REMS Access program for certain fentanyl formulations (transmucosal lozenge, buccal tablet, buccal film, intranasal, sublingual tablet, sublingual spray), careful titration with patch
tramadol (Ultram, Ryzolt)	Extended release capsule, extended release tablet, topical cream, oral suspension, immediate release oral tablet	Agonizes mu-opioid receptors; blocks the reuptake of norepinephrine and serotonin in nerves	Moderate to severe musculoskeletal pain, neuropathic pain	Concern for serotonin syndrome and increased risk for seizures

(Continued)

Table 8.3 (Continued)

Generic Name (Brand Name)[a]	Available Formulations	Mechanism of Action	Role in Pain Management[b]	Specific Risks or Adverse Effects[c]
tapentadol (Nucynta)	Immediate release tablet, extended release tablet	Agonizes mu-opioid receptors; blocks the reuptake of norepinephrine in nerves	Severe musculoskeletal pain; neuropathic pain	Concern for serotonin syndrome
buprenorphine (Butrans)	Patch, sublingual tablet, buccal film, intradermal implant	Agonizes mu-opioid receptors and blocks kappa-opioid receptors	Severe musculoskeletal pain	Sublingual tablet is most often used for treatment of substance use disorder (requires special DEA number); patch is most often used for pain

All agents are controlled substances as classified by the DEA and require a valid prescription.

DEA = Drug Enforcement Administration; NMDA = N-methyl-D-aspartate; REMS = Risk Mitigation and Evaluation Strategy

[a] Includes most commonly known brand names, may not be exhaustive
[b] Opioids should only be used if pain is non-responsive to non-opioid analgesics
[c] See Table 8.1: "Opioid Adverse Effects"

References:

Lexicomp Inc. (n.d.). Lexicomp Online(R). Hudson, OH. Accessed March 26, 2018.

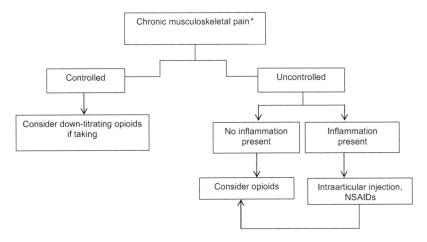

Figure 8.1   Treatment of Musculoskeletal Pain

All patients should be given trial of oral acetaminophen and topical analgesics if not previously or appropriately trialed at the most efficacious dose before oral NSAIDs or opioids.

NSAID = nonsteroidal anti-inflammatory drug

References:

Dowell, D., Haegerich, T. M., & Chou, R. (2016). CDC guideline for prescribing opioids for chronic pain—United States, 2016. MMWR. Recommendations and Reports, 65(1), 1–49. http://doi.org/10.15585/mmwr.rr6501e1er

theoretically are beneficial for neuropathic pain, studies to date have not supported their use in patients without cancer-related pain (Aiyer, Mehta, Gungor, & Gulati, 2018; Altier, Dion, Boulanger, & Choinière, 2005; Haroutounian, McNicol, & Lipman, 2012; McNicol, Ferguson, & Schumann, 2017). When present, spasm pain most often occurs in conjunction with musculoskeletal pain and is treated with muscle relaxants or antispasmodics. (See Table 8.4 for a description of muscle relaxants and antispasmodics.) Studies to date provide limited evidence to support the efficacy of muscle relaxants, antispasmodics, and benzodiazepines in the chronic pain population beyond their sedative effects (See & Ginzburg, 2008).

Consideration 2: Select a Medication Based Upon Age and Organ Function

Pediatric, elderly adults, and patients with diminished organ function require special considerations when selecting a pain medication due to differences in medication absorption, distribution, metabolism, and elimination, which ultimately alter serum concentrations of the drug. Pediatric management of chronic pain is beyond the scope of this chapter and will not be discussed.

Table 8.4 Non-opioid Medications Used to Treat Musculoskeletal Pain (Lexicomp Inc., n.d.)

Pharmacologic Class	Generic Name (Brand Name)[a]	Prescription Status[b]	Available Formulations	Mechanism of Action	Specific Risks or Adverse Effects
Topical counterirritants	Menthol methyl salicylate (Icy Hot) camphor capsaicin (Zostrix, Qutenza)	OTC capsaicin 8% patch is prescription only	Topical cream, topical gel, topical liquid, patch, balm, oil, stick, gel	Blocks various receptors in skin to block pain perception; causes surface irritation which counteracts underlying pain	Capsaicin patch must be administered in a prescriber's office; use gloves while applying or wash hands after use
Analgesic	acetaminophen (Tylenol)	OTC and prescription	Caplet, capsule, tablet, injection oral solution, oral suspension, oral liquid, oral syrup, rectal suppository	Mechanism unknown	Maximum dose of acetaminophen is 4,000 mg/day, metabolized by liver; Caution with alcohol consumption and liver disease
Salicylate analgesic	aspirin (Bayer)	OTC	Caplet, capsule extended release, rectal suppository, tablet	Irreversibly blocks COX-1 and COX-2 enzymes from making chemicals that mediate pain (like prostaglandins)	Increased risk for bleeding, gastrointestinal side effects

| Nonsteroidal anti-inflammatory drug | ibuprofen (Motrin, Advil) naproxen (Naproxen) etodolac (Lodine) ketoprofen ketorolac (Toradol) meloxicam (Mobic) celecoxib (Celebrex) diclofenac (Voltaren) nabumetone (Relafen) piroxicam (Feldene) sulindac (Clinoril) | OTC and prescription | Capsule, tablet, oral suspension, oral packet, delayed/extended release tablet, injection solution, cream | Reversibly blocks COX-1 and COX-2 enzymes from making chemicals that mediate pain (like prostaglandins) | May increase the risk for kidney injury and increase blood pressure; increased risk of gastrointestinal bleeds, and cardiovascular disease; ketorolac use should be limited to five days |
| Local anesthetic | lidocaine (Lidoderm) | OTC and prescription | Cream, gel, lotion, liquid, ointment, solution, patch, intradermal injection | Blocks sodium channels to block pain transmission | Patch must stay in place for 12 hours then remove for 12 hours; use gloves while applying or wash hands after use; may use up to 3 patches at a time; due to a special formulation the patches can be cut |

(Continued)

Table 8.4 (Continued)

Pharmacologic Class	Generic Name (Brand Name)[a]	Prescription Status[b]	Available Formulations	Mechanism of Action	Specific Risks or Adverse Effects
Skeletal muscle relaxants	cyclobenzaprine (Flexeril) methocarbamol (Robaxin) metaxalone (Skelaxin) carisoprodol (Soma) tizanidine (Zanaflex)	Prescription carisoprodol-CIV	Extended release capsule, oral suspension, oral tablet, cream, injection solution	Cyclobenzaprine: reduces muscle motor activity; methocarbamol/ metaxalone/ carisoprodol: CNS depression; tizanidine: α-2 agonist blocks release of excitatory chemicals	All can cause CNS depression; cyclobenzaprine is structurally similar to tricyclic antidepressants (see Table 8.5) and should not be used for a period longer than two weeks; carisoprodol has active metabolite similar to benzodiazepines with addictive potential— avoid use if possible
Antispasmodic	baclofen (Lioresal)	Prescription	Tablet, oral suspension, cream, injection solution, pump	Blocks transmission at the spinal cord	Can cause CNS depression and severe withdrawal if abruptly discontinued at high doses or with injection solution

CIV = controlled prescription class 4; CNS = central nervous system; COX = cyclooxygenase; OTC = over-the-counter

[a] Includes most commonly known brand names, may not be exhaustive
[b] Refers to prescription or over-the-counter status, controlled (with the appropriate class) or non-controlled substance status
[c] Higher doses required for pain/inflammation treatment than cardioprotective doses

References:

Lexicomp Inc. (n.d.). Lexicomp Online(R). Hudson, OH. Accessed March 26, 2018.

Table 8.5 Non-opioid Medications Used to Treat Neuropathic Pain

Pharmacologic Class	Generic Name (Brand Name)[a]	Prescription Status[b]	Available Formulations	Mechanism of Action	Specific Risks or Adverse Effects
Gabapentinoids[c]	gabapentin (Neurontin) pregabalin (Lyrica)	Prescription (pregabalin—CV)	Capsule, tablet, solution, suspension, extended release tablet, cream	Disrupts voltage-gated calcium channels	May cause edema, dizziness, or falls; concern for abuse especially with pregabalin; caution in elderly and patients with renal dysfunction
SNRIs	duloxetine (Cymbalta) venlafaxine (Effexor)	Prescription	Delayed/extended release capsule, tablet	Norepinephrine reuptake inhibitor, serotonin reuptake inhibitor	Potential for serotonin syndrome; may increase blood pressure and heart rate
TCAs	nortriptyline (Pamelor) amitriptyline (Elavil) imipramine (Tofranil) desipramine (Norpramin)	Prescription	Capsule, tablet, oral solution	Norepinephrine reuptake inhibitor, serotonin reuptake inhibitor, blocks sodium channels	Anticholinergic side effects; cardiovascular side effects; caution in the elderly
Anticonvulsants	carbamazepine (Tegretol)	Prescription	Tablet, extended release tablet, extended release capsule, oral suspension	Limits the influx of sodium across cell membranes; blocks pain transmission	May cause hyponatremia; caution in elderly; carbamazepine has many drug interactions

CV = controlled prescription class 5; SNRI = serotonin norepinephrine reuptake inhibitor; TCA = tricyclic antidepressant

[a] Includes most commonly known brand names, not an exhaustive list
[b] Refers to prescription or over-the-counter status, controlled (with the appropriate class) or non-controlled substance status
[c] Gabapentinoids are considered anticonvulsants

References:

Dick, I. E., Brochu, R. M., Purohit, Y., Kaczorowski, G. J., Martin, W. J., & Priest, B. T. (2007). Sodium channel blockade may contribute to the analgesic efficacy of antidepressants. The Journal of Pain, 8(4), 315–324. http://doi.org/10.1016/j.jpain.2006.10.001

Lexicomp Inc. (n.d.). Lexicomp Online(R). Hudson, OH. Accessed March 26, 2018.

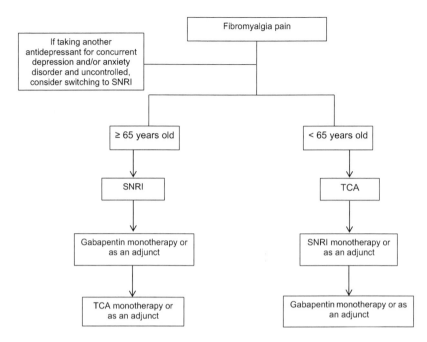

Figure 8.2 Treatment of Fibromyalgia

If partial response achieved at max dose, move to next step. If no response at therapeutic dose after two weeks, stop therapy and move to next step.

SNRI = serotonin norepinephrine reuptake inhibitor; TCA = tricyclic antidepressant

References:

Häuser, W., Petzke, F., & Sommer, C. (2010). Comparative efficacy and harms of duloxetine, milnacipran, and pregabalin in fibromyalgia syndrome. The Journal of Pain: Official Journal of the American Pain Society, 11(6), 505–521. http://doi.org/10.1016/j.jpain.2010.01.002

Häuser, W., Wolfe, F., Tölle, T., Üçeyler, N., & Sommer, C. (2012). The role of antidepressants in the management of fibromyalgia syndrome. CNS Drugs, 26(4), 297–307. http://doi.org/10.2165/11598970-000000000-00000

Older adults, most often defined as 65 years of age or older, are at higher risk of adverse effects associated with many pain medications as a result of inherent changes associated with aging. As the body ages, reduced absorption from the intestines, increased fat stores, reduced liver enzymes, and reduced kidney function alter the way that the body absorbs, processes, and eliminates drugs from the body. Older adults are more sensitive to the same dose of drugs when compared to younger adults, and they have lower physiologic reserve to handle adverse effects that occur. As such, lower than usual doses should be initiated whenever possible with older adults; drugs with potential to increase fall risk should be avoided whenever possible. The American Geriatrics Society Beers Criteria is an excellent

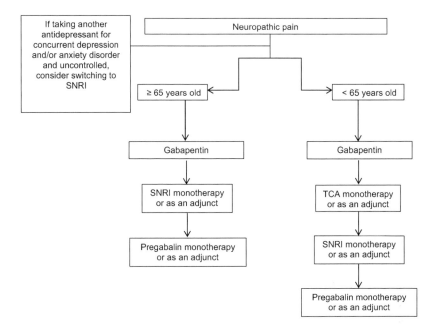

Figure 8.3 Treatment of Neuropathic Pain

If partial response achieved at max dose, move to next step. If no response at therapeutic dose after two weeks, stop therapy and move to next step.

SNRI = serotonin norepinephrine reuptake inhibitor; TCA = tricyclic antidepressant

References:

Chaparro, L.E., Wiffen, P.J., Moore, R.A., & Gilron, I. (2012). Combination pharmacotherapy for the treatment of neuropathic pain in adults. Cochrane Database of Systematic Reviews, (7), CD008943. PMID: 22786518

Dowell, D., Haegerich, T.M., & Chou, R. (2016). CDC guideline for prescribing opioids for chronic pain—United States, 2016. MMWR Recomm Reports, 65(1), 1–49. http://doi.org/10.15585/mmwr.rr6501e1er

Finnerup, N.B., Attal, N., Haroutounian, S., McNicol, E., Baron, R., Dworkin, R.H., Gilron, I., Haanpää, M., Hansson, P., Jensen, T.S., Kamerman, P.R., Lund, K., Moore, A., Raja, S.N., Rice, A.S.C., Rowbotham, M., Sena, E., Siddall, P., Smith, B.H., & Wallace, M. (2015). Pharmacotherapy for neuropathic pain in adults: A systematic review and meta-analysis. Lancet Neurology, 14(2):162–173. PMID: 25575710

Gilron, I., Baron, R., & Jensen, T. (2015). Neuropathic pain: Principles of diagnosis and treatment. Mayo Clinic Proceedings, 90(4), 532–545. PMID: 25841257

Häuser, W., Petzke, F., & Sommer, C. (2010). Comparative efficacy and harms of duloxetine, milnacipran, and pregabalin in fibromyalgia syndrome. The Journal of Pain: Official Journal of the American Pain Society, 11(6), 505–521. http://doi.org/10.1016/j.jpain.2010.01.002

Häuser, W., Wolfe, F., Tölle, T., Üçeyler, N., & Sommer, C. (2012). The role of antidepressants in the management of fibromyalgia syndrome. CNS Drugs, 26(4), 297–307. http://doi.org/10.2165/11598970-000000000-00000.

resource for medications, including medications used for pain (e.g., opioids and tricyclic antidepressants (TCAs)) that should be avoided in the elderly because of fall risk, central nervous system depression, or anticholinergic effects (American Geriatrics Society, 2012; Beers Criteria Update Expert Panel, Campanelli, 2012).

Diminished organ function can augment the effects of certain pain medications that are metabolized or eliminated by the liver or kidney. Augmentation of effect can result in greater pain control and/or increased adverse effects. Careful consideration of whether drugs should be avoided or dose-adjusted in the setting of liver or kidney dysfunction is critical to avoiding unnecessary adverse effects. One common example is the need to dose adjust gabapentin for different degrees of chronic kidney disease and to avoid using long-acting gabapentin formulations with hemodialysis. For pain medications, kidney function is estimated using the Cockcroft-Gault equation (http://nephron.com/cgi-bin/CGSI.cgi). Tertiary drug information references such as Micromedex®, Epocrates®, and others provide clinically relevant directions on whether liver or kidney function impacts a given medication. Clinicians may also reach out to pharmacists to seek guidance whenever necessary.

Consideration 3: Select a Medication Based Upon Concurrent and Past Medication Use

Whether prescribing an opioid or other pain medication, the clinician's consideration of potential drug interactions is critical. Drug interactions can be categorized as pharmacokinetic or pharmacodynamic. Pharmacokinetic drug interactions impact the serum concentrations of medications and are the result of changes in metabolism, elimination, or absorption (Cascorbi, 2012). For example, using methadone and carbamazepine together can decrease the serum concentration of methadone, which would decrease the efficacy of methadone. Pharmacodynamic drug interactions occur when two or more drugs influence the effect of a drug (Cascorbi, 2012). For example, methadone can increase the risk of serotonin syndrome, so when used in combination with amitriptyline, the risk of serotonin syndrome increases.

Past responses to medications also should influence pain medication selection. Opioids vary in structure and natural proximity from the most natural opiate, opium. Morphine and codeine are derived from the opium poppy plant and are considered natural opiates. The other opioids are considered semi-synthetic or synthetic, with fentanyl representing the most synthetic of the commercially available opioids (Baldo & Pham, 2012).

There is low risk of recurrent allergy if an opioid with a different chemical structure is used in a patient with an allergy to a particular opioid. For example, if a patient has an allergy to oxycodone, it would be reasonable to try hydromorphone or morphine. However, an allergy or intolerance is not always a contraindication (i.e., an instance where risk clearly outweighs benefit) and may be a precaution when considering using a given medication or medication within the same class. For example, if a patient reported an allergy or intolerance to gabapentin in the past, clinicians would avoid using gabapentin again with that patient. However, if a patient had lower-extremity swelling with gabapentin in the past, it would be reasonable to try it again at a low dose if it originally was started at a higher-than-recommended initial dose.

Consideration 4: Select a Medication Based Upon Comorbidities

Acute and chronic comorbidities can be affected by or change the effect of some pain medications. For example, NSAIDs are discouraged and should be used with caution in patients with chronic kidney disease because they can worsen kidney function. However, NSAIDs are contraindicated with acute kidney injury because NSAIDs can further exacerbate acute kidney injury and lead to renal failure and dialysis. Further, NSAIDs also can increase blood pressure and should be avoided if possible in patients with hypertension. Other conditions that can worsen as the result of certain pain medications include heart failure, prolonged QTc interval, gastroesophageal reflux disease, alcohol or substance use and abuse, and epilepsy. In contrast, patients with comorbid depression likely will benefit from an antidepressant for both their pain and depression, given that depression can exacerbate pain (Dowell et al., 2016).

Consideration 5: Select a Medication Based Upon Severity and Location

The severity and location of pain can influence the selection of a medication. If the pain is minimal and having little or no impact on a patient's functionality, then the benefits of starting a medication with a high-risk profile (such as opioids) likely does not outweigh the risks. Further, if the pain is limited to an area such as the lower back, a non-systemic pain medication such as a lidocaine patch or topical NSAID (see Table 8.4) may be preferred. Avoiding systemic effects of oral medications can help minimize potential adverse drug effects.

Consideration 6: Select a Medication Based Upon Patient Preference

Once medication options have been identified using the aforementioned considerations 1–5 based upon evidence-based decision-making, present these options to the patient. Shared decision-making ensures that patient values, preferences, and priorities are considered (Dowell et al., 2016), which ultimately leads to higher patient engagement and satisfaction with care (Pryzbylkowski & Ashburn, 2015).

Patients need to understand the risks, benefits, and potential outcomes of different treatment courses and must be willing and able to engage in their medication treatment plans. Some patients may resist starting an antidepressant or non-opioid medication for chronic pain because of cultural or other beliefs, preconceived opinions of certain drug class superiority, or unfortunate negative stigma associated with some drug classes (most often antidepressants) (Aggarwal, 2012). In addition, financial constraints may limit the use of particular medications, and some patients may not have transportation to facilitate needed monitoring, such as frequent echocardiograms with methadone. When informed of potential adverse effects (see Tables 8.1, 8.4, and 8.5), patients may express apprehension, such as due to sexual dysfunction with opioids.

Medication Dose Initiation

Start medications at the lowest effective dose; when initiated for specific populations (e.g., children, older adults, people with diminished organ function), the lowest possible dose should be considered (Manchikanti et al., 2012). The lowest effective dose and the lowest possible dose may differ for some medications, such as starting tramadol at 25 mg daily (half of the 50 mg tablet) instead of the recommended starting dose of 50 mg (Ortho-McNeil Pharmaceutical, 2008). When initiating opioids, use short-acting formulations initially.

Medication Dose Escalation

Dose escalation is performed based upon the effectiveness and safety of the medications and patient factors (e.g., willingness, adherence, functionality, side effects). If the patient does not respond adequately and the benefits of escalation outweigh the risks, dose escalation may be indicated. The approach to dose escalation depends upon the specific medication.

In general, maximum Food and Drug Administration (FDA)-recommended doses of non-opioid medications should be followed, and dose escalation should be individualized based upon the response. If a patient experiences adverse effects or adequate relief at a lower dose than the maximum FDA-recommended dose, then do not increase the dose further. Given that many non-opioid pain medications also are used for indications other than pain (e.g., epilepsy, depression), the doses used in clinical studies to treat chronic pain that were found to optimize safety and effectiveness should be used. For example, the maximum FDA-recommended dose of duloxetine for depression treatment is 120 mg daily, but the maximum recommended dose for chronic pain is 60 mg daily because clinical studies in the pain population found no greater benefit beyond 60 mg daily (Eli Lilly and Company, 2010). These dosing nuances often are stated in tertiary references such Micromedex® or Epocrates®.

TCAs also have important dosing considerations. Although TCAs can be used for both chronic neuropathic pain or fibromyalgia, as well as for mental health disorders such as anxiety, depression, and insomnia, the doses that are effective for pain management are lower than those generally used for other indications; studies have found higher doses of TCAs are not more effective than lower doses for treating pain (Moore, Derry, Aldington, Cole, & Wiffen, 2015; Nishishinya et al., 2008).

Unlike other pain medications, opioids generally do not have maximum doses, with the exceptions of tapentadol and tramadol (Ortho-McNeil-Janssen Pharmaceuticals, 2010; Ortho-McNeil Pharmaceutical, 2008). When dose escalation is warranted, increase opioid doses slowly based upon a percentage of the total daily dose. Typically, opioids are increased by 25–50% of the total daily dose every one to four weeks. For example, if a patient is taking oxycodone immediate release 5 mg every six hours and needs a dose increase, a 25% increase would be an additional 5 mg daily, and a 50% increase would be an additional 10 mg daily. Based upon available strength formulations of oxycodone immediate release, the patient's prescription may be increased appropriately to 7.5 mg every six hours, which is an increase of 10 mg daily, or 50%.

Historically, with dose escalation, patients were transitioned to a regimen of short- and long-acting opioids. Ideally, patients should take 10–30% of their total daily opioid dose in short-acting formulations, and the remaining 70–90% should be administered in long-acting formulations. The rationale behind this strategy is: 1) long-acting opioids curb the peaks and troughs that are more prevalent with short-acting opioids, which can precipitate euphoric sensations that can enable misuse or abuse behaviors; and 2) long-acting opioids prevent pain from escalating between doses, thereby reducing the amount of opioid needed throughout the day. Although this practice is still common, some guidelines discourage the combination use of short- and long-acting opioids, stating there is limited evidence for improvements in pain management and larger evidence to justify concerns regarding increased risks for respiratory depression, central nervous system depression, and overdose (Dowell et al., 2016). Clinicians may wish to discuss these risks and benefits with the patients to inform a shared decision regarding treatment strategies.

Monitoring for Efficacy and Safety

After initiation, monitor the benefits and risks of opioid therapy closely. Monitoring frequency depends upon the choice of medication. Re-evaluate the decision to continue opioid therapy every three months. A commonly used approach to monitoring and evaluating chronic pain treatment is the "four As" of pain treatment: analgesia, activities of daily living, adverse effects, and aberrant behavior (Passik & Weinreb, 2000). Regularly monitor and document within the patient's medical record the four As, as described below. Beyond the four As, there are many tools used to evaluate effectiveness and safety, some validated for use in clinical settings. (See Chapter 2.)

Efficacy assessment includes evaluation of analgesia and activities of daily living. Analgesia is the amount of pain relief conferred to the patient by medication and/or non-medication strategies, whereas activities of daily living refers to the psychosocial functioning experienced in the patient's everyday life. As described previously, the goal is to reduce pain with medications, not eliminate it (Manchikanti et al., 2012). Most importantly, when assessing whether the benefits outweigh the risks, the treatment goals should center on improving psychosocial functioning rather than subjective assessments of pain relief (Passik & Weinreb, 2000). Function can include physical function, mood, family or social relationships, sleep quality, and overall subjective assessments of function. Encourage the patient to identify which functionality he or she wishes to improve with pain management. The clinician should assess the patient's ability to complete these functions as pain management progresses with or without medication.

Safety includes evaluations of adverse effects and aberrant behavior. Adverse effects are unintended consequences of a drug, such as constipation, falls, or lethargy associated with opioids. Counsel patients on common or serious adverse effects with pain medications (see Tables 8.1, 8.4, and 8.5); clinicians should proactively screen their patients for emergence of adverse effects. Aberrant behavior, which suggests misuse or abuse behaviors, is most pertinent to opioids and other controlled substances with potential for abuse (such as gabapentin, pregabalin, benzodiazepines, and carisoprodol). Such behaviors can include, but are not limited to, increased use without clinician approval; early refill requests; using medications left over from old prescriptions; illegal purchase of medication from non-reputable sources; evidence of illegal or non-prescribed drug use in urine drug screens; using multiple physicians or pharmacies to obtain drugs; and sharing medication with friends or family members. See the "Risk Mitigation Strategies and Considerations" section for information on how to reduce medicolegal liability when prescribing and monitoring controlled substances such as opioids.

Opioid Tapering and Discontinuation

When opioid therapy is no longer warranted, patients are aberrant, or hyperalgesia or adverse effects arise, then tapering or discontinuation is appropriate (see Figure 8.4) Many guidelines promote the reduction of opioid doses; however, there is little consensus, evidence, or guidance for the most appropriate opioid reduction strategy, often called an opioid "taper." An opioid taper includes both dose reduction and complete opioid discontinuation. Goals of opioid tapering include reduction of reliance on opioids for pain management, reduction of opioid burden, minimization of adverse effects of opioid use and tapering, and addressing the risks of opioid treatment. Patients may experience opioid withdrawal symptoms while tapering or discontinuing. Although uncomfortable, these symptoms are short-lived and not life-threatening. The Clinical Opiate Withdrawal Scale (COWS) assesses the severity of withdrawal symptoms and level of physical dependence on opioid therapy. It can be used in inpatient or outpatient settings (Wesson & Ling, 2003). The spectrum and severity of withdrawal symptoms seen on clinical presentation is influenced by the duration of opioid exposure, amount of daily opioid burden, speed of tapering, concomitant medications, and other psychosocial factors. The range of withdrawal symptoms includes anxiety,

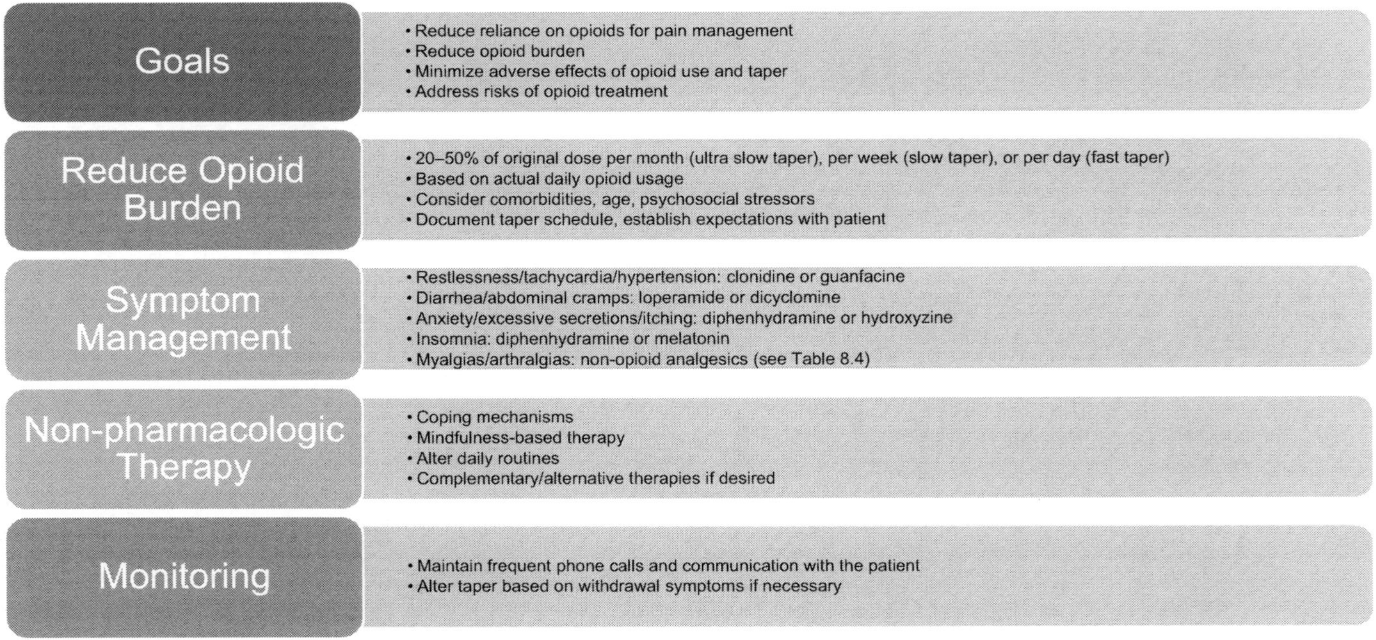

Goals
- Reduce reliance on opioids for pain management
- Reduce opioid burden
- Minimize adverse effects of opioid use and taper
- Address risks of opioid treatment

Reduce Opioid Burden
- 20–50% of original dose per month (ultra slow taper), per week (slow taper), or per day (fast taper)
- Based on actual daily opioid usage
- Consider comorbidities, age, psychosocial stressors
- Document taper schedule, establish expectations with patient

Symptom Management
- Restlessness/tachycardia/hypertension: clonidine or guanfacine
- Diarrhea/abdominal cramps: loperamide or dicyclomine
- Anxiety/excessive secretions/itching: diphenhydramine or hydroxyzine
- Insomnia: diphenhydramine or melatonin
- Myalgias/arthralgias: non-opioid analgesics (see Table 8.4)

Non-pharmacologic Therapy
- Coping mechanisms
- Mindfulness-based therapy
- Alter daily routines
- Complementary/alternative therapies if desired

Monitoring
- Maintain frequent phone calls and communication with the patient
- Alter taper based on withdrawal symptoms if necessary

Figure 8.4 Opioid Tapering

restlessness, dizziness, hot flashes, sweating, shivering, tremors, hyperalgesia, myalgias, arthralgias, nausea, diarrhea, abdominal cramping, anorexia, hypertension, tachycardia, tear production, mucus production, itching, insomnia, and yawning. The symptom timeline is relative to the last dose of the opioid. Symptoms appear within 2 to 3 half-lives, peak within 4 to 5 half-lives, and resolve within 7 to 14 days (Berna, Kulich, & Rathmell, 2015; Mattick & Hall, 1996).

Non-pharmacologic and non-opioid pharmacologic strategies can help mitigate breakthrough pain, withdrawal symptoms, and anxiety associated with opioid tapering. Many withdrawal symptoms associated with opioid tapering are due to a rush of neurotransmitters that induce a "fight or flight" response (symptoms such as tachycardia, hypertension, anxiety, and restlessness). Medications that block this response include prescription α_2 agonists such as clonidine (oral or transdermal) and guanfacine.

In addition, adverse effects that occur in the presence of opioids may be replaced by the opposite extreme during withdrawal, such as diarrhea in place of opioid-induced constipation. Diarrhea and abdominal cramps may be managed with loperamide, an over-the-counter antidiarrheal agent, or dicyclomine, an oral prescription antispasmodic. Antihistamines such as diphenhydramine or hydroxyzine can be used to assist with excessive secretions (mucus production, tear production, sweating), itching, insomnia, and anxiety. Where appropriate, oral and topical non-opioid analgesics can assist with transient hyperalgesia, myalgias, or arthralgias (see Table 8.4).

Additional opioid and benzodiazepine therapy should not be used to manage withdrawal symptoms outside of inpatient, monitored detoxification programs (United States Department of Veterans Affairs and Department of Defense, 2013; Utah Department of Health, 2009; Washington State Agency Medical Directors' Group, 2010). Counsel and coach the patient on coping mechanisms, mindfulness-based therapy, or other non-pharmacological strategies to mitigate stress associated with pain and withdrawal symptoms. Daily routines can be altered to mitigate symptoms of withdrawal, such as bathing with Epsom salts or showering for itching symptoms, keeping the mind engaged with activities and distracted, and improving sleep hygiene. Other complementary or alternative therapies (such as acupuncture) do not have robust evidence but should be encouraged if the patient is willing to try or previously has experienced relief from such modalities. If the patient experiences extreme discomfort during the taper that is refractory to all of these measures, admission to an intensive, inpatient detoxification unit may be necessary.

No randomized trials have been conducted to compare taper strategies external of patients with substance use disorders. In the absence of validated protocols, expert recommendations are used with patient-specific modifications where pertinent. Taper calculations should be performed based upon the patient's actual daily opioid usage. A tapering strategy of 20–50% of the original dose per week (slow taper) or per day (fast taper) has been suggested. This can be further refined by performing the taper to a specific goal dose (usually half the original dose) or date, then executing a more rapid taper of the dose by decreasing 20–50% of the dose every two to five days (United States Department of Veterans Affairs and Department of Defense, 2013). To assist with calculations, the University of Washington has developed a publicly available calculator (Washington State Department of Social and Human Services, n.d.). For example, if a patient is taking a total of oxycodone 60 mg daily and the clinician chooses a slow taper, he or she may have the patient reduce their weekly intake by 15 mg (25% of the original dose) until they are no longer taking any opioid. The entire taper would take approximately one month to complete.

Patients who have been on opioid therapy for longer than two years may require ultra-slow tapers, with dose reduction every one to two months. Slower tapers also may be needed in older patients, patients with multiple comorbidities, patients with failed taper experience, or patients experiencing significant psychosocial stress or withdrawal symptoms. If possible, attempt to obtain patient buy-in to the taper plan prior to executing the plan; however, this may not always be feasible if the patient is unwilling. A decision to taper or discontinue therapy should be communicated clearly to the patient with the rationale for doing so. One possible way of obtaining patient buy-in is by providing the patient with multiple options for a taper plan and asking the patient for his or her preference. For example, for patients taking long- and short-acting opioid formulations, there is no consensus on whether the long-acting or short-acting formulation should be tapered first, or whether the two should be tapered in concert. The patient may provide insight on which option he or she would prefer.

The long-acting opioid formulations have a longer half-life and will not induce withdrawal symptoms as readily; therefore, patients may opt to taper short-acting formulations first. Emphasize the amount of non-pharmacological and non-opioid support that will be provided to the patient to make the taper successful. Implement frequent patient contact via phone or office visits in order to track symptoms, pain management, and appropriate taper dosing, as well as to provide encouragement. Studies demonstrate that opioid tapering is successful in patients who are physiologically stable, experience minimal discomfort, feel treated with dignity and respect, and complete the entire taper schedule (United States Department of Veterans Affairs and Department of Defense, 2013).

Tapering is easiest when the opioid is changed to the smallest commonly available dosage unit. This enables the patient to fill one prescription to perform the taper rather than filling multiple prescriptions, paying multiple co-pays, and creating confusion with multiple pill bottles. Document a full taper schedule in the patient's chart for future reference; give the schedule to the patient in order to establish goals and realistic expectations. When documenting an opioid taper, avoid using the word "detoxification" unless in a licensed addiction treatment setting. If addiction or misuse are of concern, the clinician may opt to consult an addiction specialist before proceeding with the taper. Many clinicians opt to discontinue prescribing opioids abruptly (without tapering) if opioid abuse is confirmed through patient questioning or urine drug screening. While withdrawal symptoms are likely to occur with abrupt discontinuation, the risks of enabling continued opioid abuse generally outweigh the short-lived discomfort of withdrawal symptoms. The decision to discontinue therapy abruptly should be made by the primary pain management provider with appropriate documentation.

Conclusion

Chronic pain is prevalent and requires appropriate assessment, treatment, and monitoring to achieve the goals of therapy. Successful patient outcomes require collaboration between many professionals to manage pain effectively with medications and non-medication therapies. While opioids were once the mainstay of treatment, there are significant risks associated with their use. While mitigation strategies can help minimize the risks, the benefits of opioid use do not outweigh the risks for all patients. To minimize risks with opioids, non-opioid and non-pharmacologic therapies should be tried before opioids, and the dose and duration of opioids should be limited.

References

Acute Pain Management Guideline Panel. (1992). *Acute pain management: Operative or medical procedures and trauma (Clinical Practice Guideline)* (1st ed.). Rockyville, MD: US Department of Health. Retrieved from http://archive.ahrq.gov/clinic/medtep/acute.htm

Aggarwal, A. (2012). Challenges of pain medicine: The stigma associated with using tricyclical anti-depressants—it's not all in the mind. *Journal of Clinical Trials, 2*(24), e108. https://doi.org/10.4172/2167-0870.1000e108

Aiyer, R., Mehta, N., Gungor, S., & Gulati, A. (2018). A systematic review of NMDA receptor antagonists for treatment of neuropathic pain in clinical practice. *The Clinical Journal of Pain, 34*(5), 450–467. https://doi.org/10.1097/AJP.0000000000000547

Altier, N., Dion, D., Boulanger, A., & Choinière, M. (2005). Management of chronic neuropathic pain with methadone: A review of 13 cases. *The Clinical Journal of Pain, 21*(4), 364–369. https://doi.org/10.1097/01.ajp.0000125247.95213.53

American Geriatrics Society 2012 Beers Criteria Update Expert Panel, Campanelli, C. (2012). American Geriatrics Society updated Beers Criteria for potentially inappropriate medication use in older adults. *Journal of the American Geriatrics Society, 60*(4), 616–631. https://doi.org/10.1111/j.1532-5415.2012.03923.x

American Psychiatric Association. (2013). *Diagnostic and statistical manual of mental health disorders* (5th ed.). Arlington, VA: American Psychiatric Publishing. https://doi.org/10.1176/appi.books.9781585629992

American Society of Anesthesiologists and the American Society of Regional Anesthesia and Pain Medicine. (2010). Practice guidelines for chronic pain management. *Anesthesiology, 112*(4), 810–833. https://doi.org/10.1097/00000542-199704000-00032

Baldo, B. A., & Pham, N. H. (2012). Histamine-releasing and allergenic properties of opioid analgesic drugs: Resolving the two. *Anaesthesia and Intensive Care, 40*(2), 216–235.

Banta-Green, C. J., Merrill, J. O., Doyle, S. R., Boudreau, D. M., & Calsyn, D. A. (2009). Opioid use behaviors, mental health and pain-development of a typology of chronic pain patients. *Drug and Alcohol Dependence, 104*(1–2), 34–42. https://doi.org/10.1016/j.drugalcdep.2009.03.021

Basbaum, A. I., Bautista, D. M., Scherrer, G., & Julius, D. (2009, October 16). Cellular and molecular mechanisms of pain. *Cell, 139*(2), 267–284. https://doi.org/10.1016/j.cell.2009.09.028

Berna, C., Kulich, R. J., & Rathmell, J. P. (2015). Tapering long-term opioid therapy in chronic noncancer pain: Evidence and recommendations for everyday practice. *Mayo Clinic Proceedings, 90*(6), 828–842. https://doi.org/10.1016/j.mayocp.2015.04.003

Binswanger, I. A., Nowels, C., Corsi, K. F., Glanz, J., Long, J., Booth, R. E., & Steiner, J. F. (2012). Return to drug use and overdose after release from prison: A qualitative study of risk and protective factors. *Addiction Science & Clinical Practice, 7*(3), 1–9. https://doi.org/10.1186/1940-0640-7-3

Bohnert, A. S. B., Valenstein, M., Bair, M. J., Ganoczy, D., McCarthy, J. F., Ilgen, M. A., & Blow, F. C. (2011). Association between opioid prescribing patterns and opioid overdose-related deaths. *JAMA, 305*(13), 1315–1321. https://doi.org/10.1001/jama.2011.370

Boscarino, J., Kirchner, H. L., Pitcavage, J., Nadipelli, V., Ronquest, N., Fitzpatrick, M., & Han, J. (2016). Factors associated with opioid overdose: A 10-year retrospective study of patients in a large integrated health care system. *Substance Abuse and Rehabilitation, 7*, 131–141. https://doi.org/10.2147/SAR.S108302

Boscarino, J. A., Rukstalis, M. R., Hoffman, S. N., Han, J. J., Erlich, P. M., Ross, S., . . . Stewart, W. F. (2011). Prevalence of prescription opioid-use disorder among chronic pain patients: Comparison of the DSM-5 vs. DSM-4 diagnostic criteria. *Journal of Addictive Diseases, 30*(3), 185–194. https://doi.org/10.1080/10550887.2011.581961

Cascorbi, I. (2012). Drug interactions—principles, examples and clinical consequences. *Deutsches Arzteblatt International, 109*(33–34), 546–555; quiz 556. https://doi.org/10.3238/arztebl.2012.0546

Cheatle, M. D. (2015). Prescription opioid misuse, abuse, morbidity, and mortality: Balancing effective pain management and safety. *Pain Medicine, 16*, S3–S8. https://doi.org/10.1111/pme.12904

Chou, R., Fanciullo, G. J., Fine, P. G., Adler, J. A., Ballantyne, J. C., Davies, P., . . . Miaskowski, C. (2009). Clinical guidelines for the use of chronic opioid therapy in chronic noncancer pain. *The Journal of Pain, 10*(2), 113–130. https://doi.org/10.1016/j.jpain.2008.10.008

Chou, R., Turner, J. A., Devine, E. B., Hansen, R. N., Sullivan, S. D., Blazina, I., . . . Deyo, R. A. (2015). The effectiveness and risks of long-term opioid therapy for chronic pain: A systematic review for a national institutes of health pathways to prevention workshop. *Annals of Internal Medicine, 162*(4), 276–286. https://doi.org/10.7326/M14-2559

Cicero, T. J., & Ellis, M. S. (2015). Abuse-deterrent formulations and the prescription opioid abuse epidemic in the United States. *JAMA Psychiatry, 72*(5), 424–430. https://doi.org/10.1001/jamapsychiatry.2014.3043

Clark, H. W., & Sees, K. L. (1993). Opioids, chronic pain, and the law. *Journal of Pain and Symptom Management, 8*(5), 297–305.

Cochran, G., Hruschak, V., DeFosse, B., & Hohmeier, K. C. (2016). Prescription opioid abuse: Pharmacists' perspective and response. *Integrated Pharmacy Research and Practice, 5*, 65–73. https://doi.org/10.2147/IPRP.S99539

Dasgupta, N., Funk, M. J., Proescholdbell, S., Hirsch, A., Ribisl, K. M., & Marshall, S. (2016). Cohort study of the impact of high-dose opioid analgesics on overdose mortality. *Pain Medicine, 17*, 85–98. https://doi.org/10.1111/pme.12907

Doran, G. (1981). There's a S.M.A.R.T. way to write management's goals and objectives. *Management Review, 70*(11), 35–36.

Dowell, D., Haegerich, T. M., & Chou, R. (2016). CDC guideline for prescribing opioids for chronic pain—United States, 2016. *MMWR. Recommendations and Reports, 65*(1), 1–49. https://doi.org/10.15585/mmwr.rr6501e1er

Dunn, K. M., Saunders, K. W., Rutter, C. M., Banta-Green, C. J., Merrill, J. O., Sullivan, M. D., . . . Von Korff, M. (2010). Opioid prescriptions for chronic pain and overdose. *Annals of Internal Medicine, 152*(2), 85–92. https://doi.org/10.7326/0003-4819-152-2-201001190-00006

Eli Lilly and Company. (2010). *Cymbalta(R) [package insert]*. Indianapolis, IN. Retrieved from www.accessdata.fda.gov/drugsatfda_docs/label/2010/022516lbl.pdf

Fishman, S. M. (2005). Trust and pharmacovigilance in pain medicine. *Pain Medicine*, 6(5), 392. https://doi.org/10.1111/j.1526-4637.2005.00068.x

Fishman, S. M., Bandman, T. B., Edwards, A., & Borsook, D. (1999). The opioid contract in the management of chronic pain. *Journal of Pain and Symptom Management*, 18(1), 27–37.

Fishman, S. M., Wilsey, B., Yang, J., Reisfield, G. M., Bandman, T. B., & Borsook, D. (2000). Adherence monitoring and drug surveillance in chronic opioid therapy. *Journal of Pain and Symptom Management*, 20(4), 293–307.

Foley, K. (1979). The management of pain of malignant origin. *Current Neurology*, 279–302.

Gasior, M., Bond, M., & Malamut, R. (2016). Routes of abuse of prescription opioid analgesics: A review and assessment of the potential impact of abuse-deterrent formulations. *Postgraduate Medicine*, 128(1), 85–96. https://doi.org/10.1080/00325481.2016.1120642

Gaskin, D. J., & Richard, P. (2012). The economic costs of pain in the United States. *The Journal of Pain*, 13(8), 715–724. https://doi.org/10.1016/j.jpain.2012.03.009

Gomes, T., Mamdani, M. M., Dhalla, I. A., Paterson, J. M., & Juurlink, D. N. (2011). Opioid Dose and drug-related mortality in patients with nonmalignant pain. *Archives of Internal Medicine*, 171(7), 686–691. https://doi.org/10.1001/archinternmed.2011.117

Gourlay, D., & Heit, H. (2006). Universal precautions: A matter of mutual trust and responsibility. *Pain Medicine*, 7(2), 210–211. https://doi.org/10.1111/j.1526-4637.2006.00114.x

Gourlay, D., Heit, H., & Almahrezi, A. (2005). Universal precautions in pain medicine: A rational approach to the treatment of chronic pain. *Pain Medicine*, 6(2), 107–112. https://doi.org/10.1111/j.1526-4637.2005.05031.x

Hahn, K. (2011). Strategies to prevent opioid misuse, abuse, and diversion that may also reduce the associated costs. *American Health & Drug Benefits*, 4(2), 107–114.

Hale, M. E., Moe, D., Bond, M., Gasior, M., & Malamut, R. (2016). Pain Management Abuse-deterrent formulations of prescription opioid analgesics in the management of chronic noncancer pain. *Pain Management*, 6(5), 497–508. https://doi.org/10.2217/pmt-2015-0005

Hanks, S. (2008). The law of unintended consequences: When pain management leads to medication errors. *P & T : A Peer-Reviewed Journal for Formulary Management*, 33(7), 420–425.

Haroutounian, S., McNicol, E. D., & Lipman, A. G. (2012). Methadone for chronic noncancer pain in adults. *Cochrane Database of Systematic Reviews*, 11, CD008025. https://doi.org/10.1002/14651858.CD008025.pub2

Hedegaard, H., Warner, M., & Miniño, A. M. (2017). Drug overdose deaths in the United States, 1999–2015. *NCHS Data Brief*, 2010, (273), 1–8. Retrieved from www.cdc.gov/nchs/data/databriefs/db273.pdf

Hegyi, N. (2017, April). *Cherokee Nation Sues Wal-Mart, CVS, Walgreens Over Tribal Opioid Crisis*. Retrieved April 5, 2018, from www.npr.org/sections/codeswitch/2017/04/25/485887058/cherokee-nation-sues-wal-mart-cvs-walgreens-over-tribal-opioid-crisis

Højsted, J., & Sjøgren, P. (2007). Addiction to opioids in chronic pain patients: A literature review. *European Journal of Pain*, 11, 490–518. https://doi.org/10.1016/j.ejpain.2006.08.004

Ingersoll, S. (2018, March 27). Opioid lawsuit: Montgomery county sues makers, distributors. *The Leaf Chronicle*. Retrieved from www.theleafchronicle.com/story/news/2018/03/27/opioid-lawsuits-montgomery-county-sues-makers-distributors/461894002/

Institute of Medicine Committee on Advancing Pain Research Care and Education. (2011). *Relieving pain in America: Relieving pain in America: A blueprint for transforming prevention, care, education, and research*. Washington, DC: National Academies Press. https://doi.org/10.17226/13172

International Association for the Study of Pain. (1994). IASP Taxonomy. In H. Merskey & N. Bogduk (Ed.), *Classification of chronic pain* (2nd ed., pp. 209–214). Seattle: IASP Press. Retrieved from https://doi.org/www.iasp-pain.org/Taxonomy

International Narcotics Control Board. (2014). *Report of the international narcotics control board for 2014.* New York, NY. Retrieved from www.incb.org/documents/Publications/AnnualReports/AR2014/English/AR_2014.pdf

Jamison, R. N., Sheehan, K. A., Scanlan, E., Matthews, M., & Ross, E. L. (2014). Beliefs and attitudes about opioid prescribing and chronic pain management: Survey of primary care providers. *Journal of Opioid Management, 10*(6), 375–382. https://doi.org/10.5055/jom.2014.0234

Jones, C. M., Mack, K., & Paulozzi, L. (2013). Pharmaceutical overdose deaths, United States, 2010. *JAMA, 309*(7), 657–659. https://doi.org/10.1001/jama.2013.272

Julius, D., & Basbaum, A. I. (2001). Molecular mechanisms of nociception. *Nature, 413*(6852), 203–210. https://doi.org/10.1038/35093019

Kamdar, M. M. (2010). Principles of analgesic use in the treatment of acute pain and cancer pain. *Journal of Palliative Medicine, 13*(2), 217–218. https://doi.org/10.1089/jpm.2010.9854

Lanser, P., & Gesell, S. (2001). Pain management: The fifth vital sign. *Healthcare Benchmarks, 8*(6), 68–70, 62.

Larochelle, M. R., Liebschutz, J. M., Zhang, F., Ross-Degnan, D., & Wharam, J. F. (2016). Opioid prescribing after nonfatal overdose and association with repeated overdose: A cohort study. *Annals of Internal Medicine, 164*(1), 1–9. https://doi.org/10.7326/M15-0038

Lee, M., Silverman, S., Hansen, H., Patel, V., & Manchikanti, L. (2011). A comprehensive review of opioid-induced hyperalgesia. *Pain Physician, 14*, 145–161.

Lee, Y-H., Brown, D., & Chen, H-Y. (2017). Current impact and application of abuse-deterrent opioid formulations in clinical practice. *Pain Physician, 20*(7), E1003–E1023.

Lembke, A., Humphreys, K., & Newmark, J. (2016). Weighing the risks and benefits of chronic opioid therapy. *American Family Physician, 93*(12), 982–990.

Levy, B., Paulozzi, L., Mack, K. A., & Jones, C. M. (2015). Trends in opioid analgesic-prescribing rates by specialty, U.S., 2007–2012. *American Journal of Preventive Medicine, 49*(3), 409–413. https://doi.org/10.1016/j.amepre.2015.02.020

Luo, J., Feng, J., Liu, S., Walters, E. T., & Hu, H. (2015). Molecular and cellular mechanisms that initiate pain and itch. *Cellular and Molecular Life Sciences, 72*(17), 3201–3223. https://doi.org/10.1007/s00018-015-1904-4

Maincent, J., & Zhang, F. (2016). Recent advances in abuse-deterrent technologies for the delivery of opioids. *International Journal of Pharmaceutics, 510*, 57–72. https://doi.org/10.1016/j.ijpharm.2016.06.012

Manchikanti, L. (2007). National drug control policy and prescription drug abuse: Facts and fallacies. *Pain Physician, 10*(3), 399–424. https://doi.org/10.1111/j.1360-0443.2010.03017.x

Manchikanti, L., Abdi, S., Atluri, S., Balog, C. C., Benyamin, R. M., Boswell, M.V, . . . Wargo, B. W. (2012). American Society of Interventional Pain Physicians (ASIPP) guidelines for responsible opioid prescribing in chronic non-cancer pain: Part 2 -Guidance. *Pain Physician, 15*(3 Suppl), S67–S116.

Mantyh, P.W. (2014). The neurobiology of skeletal pain. *The European Journal of Neuroscience, 39*(3), 508–519. https://doi.org/10.1111/ejn.12462

Marks, R. M., & Sachar, E. J. (1973). Undertreatment of medical inpatients with narcotic analgesics. *Annals of Internal Medicine, 78*(2), 173–181. https://doi.org/10.7326/0003-4819-78-2-173

Mastropietro, D. J., & Omidian, H. (2015a). Abuse-deterrent formulations: Part 1—development of a formulation-based classification system. *Expert Opinion on Drug Metabolism & Toxicology, 11*(2), 193–204. https://doi.org/10.1517/17425255.2015.979786

Mastropietro, D. J., & Omidian, H. (2015b). Abuse-deterrent formulations: Part 2: Commercial products and proprietary technologies. *Expert Opinion on Pharmacotherapy, 16*(3), 305–323. https://doi.org/10.1517/14656566.2014.970175

Mattick, R. P., & Hall, W. (1996). Are detoxification programmes effective? *The Lancet, 347,* 97–100.

McGivney, W. T., & Crooks, G. M. (1984). The care of patients with severe chronic pain in terminal illness. *JAMA, 251*(9), 1182–1188.

McNicol, E., Ferguson, M., & Schumann, R. (2017). Methadone for neuropathic pain in adults. *Cochrane Database of Systematic Reviews,* (5), CD012499. https://doi.org/10.1002/14651858.CD012499.pub2.www.cochranelibrary.com

Miller, M., Barber, C. W., Leatherman, S., Fonda, J., Hermos, J. A., Cho, K., & Gagnon, D. R. (2015). Prescription opioid duration of action and the risk of unintentional overdose among patients receiving opioid therapy. *JAMA Internal Medicine, 175*(4), 608–615. https://doi.org/10.1001/jamainternmed.2014.8071

Moore, R. A., Derry, S., Aldington, D., Cole, P., & Wiffen, P. J. (2015). Amitriptyline for neuropathic pain in adults. *The Cochrane Database of Systematic Reviews,* (7), CD008242. https://doi.org/10.1002/14651858.CD008242.pub3.www.cochranelibrary.com

Naliboff, B. D., Wu, S. M., Schieffer, B., Bolus, R., Pham, Q., Baria, A., . . . Shekelle, P. (2011). A randomized trial of 2 prescription strategies for opioid treatment of chronic nonmalignant pain. *The Journal of Pain, 12*(2), 288–296. https://doi.org/10.1016/j.jpain.2010.09.003

National Alliance for Model State Drug Laws. (2015). *Naloxone access: Status of state laws maps.* Charlottesville, VA. Retrieved from www.namsdl.org/ControlledSubstancesPrescriptionDrugs/Naloxone/Naloxone-Maps-9-21-15.pdf

National Alliance for Model State Drug Laws. (2017a). *Established and operational Prescription Drug Monitoring Programs (PMPs).* Charlottesville, VA. Retrieved from www.namsdl.org/Maps/Status of PMPs-Established-Operational Map REV 7-21-17.pdf

National Alliance for Model State Drug Laws. (2017b). *Mandated registration with prescription drug monitoring programs (PMPs).* Charlottesville, VA. Retrieved from www.namsdl.org/Maps/Mandated Registration with PMPs—State Map 7–24–17.pdf

National Alliance for Model State Drug Laws. (2018). *Mandated use of prescription drug monitoring programs (PMPs).* Charlottesville, VA. Retrieved from www.namsdl.org/Maps/Mandated Use of PMPs—State Map (1–2–18).pdf

Nguyen, V., Raffa, R. B., Taylor, R., & Pergolizzi, J. V. (2015). The role of abuse-deterrent formulations in countering opioid misuse and abuse. *Journal of Clinical Pharmacy and Therapeutics, 40*(6), 629–634. https://doi.org/10.1111/jcpt.12337

Nishishinya, B., Urruia, G., Walitt, B., Rodriguez, A., Bonfill, X., Alegre, C., & Darko, G. (2008). Amitriptyline in the treatment of fibromyalgia: A systematic review of its efficacy. *Rheumatology, 47*(12), 1741–1746. https://doi.org/10.1093/rheumatology/ken317

Nuckols, T. K., Anderson, L., Popescu, I., Diamant, A. L., Doyle, B., Di Capua, P., & Chou, R. (2013). Opioid prescribing: A systematic review and critical appraisal of guidelines for chronic pain. *Annals of Internal Medicine, 160*(1), 38–47. https://doi.org/10.7326/0003-4819-160-1-201401070-00732

Ortho-McNeil-Janssen Pharmaceuticals, I. (2008). *Ultram(R) [package insert].* Raritan, NJ. Retrieved from www.accessdata.fda.gov/drugsatfda_docs/label/2009/020281s032s033lbl.pdf

Ortho-McNeil-Janssen Pharmaceuticals, I. (2010). *Nucynta (R) [package insert].* Raritan, NJ. Retrieved from www.accessdata.fda.gov/drugsatfda_docs/label/2010/022304s003lbl.pdf

Passik, S. D., & Weinreb, H. J. (2000). Managing chronic nonmalignant pain: Overcoming obstacles to the use of opioids. *Advances in Therapy, 17*(2), 70–83.

Pembroke, M. (2017). *Everette files lawsuit against Purdue pharma.* Retrieved April 5, 2018, from https://everettwa.gov/DocumentCenter/View/9018

Pergolizzi, J. V, Raffa, R. B., Taylor, R., Vacalis, S. (2018). Abuse-deterrent opioids: An update on current approaches and considerations. *Current Medical Research and Opinion, 34*(4), 711–723. https://doi.org/10.1080/03007995.2017.1419171

Phillips, K., & Clauw, D. J. (2011). Central pain mechanisms in chronic pain states—maybe it is all in their head. *Best Practice & Research. Clinical Rheumatology, 25*(2), 141–154. https://doi.org/10.1016/j.berh.2011.02.005

Portenoy, R. K. (1990). Chronic opioid therapy in nonmalignant pain. *Journal of Pain and Symptom Management, 5*(1 Suppl), S46–S62.

Portenoy, R. K., & Foley, K. M. (1986). Chronic use of opioid analgesics in non-malignant pain: Report of 38 cases. *Pain, 25*(2), 171–186. https://doi.org/10.1016/0304-3959 (86)90091-6

Porter, J., & Jick, H. (1980). Addiction rare in patients treated with narcotics. *New England Journal of Medicine, 302*(2), 123–123. https://doi.org/10.1056/NEJM198001103020221

Pryzbylkowski, P., & Ashburn, M. A. (2015). The pain medical home: A patient-centered medical home model of care for patients with chronic pain. *Anesthesiology Clinics, 33*(4), 785–793. https://doi.org/10.1016/j.anclin.2015.07.009

Qaseem, A., Wilt, T. J., McLean, R. M., & Forciea, M. A. (2017). Noninvasive treatments for acute, subacute, and chronic low back pain: A clinical practice guideline from the American College of Physicians. *Annals of Internal Medicine, 166*(7), 514–530. https://doi.org/10.7326/M16-2367

Ray, W. A., Chung, C. P., Murray, K. T., Cooper, W. O., Hall, K., & Stein, C. M. (2015). Out-of-hospital mortality among patients receiving methadone for noncancer pain. *JAMA Internal Medicine, 175*(3), 420–427. https://doi.org/10.1001/jamainternmed.2014.6294

Ray, W. A., Chung, C. P., Murray, K. T., Hall, K., & Stein, C. M. (2016). Prescription of long-acting opioids and mortality in patients with chronic noncancer pain. *JAMA, 315*(22), 2415–2423. https://doi.org/10.1001/jama.2016.7789

Raymond, N. (2018, March 29). Arkansas sues opioid manufacturers for roles in epidemic. *Thomson Reuters.* Retrieved from www.reuters.com/article/us-usa-opioids-litigation/arkansas-sues-opioid-manufacturers-for-roles-in-epidemic-idUSKBN1H535T

Ready, L. B., Edwards, W. T., & International Association for the Study of Pain. Task Force on Acute Pain. (1992). *Management of acute pain: A practical guide.* IASP Publications. Retrieved from https://books.google.it/books?id=wV5qAAAAMAAJ

Roland, C., Setnik, B., & Brown, D. (2017). Assessing the impact of Abuse-Deterrent Opioids (ADOs): Identifying epidemiologic factors related to new entrants with low population exposure. *Postgraduate Medicine, 129*(1), 12–21. https://doi.org/10.1080/003254 81.2017.1272397

Savage, S. R. (1996). Long-term opioid therapy: Assessment of consequences and risks. *Journal of Pain and Symptom Management, 11*(5), 274–286. https://doi.org/10.1016/0885-3924(95)00202-2

Schofferman, J. (1993). Long-term use of opioid analgesics for the treatment of chronic pain of non malignant origin. *Journal of Pain and Symptom Management, 8*(5), 279–288.

Schuchat, A., Houry, D., & Guy, G. P. (2017). New data on opioid use and prescribing in the United States. *JAMA, 318*(5), 425–426. https://doi.org/10.1001/jama.2017.8913.

Schug, S. A., Merry, A. F., & Acland, R. H. (1991). Treatment principles for the use of opioids in pain of nonmalignant origin. *Drugs, 42*(2), 228–239. https://doi.org/10.2165/00003495-199142020-00005

Schweers, J. (2018, April 3). *Florida agencies sue Big Pharma to recoup millions in treatment costs.* Retrieved April 5, 2018, from www.tallahassee.com/story/news/2018/04/03/big-bend-community-based-care-other-florida-mental-health-providers-join-nationwide-opioid-lawsuit-c/481889002/

See, S., & Ginzburg, R. (2008). Skeletal muscle relaxants. *Pharmacotherapy, 28*(2), 207–213. https://doi.org/10.1592/phco.28.2.207

Semuels, A. (2017, June). *Are pharmaceutical companies to blame for the opioid epidemic?* Retrieved April 5, 2018, from www.theatlantic.com/business/archive/2017/06/lawsuit-pharmaceutical-companies-opioids/529020/

Shipton, E. E., Shipton, A. J., Williman, J. A., & Shipton, E. A. (2017). Deaths from opioid overdosing: Implications of coroners' inquest reports 2008–2012 and annual rise in opioid prescription rates: A population-based cohort study. *Pain and Therapy, 6*(2), 203–215. https://doi.org/10.1007/s40122-017-0080-7

Smith, L. H. (2007). Opioid safety: Is your patient at risk for respiratory depression? *Clinical Journal of Oncology Nursing, 11*(2), 293–296. https://doi.org/10.1188/07.CJON.293-296

Smith, M., & Davey, M. (2017, December 20). With overdoses on rise, cities and counties look for someone to blame—The New York Times. *The New York Times.* Retrieved from www.nytimes.com/2017/12/20/us/opioid-cities-counties-lawsuits.html

Stein, C., & Lang, L. (2009). Peripheral mechanisms of opioid analgesia. *Current Opinion in Pharmacology, 9*, 3–8. https://doi.org/10.1016/j.coph.2008.12.009

Surescripts. (2018). *E-prescribing of controlled substances.* Retrieved April 6, 2018, from http://surescripts.com/enhance-prescribing/e-prescribing/e-prescribing-of-controlled-substances/

Sweis, G., Huffman, K., Shella, E., & Scheman, J. (2012). Longitudinal treatment outcomes of patients with comorbid chronic pain and substance dependence within a multidisciplinary chronic pain program [abstract]. *The Journal of Pain, 13*(4), S107. https://doi.org/10.1016/j.jpain.2012.01.443

Tompkins, D. A., Hobelmann, J. G., Compton, P., & Bonica, J. J. (2017). Providing chronic pain management in the Fifth Vital Sign: Historical and treatment perspectives on a modern-day medical dilemma. *Drug and Alcohol Dependence, 173*, S11–S21. https://doi.org/10.1016/j.drugalcdep.2016.12.002

Trinkley, K. E., & Nahata, M. C. (2014). Medication management of irritable bowel syndrome. *Digestion, 89*(4), 253–267. https://doi.org/10.1159/000362405

Turner, J. A., Saunders, K., Shortreed, S. M., Rapp, S. E., Thielke, S., LeResche, L., . . . Von Korff, M. (2014). Chronic opioid therapy risk reduction initiative: Impact on urine drug testing rates and results. *Journal of General Internal Medicine, 29*(2), 305–311. https://doi.org/10.1007/s11606-013-2651-6

United States Department of Veterans Affairs and Department of Defense. (2013). *Tapering and discontinuing opioids fact sheet.* Retrieved March 15, 2018, from www.healthquality.va.gov/guidelines/Pain/cot/OpioidTaperingFactSheet23May2013v1.pdf

Utah Department of Health. (2009). *Utah clinical guidelines on prescribing opioids for treatment of pain.* Salt Lake City, UT. Retrieved from https://dopl.utah.gov/licensing/forms/OpioidGuidlines.pdf

Van Zee, A. (2009). The promotion and marketing of Oxycontin: Commercial triumph, public health tragedy. *American Journal of Public Health, 99*(2), 221–227. https://doi.org/10.2105/AJPH.2007.131714

Vardeh, D., Mannion, R. J., & Woolf, C. J. (2016). Towards a mechanism-based approach to pain diagnosis. *The Journal of Pain, 17*(9 Suppl), T50–T69. https://doi.org/10.1016/j.jpain.2016.03.001

Volkow, N. D., & McLellan, A. T. (2016). Opioid abuse in chronic pain—misconceptions and mitigation strategies. *New England Journal of Medicine, 374*(13), 1253–1263. https://doi.org/10.1056/NEJMra1507771

Volkow, N. D., McLellan, T. A., Cotto, J. H., Karithanom, M., & Weiss, S. R. B. (2011). Characteristics of opioid prescriptions in 2009. *JAMA, 305*(13), 1299–1301. https://doi.org/10.1001/jama.2011.401

Washington State Agency Medical Directors' Group (AMDG). (2010). *Interagency guideline on opioid dosing for chronic non-cancer pain: What is new in this revised guideline.* Olympia, WA. Retrieved from www.agencymeddirectors.wa.gov/Files/OpioidGdline.pdf

Washington State Department of Social and Human Services. (n.d.). *Taper dosing calculator.* Retrieved from www.partnershiphp.org/Providers/HealthServices/Documents/Managing Pain Safely/Taper Dosing Calculator.xls

Wesson, D. R., & Ling, W. (2003). The Clinical Opiate Withdrawal Scale (COWS). *Journal of Psychoactive Drugs, 35*(2), 253–259. https://doi.org/10.1080/02791072.2003.10400007

Wilson, H. D., Dansie, E. J., Kim, M. S., Moskovitz, B. L., Chow, W., & Turk, D. C. (2013). Clinicians' attitudes and beliefs about opioids survey (CAOS): Instrument development and results of a national physician survey. *The Journal of Pain, 14*(6), 613–627. https://doi.org/10.1016/j.jpain.2013.01.769

Zedler, B., Xie, L., Wang, L., Joyce, A., Vick, C., Kariburyo, F., . . . Murrelle, L. (2014). Risk factors for serious prescription opioid-related toxicity or overdose among veterans health administration patients. *Pain Medicine, 15*(11), 1911–1929. https://doi.org/10.1111/pme.12480

9

Chronic Back Pain

Emily J. Ross, Jeffrey E. Cassisi, and
Kenneth R. Lofland

Background and Public Health Perspective

Evidence suggests that human beings have suffered from back pain since the origin of our species. The "rapid" evolution of homo sapiens to bipedalism may have led to fundamental design flaws in the spine (Plomp, Viðarsdóttir, Weston, Dobney, & Collard, 2015). Thus, the advantages of walking upright came with the cost of susceptibility to spinal injuries and vulnerability to back pain. Indeed, archaeological studies and comparative analyses cross-species indicate that knuckle-walking apes do not exhibit the signs of orthopedic spinal degeneration often seen in humans (Plomp et al., 2015).

Chronic back pain in modern-day humans is defined as pain that is prolonged for more than 12 weeks and that occurs frequently or daily (NIH, 2015). It continues to be one of the most prevalent, disabling, and burdensome global health problems, with a global mean prevalence rate of 31% (Hoy et al., 2014). Over the last three decades, there has been a significant increase in the global prevalence of reported chronic low back pain symptoms and rising expenditures (Meucci, Fassa, & Faria, 2015), perhaps attributable to sedentariness and degenerative processes that occur with increased lifespan (Freburger et al., 2009; Meucci et al., 2015). Chronic back pain's etiology, clinical presentation, treatment, and outcomes are extremely heterogeneous. This is illustrated by the M54 codes in the ICD-10-CM available for Dorsalgia (the group of disorders characterized by mild to moderate or intense pain emerging from muscles, nerves, or joints associated with the spine); over 30 regions and subtypes are listed.

Low back pain represents the most common type of chronic pain in the United States, with up to 60 million adults endorsing it at any given time. In the 2010 National Health Survey, 42% of respondents endorsed chronic low back pain, and it was the most frequently endorsed type of pain overall in every age group. A Centers for Disease Control (CDC) study has estimated that 7–10% of all cases of low back pain will develop into chronic pain, and it is the number one cause of long-term disability (CDC, 2006; Kennedy, Roll, Schraudner, Murphy, & McPherson, 2014). Much of the empirical literature discussed in this chapter is derived from research on low back pain but is applicable to other related chronic back pain conditions.

Chronic back pain substantially impacts all age groups, though its occurrence in the U.S. population increases with age and peaks in the elderly (CDC, 2015; Hoy et al., 2014). Studies have estimated 24.2% of Americans aged 18–44 years, 32.1% aged 45–64 years, and 33.3% aged 65 and older report chronic back pain during the past three months (CDC, 2015). The aging population in the United States will contribute to the increasing prevalence of chronic back pain, with associated greater burden on healthcare services and higher rates of disability.

Prevalence rates for chronic back pain consistently are higher for women than men (Sheffer, Cassisi, Ferraresi, Lofland, & McCracken, 2002). Epidemiologic studies identify subtle ethnic and racial differences for chronic low back pain. Incidence rates in the U.S. population for 2015 are as follows: 28.7% White, 28.4% Black or African American, 28.9% American Indian or Alaska Native, 17.6% Asian, 35.2% for two or more races, 26.9% Hispanic or Latino, 26.5% Mexican, and 28.4% for Not Hispanic or Latino individuals (CDC, 2015). Chronic low back pain impacts both urban and rural populations, as well as countries across the income spectrum.

Individuals who experience chronic back pain are at a high risk for mental health comorbidities. Strong associations between chronic back pain, depression, and anxiety have been indicated in several research studies (Fernandez et al., 2017; Sagheer, Khan, & Sharif, 2013). Additionally, chronic back pain is a significant risk factor for suicidality, with 20% of patients with musculoskeletal chronic pain conditions reporting suicidal ideation (CDC, 2006; Hassett, Aquino, & Ilgen, 2014; Tang & Crane, 2006). In comparison to other chronic pain conditions such as neuropathic pain and fibromyalgia, chronic back pain is associated with a higher risk for suicide, and greater pain severity is a risk factor for suicide mortality even after controlling for many key covariates (Hassett et al., 2014; Ilgen et al., 2010; Tang & Crane, 2006). One population-based study found that of 2,310 people who died by suicide, 21.3% were identified as experiencing hospital-treated musculoskeletal pain (Löfman, Räsänen, Hakko, & Mainio, 2011).

Etiological Patterns

Many etiologies for chronic back pain have been identified, and labeling patients using specific anatomical diagnoses is unlikely to improve outcomes in most cases of back pain (Deyo, 1993). The Joint Practice Guidelines from the American College of Physicians and the American Pain Society (Fillingim et al., 2014) organize back pain into three broad categories. The first and largest category is "nonspecific back pain." More than 85% of patients who present to primary care with chronic back pain have nonspecific pain, and their pain cannot reliably be attributed to a single disease or spinal abnormality. Muscular pain disorders usually fall into this category. The second largest category is "back pain associated with radiculopathy or spinal stenosis," which is sometimes also referred to as "mechanical spinal pain." Mechanical etiologies include radiculopathy, spondylosis, disc and facet motion segment degeneration, radiculopathy due to structural impingement, and discogenic pain (with or without radicular symptomatology). These specific mechanical spinal disorders include vertebral compression, spinal trauma, disc herniation, lumbar spondylosis, spinal stenosis, spondylolisthesis, and cauda equina syndrome (Patrick, Emanski, & Knaub, 2014). The third category, which accounts for less than 10% of cases, is "other specific spinal disorders." This category includes infection (epidural abscess, osteomyelitis), fractures, neurologic syndromes, systemic disorders, inflammation, or malignancy (Wheeler, 2016).

Nonspecific back pain is extremely complicated because several pain pathways in the back may be implicated simultaneously. These include ligaments, facet joints, the vertebral periosteum, blood vessels, spinal nerve roots, and the paravertebral muscles (Deyo & Weinstein, 2001). Muscle strain may occur when the muscle fibers around the spine are overstretched or overused. Lumbar sprain occurs when ligaments are torn or overstretched; both types of low back strain lead to pain. Research has indicated that 97% of low back pain may have musculoskeletal involvement (Deyo & Weinstein, 2001; Weinstein et al., 2010).

There are physical, psychosocial, genetic, environmental, and biomechanical risk factors for back pain developing into a chronic condition (Adams, 2004). Some identified premorbid factors include heavy lifting and twisting, bodily vibration, obesity, poor conditioning, minimal engagement in physical activity, age over 30 years, and comorbid or subclinical psychosocial difficulties such as chronic stress or depressive and anxious symptoms (Andersson, 1999; NIH, 2015). The complex neurological, orthopedic, musculoskeletal, and psychosocial factors interact, requiring personalized interdisciplinary interventions at each level of care.

Disability and Cost

Chronic back pain results from an occupational injury or other type of accident more frequently than do other medical conditions. Thus, individuals with chronic back pain are at greater risk for an unexpected major disability and absence from work, and lost productivity. Chronic back pain is one of the top eight conditions with the highest associated number of years lived with disability (YLDs) (Hoy et al., 2014). In addition, musculoskeletal disorders are among the top 15 leading diseases and risk factors contributing to disability-adjusted life years (DALYs) (Murray et al., 2013). These patients have high unemployment rates; 12.8% receive income from disability that is tied to their back pain, compared with 4.6% of patients with other chronic conditions (Shmagel, Foley, & Ibrahim, 2016). Two-thirds of the estimated total cost of chronic low back pain ($100 to 200 billion per year) is due to decreased productivity, lost wages, and 149 million lost work days (Katz, 2006; Rubin, 2007).

Sex differences have been observed in disability costs, with lower expenditures for women. Ironically, because of wage inequalities, women with chronic low back pain may simply not derive the same financial and psychosocial benefits from employment as do men. Interestingly, marriage has been associated with more household work for women with back pain and less for men with the same diagnoses (Sheffer et al., 2002).

Individuals reporting chronic back pain are three times as likely to have fair or poor health status; thus, they can be heavy utilizers of medical services (CDC, 2006). A 2010 analysis of the medical care costs for various pain diagnoses found the total direct cost of back pain to be over $34 billion, which was a significant proportion of the almost $47 billion in direct costs of medical treatment for various chronic pain conditions (IOM, 2011).

Biopsychosocial Factors in Chronic Back Pain

There are as many theories addressing the natural history of chronic back pain as there are specific treatments. This fact alone suggests that the assessment and treatment of chronic back pain requires an integrative and/or interdisciplinary team approach. One of the most robust models with clinical utility is the biopsychosocial model, which shifted discussions about chronic pain from tissue damage on the periphery and a preoccupation with nociception to a focus on interactions between the central nervous system and multiple internal and external factors (Engel, 1978). One component of this model describes how a physical injury leads to psychological distress, illness behavior, and the adoption of the "sick role." This model emphasizes the meaning that patients attribute to injury and how this impacts subsequent illness behavior.

One of the first models of the pain experience that is consistent with the biopsychosocial perspective was Melzack and Wall's gate control theory of pain (1965). This theory stipulates that nerve impulses from the peripheral nervous system undergo modulations in the spinal cord in a gate-like manner. Descending pathways from the brain send signals down the spinal cord to open and close "gates," which allow or prevent pain signals to be centrally processed (Campbell, Johnson, & Zernicke, 2013; Melzack & Wall, 1965; Wall, 1978). It is helpful to emphasize that the opening of pain gates may occur from cognitive and affective factors such as anger, depression, hopelessness, stress, anxiety, frustration, and rumination. Conversely, emotional and cognitive factors such as positive affect, stress-management skills, and adaptive coping thoughts can help close these gates. Figure 9.1 may be useful as a patient handout to facilitate discussion of these concepts, and introducing these models may also provide a simple, non-threatening rationale for the presence of psychologists on the team (Ross, 2018).

Recently, the biopsychosocial model of chronic pain has been advanced by the concept of central sensitivity (CS) theory (Woolf, 2011). This approach posits that

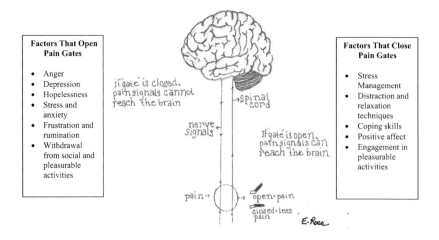

Figure 9.1 Melzack and Wall's (1965) Gate Control Theory of Pain

Illustrated by E.M. Ross

genetic factors, physical injuries, depression, sleep disturbance, fear avoidance, and social factors can cause hypersensitivity and amplification of the interoception of pain. This approach is squarely in the tradition of the study of somatization and much of Melzack's work. CS theory suggests that there are common mechanisms for pain hypersensitivity across many intractable syndromes, including fibromyalgia, chronic fatigue syndrome, irritable bowel syndrome, migraine and tension headache, and temporomandibular joint disorder, among others (Neblett et al., 2017). CS recently has been applied to musculoskeletal complaints such as back pain (Sanzarello et al., 2016).

Particularly relevant to the chronic back pain population is the observation that depression and chronic pain frequently co-occur (Doan, Manders, & Wang, 2015). One recent study (Elfering, Käser, & Melloh, 2014), using cross-lagged analyses, found a bidirectional cycle between depression and pain levels such that depression ratings at intake predicted higher pain ratings at the next meeting; higher pain ratings at the next meeting in turn predicted higher depression levels at the next. As a result, the authors recommend that health practitioners screen for and treat depressive symptoms as early as possible in order to increase the chances of successful intervention.

Further, research has shown overlapping pathways between depression and pain at the neurological and neurotransmitter levels. The neurotransmitters for these pathways are serotonin, norepinephrine, glutamate, and GABA. In short, depression may predispose an individual to experience chronic pain and subsequently worsen pain symptomatology (Doan et al., 2015). There are also many behavioral factors that contribute to the pain–depression relationship. For example, patients with chronic back pain may withdraw from social contact and enjoyable activities, thereby contributing to depressed mood, decreased functioning, and disability.

Sleep and Chronic Back Pain

Most chronic pain patients have at least one sleep complaint, such as longer sleep-onset latency, more sleep awakenings, shorter total sleep time, and less restful sleep than people who do not have pain (McCracken & Iverson, 2002). Chronic back pain patients are no exception; approximately 55–60% report impaired sleep (Alsaadi, McAuley, Hush, & Maher, 2011; Marin, Cyhan, & Miklos, 2006), and over half suffer from clinical insomnia (Tang, Wright, & Salkovskis, 2007). Several studies have found a bidirectional relationship between back pain and insomnia, such that nights with worse sleep quality are followed by days with higher pain severity, and days with higher pain severity are followed by nights with poorer sleep quality (Alsaadi et al., 2014). However, a recent study using time-lagged analyses of daily diary data found a stronger directional relationship in that poor sleep quality was predictive of higher pain ratings, lower physical functioning, and greater pain catastrophizing the following day, especially during the early part (Gerhart et al., 2017).

Sleep plays a pivotal role in both pain and depression. Research has indicated that targeting sleep can improve functioning in chronic back pain patients and reduce their risk of experiencing an onset of depression (Tang, Goodchild, Hester, & Salkovskis, 2012). These findings suggest that treating sleep disturbances in chronic back pain patients should be made part of routine clinical practice, an area only beginning to be explored (Jungquist et al., 2010).

Anxiety and Chronic Back Pain

Anxiety disorders are among the most common psychiatric diagnoses for patients with chronic back pain, and prevalence rates for anxiety are higher in this clinical population than in the general population (Sagheer et al., 2013). One study, using the Hospital Anxiety and Depressive Scale (HADS), found that 38.5% and 16.4% of back pain patients had borderline abnormal and abnormal anxiety scores, respectively (Sagheer et al., 2013). Further, anxiety severity is significantly associated with higher ratings of disabling pain (de Heer et al., 2014). The Anxiety and Depression Association of America (2016) also emphasizes that individuals with co-occurring chronic back pain and anxiety disorders may be more difficult to treat, have a lower threshold for pain, show more fear of taking medications and of their side effects, and exhibit a greater fear response to the experience of pain. One study examined whether anxiety sensitivity (i.e., fears concerning the behaviors or sensations that accompany the experience of anxiety) influences affective and pain-related anxiety in patients without a demonstrable organic pathology for their chronic back pain (Asmundson & Norton, 1995). Findings indicated that patients with high anxiety sensitivity were impacted more negatively by pain, experienced pain-related cognitive and affective disruptions that were independent of pain severity, endorsed increased fear of negative consequences related to pain, and had greater negative affect.

High anxiety sensitive chronic back pain patients also reported significantly greater use of analgesic medication compared to moderate or low anxiety sensitive patients. Different elements of anxiety (health anxiety, trait anxiety, pain-related anxiety, and anxiety sensitivity) also have been examined in musculoskeletal patients. A longitudinal study revealed that at first medical visit, pain-related anxiety uniquely predicted both disability and negative emotions; trait anxiety uniquely predicted negative emotions and perceptions of control; and anxiety sensitivity uniquely predicted negative emotions. At the three-month follow-up, health anxiety uniquely predicted disability and negative emotions. In addition, anxiety sensitivity also contributes to negative emotions. The resulting relationships were established even after controlling for pain severity as a covariate (Hadjistavropoulos, Asmundson, & Kowalyk, 2004).

The Fear and Avoidance Model is one of the most well-known mechanism-oriented chronic pain models applied to chronic back pain. It is widely used to conceptualize the cognitive, behavioral, and affective processes involved in chronic back pain's persistence, as well as central mechanisms of disability and deconditioning (Crombez, Eccleston, Van Damme, Vlaeyen, & Karoly, 2012; Edwards, Dworkin, Sullivan, Turk, & Wasan, 2016). This theory posits that a patient's beliefs about chronic pain (e.g., it is worsening and harmful) will lead to the avoidance of physical exertion and movement (Crombez et al., 2012; Philips, 1987). Over time, the consequences of fear and avoidance can lead to neurophysiological changes, such as decreasing amounts of stimulation needed to produce a pain response (Edwards et al., 2016; Rabey, 2001; Vlaeyen & Linton, 2000). The specific interrelationships involved in the Fear and Avoidance Model are illustrated in Figure 9.2.

The Continuum of Care

The management of chronic back pain can be organized by levels of care (primary, secondary, and tertiary care settings; Figure 9.3), with behavioral health providers essential at each level. Many professional medical associations, such as the American College of Physicians and APS (Chou et al., 2007), have published guidelines for evaluating and treating back pain. These guidelines consistently stress the adoption of *conservative outpatient management* as the first-line approach. However, a recent review of the literature using data from the National Ambulatory Medical Care Survey and the National Hospital Medical Care Survey found that management of back pain in the United States often does not comport to any published guidelines (Mafi, McCarthy, Davis, & Landon, 2013a). The authors conclude that this is a major factor in the low quality of care and the high cost to the healthcare system for these disorders.

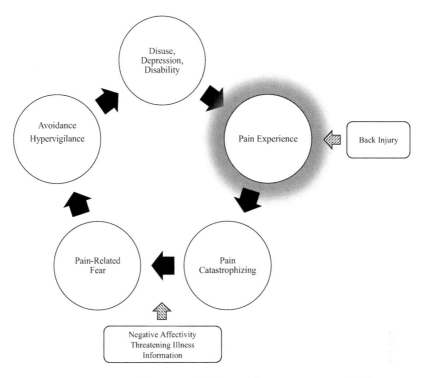

Figure 9.2   Fear and Avoidance Model of Pain (Vlaeyen & Linton, 2000)

Primary Care

Ideally, primary care is comprehensive, coordinated, continuous, and accessible; it is often the first point of contact for patients presenting with any given illness (Mills, Torrance, & Smith, 2016). Approximately 65% of chronic pain patients presently see their primary care physician for treatment (Chou et al., 2007). More than 10% of primary care visits relate to back pain, which is the fifth most common reason for all medical visits (Deyo, Mirza, Turner, & Martin, 2009; Hart, Deyo, & Cherkin, 1995; Mafi et al., 2013; Martell et al., 2007; Martin et al., 2008). Additionally, more than 85% of these patients have nonspecific low back pain (Chou et al., 2007).

Most patients with back pain recover within one month with minimal treatment, and the physical examination is the primary method used to rule out cases of unambiguous serious pathology. Plain radiography and advanced imaging are not associated with improved diagnosis or better outcomes. Imaging is, however, associated with increased exposure to ionizing radiation and increased healthcare costs. Therefore, according to published guidelines (Chou et al., 2007), diagnostic imaging is not recommended in the absence of specific signs that are elicited

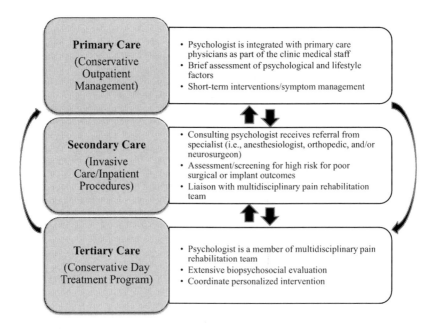

Figure 9.3 Psychological Services: Continuum of Care

during the physical exam. A detailed description of the physical exam for back pain is found in Atlas and Deyo (2001).

Evaluating mechanical, non-mechanical, and neurological components of back pain entails inspection of the spine, testing the patient's range of motion, and utilizing palpation to evaluate any soft-tissue abnormalities and tenderness. Incorporating simple techniques suggested by Waddell (Waddell, McCulloch, Kummel, & Venner, 1980) during the physical exam may help detect symptom exaggeration in occupational medicine clinics or in cases of litigation. The "Waddell" techniques include a simulated rotation of the hips or light pressure on the head or superficial tissues, which should not normally elicit a pain response. A psychologist consulting with a primary care physician may recommend these techniques to ascertain the presence of embellishment in the patient's pain reports (Waddell et al., 1980).

Presenting factors that prompt referral to a secondary level of care include the following: trauma related to age or accident (especially with osteoporosis); progressive motor or sensory deficits consistent with established dermatomes (an area of skin from which a nerve innervates) and myotomes (a group of muscles from which a single spinal nerve innervates); bowel or bladder incontinence or urinary retention; history of cancer; and/or suspected spinal infection. In cases where risk factors such as these are not present, first-line treatment for patients begins with conservative outpatient management in the primary care setting. Medically, this includes use of acetaminophen and nonsteroidal anti-inflammatory (NSAIDS) drugs. Muscle relaxants and antidepressants should be used sensibly and opiates are to be avoided in virtually all cases.

A recent meta-analysis revealed there has been a rapid increase in narcotic prescriptions, yet narcotic use does not demonstrate long-term efficacy in treating chronic back pain (Martell et al., 2007). Furthermore, up to 24% of patients prescribed opioids for back pain have comorbid substance use disorders and atypical medication-taking behaviors (Martell et al., 2007). Emerging European standards recommend introducing outpatient physical therapy and integrated behavioral services in the primary care setting soon after the patient's first presentation (Pinnington, Miller, & Stanley, 2004; Taloyan, Alinaghizadeh, & Lofvander, 2013).

The primary care setting is an ideal place for the ongoing management of many patients' back pain needs, which often can be addressed before they escalate or become more complex. However, primary care providers frequently find chronic pain patients difficult to assess and treat. Often, primary care physicians do not emphasize the physical exam enough, rely solely on medical tests, and overlook the utility of psychometrically sound psychological questionnaires. One study examined clinical actions and treatment approaches for patients with back pain among 381 primary care physicians—results indicated there were subtle biases (grouping patients as drug- or compensation-seeking) in the primary care physicians' responses to patients with back pain, and few utilized the interdisciplinary approach endorsed by the biopsychosocial model for the treatment of pain (Phelan, van Ryn, Wall, & Burgess, 2009).

Psychosocial Assessment of Patients With Back Pain in Primary Care

The use of self-report psychological instruments is associated with improved clinical outcomes in primary care settings (Lewis, Sharp, Bartholomew, & Pelosi, 1996). In addition, studies suggest that between 80% and 90% of primary care patients react positively to brief questionnaires regarding their psychosocial status in this setting (Dobscha et al., 2009; Hunter, Goodie, Oordt, & Dobmeyer, 2017; Zimmerman et al., 1996). In an era of increasingly shorter facetime with physicians during medical visits, patients appreciate the opportunity to have expanded communications with various members of the integrated team. These assessments give patients a sense of receiving thorough personalized care, encourage their engagement, and are a major advantage of the patient-centered medical home.

The specific areas assessed in the primary care context differ little from other settings. The main difference is the reliance on brief screening instruments instead of longer, more thorough versions. The use of brief screeners for depression and anxiety, such as the Patient Health Questionnaire-9, PHQ-9 (Löwe, Unützer, Callahan, Perkins, & Kroenke, 2004), and the Generalized Anxiety Disorder-7, GAD-7 (Spitzer, Kroenke, Williams, & Löwe, 2006), are now part of national guidelines stipulated by such organizations as U.S. Preventative Services Task

Force (USPSTF) and multiple state health organizations. Currently, the PHQ-9 and the GAD-7 often are incorporated into the electronic medical record, with more examples on the horizon (e.g., the Patient-Reported Outcomes Measurement Information System [PROMIS]; Ader, 2007).

Important and specific assessment domains are recommended by the APS Pain Taxonomy working group, and these are applicable to the chronic back pain population (Fillingim et al., 2014). These domains include the assessment of 1) sensory, 2) affective, 3) temporal quality, 4) pain location, 5) pain behavior and coping, 6) social support, and 7) substance use. See Chapters 2 and 7 for more information regarding assessment instruments appropriate to the primary care setting. Established instruments such as the McGill Pain Questionnaire—Short Form (Melzack, 1987) are familiar standards, but exciting new instruments are emerging that are tailored to primary care. These new instruments are optimized for electronic administration and often provide rapid automated scoring on iPads and similar devices at little or no cost.

One new instrument tailored to the primary care setting is the Profile of Chronic Pain: Screen (PCP:S) (Karoly, Ruehlman, Aiken, Todd, & Newton, 2006). This 15-item, cost-effective, psychometrically sound questionnaire has three sub-scales, each of which can be scored separately: pain severity, pain interference, and emotional burden. The pain severity (intensity) dimension is evaluated with four items; the pain interference dimension (impact of pain on self-care and cognition) is evaluated with six items; and emotional burden (distress, sadness, anger, withdrawal, etc.) is evaluated with five items. This measure also is useful in identifying patients who may require further psychosocial evaluation and treatment and can be utilized to evaluate change in each specific dimension in response to brief psychosocial intervention.

The National Institute of Health (NIH) funded the development of the Patient Reported Outcomes Measurement Information System (PROMIS) in the early 2000s to inform recommendations for researchers and clinicians to use standardized measurement of health outcomes across various chronic diseases ([NIH], 2018; Ader, 2007; David Cella et al., 2010; D. Cella et al., 2007). The pain-related domains in the PROMIS include static and adaptive item banks for pain intensity, quality, interference, and behavior (Amtmann et al., 2010; Cook et al., 2013; Revicki et al., 2009). A PROMIS pain behavior short-form scale is available, and the recently developed Pain Behaviors Self-Report (PaB-SR) may provide more comprehensive assessment of pain behaviors (Cook et al., 2013). The PROMIS approach is still under development, and psychometric evaluation of multiple item banks for assessing health domains, including pain-related outcomes, continues to this day. Other PROMIS measures (e.g., fatigue, physical function, social function, depression, etc.) also are applicable to many chronic pain patients.

Generally speaking, empirically supported screening measures are good predictors of patient-treatment outcomes and often exceed the predictive power of typical medical tests, such as MRIs or discography (Disorbio, Bruns, & Barolat, 2006). We suggest incorporating both standardized pain assessment measures and psychosocial screening measures into chronic back pain initial evaluation and treatment planning, as well as into ongoing care to objectively track functioning and somatic complaints over time, and to help inform when to escalate the level of care.

Psychological Treatment in the Primary Care Setting

Treatment recommendations for chronic back pain patients in primary care emphasize the provision of brief behavioral health consultation and interventions, non-pharmacological therapies, and symptom management. Psychosocial services are integrated into the continuum of care in the primary care setting as part of one service delivery system. If the patient is not improving and needs a higher level of care following the completion of brief behavioral health interventions, a secondary specialist referral can be made (DeBar et al., 2012).

Cognitive-behavioral therapy (CBT) components are among the most utilized and effective brief psychosocial treatments in primary care (Robinson & Reiter, 2007). CBT delivered in primary care typically is brief, with goals of reducing the patient's psychological distress and pain experience and improving physical and role functioning through addressing adaptive behaviors, thoughts, and beliefs. These CBT targets promote self-efficacy by involving the patient as an active participant in his/her own pain management. CBT may be used to target subclinical or comorbid psychological conditions prevalent in this population, such as anxiety, depressive, or sleep disorders, and may focus less on pain severity (Roditi & Robinson, 2011).

The psychologist works actively and empathically with each patient and ensures the patient's values and beliefs are incorporated into the brief intervention treatment plan. The psychologist often serves as a coach or teacher (Robinson & Reiter, 2007; Roditi & Robinson, 2011). This approach also endorses tracking progress and measurable outcomes, so patients see tangible evidence of their progress toward goals. The cognitive techniques of CBT focus on reducing distress, suffering, and pain interference (Ehde, Dillworth, & Turner, 2014). The CBT interventions summarized in Table 9.1 adhere to recommendations by Gatchel and Rollings (Robert, Gatchel & Rollings, 2008) and are guided by the CBT phases outlined by Turk and Flor (Turk, Meichenbaum, Melzack, & Wall, 2000). These brief, evidence-based interventions entail up to six to eight sessions, but are often accomplished in three.

CBT has demonstrated effectiveness in primary settings for patients with low back pain. In one study, 399 patients who received brief CBT (six sessions in group format) had improved disability ratings; reduced pain severity and depressive symptoms; and higher quality of life one year after the intervention when compared to those who received care as usual (Lamb et al., 2010). Further, self-management programs in primary care also are associated with improvements in mood and pain severity, in addition to enhancement of functional capabilities. These programs target the three-dimensional approaches to pain management

Table 9.1 Brief Psychosocial Treatment of Chronic Back Pain in Primary Care

Treatment Component	Treatment Targets
Introduction	• Use motivational interviewing (MI) to start patient at their level of readiness for change
Patient Psychoeducation	• Information is provided about: CBT, behavioral health services, the patient's presenting chronic back pain syndrome, the biopsychosocial model, guiding principles; realistic expectations set about pain, pain management, rehabilitation, and treatment
Self-Monitoring and Homework	Self-report, self-monitoring of skills and homework assignments are given throughout intervention • Track mood, cognitions, thoughts • Track functional behaviors and activities • Track pain severity and interference • Cognitive restructuring and other exercises to be used at home
Coping Skills Training	• Relaxation training • Distraction • Acceptance and commitment therapy (ACT) skills • Yoga
Lifestyle Modification	The following areas are targeted as appropriate: • Low impact exercise (i.e., walking) • Diet • Sleep hygiene (with CBT-I, if insomnia present)
Activity Management	• Stretching exercises • Increase existing adaptive behaviors and activities • Pacing of physical activity • Decrease avoidance of physical exercise • Patient activation to reduce fear through exposure
Skill Consolidation, Generalization, and Maintenance	• Coping and problem-solving skills generalized into patient's day-to-day lives • Focus is on future pain management and maintenance of skills acquired in the post-treatment phase
Post-Treatment Assessment and Follow-Up	• Evaluate post-treatment outcomes and improvement • Evaluate patients' application of CBT skills to their lives • Treatment summary is provided to primary care physician

(emotional, cognitive, and behavioral) by promoting activities and empowering the patient to manage chronic pain.

Fear-reducing and activity-inducing interventions also have demonstrated benefits for chronic back pain patients, including significant decreases in patient fears, activity limitations related to back pain, and days missed from usual activities attributable to pain (Von Korff et al., 2005). Promoting positive communication between patients with chronic back pain and their primary care physicians contributes to improved patient outcomes, understanding of treatment and diagnosis, and adherence to treatment plans (Von Korff et al., 2005). Patients value physician communication that validates pain experiences, and primary care physicians who listen with empathic presence, conduct assessments, work in a collaborative manner, and provide well-defined clinical diagnostic information (Evers et al., 2017).

Secondary Care

Secondary care typically is led by physician specialists, including but not limited to anesthesiologists, neurosurgeons, or orthopedic surgeons. At this level of treatment, patients may receive recommendations for nerve blocks or a specific surgical treatment. Notably, a recent study found a 106% increase over the past decade in referrals of chronic back pain patients by primary care physicians to secondary specialty physicians, contributing to an increased rate of surgeries (Mafi et al., 2013a). Non-primary care physicians are more likely to order advanced imaging such as x-ray with or without contrast, computerized tomography (CT), and/or magnetic resonance imaging (MRI). Furthermore, receiving an MRI is associated with an eight-fold increased likelihood of the patient receiving surgery (Lurie, Birkmeyer, & Weinstein, 2003; Mafi et al., 2013b; Webster & Cifuentes, 2010).

Invasive treatments initially may be recommended in cases such as disc hernia, spinal instability, and spinal tumor. Specific interventions for these conditions include: laminectomy, laminotomy, spinal fusion therapy, and spinal cord stimulators (SCS). Despite generally positive outcomes, surgical interventions are not without controversy. Spinal surgery is performed in the U.S. at a rate up to five times higher than in other developed countries, even though spinal disease and injury are no more prevalent (Chan & Peng, 2011). In one study, even though surgery was "objectively" successful in 84% of patients, 49% of patients reported worse pain following surgery, 44% were dissatisfied with the outcome, and 38% were significantly disabled at follow-up (LaCaille, DeBerard, Masters, Colledge, & Bacon, 2005). Another study found that opioid pain medication use, taken more than 90 days post-operatively, actually increased following surgery (Nguyen, Randolph, Talmage, Succop, & Travis, 2011). Therefore, even when the surgeon has labeled the spinal surgery a success, it does not necessarily improve patient functioning or satisfaction with care. With every intervention, the probability of success decreases and the pain syndrome can become more complex.

Treatment-Resistant Back Pain

Spine surgery, as with any invasive procedure requiring anesthesia, has considerable risks. These include the risk of infection, nerve injury, blood loss, worse pain, urinary/bowel disturbances, and sensorimotor dysfunction (Deyo et al., 2009; Deyo, Nachemson, & Mirza, 2004; Fritzell, Hagg, & Nordwall, 2003; Thomsen et al., 1997). Beginning in the 1980s, the disabling chronic syndrome associated with the iatrogenic effects of spine surgery was sometimes labeled failed back surgery syndrome, or FBSS (Thomson, 2013). Thus, the intractable worsening of symptoms following surgery was common enough to become a diagnosis in its own right. Currently, there is debate about the appropriateness of this label among surgeons. To some, the label seems to imply that the patient is being difficult or has failed, and to others it seems to place the blame on the surgeon for the patient's worsening condition (Lucas, 2012). We are critical of the FBSS label because it tells little about pain mechanisms other than that previous surgeries have been attempted without success. Clearly, poor outcomes have multiple and complex causes. As such, we advocate for use of the term "treatment-resistant back pain." This label recognizes multiple causes, including patient variables and treatment history.

Since invasive spinal procedures may not help a substantial subgroup of patients, the cautious specialist often consults with psychologists in the secondary care setting to conduct presurgical psychological screening (PPS) to predict the patient's response to treatment and risk of developing treatment-resistant back pain and to reduce failure rates. Indeed, the United States Preventive Services Task Force (USPSTF) recommends PPS for patients undergoing back surgery (Young, Young, Riley, & Skolasky, 2014). This guideline is a culmination of many years of effort in the field, and a number of individuals have contributed to the PPS literature, including Andrew Block, Robert Gatchel (Marek, Block, & Ben-Porath, 2017) and Daniel Bruns (Bruns & Disorbio, 2009).

A recent survey of approximately 100 surgeons found the PPS was most commonly used to screen for depression (100%) or anxiety (85%). Referral for a PPS was highest among surgeons with more experience, higher annual volume, and, counter-intuitively, no university affiliation. The majority of surgeons surveyed acknowledged a connection between psychological factors and pain relief, adherence to therapy, and return to work. Despite this belief, the ability of the PPS to predict successful return to work at follow-up was only moderate (Young et al., 2014). Other studies suggest that psychological tests, such as the Minnesota Multiphasic Personality Inventory-2 Revised Form (MMPI-2-RF), can outperform medical tests at predicting poor response to back surgery (Carragee & Hannibal, 2004; Meyer et al., 2001).

There is general agreement on the starting point for the PPS and which specific patient risk factors predict an unsuccessful treatment outcome. Differences exist in the specific assessment instruments recommended and how to calculate risk. The PPS starts with a medical chart review of the patient's treatment history, medication use, compliance, and pain levels. As Turk and Meichenbaum (1984) originally noted, three central questions should guide the assessment of chronic pain:

1. What is the extent of the patient's disease or injury (physical impairment)?
2. What is the magnitude of the illness? That is, to what extent is the patient suffering, disabled, and unable to enjoy usual activities?
3. Does the individual's behavior seem appropriate to the disease or injury, or is there evidence of amplification of symptoms for any of a variety of psychosocial reasons? (Turk, 1984, pp. 787–794)

The PPS also includes a standard psychological interview, which provides an opportunity for behavioral observations and for the patient to give a narrative in his/her own words. (See Chapter 2 for more information on conducting a structured interview assessing chronic pain.) It can be helpful to use a Pain Location Drawing at the interview stage of the PPS. Patients indicate their pain on a drawn figure. The pain drawing, which has qualitative features and allows the patient to use his/her own words to describe the pain, has been shown to be influenced by emotional distress (Ransford, Cairns, & Mooney, 1976). A recent qualitative systematic review demonstrated pain drawings are comprehensive, reliable, valid, and relevant to multiple, diverse constructs (Hartzell, Liegey-Dougall, Kishino, & Gatchel, 2016). The review also revealed that pain drawings are useful for screening for psychosocial, disability, occupational, medicinal, cognitive, and quality of life outcomes in the chronic pain patient population (Hartzell et al., 2016).

Figures 9.4 and 9.5 provide examples of Pain Location Drawings. In Figure 9.4, the pain drawing indicates a patient with pain localized in the back, but with significant bilateral radiating pain. The patient's pain report is limited to these areas and there is no evidence in the drawing of particular psychological investment or amplification of symptoms. In sharp contrast, Figure 9.5 indicates a patient with diffuse severe pain and significant distress associated with his pain experience. Additionally, the location of the pain is hard to determine and there is evidence in the drawing of particular psychological investment or amplification of symptoms associated with the pain experience.

In general, the PPS designates risk factors in two categories. Primary risk factors are referred to as "red flags" due to their strong association with negative treatment outcomes. Primary risk factors are diagnosable psychiatric conditions that lead to severe psychological instability. Examples of the most severe primary risk factors include suicidal and homicidal ideation and/or behavior, psychotic behavior, violent ideation toward the physician, or acute intoxication (Fishbain, Bruns, Disorbio, & Lewis, 2009; Fishbain et al., 2011). More commonly seen red flags include clinical depression, anxiety, and substance use disorders. In most cases, if a primary risk factor is present, the psychologist would recommend delaying the elective surgery until it is resolved or accommodated. This recommendation is supported by at least one study that documented poor prognosis when

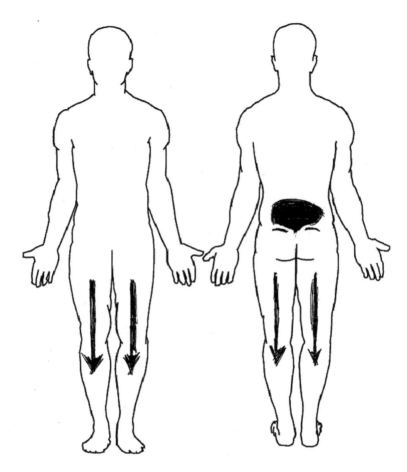

Figure 9.4 Pain Location Drawing 1

patients with back pain have multiple psychiatric diagnoses. Schofferman (1992) observed a 95% positive surgical outcome in cases where no co-occurring psychiatric diagnoses were present (Schofferman, Anderson, Hines, Smith, & White, 1992). However, observed success rates dropped precipitously to 73% when one or two psychiatric diagnoses were present, and to 15% if three or more were present. Subsequent cumulative empirical findings have demonstrated similar findings concerning the role of psychological factors and surgical outcomes (Block, Marek, Ben-Porath, & Kukal, 2017).

Secondary or "yellow flag" risk factors are much more common and have less direct and individual predictive value. Examples of "yellow flag" risk factors include poor physical functioning, job dissatisfaction, somatization, and poor coping. Nonetheless, a considerable amount of research indicates secondary risk factors play a significant role in surgical outcomes when present in combination

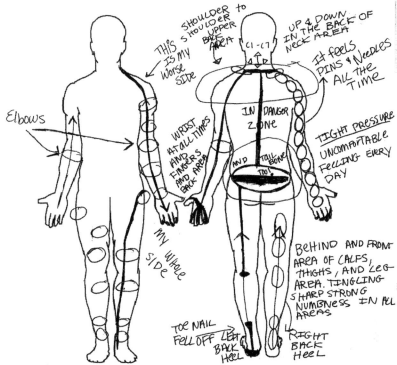

Figure 9.5 Pain Location Drawing 2

(Block, Ohnmeiss, Ben-Porath, & Burchett; Block et al., 2017; Andrew Block, Marek, Ben-Porath, & Ohnmeiss, 2014; Bruns & Disorbio, 2009; Mannion & Elfering, 2006). The presence of four or more secondary psychosocial risk factors doubles the chances of failure to return to work after medical treatment of back pain patients (Gatchel, 2006).

Psychological tests are also used to assess risk factors in the PPS. Two of the most common psychological tests used for the diagnosis of psychopathology in PPS assessments are the MMPI-2-RF and the Battery for Health Improvement 2 (BHI2).

The MMPI-2-RF is the current version of one of the most iconic psychological tests. It has gone through several updates since it was first developed in the 1940s and has been used in medical settings since its inception. The version of the test appropriate for the PPS is the MMPI-2-RF, which has 338 true/false items and takes 35–50 minutes to administer (Marek et al., 2017). This instrument is well normed and contains many scales that are relevant to the medical setting, including nine Validity Scales, 12 Higher-Order (H-O) and Restructured Clinical (RC) Scales, 14 Somatic/Cognitive and Internalizing Scales, 11 Externalizing, Interpersonal, and Interest Scales, and five Personality Psychopathology Five (PSY-5) Scales. The MMPI-2-RF is especially good at identifying the likely presence of psychiatric symptoms and pathological processes, as well as suggesting formal clinical diagnoses. It provides insights into the way the patient communicates with the treatment team (forthright, defensive, exaggerating, etc.). A complete description of the scales and their use in medical settings, while beyond the scope of this chapter, is available in the test manual. The MMPI-2-RF has significant costs associated with its use and is available from the publisher to qualified users.

The original MMPI, MMPI-2, and most recently, the MMPI-2-RF have been empirically studied in relation to spinal surgery outcomes. In one study of 172 men and 210 women who underwent a comprehensive PPS, the MMPI-2-RF scale scores predicted early surgical outcomes independent of other presurgical risk factors (Marek et al., 2017). The MMPI-2-RF accounted for up to 11% of additional variance in measures of early postoperative functioning. The specific MMPI-2-RF scales that contributed most to poorer outcomes were emotional/internalizing problems, demoralization, somatoform dysfunction, and interpersonal problems. The MMPI-2-RF results should not be applied carelessly or automatically. For example, specific injury or disease processes may be responsible for a patient's widespread and general neurological complaints. No assessment instrument should ever replace the clinical judgment of a trained clinician.

The Battery for Health Improvement 2 (BHI2; Bruns & Disorbio, 2014) is another psychological test often used as part of PPS. It was designed for the biopsychosocial assessment of medical patients who suffer from pain or injury. It is a 217-item, self-report inventory with three validity measures, 16 clinical scales, and a multidimensional assessment of pain. This instrument was developed to evaluate medical patients, and the norm reference groups are targeted more narrowly. The BHI2 has two validity scales, Self-Disclosure and Defensiveness, and four major subscales (Physical Symptom, Character, Affective, and Psychosocial Status).

The BHI2 can generate a Medical Intervention Risk (MIR) report, which summarizes five psychosocial risk factors impacting a patient's response to treatment: Primary Risk, Presurgical Risk, Rehabilitation Risk, Addiction History Risk, and Addiction Potential Risk. This report also generates an overall Outcome Risk Level (ORL). In addition, the MIR report measures several other scales that include catastrophizing and kinesiophobia, two non-adaptive coping styles that can interfere with medical outcomes. Finally, the MIR report assesses suicidal and violent ideation and suggests behavioral interventions that may prove helpful in reducing a patient's risk for medical treatment.

Extensive literature demonstrates that psychosocial factors are associated with spine surgery outcomes (reviewed in Bruns & Disorbio, 2009). The two instruments reviewed here are not the only ones that have been used during PPS evaluations. Many psychologists prefer to use a battery approach, choosing measures that target a patient's presenting situation. Several algorithms have been offered for combining measures to yield empirically supported recommendations.

Marek, Block, and Porath conducted a validation of one of the most widely used psychological screening algorithms for predicting spine surgery outcomes, including a worksheet to calculate and apply the algorithm (Marek et al., 2017). In this study, 603 patients underwent a PPS, including a diagnostic interview, psychometric testing (MMPI-2-RF, Patient Self-Reported Survey Data, Owestry Disability Index, and Pain and Impairment Relationship Scale), and review of medical records. A third-party evaluator utilized the PPS algorithm (Block, 2014) for patients by assigning them into prognosis categories. The resulting categories of patients were organized into three prognosis groups: Excellent, Good, and Fair to Very Poor. The patients categorized as having an "Excellent" prognosis attained the best results following surgery, while those in the "Fair" to "Very Poor" category had the worst surgical outcomes. Analyses of specific mechanisms of the PPS algorithm revealed that algorithm items were modestly associated with reduced spinal surgery outcomes. This study supports employing the PPS algorithm for the short-term prediction of spinal surgical outcomes and patient satisfaction (Block, 2014).

Tertiary Treatment and Interdisciplinary Pain Rehabilitation

Patients who have not responded to primary and secondary treatment interventions, or who are suffering from treatment-resistant back pain (Bruce & Quinlan, 2011; Macrae, 2001), are referred to tertiary treatment settings. These settings may specialize in repeat surgery if necessary, spinal cord stimulators (SCS), or a pain rehabilitation program that follows one of several models. Ideally, all levels of care work together to improve the patient's condition. For example, after surgery the patient is returned to the primary care level for long-term monitoring and treatment maintenance. Improvement often takes a long time with a treatment team carefully tracking patient progress (Gawande, 2017).

There are different types of rehabilitation programs currently defined and accredited by the Commission for Accreditation of Rehabilitation Facilities (CARF). Historically, CARF has required that a psychologist be on the treatment team for most rehabilitation programs. Three types of programs are particularly relevant to this discussion: 1) comprehensive integrated inpatient rehabilitation; 2) outpatient medical rehabilitation; and 3) interdisciplinary pain rehabilitation. Notably, estimates of opiate use in pain rehabilitation settings range from 30%

to over 90% (Manchikanti, 2006; Manchikanti, Damron, McManus, & Barnhill, 2004). Thus, if addiction is present, inpatient treatment may be required prior to, or as a part of, the patient's participation in these programs. Outpatient day treatment programs are often preferred by third-party payers due to the high cost of hospitalization.

The Functional Restoration Approach

The interdisciplinary pain management orientation we will focus on here is often termed the functional restoration (FR) approach. According to Gatchel and Okifuji (2006), essential characteristics of FR are:

- Formal, repeated quantification of physical deficits to monitor physical training progress
- Psychosocial and socioeconomic assessment to monitor functional outcomes
- Multimodal disability management programs using cognitive-behavioral approaches
- Psychopharmacological interventions for detoxification and psychological management
- Interdisciplinary, medically directed team approach with frequent team conferences
- Ongoing outcome assessment using standardized objective criteria

---

Different practitioners who are part of the functional restoration team include medical providers, physical therapists, occupational therapists, case managers, nurses, vocational therapists, pain management specialists, nurses, and psychologists. The FR approach begins with education and orientation sessions provided by the leadership of the program, preferably the entire team. By definition, patients with back pain in the tertiary setting already have been exposed to other interventions and may have received inaccurate information about their chronic condition and prognosis. For example, patients often received lifting restrictions that they continue to follow for years after the necessity has lapsed or were prescribed bed rest in an acute care setting and continue to adhere to this long after helpful (Feinberg, Gatchel, Stanos, Feinberg, & Johnson-Montieth, 2015).

The elements of FR can be grouped generally into both physical and psychological approaches. Physical approaches include assessment of strength, sensation, range of motion, aerobic capacity, and endurance, as well as measures of work-related activities and activities of daily living (ADLs). Physical therapy goals of these programs focus on restoring joint mobility and posture, as well as increasing muscle strength, endurance, conditioning, and cardiovascular fitness. Physical therapists aim to train patients in exercise techniques that they later can do regularly and independently in the home environment without close supervision.

The psychologist has an important role in the physical therapies that are part of the FR approach and works closely with the physical and occupational therapists. For example, psychologists often apply biofeedback techniques based on electromyography and respiration. These techniques can directly impact pain mechanisms by reducing autonomic arousal and muscle tension, restoring paraspinal muscle symmetry, improving posture, and encouraging relaxation and coping strategies (Cram, 1990; Neblett, 2016). Biofeedback facilitates the development of patient self-efficacy over body control and particularly is effective with patients who are initially receptive to somatic explanations of their condition and resistant to psychological approaches.

Practicing ADLs, strengthening, and conditioning are integral parts of physical treatment. In addition, if done correctly, these exercises also provide a natural exposure therapy for kinesiophobia. Patients judge the threat value of the various activities prior to commencing, begin with the least fear-inducing exercises, and advance gradually through the hierarchy to the most feared. If a patient reaches a subjective unit of distress (SUDS) rating level in their fear of injury or pain hierarchy they can no longer tolerate, then they take breaks and use relaxation and coping techniques practiced with the psychologist.

Given the progressively challenging physical activities that are an inherent part of these programs, flare-ups are inevitable. Flare-ups are a precipitous worsening of chronic pain that can feel unmanageable and can be extremely demoralizing for even the most motivated patient. The physical reactions to these flare-ups may include disrupted breathing, muscle spasms, tightening of chest and stomach muscles, and nausea. Psychological reactions may include anxiety, panic, catastrophizing, and anger. The treatment team encourages patient self-management during flare-ups with tools that include ice packs, TENS, diaphragmatic breathing, relaxation techniques, distraction, and visual imagery.

Activity pacing is one of the most important skills taught within the context of fear exposure and the avoidance of flare-ups. Patients often have a history of alternating between excessive exertion before they are physically ready, and complete helplessness and avoidance of activity after perceived failure. Pacing requires that the patient regulate daily activities so as to not over-exert themselves in the moment, and to increase tolerance gradually by increasing activity. Pacing requires the patient to plan for an activity, anticipate its duration, and break it into active and rest periods as necessary. The psychologist guides the individual to be mindful in scheduling his/her day, structuring any physical activity, and avoiding impulsivity. Activity pacing often is applied to daily exercises and work simulations that ultimately generalize to the home and work environments.

The psychologist often is involved in interventions targeting social and interpersonal variables, as one of the most significant causes of suffering in patients with chronic pain is stark social isolation (Carr & Moffett, 2005; Oliveira et al., 2015). Many chronic pain patients have had to quit work and their worlds have shrunk to the boundaries of their homes; at the same time, family members continue their daily occupational and school activities. Therefore, the FR program becomes analogous to a full-time job and provides a daily structure and schedule. Group classes provide a context for rehearsal and feedback for social interactions with individuals other than family members.

Social interventions also include the family. Spouses are asked to attend some sessions to provide them with updates about the pain management exercises and techniques the patient is learning. Family involvement throughout the program helps ensure treatment generalization. For example, significant others often are unaware of their enabling and punishing responses that maintain the patient's state. Enabling responses are termed "solicitousness" and include avoiding conflict and performing simple activities for the patient (McCracken, 2005). Like bed rest, solicitous responses may be helpful during the acute phase of injury, but they undermine recovery in the long term. Research indicates that family solicitousness actually interferes with patients developing healthy coping techniques and is associated with higher overt pain behavior and maladaptive thinking such as catastrophizing (McCracken, 2005).

The type of psychological intervention emphasized in FR is CBT. CBT in the tertiary treatment setting is more intense and often includes the exposure techniques described above. It focuses on how beliefs, negative moods, unhealthy behaviors, and attitudes undermine the patient's progress toward a constructive and adaptive lifestyle. The goals of CBT in FR include the following (Feinberg et al., 2015):

- Combat demoralization by helping patients change their perceptions of pain from overwhelming to manageable
- Teach patients coping strategies and techniques to help them adapt and respond to pain and secondary negative functional impacts
- Assist patients with reconceptualizing themselves as active, resourceful, and competent
- Teach patients the associations between thoughts, feelings, and behaviors, and subsequently how to identify and alter automatic, maladaptive patterns
- Encourage utilization of more adaptive ways of thinking, feeling, and behaving
- Bolster self-efficacy and patients' attribution of successful outcomes to their own efforts
- Help patients anticipate problems proactively and generate solutions, thereby facilitating maintenance and generalization

Psychological and pain measures used in FR are the same as those utilized at the other levels of intervention presented elsewhere in this chapter. Here we broadly outline various disability self-report measures used to evaluate FR outcomes, as they are frequently used in this context. These self-report measures are used to quantify functional disability and activities of daily living and to monitor progress for chronic back pain patients in FR programs (Table 9.2).

At the end of the FR restoration program, the patient typically is released with a Functional Capacity Evaluation (FCE) resulting from a systematic assessment of

Table 9.2 Self-Report Measures of Disability, Activities of Daily Living, and Functional Outcomes Used in FR

Name of Measure	Description	Number of Items	Author
Roland-Morris Disability Questionnaire	Covers daily physical activities and functions: housework, sleeping, mobility, dressing, getting help, appetite, irritability, and pain severity that may be impacted by chronic back pain	24	Roland and Morris (1983)
Oswestry Disability Index	Covers pain severity and daily physical activities, such as social engagement, lifting, walking, sleep, personal care, sex life, etc.	10	Fairbank and Pynsent (2000)
Pain Disability Index	Evaluate pain in several areas: social, sexual, and occupational functioning, self-care, family/home, and recreation	7	Tait, Chibnall, and Krause (1990)
Low Back Pain Rating Scale (LBPRS)	Measures three components of low back pain: pain (back and leg), disability, and physical impairment	21	Manniche et al. (1994)
Quebec Back Pain Disability Scale	Daily physical activities classified into six domains of activity affected by back pain: bed/rest, sitting/ standing, ambulation, movement, bending/ stooping, and handling of large/heavy objects	20	Kopec et al. (1995)
The Fear-Avoidance Components Scale (FACS)	A patient-reported measure evaluating pain-related fear and avoidance in patients with chronic and painful medical conditions	20	Neblett et al. (2017)

the individual's physical capacities and functional abilities completed over several days. Physical and/or occupational therapists with specialized training in this area of assessment are the key personnel who administer FCE testing, which includes direct observation and performance testing. An FCE's main goal is to measure the patient's physical capabilities and performance level within the context of work demands. As such, it is readily used by vocational counselors employed by third parties for job placement, occupational disability, and return to work status. FCE testing may answer questions about whether a patient needs occupational accommodations, restrictions, or modifications, or if there is residual physical disability and impairment (Feinberg & Brigham, 2015).

Evidence for Functional Restoration

The preponderance of studies published over several decades strongly supports the effectiveness of interdisciplinary pain rehabilitation and FR. A systematic literature review of randomized controlled trials of a total of 1,964 patients with disabling back pain revealed that an intensive interdisciplinary rehabilitation with an FR orientation improved overall functioning and reduced pain compared to outpatient non-multidisciplinary rehabilitation or usual care (Guzmán et al., 2001). There are now numerous systematic reviews showing the overall effectiveness of FR programs, rating them as a "strong recommendation, high-quality evidence" (Bosy, Etlin, Corey, & Lee, 2010; Chou et al., 2009).

Long-term savings also are associated with interdisciplinary care. One study found that patients who received chronic pain treatment from comprehensive pain clinics had fewer emergency room and primary care visits than patients receiving treatment in other settings (Rodríguez & García, 2007). Further, patients have significantly decreased medication and healthcare utilization (including surgeries) and fewer sick days from work when involved in comprehensive pain programs (Cunningham, Rome, Kerkvliet, & Townsend, 2009; Ektor-Andersen, Ingvarsson, Kullendorff, & Orbaek, 2008). As such, patients conceivably could save hundreds of thousands of dollars of healthcare costs related to long-term disability (Cunningham et al., 2009; Ektor-Andersen et al., 2008; Gatchel, McGeary, McGeary, & Lippe, 2014).

The effectiveness of pain rehabilitation programs has been called into question recently with a meta-analysis that suggests weak effects being attributed to the behavioral and psychological aspects of the FR program compared to treatment as usual (O'Keeffe et al., 2016). Gatchel and Licciardone (2017) have responded that the O'Keeffe et al. (2016) meta-analysis included many "multidisciplinary" programs that "carved-out" two or three interventions that were provided at different locations to reduce costs. They argue this results in fragmentation and incomplete care and does not represent true FR. This debate undoubtedly will continue as long as outcomes are based on self-report disability measures with limited scope and generalizability. In the future, FR outcomes should be evaluated and compared using a standardized set of performance measures, such as what is obtained in the FCE (Gatchel & Licciardone, 2017).

Conclusions

Chronic back pain is a worldwide health problem that impacts many individuals' adaptive functioning and quality of life and is associated with significant economic and occupational burdens. In this chapter, we have described different intervention approaches across the continuum of care anchored in the biopsychosocial model. The preponderance of studies published over several decades strongly supports the effectiveness of psychosocial interventions used in chronic back pain treatment and management. Psychological services add value at primary, secondary, and tertiary levels of care. The continuum of care provides many opportunities to implement psychological assessment and treatment, including CBT, PPS, and interdisciplinary pain rehabilitation to improve treatment outcomes, coordinate personalized intervention, and promote quality of life.

References

AdAA. (2015). *Facts & statistics*. Anxiety and Depression Association of America, ADAA. Retrieved from http://www.adaa.org/about-adaa/press-room/facts-statistics

Adams, M. A. (2004). Biomechanics of back pain. *Acupuncture in Medicine*, 22(4), 178–188.

Ader, D. N. (2007). Developing the Patient-Reported Outcomes Measurement Information System (PROMIS). *Medical Care*, 45(5), S1–S2. doi:10.1097/01.mlr.0000260537.45076.74

Alsaadi, S. M., McAuley, J. H., Hush, J. M., Lo, S., Bartlett, D. J., Grunstein, R. R., & Maher, C. G. (2014). The bidirectionl relationship between pain intensity and sleep disturbance/quality in patients with low back pain. *Clinical Journal of Pain*, 30(9), 755–765. doi:10.1097/ajp.0000000000000055

Alsaadi, S. M., McAuley, J. H., Hush, J. M., & Maher, C. G. (2011). Prevalence of sleep disturbance in patients with low back pain. *European Spine Journal*, 20(5), 737–743. doi:10.1007/s00586-010-1661-x

Amtmann, D., Cook, K. F., Jensen, M. P., Chen, W-H., Choi, S., Revicki, D., . . . Callahan, L. (2010). Development of a PROMIS item bank to measure pain interference. *Pain*, 150(1), 173–182. doi:10.1016/j.pain.2010.04.025

Andersson, G. B. (1999). Epidemiological features of chronic low-back pain. *Lancet*, 354(9178), 581–585. doi:10.1016/s0140-6736(99)01312-4

Asmundson, G. J. G., & Norton, G. R. (1995). Anxiety sensitivity in patients with physically unexplained chronic back pain: A preliminary report. *Behaviour Research and Therapy*, 33(7), 771–777. https://doi.org/10.1016/0005-7967(95)00012-M

Atlas, S. J., & Deyo, R. A. (2001). Evaluating and managing acute low back pain in the primary care setting. *Journal of General Internal Medicine*, 16(2), 120–131. doi:10.1111/j.1525-1497.2001.91141.x

Block, A., Ohnmeiss, D., Ben-Porath, Y., & Burchett, D. (2011). Presurgical psychological screening: A new algorithm, including the MMPI-2-RF, for predicting surgery results. *The Spine Journal*, 11(10), S137–S138. doi:10.1016/j.spinee.2011.08.333

Block, A. R., Marek, R. J., Ben-Porath, Y. S., & Kukal, D. (2017). Associations between pre-implant psychosocial factors and spinal cord stimulation outcome: Evaluation using the MMPI-2-RF. *Assessment*, 24(1), 60–70. doi:10.1177/1073191115601518

Block, A. R., Marek, R. J., Ben-Porath, Y. S., & Ohnmeiss, D. D. (2014). Associations between Minnesota Multiphasic Personality Inventory-2-Restructured Form (MMPI-2-RF) scores, workers' compensation status, and spine surgery outcome. *Journal of Applied Biobehavioral Research*, 19(4), 248–267. doi:10.1111/jabr.12028

Bosy, D., Etlin, D., Corey, D., & Lee, J. W. (2010). An interdisciplinary pain rehabilitation programme: Description and evaluation of outcomes. *Physiotherapy Canada, 62*(4), 316–326. doi:10.3138/physio.62.4.316

Bruce, J., & Quinlan, J. (2011). Chronic post surgical pain. *Reviews in Pain, 5*(3), 23–29. doi:10.1177/204946371100500306

Bruns, D., & Disorbio, J. M. (2009). Assessment of biopsychosocial risk factors for medical treatment: A collaborative approach. *Journal of Clinical Psychology in Medical Settings, 16*(2), 127–147. doi:10.1007/s10880-009-9148-9

Bruns, D., & Disorbio, J. M. (2014). The psychological evaluation of patients with chronic pain: A review of BHI 2 clinical and forensic interpretive considerations. *Psychological Injury and Law, 7*(4), 335–361.

Campbell, T. S., Johnson, J. A., & Zernicke, K. A. (2013). Gate control theory of pain. In M. D. Gellman & J. R. Turner (Eds.), *Encyclopedia of behavioral medicine* (pp. 832–834). New York, NY: Springer.

Carr, J. L., & Moffett, J. A. (2005). The impact of social deprivation on chronic back pain outcomes. *Chronic Illness, 1*(2), 121–129. doi:10.1177/17423953050010020901

Carragee, E. J., & Hannibal, M. (2004). Diagnostic evaluation of low back pain. *Orthopedic Clinics of North America, 35*(1), 7–16. doi:10.1016/s0030-5898(03)00099-3

CDC. (2006). *National center for health statistics chartbook on trends in the health of Americans.* Retrieved from www.cdc.gov/nchs/data/hus/hus06.pdf.

CDC. (2015). *National center for health statistics, United States, 2015: With special feature on racial and ethnic health disparities.* Retrieved from https://www.cdc.gov/nchs/data/hus/hus15.pdf

Cella, D., Riley, W., Stone, A., Rothrock, N., Reeve, B., Yount, S., . . . Hays, R. (2010). Initial adult health item banks and first wave testing of the Patient-Reported Outcomes Measurement Information System (PROMIS(™)) network: 2005–2008. *Journal of Clinical Epidemiology, 63*(11), 1179–1194. doi:10.1016/j.jclinepi.2010.04.011

Cella, D., Yount, S., Rothrock, N., Gershon, R., Cook, K., Reeve, B., . . . Rose, M. (2007). The Patient-Reported Outcomes Measurement Information System (PROMIS): Progress of an NIH roadmap cooperative group during its first two years. *Medical Care, 45*(5 Suppl 1), S3–S11. doi:10.1097/01.mlr.0000258615.42478.55

Chan, C-W., & Peng, P. (2011). Failed back surgery syndrome. *Pain Medicine, 12*(4), 577–606. doi:10.1111/j.1526-4637.2011.01089.x

Chou, R., Loeser, J. D., Owens, D. K., Rosenquist, R. W., Atlas, S. J., Baisden, J., . . . Wall, E. M. (2009). Interventional therapies, surgery, and interdisciplinary rehabilitation for low back pain: An evidence-based clinical practice guideline from the American pain society. *Spine (Phila Pa 1976), 34*(10), 1066–1077. doi:10.1097/BRS.0b013e3181a1390d

Chou, R., Qaseem, A., Snow, V., Casey, D., Cross, J. T. Jr., Shekelle, P., & Owens, D. K. (2007). Diagnosis and treatment of low back pain: A joint clinical practice guideline from the American college of physicians and the American pain society. *Annals of Internal Medicine, 147*(7), 478–491.

Cook, K. F., Keefe, F., Jensen, M. P., Roddey, T. S., Callahan, L. F., Revicki, D., . . . Amtmann, D. (2013). Development and validation of a new self-report measure of pain behaviors. *Pain, 154*(12), 2867–2876. doi:10.1016/j.pain.2013.08.024

Cram, J. R. (1990). *Clinical EMG for surface recordings: Volume 2* (Vol. 2): Aspen Publishers.

Crombez, G., Eccleston, C., Van Damme, S., Vlaeyen, J. W., & Karoly, P. (2012). Fear-avoidance model of chronic pain: The next generation. *The Clinical Journal of Pain, 28*(6), 475–483. doi:10.1097/AJP.0b013e3182385392

Cunningham, J. L., Rome, J. D., Kerkvliet, J. L., & Townsend, C. O. (2009). Reduction in medication costs for patients with chronic nonmalignant pain completing a pain rehabilitation program: A prospective analysis of admission, discharge, and 6-month follow-up medication costs. *Pain Medicine, 10*(5), 787–796. doi:10.1111/j.1526-4637.2009.00582.x

DeBar, L. L., Kindler, L., Keefe, F. J., Green, C. A., Smith, D. H., Deyo, R. A., . . . Feldstein, A. (2012). A primary care-based interdisciplinary team approach to the treatment of chronic pain utilizing a pragmatic clinical trials framework. *Translational Behavioral Medicine, 2*(4), 523–530. doi:10.1007/s13142-012-0163-2

de Heer, E. W., Gerrits, M. M. J. G., Beekman, A. T. F., Dekker, J., van Marwijk, H. W. J., de Waal, M. W. M., . . . van der Feltz-Cornelis, C. M. (2014). The association of depression and anxiety with pain: A study from NESDA. *PLoS One, 9*(10), e106907. doi:10.1371/journal.pone.0106907

Deyo, R. A. (1993). Practice variations, treatment fads, rising disability: Do we need a new clinical research paradigm? *Spine (Phila Pa 1976), 18*(15), 2153–2162.

Deyo, R. A., Mirza, S. K., Turner, J. A., & Martin, B. I. (2009). Overtreating chronic back pain: Time to back off? *Journal of the American Board of Family Medicine: JABFM, 22*(1), 62–68. doi:10.3122/jabfm.2009.01.080102

Deyo, R. A., Nachemson, A., & Mirza, S. K. (2004). Spinal-fusion surgery—the case for restraint. *New England Journal of Medicine, 350*(7), 722–726. doi:10.1056/NEJMsb031771

Deyo, R. A., & Weinstein, J. N. (2001). Low back pain. *New England Journal of Medicine, 344*(5), 363–370. doi:10.1056/nejm200102013440508

Disorbio, J. M., Bruns, D., & Barolat, G. (2006). Assessment and treatment of chronic pain. *Practical Pain Management, 6*(2), 1–10.

Doan, L., Manders, T., & Wang, J. (2015). Neuroplasticity underlying the comorbidity of pain and depression. *Neural Plasticity, 504691.* doi:10.1155/2015/504691

Dobscha, S. K., Corson, K., Perrin, N. A., Hanson, G. C., Leibowitz, R. Q., Doak, M. N., . . . Gerrity, M. S. (2009). Collaborative care for chronic pain in primary care: A cluster randomized trial. *JAMA, 301*(12), 1242–1252. doi:10.1001/jama.2009.377

Edwards, R. R., Dworkin, R. H., Sullivan, M. D., Turk, D. C., & Wasan, A. D. (2016). The role of psychosocial processes in the development and maintenance of chronic pain. *The Journal of Pain, 17*(9 Suppl), T70–92. doi:10.1016/j.jpain.2016.01.001

Ehde, D. M., Dillworth, T. M., & Turner, J. A. (2014). Cognitive-behavioral therapy for individuals with chronic pain: Efficacy, innovations, and directions for research. *American Psychologist, 69*(2), 153.

Ektor-Andersen, J., Ingvarsson, E., Kullendorff, M., & Orbaek, P. (2008). High cost-benefit of early team-based biomedical and cognitive-behaviour intervention for long-term pain-related sickness absence. *Journal of Rehabilitation Medicine, 40*(1), 1–8. doi:10.2340/16501977-0127

Elfering, A., Käser, A., & Melloh, M. (2014). Relationship between depressive symptoms and acute low back pain at first medical consultation, three and six weeks of primary care. *Psychology, Health & Medicine, 19*(2), 235–246. doi:10.1080/13548506.2013.780131

Engel, G. L. (1978). The biopsychosocial model and the education of health professionals. *Annals of the New York Academy of Sciences, 310,* 169–187.

Evers, S., Hsu, C., Sherman, K. J., Balderson, B., Hawkes, R., Brewer, G., . . . Cherkin, D. (2017). Patient perspectives on communication with primary care physicians about chronic low back pain. *The Permanente Journal, 21,* 16–177. doi:10.7812/TPP/16-177

Fairbank, J. C., & Pynsent, P. B. (2000). The Oswestry disability index. *Spine, 25*(22), 2940–2953.

Feinberg, S. D., & Brigham, C. R. (2015). Assessing disability in the pain patient. In *Treatment of chronic pain by integrative approaches* (pp. 285–297). New York, NY: Springer.

Feinberg, S. D., Gatchel, R. J., Stanos, S., Feinberg, R., & Johnson-Montieth, V. (2015). Interdisciplinary functional restoraion and pain programs. In *Treatment of chronic pain by integrative approaches* (pp. 169–182). New York, NY: Springer.

Fernandez, M., Colodro-Conde, L., Hartvigsen, J., Ferreira, M. L., Refshauge, K. M., Pinheiro, M. B., . . . Ferreira, P. H. (2017). Chronic low back pain and the risk of depression or anxiety symptoms: Insights from a longitudinal twin study. *The Spine Journal, 17*(7), 905–912. doi:10.1016/j.spinee.2017.02.009

Fillingim, R. B., Bruehl, S., Dworkin, R. H., Dworkin, S. F., Loeser, J. D., Turk, D. C., . . . Wesselmann, U. (2014). The ACTTION-American Pain Society Pain Taxonomy (AAPT): An evidence-based and multidimensional approach to classifying chronic pain conditions. *The Journal of Pain, 15*(3), 241–249. doi:10.1016/j.jpain.2014.01.004

Fishbain, D. A., Bruns, D., Disorbio, J. M., & Lewis, J. E. (2009). Correlates of self-reported violent ideation against physicians in acute- and chronic-pain patients. *Pain Medicine, 10*(3), 573–585. doi:10.1111/j.1526-4637.2009.00606.x

Fishbain, D. A., Bruns, D., Lewis, J. E., Disorbio, J. M., Gao, J., & Meyer, L. J. (2011). Predictors of homicide-suicide affirmation in acute and chronic pain patients. *Pain Medicine, 12*(1), 127–137. doi:10.1111/j.1526-4637.2010.01013.x

Freburger, J. K., Holmes, G. M., Agans, R. P., Jackman, A. M., Darter, J. D., Wallace, A. S., . . . Carey, T. S. (2009). The rising prevalence of chronic low back pain. *Archives of Internal Medicine, 169*(3), 251–258. doi:10.1001/archinternmed.2008.543

Fritzell, P., Hagg, O., & Nordwall, A. (2003). Complications in lumbar fusion surgery for chronic low back pain: Comparison of three surgical techniques used in a prospective randomized study. A report from the Swedish lumbar Spine study group. *European Spine Journal, 12*(2), 178–189. doi:10.1007/s00586-002-0493-8

Gatchel, R. J., & Okifuji, A. (2006). Evidence-based scientific data documenting the treatment and cost-effectiveness of comprehensive pain programs for chronic nonmalignant pain. *The Journal of Pain, 7*(11), 779–793. doi:10.1016/j.jpain.2006.08.005

Gatchel, R. J., & Licciardone, J. C. (2017). Potential problems with systematic reviews and meta-analyses. *Journal of Pain, 18*(2), 228–229. doi:10.1016/j.jpain.2016.09.006

Gatchel, R. J., McGeary, D. D., McGeary, C. A., & Lippe, B. (2014). Interdisciplinary chronic pain management: Past, present, and future. *American Psychologist, 69*(2), 119–130. doi:10.1037/a0035514

Gatchel, R. J., & Rollings, K. H. (2008). Evidence informed management of chronic low back pain with cognitive behavioral therapy. *The Spine Journal: Official Journal of the North American Spine Society, 8*(1), 40–44. doi:10.1016/j.spinee.2007.10.007

Gawande, A. (2017, January 23). The heroism of incremental care. *The New Yorker.*

Gerhart, J. I., Burns, J. W., Post, K. M., Smith, D. A., Porter, L. S., Burgess, H. J., . . . Keefe, F. J. (2017). Relationships between sleep quality and pain-related factors for people with chronic low back pain: Tests of reciprocal and time of day effects. *Annals of Behavioral Medicine, 51*(3), 365–375. doi:10.1007/s12160-016-9860-2

Guzmán, J., Esmail, R., Karjalainen, K., Malmivaara, A., Irvin, E., & Bombardier, C. (2001). Multidisciplinary rehabilitation for chronic low back pain: Systematic review. *British Medical Journal, 322*(7301), 1511–1516. doi:10.1136/bmj.322.7301.1511

Hadjistavropoulos, H. D., Asmundson, G. J., & Kowalyk, K. M. (2004). Measures of anxiety: Is there a difference in their ability to predict functioning at three-month follow-up among pain patients? *European Journal of Pain, 8*(1), 1–11. doi:10.1016/s1090-3801(03)00059-4

Hart, L. G., Deyo, R. A., & Cherkin, D. C. (1995). Physician office visits for low back pain. Frequency, clinical evaluation, and treatment patterns from a US national survey. *Spine, 20*(1), 11–19.

Hartzell, M. M., Liegey-Dougall, A., Kishino, N. D., & Gatchel, R. J. (2016). Utility of pain drawings rated for non-organic pain in chronic low back pain populations: A qualitative systematic review. *Journal of Applied Biobehavioral Research, 21*(3), 162–187. doi:10.1111/jabr.12048

Hassett, A. L., Aquino, J. K., & Ilgen, M. A. (2014). The risk of suicide mortality in chronic pain patients. *Current Pain Headache Reports, 18*(8), 436. doi:10.1007/s11916-014-0436-1

Hoy, D., March, L., Brooks, P., Blyth, F., Woolf, A., Bain, C., . . . Buchbinder, R. (2014). The global burden of low back pain: Estimates from the global burden of disease 2010 study. *Annals of the Rheumatic Disease, 73*(6), 968–974. doi:10.1136/annrheumdis-2013-204428

Hunter, C. L., Goodie, J. L., Oordt, M. S., & Dobmeyer, A. C. (2017). *Integrated behavioral health in primary care: Step-by-step guidance for assessment and intervention, 2nd ed.* Washington, DC, US: American Psychological Association.

Ilgen, M. A., Zivin, K., Austin, K. L., Bohnert, A. S., Czyz, E. K., Valenstein, M., & Kilbourne, A. M. (2010). Severe pain predicts greater likelihood of subsequent suicide. *Suicide Life Threat Behav, 40*(6), 597–608. doi:10.1521/suli.2010.40.6.597

IOM. (2011). *Relieving pain in America: A blueprint for transforming prevention, care, education, and research.* Washington, DC: The National Academies Press.

Jungquist, C. R., O'Brien, C., Matteson-Rusby, S., Smith, M. T., Pigeon, W. R., Xia, Y., . . . Perlis, M. L. (2010). The efficacy of cognitive-behavioral therapy for insomnia in patients with chronic pain. *Sleep Medicine, 11*(3), 302–309. doi:10.1016/j.sleep.2009.05.018

Karoly, P., Ruehlman, L. S., Aiken, L. S., Todd, M., & Newton, C. (2006). Evaluating chronic pain impact among patients in primary care: Further validation of a brief assessment instrument. *Pain Medicine, 7*(4), 289–298. doi:10.1111/j.1526-4637.2006.00182.x

Katz, J. N. (2006). Lumbar disc disorders and low-back pain: Socioeconomic factors and consequences. *The Journal of Bone Joint Surgery American, 88* (Suppl 2), 21–24. doi:10.2106/jbjs.e.01273

Kennedy, J., Roll, J. M., Schraudner, T., Murphy, S., & McPherson, S. (2014). Prevalence of persistent pain in the U.S. adult population: New data from the 2010 national health interview survey. *The Journal of Pain, 15*(10), 979–984. https://doi.org/10.1016/j.jpain.2014.05.009

Kopec, J. A., Esdaile, J. M., Abrahamowicz, M., Abenhaim, L., Wood-Dauphinee, S., Lamping, D. L., & Williams, J. I. (1995). The Quebec Back Pain Disability Scale. Measurement properties. *Spine, 20*(3), 341–352.

LaCaille, R. A., DeBerard, M. S., Masters, K. S., Colledge, A. L., & Bacon, W. (2005). Presurgical biopsychosocial factors predict multidimensional patient: Outcomes of interbody cage lumbar fusion. *Spine, 5*(1), 71–78. doi:10.1016/j.spinee.2004.08.004

Lamb, S. E., Hansen, Z., Lall, R., Castelnuovo, E., Withers, E. J., Nichols, V., . . . Underwood, M. R. (2010). Group cognitive behavioural treatment for low-back pain in primary care: A randomised controlled trial and cost-effectiveness analysis. *Lancet, 375*(9718), 916–923. doi:10.1016/s0140-6736(09)62164-4

Lewis, G., Sharp, D., Bartholomew, J., & Pelosi, A. J. (1996). Computerized assessment of common mental disorders in primary care: Effect on clinical outcome. *Family Practice, 13*(2), 120–126.

Löfman, S., Räsänen, P., Hakko, H., & Mainio, A. (2011). Suicide among persons with back pain: A population-based study of 2310 suicide victims in Northern Finland. *Spine (Phila Pa 1976), 36*(7), 541–548. doi:10.1097/BRS.0b013e3181f2f08a

Löwe, B., Unützer, J., Callahan, C. M., Perkins, A. J., & Kroenke, K. (2004). Monitoring depression treatment outcomes with the patient health questionnaire-9. *Medical Care, 42*(12), 1194–1201.

Lucas, A. J. (2012). Failed back surgery syndrome: Whose failure? Time to discard a redundant term. *British Journal of Pain, 6*(4), 162–165. doi:10.1177/2049463712466517

Lurie, J. D., Birkmeyer, N. J., & Weinstein, J. N. (2003). Rates of advanced spinal imaging and spine surgery. *Spine (Phila Pa 1976), 28*(6), 616–620. doi:10.1097/01.brs.0000049927.37696.dc

Macrae, W. A. (2001). Chronic pain after surgery. *BJA: British Journal of Anaesthesia, 87*(1), 88–98. doi:10.1093/bja/87.1.88

Mafi, J. N., McCarthy, E. P., Davis, R. B., & Landon, B. E. (2013). Worsening trends in the management and treatment of back pain. *JAMA Internal Medicine, 173*(17), 1573–1581. doi:10.1001/jamainternmed.2013.8992

Manchikanti, L. (2006). Prescription drug abuse: What is being done to address this new drug epidemic? Testimony before the subcommittee on criminal justice, drug policy and human resources. *Pain Physician, 9*(4), 287–321.

Manchikanti, L., Damron, K. S., McManus, C. D., & Barnhill, R. C. (2004). Patterns of illicit drug use and opioid abuse in patients with chronic pain at initial evaluation: A prospective, observational study. *Pain Physician, 7*(4), 431–437.

Manniche, C., Asmussen, K., Lauritsen, B., Vinterberg, H., Kreiner, S., & Jordan, A. (1994). Low Back Pain Rating scale: Validation of a tool for assessment of low back pain. *Pain, 57*(3), 317–326.

Mannion, A. F., & Elfering, A. (2006). Predictors of surgical outcome and their assessment. *European Spine Journal, 15*(Suppl 1), S93–S108. doi:10.1007/s00586-005-1045-9

Marek, R. J., Block, A. R., & Ben-Porath, Y. S. (2017). Validation of a psychological screening algorithm for predicting spine surgery outcomes. *Assessment.* doi:10.1177/1073191117719512

Marin, R., Cyhan, T., & Miklos, W. (2006). Sleep disturbance in patients with chronic low back pain. *Am J Phys Med Rehabil, 85*(5), 430–435. doi:10.1097/01.phm.0000214259.06380.79

Martell, B. A., O'Connor, P. G., Kerns, R. D., Becker, W. C., Morales, K. H., Kosten, T. R., & Fiellin, D. A. (2007). Systematic review: Opioid treatment for chronic back pain: Prevalence, efficacy, and association with addiction. *Annals of Internal Medicine, 146*(2), 116–127.

Martin, B. I., Deyo, R. A., Mirza, S. K., Turner, J. A., Comstock, B. A., Hollingworth, W., & Sullivan, S. D. (2008). Expenditures and health status among adults with back and neck problems. *JAMA, 299*(6), 656–664. doi:10.1001/jama.299.6.656

McCracken, L. M. (2005). Social context and acceptance of chronic pain: The role of solicitous and punishing responses. *Pain, 113*(1–2), 155–159. doi:10.1016/j.pain.2004.10.004

McCracken, L. M., & Iverson, G. L. (2002). Disrupted sleep patterns and daily functioning in patients with chronic pain. *Pain Research Management, 7*(2), 75–79.

McMahon, S. B., Koltzenburg, M., Tracey, I., & Turk, D. (2013). *Wall & Melzack's textbook of pain: Expert consult-online and print.* Philadelphia, PA: Elsevier Health Sciences.

Melzack, R. (1987). The short-form McGill pain questionnaire. *Pain, 30*(2), 191–197.

Melzack, R., & Wall, P. D. (1965). Pain mechanisms: A new theory. *Science, 150*(3699), 971–979.

Meucci, R. D., Fassa, A. G., & Faria, N. M. X. (2015). Prevalence of chronic low back pain: Systematic review. *Revista de Saúde Pública, 49*, 1–1. doi:10.1590/S0034-8910.2015049005874

Meyer, G. J., Finn, S. E., Eyde, L. D., Kay, G. G., Moreland, K. L., Dies, R. R., . . . Reed, G. M. (2001). Psychological testing and psychological assessment. A review of evidence and issues. *American Psychologist, 56*(2), 128–165.

Mills, S., Torrance, N., & Smith, B. H. (2016). Identification and management of chronic pain in primary care: A review. *Current Psychiatry Report, 18*(2), 22. doi:10.1007/s11920-015-0659-9

Murray, C. J., Atkinson, C., Bhalla, K., Birbeck, G., Burstein, R., Chou, D., . . . Murray. (2013). The state of US health, 1990–2010: Burden of diseases, injuries, and risk factors. *Jama, 310*(6), 591–608. doi:10.1001/jama.2013.13805

Neblett, R. (2016). Surface electromyographic (SEMG) biofeedback for chronic low back pain. *Healthcare, 4*(2), 27. doi:10.3390/healthcare4020027

Neblett, R., Hartzell, M. M., Williams, M., Bevers, K. R., Mayer, T. G., & Gatchel, R. J. (2017). Use of the Central Sensitization Inventory (CSI) as a treatment outcome measure for patients with chronic spinal pain disorder in a functional restoration program. *Spine, 17*(12), 1819–1829. doi:10.1016/j.spinee.2017.06.008

Nguyen, T. H., Randolph, D. C., Talmage, J., Succop, P., & Travis, R. (2011). Long-term outcomes of lumbar fusion among workers' compensation subjects: A historical cohort study. *Spine (Phila Pa 1976), 36*(4), 320–331. doi:10.1097/BRS.0b013e3181ccc220

[NIH], N. I. o. H. (2015). *Low back pain fact sheet*. Retrieved from www.ninds.nih.gov/ Disorders/Patient-Caregiver-Education/Fact-Sheets/Low-Back-Pain-Fact-Sheet

[NIH], N. I. o. H. (2018). *Health measures PROMIS*. Retrieved from www.healthmeasures. net/explore-measurement-systems/promis

O'Keeffe, M., Purtill, H., Kennedy, N., Conneely, M., Hurley, J., O'Sullivan, P., . . . O'Sullivan, K. (2016). Comparative effectiveness of conservative interventions for nonspecific chronic spinal pain: Physical, behavioral/psychologically informed, or combined? A systematic review and meta-analysis. *Journal of Pain, 17*(7), 755–774. doi:10.1016/j. jpain.2016.01.473

Oliveira, V. C., Ferreira, M. L., Morso, L., Albert, H. B., Refshauge, K. M., & Ferreira, P. H. (2015). Patients' perceived level of social isolation affects the prognosis of low back pain. *European Journal of Pain, 19*(4), 538–545. doi:10.1002/ejp.578

Patrick, N., Emanski, E., & Knaub, M. A. (2014). Acute and chronic low back pain. *Medical Clinics of North America, 98*(4), 777–789, xii. doi:10.1016/j.mcna.2014.03.005

Phelan, S. M., van Ryn, M., Wall, M., & Burgess, D. (2009). Understanding primary care physicians' treatment of chronic low back pain: The role of physician and practice factors. *Pain Medicine, 10*(7), 1270–1279. doi:10.1111/j.1526-4637.2009.00717.x

Philips, H. C. (1987). Avoidance behaviour and its role in sustaining chronic pain. *Behaviour Research and Therapy, 25*(4), 273–279. doi:https://doi.org/10.1016/0005-7967 (87)90005-2

Pinnington, M. A., Miller, J., & Stanley, I. (2004). An evaluation of prompt access to physiotherapy in the management of low back pain in primary care. *Family Practice, 21*(4), 372–380. doi:10.1093/fampra/cmh406

Plomp, K. A., Viðarsdóttir, U. S., Weston, D. A., Dobney, K., & Collard, M. (2015). The ancestral shape hypothesis: An evolutionary explanation for the occurrence of intervertebral disc herniation in humans. *BMC Evolutionary Biology, 15*(1), 68. doi:10.1186/ s12862-015-0336-y

Rabey, M. (2001). Interaction between pain physiology and movement-based therapy: Opinion. *Physiotherapy, 87*(7), 338–340. https://doi.org/10.1016/S0031-9406(05)60865-6

Ransford, A. O., Cairns, D., & Mooney, V. (1976). The pain drawing as an aid to the psychologic evaluation of patients with low-back pain. *Spine, 1*(2), 127–134.

Revicki, D. A., Chen, W. H., Harnam, N., Cook, K. F., Amtmann, D., Callahan, L. F., . . . Keefe, F. J. (2009). Development and psychometric analysis of the PROMIS pain behavior item bank. *Pain, 146*(1–2), 158–169. doi:10.1016/j.pain.2009.07.029

Robinson, P., & Reiter, J. (2007). *Behavioral consultation and primary care*. Springer Science+ Business Media, LLC.

Roditi, D., & Robinson, M. E. (2011). The role of psychological interventions in the management of patients with chronic pain. *Psychology Research and Behavior Management, 4*, 41–49. doi:10.2147/PRBM.S15375

Rodríguez, M. J., & García, A. J. (2007). A registry of the aetiology and costs of neuropathic pain in pain clinics. *Clinical Drug Investigation, 27*(11), 771–782. doi:10.2165/00044011-200727110-00004

Roland, M., & Morris, R. (1983). A study of the natural history of low-back pain. Part II: Development of guidelines for trials of treatment in primary care. *Spine* (Phila Pa 1976), *8*(2), 145–150.

Ross, E. M. (2018). *Figure 1 Melzack and Wall's (1965) Gate Control Theory of Pain* [Hand Illustration].

Rubin, D. I. (2007). Epidemiology and risk factors for spine pain. *Neurologic Clinics, 25*(2), 353–371. doi:10.1016/j.ncl.2007.01.004

Sagheer, M. A., Khan, M. F., & Sharif, S. (2013). Association between chronic low back pain, anxiety and depression in patients at a tertiary care centre. *Journal of Pakistan Medical Association, 63*(6), 688–690.

Sanzarello, I., Merlini, L., Rosa, M. A., Perrone, M., Frugiuele, J., Borghi, R., & Faldini, C. (2016). Central sensitization in chronic low back pain: A narrative review. *Journal of Back and Musculoskeletal Rehabilitation, 29*(4), 625–633. doi:10.3233/bmr-160685

Schofferman, J., Anderson, D., Hines, R., Smith, G., & White, A. (1992). Childhood psychological trauma correlates with unsuccessful lumbar spine surgery. *Spine (Phila Pa 1976), 17*(6 Suppl), S138–144.

Sheffer, C. E., Cassisi, J. E., Ferraresi, L. M., Lofland, K. R., & McCracken, L. M. (2002). Sex differences in the presentation of chronic low back pain. *Psychology of Women Quarterly, 26*(4), 329–340.

Shmagel, A., Foley, R., & Ibrahim, H. (2016). Epidemiology of chronic low back pain in US adults: Data from the 2009–2010 national health and nutrition examination survey. *Arthritis Care Res (Hoboken), 68*(11), 1688–1694. doi:10.1002/acr.22890

Spitzer, R. L., Kroenke, K., Williams, J. B., & Löwe, B. (2006). A brief measure for assessing generalized anxiety disorder: The GAD-7. *Archives of Internal Medicine, 166*(10), 1092–1097.

Tait, R. C., Chibnall, J. T., & Krause, S. (1990). The pain disability index: psychometric properties. *Pain, 40*(2), 171–182.

Taloyan, M., Alinaghizadeh, H., & Lofvander, M. (2013). Short-term cognitive-behavioral treatment in multicultural primary care of patients with longstanding backache. *Scandinavian Journal of Psychology, 54*(5), 371–375. doi:10.1111/sjop.12061

Tang, N. K., & Crane, C. (2006). Suicidality in chronic pain: A review of the prevalence, risk factors and psychological links. *Psychological Medicine, 36*(5), 575–586. doi:10.1017/s0033291705006859

Tang, N. K., Goodchild, C. E., Hester, J., & Salkovskis, P. M. (2012). Pain-related insomnia versus primary insomnia: A comparison study of sleep pattern, psychological characteristics, and cognitive-behavioral processes. *Clinical Journal of Pain, 28*(5), 428–436. doi:10.1097/AJP.0b013e31823711bc

Tang, N. K., Wright, K. J., & Salkovskis, P. M. (2007). Prevalence and correlates of clinical insomnia co-occurring with chronic back pain. *Journal of Sleep Research, 16*(1), 85–95. doi:10.1111/j.1365-2869.2007.00571.x

Thomsen, K., Christensen, F. B., Eiskjaer, S. P., Hansen, E. S., Fruensgaard, S., & Bunger, C. E. (1997). 1997 Volvo award winner in clinical studies. The effect of pedicle screw instrumentation on functional outcome and fusion rates in posterolateral lumbar spinal fusion: A prospective, randomized clinical study. *Spine (Phila Pa 1976), 22*(24), 2813–2822.

Thomson, S. (2013). Failed back surgery syndrome—definition, epidemiology and demographics. *British Journal of Pain, 7*(1), 56–59. doi:10.1177/2049463713479096

Turk, D. C., & Meichenbaum, D. (1984). A cognitive-behavioral approach to pain management. In P. D. Wall, & R. Melzack. (Eds.), *Textbook of pain* (pp. 787–794). New York, NY: Churchill-Livingstone.

Turk, D. C., Meichenbaum, D., Melzack, R., & Wall, P. (2000). *A cognitive-behavioral approach to pain management*. In P. D. Wall, & R. Melzack (Eds.), *Textbook of pain*, (3rd ed.) (pp. 1337–1349). New York, NY: Churchill Livingstone.

Vlaeyen, J. W. S., & Linton, S. J. (2000). Fear-avoidance and its consequences in chronic musculoskeletal pain: A state of the art. *Pain, 85*(3), 317–332. https://doi.org/10.1016/S0304-3959(99)00242-0

Von Korff, M., Balderson, B. H., Saunders, K., Miglioretti, D. L., Lin, E. H., Berry, S., . . . Turner, J. A. (2005). A trial of an activating intervention for chronic back pain in primary care and physical therapy settings. *Pain, 113*(3), 323–330. doi:10.1016/j.pain.2004.11.007

Waddell, G., McCulloch, J. A., Kummel, E., & Venner, R. M. (1980). Nonorganic physical signs in low-back pain. *Spine (Phila Pa 1976)*, *5*(2), 117–125.

Wall, P. D. (1978). The gate control theory of pain mechanisms: a re-examination and re-statement. *Brain*, *101*(1), 1–18. doi:10.1093/brain/101.1.1

Webster, B. S., & Cifuentes, M. (2010). Relationship of early magnetic resonance imaging for work-related acute low back pain with disability and medical utilization outcomes. *Journal of Occupational and Environmental Medicine*, *52*(9), 900–907. doi:10.1097/JOM.0b013e3181ef7e53

Weinstein, J. N., Tosteson, T. D., Lurie, J. D., Tosteson, A., Blood, E., Herkowitz, H., . . . An, H. (2010). Surgical versus nonoperative treatment for lumbar spinal stenosis four-year results of the Spine patient outcomes research trial. *Spine (Phila Pa 1976)*, *35*(14), 1329–1338. doi:10.1097/BRS.0b013e3181e0f04d

Wheeler, A. H. (2016). *Low back pain and sciatica medscape*. Retrieved from https://emedicine.medscape.com/article/1144130-overview

Woolf, C. J. (2011). Central sensitization: Implications for the diagnosis and treatment of pain. *Pain*, *152*(3 Suppl), S2–15. doi:10.1016/j.pain.2010.09.030

Young, A. K., Young, B. K., Riley, L. H., 3rd, & Skolasky, R. L. (2014). Assessment of presurgical psychological screening in patients undergoing spine surgery: Use and clinical impact. *Journal of Spinal Disorders & Techniques*, *27*(2), 76–79. doi:10.1097/BSD.0b013e31827d7a92

Zimmerman, M., Lush, D. T., Farber, N. J., Hartung, J., Plescia, G., Kuzma, M. A., & Lish, J. (1996). Primary care patients' reactions to mental health screening. *The International Journal of Psychiatry in Medicine*, *26*(4), 431–441. doi:10.2190/8krc-fjlb-ucga-6caq

10

Cancer-Related Pain

Jinsoon Lee, Amy Wachholtz, Beverly S. Shieh,
and Michael Tees

Introduction

Cancer is a significant public health concern worldwide and is the second leading cause of death in the United States behind heart disease (Centers for Disease Control and Prevention, 2017). In 2016, more than 4,600 Americans were diagnosed with cancer each day (Siegel, Miller, & Jemal, 2016), and the World Health Organization (2017) expects a 70% increase in new cancer diagnoses over the next two decades. Despite increases in cancer prevalence, advances in the fields of oncology, radiation oncology, immunotherapy, and cellular therapy have contributed to remarkable improvements in treatment outcomes; the five-year survival rate for all cancers combined has increased approximately 20% over the past three decades (Siegel et al., 2016). As mortality rates decrease, there is a greater emphasis being placed on improving quality of life during survivorship, including reducing pain. Indeed, pain is one of the most common symptoms reported by patients with a cancer diagnosis and can affect patients at any stage of the disease process, including long into survivorship.

In 1986, the World Health Organization (WHO) developed a systematic approach for treating adult cancer pain, eventually expanding it to include pediatric pain and non-cancer pain (WHO, 1986, 1996, 1998, 2017). Widely known as the 3-Step Ladder, this system summarizes strategies to alleviate cancer-related pain utilizing various medications that include non-opioid, opioid, and adjuvant drugs. It has been used continuously since its original release. The WHO states that this approach is effective in managing 80–90% of cancer-related pain (WHO, 2017, 1986). However, research studies indicate that 25–63% of cancer patients, and up to 90% of advanced stage cancer patients, experience pain (Gardner-Nix & Mercadante, 2010; Pina, Sabri, & Lawlor, 2015; Xia, 2017).

Pain also is a common symptom during cancer survivorship, when it often becomes more chronic in nature. For example, 33% of patients report pain *after* curative therapy, potentially contributing to "treatment inertia" in other areas of treatment such as not engaging in behavioral activation or psychotherapy, dropping out of physical therapy, or having difficulty managing chronic pain effectively (Pergolizzi, Gharibo, & Ho, 2015; van den Beuken-van Everdingen et al., 2007). In this chapter, we discuss mechanisms of chronic pain commonly experienced by cancer patients and survivors, the complex biopsychosocial factors associated with cancer pain, and evidence-based psychological interventions for cancer-related pain.

Pathophysiological Mechanisms of Cancer-Related Pain

Although the classification of cancer pain syndromes is imprecise (Caraceni & Weinstein, 2001), understanding the etiology of cancer-related pain facilitates the determination of appropriate interventions. In general, two pathophysiologic pain mechanisms exist in the cancer patient: nociceptive and neuropathic. Nociceptive and neuropathic pain in cancer patients can be directly associated with disease processes or with the cancer treatments themselves. Additionally, pain may occur prior to or early after diagnosis, during treatment, during survivorship, and/or at the end of life.

Nociceptive

Nociceptive pain is derived from tissue and structural damage that results in activation of nociceptors found in skin, muscle, connective tissue, and visceral structures. Somatic nociceptive pain is described as sharp, localized, and throbbing, and often is present as metastatic bone pain or pain after a surgical intervention (Falk & Dickenson, 2014). Visceral nociceptive pain is described as diffuse, aching, and cramping, and can be present with infiltrating disease or abdominal distention (Portenoy, 1989). A recent study indicates that approximately 30% of cancer patients experience nociceptive visceral pain, 40% of cancer patients experience nociceptive bone pain, and 59% of cancer patients complain of soft-tissue nociceptive pain (Pina et al., 2015).

Neuropathic

Neuropathic pain results from injury to the peripheral or central nervous system, such as pain described within the context of disc herniation, radiation therapy, or chemotherapy (e.g., vincristine or brentuximab vedotin). Neuropathic pain usually is described as shooting or burning sensations, and between 19% and 39% of cancer patients experience this type of pain (Bennett et al., 2012; Waldman, 2010b). Patients with neuropathic pain often experience extreme pain sensations with temperature changes or stimuli that typically evoke normal mild levels of discomfort (Fallon, 2013). Neuropathic pain can occur simultaneously with nociceptive pain, highlighting the importance of identifying the etiologies of pain in order to tailor interventions (Epstein, Wilkie, Fischer, Kim, & Villines, 2009).

Disease-Related Cancer Pain

In patients with persistent disease, tumor infiltration into local tissues may cause a myriad of pain syndromes, such as plexopathies, or tumor invasion into a network of nerves. Plexopathies may cause chronic pain as well as motor and sensory deficits and are diagnosed via electrodiagnostic studies (EMG). Similar to acute cancer pain, the location of the lesion(s) typically drives discomfort. However, the complexity of the nervous system can cause pain to be referred to other locations. For example, in patients with malignancy involving the pelvis, pain can be referred to the lumbar region or upper legs. In certain blood cancer patients with disease involvement in the bone marrow, or in patients with metastatic malignancies with bony involvement, a significant amount of pain can exist in multiple areas of the body (Falk & Dickenson, 2014).

Treatment-Related Cancer Pain

Treatment-related chronic pain in cancer patients can be neuropathic, nociceptive, or mixed. Neuropathic pain is more prevalent, and patients may complain of pain at a site of surgical intervention for years due to local nerve injury. In lung cancer patients requiring surgical resection, post-thoracotomy pain syndrome is well described as a longer-term complication (Hopkins et al., 2015). Post-mastectomy patients have described phantom breast pain, which is thought to develop from local nerve injury followed by abnormal somatosensory cortex reorganization (Hsu & Cohen, 2013; Kroner, Knudsen, Lundby, & Hvid, 1992). In some patients, chronic nociceptive pain can occur at the site of tissue damage from a past surgical procedure (Nersesyan & Slavin, 2007). For example, post-nephrectomy patients may experience chronic pain at the site of intervention (Alper & Yüksel, 2016).

Chemotherapy-induced peripheral neuropathy (CIPN) is a longer-term complication associated with certain chemotherapeutic agents. Platinum-based agents, vinca alkaloids, taxanes, and proteasome inhibitors are classic culprits. Newer antibody-drug conjugates (e.g., brentuximab vedotin) also are associated with peripheral neuropathy. While the onset may manifest within weeks of therapy, symptoms may last for years (Kim, Dougherty, & Abdi, 2015). A large meta-analysis reported the prevalence of CIPN as 68.1% (57.7–78.4) in the first month, 60.0% (36.4–81.6) at three months, and 30.0% (6.4–53.5) at six months or longer from the start of chemotherapy (Seretny et al., 2014). Of the studies reviewed, a majority of patients were treated for colorectal cancer, breast cancer, lung cancer, and multiple myeloma, reflecting the common side effect of neuropathy from the treatments typically used for these diseases. A paucity of data exists on the rate of resolution or improvement in patients with symptoms beyond six months.

Patients receiving immunosuppressive therapy (e.g., chemotherapy, radiation, or steroids) have a higher risk of varicella zoster virus (VZV) reactivation or shingles (Hansson, Forbes, Langan, Smeeth, & Bhaskaran, 2017). Lymphoma patients and those older than 60 years of age also have a higher risk of VZV reactivation (Chua & Chen, 2010). Pain associated with shingles can be quite severe and progress from a dull, aching sensation to hyperalgesia, classically following certain nerve distributions (Waldman, 2010a). After viral reactivation and resolution, many patients can develop postherpetic neuralgia, ranging from mild and self-resolving to severe and debilitating. Patients report persistent burning pain, paresthesia, hypersensitivity, or shock-like pain (Kost & Straus, 1996).

Another form of chronic pain impacting a subpopulation of cancer patients is secondary to chronic graft versus host disease (GVHD). Recipients of an allogeneic stem cell transplant for hematologic malignancies or disorders can experience this longer-term complication when the donor immune system develops an aberrant response against the recipient. In some advanced patients, this may manifest as myofascial or sclerodermatous changes, causing skin or joint tightness and painful skin breakdown. Other manifestations include painful and hypersensitive oral mucosa in oral GVHD, and dyspareunia associated with vaginal GVHD in women (Flowers & Martin, 2015). While treatment to suppress the immune response (e.g., immunosuppression, extracorporeal photopheresis) may reduce the severity of, and possibly reverse, the damage, patient education on the early signs of the disease as well as close follow-up can avoid more severe complications.

Although a discussion of acute and breakthrough pain in cancer patients is outside the scope of this chapter, it is worth mentioning that between 40% and 86% of cancer patients may develop breakthrough pain (Mishra, Bhatnagar, Chaudhary, & Rana, 2009), defined as an acute pain event in the setting of chronic pain control. Patients with breakthrough pain report more overall pain intensity, which contributes to increased overall cost of care through more visits to the clinic, emergency department, and hospital compared to people with controlled pain (Daeninck et al., 2016).

Biopsychosocial Considerations

Chronic pain, including cancer-related chronic pain, is now primarily understood to be a biopsychosocial experience and not simply a physiological phenomenon. Dame Cicely Saunders, founder of the modern hospice movement, coined the term "Total Pain" to describe the biopsychosocial-spiritual influences on a pain experience (Richmond, 2005). In short, biological, psychological, social, and spiritual qualities can impact the patient's pain experience and effectively exacerbate or ameliorate pain.

Psychological Factors Impacting Cancer-Related Pain

Psychological variables that may serve as precipitating or aggravating factors in the pain experiences of cancer patients include mood disturbances, such as anxiety or depression, and overall emotional distress (Breitbart, 1998; Kwon et al., 2013; Wong-Kim & Bloom, 2005). Depression and anxiety are the most common psychological comorbidities, diagnosed in approximately 42% of patients with cancer pain (Dureja, Iyer, Das, Ahdal, & Narang, 2017; Khalil et al., 2016). More generally, studies have demonstrated that negative emotions and stress are associated with increased contraction of muscle tissue through a sympathoexcitatory reaction, likely leading to increased sensations of pain, while positive emotional states reduce the perception of pain intensity and experience (Lumley et al., 2011; Rainville, Bao, & Chretien, 2005).

A patient's negative affect, as well as maladaptive thoughts and beliefs about cancer pain management, may lead to increased pain intensity and increased use of pain medications. A systematic review indicated that cancer patients' misconceptions or maladaptive thoughts toward cancer pain management mediate their analgesic use and ability to communicate effectively with treatment providers about pain, which in turn impacts their ability to manage cancer pain (Jacobsen, Møldrup, Christrup, & Sjøgren, 2009). Specifically, cancer patients' cognitive factors mediating pain management include knowledge, beliefs, attitudes, and concerns about treatment or medication for cancer-related pain (Davis & Walsh, 2004; Sun et al., 2007). For example, if patients believe that a cancer diagnosis means they need to quit their job, lose their friends, and die alone (despite their treatment team providing information to the contrary), then they are more likely to have stronger pain experiences and request more analgesic medications.

Cancer-Related Pain and Substance Abuse

A recent literature review suggests a rising concern about co-occurring substance abuse disorders, which occur in approximately 7.7% of cancer patients and survivors (Pergolizzi et al., 2015). Some patients may have had substance use disorders prior to cancer, while others may develop dependence and/or abuse issues with opioids and/or benzodiazepines during or after cancer treatment. General guidelines and restrictions for opioid prescribing for chronic pain typically exclude patients in active cancer treatment and/or end-of-life care (Centers for Disease Control and Prevention, 2016). Accordingly, many cancer patients are prescribed opioids during active treatment in response to pain (Chwistek & Ewerth, 2016), which may make cancer survivors uniquely at risk for longer-term dependency concerns. Sutradhar, Lokku, and Barbera (2017) found that the opioid prescription rate for cancer survivors was 1.22 times higher than the healthy population. They also identified that low income, younger adult age, rural living environment, and being diagnosed over ten years ago predicted higher rates of opioid use. Koyyalagunta and colleagues (2013) found that nearly 30% of cancer patients were identified as at risk for long-term opioid misuse. Of those in the at-risk population, 27% currently were using alcohol and 54% reported a history of alcohol use.

Cancer-Related Pain and Delirium

Delirium is one of the most common neuropsychological complications in cancer patients, occurring in 33–49% (Gagnon, Allard, Gagnon, Merette, & Tardif, 2010). Reducing risk of delirium in this population is particularly challenging because it may emerge secondary to both pain and pain treatment. Specifically, undertreatment of cancer pain may be associated with delirium (Breitbart, 1998; Coyle, Breitbart, Weaver, & Portenoy, 1994; Kwon et al., 2013). Conversely, de la Cruz et al. (2015) found that opioid use is the most common etiology of delirium experienced among cancer patients. Delirium may be under-recognized in many cancer patients. In de la Cruz and colleagues' study, 61% of the cancer patients with delirium were not diagnosed, and providers were more likely to miss the diagnosis when the patients reported pain.

Cancer-Related Pain and Mortality

Some studies indicate a link between uncontrolled cancer pain and risk of mortality. For example, Halabi and colleagues (2008) investigated the impact of pain interference (i.e., the impact of pain on a patient's ability to engage in activities of daily living) on overall survival among patients with refractory prostate cancer with bone metastases. In this study, the authors identified that the patients with high levels of pain interference at baseline had significantly worse prognostic outcomes compared to those with low levels of pain interference regardless of initial disease status (median survival time = 10.2 months versus 17.6 months, respectively). Inadequate pain management also can contribute to suicidal ideation, which is present in as many as 32% of cancer patients (Daeninck et al., 2016; Syrjala et al., 2014). Cheung, Douwes, and Sundram (2017) investigated potential factors related to increasing rates of suicide among older cancer patients; the majority who died by suicide suffered from uncontrolled pain.

Interpersonal Factors Impacting Cancer-Related Pain

A systematic review of psychosocial factors impacting cancer pain found that variables related to the caregiver often impact the cancer patient's pain experience (Smyth, Dempster, Warwick, Wilkinson, & McCorry, 2018). Specifically, important interpersonal factors influencing the patient's pain levels included the caregiver's knowledge of cancer pain management, the level of burden put on caregivers, relationship distress between the patient and caregiver, and patient satisfaction with the treatment team. However, the authors note that even these identified factors often have been examined only by a single study and that more quantitative research in this area is needed. Additional studies have explored the role of general social support on psychological and biological factors that directly influence the patient's pain experience, such as depressive symptoms and inflammation (Hughes et al., 2014). While not yet studied specifically within the context of cancer pain, positive social support has long been identified as a factor in many other pain conditions that decrease activation levels in biological stress mechanisms (e.g., hypothalamus-pituitary-adrenal axis, cortisol, and pro-inflammatory cytokines) and that contribute to reductions in inflammation, pain, and depression (Uchino, 2006; Slavich & Irwin, 2014).

Notably, the impact of social support on the cancer patient's pain experience appears to depend on both the quantity *and* quality of the social interactions. For example, if a caregiver experiences depression, anxiety, or low self-efficacy, the resultant low quality of interactions can impact the patient's mental and physical health outcomes, including pain (Kershaw et al., 2015). Therefore, providing psychosocial support to cancer caregivers is an important component of overall cancer care.

In general, poorly managed cancer pain impacts patients' well-being and influences their social relationships. Some patients and caregivers develop a closer relationship following a cancer diagnosis; however, others do not. When cancer patients live with significant pain, caregivers can develop resentment secondary to role changes, diverted attention away from other aspects of their lives, and a sense of uncertainty (McPherson, Hadjistavropoulos, Lobchuk, & Kilgour, 2013).

Provider and Healthcare System Factors

Provider-level factors that impact pain control include lack of adequate training and knowledge about cancer pain management among healthcare professionals involved with cancer treatment (Jho, Myung, Chang, Kim, & Ko, 2013; Xia, 2017; Zaza, Sellick, Willan, Reyno, & Browman, 1999); lack of standardized pain management protocols, including systematic pain assessment; and multiple providers overseeing a patient's pain management (Kim et al., 2015; Sun et al., 2007). Sun and colleagues (2007) found that only 7.8% of the cancer patients in their study consistently were screened for pain at each clinic visit during a one-month period.

Healthcare system-level variables also can negatively impact cancer-related pain management. These include shortage of trained healthcare providers skilled in cancer pain management; lack of adequate referral systems; and financial issues that include the cost, insurance, and reimbursement challenges associated with pain management (Jacobsen et al., 2009; Javier et al., 2016; Kim et al., 2015; Linklater, Leng, Tiernan, Lee, & Chambers, 2002; Sun et al., 2007).

Spiritual Factors

The biopsychosocial-spiritual model recognizes the potential mediating role of spiritual and religious variables in cancer-related pain. It is arguable that the cancer-related pain experience, even compared to other forms of chronic pain, is likely to contain an existential or spiritual component due to the real or perceived life-threatening nature of many cancers. Spirituality is a major component in the lives of cancer patients. A series of large meta-analyses showed that cancer patients who routinely engaged in religious or spiritual activities had improved physical well-being and emotional well-being (Jim et al., 2015; Salsman et al., 2015).

Non-theistic psychospiritual meaning-making among chronic pain patients reduces the experience of chronic pain via a reduction of inflammation and an increase in self-efficacy, which results in a lessened pain experience (Dezutter et al., 2013; Dezutter, Luyckx, & Wachholtz, 2015; Lysne & Wachholtz, 2011). This has been shown in both short-term and longitudinal studies (Dezutter et al., 2013; Dezutter, Luyckx, & Wachholtz, 2015). Conversely, patients unable to engage in adaptive meaning-making (and who, as a result, struggle spiritually) likely will experience increased physiological stress that, if not resolved, promotes increased morbidity and mortality over the subsequent two years (Pargament, Koenig, Tarakeshwar, & Hahn, 2001).

Notably, traditional religious frameworks may be less accessible to many patients as society becomes increasingly secular, although many cancer patients continue to report high levels of spirituality (Jim et al., 2015). The lack of pre-established routes of religious tradition to meaning-making leads some individuals to maladaptive approaches for interpreting suffering (e.g., cancer is punishment from God), which in turn negatively impacts quality of life. Ironically, maladaptive searches for psychospiritual meaning, or a sense of lacking meaning, may cause more psychophysiological stress than failing to search at all (Dezutter et al., 2015). Therefore, a psychotherapist trained in existential psychotherapy may be useful for patients who do not have an established faith background but struggle with existential issues that influence their pain experience (Dezutter et al., 2015).

Assessment Measures Useful to Assess Cancer-Related Pain

Brief Pain Inventory

The Brief Pain Inventory (BPI) is an 11-item questionnaire developed by Cleeland and colleagues in the 1970s to assess cancer-related pain and facilitate cancer pain management (Cleeland & Ryan, 1991). Four items assess pain intensity using a 0–10 numerical rating scale. The remaining seven items assess the degree of pain interference using the same 0–10 scale. In clinical settings, the short version of the BPI (a 9-item questionnaire) is widely used with a variety of patient populations, including non-cancer patients, and has become one of the most commonly used pain assessment measures (Atkinson et al., 2011).

Edmonton Symptom Assessment Scale

The Edmonton Symptom Assessment Scale—revised (ESAS-r) is a 10-item questionnaire originally developed by Bruera and colleagues in 1991 (Bruera, Kuehn, Miller, Selmser, & Macmillan, 1991). This assessment uses an 11-point numerical rating scale (0 = "no symptom" to 10 = "the worst possible") to measure ten domains of symptom burden typically endorsed by cancer patients: pain, fatigue, nausea, depression, anxiety, drowsiness, appetite concern, sense of well-being, shortness of breath, and "other concerns." Patients and/or caregivers complete the questionnaire and rate the patient's experience at the time of the assessment. A systematic review suggests that the cutoff for moderate symptom burden ranges from 4 to 5, while the cutoff for severe symptom burden ranges from 7 to 8 (Oldenmenger, de Raaf, de Klerk, & van Der Rijt, 2013). The assessment is available publicly and has been translated into over 20 languages.

Barriers Questionnaire

Barriers Questionnaire II (BQ-II) is a 27-item questionnaire assessing cancer patients' various beliefs and concerns about their cancer pain management (Gunnarsdottir, Donovan, Serlin, Voge, & Ward, 2002). The measure originally was developed by Ward and associates (1993) and includes eight categories that may mediate effective cancer pain management and communication with healthcare providers. These include concerns and beliefs about 1) addiction; 2) analgesics tolerance; 3) side effects; 4) fatalism (e.g., cancer pain is impossible to control); 5) diminished immune system; 6) inability to monitor own symptoms; 7) "good patients" should tolerate pain; and 8) distracting the medical team. Patients rate each item on a Likert scale ranging from 0 ("do not agree at all") to 5 ("agree very much"). The authors suggest calculating the mean score of the total items and subscales to better understand the patient's attitudes and beliefs about cancer pain management. The BQ-II, which has been used primarily in research settings over the years, is identified as a valid and reliable measure (Ward et al., 2009; Wells, Johnson, & Wujeik, 1998). Concurrently, some researchers recognized challenges with the measure, such as its length and floor effect, which led to the development of short versions for clinical use (Boyd-Seale et al., 2010; Ward, Wang, Serlin, Peterson, & Murray, 2009; Wells et al., 1998).

Spiritual Assessment

Multiple spiritual assessment tools have been tried in clinical practice, ranging from the simple (e.g., spiritual distress thermometer) to the more complex (e.g., OASIS interview). Including a spiritual assessment helps the provider identify when to refer the patient for interdisciplinary interventions to address spiritual or existential concerns. To date, the only empirically validated interview is the OASIS (Oncologist Assisted Spiritual Intervention Study), which consists of seven questions designed to lead an oncologist in (and out) of a brief interview to assess spiritual distress, resources, and needs. It has been shown to be acceptable to both patients and physicians, even among those who do not have religious or spiritual beliefs (Kristeller, Rhodes, Cripe, & Sheets, 2005). See Table 10.1.

In a clinical setting, brief quantitative screening tools may be more useful than interviews when assessing patient spiritual-level variables. Empirically validated tools that are widely used for both clinical and research assessment include the Religious/Spiritual Coping Short Form (Brief RCOPE) and the Functional Assessment of Chronic Illness Therapy—Spiritual Well-Being (FACIT-SP; Pargament, Smith, Koenig, & Perez, 1998; Peterman, Fitchett, Brady, Hernandez, & Cella, 2002, respectively). These quantitative questionnaires have utility in light of empirical research indicating connections between spiritual coping style and the pain experience (Bush et al., 1999; Wachholtz, Pearce, & Koenig, 2007).

Evidence-Based Psychological Interventions for Treating Cancer-Related Pain

Psychological interventions are essential components of cancer-related pain management anchored in the biopsychosocial model (Gordon, Dahl, & Miaskowski, 2005). Utilizing psychosocial interventions has been shown empirically to reduce pain associated with cancer (Gorin et al., 2012; Devine & Westlake, 1995; Luebbert, Dahme, & Hasenbring, 2001; Devine, 2003; Tatrow & Montgomery, 2006; Jho et al., 2013; Johannsen, Farver, Beck, & Zachariae, 2013). Additionally, studies report decreases in pain and functional impairments, as well as increases in patient satisfaction, when cancer patients receive pain management with both an individualized and collaborative team approach (e.g., Peng, Wu, Sun, Chen, & Huang, 2006). Interventions targeting patients' adjustment to, and coping with, cancer-related pain are often education- and skills-based (Keefe, Abernethy, & Campbell, 2005; Allard, Maunsell, Labbé, & Dorval, 2001) and are reviewed below.

Education

A patient's lack of knowledge about cancer pain and misconceptions about self-management, medications, and other forms of treatment often serve as barriers to effective pain management (Ward et al., 1993; Kwon, 2014). In education-based intervention, the patient is provided with resources to increase knowledge and awareness about these areas; patient education has been shown to enable people with chronic disease to manage their illnesses and achieve optimal pain control (Gureje, Von Korff, Simon, & Gater, 1998; Hibbard, 2003). Education modalities include face-to-face psychoeducational/didactic individual or group sessions, booklets or other written materials, having the patient act out learned materials (e.g., practice what questions to ask healthcare professionals), and video or audio recordings. Pain education also empowers patients to actively participate in pain management decision-making (Gordon et al., 2005; Hibbard, 2003), facilitating active coping and self-efficacy through open communication and collaborative treatment planning.

In Prevost, Delorme, Grach, Chvetzoff, and Hureau (2015) literature review of 44 published articles on cancer pain education programs (PEPs), more than 80% of the studies found that PEPs improve beliefs regarding cancer pain and its treatment. Specifically, PEPs improve comprehension about medication and its adverse effects, facilitate treatment adherence and opioid dose adjustment, and increase patient satisfaction with cancer pain treatment.

Several studies have investigated which types of education modalities are most effective for cancer-related pain management. Green et al. (2010) analyzed major evidence-based clinical practice guidelines for cancer-related pain and determined that educational interventions should focus on addressing myths and misconceptions about pain, encourage family involvement in pain management, and utilize teaching materials appropriate to age and language (e.g., materials in the patient's first language). Extensive meta-analyses (Cummings et al., 2011; Jho et al., 2013) found the most effective educational interventions to be individualized and tailored face-to-face sessions approximately 30–60 minutes in length with video presentation and written materials.

Technologies such as smartphones, computers, and tablets increasingly are utilized as modalities that make educational materials accessible to wider numbers of people. Several smartphone apps currently in use can increase education (e.g., accessing medical records and pain management instructions/educational materials via online portals) and facilitate behaviors that contribute to cancer-related pain management (e.g., medication compliance reminders, coping skills practice reminders, guided meditations, etc.).

For example, CareZone (Care Zone Inc., 2018) enables patients to track medical appointments, record medications, set medication reminders, and add dictations from medical appointments. The Pocket Cancer Care Guide (National Coalition for Cancer Survivorship, 2015) provides cancer patients with answers to common questions for each stage of cancer and pain management. It also provides patients with an extensive glossary of the medical terms commonly used in cancer treatment. Other common pain management smartphone apps help increase awareness of pain and provide education. Many smartphone apps target pain management by educating patients on ways to track pain triggers and to engage in coping behaviors that help decrease the pain. These apps include CatchMyPain (Sanovation AG, 2016), My Pain Diary (DamoLab, LLC., 2018), and the Pain Scale (Boston Scientific, 2018). Unfortunately, there remains a paucity of research literature examining these apps' efficacy and effectiveness.

Cognitive-Behavioral Therapy

Patients often endorse cognitive, behavioral, and psychological symptoms in response to experiencing cancer-related pain (Syrjala et al., 2014; Gorin et al., 2012). These symptoms correlate with diagnoses of depression, anxiety, and other emotional distress concerns related to the experience of cancer and pain (National Comprehensive Cancer Network Distress Management Panel, 2005). In skills-based interventions, the patient learns pain management techniques to change behaviors and thoughts and to increase coping skills.

Cognitive-behavioral therapy (CBT) is considered a gold standard in pain management. It is highly recommended as part of a comprehensive cancer-related pain management regimen in adjunct to medication and has been shown to be effective for reducing distress and pain (Keefe, 2000; Dalton, Keefe, Carlson, & Youngblood, 2004; American Pain Society, 2005; National Comprehensive Cancer Network, 2006). A variety of techniques fall under the umbrella of CBT, including guided imagery, relaxation, meditation, progressive muscular relaxation (PMR), coping skills training, biofeedback, cognitive restructuring, stress-management techniques, and supportive individual and group therapy (Lebovits, 2007). A meta-analysis of studies utilizing CBT in breast cancer patients demonstrated a significant decrease in pain and distress (Tatrow & Montgomery, 2006). The most evidence-based components of CBTs in cancer patient populations are relaxation and guided imagery, with demonstrated decreases in nausea and anxiety, and improved overall mood states (Luebbert et al., 2001). A randomized controlled study of advanced cancer patients found guided imagery and relaxation techniques to reduce acute pain, fatigue, and sleep symptoms (Kwekkeboom et al., 2012). Dalton et al. (2004) studied standard CBT and profile-tailored CBT to determine the value of matching CBT techniques with cancer patients' profiles. Patient-treatment matching was conducted by administering the Biobehavioral Pain Profile (Dalton, Feuerstein, Carlson, & Roghman, 1994) to assess patient characteristics and needs (e.g., sense of loss of control, avoidance behaviors, perception of past experiences, and beliefs about the disease). CBT techniques subsequently were selected to focus on each patient's characteristics and needs as indicated by this assessment. Patients who received profile-tailored CBT demonstrated greater improvement in overall pain and functionality from baseline to one month post-intervention. However, at six months post-intervention, those who received standard CBT showed greater improvements in pain, overall distress, and quality of life.

Acceptance and Commitment Therapy

Negative beliefs and distress surrounding illness and pain are common in cancer patients, and in some situations working toward tolerating and accepting these symptoms and distress may be more effective long term than altering cognitions (Graham, Simmons, Stuart, & Rose, 2015; Low et al., 2012). A "third-wave" form of CBT called acceptance and commitment therapy (ACT) is being widely incorporated into treatment plans for chronic conditions such as cancer-related pain (Low et al., 2012; Greco, Lambert, & Baer, 2008). ACT does not aim to distract from or reconstruct negative thoughts, but rather focuses on decreasing behavioral impact through acceptance of *all* experiences and by realigning with personal values even amid adversity (Thewes et al., 2014).

ACT has been applied to many long-term conditions such as cancer (Feros, Lane, Ciarrochi, & Blackledge, 2013; Hawkes et al., 2013; Hawkes, Pakenham, Chambers, Patrao, & Courneya, 2014; Rost, Wilson, Buchanan, Hildebrandt, & Mutch, 2012) and chronic pain (Scott, Hann, & McCracken, 2016) and has been shown to improve functioning and distress (Dindo, Recober, Marchman,

Turvey, & O'Hara, 2012; Hann & McCracken, 2014). A pre-post finding of an ACT treatment delivered to participants who completed cancer treatment noted a medium to large improvement in physical pain (Arch & Mitchell, 2015), while other studies also have demonstrated ACT's effectiveness in decreasing pain levels and improving quality of life for cancer patients (Low et al., 2012; Hulbert-Williams, Storey, & Wilson, 2015).

Mindfulness, Meditation, and Hypnosis

Mindfulness often is integrated with CBT and ACT to decrease distress through increased awareness of the present moment in an active, calm, and nonjudgmental manner (Kabat-Zinn, 1990). Mindfulness techniques frequently are used to treat patients with chronic medical conditions such as cancer and pain (Gunaratana, 2002). Several approaches fall within the realm of mindfulness, including meditation and hypnosis. All aim to cultivate an increased or altered state of awareness, to increase openness and acceptance, and to facilitate reframing of current distress (Shennan, Payne, & Fenlon, 2011).

A structured eight- to ten-week group program called mindfulness-based stress reduction (MBSR) originally was created to help patients cope with medical illnesses by targeting emotional management through mindfulness techniques (Bishop, 2002). The program's primary goals include increasing awareness of thoughts and feelings and altering one's reactions and approach to them in order to decrease distress in a stressful situation. The program usually begins with psychoeducation about the psychophysiological connection between stress and emotions, followed by practice of mindfulness skills and meditation. A meta-analysis investigated 64 empirical studies on the health benefits of MBSR in a variety of populations, including people with chronic pain and cancer (Grossman, Niemann, Schmidt, & Walach, 2004). Benefits were found both with quality of life and with physical well-being and medical symptoms (such as sensory pain and physical impairment).

Hypnosis, another approach that facilitates altered awareness, is characterized by inducing a state of suggestibility, absorption, and dissociation (Elkins, Barabasz, Council, & Spiegel, 2015; Spiegel & Spiegel, 2004). Hypnosis has effectively reduced cancer-related pain, particularly when combined with CBT (Wortzel & Spiegel, 2017; US National Institutes of Health, 1995). Studies also have shown benefit when cancer patients engage in self-hypnosis during their treatment to decrease pain (Butler et al., 2009). Self-hypnosis often requires extensive practice and written summaries or audio recordings.

Three fundamental principles have proven effective in achieving hypnotic analgesia: sensory transformation, sensory accommodation, and imagination (Wortzel & Spiegel, 2017). During sensory transformation, the patient focuses on a competing stimulus to combat a painful stimulus (e.g., focus on warmth or tingling in the painful area). With sensory accommodation, the patient's awareness of the pain signal increases and the fear of the pain decreases as the patient begins to understand the function of the pain. In imagination, patients envision themselves in a different environment, such as the beach or the snow. The goal is to detach from the current environment and painful experience.

Spiritual-Based Interventions

Spirituality is increasingly recognized as an important component of psychosocial interventions for cancer-related pain (McClain, Rosenfield, & Breitbart, 2003). However, spirituality continues to be among the components most overlooked in cancer treatment protocols (Breitbart, 2005). Patients diagnosed with cancer often experience both distress over mortality and increased spiritual and existential questioning related to faith, life, death, purpose, and meaning (Taylor, 2000; Rettger et al., 2015).

Psychospiritual integration and transformation (PSIT) is an example of a spiritually based intervention that provides both psychological and spiritual resources to help cancer patients seeking meaning and purpose (Lee et al., 2015). In PSIT, patients in a group treatment format focus on attaining their life purpose, as well as identifying factors that may be hindering that attainment. Awareness increases as they begin to accept their initial reactions (emotions, thoughts, body sensations) and share their experience with the group. Patients are encouraged to increase awareness by utilizing spiritual text, meditation, lyrics, and poems. The spiritual practice in PSIT focuses on building a personal sense of the sacred as a source of motivation and internal support. A systematic literature review conducted by Wei, Liu, Chen, Zhou, and Hu (2016) reviewed the emotional and physical benefits of spiritual intervention among breast cancer survivors. That review found a correlation between spiritual intervention, including PSIT, and several health benefits, including reduced cancer-related chronic pain, increased coping, and higher reported quality of life.

Meaning-making is a specific spiritual-based intervention useful for cancer pain management (Park, 2010a; Park, 2010b). With chronic illnesses, patients often experience distress as they struggle with questions of mortality and questions regarding the impact of the illnesses on their lives. It can be challenging for patients to make meaning of their illness, and meaning-making intervention can assist patients who strive to assimilate or accommodate their current experiences with their pre-illness understandings of life (Lepore, 2001). Helping a patient incorporate his or her experiences with cancer-related pain into a greater sense of purpose may help decrease overall distress (e.g., "I am experiencing pain because it is my body's way of telling me that it is going through changes").

Family and Couple Interventions

Studies show that caregivers and significant others play important roles in cancer pain management. These individuals provide logistical support by aiding with medication management, prompting medication adherence, and supplying massages, cold/heat packs, ointments, and lotions. They provide emotional support through encouragement and distraction (Ferrell, Coehn, Rhiner, & Rozek, 1991). A study conducted by Keefe et al. (2005) investigated the effects of partner-guided cancer pain management on the patient's overall quality of life and pain level. They found a decrease in patient pain, an increase in quality of life, and an increase in the partner's sense of self-efficacy. Interventions most useful to both partner and patient included behavioral rehearsal (role play) with coping skills, relaxation tapes and handouts (with specific directions on coping strategies), and cognitive-behavioral interventions for pain management.

Cancer-related pain affects the patient, his or her primary caregivers, and the patient's significant others (Hodges, Humphris, & Macfarlane, 2005). Hopkins et al. (2015) conducted a systematic literature review on patient family/caregiver interventions and their impact on patient cancer care. These interventions included providing the family with problem-solving, coping, and cognitive-behavioral skills, as well as improving communication skills between caregivers and patients. Specific pain management skills included psychoeducation about pain, tools for assessing pain, pain-coping strategies, and surgical wound care management. Demonstrated improvements included depression and anxiety, quality of life, and patient–caregiver relationship. There also were demonstrated improvements in the patients' pain management and the patients' open reporting of pain to caregivers.

Table 10.1

Action	Example
Introduce spirituality in a neutral manner	"When dealing with chronic pain, many people draw on religious or spiritual beliefs to help cope. It would be helpful to me to know how you feel about this."
Inquire further, adjusting to patient response	1. Positive active faith response 2. Neutral receptive faith response 3. Spiritually distressed faith response 4. Defensive/rejecting faith response "I see, can you tell me more about . . ."
Inquire about ways of finding meaning and sense of peace	"Is there some way in which you are able to find a sense of meaning or peace in the midst of this?"
Inquire about resources	"Whom do you have to talk to about this/these concerns?"
Offer assistance to locate resources	"Perhaps we can arrange for you to talk to someone . . ."; ". . . there's a support group."
Bring inquiry to a close	"I appreciate you discussing these issues with me. May I ask about it again?"

From Kristeller, J. L., Rhodes, M., Cripe, L. D., & Sheets, V. (2005). Oncologist assisted spiritual intervention study (OASIS): Patient acceptability & initial evidence of effects. *The International Journal of Psychiatry in Medicine*, 35(4), 329–347.

Conclusion

Cancer pain is complex, impacted by multiple biopsychosocial-spiritual factors. Managing cancer pain can be challenging due to disease progression and/ or pain exacerbation from cancer treatment. Effective psychosocial intervention focuses on empowering patients to self-manage their cancer-related pain using expanded coping strategies, and often involves caregivers and loved ones. Incorporating psychologists into an integrated cancer care setting helps maximize the comprehensiveness and effectiveness of cancer-related pain management.

References

Allard, P., Maunsell, E., Labbé, J., & Dorval, M. (2001). Educational interventions to improve cancer pain control: A systematic review. *Journal of Palliative Medicine, 4*(2), 191–203.

Alper, I., & Yüksel, E. (2016). Comparison of acute and chronic pain after open nephrectomy versus laparoscopic nephrectomy: A prospective clinical trial. *Medicine, 95*(16), e3433.

American Pain Society. (2005). *Guideline for the management of cancer pain in adults and children.* Glenview, IL: American Pain Society.

Arch, J., & Mitchell, J. (2015). An Acceptance and Commitment Therapy (ACT) group intervention for cancer survivors experiencing anxiety at re-entry. *Psycho-Oncology, 25*(5), 610–615.

Atkinson, T. M., Rosenfield, B. D., Sit, L., Mendoza, T., Fruscione, M., Lavene, D., . . . Basch, E. (2011). Using confirmatory factor analysis to evaluate construct validity on the Brief Pain Inventory (BPI). *Journal of Pain and Symptom Management, 41*(3), 559–565.

Bennett, A., Rayment, C., Hjermstad, M., Aass, N., Caraceni, A., & Kaasa, S. (2012). Prevalence and aetiology of neuropathic pain in cancer patients: A systematic review. *Pain, 153*, 359–365.

Bishop, S. R. (2002). What do we really know about mindfulness-based stress reduction? *Psychosomatic Medicine, 64*(1), 71–83.

Boston Scientific. (2018). *Pain scale-chronic pain coach [Mobile Application Software].* Retrieved from www.painscale.com.

Boyd-Seale, D., Wilkie, D. J., Kim, Y. O., Suarez, M. L., Lee, H., Molokie, R., . . . Zong, S. (2010). Pain barriers: Psychometrics of a 13-item questionnaire. *Nursing Research, 59*(2), 93–101.

Breitbart, W. (1998). Psychotropic adjuvant analgesics for pain in cancer and AIDS. *Psycho-Oncology, 7*, 333–345.

Breitbart, W. (2005). Spirituality and meaning in cancer. *Revue Francophone de Psycho-Oncologie, 4*(4), 237–240.

Bruera, E., Kuehn, N., Miller, M. J., Selmser, P., & Macmillan, K. (1991). The Edmonton Symptom Assessment System (ESAS): A simple method for the assessment of palliative care patients. *Journal of Palliative Care, 7*(2), 6–9. PMID: 1714502.

Bush, E., Rye, M., Brant, C., Emery, E., Pargament, K., & Riessinger, C. (1999). Religious coping with chronic pain. *Applied Psychophysiology and Biofeedback, 24*(4), 249–260.

Butler, L., Koopman, C., Neri, E., Giese-Davis, J., Palesh, O., Thorne-Yocam, K., . . . Spiegel, D. (2009). Effects of supportive-expressive group therapy on pain in women with metastatic breast cancer. *Health Psychology, 28*(5), 579–587. doi:10.1037/a0016124

Caraceni, A., & Weinstein, S. M. (2001). Classification of cancer pain syndromes. *Oncology, 15*(12), 1627–1647.

Care Zone Inc. (2018). *CareZone [Mobile Application Software]*. Retrieved from https://carezone.com/home.

Centers for Disease Control and Prevention. (2016). *CDC guideline for prescribing opioids for chronic pain—United States*. Retrieved from www.cdc.gov/mmwr/volumes/65/rr/rr6501e1.htm

Centers for Disease Control and Prevention. (2017). *Report of death and mortality*. Retrieved from www.cdc.gov/nchs/fastats/deaths.htm

Cheung, G., Douwes, G., & Sundram, F. (2017). Late-life suicide in terminal cancer: A rational act or under-diagnosed depression? *Journal of Pain and Symptom Management, 54*(6), 835–842.

Chwistek, M., & Ewerth, N. (2016). Opioids and chronic pain in cancer survivors: Evolving practice for palliative care clinics. *Journal of Palliative Medicine, 19*(3), 254.

Chua, J.V., & Chen, W. H. (2010). Herpes zoster vaccine for the elderly: Boosting immunity. *Aging Health, 6*(2), 169–176.

Cleeland, C. S., & Ryan, K. M. (1991). The brief pain inventory. *Pain Research Group*, 1–38.

Coyle, N., Breitbart, W., Weaver, S., & Portenoy, R. (1994). Delirium as a contributing factor to "crescendo" pain: Three case reports. *Journal of Pain Symptom Management, 9*(1), 44–47.

Cummings, G. G, Olivo, S. A., Biondo, P. D., Stiles, C. R., Yurtseven, O., Fainsinger, R. L., & Hagen, N. A. (2011). Effectiveness of knowledge translation interventions to improve cancer pain management. *Journal of Pain Symptom Management, 41*(5), 915–939.

Daeninck, P., Gagnon, B., Gallagher, R., Henderson, J. D., Shir, Y., Zimmermann, C., & Lapointe, B. (2016). Canadian recommendations for the management of breakthrough cancer pain. *Current Oncology, 23*(2), 96–108.

Dalton, J. A., Feuerstein, M., Carlson, J., & Roghman, K. (1994). Biobehavioral pain profile: Development and psychometric properties. *Pain, 57*(1), 95–107.

Dalton, J. A., Keefe, F., Carlson, J., & Youngblood, R. (2004). Tailoring cognitive-behavioral treatment for cancer pain. *Pain Management Nursing, 5*(1), 3–18.

DamoLab, LLC. (2018). *My pain diary [Mobile Application Software]*. Retrieved from http://mypaindiary.com.

Davis, M. P., & Walsh, D. (2004). Epidemiology of cancer pain and factors influencing poor pain control. *The American Journal of Hospice & Palliative Care, 21*(2), 137–142. https://doi:10.1177/104990910402100213

De la Cruz, M., Fan, J., Yennu, S., Tanco, K., Shin, S. H., Wu, J., . . . Bruera, E. (2015). The frequency of missed delirium in patients referred to palliative care in a comprehensive cancer center. *Supportive Care in Cancer, 23*(8), 2427–2433. https://doi.org/10.1007/s00520-015-2610-3

Devine, E. (2003). Meta—analysis of the effect of psychoeducational interventions on pain in adults with cancer. *Oncology Nursing Forum, 30*(1), 75–89.

Devine, E., & Westlake, S. (1995). The effects of psychoeducational care provided to adults with cancer: Meta—analysis of 116 studies. *Oncology Nursing Forum, 22*(9), 1369–1381.

Dezutter, J., Casalin, S., Wachholtz, A., Luyckx, K., Hekking, J., & Vandewiele, W. (2013). Meaning in life: An important factor for the psychological well-being of chronically ill patients? *Rehabilitation Psychology, 58*(4), 334–341.

Dezutter, J., Luyckx, K., & Wachholtz, A. (2015). Meaning in life in chronic pain patients over time: Associations with pain experience and psychological well-being. *Journal of Behavioral Medicine, 38*, 384–396. doi:10.1007/s10865-014-9614-1

Dindo, L., Recober, A., Marchman, J., Turvey, C., & O'Hara, M. (2012). One-day behavioral treatment for patients with comorbid depression and migraine: A pilot study. *Behaviour Research and Therapy, 50*(9), 537–543.

Dureja, G. P., Iyer, R. N., Das, G., Ahdal, J., & Narang, P. (2017). Evidence and consensus recommendations for the pharmacological management of pain in India. *Journal of Pain Research, 10*, 709–736. doi: 10.2147/JPR.S128655

Elkins, G., Barabasz, A., Council, J., & Spiegel, D. (2015). Advancing research and practice: The revised APA division 30 definition of hypnosis. *International Journal of Clinical Experimental Hypnosis*, *63*(1), 1–9. doi:10.1080/00207144.2014.961870

Epstein, J. B., Wilkie, D. J., Fischer, D. J., Kim, Y-O., & Villines, D. (2009). Neuropathic and nociceptive pain in head and neck cancer patients receiving radiation therapy. *Head & Neck Oncology*, *1*(1), 26.

Falk, S., & Dickenson, A. H. (2014). Pain and nociception: Mechanisms of cancer-induced bone pain. *Journal of Clinical Oncology*, *32*(16), 1647–1654.

Fallon, M. T. (2013). Neuropathic pain in cancer. *British Journal of Anaesthesia*, *111*(1), 105–111.

Feros, D., Lane, L., Ciarrochi, J., & Blackledge, J. (2013). Acceptance and Commitment Therapy (ACT) for improving the lives of cancer patients: A preliminary study. *Psycho-Oncology*, *22*(2), 459–464. http://dx.doi.org/10.1002/pon.2083.

Ferrell, B. R., Cohen, M. Z., Rhiner, M., & Rozek, A. (1991). Pain as a metaphor for illness. Part II: Family caregivers' management of pain. *Oncology Nursing Forum*, *18*(8), 1315–1321.

Flowers, M. E. D., & Martin, P. J. (2015). How we treat chronic graft-versus-host disease. *Blood*, *125*(4), 606–615. doi:10.1182/blood-2014-08-551994

Gagnon, P., Allard, P., Gagnon, B., Merette, C., & Tardif, F. (2012). Delirium prevention in terminal cancer: Assessment of a multicomponent intervention. *Psycho-Oncology*, *21*, 187–194.

Gardner-Nix, J., & Mercadante, S. (2010). The role of OROS® Hydromorphone in the management of cancer pain. *Pain Practice: The Official Journal of World Institute of Pain*, *10*(1), 72–77. doi:10.1111/j.1533-2500.2009.00313.x

Gordon, D., Dahl, J., & Miaskowski, C. (2005). American pain society recommendations for improving the quality of acute and cancer pain management: American pain society quality of care task force. *Archives of Internal Medicine*, *165*(14), 1574–1580.

Gorin, S., Krebs, P., Badr, H., Janke, E., Jim, H., Spring, B., & Jacobson, P. B. (2012). Meta-analysis of psychosocial interventions to reduce pain in patients with cancer. *Journal of Clinical Oncology*, *30*(5), 539–547.

Graham, C., Simmons, Z., Stuart, S., & Rose, M. (2015). The potential of psychological interventions to improve quality of life and mood in muscle disorders. *Muscle & Nerve*, *52*(1), 131–136. http://dx.doi.org/10.1002/mus.24487.

Greco, L., Lambert, W., & Baer, R. (2008). Psychological inflexibility in childhood and adolescence: Development and evaluation of the avoidance and fusion questionnaire for youth. *Psychological Assessment*, *20*, 93–102.

Green, E., Zwaal, C., Beals, C., Beals, C., Fitzgerald, B., Harle, I., . . . Wiernikowski, J. (2010). Cancer-related pain management: A report of evidence-based recommendations to guide practice. *Clinical Journal of Pain*, *26*(6), 449–462.

Grossman, P., Niemann, L., Schmidt, S., & Walach, H. (2004). Mindfulness-based stress reduction and health benefits: A meta-analysis. *Journal of Psychosomatic Research*, *57*(1), 35–43.

Gunaratana, H. (2002). *Mindfulness in plain English*. Boston, MA: Wisdom Publications.

Gunnarsdottir, S., Donovan, H. S., Serlin, R. C., Voge, C., & Ward, S. (2002). Patient-related barriers to pain management: The barriers questionnaire II (BQ-II). *Pain*, *99*, 385–396.

Gureje, O., Von Korff, M., Simon, G., & Gater, R. (1998). Persistent pain and well-being: A world health organization study in primary care. *Journal of American Medical Association*, *280*(2), 147–151.

Halabi, S., Vogelzang, N. J., Kornblith, A. B., Ou, S. S., Kantoff, P. W., Dawson, N. A., & Small, E. J. (2008). Pain predicts overall survival in men with metastatic castration-refractory prostate cancer. *Journal of Clinical Oncology*, *26*(15), 2544–2549.

Hann, K., & McCracken, L. (2014). A systematic review of randomized controlled trials of acceptance and commitment therapy for adults with chronic pain: Outcome domains, design quality, and efficacy. *Journal of Contextual Behavioral Science, 3*(4), 217–227.

Hansson, E., Forbes, H. J., Langan, S. M., Smeeth, L., & Bhaskaran, K. (2017). Herpes zoster risk after 21 specific cancers: Population-based case-control study. *British Journal of Cancer, 116*(12):1643–1651.

Hawkes, A., Chambers, S., Pakenham, K., Patrao, T., Baade, P., Lynch, B., . . . Courneya, K. S. (2013). Effects of a telephone-delivered multiple health behavior change intervention (Can Change) on health and behavioral outcomes in survivors of colorectal cancer: A randomized controlled trial. *Journal of Clinical Oncology, 31*(18), 2313–2321.

Hawkes, A., Pakenham, K., Chambers, S., Patrao, T., & Courneya, K. (2014). Effects of a multiple health behavior change intervention for colorectal cancer survivors on psychosocial outcomes and quality of life: A randomized controlled trial. *Annals of Behavioral Medicine, 48*(3), 359–370. http://dx.doi.org/10.1007/s12160-014-9610-2.

Hibbard, J. (2003). Engaging healthcare consumers to improve the quality of care. *Medical Care, 41*(1), 161–170.

Hodges, L. J., Humphris, G. M., & Macfarlane, G. (2005). A meta-analytic investigation of the relationship between the psychological distress of cancer patients and their carers. *Social Science & Medicine, 60*(1), 1–12.

Hopkins, K. G., Hoffman, L. A., Dabbs Ade, V., Ferson, P. F., King, L., Dudjak, L. A., . . . Rosenzweig, M. Q. (2015). Postthoracotomy pain syndrome following surgery for lung cancer: Symptoms and impact on quality of life. *Journal of Advanced Practical Oncology, 6*(2), 121–132.

Hsu, E., & Cohen, S. P. (2013). Postamputation pain: Epidemiology, mechanisms, and treatment. *Journal of Pain Research, 6*, 121–136.

Hughes, S., Jaremka, L. M., Alfano, C. M., Glaser, R., Povoski, S. P., Lipari, A. M., . . . Kiecolt-Glaser, J. K. (2014). Social support predicts inflammation, pain, and depressive symptoms: Longitudinal relationships among breast cancer survivors. *Psychoneuroendocrinology, 42*, 38–44.

Hulbert-Williams, N., Storey, L., & Wilson, K. (2015). Psychological interventions for patients with cancer: Psychological flexibility and the potential utility of Acceptance and Commitment Therapy. *European Journal of Cancer Care, 24*(1), 15–27.

Jacobsen, R., Møldrup, C., Christrup, L., & Sjøgren, P. (2009). Patient-related barriers to cancer pain management: a systematic exploratory review. *Scandinavian Journal of Caring Sciences, 23*(1), 190–208. doi: 10.1111/j.1471-6712.2008.00601.x

Javier, F. O., Irawan, C., Mansor, M. B., Sriraj, W., Tan, K. H., & Thinh, D. H. Q. (2016). Cancer pain management insights and reality in Southeast Asia: Expert perspectives from six countries. *Journal of Global Oncology, 2*(4), 235–243. doi:10.1200/JGO.2015.001859

Jho, H., Myung, S., Chang, Y., Kim, D., & Ko, D. (2013). Efficacy of pain education in cancer patients. *Supportive Care in Cancer, 21*(7), 1963–1971.

Jim, H. S. L., Pustejovsky, J. E., Park, C. L., Danhauer, S. C., Sherman, A. C., Fitchett, G., . . . Salsman, J. M. (2015). Religion, spirituality, and physical health in cancer patients: A meta-analysis. *Cancer, 121*, 3760–3768.

Johannsen, M., Farver, I., Beck, N., & Zachariae, R. (2013). The efficacy of psychosocial intervention for pain in breast cancer patients and survivors: A systematic review and meta-analysis. *Breast Cancer Research and Treatment, 138*(3), 675–690.

Kabat-Zinn, J. (1990). *Full catastrophe living: Using the wisdom of your body and mind to face stress, pain, and illness.* New York, NY: Delacourt.

Keefe, F. (2000). Can cognitive-behavioral therapies succeed where medical treatments fail? In M. Devor, M. C. Rowbotham, & Z. Wiesenfeld-Hallin (Eds.), *Proceedings of the 9th world congress on pain* (Vol. 16, pp. 1069–1084). Seattle, Washington, DC: International Association for the Study of Pain Press.

Keefe, F. J., Abernethy, A. P., & Campbell, L. (2005). Psychological approaches to understanding and treating disease-related pain. *Annual Review of Psychology, 56*, 601–630. doi:10.1146/annurev.psych.56.091103.070302.

Kershaw, T., Ellis, K., Yoon, H., Schafenacker, A., Katapodi, M., & Northouse, L. (2015). The interdependence of advanced cancer patients' and their family caregivers' mental health, physical health, and self-efficacy over time. *Annals of Behavioral Medicine, 49*(6), 901–911.

Khalil, A., Faheem, M., Fahim, A., Innocent, H., Mansoor, Z., Rizvi, S., Farrukh, H. (2016). Prevalence of depression and anxiety amongst cancer patients in a hospital setting: A cross-sectional study. *Psychiatry Journal*, 2016, 1–6.

Kim, J. H., Dougherty, P. M., & Abdi, S. (2015). Basic science and clinical management of painful and non-painful chemotherapy-related neuropathy. *Gynecologic Oncology, 136*(3), 453–459. doi:10.1016/j.ygyno.2015.01.524

Kost, R. G., & Straus, S. E. (1996). Postherpetic neuralgia—pathogenesis, treatment, and prevention. *New England Journal of Medicine, 335*(1), 32–42. doi:10.1056/nejm199607043350107

Koyyalagunta, D., Bruera, E., Aigner, C., Nusrat, H., Driver, L., & Novy, D. (2013). Risk stratification of opioid misuse among patients with cancer pain using the SOAPP-SF. *Pain Medicine, 14*, 667–675.

Kristeller, J. L., Rhodes, M., Cripe, L. D., & Sheets, V. (2005). Oncologist assisted spiritual intervention study (OASIS): Patient acceptability & initial evidence of effects. *The International Journal of Psychiatry in Medicine, 35*(4), 329–347.

Kroner, K., Knudsen, U. B., Lundby, L., & Hvid, H. (1992). Long-term phantom breast syndrome after mastectomy. *Clinical Journal of Pain, 8*(4), 346–350.

Kwekkeboom, K., Abbott-Anderson, K., Cherwin, C., Roiland, R., Serlin, R. C., & Ward, S. E. (2012). Pilot randomized controlled trial of a patient-controlled cognitive-behavioral intervention for the pain, fatigue, and sleep disturbance symptom cluster in cancer. *Journal of Pain and Symptom Management, 44*(6), 810–822.

Kwon, J. H. (2014). Overcoming barriers in cancer pain management. *Journal of Clinical Oncology, 32*(16), 1727–1733. doi:10.1200/JCO.2013.52.4827.

Kwon, J. H., Hui, D., Chisholm, G., Hong, W. T., Nguyen, L., & Bruera, E. (2013). Experience of barriers to pain management in patients receiving outpatient palliative care. *Journal of Palliative Medicine, 16*(8), 908–914.

Lebovits, A. (2007). Cognitive-behavioral approaches to chronic pain. *Primary Psychiatry, 14*(9), 48–54.

Lee, Y., Wu, C., Chiu, T., Chen, C., Morita, T., Hung, S., . . . Tsai, J. (2015). The relationship between pain management and psychospiritual distress in patients with advanced cancer following admission to a palliative care unit. *BMC Palliative Care, 14*(1), 69.

Lepore, S. (2001). A social-cognitive processing model of emotional adjustment to cancer. In A. Baum & B. Anderson (Eds.), *Psychosocial interventions for cancer* (pp. 99–118). Washington, DC: American Psychological Association.

Linklater, G. T., Leng, M. E. F., Tiernan, E. J. J., Lee, M. A., & Chambers, W. A. (2002). Pain management services in palliative care: A national survey. *Pain Reviews, 9*(3–4), 135–140. doi:10.1191/0968130202pr195oa

Low, J., Davis, S., Drake, R., King, M., Tookman, A., Turner, K., . . . Jones, L. (2012). The role of acceptance in rehabilitation in life-threatening illness. *Journal of Pain and Symptom Management, 43*(1), 20–28. doi:10.1016/j.jpainsymman.2011.03.020.

Luebbert, K., Dahme, B., & Hasenbring, M. (2001). The effectiveness of relaxation training in reducing treatment-related symptoms and improving emotional adjustment in acute non-surgical cancer treatment: A meta-analytical review. *Psycho-Oncology, 10*, 490–502.

Lumley, M. A., Cohen, J. L., Borszcz, G. S., Cano, A., Radcliffe, A. M., Porter, L. S., . . . Keefe, F. J. (2011). Pain and emotion: A biopsychosocial review of recent research. *Journal of Clinical Psychology, 67*(9), 942–968. doi:10.1002/jclp.20816

Lysne, C. J., & Wachholtz, A. B. (2011). Pain, spirituality, and meaning making: What can we learn from the literature? *Religions*, *2*, 1–16. doi:10.3390/rel2010001

McClain, C., Rosenfield, B., & Breitbart, W. (2003). Effect of spiritual well-being on end-of-life despair in terminally-ill cancer patients. *Lancet*, *361*, 1603–1607.

McPherson, C. J., Hadjistavropoulos, T., Lobchuk, M. M., & Kilgour, K. N. (2013). Cancer-related pain in older adults receiving palliative care: Patients and family caregiver perspectives on the experience of pain. *Pain Research and Management*, *18*(6), 293–300.

Mishra, S., Bhatnagar, S., Chaudhary, P., & Rana, S. P. S. (2009). Breakthrough cancer pain: Review of prevalence, characteristics and management. *Indian Journal Palliative Care*, *15*(1):14–18.

National Coalition for Cancer Survivorship. (2015). *Pocket cancer care guide [Mobile Application Software]*. Retrieved from www.canceradvocacy.org/resources/pocket-care-guide/.

National Comprehensive Cancer Network Distress Management Panel. (2005, February 24). *Clinical practice guidelines in oncology: Distress management* (Vol. 1) [Data file]. Retrieved from NCCN Web site www.nccn.org

National Comprehensive Cancer Network. NCCN clinical practice guidelines in oncology: Acute cancer pain (Version 1.2006). Retrieved November 20, 2006, from www.nccn.org

Nersesyan, H., & Slavin, K. V. (2007). Current approach to cancer pain management: Availability and implications of different treatment options. *Therapeutics and Clinical Risk Management*, *3*(3), 381–400.

Oldenmenger, W. H., de Raaf, P. J., de Klerk, C., & ven der Rijt, C. C. D. (2013). Cut points on 0–10 numeric rating scales for symptoms included in the Edmonton symptom assessment scale in cancer patients: A systematic review. *Journal of Pain and Symptom Management*, *45*(6), 1083–1093.

Pargament, K. I., Koenig, H. G., Tarakeshwar, N., & Hahn, J. (2001). Religious struggle as a predictor of mortality among medically ill elderly patients. *Archives of Internal Medicine*, *161*, 1881–1885.

Pargament, K. I., Smith, B., Koenig, H. G., & Perez, L. (1998). Patterns of positive and negative religious coping with major life stressors. *Journal for the Scientific Study of Religion*, *37*(4), 710–724.

Park, C. (2010a). Making sense of the meaning literature: An integrative review of meaning making and its effects on adjustment to stressful life events. *Psychological Bulletin*, *136*, 257–301. doi:10.1037/a0018301

Park, C. (2010b). Stress, coping, and meaning. In S. Folkman (Ed.), *Oxford handbook of stress, health, and coping* (pp. 227–241). New York, NY: Oxford University Press.

Peng, W. L., Wu, G. J., Sun, W. Z., Chen, J. C., & Huang, A. T. (2006). Multidisciplinary management of cancer pain: A longitudinal retrospective study on a cohort of end-stage cancer patients. *Journal of pain and symptom management*, *32*(5), 444–452.

Pergolizzi, J. V., Gharibo, C., & Ho, K-Y. (2015). Treatment considerations for cancer pain: A global perspective. *Pain Practice: The Official Journal of World Institute of Pain*, *15*(8), 778–792. doi:10.1111/papr.12253

Peterman, A., Fitchett, G., Brady, M., Hernandez, L., & Cella, D. (2002). Measuring spiritual well-being in people with cancer: The Functional Assessment of Chronic Illness Therapy-Spiritual Well-Being Scale (FACIT-Sp). *Annals of Behavioral Medicine*, *24*(1), 49–58.

Pina, P., Sabri, E., & Lawlor, P. G. (2015). Characteristics and associations of pain intensity in patients referred to a specialist cancer pain clinic. *Pain Research & Management: The Journal of the Canadian Pain Society*, *20*(5), 249–254. Retrieved from www.ncbi.nlm.nih.gov/pubmed/26291125

Portenoy, R. K. (1989). Cancer pain. Epidemiology and syndromes. *Cancer*, *63*(11 Suppl), 2298–2307.

Prevost, V., Delorme, C., Grach, M.-C., Chvetzoff, G., & Hureau, M. (2015). Therapeutic education in improving cancer pain management: A synthesis of available studies. *American Journal of Hospice and Palliative Medicine, 33*(6), 599–612. https://doi.org/10.1177/1049909115586394

Rainville, P., Bao, Q.V., & Chretien, P. (2005). Pain-related emotions modulate experimental pain perception and autonomic responses. *Pain, 118*(3), 306–318.

Rettger, J., Wall, K., Corwin, D., Davidson, A., Lukoff, D., & Koopman, C. (2015). In psychospiritual integrative therapy for women with primary breast cancer, what factors account for the benefits? Insights from a multiple case analysis. *Healthcare, 3*(2), 263–283.

Richmond, C. (2005). Dame Cicely Saunders. *British Medical Journal, 33,* 238–239.

Rost, A., Wilson, K., Buchanan, E., Hildebrandt, M., & Mutch, D. (2012). Improving psychological adjustment among late-stage ovarian cancer patients: Examining the role of avoidance in treatment. *Cognitive and Behavioral Practice, 19*(4), 508–517. http://dx.doi.org/10.1016/j.cbpra.2012.01.003

Salsman, J. M., Pustejovsky, J. E., Jim, H. S. L., Munoz, A. R., Merluzzi, T.V., George, L., . . . Fitcherr, G. (2015). A meta-analytic approach to examining the correlation between religion/spirituality and mental health in cancer. *Cancer, 121,* 3769–3778.

Sanovation, A. G. (2016). *CatchMyPain [Mobile Application Software].* Retrieved from www.catchmypain.com

Scott, W., Hann, K., & McCracken, L. (2016). A comprehensive examination of changes in psychological flexibility following acceptance and commitment therapy for chronic pain. *Journal of Contemporary Psychotherapy, 46*(3), 139–148.

Seretny, M., Currie, G. L., Sena, E. S., Ramnarine, S., Grant, R., MacLeod, M. R., . . . Fallon, M. (2014). Incidence, prevalence, and predictors of chemotherapy-induced peripheral neuropathy: A systematic review and meta-analysis. *Pain, 155*(12), 2461–2470. doi:10.1016/j.pain.2014.09.020

Shennan, C., Payne, S., & Fenlon, D. (2011). What is the evidence for the use of mindfulness-based interventions in cancer care? A review. *Psycho-Oncology, 20*(7), 681–697.

Siegel, R. L., Miller, K. D., & Jemal, A. (2016). Cancer statistics, 2016. *CA: A Cancer Journal for Clinicians, 66*(1), 7–30. https://doi.org/10.3322/caac.21332

Slavich, G. M., & Irwin, M. R. (2014). From stress to inflammation and major depressive disorder: A social signal transduction theory of depression. *Psychological Bulletin, 140*(3), 774–815. http://dx.doi.org/10.1037/a0035302

Smyth, J. A., Dempster, M., Warwick, I., Wilkinson, P., & McCorry, N. K. (2018). A systematic review of the patient and carer related factors affecting the experience of pain for advanced cancer patients cared for at home. *Journal of Pain and Symptom Management, 55*(2), 296–507.

Spiegel, H., & Spiegel, D. (2004). *Trance and treatment: Clinical uses of hypnosis.* Washington, DC: American Psychiatric Publishing.

Sun, V. C.-Y., Borneman, T., Ferrell, B., Piper, B., Koczymas, M., & Choi, K. (2007). Overcoming barriers to cancer pain management: An institutional change model. *Journal of Pain and Symptom Management, 34*(4), 359–369.

Sutradhar, R., Lokku, A., & Barbera, L. (2017). Cancer survivorship and opioid prescribing rates: A population-based matched cohort study among individuals with and without a history of cancer. *Cancer, 123*(21), 4286–4293.

Syrjala, K. L., Jensen, M. P., Mendoza, M. E., Yi, J. C., Fisher, H. M., & Keefe, F. J. (2014). Psychological and behavioral approaches to cancer pain management. *Journal of Clinical Oncology, 32*(16), 1703–1711.

Tatrow, K., & Montgomery, G. H. (2006). Cognitive behavioral therapy techniques for distress and pain in breast cancer patients: A meta-analysis. *Journal of Behavioral Medicine, 29*(1), 17–27.

Taylor, E. (2000). Transformation of tragedy among women surviving breast cancer. *Oncology Nursing Forum, 27*(5), 781–788.

Thewes, B., Brebach, R., Dzidowska, M., Rhodes, P., Sharpe, L., & Butow, P. (2014). Current approaches to managing fear of cancer recurrence: A descriptive survey of psychosocial and clinical health professionals. *Psycho-Oncology, 23*(4), 390–396. http://dx.doi.org/10.1002/pon.3423.

Uchino, B. N. (2006). Social support and health: A review of physiological processes potentially underlying links to disease outcomes. *Journal of Behavioral Medicine, 29*(4), 377–387.

US National Institutes of Health. (1995). Integration of behavioral and relaxation approaches into the treatment of chronic pain and insomnia. NIH technology assessment panel on integration of behavioral and relaxation approaches into the treatment of chronic pain and insomnia. *Journal of American Medical Association, 276*(4), 313–318.

van den Beuken-van Everdingen, M. H., de Rijke, J. M., Kessels, A. G., Schouten, H. C., van Kleef, M., & Patijn, J. (2007). Prevalence of pain in patients with cancer: A systematic review of the past 40 years. *Annals of Oncology, 18*(9), 1437–1449. doi:10.1093/annonc/mdm056

Wachholtz, A. B., Pearce, M. J., & Koenig, H. G. (2007). Exploring the relationship between spirituality, coping, and pain. *Journal of Behavioral Medicine, 30*(4), 311–318. doi:10.1007/s10865-007-9114-7

Waldman, S. D. (2010a). Acute herpes zoster and postherpetic neuralgia. In S. D. Waldman (Ed.), *Pain management* (2nd ed., pp. 268–271). Philadelphia, PA: Elsevier.

Waldman, S. D. (2010b). Identification and treatment of cancer pain syndromes. In S. D. Waldman (Ed.), *Pain management* (2nd ed., pp. 302–311). Philadelphia, PA: Elsevier.

Ward, S., Goldberg, N., Miller-McCauley, V., Mueller, C. Nolan, A. Pawlik-Plank, D., . . . Weissman, D. E. (1993). Patient-related barriers to management of cancer pain. *Pain, 52*(3), 319–324.

Ward, S., Wang, K., Serlin, R. C., Peterson, S. L., & Murray, M. E. (2009). A randomized trial of a tailored barriers intervention for Cancer Information Service (CIS) callers in pain. *Pain, 144*, 49–56.

Wei, D., Liu, X. Y., Chen, Y. Y., Zhou, X., & Hu, H. P. (2016). Effectiveness of physical, psychological, social, and spiritual intervention in breast cancer survivors: An integrative review. *Asia-Pacific Journal of Oncology Nursing, 3*(3), 226.

Wells, N., Johnson, R. L., & Wujeik, D. (1998). Development of a short version of the barrier questionnaire. *Journal of Pain and Symptom Management, 15*(5), 294–298.

Wong-Kim, E. C., & Bloom, J. R. (2005). Depression experienced by young women newly diagnosed with breast cancer. *Psycho-Oncology, 14*(7), 564–573. doi: 10.1002/pon.873

World Health Organization. (1986). *World Health Organization: Cancer pain relief.* Retrieved May 21, 2018, from www.who.int/cancer/palliative/painladder/en/

World Health Organization. (1996). *Cancer pain relief. With a guide to opioid availability* (2nd ed.). Geneva: WHO. ISBN 92-4-154482-1

World Health Organization. (1998). *Cancer pain relief and palliative care in children.* Geneva: WHO. ISBN 978-92-4-154512-9

World Health Organization. (2017). *Cancer. WHO's cancer pain ladder for adults.* Retrieved November 10, 2017, from www.who.int/cancer/palliative/painladder/en/

Wortzel, J., & Spiegel, D. (2017). Hypnosis in cancer care. *American Journal of Clinical Hypnosis, 60*(1), 4–17.

Xia, Z. (2017). Cancer pain management in China: Current status and practice implications based on the ACHEON survey. *Journal of Pain Research, 10*, 1943–1952. doi:10.2147/JPR.S128533

Zaza, C., Sellick, S. M., Willan, A., Reyno, L., & Browman, G. P. (1999). Health care professionals' familiarity with non-pharmacological strategies for managing cancer pain. *Psycho-Oncology, 8*(2), 99–111. doi:10.1002/(SICI)1099-1611

11

Chronic GI Disorders

Melissa Hunt

Chronic GI disorders fall into three large subgroups: functional GI disorders (FGIDs such as irritable bowel syndrome [IBS], functional dyspepsia, functional heartburn, functional chest pain of presumed esophageal origin); motility disorders (e.g., gastroparesis, intestinal pseudo-obstruction); and organic (structural) disorders in which tissue pathology and other pathognomonic indicators can actually be identified (e.g., inflammatory bowel disease [IBD], including Crohn's disease and ulcerative colitis). Patients suffering from these chronic GI conditions can benefit from psychosocial interventions (including cognitive-behavioral therapy, hypnosis, and mindfulness-based interventions) that target pain, symptom management, and coping, with clinical benefits having been demonstrated in IBS and IBD patients in particular (Ballou & Keefer, 2017).

While most of these disorders have pain as part of their symptom profiles, impaired health-related quality of life, distress, and disability also are highly associated with anxiety, depression, catastrophizing, fear of food, and maladaptive avoidance. As such, cognitive-behavioral therapy is well positioned to address many of the factors that contribute to poor quality of life in these patient populations. In the case of the functional disorders, CBT can actually reduce symptom severity and pain as well. This chapter focuses primarily on elucidating the etiology of pain in IBS and on empirically supported, evidence-based behavioral health interventions for IBS and IBD.

Irritable Bowel Syndrome

Diagnosis

Functional GI disorders are defined by the Rome IV diagnostic criteria and are characterized by biopsychosocial models as disturbances of neurogastroenterology or brain–gut interaction (Drossman, 2016). In the absence of pathognomonic indicators, FGIDs are diagnosed primarily in terms of symptoms. Those symptoms almost always occur in the context of visceral hypersensitivity and also may be associated with disturbed motility, altered mucosal and immune function, altered gut microbiota (dysbiosis), and altered central-enteric (gut) nervous system processing (Drossman, 2016).

Irritable bowel syndrome (IBS) is one of the most common FGIDs. The Rome IV criteria for IBS include recurrent abdominal pain that occurs at least four times per month, or about once a week. The pain should be related to defecation and is associated with changes in the form of stool and/or the frequency of defecation. Onset must have been at least six months prior, but pain must have been recurrent over at least three months. These criteria were promulgated in May of 2016 and were an update from the prior Rome III criteria that had been in place since 2006 (Longstreth et al., 2006). They clarify and tighten the criteria, eliminating vague words like "discomfort" and improving the specificity of the diagnosis by increasing the frequency criteria from three days per month to once per week. This led prevalence estimates in United States adults to drop somewhat, typically from 10% using Rome III criteria to around 6% using Rome IV (Palsson, van Tiburg, Simrén, Sperber & Whitehead, 2016). Women are approximately twice as likely as men to meet criteria for IBS, and older individuals are less likely to report IBS (Palsson et al., 2016). Moreover, in a survey of individuals who had previously met Rome III criteria, individuals who also met Rome IV criteria were more likely to be younger, female, and to report more psychological comorbidity (Vork et al., 2018). IBS has three different presentations: diarrhea predominant (IBS-D), constipation predominant (IBS-C), and a mixed presentation; however, abdominal pain is the single unifying symptom and cardinal feature of IBS from the medical perspective (Lacy, 2016a).

In practice, IBS patients suffer from a host of related difficulties beyond pain that substantially impair health-related quality of life and functioning. Fecal urgency and fear of fecal incontinence (FI) are significant concerns for many IBS patients, particularly those who suffer from diarrhea. Two recent population studies have examined the actual prevalence of fecal incontinence in IBS. One study reported that rates of FI of more than once per month in approximately 20% of IBS patients, with even higher rates (43%) if patients with less frequent FI were included (Simrén et al., 2017). The other (Hunt, Wong, Aajmain & Dawodu, 2018) reported that about 60% of people with IBS reported experiencing at least one lifetime episode of FI, with just over half of those experiencing between two and five lifetime episodes. Not surprisingly, fear of FI (even in individuals who have never actually experienced it) has an adverse impact on quality of life, psychological symptoms, and work productivity.

Bloating, gas, and flatulence also afflict many, if not most, IBS patients and can lead to significant physical discomfort as well as to embarrassment and fear of humiliation. Many IBS patients develop substantial fear of foods that they believe trigger their GI symptoms (Hunt, Zickgraf, Gibbons & Loftus, 2018), and self-reported food intolerance and avoidance are associated with more severe symptom burden and reduced quality of life (Böhn, Störsrud, Törnblom, Bengtsson & Simrén, 2013). This in turn leads to trying various restrictive diets and to avoiding food and food-related social situations, which further reduces quality of life and contributes to isolation.

Because the symptoms of IBS are fairly nonspecific and are not associated with abnormal radiologic or endoscopic abnormalities or with any reliable biomarkers, differential diagnosis can be tricky and is typically made on clinical grounds (Ford, Moayyedi et al., 2014). Indeed, current evidence suggests that performing multiple diagnostic tests (especially invasive testing such as colonoscopy) typically is not warranted (Cash, Schoenfeld & Chey, 2002). Nevertheless, most IBS patients will visit multiple doctors and have some testing done before the diagnosis is confirmed (Lacy et al., 2016). Some rule-outs are important to make, especially in IBS-D cases, and some "alarm" symptoms suggest that whatever is going on is not IBS (Lacy, 2016b). Alarm symptoms include fever, pain that wakes people out of a sound sleep, high white count, anemia, and blood in the stool. Two of the most important conditions to rule out are celiac disease and inflammatory bowel disease. A basic work-up for IBS should include bloodwork to check for elevated white count (an indication of inflammation) and for nutritional deficiencies such as anemia and B12 insufficiency, both of which suggest a diagnosis other than IBS since they indicate that the gut is actually failing to absorb nutrients appropriately. Testing also should include bloodwork to rule out celiac specific antibodies. Celiac disease is an autoimmune disorder in which the body becomes sensitized to gluten and the immune system attacks the tissues of the gut when gluten is present.

Other important tests include fecal occult tests to rule out blood in the stool (which could suggest intestinal bleeding due to the ulcerations of IBD) and the fecal calprotectin test, which is fairly sensitive to inflammatory markers consistent with IBD in the large intestine and is a useful, noninvasive way to differentiate IBD from IBS (Walsham & Sherwood, 2016), though it sometimes misses ileal or small bowel disease (Ye et al., 2017). One final ruleout is bile acid malabsorption, which is a common result of long-term nonsteroidal anti-inflammatory (NSAID) use. Long-term NSAID use, especially at relatively high doses, can result in subtle enteropathy (Shin, Noh, Lim, Lee & Lee, 2017) that reduces the ability of the intestines to reabsorb bile acid. Excess bile acid leads to diarrhea that can mimic IBS, because it causes increased water and electrolyte imbalance in the large intestine, which in turn results in watery diarrhea and decreased transit time for food to move through the bowel, resulting in urgency. Each of these conditions needs to be managed medically.

In the case of celiac disease, patients must adhere to a strict gluten-free diet. In the case of IBD, there are multiple medical measures that will reduce inflammation. In the case of bile acid malabsorption, the simple expedients of taking B12 supplements and a bile acid sequestrant will often lead to symptom resolution (Walters & Pattni, 2010).

Etiology

The etiology of IBS is important to understand and to explain to patients, in part to get their "buy in" for the utility of psychological interventions. IBS patients understandably resent the suggestion that their problems are "all in their head." Unfortunately, many IBS patients have experienced significant dissatisfaction in their encounters with physicians, and physicians often share frustration with patients over their inability to point to positive lab results or tests and to the lack of effective medical treatments (Chang et al., 2006). Moreover, IBS patients often feel insufficiently informed and harbor numerous distorted, incorrect, and even catastrophic beliefs about IBS (Halpert et al., 2007).

Nevertheless, there *are* explanatory models for IBS that are emerging. One of the most important etiological processes is the development of *visceral hypersensitivity* (Camilleri, Coulie & Tack, 2001). Visceral hypersensitivity refers to abnormal endogenous pain modulation and has been clearly identified as an underlying mechanism in IBS (e.g., Wilder-Smith & Robert-Yap, 2007). In sum, patients with IBS feel normal gut sensations that most people would be unaware of and experience many of those sensations as more painful than healthy controls. Visceral hypersensitivity can be measured objectively with balloon distension (of the gastric fundus, descending colon, or rectum) and is clearly correlated with IBS symptom severity above and beyond symptoms of depression and anxiety (Simrén et al., 2018). While the underlying neurological mechanisms mediating visceral hypersensitivity remain under investigation in both animals (e.g., Asano & Takenaga, 2017) and humans (Wouters et al., 2016), the important point is that, similar to anxiety sensitivity in panic patients, visceral hypersensitivity leads to a vicious cycle of vigilance, stress, increasing pain, and increasing vigilance. Fortunately, there is an excellent self-report measure available for the assessment of visceral sensitivity and anxiety in IBS patients—the Visceral Sensitivity Index (Labus et al., 2004; Labus, Mayer, Chang, Bolus & Naliboff, 2007). The VSI is included in Appendix 1.

The metaphor this author uses with patients when discussing visceral hypersensitivity is an overly sensitive smoke detector. Pain is supposed to be a useful signal that damage is occurring or that something is wrong that needs to be addressed. A good smoke detector reacts to the presence of actual smoke (and fire) and alerts you that you need to take action. An overly sensitive smoke detector, however, might go off in the presence of water vapor—say steam from a shower or a boiling pot of pasta. At best, this is annoying. At worst, it would send the entire family fleeing the house every time they tried to bathe or cook dinner. This author explains to patients that the pain sensors in their gut have turned into overly sensitive smoke detectors, and that they are spending a significant amount of time and energy reacting to sensations that are really benign. Pain receptors in the gut are supposed to tell us when we have a serious infection, an ulcer or fistula, an obstruction, or have eaten something dangerous. They are NOT supposed to overreact to basically benign foods, and they certainly are not supposed to overreact to environmental and psychological stressors.

Stress itself clearly plays a role in the onset and maintenance of IBS symptoms. Stress often precedes and subsequently exacerbates IBS symptoms (Blanchard et al., 2008). In animal models, early life stress has been shown to induce visceral hypersensitivity in mice (Moloney et al., 2012). IBS patients have been shown to have sustained HPA axis responses to acute psychosocial stress, followed by an increase in problematic GI symptoms (Bhatia & Tandon, 2004; Kennedy, Cryan, Quigley, Dinan & Clarke, 2014). Moreover, *perceived* stress in IBS patients correlates with self-reported average pain, worst pain, fatigue, and sleep disturbance, as well as overall health-related and mental health-related quality of life (Edman et al., 2017).

Given the role of stress (and the involvement of HPA axis dysregulation) in the onset and exacerbation of IBS, it is not surprising that low grade inflammation has been hypothesized to play an etiological role (Barbara, De Giorgio, Stanghellini, Cremon & Corinaldesi, 2002). Investigated mechanisms suggest a major role of hypothalamic corticotropin-releasing hormone (CRH—also known as corticotropin-releasing factor or CRF) in stress-related pathophysiology of IBS and possibly in inflammation of the intestinal mucosa (Fukudo, 2007). Stress also may reactivate previous inflammation when applied in conjunction with a small luminal stimulus. This reactivation triggers increased permeability and immune system alterations (Collins, 2001; Öhman & Simrén, 2010).

Another important aspect of IBS's etiology is almost certainly the role of dysbiosis, or disruption in the normal balance of flora in the microbiome of the gut (Collins, 2014). A recent surge of research suggests that dysbiosis may underlie a wide range of health problems, including everything from depression to obesity, through neural, endocrine, and immune pathways (Cryan & Dinan, 2012). Thus, dysbiosis may help explain the complex dysregulation of the brain–gut axis in IBS, and the links between chronic stress, psychiatric disorders such as depression, and IBS (Dinan & Cryan, 2013). Indeed, there clearly are links between stress, the microbiome–gut–brain axis and visceral pain (Moloney et al., 2016). Interestingly, treatment with probiotics has been found to reduce pain and other symptom severity scores in IBS without adverse effects (Didari, Mozaffari, Nikfar & Abdollahi, 2015).

Psychiatric Comorbidity

As many as 65% of IBS patients suffer from psychiatric comorbidities, most predominantly anxiety and mood disorders (Stanculete & Dumitrascu, 2016). In a rigorous population-based study that employed structured clinical interviewing, 50% of IBS patients had a lifetime mood or anxiety disorder (Mykletun et al., 2010). In IBS patients who actively seek treatment, upwards of 90% may present with psychiatric comorbidity (Lydiard, 2001), including mood, anxiety, and trauma disorders. With respect to depression, IBS patients have high rates of comorbid depression, but depressed patients *also* have high rates of comorbid IBS (Masand et al., 1995). Of particular interest for this volume, it has been found that pain catastrophizing (that is, distorted, negative beliefs about pain) mediates the link between IBS symptom severity and depression (Lackner, Quigley & Blanchard, 2004). In general, psychiatric comorbidity is associated with greater distress, reduced HRQL, and more severe symptoms in IBS (Lackner et al., 2013).

Perhaps more importantly, IBS overlaps considerably with both panic and agoraphobia and with social anxiety (Gros, Antony, McCabe & Swinson, 2009). Many IBS patients develop catastrophic distortions about the social and occupational implications of their GI symptoms (Hunt, Ertel, Coello & Rodriguez, 2014a). For example, they become acutely self-conscious about the possibility of their gut rumbling or gurgling in public, of flatulence, or of drawing attention to themselves if they need to exit a meeting or interrupt a car ride in order to use a bathroom. Similar to individuals with social anxiety disorder, they overestimate the degree to which others are noticing and judging such behaviors. Indeed, there is evidence that IBS patients do not even talk openly with intimate partners and family members about their experiences with IBS for fear of embarrassment and humiliation, and that communication apprehension and topic avoidance are correlated with more severe GI symptoms and pain (Bevan, 2009).

IBS patients also overlap significantly with panic disorder patients, especially in the way they catastrophize the physical sensations and symptoms they experience. Indeed, there is evidence that IBS patients catastrophize GI-specific sensations *more* than panic disorder patients do (Hunt, Milonova & Moshier, 2009). The GI-Cognitions Questionnaire (GI-Cog; Hunt et al., 2014a), which is a validated self-report measure that allows clinicians to determine quickly the degree of distorted, catastrophic, GI-specific cognitions their IBS patients may hold, is included in Appendix 2.

Avoidance in IBS

Many IBS patients easily can meet DSM-5 (APA, 2013) criteria for agoraphobia, where the definition includes avoidance secondary to fear of incapacitating or embarrassing symptoms, including fear of incontinence. Avoided activities (including travel, recreational activities, social activities) typically focus on situations in which it might be difficult or embarrassing to get to a bathroom quickly. Indeed, panic patients with comorbid IBS (especially the IBS-D subtype) are more likely to develop agoraphobia, avoid a greater number of situations, and develop a more severe form of agoraphobia than panic patients without IBS (Sugaya et al., 2013; Sugaya, Kaiya, Kumano & Nomura, 2008).

In addition to obvious avoidance, IBS patients also engage in considerable subtle avoidance (Ljótsson et al., 2010). These patients may engage in activities, but only if they employ numerous safety utilization behaviors. Some of these are similar to those used by panic patients, such as always sitting in the back or on the aisle of a crowded classroom, movie theater, or place of worship. Other behaviors are more specific to IBS. Patients who experience urgency often will scope out the location and proximity of bathrooms either on-site or in advance by using a "bathroom finder" website or app. IBS patients often wear only loose, comfortable clothes that do not press on the abdomen. Some routinely carry a change of clothes and wet wipes "just in case" they have an accident, even if they have never experienced a single actual episode of FI.

Many IBS patients take steps to avoid experiencing visceral sensations or having to defecate at all during certain periods. For example, they will "pre-load" by taking multiple doses of antidiarrheal medications before heading out for the day, or by the simple expedient of *not eating* all day until they are back in the safety of their home. Some patients carry quick-acting, dissolvable antidiarrheal medication with them, the same way that panic patients carry clonazepam wafers "just in case" they begin to experience symptoms. Of course, using antidiarrheals and fasting have adverse effects. While antidiarrheal medications generally are quite safe and typically do not promote tolerance, they *do* cause constipation. This can lead to straining, hemorrhoids, bloating and more gas pain, and ironically may require laxative medication to resolve (leading to a return of urgency). Fasting is another strategy that many IBS patients feel is warranted. But if a patient was told that a new treatment's side effects included dizziness, nausea, headache, irritability, slowed reaction time, reduced concentration, memory impairment, and learning deficits, most patients would refuse it. Yet that is exactly what hunger does! While all of these subtle avoidance behaviors feel perfectly reasonable to IBS sufferers, they end up maintaining the cycle of visceral hypersensitivity, anxiety, and catastrophizing, and thereby ironically tend to exacerbate symptoms and disability long term.

Restrictive Diets

Unfortunately, the most common solution IBS patients try is dietary restriction, attempting to eliminate "dangerous trigger" foods that cause unwanted visceral sensations in the context of visceral hypersensitivity (e.g., Böhn et al., 2013). Even a cursory review of online message groups and blogs serves up an astounding array of (often contradictory) advice to IBS sufferers. Lists of dangerous foods include dairy, meat, eggs, gluten, legumes, leafy greens, cruciferous vegetables, fiber, fat, spicy food, caffeine, sugar, alcohol, sorbitol, fructose; the list goes on and on. If a patient followed all the advice available online, they would end up with nothing on their plate but a pile of plain white rice and a probiotic pill—not a very appetizing, nourishing, or satisfactory diet. Indeed, for many IBS patients, fear of food explains a great deal of the variance in impaired quality of life. Fear of food has several components, including fear of GI symptoms after consuming particular foods, fear and avoidance of foods themselves, social impairment, and distress about loss of pleasure in eating. The Fear of Food Questionnaire (FFQ; Hunt, Zickgraf et al., 2018) is a brief, validated self-report measure that captures all of these domains and is included in Appendix 3.

The restrictive diet with the most empirical support for its efficacy is the low FODMAP diet (Gibson & Shepherd, 2010). FODMAP stands for Fermentable

Oligo-Di-Monosaccharides and Polyols, which are short chain carbohydrates that are co-digested by symbiotic bacteria in the small bowel. In fact, FODMAPs are the "prebiotic" foods that "feed" the symbiotic bacteria that make up our microbiome and are essential for good health. High FODMAP foods *do* reliably cause more gas and water content in the gut as a by-product of the fermentation process (Ong, Mitchell, Barrett et al., 2010). However, this is only problematic in the context of visceral hypersensitivity, and only IBS patients (and some IBD patients) are particularly bothered by it (Staudacher, Irving, Lomer & Whelan, 2014). There is mounting evidence that restricting high FODMAP foods does indeed reduce acute GI discomfort for people with IBS (e.g., Halmos, Power, Shepherd et al., 2014; Rao, Yu & Fedewa, 2015). However, the long-term effects of this restrictive diet are concerning, particularly with respect to evidence that it increases dysbiosis by starving whole species of symbiotic bacteria such as bifidus (Staudacher, Lomer, Anderson et al., 2012).

Moreover, without the guidance of a specialized registered dietician, it is very difficult to maintain the diet and ensure good nutrition while on it (Nanayakkara, Skidmore, O'Brien et al., 2016). In practice, many patients report receiving a one-page handout from a physician listing the FODMAP foods they should avoid and do not follow-up with a dietician. The diet is *extremely* restrictive and eliminates all dairy, all legumes, including soy, most grains, many fruits (including apples and all fruits with pits) and many vegetables, including onions and garlic (Shepherd & Gibson, 2013). Ideally, patients are instructed to eliminate all high FODMAP foods for six weeks, and then go through a systematic reintroduction phase with small, test amounts of restricted foods to see what they can tolerate. Long-term restriction of FODMAPs may lead to as yet unknown adverse effects (Nanayakkara et al., 2016). Although patients do report significant IBS symptom relief on the diet, overall quality of life generally is *not* improved (Pedersen, Andersen, Végh et al., 2014), and initial and long-term adherence rates are quite low, in the range of about 30% and 16% respectively (Maagaard, Ankersen, Végh et al., 2016). Finally, it is unclear whether a low FODMAP diet actually results in any greater symptom improvement than far less restrictive modified diets (Böhn, Störsrud, Liljebo et al., 2015).

From a behavioral health perspective, the problem with restrictive diets is that they are, at their core, *avoidance strategies*. The goal of all of these diets (and symptom-based pharmacological interventions for IBS such as antispasmodic, antigas, and antidiarrheal medications) is to minimize or eliminate visceral sensations. From both cognitive-behavioral and acceptance/mindfulness-based perspectives, experiential avoidance almost always backfires, giving the feared sensations, thoughts, or feelings greater salience and exacerbating the underlying hypervigilance toward, anxiety about, and reactivity to them (Chawla & Ostafin, 2007).

Psychotherapeutic Approaches to IBS

In contrast, successful psychotherapeutic approaches to IBS take an entirely different approach, generally by encouraging patients to learn effective stress management and relaxation strategies (to reduce HPA axis reactivity that contributes to visceral hypersensitivity and GI symptoms), but *also* by encouraging patients to expose themselves to feared sensations and situations, to de-catastrophize their symptoms, and to reduce cognitive distortions about the social and occupational implications of their symptoms. Increasingly, gastroenterologists recognize that IBS patients often show inadequate response to usual medical care and that psychological treatments (including CBT and gut-directed hypnosis) should be considered in many cases (Palsson & Whitehead, 2013). Indeed, there is growing recognition that such complementary approaches typically result in far better treatment outcomes and improved quality of life for IBS sufferers over and above traditional medical care and dietary management (Grundmann & Yoon, 2014).

Hypnotherapy

Gut-directed hypnotherapy, originally developed by Whorwell and colleagues (Whorwell, Prior & Faragher, 1984; Whorwell, Prior & Faragher, 1987), has been tested and reviewed and found to be an efficacious treatment for IBS (Tan, Hammon & Gurrala, 2005) with reasonable, but not robust, long-term follow-up efficacy (Lindfors, Unge, Nyhlin et al., 2012). In a typical protocol, hypnotic induction (including arm levitation) is followed by basic psychoeducation about the functioning of the gut and guided imagery of a smoothly functioning gut while the patient places their hands on their abdomen. A typical course of treatment is 7 to 12 sessions, delivered over two to three months. Outcomes include not only reductions in abdominal pain, constipation, and diarrhea but also improved quality of life (which highly restrictive diets typically do not afford).

Overall, hypnosis appears to reduce rectal hypersensitivity and psychological distress in response to visceral sensory perception (Tan et al., 2005). The most recent review (Palsson, 2015) found strong support for hypnotherapy as highly efficacious in reducing bowel symptoms and providing relief to IBS patients. The question of mechanism of action remains. During hypnotic induction, various aspects of GI functioning are altered in measurable ways. For example, hypnotic suggestions for reduced pain sensation in the gut can suppress evoked viscerosensory brain potentials (Watanabe, Hattori, Kanazawa, Kano & Fukudo, 2007) and also slow GI smooth muscle activity, reducing cramping and urgency (Whorwell, Houghton, Taylor & Maxton, 1992). Moreover, hypnosis appears to normalize visceral discomfort thresholds (Lea, Houghton, Calvert et al., 2003). It seems plausible that gut-directed hypnotherapy combines the benefits of relaxation training (which will quiet HPA axis activity) with the benefits of mild exposure to and reinterpretation of feared GI sensations, which will break the cycle of experiential avoidance that paradoxically was maintaining visceral hypersensitivity. It also can be effectively delivered in group format (Gerson, Gerson & Gerson, 2013).

Mindfulness

Another psychotherapeutic approach to IBS that emphasizes decreasing experiential avoidance is mindfulness. Mindfulness training, which typically involves helping people attend to present-moment experience in a nonjudgmental way, was developed by Kabat-Zinn and colleagues to treat a variety of chronic pain conditions (e.g., Kabat-Zinn, Lipworth, Burney & Sellers, 1986). Mindfulness-based interventions (or MBIs) have been applied to IBS with considerable success. For example, Gaylord, Palsson, Garland et al. (2011) found that mindfulness training had a substantial effect on bowel symptom severity, relative to a support group, and improved health-related quality of life and reduced distress. Similarly, Zernicke, Campbell, Blustein et al. (2013) found that a mindfulness-based stress reduction (MBSR) program resulted in significant improvement in symptom severity, compared to a waitlist control, as well as significant improvements in quality of life and overall mood that were maintained six months following treatment. Bridging the gap between mindfulness and CBT with its explicit exposure component, Ljótsson and colleagues (Ljótsson et al., 2010; Ljótsson et al., 2011) delivered a combination of mindfulness and exposure to IBS patients via the internet. Even with very limited interaction with therapists, the intervention resulted in significant improvement in IBS symptoms, quality of life, and anxiety related to GI symptoms. Gains were generally maintained over a year later.

Cognitive-Behavioral Therapy

While hypnotherapy and mindfulness clearly are efficacious approaches to IBS, the psychological approach to IBS with the most empirical support is cognitive-behavioral therapy (Kinsinger, 2017). CBT has been tested rigorously in a number of randomized controlled trials and typically results in substantial improvements in GI symptom severity *and* health-related quality of life, gains which are typically maintained and consolidated over time (Laird, Tanner-Smith, Russell, Hollon & Walker, 2016). A number of protocols delivering CBT for IBS have been developed and tested in randomized controlled trials. They typically include substantial psychoeducation about the brain–gut axis, the role of stress and arousal in exacerbating GI symptoms, relaxation training, the role of visceral hypersensitivity, and the degree to which experiential and behavioral avoidance maintain and exacerbate disability and distress. Some focus primarily on interoceptive exposure (e.g., Craske et al., 2011). Others combine mindfulness and acceptance with interoceptive and in vivo exposure (Ljótsson et al., 2010). Still others combine interoceptive and in vivo exposure with explicit cognitive restructuring to reduce catastrophizing about IBS symptoms.

For example, Moss-Morris, McAlpine, Didsbury & Spence (2010) developed a manualized self-management intervention incorporating modules on recognizing and managing unhelpful thoughts and reducing perfectionism and all or nothing thinking. Hunt, Moshier and Milonova (2009) developed a brief CBT treatment with modules that teach patients to challenge negative automatic thoughts and GI-specific catastrophizing. The efficacy of CBT for IBS has been shown to be partially mediated by reductions in visceral sensitivity (Wolitzky-Taylor, Craske, Labus, Mayer & Naliboff, 2012; Hunt, Moshier et al., 2009; Hunt, Ertel, Coello & Rodriguez, 2014b) and by reductions in maladaptive, illness-related cognitions (Chilcot & Moss-Morris, 2013) and GI-specific catastrophizing (Hunt et al., 2014b). Exposure to IBS symptoms and related situations seems to be a core component of effective treatment (Ljótsson et al., 2014) and works in large part by reducing gastrointestinal-specific anxiety (Ljótsson et al., 2013).

Ljótsson and colleagues (Ljótsson et al., 2014) detail a number of different types of exposure exercises that IBS patients can undertake: 1) efforts to provoke GI symptoms by engaging in activities such as eating certain foods, wearing tight clothes, physical activity, and stressful situations; 2) reduction in use of safety and control behaviors, such as distraction, repeated toilet visits, avoiding or preferentially consuming certain foods, resting, and taking unprescribed medications; 3) exposure to situations where symptoms are unwanted, such as attending a meeting when experiencing abdominal pain or riding the bus with fear of losing control of the bowels; 4) for IBS-C participants, scheduling of toilet visits; 5) for IBS-D participants, gradual increase in time between onset of urgency and toilet visits.

In a case example from the author's own practice, an IBS patient had developed elaborate rituals with food that she would undertake before "risking" going out with friends. For example, she would eat exactly two-thirds of a packet of instant oatmeal and one hard-boiled egg during the day. Before leaving work, she would ensure that she had visited the restroom at least three times in the hour before departing. On arriving at a restaurant or bar to meet friends, she would immediately consume three saltine crackers and a half a glass of water. She would then wait 30 minutes before allowing herself to eat or drink anything further. She was convinced that this ritual would stave off acute nausea and/or bowel discomfort and diarrhea. Exposure therapy involved helping her abandon these specific safety behaviors and broaden her dietary choices and the timing of eating while still going out to meet friends.

Despite the efficacy of CBT for IBS, one of the main barriers to dissemination remains the lack of sufficient numbers of practitioners knowledgeable about both GI processes and CBT (Kinsinger, 2017). Researchers have tested variants of CBT for IBS, including group CBT (Toner et al., 1998) and CBT with limited or distant (e.g., via e-mail) therapist involvement (e.g., Ljótsson et al., 2010, 2011; Hunt, Moshier et al., 2009), and typically obtain robust effect sizes. Several treatment manuals and self-help books are available that detail the CBT treatment approach. One (*Cognitive-Behavioral Treatment of Irritable Bowel Syndrome: The Brain-Gut Connection*; Toner, Segal, Emmott & Myran, 2000) is a manual written for clinicians. Another (*Controlling IBS the Drug-Free Way: A 10-Step Plan for Symptom Relief*; Lackner, 2007) is written for consumers.

The third (*Reclaim Your Life from IBS*; Hunt, 2016), which also is written for consumers, is unique in that it actually was tested as a stand-alone, self-help therapy with no therapist guidance in a randomized, controlled clinical trial (Hunt et al., 2014b). Participants had six weeks to work through the book, at which point post-treatment assessments were completed. Treatment completers showed statistically and clinically significant improvement in GI symptom severity and health-related quality of life, mediated by substantial reductions in both visceral sensitivity and GI-specific catastrophizing, with effect sizes in the large to very large ranges. Gains were typically maintained at three-month follow-up.

Thus, there are a number of resources available to interested clinicians and patients that can be used as stand-alone self-help treatments or in conjunction with in-person work with behavioral health specialists. It is particularly worth noting that interdisciplinary, collaborative treatment that includes both skilled medical management by a gastroenterologist and early referral to and inclusion of psychological intervention by behavioral health specialists may well yield the best outcome for IBS patients (Gerson & Gerson, 2003). Gerson and Gerson (2012) also recommend including partners, spouses, and other family members in treatment in the early stages in order to increase social support and to help to educate loved ones about the nature of the disorder and treatment strategies.

Inflammatory Bowel Disease

Phenomenology

The inflammatory bowel diseases, including Crohn's disease (CD) and ulcerative colitis (UC), are autoimmune disorders in which the body starts to attack the tissues of the digestive tract. The etiology and medical management of these disorders is complex and well beyond the scope of this chapter. See Zhang and Li (2014), Ford et al. (2011) and others for comprehensive reviews of these issues. Of concern is that the prevalence of IBDs has been increasing steadily with time, particularly in the developed world (Molodecky et al., 2012), with the highest reported prevalence in Europe and North America (approximately 320 per 100,000 persons for CD and between 250 and 500 per 100,000 persons for UC). For the purposes of this volume, it is important to understand that the primary symptoms of IBD include abdominal pain and cramping, diarrhea, fatigue, bloody stool, and weight loss. Complications can be serious (e.g., fistulas, which are holes or tubes that form through the wall of the digestive tract to other body parts) and even life-threatening (e.g., small bowel obstructions due to narrowing of the intestines secondary to inflammation or scar tissue). Up to 40% of CD patients and 30% of UC patients will require corrective surgery at some point during their lifetimes (Ferrari, Krane & Fichera, 2016).

Stress and HRQL in IBD

Like IBS, IBD can significantly impair an individual's HRQL (Zhou, Ren, Irvine & Yang, 2010). Additionally, individuals who have IBD are much more likely to suffer from anxiety and depression compared with the general population (Goodhand, Wahed, Mawdsley et al., 2012; Graff, Walker & Bernstein, 2009). Overall, the prevalence of psychiatric comorbidity approaches 24–27%, which is about three times higher than in a control population (Walker et al., 2008). The existence of a comorbid psychological disorder further reduces HRQL in individuals with IBD regardless of the medical severity of their condition (Guthrie, 2002; Iglesias-Rey et al., 2014).

The relationship between psychological distress and disease activity appears to be bidirectional. Psychological distress may be a response to disease activity itself (Sewitch, 2001), and long-term stress and depression also may worsen or exacerbate the disease (Levenstein, 2000; Maunder & Levenstein, 2008; Graff, Walker & Bernstein, 2009; Bernstein, Singh, Graff, Walker & Cheang, 2011). Persoons et al. (2005) found that major depressive disorder was predictive of failure to achieve remission while using infliximab for the medical management of CD. Bitton et al. (2008) showed that psychosocial variables, including high levels of perceived stress, especially in combination with avoidant coping, as well as biological markers, predicted relapse in IBD patients. Mittermaier et al. (2004) reported that scores on the Beck Depression Inventory correlated with the number of relapses at an 18-month follow-up.

Similar to IBS, there are a number of mechanisms by which stress and distress can affect inflammation in IBDs, including hypothalamic–pituitary axis dysfunction, alterations in bacterial-mucosal interactions, effects on mucosal mast cells, and mediators such as corticotrophin releasing factor (Mawdsley & Rampton, 2005, 2006; Bonaz & Bernstein, 2013). In addition, psychological distress is related strongly to *perceived* health in IBD patients over and above actual disease severity (Graff, Walker, Clara et al., 2009). Indeed, IBD patients are at significant risk for secondary IBS, and comorbid IBS is associated with worse quality of life in IBD patients (Mikocka-Walus, Turnbull, Andrews, Moulding & Holtmann, 2008). Thus, the assessment and treatment of psychological disorders in this population is likely to result in an improvement of HRQL and might even impact disease course. Unfortunately, these psychological disorders often remain untreated (Evertsz et al., 2012), despite the strong evidence for the value of adding psychological interventions to standard medical care (Szigethy et al., 2017; Sajadinejad, Asgari, Molavi, Kalantari & Adibi, 2012).

Psychotherapeutic Approaches to IBD

Psychotherapy and behavioral health interventions for adults with IBDs certainly are warranted, and most international guidelines for the management of IBD call for attention to psychosocial issues and psychological distress (Häuser, Moser, Klose & Miocka-Walus, 2014). Not surprisingly, CBT and hypnosis have been found to be the most useful, although there are relatively few trials of each (Knowles, Monshat & Castle, 2013). Mindfulness is a promising modality as well (Neilson et al., 2016).

251

Evertsz et al. (2012) developed a manualized CBT treatment for IBD patients with the goal of improving HRQL. Mussell, Böcker, Nagel et al. (2003) found that group CBT could be effective for both short-term and long-term management of psychological distress in IBD patients. Mikocka-Walus et al. (2015) tested the effects of face-to-face CBT or online CBT when compared to standard treatment alone on disease activity and quality of life in IBD patients. The treatment resulted in improved HRQL in the most distressed subgroups, which were most in need of treatment. Importantly, the trial did not find many significant differences between the efficacy of online CBT as opposed to face-to-face CBT. Unfortunately, this rigorous 24-month longitudinal study found that CBT did not affect disease course over time on a variety of objective measures of inflammation (Mikocka-Walus et al., 2016).

Hunt and colleagues adapted their modularized CBT treatment for IBS to IBD patients and tested it in a small pilot RCT with minimal therapist feedback (Hunt, Rodriguez & Marcelle, 2017). The treatment resulted in declines in depression and significant gains in HRQL, along with decreases in visceral anxiety and GI-specific catastrophizing. The group then turned the modularized treatment into a stand-alone self-help CBT workbook (*Coping With Crohn's and Colitis*) and tested the book against a psychoeducational control workbook in a larger RCT (Hunt, Loftus, Accardo, Keenan & Cohen, 2018). Both groups improved on a range of measures, including catastrophizing, visceral sensitivity, and quality of life, although effect sizes were more robust generally in the CBT workbook group. However, only participants in the CBT group had significant improvements in anxiety and depression. Improvements were maintained generally or consolidated at three-month follow-up. The authors hope that the book will be commercially available in 2019. In the meantime, readers may contact the author for access to the unpublished manuscript.

The key modifications of CBT for IBD versus CBT for IBS include recognition that pain may sometimes signal disease flares that require medical management or even a life-threatening emergency like a small bowel obstruction. Moreover, individuals with IBDs experience urgency to defecate that is the result of inflammatory processes, ulcerations, and tissue pathology, not centrally mediated pain processing. They also are far more likely to experience both urgency and fecal incontinence if they do not get to a bathroom in a timely fashion, and passive incontinence with no urge. Indeed, about 75% of IBD patients report episodes of FI, with about 10% experiencing it regularly (Dibley & Norton, 2013). Thus, CBT for IBD tends to focus more on problem-solving, planning, de-catastrophizing the effects of their symptoms on their lives and social networks, and reducing shame and secrecy. What might be viewed as maladaptive avoidance in an IBS patient (e.g., use of antidiarrheal medication, carrying wet wipes and a change of clothes, planning travel routes and activities with ready bathroom access) is appropriate adaptive problem-solving in an IBD patient in active flare.

Indeed, the ability to get to a bathroom "in time" and gain access to it is an issue of both patient advocacy and law. The Crohn's and Colitis Foundation

(CCF) provides and promotes the use of "I can't wait" wallet cards that IBD patients can use to establish the medical necessity for bathroom access. Many (but not all) states in the U.S. have passed versions of the Restroom Access Act (also known as Ally's Law) that require retail establishments with toilet facilities for employees to allow customers to use the facilities in the case of medical necessity such as an IBD. Encouraging IBD patients to feel free to ask to use restroom facilities across multiple situations is appropriate and therapeutic.

Fear of food also plays a role in HRQL for IBD patients. During active flares and post-surgery, IBD patients typically *will* be advised by their physicians to avoid "high residue" foods, including those high in insoluble fiber and certain stringy or chunky foods (e.g., celery, nuts, popcorn) that increase the odds of intestinal obstruction. However, this is *not* a strategy for long-term maintenance. There is evidence that a "Western" diet high in refined carbohydrates, meat, and fat, and low in fiber, fruits, and vegetables, contributes to the risk of IBD (Hou, Abraham & El-Serag, 2011), probably in part by its effect on the microbiome (Leone, Change & Devkota, 2013).

Despite the lack of scientific evidence available to make specific dietary recommendations to IBD patients (Lee et al., 2015), the vast majority of IBD patients *believe* that diet has an impact on their symptoms (Cohen et al., 2013) and pursue various dietary modifications and restrictive diets (Vagianos et al., 2014). This can be problematic in patients who already are losing weight and may be malnourished, in addition to the negative impact on HRQL and socializing (Mutlu & Gor, 2008). Clinically, some patients are so terrified of food that they resort to eating nothing but pureed baby food, even when their disease is in remission. Indeed, those who score the highest on the Fear of Food Questionnaire tend to be patients with comorbid IBD and IBS (Hunt, Zickgraf et al., 2018). Thus, targeting fear of food and encouraging patients to eat a reasonably varied, whole foods diet is an important component of behavioral health interventions for IBD.

CBT for Chronic GI Disorders

A typical course of CBT for chronic GI disorders would follow something like the protocol below.

Session 1

- Review of differential diagnosis and medical history.
  In IBS, ensure patient has had appropriate medical rule-outs (e.g., celiac disease and inflammatory bowel disease) and currently does not experience alarm symptoms. In IBD, ensure that the patient is receiving good medical care and that the disease is being managed and treated appropriately. If the patient's IBD is in remission, evaluate the possibility of secondary IBS.
- Educate the patient about the impact of stress and arousal on GI function via multiple mechanisms and pathways, including cortisol, adrenaline, sympathetic arousal, and the microbiome.

- Educate the patient about the role of visceral hypersensitivity in maintaining and exacerbating symptoms. Have the patient complete the VSI (included in Appendix 1).
- Teach effective relaxation strategies, including deep diaphragmatic breathing (which optimizes intestinal motility and activates the parasympathetic nervous system), muscle relaxation, and imagery. Some GI patients have difficulty with breathing and muscle relaxation because it focuses them on and in their body and heightens visceral awareness. If they feel like their body has become their enemy, getting the body to do what they want may seem impossible. In that case, start with imagery, but come back to other strategies later in treatment.
- Consider encouraging the addition of probiotics to their diet, since research does suggest that dysbiosis is often an underlying factor in both IBS and IBD.

Sessions 2–3

- Introduce the basic cognitive model of stress management, including negative automatic thoughts, and the link between thoughts and both emotions and physical reactivity. Teach the basic principles of cognitive restructuring. Use all components of classical cognitive therapy, including identifying situations, thoughts, and outcomes (feelings and behaviors), learning to generate benign alternatives, and examining the evidence for competing beliefs.
- Begin to explore any GI-specific catastrophic beliefs and distortions, especially those that overlap with panic disorder (such as catastrophic misinterpretation of benign bodily sensations) and social anxiety disorder (such as the "spotlight effect," and catastrophic beliefs about how others both notice and judge one's behaviors negatively).
- Have patient complete the GI-Cog and FFQ (included in Appendices 2 and 3) to gauge catastrophizing and fear of food. Be sure to explore the actual experience and fear of fecal incontinence, as many patients are acutely embarrassed by this topic and will not spontaneously report it. IBS patients may fear it despite never having experienced it. IBD patients may be justified in their concern about the probability of FI but may still have exaggerated, catastrophic fears of the implications of it. (For example, a patient who states unequivocally that if she ever experiences incontinence at work, she would have to quit that day and never return, probably is catastrophizing in a maladaptive way.)

Session 4

- Educate the patient about the role of experiential avoidance in maintaining and exacerbating impaired quality of life (because of missed experiences) and in contributing to visceral hypersensitivity and GI symptoms, including pain.
- Encourage the patient to identify avoidance behaviors in their own life and begin to make an anxiety hierarchy of situations they typically avoid.

- Explain the principles of graded exposure and agree collaboratively on some relatively easy homework assignments they can try. For example, if an IBS patient fears fecal incontinence and believes that they must always be no more than 30 seconds away from a bathroom, have them try to delay defecation by one minute in the safety of their own home. If they are able to do that successfully, increase the delay to two minutes, or three or five. This both provides exposure to feared GI sensations and also gives people a sense of mastery. If the patient has become agoraphobic about travel, have them sit in their car in the driveway or garage for half an hour. When that is easy and boring, have them drive around the block multiple times, so that they are never more than a minute away from home. This follows all the basic principles of graded exposure therapy but applies them specifically to GI-specific feared sensations, situations, and outcomes.
- If an IBD patient has been avoiding public places like the mall or the movie theater, agree on graded exposures they can try to achieve mastery. For example, they could look up the mall online, figure out where the bathrooms are, and then shop for half an hour in a store close by. They can also practice asking to use restrooms in facilities that do not normally allow the public access. It's a good idea to practice this when they don't *actually* have to go.

Sessions 5–6

- Continue reviewing reinterpretation of experiences and beliefs using thought records.
- Continue in-session exposure (e.g., have an IBS patient wear tight clothing that presses on the abdomen) and discussion of out-of-session exposure assignments.
- Begin to explore whether an IBS patient is engaging in *subtle* avoidance (e.g., prophylactic use of antidiarrheal medication, fasting, food rituals, scoping out bathrooms in advance, preferential seating near exits). Encourage patient to begin curtailing subtle avoidance.
- Encourage continued acceptance and reinterpretation of visceral sensations as uncomfortable but not dangerous or illness-related. In IBD patients, encourage appropriate symptom management but remind them that not *all* visceral sensations are necessarily problematic or illness-related.
- Encourage the patient to begin experimenting with eating a wider range of foods, including foods they have been avoiding for fear of triggering GI sensations and symptoms.

Sessions 7–8

- Explore any remaining catastrophic beliefs and explain the concept of behavioral experiments. This is good time to explore whether shame and secrecy play a role in experiential avoidance. Many GI patients believe that others in their lives would be disgusted or repulsed if they knew "the truth" about their GI issues and therefore take great pains to disguise their issues, make up excuses for absences or for avoiding social gatherings, and so on. A good behavioral experiment to encourage is having the patient choose one trusted person in their life and tell them the truth about having chronic GI issues. Since the vast majority of people are actually compassionate, curious, and concerned, patients typically are very positively surprised.

- Continue to encourage curtailing avoidance and engaging in life fully, including eating a variety of healthful foods and participating in activities that involve food or situations in which getting to a bathroom instantly might be difficult. Remind patients that even if they experience some GI symptoms, their quality of life still will be far better if they engage in life rather than giving in to the urge to avoid. If IBD patients *are* medically restricted to low residue diets, have them invite a friend over for a meal they have cooked, or go to a friend's house but offer to bring a dish they know they can eat. Honesty, humor, and problem-solving go a long way toward reducing the shame, embarrassment, and social isolation an IBD can cause.

- End with relapse prevention and planning. Remind patients that *everyone* experiences occasional GI discomfort, episodes of diarrhea or constipation, gas, and flatulence. Encourage patients to normalize those experiences, rather than catastrophize them.

- Encourage IBD patients to learn the difference between normative visceral sensations and discomfort and pain that signals an active flare.

In many behavioral medicine settings, especially those entailing consultation and liaison services and/or integrated primary care, therapists may be limited in the number of sessions they can provide, and in the length of those sessions. Thus, although six to eight hour-long sessions may be a relatively short treatment protocol, not all providers will have the luxury of even that many service contacts. In such cases, the most important points to convey are that effective stress-management strategies (not simply avoiding stress) and reducing behavioral avoidance are the two most important components of improving quality of life. Most patients are quick to acknowledge, when it is pointed out, that avoidant coping is not really "working" for them, in that it doesn't actually eliminate physical discomfort and it ends up greatly reducing HRQL. Doing some quick psychoeducation about the impact of stress on GI functioning, followed by some basic strategies for reducing avoidance (including de-catastrophizing or asking "What's the worst thing that could realistically happen? What would be so bad about that?") and then encouraging graded exposure to feared foods, sensations, and situations can go a long way for many patients.

Patients with complex psychiatric comorbidities may need much longer treatment protocols. Depression, severe social anxiety, trauma disorders, and more severe variants of agoraphobia all require skillful application of empirically supported treatment strategies and evidence-based practice. Fortunately, evidence is accruing that transdiagnostic approaches incorporating numerous empirically supported *principles* of effective treatment are helpful for patients with multiple comorbidities (e.g., Craske, 2012). CBT for IBS utilizes many such core principles (e.g., de-catastrophizing, exposure to reduce experiential avoidance) and is easily incorporated into a more general transdiagnostic approach to any existing comorbid disorders that the patient might present with. Such approaches have been shown to reduce both the target and the comorbid diagnoses (e.g., Norton et al., 2013).

Adjunctive Medication

In some GI patients, adjunctive treatment with psychiatric medication will be warranted. There is evidence from multiple RCTs supporting the usefulness in IBS of both SSRIs and tricyclics (Ford et al., 2014) and some open-label trials that show promise with the SNRI duloxetine (e.g., Kaplan, Franzen, Nickell, Ransom & Lebovitz, 2014; Lewis-Fernández et al., 2016). Duloxetine also has been shown to be useful in IBD patients (Daghaghzadeh et al., 2015). The medications can be helpful for any comorbid anxiety or depression but *also* have a modulating effect on visceral sensation in the gut (Camilleri, 2002). All of these drugs can modulate pain perception by modulating central regulatory mechanisms and visceral hypersensitivity (Sperber & Drossman, 2011; Dekel, Drossman & Sperber, 2013). Indeed, when introducing the possibility of medication to patients, it can be helpful to describe them as "neuromodulators" rather than as "antidepressants" or "anti-anxiety" drugs.

Each of the three major classes (SSRIs, SNRIs, and tricyclics) has advantages and disadvantages for patients with chronic GI disorders. SSRIs can induce nausea and diarrhea, which are sometimes intolerable to IBS-D patients. They may not be willing or able to tolerate the GI side effects long enough to experience the possible therapeutic effects. Tricyclic medications tend to be constipating, which is often a relief for IBS-D and IBD patients, but can be problematic for IBS-C patients. The SNRIs have shown some analgesic efficacy for pain in a variety of patients, including those with diabetic neuropathy (Yarnitsky, Granot, Nahman-Averbuch, Khamaisi & Granovsky, 2012) and fibromyalgia (Cording, Derry, Phillips, Moore & Wiffen, 2015); animal models suggest that they may have analgesic effects in abdominal visceral pain specifically (Depoortère et al., 2011). The GI side effect profile of SNRIs tends to mimic those of SSRIs at low doses followed by noradrenergic side effects at higher doses and over longer use (Sansone & Sansone, 2014). The advantage for IBS and IBD patients is that the two sets of GI side effects tend to either cancel each other out or land on the side of slightly constipating, providing relief from diarrhea and urgency that are so troubling to many patients.

Summary

Patients with chronic GI disorders, including IBS and IBD, are troubled by recurrent abdominal pain but also by urgency, diarrhea, flatulence, and fear of fecal incontinence. Many patients engage in substantial avoidance behaviors that can meet criteria for agoraphobia, and both IBS and IBD patients are at increased risk for comorbid psychiatric disorders, especially anxiety disorders and depression. Many develop substantial fear and avoidance of food and restrict their diets substantially, leading to loss of social opportunities and hedonic pleasure and, in some cases, compromised nutrition and/or increasing dysbiosis.

Medical management is crucial in the case of IBD, but traditional medical management often is unsatisfactory in the case of IBS. Both groups of patients are at risk for greatly reduced health-related quality of life, even with highly competent medical care. Fortunately, psychosocial, behavioral health treatments have been developed that benefit both groups. Hypnotherapy, mindfulness-based interventions, and cognitive-behavioral therapy are evidence-based treatments for chronic GI disorders that have considerable empirical support for their efficacy. All three approaches discourage experiential avoidance and teach patients to approach and think about their symptoms in less catastrophic ways. CBT protocols for both IBS and IBD have been modularized and adapted as self-help workbooks that can be used as standalone treatments or as adjunctive bibliotherapy in work with a therapist. This should increase the dissemination of such treatments and make it easier for healthcare professionals from various disciplines (psychology, counseling, social work, medical providers) to incorporate GI-informed psychotherapeutic interventions into their work with GI patients. Given that we know that patients can benefit from complementary approaches to reduce pain and improve quality of life, it is my fervent hope that together we can improve patient access to these effective treatments.

References

American Psychiatric Association. (2013). *Diagnostic and statistical manual of mental disorders* (5th ed.). Arlington, VA: American Psychiatric Publishing.

Asano, T., & Takenaga, M. (2017). Chlorpromazine hydrochloride suppresses visceral hypersensitivity to colorectal distension in a rat model of irritable bowel syndrome. *The FASEB Journal, 31*(S1), 666.

Ballou, S., & Keefer, L. (2017). Psychological interventions for irritable bowel syndrome and inflammatory bowel diseases. *Clinical and Translational Gastroenterology, 8*, e214. doi:10.1038/ctg.2016.69

Barbara, G., De Giorgio, R., Stanghellini, V., Cremon, C., & Corinaldesi, R. (2002). A role for inflammation in irritable bowel syndrome? *Gut, 51* (Suppl 1); London, i41–i44.

Bernstein, C. N., Singh, S., Graff, L. A., Walker, J. R., & Cheang, M. (2011). A prospective population-based study of triggers of symptomatic flares in IBD. *American Journal of Gastroenterology, 105*(9), 1994–2002.

Bevan, J. L. (2009). Interpersonal communication apprehension, topic avoidance, and the experience of irritable bowel syndrome. *Personal Relationships, 16*(2), 147–165.

Bhatia, V., & Tandon, R. K. (2004). Stress and the gastrointestinal tract. *Journal of Gastroenterology & Hepatology, 20*(3), 332–339.

Bitton, A., Dobkin, P. L., Edwardes, M. D., Sewitch, M. J., Meddings, J. B., Rawal, S., . . . Wild, G. E. (2008). Predicting relapse in Crohn's disease: A biopsychosocial model. *Gut, 57*(10), 1386–1392.

Blanchard, E. B., Lackner, J. M., Jaccard, J., Rowell, D., Carosella, A. M., Powell, C., . . . & Kuhn, E. (2008). The role of stress in symptom exacerbation among IBS patients. *Journal of Psychosomatic Research, 64*(2), 119–128.

Böhn, L., Störsrud, S., Liljebo, T., Collin, L., Lindfors, P., Törnblom, H., & Simrén, M. (2015). Diet low in FODMAPs reduces symptoms of irritable bowel syndrome as well as traditional dietary advice: A randomized controlled trial. *Gastroenterology, 149*(6), 1399–1407.

Böhn, L., Störsrud, S., Törnblom, H., Bengtsson, U., & Simrén, M. (2013). Self-reported food-related gastrointestinal symptoms in IBS are common and associated with more severe symptoms and reduced quality of life. *The American Journal of Gastroenterology, 108*(5), 634–641.

Bonaz, B. L., & Bernstein, C. N. (2013). Brain-gut interactions in inflammatory bowel disease. *Gastroenterology, 144*(1), 36–49.

Camilleri, M. (2002). Serotonergic modulation of visceral sensation: Lower gut. *Gut, 51*, i81–i86.

Camilleri, M., Coulie, B., & Tack, J. F. (2001). Visceral hypersensitivity: Facts, speculations, and challenges. *Gut, 48*(1), 125–131.

Cash, B. D., Schoenfeld, P., & Chey, W. D. (2002). The utility of diagnostic tests in irritable bowel syndrome patients: A systematic review. *The American Journal of Gastroenterology, 97*(11), 2812–2819.

Chang, L., Toner, B. B., Fukudo, S., Guthrie, E., Locke, G. R., Norton, N. J., & Sperber, A. D. (2006). Gender, age, society, culture, and the patient's perspective in the functional gastrointestinal disorders. *Gastroenterology, 130*(5), 1435–1446.

Chawla, N., & Ostafin, B. (2007). Experiential avoidance as a functional dimensional approach to psychopathology: An empirical review. *Journal of Clinical Psychology, 63*(9), 871–890.

Chilcot, J., & Moss-Morris, R. (2013). Changes in illness-related cognitions rather than distress mediate improvements in Irritable Bowel Syndrome (IBS) symptoms and disability following a brief cognitive behavioural therapy intervention. *Behaviour Research and Therapy, 51*(10), 690–695. doi:10.1016/j.brat.2013.07.007.

Cohen, A. B., Lee, D., Long, M. D., Kappelman, M. D., Martin, C. F., Sandler, R. S., & Lewis, J. D. (2013). Dietary patterns and self-reported associations of diet with symptoms of inflammatory bowel disease. *Digestive Diseases and Sciences, 58*(5), 1322–1328.

Collins, S. M. (2001). Modulation of intestinal inflammation by stress: Basic mechanisms and clinical relevance. *American Journal of Physiology-Gastrointestinal and Liver Physiology, 280*, G315–G318.

Collins, S. M. (2014). A role for the gut microbiota in IBS. *Nature Reviews Gastroenterology & Hepatology, 11*, 497–505.

Cording, M., Derry, S., Phillips, T., Moore, R. S., & Wiffen, P. J. (2015). Milnacipran for pain in fibromyalgia in adults. *The Cochrane Database of Systematic Reviews, 20*(10). doi:10.1002/14651858.CD008244.pub3

Craske, M. G. (2012). Transdiagnostic treatment for anxiety and depression. *Depression and Anxiety, 29*(9), 749–753.

Craske, M. G., Wolitzky-Taylor, K. B., Labus, J., Wu, S., Frese, M., Mayer, E. A., & Naliboff, B.D. (2011). A cognitive-behavioral treatment for irritable bowel syndrome using interoceptive exposure to visceral sensations. *Behaviour Research and Therapy, 49*(6–7), 413–421. doi:10.1016/j.brat.2011.04.001

Cryan, J. F., & Dinan, T. G. (2012). Mind-altering microorganisms: The impact of the gut microbiota on brain and behavior. *Nature Reviews Neuroscience, 13*, 701–712.

Daghaghzadeh, H., Naji, F., Afshar, H., Sharbafchi, M. R., Faizi, A., Maroufi, M., . . . Tavakoli, H. (2015). Efficacy of duloxetine add on in treatment of inflammatory bowel disease patients: A double-blind controlled study. *Journal of Research in Medical Sciences, 20*(6), 595–601.

Dekel, R., Drossman, D. A., & Sperber, A. D. (2013). The use of psychotropic drugs in irritable bowel syndrome. *Expert Opinion on Investigational Drugs, 22*(3), 329–339.

Depoortère, R., Meleine, M., Bardin, L., Aliaga, M., Muller, E., Ardid, D., & Newman-Tancredi, A. (2011). Milnacipran is active in models of irritable bowel syndrome and abdominal visceral pain in rodents. *European Journal of Pharmacology, 672*(1–3), 83–87.

Dibley, L., & Norton, C. (2013). Experiences of fecal incontinence in people with inflammatory bowel disease: Self-reported experiences among a community sample. *Inflammatory Bowel Diseases, 19*(7), 1450–1462.

Didari, T., Mozaffari, S., Nikfar, S., & Abdollahi, M. (2015). Effectiveness of probiotics in irritable bowel syndrome: Updated systematic review with meta-analysis. *World Journal of Gastroenterology, 21*(10), 3027–3084.

Dinan, T. G., & Cryan, J. F. (2013). Melancholic microbes: A link between gut microbiota and depression? *Neurogastroenterology and Motility, 25*(9), 713–719.

Drossman, D. A. (2016). Functional gastrointestinal disorders: History, pathophysiology, clinical features, and Rome IV. *Gastroenterology, 150*(6), 1262–1279.

Edman, J. S., Greeson, J. M, Roberts, R. S., Kaufman, A. B., Abrams, D. I., Dolor, R. J., & Wolever, R. Q. (2017). Perceived stress in patients with common gastrointestinal disorders: Associations with quality of life, symptoms and disease management. *Explore: The Journal of Science and Healing, 13*(3), 124–128.

Evertsz, F. B., Thijssens, N., Stokkers, P., Grootenhuis, M., Bockting, C., Nieuwkerk, P., & Sprangers, M. (2012). Do inflammatory bowel disease patients with anxiety and depressive symptoms receive the care they need? *Journal of Crohn's and Colitis, 6*(1), 68–76. doi:10.1016/j.crohns.2011.07.006

Ferrari, L., Krane, M. K., & Fichera, A. (2016). Inflammatory bowel disease surgery in the biologic era. *World Journal of Gastroenterology, 8*(5), 363–370.

Ford, A. C., Moayyedi, P., Lacy, B. E., Lembo, A. J., Saito, Y. A., Schiller, L. R., . . . Quigley, E. M. M. (2014). American college of gastroenterology monograph on the management of irritable bowel syndrome and chronic idiopathic constipation. *The American Journal of Gastroenterology, 109*, S2–S26.

Ford, A. C., Quigley, E. M. M., Lacy, B. E., Lembo, A. J., Saito, Y. A., Schiler, L. R., . . . Moayyedi, P. (2014). Effect of antidepressants and psychological therapies, including hypnotherapy, in irritable bowel syndrome: Systematic review and meta-analysis. *American Journal of Gastroenterology, 109*, 1350–1365.

Ford, A. C., Sandborn, W. J., Kahn, K. J., Hanauer, S. B., Talley, N. J., & Moayyedi, P. (2011). Efficacy of biological therapies in inflammatory bowel disease: Systematic review and meta-analysis. *The American Journal of Gastroenterology, 106*, 644–659.

Fukudo, S. (2007). Role of corticotropin-releasing hormone in irritable bowel syndrome and intestinal inflammation. *Journal of Gastroenterology, 42*(S17), 48–51.

Gaylord, S. A., Palsson, O. S., Garland, E. L., Faurot, K. R., Coble, R. S., Mann, J. D., Frey, W., Leniek, K., & Whitehead, W. E. (2011). Mindfulness training reduces the severity of irritable bowel syndrome in women: Results of a randomized controlled trial. *American Journal of Gastroenterology, 106*, 1678–1688.

Gerson, C. D., & Gerson, M. J. (2003). A collaborative health care model for the treatment of irritable bowel syndrome. *Clinical Gastroenterology and Hepatology, 1*(6), 446–452.

Gerson, C. D., Gerson, M. J., & Gerson, M. J. (2013). Group hypnotherapy for irritable bowel syndrome with long-term follow-up. *International Journal of Clinical and Experimental Hypnotherapy, 61*(1), 38–54.

Gerson, M. J., & Gerson, C. D. (2012). The importance of relationships in patients with irritable bowel syndrome: A review. *Gastroenterology Research and Practice, V2012*, 1–5. http://dx.doi.org/10.1155/2012/157340

Gibson, P. R., & Shepherd, S. J. (2010). Evidence-based dietary management of functional gastrointestinal symptoms: The FODMAP approach. *Journal of Gastroenterology and Hepatology, 25*, 252–258.

Goodhand, J. R., Wahed, M., Mawdsley, J. E., Farmer, A. D., Aziz, Q., & Rampton, D. S. (2012). Mood disorders in inflammatory bowel disease: Relation to diagnosis, disease activity, perceived stress, and other factors. *Inflammatory Bowel Diseases, 18*(12), 2301–2309. doi:10.1002/ibd.22916

Graff, L. A., Walker, J. R., & Bernstein, C. N. (2009). Depression and anxiety in inflammatory bowel disease: A review of comorbidity and management. *Inflammatory Bowel Diseases, 15*(7), 1105–1118. doi:10.1002/ibd.20873

Graff, L. A., Walker, J. R., Clara, I., Lix, L., Miller, N., Rogala, L., . . . & Bernstein, C. N. (2009). Stress coping, distress, and health perceptions in inflammatory bowel disease and community controls. *American Journal of Gastroenterology, 104*(12), 2959–2969. doi:10.1038/ajg.2009.529

Gros, D. F., Antony, M. M., McCabe, R. E., & Swinson, R. P. (2009). Frequency and severity of the symptoms of irritable bowel syndrome across the anxiety disorders and depression. *Journal of Anxiety Disorders, 23*(2), 290–296.

Grundmann, O., & Yoon, S. L. (2014). Complementary and alternative medicines in irritable bowel syndrome: An integrative view. *World Journal of Gastroenterology, 20*(2), 346–362.

Guthrie, E. (2002). Psychological disorder and severity of inflammatory bowel disease predict health-related quality of life in ulcerative colitis and Crohn's disease. *The American Journal of Gastroenterology, 97*(8), 1994–1999. doi:10.1016/s0002-9270(02)04198-9

Halmos, E. P., Power, V. A., Shepherd, S. J., Gibson, P. R., & Muir, J. G. (2014). A diet low in FODMAPs reduces symptoms of irritable bowel syndrome. *Gastroenterology, 146*(1), 67–75.

Halpert, A., Dalton, C. B., Palsson, O., Morris, C., Hu, Y., Bangdiwala, S., . . . Drossman, D. (2007). What patients know about Irritable Bowel Syndrome (IBS) and what they would like to know. National survey on patient educational needs in IBS and development and validation of the Patient Educational Needs Questionnaire (PEQ). *American Journal of Gastroenterology, 102*, 1972–1982.

Häuser, W., Moser, G., Klose, P., & Miocka-Walus, A. (2014). Psychosocial issues in evidence-based guidelines on inflammatory bowel diseases: A review. *World Journal of Gastroenterology, 20*(13), 3663–3671.

Hou, J. K., Abraham, B., & El-Serag, H. (2011). Dietary intake and risk of developing inflammatory bowel disease: A systematic review of the literature. *The American Journal of Gastroenterology, 106*, 563–573.

Hunt, M. (2016). *Reclaim your life from IBS: A scientifically proven plan for relief without restrictive diets*. New York, NY: Sterling Publishing Co.

Hunt, M., Ertel, E., Coello, J., & Rodriguez, L. (2014a). Development and validation of the GI-cognitions questionnaire. *Cognitive Therapy and Research, 38*(4), 472–482. Retrieved from www.springerlink.com/openurl.asp?genre=article&id=doi:10.1007/s10608-014-9607-y

Hunt, M., Ertel, E., Coello, J., & Rodriguez, L. (2014b). Empirical support for a self-help treatment for IBS. *Cognitive Therapy and Research, 39*, 215–227.

Hunt, M., Loftus, P., Accardo, M, Keenan, M., & Cohen, L. (2018). *Coping with Crohn's and colitis: Three-month follow-up for a randomized controlled trial comparing a CBT self-help book to an active psychoeducational control*. Poster presented at the anxiety and depression association of America annual meeting.

Hunt, M., Milonova, M., & Moshier, S. (2009). Catastrophic consequences of GI symptoms in irritable bowel syndrome. *Journal of Cognitive Psychotherapy, 23*(2), 160–173.

Hunt, M., Moshier, S., & Milonova, M. (2009). Brief cognitive-behavioral internet therapy for irritable bowel syndrome. *Behaviour Research and Therapy, 47*(9), 797–802.

Hunt, M., Rodriguez, L., & Marcelle, E. (2017). A cognitive behavioral therapy workbook delivered online with minimal therapist feedback improves quality of life for inflammatory bowel disease patients. *Internal Medicine Review, 3*(10), 1–16.

Hunt, M., Wong, C, Aajmain, S., & Dawodu, I., (2018). Fecal incontinence in people with self-reported irritable bowel syndrome: Prevalence and quality of life. *Journal of Psychosomatic Research, 113*, 45–51, doi:10.1016/j.jpsychores.2018.07.015

Hunt, M., Zickgraf, H., Gibbons, B., & Loftus, P. (2018). *Development and validation of the Fear of Food Questionnaire (FFQ).* Poster presented at the annual meeting of the anxiety and depression association of America. Washington, DC.

Iglesias-Rey, M., Barreiro-de Acosta, M., Caamaño-Isorna, F., Rodriguez, I.V., Ferreiro, R., Lindkvist, B., . . . Dominguez-Munoz, J. E. (2014). Psychological factors are associated with changes in the health-related quality of life in inflammatory bowel disease. *Inflammatory Bowel Diseases, 20*(1), 92–102. doi:10.1097/01.MIB.0000436955.78 220.bc.

Kabat-Zinn, J., Lipworth, L., Burney, R., & Sellers, W. (1986). Four-year follow-up of a meditation-based program for the self-regulation of chronic pain: Treatment outcomes and compliance. *Clinical Journal of Pain, 2*, 159–173.

Kaplan, A., Franzen, M. D., Nickell, P.V., Ransom, D., & Lebovitz, P. J. (2014). An open-label trial of duloxetine in patients with irritable bowel syndrome and comorbid generalized anxiety disorder. *International Journal of Psychiatry in Clinical Practice, 18*(1), 11–15. doi.org/10.3109/13651501.2013.838632

Kennedy, P. J., Cryan, J. F., Quigley, E. M. M., Dinan, T. G., & Clarke, G. (2014). A sustained hypothalamic—pituitary—adrenal axis response to acute psychosocial stress in irritable bowel syndrome. *Psychological Medicine, 44*, 3123–3134.

Kinsinger, S. W. (2017). Cognitive-behavioral therapy for patients with irritable bowel syndrome: Current insights. *Psychology Research and Behavior Management, 10*, 231–237.

Knowles, S. R., Monshat, K., & Castle, D. J. (2013). The efficacy and methodological challenges of psychotherapy for adults with inflammatory bowel disease: A review. *Inflammatory Bowel Diseases, 19*(12), 2704–2715.

Labus, J. S., Bolus, R., Chang, L., Wiklund, I., Naesal, J., Mayer, E. A., & Naliboff, B. D. (2004). The visceral sensitivity index: Development and validation of a gastrointestinal symptom-specific anxiety scale. *Alimentary Pharmacology & Therapeutics, 20*(1), 89–97.

Labus, J. S., Mayer, E. A., Chang, L., Bolus, R., & Naliboff, B. D. (2007). The central role of gastrointestinal-specific anxiety in irritable bowel syndrome: Further validation of the visceral sensitivity index. *Psychosomatic Medicine, 69*(1), 89–98.

Lackner, J. M. (2007). *Controlling IBS the drug-free way: A 10-step plan for symptom relief.* New York, NY: Harry N. Abrams Publisher.

Lackner, J. M., Ma, C. X., Keefer, L., Brenner, D. M., Gudleski, G. D., Satchidanand, N., . . . Mayer, E. A. (2013). Type, rather than number, of mental and physical comorbidities increases the severity of symptoms in patients with irritable bowel syndrome. *Clinical Gastroenterology and Hepatology, 11*(9), 1147–1157.

Lackner, J. M., Quigley, B. M., & Blanchard, E. B. (2004). Depression and abdominal pain in IBS patients: The mediating role of catastrophizing. *Psychosomatic Medicine, 66*(3), 435–441.

Lacy, B. E. (2016a). Perspective: An easier diagnosis. *Nature, 533*, S107, doi:10.1038/533S107a

Lacy, B. E. (2016b). Diagnosis and treatment of diarrhea-predominant irritable bowel syndrome. *International Journal of General Medicine, 9*, 7–17.

Lacy, B., Patel, H., Guérin, A., Dea, K., Scopel, J. L., Alaghband, R., . . . & Mody, R. (2016). Regional variation of care for irritable bowel syndrome in the United States. *PLoS ONE, 11*(4): e0154258. https://doi.org/10.1371/journal.pone.0154258

Laird, K. T., Tanner-Smith, E. E., Russell, A. C., Hollon, S. D., & Walker, L. S. (2016). Short-term and long-term efficacy of psychological therapies for irritable bowel syndrome:

A systematic review and meta-analysis. *Clinical Gastroenterology and Hepatology*, *14*(7), 937–947.

Lea, R., Houghton, L. A., Calvert, E. L., Larder, S., Gonsalkorale, W. M., Whelan, V., Randles, J., Cooper, P., Cruickshanks, P., Miller, V., & Whorwell, P.J. (2003). Gut-focused hypnotherapy normalizes disordered rectal sensitivity in patients with irritable bowel syndrome. *Alimentary Pharmacology and Therapeutics*, *17*, 635–642. doi:10.1046/j.1365-2036.2003.01486.x

Lee, D., Albenberg, L., Compher, C., Baldassano, R., Piccoli, D., Lewis, J. D., & Wu, G. D. (2015). Diet in the pathogensis and treatment of inflammatory bowel diseases. *Gastroenterology*, *148*(6), 1087–1106.

Leone, V., Change, E. B., & Devkota, S. (2013). Diet, microbes, and host genetics: The perfect storm in inflammatory bowel diseases. *Journal of Gastroenterology*, *48*(3), 315–321.

Levenstein, S. (2000). Stress and exacerbation in ulcerative colitis: A prospective study of patients enrolled in remission. *The American Journal of Gastroenterology*, *95*(5), 1213–1220. doi:10.1016/s0002-9270(00)00804-2

Lewis-Fernández, R., Lam, P., Lucak, S., Galfalvy, H., Jackson, E., Fried, J., . . . Schneier, F. (2016). An open-label pilot study of duloxetine in patients with irritable bowel syndrome and comorbid major depressive disorder. *Journal of Clinical Psychopharmacology*, *36*(6), 710–715.

Lindfors, P., Unge, P., Nyhlin, H., Ljótsson, B., Björnsson, E. S., Abrahamsson, H., & Simrén, M. (2012). Long-term effects of hypnotherapy in patients with refractory irritable bowel syndrome. *Scandinavian Journal of Gastroenterology*, *47*, 413–420.

Ljótsson, B., Falk, L., Vesterlund, A. W., Hedman, E., Lindfors, P., Rück, C., . . . Andersson, G. (2010). Internet-delivered exposure and mindfulness based therapy for irritable bowel syndrome—A randomized controlled trial. *Behaviour Research and Therapy*, *48*(6), 531–539.

Ljótsson, B., Hedman, E., Lindfors, P., Hursti, T., Lindefors, N., Andersson, G., & Rück, C. (2011). Long-term follow-up of internet-delivered exposure and mindfulness based treatment for irritable bowel syndrome. *Behaviour Research and Therapy*, *49*(1), 58–61.

Ljótsson, B., Hesser, H., Andersson, E., Lindfors, P., Hursti, T., Rück, C., . . . Hedman, E. (2013). Mechanisms of change in an exposure-based treatment for irritable bowel syndrome. *Journal of Consulting and Clinical Psychology*, *81*(6), 1113–1126. http://dx.doi.org/10.1037/a0033439

Ljótsson, B., Hesser, H., Andersson, E., Lackner, J. M., Alaoui, S. E., Falk, L., . . . Hedman, E. (2014). Provoking symptoms to relieve symptoms: A randomized controlled dismantling study of exposure therapy in irritable bowel syndrome. *Behaviour Research and Therapy*, *55*, 27–39.

Longstreth, G. F., Thompson, W. G., Chey, W. D., Houghton, L. A., Mearin, F., & Spiller, R. C. (2006). Functional bowel disorders. *Gastroenterology*, *130*, 1480–1491.

Lydiard, R. B. (2001). Irritable bowel syndrome, anxiety, and depression: What are the links? *Journal of Clinical Psychiatry*, *62* (Suppl 8), 38–45.

Maagaard, L., Ankersen, D. V., Végh, Z., Burisch, J., Jensen, L., Pedersen, N., & Munkholm, P. (2016). Follow-up of patients with functional bowel symptoms treated with a low FODMAP diet. *World Journal of Gastroenterology*, *22*(15), 4009–4019.

Masand, P. S., Kaplan, D. S., Gupta, S., Bhandary, A. N., Nasra, G. S., Kline, M. D., & Margo, K. L. (1995). Major depression and irritable bowel syndrome: Is there a relationship? *The Journal of Clinical Psychiatry*, *56*(8), 363–367.

Maunder, R. G., & Levenstein, S. (2008). The role of stress in the development and clinical course of inflammatory bowel disease: Epidemiological evidence. *Current Molecular Medicine*, *8*(4), 247–252.

Mawdsley, J. E., & Rampton, D. S. (2005). Psychological stress in IBD: New insights into pathogenic and therapeutic implications. *Gut*, *54*(10), 1481–1491. doi:10.1136/gut.2005.064261

Mawdsley, J. E., & Rampton, D. S. (2006). The role of psychological stress in inflammatory bowel disease. *Neuroimmunomodulation, 13*(5–6), 327–336. doi:10.1159/000104861

Mikocka-Walus, A., Bampton, P., Hetzel, D., Hughes, P., Esterman, A., & Andrews, J. M. (2015). Cognitive-behavioural therapy has no effect on disease activity but improves quality of life in subgroups of patients with inflammatory bowel disease: A pilot randomised controlled trial. *BMC Gastroenterology, 15*(1), 54. doi:10.1186/s12876-015-0278-2

Mikocka-Walus, A., Bampton, P., Hetzel, D., Hughes, P., Esterman, A., & Andrews, J. M. (2016). Cognitive-behavioural therapy for inflammatory bowel disease: 24-Month data from a randomised controlled trial. *International Journal of Behavioral Medicine, 24*(1), 127–135. doi:10.1007/s12529-016-9580-9

Mikocka-Walus, A., Turnbull, D. A., Andrews, J. M., Moulding, N. T., & Holtmann, G. J. (2008). The effect of functional gastrointestinal disorders on psychological comorbidity and quality of life in patients with inflammatory bowel disease. *Alimentary Pharmacology and Therapeutics, 28*(4), 475–483.

Mittermaier, C., Dejaco, C., Waldhoer, T., Oefferlbauer-Ernst, A., Miehsler, W., Beier, M., . . . Moser, G. (2004). Impact of depressive mood on relapse in patients with inflammatory bowel disease: A prospective 18-month follow-up study. *Psychosomatic Medicine, 66*(1), 79–84. doi:10.1097/01.psy.0000106907.24881.f2

Molodecky, N. A., Soon, I. S., Rabi, D. M., Ghali, W. A., Ferris, M., Chernoff, G., . . . Kaplan, G. G. (2012). Increasing incidence and prevalence of the inflammatory bowel diseases with time, based on systematic review. *Gastroenterology, 142*(1), 46–54.

Moloney, R. D., Johnson, A. C., O'Mahony, S. M., Dinan, T. G., Greenwood-Van Meerveld, B., Cryan, J. F. (2016). Stress and the microbiota-gut-brain axis in visceral pain: Relevance to irritable bowel syndrome. *CNS Neuroscience & Therapeutics, 22*(2), 102–117.

Moloney, R. D., O'Leary, O. F., Felice, D., Bettler, B., Dinan, T. G., & Cryan, J. F. (2012). Early-life stress induces visceral hypersensitivity in mice. *Neuroscience Letters, 512*, 99–102.

Moss-Morris, R., McAlpine, L., Didsbury, L. P., & Spence, M. J. (2010). A randomized controlled trial of a cognitive behavioural therapy-based self-management intervention for irritable bowel syndrome in primary care. *Psychological Medicine, 40*(1), 85–94. doi:10.1017/S0033291709990195

Mussell, M., Böcker, U., Nagel, N., Olbrich, R., & Singer, M. (2003). Reducing psychological distress in patients with inflammatory bowel disease by cognitive-behavioural treatment: Exploratory study of effectiveness. *Scandinavian Journal of Gastroenterology, 38*(7), 755–762. doi:10.1080/00365520310003110

Mutlu, E. A., & Gor, N. (2008). To diet or not if you have inflammatory bowel disease. *Expert Review of Gastroenterology & Hepatology, 2*(5), 613.

Mykletun, A., Jacka, F., Williams, L., Pasco, J., Henry, M. Nicholson, G. C., . . . Berk, M. (2010). Prevalence of mood and anxiety disorder in self-reported irritable bowel syndrome (IBS). An epidemiological population based study of women. *BMC Gastroenterology, 10*, 88.

Nanayakkara, W. S., Skidmore, P. M. L., O'Brien, L., Wilkinson, T. J., & Gearry, R. B. (2016). Efficacy of the low FODMAP diet for treating irritable bowel syndrome: The evidence to date. *Clinical and Experimental Gastroenterology, 9*, 131–142.

Neilson, K., Ftanou, M., Monshat, K., Salzberg, M., Bell, S., Kamm, M. A., . . . Castle, D. (2016). A controlled study of a group mindfulness intervention for individuals living with inflammatory bowel disease. *Inflammatory Bowel Diseases, 22*(3), 694–701. doi:10.1097/mib.0000000000000629

Norton, P. J., Barrera, T. L., Mathew, A. R., Chamberlain, L. D., Szafranski, D. D., Reddy, R., & Smith, A. H. (2013). Effect of transdiagnostic CBT for anxiety disorders on comorbid diagnoses. *Anxiety and Depression, 30*(2), 168–173.

Öhman, L., & Simrén, M. (2010). Pathogenesis of IBS: Role of inflammation, immunity and neuroimmune interactions. *Nature Reviews Gastroenterology & Hepatology, 7*, 163–173.

Ong, D. K., Mitchell, S. B., Barrett, J. S., Shepherd, S. J., Irving, P. M., Biesiekierski, J. R., ... Muir, J. G. (2010). Manipulation of dietary short chain carbohydrates alters the pattern of gas production and genesis of symptoms in irritable bowel syndrome. *Journal of Gastroenterology and Hepatology, 25*, 1366–1373.

Palsson, O. S. (2015). Hypnosis treatment of gastrointestinal disorders: A comprehensive review of the empirical evidence. *American Journal of Clinical Hypnosis, 58*(2), 134–158. doi:10.1080/00029157.2015.1039114

Palsson, O. S., van Tiburg, M. A., Simren, M., Sperber, A. D., & Whitehead, W. E. (2016). Mo1642 population prevalence of Rome IV and Rome III Irritable Bowel Syndrome (IBS) in the United States (US), Canada and the United Kingdom (UK). *Gastroenterology, 150*(4 Suppl 1), S739–S740.

Palsson, O. S., & Whitehead, W. E. (2013). Psychological treatments in functional gastrointestinal disorders: A primer for the gastroenterologist. *Clinical Gastroenterology and Hepatology, 11*(3), 208–216.

Pedersen, N., Andersen, N. N., Végh, Z., Jensen, L., Andersen, D.V., Felding, M., ... Munkholm, P. (2014). Ehealth: Low FODMAP diet vs *Lactobacillus rhamnosus* GG in irritable bowel syndrome. *World Journal of Gastroenterology, 20*(43), 16215–16226.

Persoons, P., Vermeire, S., Demyttenaere, K., Fischler, B., Vandenberghe, J., Oudenhove, L.V., ... Rutgeerts, P. (2005). The impact of major depressive disorder on the short-and long-term outcome of Crohn's disease treatment with infliximab. *Alimentary Pharmacology and Therapeutics, 22*(2), 101–110. doi:10.1111/j.1365-2036.2005.02535.x

Rao, S. S. C., Yu, S., & Fedewa, A. (2015). Systematic review: Dietary fibre and FODMAP-restricted diet in the management of constipation and irritable bowel syndrome. *Alimentary Pharmacology and Therapeutics, 41*(12), 1256–1270.

Sajadinejad, M. S., Asgari, K., Molavi, H., Kalantari, M., & Adibi, P. (2012). Psychological issues in inflammatory bowel disease: An overview. *Gastroenterology Research and Practice*, 1–11. doi:10.1155/2012/106502

Sansone, R. A., & Sansone, L. A. (2014). Serotonin norepinephrine reuptake inhibitors: A pharmacological comparison. *Innovations in Clinical Neuroscience, 11*(3–4), 37–42.

Sewitch, M. (2001). Psychological distress, social support, and disease activity in patients with inflammatory bowel disease. *The American Journal of Gastroenterology, 96*(5), 1470–1479. doi:10.1016/s0002-9270(01)02363-2

Shepherd, S., & Gibson, P. (2013). *The complete low-FODMAP diet book: A revolutionary plan for managing IBS and other digestive disorders.* New York, NY: The Experiment Publishing, LLC.

Shin, S. J., Noh, C., Lim, S. G., Lee, K. M., & Lee, K. J. (2017). Non-steroidal anti-inflammatory drug-induced enteropathy. *Intestinal Research, 15*(4), 446–455.

Simrén, M., Palsson, O. S., Heymen, S., Bajor, A., Törnblom, H., & Whitehead, W. E. (2017). Fecal incontinence in irritable bowel syndrome: Prevalence and associated factors in Swedish and American patients. *Neurogastroenterology & Motility, 29*(2), e12919, doi:10.1111/nmo.12919

Simrén, M., Törnblom, H., Palsson, O. S., van Tilgurg, M. A., van Oudenhove, L., Tack, J., & Whitehead, W. E. (2018). Visceral hypersensitivity is associated with GI symptom severity in functional GI disorders: Consistent findings from five different patient cohorts. *Gut, 67*(2), 255–262.

Sperber, A. D., & Drossman, D. A. (2011). Review article: The functional abdominal pain syndrome. *Alimentary Pharmacology and Therapeutics, 33*, 514–524.

Stanculete, M. F., & Dumitrascu, D. L. (2016). Psychiatric comorbidities in IBS patients. *Journal of Psychosomatic Research, 85*, 81.

Staudacher, H. M., Irving, P. M., Lomer, M. C. E., & Whelan, K. (2014). Mechanisms and efficacy of dietary FODMAP restriction in IBS. *Nature Reviews Gastroenterology & Hepatology, 11*, 256–266.

Staudacher, H. M., Lomer, M. C., Anderson, J. L, Barrett, J. S., Muir, J. G., Irving, P. M., & Whelan, K. (2012). Fermentable carbohydrate restriction reduces luminal bifidobacteria and gastrointestinal symptoms in patients with irritable bowel syndrome. *Journal of Nutrition, 142*, 1510–1518.

Sugaya, N., Kaiya, H., Kumano, H., & Nomura, S. (2008). Relationship between subtypes of irritable bowel syndrome and severity of symptoms associated with panic disorder. *Scandinavian Journal of Gastroenterology, 43*(6), 675–681.

Sugaya, N., Yoshida, E., Yasuda, S., Tochigi, M., Takei, K., Ohtani, T., . . . Sasaki, T. (2013). Irritable bowel syndrome, its cognition, anxiety sensitivity, and anticipatory anxiety in panic disorder patients. *Psychiatry and Clinical Neurosciences, 67*(6), 397–404.

Szigethy, E. M., Allen, J. I., Reiss, M., Cohen, W., Perera, L. P., Brillstein, L., . . . Regueiro, M. D. (2017). The impact of mental and psychosocial factors on the care of patients with inflammatory bowel disease. *Clinical Gastroenterology and Hepatology, 15*(7), 986–997.

Tan, G., Hammon, D. C., & Gurrala, J. (2005). Hypnosis and irritable bowel syndrome: A review of efficacy and mechanism of action. *American Journal of Clinical Hypnosis, 47*(3), 161–178.

Toner, B., Segal, Z. V., Emmott, S. D., & Myran, D. (2000). *Cognitive-behavioral treatment of irritable bowel syndrome: The brain-gut connection.* New York, NY: The Guilford Press.

Toner, B., Segal, Z. V., Emmott, S., Myran, D., Ali, A., Digasbarro, I., & Stuckless, N. (1998). Cognitive-behavioral group therapy for patients with irritable bowel syndrome. *International Journal of Group Psychotherapy, 48*(2), 215–243.

Vagianos, K., Clara, I., Carr, R., Graff, L. A., Walker, J. R., Targownik, L. E., . . . Bernstein, C. N. (2014). What are adults with inflammatory bowel disease (IBD) eating? A closer look at the dietary habits of a population-based Canadian IBD cohort. *Journal of Perenteral and Enteral Nutrition, 40*(3), 405–411.

Vork, L., Weerts, Z. Z. R. M., Mujagic, Z., Kruimel, J. W., Hesselink, M. A. M., Muris, J. W. M., . . . Masclee, A. A. M. (2018). Rome III vs Rome IV criteria for irritable bowel syndrome: A comparison of clinical characteristics in a large cohort study. *Neurogastroenterology and Motility, 30*(2). doi:https://doi.org/10.1111/nmo.13189

Walker, J. R., Ediger, J. P., Graff, L. A., Greenfeld, J. M., Clara, I., Lix, L., . . . Bernstein, C. N. (2008). The Manitoba IBD cohort study: A population-based study of the prevalence of lifetime and 12-month anxiety and mood disorders. *American Journal of Gastroenterology, 103*(8), 1989–1997.

Walsham, N. E., & Sherwood, R. A. (2016). Fecal calprotectin in inflammatory bowel disease. *Clinical Experimental Gastroenterology, 9*, 21–29.

Walters, J. R. F., & Pattni, S. S. (2010). Managing bile acid diarrhea. *Therapeutic Advances in Gastroenterology, 3*(6), 349–357.

Watanabe, S., Hattori, T., Kanazawa, M., Kano, M., & Fukudo, S. (2007). Role of histaminergic neurons in hypnotic modulation of brain processing of visceral perception. *Neurogastroenterology & Motility, 19*, 831–838. doi:10.1111/j.1365-2982.2007.00959.x

Whorwell, P. J., Houghton, L. A., Taylor, E. E., & Maxton, D. G. (1992). Physiological effects of emotion: Assessment via hypnosis. *Lancet, 340*, 69–72. doi:10.1016/0140-6736(92)90394-I

Whorwell, P., Prior, A., & Colgan, S. (1987). Hypnotherapy in severe irritable bowel syndrome: Further experience. *Gut, 28*(4), 423–425.

Whorwell, P., Prior, A., & Faragher, E. (1984). Controlled trial of hypnotherapy in the treatment of severe refractory irritable bowel syndrome. *The Lancet, 2*, 1232–1234.

Wilder-Smith, C. H., & Robert-Yap, J. (2007). Abnormal endogenous pain modulation and somatic and visceral hypersensitivity in female patients with irritable bowel syndrome. *World Journal of Gastroenterology, 13*(27), 3699–3704.

Wolitzky-Taylor, K., Craske, M. G., Labus, J. S., Mayer, E. A., & Naliboff, B. D. (2012). Visceral sensitivity as a mediator of outcome in the treatment of irritable bowel syndrome. *Behaviour Research and Therapy, 50*(10), 647–650. doi:10.1016/j.brat.2012.05.010

Wouters, M. M., Balemans, D., Van Wanrooy, S. V., Dooley, J., Ciber-Goton, V., Alpizar, Y.A., . . . Boeckxstaens, G. E. (2016). Histamine receptor H1-mediated sensitization of TRPV1 mediates visceral hypersensitivity and symptoms in patients with irritable bowel syndrome. *Gastroenterology*, *150*(4), 875–887.

Yarnitsky, D., Granot, M., Nahman-Averbuch, H., Khamaisi, M., & Granovsky, Y. (2012). Conditioned pain modulation predicts duloxetine efficacy in painful diabetic neuropathy. *Pain*, *153*(6), 1193–1198.

Ye, L., Chen, W., Chen, B., Lan, X., Wang, S., Wu, X. C., . . . Wang, F. Y. (2017). Levels of faecal calprotectin and magnetic resonance enterocolonography correlate with severity of small bowel crohn's disease: A retrospective cohort study. *Scientific Reports*, *7*(1), 1970. doi:10.1038/s41598-017-02111-6

Zernicke, K. A., Campbell, T. S., Blustein, P. K., Fung, T. S., Johnson, J. A., Bacon, S. L., & Carlson, L. E. (2013). Mindfulness-based stress reduction for the treatment of irritable bowel syndrome symptoms: A randomized wait-list controlled trial. *International Journal of Behavioral Medicine*, *20*(3), 385–396.

Zhang, Y. Z., & Li, Y. Y. (2014). Inflammatory bowel disease: Pathogenesis. *World Journal of Gastroenterology*, *20*(1), 91–99.

Zhou, Y., Ren, W., Irvine, E. J., & Yang, D. (2010). Assessing health-related quality of life in patients with inflammatory bowel disease in Zhejiang, China. *Journal of Clinical Nursing*, *19*(1–2), 79–88. doi:10.1111/j.1365-2702.2009.03020.x

Appendix 1

Visceral Sensitivity Index (VSI)

Labus, J. (2007). The central role of gastrointestinal-specific anxiety in IBS: Further validation of the Visceral Sensitivity Index. *Psychosomatic Medicine, 69*: 89–98.

Below are statements that describe how some people respond to symptoms or discomfort in their belly or lower abdomen. These may include pain, diarrhea, constipation, bloating, or sense of urgency. Please answer *how strongly you agree or disagree* with each of these statements, AS THEY RELATE TO YOU. Answer all of the statements as honestly and thoughtfully as you can.

Item	Strongly Disagree	Moderately Disagree	Mildly Disagree	Mildly Agree	Moderately Agree	Strongly Agree
I worry that whenever I eat during the day, bloating and distension in my belly will get worse.	0	1	2	3	4	5
I get anxious when I go to a new restaurant.	0	1	2	3	4	5
I often worry about problems in my belly.	0	1	2	3	4	5
I have a difficult time enjoying myself because I cannot get my mind off of discomfort in my belly.	0	1	2	3	4	5

Item	Strongly Disagree	Moderately Disagree	Mildly Disagree	Mildly Agree	Moderately Agree	Strongly Agree
I often fear that I won't be able to have a normal bowel movement.	0	1	2	3	4	5
Because of fear of developing abdominal discomfort, I seldom try new foods.	0	1	2	3	4	5
No matter what I eat, I will probably feel uncomfortable.	0	1	2	3	4	5
As soon as I feel abdominal discomfort I begin to worry and feel anxious.	0	1	2	3	4	5
When I enter a place I haven't been before, one of the first things I do is to look for a bathroom.	0	1	2	3	4	5
I am constantly aware of the feelings I have in my belly.	0	1	2	3	4	5
I often feel discomfort in my belly could be a sign of a serious illness.	0	1	2	3	4	5
As soon as I awake, I worry that I will have discomfort in my belly during the day.	0	1	2	3	4	5
When I feel discomfort in my belly, it frightens me.	0	1	2	3	4	5
In stressful situations, my belly bothers me a lot.	0	1	2	3	4	5

(Continued)

Item	Strongly Disagree	Moderately Disagree	Mildly Disagree	Mildly Agree	Moderately Agree	Strongly Agree
I constantly think about what is happening inside my belly.	0	1	2	3	4	5

To score the VSI, just add up the numbers you circled. My score _____
Mild: 0–10
Moderate: 11–30
Severe: 31–75

Appendix 2

GI-Cognitions Questionnaires (GI-COG)

Hunt, M.G., et al. (2014). Development and validation of the GI-Cognitions Questionnaire, *Cognitive Therapy and Research*, 38, 472–482

Please Rate the Degree to Which You Believe Each of the Following Statements

Item	Hardly at All	A Little Bit	Moderately	A Fair Bit	Very Much
If I feel the urge to defecate and cannot find a bathroom right away, I won't be able to hold it and I'll be incontinent.	0	1	2	3	4
The thought of fecal incontinence is terrifying. If it happened, I would never get over the humiliation.	0	1	2	3	4
If I fart, people around me will be disgusted.	0	1	2	3	4
If I don't drink or eat with other people, they will think I'm antisocial and no fun.	0	1	2	3	4
If I have to get up and leave an event, meeting, or social gathering to go to the bathroom, people will think there's something wrong with me.	0	1	2	3	4

(Continued)

Item	Hardly at All	A Little Bit	Moderately	A Fair Bit	Very Much
If I have to interrupt a meeting or presentation at work to go to the bathroom, it will be awful, and people will think I'm incompetent or unreliable.	0	1	2	3	4
If I have stop or leave to find a bathroom during an outing or trip, my friends and family will be frustrated and annoyed with me.	0	1	2	3	4
If I told my coworkers about my gut problems, they wouldn't understand and would think I was weak or gross.	0	1	2	3	4
When I feel my GI symptoms acting up, I'm afraid the pain will be excruciating and intolerable.	0	1	2	3	4
When my gut acts up, I have to cancel my plans and miss out on important parts of life.	0	1	2	3	4
If I'm experiencing a gut attack and feeling sick, I can't enjoy or pay attention to anything else.	0	1	2	3	4
It is unfair and horrible that I have to have these awful symptoms.	0	1	2	3	4
If people knew about my gut problems, they would think about me negatively.	0	1	2	3	4
If I leave the house without my emergency medicine(s) (e.g., Imodium, Lomotil, Pepto-Bismol, Gas-Ex, Tums) it could lead to disaster.	0	1	2	3	4
Having to deal with gut problems is incredibly embarrassing.	0	1	2	3	4
If people knew what my life was really like they would think I was crazy.	0	1	2	3	4

To score the GI-COG, just add up the numbers you circled. My score_____
Mild: 0–19
Moderate: 20–39
Severe: 40–64

Appendix 3

Fear of Food Questionnaire

Hunt, M.G., et al. (2018). Development and validation of the Fear of Food Questionnaire (FFQ). Poster presented at the annual meeting of the Anxiety and Depression Association of America. Washington, DC.

Please Rate the Degree to Which You Believe Each of the Following Statements

Item	Not at All	A Little	Somewhat	Moderately	Quite a Bit	Absolutely
1. I try hard to identify foods that trigger GI symptoms.	0	1	2	3	4	5
2. I cannot tolerate certain foods.	0	1	2	3	4	5
3. I try to avoid eating trigger foods.	0	1	2	3	4	5
4. The range of foods it feels "safe" to eat has grown pretty narrow.	0	1	2	3	4	5
5. Sometimes I don't eat in order to avoid dealing with GI symptoms.	0	1	2	3	4	5
6. If I could survive without eating, it would be a huge relief.	0	1	2	3	4	5
7. I'm afraid of experiencing GI symptoms when I eat.	0	1	2	3	4	5

(Continued)

Item	Not at All	A Little	Somewhat	Moderately	Quite a Bit	Absolutely
8. I'm afraid to eat certain foods.	0	1	2	3	4	5
9. Food sometimes feels like the enemy.	0	1	2	3	4	5
10. If a certain food triggers GI symptoms, I worry about eating it again.	0	1	2	3	4	5
11. I have lost too much weight because I avoid eating.	0	1	2	3	4	5
12. My restricted diet makes it harder to go out and socialize.	0	1	2	3	4	5
13. People in my life don't always support my efforts to eliminate trigger foods from my diet.	0	1	2	3	4	5
14. My restricted diet sometimes causes conflict with people in my life.	0	1	2	3	4	5
15. I can't enjoy food the way I used to.	0	1	2	3	4	5
16. I have had to give up foods that I enjoy.	0	1	2	3	4	5
17. I really miss eating certain foods.	0	1	2	3	4	5
18. My restrictive diet frustrates me.	0	1	2	3	4	5

To score the FFQ, just add up the numbers you circled. My score_____

None: 0–15
Mild: 16–30
Moderate: 31–45
Severe: 46–90

12

Fibromyalgia and Related Conditions

*Jessica Payne-Murphy, Stephanie Parazak Eberle,
Colleen Conry, and Abbie O. Beacham*

Introduction

Fibromyalgia syndrome (FM) is a challenging and costly chronic pain condition that impacts patients, their families, and the healthcare system. FM is defined as persistent generalized body pain/tenderness and either cognitive changes, fatigue, headaches, lower abdominal pain, waking unrefreshed, or depression, which have occurred for three months or more and which are not explained by another illness (Wolfe et al., 2016). Healthcare professionals often regard patients who present for treatment of FM and other related conditions as having a more complex, varied, and challenging constellation of symptoms than other pain patients. Probably the most challenging aspect of treating these conditions is that little is fully understood regarding their cause, definitive diagnosis, course, and treatment effectiveness, despite many hypotheses.

This chapter aims to provide clinically useful information, resources, and tools helpful to understand, case conceptualize, and treatment plan for patients who present with FM or related conditions. In terms of intervention suggestions, we intentionally select "transdiagnostic" approaches that are applicable to a variety of patient presentations and problems regardless of their "diagnosis." We present three approaches: 1) unified protocol for transdiagnostic treatment of emotional disorders (UP; Barlow & Farchione, 2018); 2) acceptance and commitment therapy (ACT; Hayes, Strosahl, & Wilson, 2012); and 3) cognitive-behavioral therapy for insomnia (CBT-I; Perlis, Aloia, & Kuhn, 2011).

Although other treatment approaches place a premium on symptom abatement as a primary (or sole) indicator of successful outcomes, our approach focuses more on the outcome of increased function in the patients' valued domains of living. By offering this approach, we hope that the reader will consider its application in accordance with the recommendations of Sackett, Straus, Richardson, Rosenberg, and Haynes (2000) and the American Psychological Association Presidential Task Force on Evidence-Based Practice (2005), which defines evidence-based practice as "the integration of the best available research with clinical expertise in the context of patient characteristics, culture, and preferences" (p. 5).

As co-authors, we want to share a bit about the spirit with which we approached this chapter. None of us would individually define ourselves as "experts" on FM. Collectively, however, we have decades of research and clinical experience with patients in primary and specialty care clinics, including many patients who have struggled with these symptoms, diagnoses, and conditions. We approached this chapter as a team endeavor. Our team is comprised of psychologists/behavioral health professionals and a physician. This work would have suffered greatly if any one member of the team had been excluded.

Accordingly, at the outset our team makes two explicit recommendations. First, we advise behavioral health professionals involved in this work to proactively partner—or at least initiate bidirectional communication—with the patient's primary care medical provider. Patients with FM who are treated by primary care clinicians have been noted to have a better prognosis than those not treated in primary care (Goldenberg, Schur, & Romain, 2017). This recommendation for interdisciplinary collaboration also applies to medical providers working with FM patients who have access to behavioral health providers. Second, we heartily recommend that clinicians consider their work with these patients to be longitudinal in nature. We believe that when patients present with these symptoms and experiences, they come to us having utilized their problem-solving repertoire to the best of their perceived abilities. Although the behavioral treatment protocols presented herein are brief and time-limited, as with all ongoing relationships, the ebb and flow of the constellation of symptoms and patient experience will fluctuate over time. In the words of Colleen Conry, one of our authors, "if you don't stick with [the patient] over time, you may not be around to see their successes."

Fibromyalgia Syndrome

Persistent generalized body pain and tenderness, fatigue, and sleep disturbances largely define FM. Due to the range of FM's symptoms that remain undetected by laboratory testing, it has been characterized as one of the Functional Somatic Syndromes (FSS) or "related syndromes that are characterized more by symptoms, suffering, and disability than by disease-specific, demonstrable abnormalities of structure or function" (Barsky & Borus, 1999, p. 910). The American College of Rheumatology diagnostic criteria have evolved since 1990 to reflect a more spectrum-based conceptualization (Clauw, 2014).

2016 FM criteria entail:

- Widespread musculoskeletal pain locations ≥ 7 (out of 19) and the presence and severity of unwanted symptoms (i.e., fatigue, waking unrefreshed, cognitive difficulties, headaches, lower abdominal pain, and/or depression) ≥ 5 (out of 9) **or**

- Widespread musculoskeletal pain in several locations = 4–6 (out of 19) and presence of ≥ 9 of the aforementioned symptoms
- Second, generalized pain must be present in four out of five body regions
- Lastly, patients must experience these symptoms for three months or more and may have co-occurring medical conditions (Wolfe et al., 2016)

Other co-occurring symptoms may include numbness, tingling, burning sensations, increased sensitivity to sound, odor, touch, and light, multiple chemical sensitivities, balance difficulties, dysmenorrhea, pelvic pain and bladder disturbances, restless legs syndrome, anxiety, depression, and "fibro fog" or other concentration or memory impairments (Goldenberg et al., 2017).

Diagnosis is rendered in clinical settings via interview, medical examination, and laboratory testing in order to rule out common comorbid diagnoses, which may better account for presenting physical symptoms such as thyroid disease, chronic pain syndromes, and inflammatory and noninflammatory rheumatologic disorders (Goldenberg et al., 2017; Wolfe et al., 2016). Notably, diagnosis often is delayed due to the fluctuating nature, complexity, and range of symptomatology. The estimated delay from symptom onset to diagnosis is 2.3 years, with an estimated 3.7 consultations from a variety of medical professionals (Choy et al., 2010).

The prevalence of FM is 2–3% worldwide, although underreporting makes estimates difficult to ascertain. FM is most common among patients 30 years or older and of lower socioeconomic status and education level. Females are impacted at up to six times the rate of males (Goldenberg et al., 2017; Queiroz, 2013). FM is thought to be present across ethnic groups; however, estimates are only reported for select countries. Therefore, inter- and intra-population variability is difficult to ascertain (Queiroz, 2013). Other pain conditions are often comorbid with FM. Studies suggest that 86% of FM patients also exhibit chronic fatigue syndrome; 32% to 81% have comorbid irritable bowel syndrome; and approximately 35% meet criteria for temporomandibular disorder (Aaron, Burke, & Buchwald, 2000; Fraga et al., 2012; Kurland, Coyle, Winkler, & Zable, 2006; Sperber et al., 1999). Both tension and migraine headache are prominent in FM patients, with an estimated 45–76% affected (Marcus, Bernstein, & Rudy, 2005).

Etiology of Fibromyalgia

Compared to chronic pain conditions in which the pain location is related to the site of prior injury, the etiology of FM persistent pain and hyperalgesia is thought to be abnormal pain processing in the central nervous system, called central sensitization (Clauw, 2014). Neurochemical differences (i.e., related to serotonin, dopamine, substance P, glutamate, and others) mirror this hypersensitivity in FM and suggest dysregulation in both the ascending and descending pain pathways among the brain, spinal cord, and peripheral nerves (Bellato et al., 2012; Clauw, Arnold, & McCarberg, 2011). Small nerve fiber neuropathy found in FM patients further may suggest pathophysiological differences in pain expression (Üçeyler et al., 2017). These neurotransmitter discrepancies also are believed to contribute to the fatigue, sensory sensitivities, and mood and sleep disturbances that so often co-exist (Phillips & Clauw, 2013).

Notably, sleep disturbances, one of the most prominent symptoms in FM, also correlate with documented increases in stage 1 and 2, or "lighter," sleep and disordered deep-wave or restorative sleep (Besteiro González et al., 2011; Burns, Crofford, & Chervin, 2008). This has implications for the deficiencies in growth hormone, important neurotransmitters involved in muscle and tissue-repair processes that occur in deep-wave sleep stages, thus highlighting the significant perpetuating cycle of pain and sleep problems (Bellato et al., 2012; Diaz-Piedra et al., 2015).

Current theory also proposes that FM is a biopsychosocial condition largely shaped by multifactorial epigenetic processes. Specifically, trauma, often physical, has been posited as a factor that can activate symptom onset in FM patients with a genetic predisposition (Clauw, 2014; Üçeyler et al., 2017). Findings suggest that an individual is 8.5 times more likely to have FM given a first-degree relative with this diagnosis (Arnold et al., 2004). Assessed prevalence risk in FM, IBS, and headache patients suggests that half may be attributed to genetic factors and half to environmental factors (Kato, Sullivan, Evengård, & Pedersen, 2009). Physical trauma, however, has been challenging to study in FM. Suspected triggers include acute injury due to motor vehicle or work-related accidents, childbirth, post-deployment in military veterans, and infectious diseases such as HIV, Hepatitis C, and Lyme disease (Jiao et al., 2015).

Psychological Comorbidities in Fibromyalgia

Patients diagnosed with FM and other FSS commonly experience psychological distress and impairment in functioning. Before 1990, FM was regarded as primarily a psychological condition (Wolfe et al., 1990). Depression, anxiety, and PTSD are the most prevalent psychiatric diagnoses in FM patients. These patients are 2.9 to 3.6 times more likely to carry a diagnosis of depression or anxiety than people without FM (Weir et al., 2006). A lifetime prevalence of depressive disorders among FM patients is thought to be 62–86% (Gracely, Ceko, & Bushnell, 2012), with an estimated incident comorbidity rate of 40% (Kato et al., 2009). Approximately 13–63.8% of those with FM are thought to have comorbid anxiety disorders (Fietta, Fietta, & Manganelli, 2007). FM patients have nearly double the prevalence of psychiatric conditions compared to patients with lupus, rheumatoid and noninflammatory rheumatic disorders. Specifically, they had the highest rates of depression (lifetime = 67%; current = 38%), substance abuse (6.1%; 0.4%), and total psychiatric illness (68.1%; 38%) (Wolfe, Michaud, Li, & Katz, 2010).

In addition, increased rates of trauma history and PTSD symptoms are found in FM patients. Although originally believed to be causative, recent large meta-analyses suggest the associations are much more complex among FM symptom severity, trauma history, and psychiatric diagnoses (Yavne, Amital, Watad, Tiosano & Amital, 2018). Retrospective self-report of trauma is significant in FM, with 31.3% of patients reporting that emotional trauma triggered symptom onset, second only to chronic stress (41.9%) (Bennett, Jones, Turk, Russell, & Matallana, 2007). One study suggested 33.8% of FM patients had a likely PTSD diagnosis and 60% had suffered at least one traumatic event (e.g., sexual abuse < age 14 years, rape, severe physical violence, severe accident, or other severe life event; Häuser et al., 2015). Among 45% of FM patients with PTSD, 66.5% experienced their most severe trauma prior to FM symptom onset (Häuser et al., 2013). Furthermore, PTSD diagnosis has been associated with higher pain severity, depression, and/or disability in FM patients (Ortiz et al., 2016).

FM symptoms are challenging to treat, with often less than optimal medical, psychological, and functional outcomes. Approximately 30% of FM patients receive disability payments and an estimated 25–50% report significant work disability. Many patients endorse work interference due to symptoms (Bennett et al., 2007; Fitzcharles, Ste-Marie, Rampakakis, Sampalis, & Shir, 2016). Prevailing theory suggests that actual or functional disability is impacted directly by self-perceptions of disability, regardless of physical functioning (Karsdorp & Vlaeyen, 2009). Perceived disability is defined as a patient's subjective account of his/her degree of impairment resulting from pain while engaging in voluntary and necessary life activities (Fordyce et al., 1984; Tait, Chibnall, & Krause, 1990). Predictors of higher perceived disability in FM include catastrophizing, low self-efficacy, and fear of pain (Dobkin et al., 2010; Karsdorp & Vlaeyen, 2009). Notably, these traits are greater in FM patients than in patients with either complex regional pain syndrome or chronic low back pain, when controlling for physical severity (Verbunt, Pernot, & Smeets, 2008).

Medical Treatment of Fibromyalgia

In descending order of efficacy, the most efficacious interventions for FM are aerobic exercise, cognitive-behavioral therapy (see Psychological Treatment Models for Fibromyalgia), and pharmaceuticals (Thieme, Mathys, & Turk, 2017). Overall, the gold standard of care is multicomponent treatment that includes all three of these treatment approaches, as well as patient education provided by the patient care team (primary care physician and/or psychologist/psychiatrist or rheumatologist/neurologist for more challenging pain or functional somatic syndrome management). Physical or occupational therapists also can be very beneficial in guiding patients to attain graduated physical activity goals. Specifically, graded low-to-moderate intensity physical activity is recommended to steadily build strength and to minimize symptom exacerbation (Clauw, 2015).

Pharmaceuticals for FM symptom management are reported to be only moderately beneficial, primarily in the short term (Häuser, Walitt, Fitzcharles, & Sommer, 2014). Targets include pain, tenderness, fatigue, sleep, dyscognition, stiffness, depressed and anxious mood, and "global multidimensional functioning" (Mease, Dundon, & Sarzi-Puttini, 2011). Evidence-based treatment guidelines recommended by the American Pain Society (APS), the Association of the Scientific Medical Societies in Germany (AWMF), the Canadian Pain Society (CPS). and the European League Against Rheumatism (EULAR) suggest that amitriptyline (a tricyclic antidepressant) and cyclobenzaprine (a muscle relaxant) are the two first-line medical treatments (Thieme et al., 2017). In addition, the CPS strongly recommends anticonvulsants (e.g., Pregabalin), fluoxetine (a selective serotonin reuptake inhibitor (SSRI)), and duloxetine or milnacipran (both serotonin norepinephrine reuptake inhibitors (SNRIs)) for FM treatment. Amitriptyline, SNRIs, and SSRIs are thought to act on the central nervous system by regulating serotonin and norepinephrine to decrease pain signaling. Notably, opioids, NSAIDs, and corticosteroids are ineffective for managing FM symptoms (Clauw, 2015).

Psychological Treatment Models for Fibromyalgia

A number of psychological and behavioral treatment approaches have been applied to chronic pain conditions, including FM. The reader may find the following treatment overview helpful. The concepts are more fully described in Payne-Murphy (2015), with updated sources cited below.

Operant Behavioral Therapy (OBT)

Wilbert Fordyce's development of the Operant Learning Theory of Pain is one of the most important advancements in chronic pain and FM treatment (Fordyce, 1976). "Pain behaviors" comprise a core element in this model and are exhibited by patients in pain. Specifically, these may include avoiding physical or social activities or eliciting sympathy or assistance, thereby communicating to others the presence of pain. Although this behavior may momentarily decrease suffering, paradoxically it is thought to maintain pain levels and, ultimately, increase functional disability and a lower quality of life. According to the general theory of operant learning, pain behaviors are susceptible to being reinforced and therefore can be shaped. OBT interventions for FM consist of group training and education in physical exercise, contingent schedules of medication use, modification of solicitous spouse behavior, and activities that decrease pain behaviors and interference of pain in life's activities using reinforcement and punishment. Engaging the patient's spouse and family members in the patient's treatment is often a mechanism for helping change and shape these conditioned responses within an OBT framework (Thieme & Gracely, 2009).

FM and pain studies examining OBT interventions indicate significant improvements in pain intensity, physical impairment, pain behaviors, solicitous spouse behaviors, affective distress, and physician visits. However, research suggests that while OBT in general is most effective for behavioral aspects, it is less beneficial in modifying affective components or other symptoms (e.g., sleep difficulties, mood, and quality of life) when compared to cognitive-behavioral therapy (Thieme & Gracely, 2009).

Cognitive and Cognitive-Behavioral Therapy (CBT)

Cognitive-behavioral therapy (CBT; Beck, 1976) is the most frequently utilized psychotherapeutic modality for many psychological and medical illnesses, with over 330 studies published as of 2006 (Hofmann, Asnaani, Vonk, Sawyer, & Fang, 2012). CBT for pain and FM emphasizes education and training to identify, evaluate, and reconceptualize maladaptive cognitions and behaviors that continue to maintain one's pain experience. Repeated momentary recognition, restructuring, and reconceptualization of thoughts then aid in improving the patient's pattern of distorted thinking, and therefore mood, over time.

Pain catastrophizing, or "an exaggerated negative 'mental set' brought to bear during painful experiences," is a well-established treatment target in CBT (Sullivan et al., 2001, p. 52). Functional MRI research in FM suggests that increased catastrophic thinking triggers neural pathways in areas involved in pain processing such as attention to pain, emotion, and motor control (Lazaridou et al., 2017). CBT interventions that target catastrophizing and other maladaptive cognitions are linked to significant mood improvements, as well as to decreases in pain and functional disability (Williams, Eccleston, & Morley, 2012).

Additional evidence-based strategies delivered via CBT for FM include goal-setting, relaxation, assertiveness training, psychoeducation regarding the psychophysiological processes in FM, and increased goal-driven work and social and physical activity balanced with activity pacing. Activity pacing and increased goal-driven activity target a common cycle found in this population: either too little or too much physical and/or mental activity often contributes to muscle atrophy or exacerbations in pain, negative mood states, and/or functional disability (Karsdorp & Vlaeyen, 2009).

Both OBT and CBT continue to be the most effective psychological treatment approaches reported for FM, with small to medium effect sizes (Bernardy, Klose, Busch, Choy, & Häuser, 2012; Hofmann et al., 2012). However, mixed empirical efficacy across symptoms is reported. Small changes in self-efficacy, perceived disability, depression, and short-term pain intensity are most frequently seen (Glombieski et al., 2010). See Chapter 4 of this volume for a detailed description of CBT applications to chronic pain in general.

Acceptance and Commitment Therapy

Acceptance and commitment therapy (ACT; Hayes et al., 2012), which is often referred to as a "third-wave" behavioral therapy, approaches relationships among cognitions, emotions, and behavior. Much like CBT, ACT pays particular attention to the cycle of how patients engage with their external and internal environments with regard to their pain. Experiential avoidance is a core concept that addresses the avoidance of pain and pain-related stimuli (e.g., tasks, locations, behaviors, thoughts, emotions). Avoidance contributes to increased pain and physical and emotional suffering. Negative interpretation of the pain experience and one's self-perception also leads to justification for disengaging from adaptive and daily life activity (McCracken & Eccleston, 2005.)

A fundamental goal in ACT consists of working toward acceptance of pain and commitment to personal values that produce action-based outcomes to create a desired life despite pain (McCracken & Vowles, 2014). ACT research has identified two core therapeutic factors particularly relevant for patients with chronic pain and FM: pain willingness and activity engagement. "Pain willingness" is defined as one's degree of willingness to experience pain and related thoughts and feelings. "Activity engagement" is the degree of willingness to engage in life's activities despite pain (Vowles, McCracken, McLeod, & Eccleston, 2008).

Additionally, there are six core ACT therapeutic processes that work together toward the overall goal of "psychological flexibility" or "the ability to contact the present moment more fully ... to change or persist in behavior in order to serve valued ends" (Luoma, Hayes, & Walser, 2007, p. 17): 1) "contacting the present moment" encourages patients to focus on the here and now; 2) "self-as-context" suggests that the mind has two distinct entities: the observing and the thinking self; 3) "defusion" encourages simply noticing and detaching from negative thoughts and memories that do not serve the patient well; 4) "acceptance" aims to allow for all of life's experiences, painful *and* joyful, as opposed to avoidance; 5) "values" identifies the factors most important to patients; and 6) "committed action" leads to goal completion (Luoma et al., 2007). Chapter 5 provides detailed information on ACT and other mindfulness-based intervention approaches for chronic pain.

Like CBT, ACT studies have demonstrated efficacy and effectiveness in improving the functional and affective outcomes of chronic pain patients, as well as other psychological concerns. Greater pain willingness and activity engagement have contributed to significant decreases in physical and psychosocial disability, pain-related anxiety, depression-related interference with functioning, pain medications, and medical utilization, as well as improved work status (Hughes, Clark, Colclough, Dale, & McMillan, 2017). When compared to active treatments, findings from 11 ACT randomized controlled trials for chronic pain suggest ACT was favored in regards to functioning, quality of life, and depression (ES = small to large). Finally, a comparison of ACT and CBT for pain found both largely equivalent in contributing to positive outcomes. However, CBT was favored slightly as the result of small effects on quality of life, depression, and pain intensity.

At the time of publication, two studies had assessed directly the efficacy of ACT for FM patients. The first found ACT to be superior in FM impact, perceived disability, self-efficacy, depression, anxiety, and mental health quality of life compared to waitlist control (ES = moderate to large; Wicksell et al., 2013). The second, a study comparing ACT to either combined pregabalin and duloxetine use or a waitlist control group, found that ACT was favored overall in terms of FM impact, catastrophizing, depression, and anxiety (ES = moderate to large; Luciano et al., 2014). Notwithstanding a smaller research base compared to CBT and a need to improve study quality, evidence suggests that ACT offers good clinical utility for FM.

Cognitive-Behavioral Therapy for Insomnia

Sleep disturbances are the most frequently experienced symptom in FM (70–96%) other than chronic body pain (Borchers & Gershwin, 2015). These include recurrent difficulties falling and staying asleep, nonrestorative slumber, early awakenings and daytime fatigue or sleepiness. Research findings suggest that over 50% of FM patients meet diagnostic criteria for insomnia as well (White, Speechley, Harth, & Ostbye, 1999). As previously described, polysomnography studies examining FM and chronic pain patients reflect greater alpha-wave intrusions both in non-REM and stage 3 sleep; reduced slow wave and REM activity; and increased leg movements. This is thought to contribute to greater sleep arousals and feeling unrefreshed. FM studies suggest that worse sleep also predicts poorer outcomes in pain, pain sensitivity, social functioning, depression, anxiety, fatigue, self-efficacy, and perceived stress and disability (Borchers & Gershwin, 2015).

Cognitive-behavioral therapy for insomnia (CBT-I) is the first-line treatment for insomnia, with robust outcomes for insomnia patients across studies (ES = moderate to large; Van Straten et al., 2018). Core components within this four- to ten-week therapy include sleep education, sleep hygiene, stimulus control, sleep restriction or compression, relaxation, and cognitive restructuring (Perlis et al., 2011). CBT-I studies also suggest substantial improvements among FM and other pain patients when pain-specific approaches are included, such as 1) pain-specific psychoeducation or 2) psychoeducation plus activity pacing, activity goal setting for pain, and visual imagery. In these studies, significant changes are seen in pain intensity, pain interference, catastrophizing, fatigue, depression, quality of life, and sleep (Martinez et al., 2014; Tang, Goodchild, & Salkovskis, 2012; Vitiello et al., 2014). Executive functioning, attention, and reaction time also improve significantly in FM patients using this treatment approach (Miró et al., 2011). These studies suggest that the additional treatment target of sleep is a highly effective method to improve sleep and cognition, as well as quality of life and pain-related factors in those with FM.

Case Study: Pat

"Pat" is a 58-year-old Caucasian female who was diagnosed with FM two years ago. Although her diagnosis is relatively recent, Pat estimates that the onset of her persistent chronic pain began ten years ago after she was in a serious car accident. Although her acute injuries from that accident have resolved, she has continued to suffer from widespread pain—worsening with the passing of time—ever since the accident. She estimates that it took at least five years of testing and "work-ups" for a medical provider to officially diagnose her with FM.

Pat endorses widespread daily musculoskeletal pain that she defines as "hard to predict" in terms of location, duration, and intensity. She notes that on a good day, her pain may only be a 3–4 (on 0–10 scale). However, if she is overactive on those days, she will "pay the price" with excessive necessary inactive time on following days. When asked to rate her pain, she notes that her average pain is 6–7/10, peak pain 10/10, and least pain 2/10. Pat also complains of cognitive symptoms, stating that she is "just not as sharp," "foggy," and unable to maintain focus in her thinking.

Pat has worked with a number of healthcare providers, often not staying with a single physician for more than a few months before becoming frustrated and seeking a new doctor. Pat states that the multiple medications prescribed by her past providers—including antidepressants—have never worked. She admits that she has never felt able to take these medications regularly (i.e., as prescribed) due to side effects. She worried about the many medications and their combined effects and feels that she was prescribed antidepressants because her doctors thought her symptoms were "all in her head." As a result, she recently began seeing a new medical provider, but states that she doubts this relationship will be any more fruitful than any of her past patient–provider relationships; this doctor will "probably just tell me it's all in my head, too" and prescribe another antidepressant. Pat believes that this is a hopeless process and that she will never regain the life she lived prior to the onset of her symptoms, and feels helpless to manage her condition.

Fatigue, negative moods (sadness and anxiety), and insomnia are the other most salient major symptoms for Pat. She states that despite feeling "exhausted" and deflated almost all day, beginning early in the day, she dreads bedtime because she knows she will end up lying awake and frustrated that she cannot get the rest she knows she needs. Sometimes she cannot sleep because she is in pain, but other times Pat struggles to identify a reason for her insomnia. She does find that the longer she lies awake, the more her thoughts begin to drift to how helpless she feels. Pat says that she feels most down and anxious during those times when she is lying awake in bed, so she usually turns on the TV when she wakes up to distract herself. About six months ago, Pat began having between two and four glasses of wine each night to help her fall asleep more quickly, but she still wakes frequently in the middle of the night.

Approximately one year ago, Pat resigned her position as a successful sales representative after several months of increasing difficulty at work. Her relationship with her supervisor had always been quite positive, but over the past year Pat received feedback that she has been making mistakes and forgetting tasks. Pat was finding it increasingly difficult to keep full-time hours and fulfill the physical demands of her job, such as standing for long periods at trade shows and client events. Ultimately, she felt that the situation was so bad that she resigned. She stated, "Of course, I feel like a complete failure. I took a lot of pride in my work and helped build that company's success." She is currently unemployed and is looking into applying for disability benefits, which feels even worse to her, as she feels it is unlikely she will ever be able to function in a work environment again.

Pat lives with her partner of 32 years and has two adult children and five grandchildren who live nearby. Pat's partner tries to be supportive but sometimes becomes frustrated and feels as though she is using FM as an "excuse" to stay home in bed. Pat states that their relationship has suffered as a result of her partner's frustration, and her loss of interest in affection, sex, and intimacy has resulted in further strain. Pat's children have become increasingly distant, and they have shared with her that they do not know how to help her because she seems like she has "given up." Most devastating to Pat is that her children no longer ask her to babysit or to attend activities with her grandchildren. Pat has lost touch with the majority of her friends, as she is too tired and in too much pain to go out much. As a result, she reports feeling down, worried, isolated, and hopeless.

Regarding health-related behaviors, Pat reports that with the exception of a brief time in high school, she has never smoked cigarettes or used other tobacco products. She only began using cannabis (edible candies) to manage her pain and insomnia within the past year. She has always informed her medical provider of the cannabis and other over-the-counter medication use. Pat was previously quite physically active including running, hiking, and aerobics. However, over the past two years she has become increasingly sedentary. This, combined with eating more to offset sometimes-unpleasant side effects of medication and increased cravings for sweets and carbohydrates, has resulted in a considerable weight gain of 40–50 lbs. Her current body mass index is 32.9 (obese). Her weight gain and physical changes are a considerable source of distress for her. Pat denies any other drug and alcohol use beyond the few glasses of wine in the evenings.

Pat has been referred for behavioral health treatment by her new medical provider for a collaborative team approach to her care. Although she is hesitant, Pat has agreed to attend a "session or two" of treatment in hopes that she can regain control of her life by better managing her FM symptoms. She ended the meeting saying, "I sure hope you can help make this go away. I have tried everything and can't make any of it better."

Assessment

Each clinician must determine how to format the most useful assessment protocol for his or her setting. In general, we espouse a three-layered assessment approach: 1) general assessment for overall function and psychological symptomatology; 2) protocol-specific objective assessment; and 3) an ideographic functional assessment to pinpoint treatment targets specific to the case presentation and treatment outcome goals.

The general assessment consists of two components: clinical interview and objective self-report measures. In our opinion, a semi-structured clinical interview is essential. Which interview is most appropriate is a matter of each clinician's preferences and selected treatment approach. In addition to the interview, in medical populations our preference is to also incorporate an adaptation of a 24-hour "Typical Day" (Rollnick, Miller, & Butler, 2007), which includes activities and ratings of pain, mood, and fatigue (see Table 12.1). This approach provides the clinician with valuable insights regarding health behavior, medication use, food/diet, and rest and activity patterns through a full 24-hour period.

Table 12.1 Case Study: 24-Hour Typical Day

Time	Activity	Pain 0 (None)–10 (Most Imaginable)	Mood 0 (None)–10 (Most Imaginable)	Fatigue 0 (None)–10 (Most Imaginable)
6–8 AM	Wakes up—due to pain. Attempts to return to sleep and may use cell phone to play games. Avoids rising due to desire to sleep longer. At 8am, she takes pain medication, coffee, and toast. Watches morning news. Will walk dog to mailbox and back.	8	9: Sad	8: Sleepy
9–11 AM	Watches morning TV and tries to relax. Will typically doze off.	5	5: Sad	7: Sleepy
Noon—3 PM	Lunch—sandwich or leftovers. Then move to craft area. Check e-mail and Facebook. Try to work on crafts for presents for grandkids and other friends. Meets friends for lunch if she feels up to it (about once per month). Typically takes another OTC pain med such as Ibuprofen and has diet soft drinks during this time.	7	6: Anxious 3: Sad	4: Physical fatigue
4–6 PM	While watching evening news, prepares dinner for partner and any other family members if feels up to it (otherwise may get carry out). Typically has leftovers from weekend meals that kids bring over. Very occasionally will go out to dinner. Partner walks dog after dinner and will go along if feels up to it.	6	6: Lonely	7: Sleepy
7–9 PM	After dinner both return to watch evening shows. Sometimes watches TV in bed if she is more fatigued.	8	9: Lonely 7: Sad	8

(Continued)

Table 12.1 (Continued)

Time	Activity	Pain 0 (None)–10 (Most Imaginable)	Mood 0 (None)–10 (Most Imaginable)	Fatigue 0 (None)–10 (Most Imaginable)
10–11 PM	Pre-bedtime routine. Answers e-mails, browses Facebook and news websites. Plays crossword on phone (before bedtime and in middle of the night). Usually takes OTC sleep medication and waits to become drowsy. May also have 2–4 glasses of wine or edible cannabis to aid in sleep and pain management.	7	10: "dread" about possibility of not being able to sleep	6
11 PM- 8 AM	Usually falls asleep fairly rapidly after going to bed (within 20–30 mins). She sleeps for about two hours and then rises to use the bathroom and returns to bed. Sometimes she will go back to sleep and other times will be awake for a couple of hours. Typically, she stays in bed reading a book or playing a game on her phone during wakeful periods. She will allow herself to sleep in until 8 or 9 if she has been up for a long time during the night.	5–6 (after wine and cannabis) 7–8 as morning approaches and can't find comfortable position for sleep	9: Frustration about poor sleep 9: Worry about her health, money, relationships, and the future	9: Sleepy

Charting the pain, mood, and other patient-identified salient symptoms throughout this timeframe informs the most impactful interventions. Objective self-report measures at this level can serve to identify additional underlying factors that may enhance or impede the success of interventions. Given the prevalence of psychological comorbidities in patients with FM, we suggest using a symptom checklist to identify any severe psychological symptoms that may need attention. It is also important to ascertain previous history of trauma and/or trauma symptoms.

As part of the general assessment we also recommend assessing key social determinants of health that may hinder higher level interventions. These are organized across five domains: 1) economic stability; 2) education; 3) health and healthcare; 4) neighborhood and built environment; and 5) social and community context. For more information, consult the *Healthy People 2020* website at www.healthypeople.gov/2020/topics-objectives/topic/social-determinants-of-health. Protocol-specific measures and approaches are described contextually in the chapter sections that follow.

Finally, we recommend Functional Assessment/Analysis of Behavior as a means of identifying and understanding what is working and not working in each patient's attempt to problem-solve and manage pain and other symptoms. Application of this approach is outlined within the treatment protocol sections.

Case Conceptualization and Treatment Plan(s)

Biopsychosocial Model

Although the biopsychosocial model was introduced over four decades ago (Engel, 1977), it still is not consistently and automatically applied in case conceptualizations of medical patients. It is especially applicable to our case of a patient presenting with FM and/or a complex interrelated constellation of symptoms. The biopsychosocial model components are not mutually exclusive factors but rather are domains that sometimes overlap and influence each other and the whole person. The model provides insight into not only physiological disease processes but also the suffering that accompanies these processes (Borrell-Carrio, Suchman, & Epstein, 2004). Viewed from this perspective, the impact of presenting problems and selected interventions can have far-reaching "generalizing" effects on the patient.

The biological domain is especially salient to patients diagnosed with FM and related disorders. In Pat's case above, some factors are modifiable or amenable to behavior change, and some are not. Among the latter are sex (female) and age (midlife). Both of these characteristics have accompanying biological variables such as natural physical changes, including hormone fluctuations. These alone may appreciably impact some of Pat's most concerning physical and psychological symptoms. It may be important to assess these factors during the initial conceptualization. Those biological factors that may be linked to behavior and are, therefore, potentially impacted by behavior change include Pat's level of physical conditioning/sedentary behavior, diet and nutrition habits, sleep dysfunction, self-medication (e.g., over-the-counter medication and alcohol), and variable adherence to prescribed medication regimen.

The psychological domain also has a diverse and reciprocal impact on other biopsychosocial domains. Representative factors in the psychological domain include fatigue, affect, mood, and cognitive function/experiences. These factors provide a context in which internal experiences are labeled. First and foremost is the subjective nature of the interpretation of pain. Pain and associated suffering are private experiences and thus are interpreted through a lens of psychological state. Conversely, pain levels have a reciprocal impact on psychological symptoms to varying degrees. Second, every variable included in the biological domain can impact the psychological domain. In Pat's case, all of these factors seem to have a noteworthy impact on her present pain experience.

In addition, the social domain reciprocally determines health on a number of levels (Bandura, 1989). Presumably, Pat's pain and other symptoms impact the way she interacts with the people in her social environment. Her confidence, motivation, and expected outcomes are influenced by her collective and recent experiences. Pat herself tells us that her work, family, and social relationships have suffered since the onset and worsening of her pain and symptoms. She avoids social situations because of her fear of worsening symptoms. The world reciprocates based upon how she interacts, thus creating a virtual feedback loop. The feedback loop and associated interactions lay a foundation for the "self-fulfilling prophecy."

Taken together, the cumulative and interrelated effect of all these domains is undoubtedly an increasing sense of despair. Pat's symptoms and experiences may seem insurmountable to her. Taking all of these elements into consideration, it is apparent that the whole of the patient experience can be far greater than the sum of the parts. However, the information gathered in the general overall assessment provides a map of important biopsychosocial factors and accordingly a vital starting point in case conceptualization.

Assessment and Treatment Plan Using Three Different FM Intervention Approaches

Approach 1: Unified Protocol for Transdiagnostic Treatment of FM and Related Symptoms

We chose the unified protocol (UP) because of the transdiagnostic nature of the approach and the emphasis on function. The UP espouses the belief that psychopathology occurs as a spectrum of multiple internal experiences. Additionally, patients who have such "disorders" often experience symptoms with greater sensitivity than persons who do not have "disorders." This approach is well-suited to the complex presentation of patients with FM and other similar conditions/

diagnoses. The UP offers intervention in a modular format that may be especially appealing to clinicians. The modules can be modified (i.e., lengthened or abbreviated) as needed to meet patients' individual needs. We present an introduction to the UP as a useful approach to treating FM patients. For a more complete review of the UP rationale, assessment, conceptualization, and treatment, consult Barlow and Farchione (2018).

UP Assessment

According to the UP, four key constructs describe ways in which patients find internal experiences to be especially aversive. According to Barlow and Farchione (2018), these are increased anxiety sensitivity, decreased mindfulness, experiential avoidance, and negative appraisals and attributions. Anxiety sensitivity is the fear of anxiety-related sensations. The Anxiety Sensitivity Index—Revised (ASI; Deacon, Abramowitz, Woods, & Tolin, 2003) assesses 1) beliefs about the harmful consequences of somatic sensations; 2) fear of publicly observable anxiety reactions; 3) fear of cognitive dyscontrol; and 4) fear of somatic sensations without explicit consequences.

Pat's completed self-report questionnaires indicate that she seems especially sensitive to her internal experiences. Her ratings of perceived pain-related disability are also high, suggesting that she perceives her level of function to be hindered markedly by her symptoms. This is also illustrated in her 24-hour Typical Day and associated functional analyses. Our assessment suggests that Pat may not be accustomed to noticing her present-moment experience, which indicates that she may be low in "mindfulness." Rather, she describes her inner experience as unacceptable and focuses on eradicating the negative aspects of it.

The Five Facet Mindfulness Questionnaire (FFMQ; Baer et al., 2006) provides a useful measure of mindfulness. The FFMQ assesses five different facets of mindfulness, including observing, describing, acting with awareness, nonjudging of inner experience, and non-reactivity to inner experience.

Notably, Pat does not endorse unusual patterns of thinking or symptoms that would suggest serious psychopathology. Her levels of depression, irritability, anxiety, and fatigue are quite high, as are her pain levels. For purposes of the UP, we would as a matter of course administer the Positive and Negative Affect Schedule (PANAS; Watson, Clark, & Tellegen, 1988) as an important indicator of her positive and negative internal experiences. Pat experiences high levels of negative affect but is lacking in positive experiences.

UP Modular Treatment Plan

Table 12.2 includes the key factors pertaining to the modular plan. The first two modules (i.e., the module entitled "Goal Setting/Motivational Enhancement" and the module entitled "Understanding Emotions") are considered to be precursors to the core modules. If a patient experiences FM with diffuse unpredictable

Table 12.2 UP Case Conceptualization and Treatment Plan

Presenting Problems:

"I sure hope you can help make this go away. I have tried everything and can't make any of it better." Diffuse and changing pain sensations. Negative mood/affect and extreme fatigue. Loss of job and career. Strain on family and personal relationships. Sleep and daily activity disruption.

Strong Uncomfortable Emotions/Sensations:

Diffuse, recurrent, and/or unremitting chronic pain (ten years) with unpredictable course. Extreme fatigue and negative moods (anxiety and depression). Fear about future prognosis and life if symptoms persist.

Aversive Reactions:

Interaction with healthcare professionals not gratifying or hopeful. [They will] "probably just tell me it's all in my head, too." Regarding loss of career and meaningful work, "I feel like a complete failure. I took a lot of pride in my work and helped build that company's success."

Avoidant Coping:

> **Situational Avoidance/Escape:** Too tired to go out with friends or family. Worries about pain flare up so stays home.
>
> **Subtle Behavioral Avoidance:** Does not engage with family when they are present. Sits back to appear "well." Pat fears interaction will make her sad.
>
> **Cognitive Avoidance:** Watches TV or plays computer games when pain increases or cannot sleep. This helps Pat avoid worry and anxiety symptoms.

Treatment Plan: Focus/Application of Sessions

Session 1˙—Setting Goals and Maintaining Motivation

> Reinforce that moving forward in small ways is foundation for larger goals. Garner support for agreement to set aside "be pain free" as the sole outcome goal. Work toward centralizing care among healthcare team members.

Session 2˙—Understanding FM Emotional and Physical Experience

> Ascertain current understanding of FM and related fluctuation of symptoms. Educate Pat about course, symptoms, and treatment anchored in biopsychosocial model. Normalize patient experience of symptoms and chronic nature of symptom management.

Session 3—Mindful Emotion/Experience Awareness

> Practice noticing internal sensations and symptom fluctuations without judgment. Exercises may enhance greater flexibility in reacting to aversive stimuli. NOTE: Pat's pain ratings suggest awareness of fluctuations in pain, fatigue, and symptoms ratings.

Session 4—Cognitive Flexibility

> Pat believes that a recent exacerbation in pain when she went on an errand indicated that she would never again be able to have a good day. She reasons that she should avoid all activity. Encourage alternative and flexible (less catastrophizing) ways of interpreting an event.

Session 5—Countering Emotional Behaviors

> A great source of distress for Pat is her belief that her loved ones don't want to be near her. She, in turn, interacts with them emotionally and negatively. Practice interpersonal interactions with partner and children with brief neutral-to-positive topics.

Session 6—Understanding and Confronting Sensations

Pat's most salient physical sensations are pain and physical fatigue. The intensity, location, and course of these symptoms is unpredictable. Exposure to physical sensations via practice noticing without attempts to avoid or change it. Practice skills describing and "sitting with" the sensation(s).

Session 7—Exposures to Emotional Experiences

Pat's physical sensations are often an antecedent of her emotional experiences. Exposure to the experience, along with "riding the wave" of the unpredictable ebb and flow of symptoms and sensations, may be especially useful.

Session 8—Recognizing Accomplishments and Looking to Future

Practice noticing and recognizing confidence in mindfully adapting flexibly to the course and intensity of symptoms. Help Pat to remind herself of her goal to engage in activities that she values on a day-to-day basis. Include relapse prevention in this module.

Adapted from Barlow and Farchione (2018) (p. 37).

NOTE: Original table format was adapted to accommodate common pain/FM presentation and characteristics. Core concepts and modules in boldface. *Sessions 1 and 2 may be reversed; Sessions 6 and 7 should incorporate evidence-based exposure protocols as described in Barlow and Farchione (2018).

symptoms, arguably these two modules may prove to be critical to the success of modules and concepts that follow.

In general, there are times in which it makes sense to present the second module before the first module. We believe that this is true for some FM patients. Often these patients have seen multiple medical providers with divergent opinions and recommendations. As a result, they may be confused about what constitutes reasonable expectations. The clinician cannot be sure what information the patient has gleaned previously.

By initially introducing Module 2, "Understanding FM," the clinician can explore the understanding and expectations brought by the patient to treatment. Additionally, the clinician can reinforce or provide additional information regarding the biopsychosocial model, along with distinguishing between acute and chronic pain management. Misinformation and questions can be noted at this juncture. Finally, it may be possible at this time to obtain patient buy-in to including a primary care provider as a consistent member of the treatment team.

Module 1, "Goal Setting/Motivational Enhancement," follows next. This can be challenging for patients living with chronic recurrent or intractable pain. Understandably, with each new provider, the hope of symptom abatement re-emerges as a primary outcome goal. However, this may be unachievable at the point of treatment entry. Paradoxically, a patient's fear of symptom exacerbation as a consequence of behavior change can stall the process before it begins.

The UP incorporates a decisional balance exercise that examines the benefits of changing as opposed to staying the same. If the patient sees that the benefits outweigh the barriers, his/her openness to change may occur and motivation may be enhanced (Rollnick, Miller, & Butler, 2007). The UP recognizes that noting positive affect and mood can be especially valuable. The explicit goal of acknowledging positive affect (e.g., joy, curiosity, interest) as well as intentional behavioral activation may be useful. This is consistent with the explicit goal of increasing function as a key outcome in FM patients.

Approach 2: Acceptance and Commitment Therapy (ACT)

Assessment

Similar to when using the CBT model, developing a tailored treatment plan within ACT depends upon a well-informed case conceptualization, completed at Session 1. This is based upon the patient's concerns, emotions, beliefs, thoughts, and behaviors and the "Typical Day" functional analysis (Table 12.1). For example, returning to the earlier case study of Pat, the results of her ACT measures (Table 12.3) suggest high experiential avoidance and psychological inflexibility (AAQ-II; Acceptance and Action Questionnaire; Bond et al. 2011). Findings from the CPAQ (Chronic Pain Acceptance Questionnaire; Vowles, McCracken, McLeod, & Eccleston, 2008) also indicate Pat's decreased engagement in life activities due to pain and related sequelae, and a low degree of willingness to experience and accept her pain. Pat's most important valued life domains are reflected in the VLQ (Valued Living Questionnaire; Wilson & Groom, 2002).

Next, inquire about the patient's primary objective for attending treatment. The answers will guide treatment monitoring and will enable a more thorough and focused intervention, recognizing that this conceptualization likely will evolve with new information (Luoma, Hayes, & Walser, 2007). More broadly, ask about multiple dimensions of the presenting problem: onset, duration, severity, attempts to manage, and the patient's overarching life goals.

The areas of assessment discussed below need not be administered in any particular order and may be garnered from the "Typical Day" functional analysis.

Table 12.3 ACT Protocol-Specific Measures

Construct	Measure	Pat's Score
Experiential Avoidance	AAQ-II	High
CP Acceptance	CPAQ—Activity Engagement	Low
	CPAQ—Willingness	Low
	CPAQ—Total	Low
Values	VLQ	Family
		Health/Physical Self-Care
		Work/Career

Emphasize building rapport, maintaining a stance of nonjudgment, and allowing questions to emerge as part of the conversation in order to truly understand the patient's conceptualization. Identify the following key factors:

1. Most prominent thoughts, feelings, situations, and memories that the patient is avoiding and/or is fused with (begin to identify other ACT processes that are contributing to the patient's stated difficulties)
2. Behaviors (internal, external, or overt emotional control) that the patient employs in efforts to avoid unwanted emotions, thoughts, or behaviors
3. Environmental factors that pose limitations to the patient's ability to create change
4. Internal factors that contribute to the patient's willingness to change
5. Patient strengths to enhance psychological flexibility

Once this information is gathered and documented, a treatment plan can emerge that includes which ACT processes may be helpful to focus upon and when (Table 12.4; Luoma et al., 2007). Treatment sessions should be offered in the order of patient readiness and preference, with the exception of Sessions 1 and 2.

Approach 3: Cognitive-Behavioral Treatment of Insomnia (CBT-I)

Assessment

In addition to pain assessment, evaluation for sleep symptoms is essential in FM. Behavioral and cognitive factors in sleep and pain can be identified from both verbal and written self-reports. A functional analysis of behavior with a focus on bedtime and nighttime factors is sufficient to identify treatment targets. See Table 12.1 for functional analysis responses found in the "Typical Day." Table 12.5 summarizes CBT-I-specific assessment.

Interpretation of the Pittsburgh Sleep Quality Inventory (PSQI; Buysse, Reynolds, Monk, Berman, & Kupfer, 1989) can reveal significant difficulties with sleep maintenance and nonrestorative sleep. For example, a selection of the DBAS (Dysfunctional Beliefs and Attitudes Towards Sleep; Morin, 1994) in Table 12.5 regarding Pat indicates her strong maladaptive beliefs.

The theory guiding case conceptualization and treatment for sleep disturbances and insomnia is the 3P Model of Insomnia: Predisposing, Precipitating, and Perpetuating factors (see Table 12.6; Spielman, Caruso, & Glovinsky, 1987). Predisposing factors include those that increase the risk of a patient developing sleep difficulties over the course of his/her lifetime. This may entail, for example, aging; the presence of another medical or sleep disorder (e.g., FM or obstructive sleep apnea); or a family history of sleep or mental health conditions. Precipitating factors are events that may trigger an acute episode of insomnia; any type of

Table 12.4 ACT Case Conceptualization

Presenting Problem and Primary Objective for Attending Treatment

"I sure hope you can help make this go away. I have tried everything and can't make any of it better."
"Nothing has worked for me and I'm tired of feeling this way. I want my life back."

Core Process	Pattern
Lack of Values Clarity	Pat engages in behaviors that serve to gain relief from suffering. These move her away from her values: family, health, and work/career.
Dominance of Conceptualized Past and Future	Thoughts of being a failure with:
Attachment to Conceptualized Self	1) comparison between her negative current experience and past success
Cognitive Fusion	2) hopelessness that her circumstances will improve
"Of course, I feel like a complete failure. I took a lot of pride in my work and helped build that company's success."	
—Weight gain and physical changes are a considerable source of distress.	
—Psychotropic medication "does not work."	
Inaction and Avoidant Persistent	**Experiential Avoidance**
Antecedents to avoidance of valued life activities: unpredictable pain, cognitive symptoms, side effects from medication, exhaustion, and depressed and anxious mood.	When Pat does not feel well, she avoids her internal experience through substance use, food (esp. sweets and carbohydrates), napping, isolation from loved ones and friends, and social media/games/TV.

Assessment and Treatment Plan:
Session 1—Assessment
See Assessment.

Session 2—Values Assessment
VLQ responses are reviewed and Pat's desired outcomes from therapy ("How would it look for you to have your life back?") are further explored. Cycle of fighting experience versus willingness to experience is normalized and discussed.

Insert early and as needed in the following sessions: Education regarding creative helplessness: willingness to stop the struggle and allow pain and suffering to accompany as she rebuilds a values-driven life.

Session 3—Context and the Power of the Language/Emotion Connection

Relational Frame Theory is discussed here using ACT metaphor. Pat is encouraged to share specific thoughts or images she experiences as part of her FM. Explore attributes that comprise Pat's "self-as-content." Enhances focus on values-driven activities despite current suffering. With increased willingness and active engagement, suffering experience changes.

Session 4—Mindfulness

Rationale is provided and guided mindfulness activity is practiced in-session. Plan is developed to maintain a daily mindfulness practice.

Session 5—Contacting the Present Moment and Defusion

Draw connections between Pat's fused thoughts, beliefs, identity, etc. and futility in continuing to engage with them in the same way.

Session 6—Experiential Avoidance and Activity Engagement

Rationale provided. Encouraging Pat's new self-as-content skills, use active listening to gently explore Pat's methods of avoidance.

Session 7—Pain Willingness Exposure and Acceptance

Rationale provided and again, invitation to willingly experience pain and all FM experiences is offered. Acceptance is discussed.

Session 8—Review, Praise, and Plan

Adapted from Luoma et al. (2007).

Table 12.5 CBT-I Protocol-Specific Measures

Construct	Measure	Pat's Score
CBT-I Protocol Specific		
Sleep	PSQI—total score	High
	Latency	25 mins
	Nighttime awakenings	1–2; 5 mins to 3 hours
	Efficiency	62.5%
	Subjective Rating of Sleep Quality	Low
Cognitive Aspects of Sleep	DBAS	—I am concerned that chronic insomnia may have serious consequences on my physical health.
		—When I have trouble falling asleep or getting back to sleep . . . I should stay in bed and try harder.
		—I am worried that I may lose control over my abilities to sleep.
		—Without an adequate night's sleep, I can hardly function the next day.
		—I get overwhelmed by my thoughts at night and often feel I have no control over this racing mind.

significant life event may prompt this. Perpetuating factors are the behaviors (e.g., late caffeine use), thoughts ("I'll die if I don't get to sleep"), emotions (anxiety), and attitudes ("there is nothing I can do to help my sleep") that contribute to maintaining these sleep disturbances.

Returning to Pat, her sleep efficiency and subjective ratings of sleep quality increased by Session 4 (notwithstanding some early challenges). This, in turn, contributed to a growing sense of progress, pride, and perceived improvement in her health status. Engaging in twice daily relaxation exercises using the provided tracks was particularly helpful. Pat reported that utilizing deep breathing when encountering unpleasant symptoms during her day helped her feel less defeated. This practice, as well as adhering to sleep guidelines that led to feeling sleepier at bedtime, also helped Pat transition away from her growing reliance on alcohol and cannabis.

By Session 7, Pat recognized improvements in her cognitive symptoms. Coupled with less daytime fatigue, Pat began to feel as though she could return to some activities she previously enjoyed with family and friends. Pat's behavioral health provider (BHP) informed her primary care physician of the progress; in turn, the primary care physician praised and reinforced Pat at her follow-up appointments. The primary care provider's efforts to support Pat's progress (and in general, to express the known efficacy of CBT-I for sleep and health outcomes)

Table 12.6 CBT-I Case Conceptualization and Treatment Plan

Presenting Problems:

FM symptoms, particularly insomnia and pain, as well as depressed and anxious mood, contribute to a daily perpetuating cycle of increasing symptomatology and poor quality of life.

Predisposing Factors:

Female gender, aging, genetic predisposition to insomnia, predisposition to and current ruminative worry; FM diagnosis.

Precipitating Event(s):

Motor vehicle accident followed by FM symptom onset and subsequent life changes including loss of employment contributing to loss of identity as a working professional and increased social isolation.

Perpetuating Factors:

Spending longer periods in bed engaging in other non-sleep activities, including blue light exposure via electronic screens (e.g., cell phone use, television, etc.); anticipatory worry pre-bedtime; ruminative worry and frustration in bed at nighttime awakenings; evening alcohol and cannabis use; inconsistent wake times; morning naps; and afternoon caffeine. Poor sleep contributes to worse pain and mood.

In sum, these factors contribute to Pat's sleep dysregulation, which therefore adversely impacts FM symptoms (pain and cognitive difficulties, in particular) as well as mood. Conversely, FM symptoms and mood contribute to poor sleep maintenance and the cycle continues.

Treatment Plan:

Session 1—Assessment

Following assessment, provide Pat with how her predisposing, precipitating, and perpetuating factors maintain sleep, pain, and mood symptoms. Encourage reflection and provide hope via efficacy of CBT-I research findings. Sleep diary is then provided at every session to record sleep schedule over the coming week and is then reviewed.

Session 2—Psychoeducation on the Basics of FM and Sleep; Sleep Hygiene Education; Stimulus Control Education and Anticipatory Problem-Solving

Given several perpetuating factors that contribute to Pat's insomnia (i.e., spending a good deal of time in bed attending to other activities aside from sleeping or sex), this initial emphasis will aid in producing early improvements to gain confidence.

Session 3**—Sleep Restriction or Compression and Pleasant Activity Scheduling

Praise adherence and problem-solve barriers. Provide rationale for session topics and collaboratively develop goals and specific plan.

(Continued)

Table 12.6 (Continued)

Session 4**—Relaxation for Pain and Sleep

Rationale is given and pain-specific guided relaxation script is administered in-session. Barriers to adherence are discussed. Homework: listen to given relaxation tracks in bed at bedtime, at nighttime awakenings, and once during the day.

Session 4—Introduction to Cognitive Therapy (CT), Sleep, and Pain Focus, Part I

Rationale for CT; collaboratively illuminate the patterns of emotions, behaviors, thoughts, and physiological responses that Pat experiences, and identify common cognitions occurring in this cycle. Review progress toward activity goals. Homework: Thought Log to identify mood and thoughts is provided. Review sleep and activity scheduling; praise and problem-solve.

Session 5—Introduction to Cognitive Therapy, Sleep, and Pain Focus, Part II: Cognitive Restructuring

Review Thought Log and relay steps for cognitive restructuring: expand to identify evidence for and against these cognitions; determine alternative (more accurate) thoughts; identify emotion and intensity. Review sleep and activity scheduling; praise and problem-solve.

Session 6—Continued Cognitive Restructuring and Activity Pacing for Pain

Education on activity pacing followed by plan development for the coming week and problem-solve barriers.

Session 7—Continued Cognitive Restructuring
Session 8—Maintenance Instruction and Graduation

Adapted from Perlis et al., 2011; Von Korff et al., 2012, p. 17

** These sessions may be reversed if 1) provider determines treatment adherence would benefit from initial reduced anxiety or 2) two weeks of sleep diaries have not been completed in order to calculate a sleep restriction/compression prescription.

increased the likelihood of adherence and success. If there are sleep- and mood-specific medications that are prescribed, it is especially important that the BHP communicate any changes in these domains to facilitate discussions regarding medication changes or tapers.

Summary

FM and related conditions are diagnostically complex, requiring great thought and commitment for effective treatment. Clinicians can offer a great deal to assist patients in living valued lives, notwithstanding the unpredictable and often debilitating symptoms they may be experiencing. A single chapter cannot provide a comprehensive document to guide understanding, conceptualization, and treatment. However, hopefully this overview has provided a useful starting point in treatment of patients with these diagnoses. It concludes by offering the following "take home" points. First, when working with FM patients, partner with a primary care physician in order to offer the most effective team-based care possible. Second, this chapter presented information regarding three transdiagnostic approaches that target important aspects of the FM symptom constellation. Whatever approach you use, hopefully a biopsychosocial model will inform your work. Finally, each of the protocols presented can be brief and time-limited. However, we recognize that the work with the patient is longitudinal, the protocol application may be repeated over time as symptoms wax and wane, and patience and an empathic approach help to remind us that gains, however small, bring much reward.

References

Aaron, L. A., Burke, M. M., & Buchwald, D. (2000). Overlapping conditions among patients with chronic fatigue syndrome, fibromyalgia, and temporomandibular disorder. *Archives of Internal Medicine, 160*(2), 221–227.

Arnold, L. M., Hudson, J. I., Hess, E. V., Ware, A. E., Fritz, D. A., Auchenbach, M. B., . . . Keck, P. E. (2004). Family study of fibromyalgia. *Arthritis & Rheumatology, 50*(3), 944–952.

Baer, R. A., Smith, G. T., Lykins, E., Button, D., Krietemeyer, J., Sauer, S., . . . Williams, J. M. G. (2008). Construct validity of the five facet mindfulness questionnaire in meditating and nonmeditating samples. *Assessment, 15*, 329–342.

Bandura, A. (1989). Human agency in social cognitive theory. *American Psychologist, 44*(9), 1175.

Barlow, D. H., & Farchione, T. J. (Eds.). (2018). *Applications of the unified protocol for transdiagnostic treatment of emotional disorders.* New York, NY: Oxford University Press.

Barsky, A. J., & Borus, J. F. (1999). Functional somatic syndromes. *Annals of Internal Medicine, 130*(11), 910–921.

Beck, A. T. (1976). *Cognitive therapy and the emotional disorders.* Oxford: International Universities Press.

Bellato, E., Marini, E., Castoldi, F., Barbasetti, N., Mattei, L., Bonasia, D. E., & Blonna, D. (2012). Fibromyalgia syndrome: Etiology, pathogenesis, diagnosis, and treatment. *Pain Research and Treatment, 2012*, 1–17.

Bennett, R. M., Jones, J., Turk, D. C, Russell, J., & Matallana, L. (2007). An Internet survey of 2,596 people with fibromyalgia. *BMC Musculoskeletal Disorders, 8*(27).

Bernardy, K., Klose, P., Busch, A. J., Choy, E. H., & Häuser, W. (2012). Cognitive behavioural therapies for fibromyalgia syndrome. *The Cochrane Database of Systematic Reviews, 9.*

Besteiro González, J. L., Suárez Fernández, T. V., Arboleya Rodríguez, L., Muñiz, J., Lemos Giráldez, S., & Álvarez Fernández, Á. (2011). Sleep architecture in patients with fibromyalgia. *Psichothema, 23*(3).

Bond, F. W., Hayes, S. C., Baer, R. A., Carpenter, K. M., Guenole, N., Orcutt, H. K., . . . Zettle, R. D. (2011). Preliminary psychometric properties of the acceptance and action questionnaire—II: A revised measure of psychological inflexibility and experiential avoidance. *Behavior Therapy, 42*(4), 676–688.

Borchers, A. T., & Gershwin, M. E. (2015). Fibromyalgia: A critical and comprehensive review. *Clinical Reviews in Allergy & Immunology, 49*(2), 100–151.

Borrell-Carrio, F., Suchman, A. L., & Epstein, R. (2004). The biopsychosocial model 25 years later: Principles, practice, and scientific inquiry. *Annals of Family Medicine, 2*(6), 576–582. doi:10.1370/afm.245

Burns, J. W., Crofford, L. J., & Chervin, R. D. (2008). Sleep stage dynamics in fibromyalgia patients and controls. *Sleep Medicine, 9*(6), 689–696.

Buysse, D. J., Reynolds, C. F., Monk, T. H., Berman, S. R., & Kupfer, D. J. (1989). The Pittsburgh sleep quality index: A new instrument for psychiatric practice and research. *Psychiatry Research, 28*(2), 193–213.

Choy, E., Perrot, S., Leon, T., Kaplan, J., Petersel, D., Ginovker, A., & Kramer, E. (2010). A patient survey of the impact of fibromyalgia and the journey to diagnosis. *BMC Health Services Research,* 10(1), 102.

Clauw, D. J. (2015). Fibromyalgia and related conditions. *Mayo Clinic Proceedings, 90*(5), 680–692.

Clauw, D. J. (2014). Fibromyalgia: A clinical review. *Journal of the American Medical Association, 311*(15), 1547–1555.

Clauw, D. J., Arnold, L. M., & McCarberg, B. H. (2011). The science of fibromyalgia. *Mayo Clinic Proceedings, 86*(9), 907–911.

Deacon, B., Abramowitz, J. S., Woods, C. M., & Tolin, D. (2003). The anxiety sensitivity index— revised: Psychometric properties and factor structure in two nonclinical samples. *Behavior Research and Therapy, 41*(12), 1427–1449.

Diaz-Piedra, C., Catena, A., Sánchez, A. I., Miró, E., Martínez, M. P., & Buela-Casal, G. (2015). Sleep disturbances in fibromyalgia syndrome: The role of clinical and polysomnographic variables explaining poor sleep quality in patients. *Sleep Medicine, 16*(8), 917–925.

Dobkin, P. L., Liu, A., Abrahamowicz, M., Ionescu-Ittu, R., Bernatsky, S., Goldberger, A., & Baron, M. (2010). Predictors of disability and pain six months after the end of treatment for fibromyalgia. *The Clinical Journal of Pain, 26*(1), 23–29.

Engel, G. L. (1977). The need for a new medical model: A challenge for biomedicine. *Science, 196*(4286), 129–136. doi:10.1126/science.847460

Fietta, P., Fietta, P., & Manganelli, P. (2007). Fibromyalgia and psychiatric disorders. *ACTA Biomedica-Ateneo Parmense, 78*(2), 88.

Fitzcharles, M. A., Ste-Marie, P. A., Rampakakis, E., Sampalis, J. S., & Shir, Y. (2016). Disability in fibromyalgia associates with symptom severity and occupation characteristics. *The Journal of Rheumatology, 43*(5), 931–936.

Fordyce, W. E. (1976). *Behavioral concepts in chronic pain and illness.* St. Louis, MO: Mosby.

Fordyce, W. E., Lansky, D., Calsyn, D. A., Shelton, J. L., Stolov, W. C., & Rock, D. L. (1984). Pain measurement and pain behavior. *Pain, 18*, 53–69.

Fraga, B. P., Santos, E. B., Neto, J. P. F., Macieira, J. C., Quintans, L. J. Jr, Onofre, A. S., . . . Bonjardim, L. R. (2012). Signs and symptoms of temporomandibular dysfunction in fibromyalgia patients. *Journal of Craniofacial Surgery, 23*(2), 615–618.

Glombieski, J. A., Sawyer, A. T., Gutermann, J., Koenig, K., Rief, W., & Hofmann, S. G. (2010). Psychological treatments for fibromyalgia: A meta-analysis. *Pain, 151*(2), 280–295.

Goldenberg, D. L., Schur, P., & Romain, P. (2017). *Clinical manifestations and diagnosis of fibromyalgia in adults*. Retrieved from https://www.uptodate.com/contents/clinical-manifestations-and-diagnosis-of-fibromyalgia-in-adults

Gracely, R. H., Ceko, M., & Bushnell, M. C. (2012). Fibromyalgia and depression. *Pain Research and Treatment, 2012*, 486590.

Häuser, W., Galek, A., Erbslöh-Möller, B., Köllner, V., Kühn-Becker, H., Langhorst, J., . . . Brähler, E. (2013). Posttraumatic stress disorder in fibromyalgia syndrome: Prevalence, temporal relationship between posttraumatic stress and fibromyalgia symptoms, and impact on clinical outcome. *PAIN, 154*(8), 1216–1223.

Häuser, W., Hoffmann, E. M., Wolfe, F., Worthing, A. B., Stahl, N., Rothenberg, R., & Walitt, B. (2015). Self-reported childhood maltreatment, lifelong traumatic events and mental disorders in fibromyalgia syndrome: A comparison of US and German outpatients. *Clinical and Experimental Rheumatology, 33*(1 Suppl 88), S86.

Häuser, W., Walitt, B., Fitzcharles, M. A., & Sommer, C. (2014). Review of pharmacological therapies in fibromyalgia syndrome. *Arthritis Research & Therapy, 16*(1), 201.

Hayes, S. C., Strosahl, K. D., & Wilson, K. G. (2012). *Acceptance and commitment therapy: The process and practice of mindful change*. New York, NY: The Guilford Press.

Hofmann, S. G., Asnaani, A., Vonk, I. J., Sawyer, A. T., & Fang, A. (2012). The efficacy of cognitive behavioral therapy: A review of meta-analyses. *Cognitive Therapy and Research, 36*(5), 427–440.

Hughes, L. S., Clark, J., Colclough, J. A., Dale, E., & McMillan, D. (2017). Acceptance and Commitment Therapy (ACT) for chronic pain. *The Clinical Journal of Pain, 33*(6), 552–568.

Jiao, J., Vincent, A., Cha, S. S., Luedtke, C. A., Kim, C. H., & Oh, T. H. (2015). Physical trauma and infection as precipitating factors in patients with fibromyalgia. *American Journal of Physical Medicine & Rehabilitation, 94*(12), 1075–1082.

Karsdorp, P. A., & Vlaeyen, J. W. (2009). Active avoidance but not activity pacing is associated with disability in fibromyalgia. *Pain, 147*(1), 29–35.

Kato, K., Sullivan, P. F., Evengård, B., & Pedersen, N. L. (2009). A population-based twin study of functional somatic syndromes. *Psychological Medicine, 39*(3), 497–505.

Kurland, J. E., Coyle, W. J., Winkler, A., & Zable, E. (2006). Prevalence of irritable bowel syndrome and depression in fibromyalgia. *Digestive Diseases and Sciences, 51*(3), 454–460.

Lazaridou, A., Kim, J., Cahalan, C. M., Loggia, M. L., Franceschelli, O., Berna, C., . . . Edwards, R. R. (2017). Effects of Cognitive-Behavioral Therapy (CBT) on brain connectivity supporting catastrophizing in fibromyalgia. *The Clinical Journal of Pain, 33*(3), 215–221.

Levant, R. F. (2005). *Report of the 2005 presidential task force on evidence-based practice*. Washington, DC: American Psychological Association.

Luciano, J. V., Guallar, J. A., Aguado, J., López-del-Hoyo, Y., Olivan, B., Magallón, R., Alda, M., Serrano-Blanco, A., Gili, M., & Garcia-Campayo, J. (2014). Effectiveness of group acceptance and commitment therapy for fibromyalgia: A 6-month randomized controlled trial (EFFIGACT study). *PAIN, 155*(4), 693–702.

Luoma, J. B., Hayes, S. C., & Walser, R. D. (2007). *Learning ACT: An acceptance and commitment therapy skills-training manual for therapists*. Oakland, CA: New Harbinger Publications.

Marcus, D. A., Bernstein, C., & Rudy, T. E. (2005). Fibromyalgia and headache: An epidemiological study supporting migraine as part of the fibromyalgia syndrome. *Clinical Rheumatology, 24*(6), 595–601.

Martínez, M. P., Miró, E., Sánchez, A. I., Díaz-Piedra, C., Cáliz, R., Vlaeyen, J. W., & Buela-Casal, G. (2014). Cognitive-behavioral therapy for insomnia and sleep hygiene in fibromyalgia: A randomized controlled trial. *Journal of Behavioral Medicine, 37*(4), 683–697.

McCracken, L. M., & Eccleston, C. (2005). A prospective study of acceptance of pain and patient functioning with chronic pain. *Pain, 118*(1–2), 164–169.

McCracken, L. M., & Vowles, K. E. (2014). Acceptance and commitment therapy and mindfulness for chronic pain: Model, process, and progress. *American Psychologist, 69*(2), 178.

Mease, P. J., Dundon, K., & Sarzi-Puttini, P. (2011). Pharmacotherapy of fibromyalgia. *Best Practice & Research Clinical Rheumatology, 25*(2), 285–297.

Miró, E., Lupiáñez, J., Martínez, M. P., Sánchez, A. I., Díaz-Piedra, C., Guzmán, M. A., & Buela-Casal, G. (2011). Cognitive-behavioral therapy for insomnia improves attentional function in fibromyalgia syndrome: A pilot, randomized controlled trial. *Journal of Health Psychology, 16*(5), 770–782.

Morin, C. M. (1994). Dysfunctional beliefs and attitudes about sleep: Preliminary scale development and description. *The Behavior Therapist*, 163–164.

Ortiz, R., Ballard, E. D., Machado-Vieira, R., Saligan, L. N., & Walitt, B. (2016). Quantifying the influence of child abuse history on the cardinal symptoms of fibromyalgia. *Clinical and Experimental Rheumatology, 34*(2 Suppl 96), 59–66.

Payne-Murphy, J. C. (2015). *Acceptance-based factors in chronic pain: A comparison between fibromyalgia and chronic pain patients in an internet support group sample* (Doctoral dissertation), University of Colorado at Denver.

Perlis, M. L., Aloia, M., & Kuhn, B. (Eds.). (2011). *Behavioral treatments for sleep disorders: A comprehensive primer of behavioral sleep medicine interventions*. London: Academic Press.

Phillips, K., & Clauw, D. J. (2013). Central pain mechanisms in the rheumatic diseases: Future directions. *Arthritis & Rheumatology, 65*(2), 291–302.

Queiroz, L. P. (2013). Worldwide epidemiology of fibromyalgia. *Current Pain and Headache Reports, 17*(8), 356.

Rollnick, S., Miller, W., & Butler, C. (2007). *Motivational interviewing in health care: Helping patients change behavior*. New York, NY: The Guilford Press.

Sackett, D. L., Straus, S. E., Richardson, W. S., Rosenberg, W., & Haynes, R. B. (2000). *Evidence based medicine: How to practice and teach EBM* (2nd ed.). London: Churchill Livingstone.

Sperber, A. D., Atzmon, Y., Neumann, L., Weisberg, I., Shalit, Y., Abu-Shakrah, M., . . . Buskila, D. (1999). Fibromyalgia in the irritable bowel syndrome: Studies of prevalence and clinical implications. *The American Journal of Gastroenterology, 94*(12), 3541–3546.

Spielman, A. J., Caruso, L. S., & Glovinsky, P. B. (1987). A behavioral perspective on insomnia treatment. *Psychiatric Clinics of North America, 10*(4), 541–553.

Sullivan, M. J., Thorn, B., Haythornthwaite, J. A., Keefe, F., Martin, M., Bradley, L. A., & Lefebvre, J. C. (2001). Theoretical perspectives on the relation between catastrophizing and pain. *The Clinical Journal of Pain, 17*(1), 52–64.

Tait, R. C., Chibnall, J. T., & Krause, S. (1990). The pain disability index: Psychometric properties. *Pain, 40*, 171–182.

Tang, N. K., Goodchild, C. E., & Salkovskis, P. M. (2012). Hybrid cognitive-behaviour therapy for individuals with insomnia and chronic pain: A pilot randomised controlled trial. *Behaviour Research and Therapy, 50*(12), 814–821.

Thieme, K., & Gracely, R. H. (2009). Are psychological treatments effective for fibromyalgia pain? *Current Rheumatology Reports, 11*(6), 443–450.

Thieme, K., Mathys, M., & Turk, D. C. (2017). Evidenced-based guidelines on the treatment of fibromyalgia patients: Are they consistent and if not, why not? Have effective psychological treatments been overlooked? *The Journal of Pain, 18*(7), 747–756.

Üçeyler, N., Burgmer, M., Friedel, E., Greiner, W., Petzke, F., Sarholz, M., . . . Häuser, W. (2017). Etiology and pathophysiology of fibromyalgia syndrome: Updated guidelines 2017, overview of systematic review articles and overview of studies on small fiber neuropathy in FMS subgroups. *Schmerz* (Berlin, Germany), *31*(3), 239–245.

Van Straten, A., van der Zweerde, T., Kleiboer, A., Cuijpers, P., Morin, C. M., & Lancee, J. (2018). Cognitive and behavioral therapies in the treatment of insomnia: A meta-analysis. *Sleep Medicine Reviews, 38*, 3–16.

Verbunt, J. A., Pernot, D. H., & Smeets, R. J. (2008). Disability and quality of life in patients with fibromyalgia. *Health Quality Life Outcomes, 6*, 8.

Vitiello, M. V., McCurry, S. M., Shortreed, S. M., Balderson, B. H., Baker, L. D., Keefe, F. J., . . . Von Korff, M. (2014). Cognitive-behavioral treatment for comorbid insomnia and osteoarthritis pain in primary care: The lifestyles randomized controlled trial. *Journal of the American Geriatrics Society, 61*(6), 947–956.

Von Korff, M., Vitiello, M. V., McCurry, S. M., Balderson, B. H., Moore, A. L., Baker, L. D., . . . Rybarczyk, B. D. (2012). Group interventions for co-morbid insomnia and osteoarthritis pain in primary care: The Lifestyles cluster randomized trial design. *Contemporary Clinical Trials, 33*, 759–768. [PubMed: 22484341]

Vowles, K. E., McCracken, L. M., McLeod, C., & Eccleston, C. (2008). The chronic pain acceptance questionnaire: Confirmatory factor analysis and identification of patient subgroups. *Pain, 140*(2), 284–291.

Watson, D., Clark, L. A., & Tellegen, A. (1988). Development and validation of brief measures of positive and negative affect: The PANAS scales. *Journal of Personality and Social Psychology, 54*(6), 1063–1079.

Weir, P. T., Harlan, G. A., Nkoy, F. L., Jones, S. S., Hegmann, K. T., Gren, L. H., & Lyon, J. L. (2006). The incidence of fibromyalgia and its associated comorbidities: A population-based retrospective cohort study based on international classification of diseases, 9th Revision codes. *JCR: Journal of Clinical Rheumatology, 12*(3), 124–128.

White, K. P., Speechley, M., Harth, M., & Ostbye, T. (1999). The London fibromyalgia epidemiology study: Comparing the demographic and clinical characteristics in 100 random community cases of fibromyalgia versus controls. *The Journal of Rheumatology, 26*(7), 1577–1585.

Wicksell, R. K., Kemani, M., Jensen, K., Kosek, E., Kadetoff, D., Sorjonen, K., Ingvar, M., & Olsson, G. L. (2013). Acceptance and commitment therapy for fibromyalgia: A randomized controlled trial. *European Journal of Pain, 17*(4), 599–611.

Williams, A. C. D. C., Eccleston, C., & Morley, S. (2012). Psychological therapies for the management of chronic pain (excluding headache) in adults. *Cochrane Database of Systematic Reviews, 11*. doi: 10.1002/14651858.CD007407

Wilson, K. G., & Groom, J. (2002). *The valued living questionnaire. Available from the first author at department of psychology.* University, MS: University of Mississippi.

Wolfe, F., Clauw, D. J., Fitzcharles, M. A., Goldenberg, D. L., Häuser, W., Katz, R. L., . . . Walitt, B. (2016). 2016 Revisions to the 2010/2011 fibromyalgia diagnostic criteria. *Seminars in Arthritis and Rheumatism, 46*(3), 319–329.

Wolfe, F., Michaud, K., Li, T., & Katz, R. S. (2010). Chronic conditions and health problems in rheumatic diseases: Comparisons with rheumatoid arthritis, noninflammatory rheumatic disorders, systemic lupus erythematosus, and fibromyalgia. *The Journal of Rheumatology, 37*(2), 305–315.

Wolfe, F., Smythe, H. A., Yunus, M. B., Bennett, R. M., Bombardier, C., Goldenberg, D. L., . . . Fam, A. G. (1990). The American college of rheumatology 1990 criteria for the classification of fibromyalgia. *Arthritis & Rheumatology, 33*(2), 160–172.

Yavne, Y., Amital, D., Watad, A., Tiosano, S., & Amital, H. (2018). A systematic review of precipitating physical and psychological traumatic events in the development of fibromyalgia. *Seminars in Arthritis and Rheumatism, 48*(1), 121–133.

13

Chronic Headache Pain

RuthAnn R. Lester, Eleanor S. Brammer,
and Allison Gray

Background

The most recent Global Burden of Disease Study identified headaches as the third most common pain condition in terms of global prevalence (the proportion of the population with the condition at any point in time) and the sixth most common in terms of global incidence (the rate of onset or new diagnoses during a period of time) (GBD 2016 Disease and Injury Incidence and Prevalence Collaborators, 2017). Headache disorders are among the ten most disabling conditions for males and the five most disabling conditions for females according to the World Health Organization (WHO) (2006). Therefore, not surprisingly, headache is among the most frequent pain complaints with which patients present to primary care in the United States, with a lifetime prevalence of greater than 90% among adults (Clinch, 2015).

The term "chronic headache" encompasses several diagnoses characterized by frequent and persistent headaches (defined as occurring on 15 days or more per month for longer than three months), with chronic migraine being the most common. Prevalence rates for chronic headache are estimated to be between 2% and 5% (Grazzi, Usai, & Bussone, 2006). Furthermore, headache disorders are prevalent throughout the world, affecting people of all ages, races, income levels, and geographical areas (WHO, 2006). Collectively, headache disorders were the third highest cause of years lost to disability worldwide as of 2013 (WHO, 2006) and represent a significant public health concern associated with substantial personal suffering, disability, and societal expenses (Smitherman, Burch, Sheikh, & Loder, 2013).

Although correctly diagnosing chronic headaches and differentiating between headache conditions is important in order to inform the most effective medical and behavioral medicine interventions, properly diagnosing and treating headache syndromes can be challenging for providers. The WHO (2006) describes headache as a condition that has been underestimated, under-recognized, and undertreated throughout the world, with a minority of headache conditions diagnosed appropriately by healthcare providers. Successful management of chronic headache patients is often complex and represents a challenge for primary care providers due to variables such as limited time for office visits and the significant expertise needed to optimally treat the often-refractory nature of chronic headaches (Becker, 2017). Treatment failure frequently is attributed to a combination of incomplete or incorrect diagnosis, important exacerbating factors that have been missed, inadequate pharmacotherapy and non-pharmacotherapy interventions, and patient factors such as unrealistic expectations and comorbidities (Lipton, Silberstein, Saper, Bigal, & Goadsby, 2003).

The use of pharmacological and non-pharmacological treatments in combination has been shown to be superior to either option alone (Holroyd, O'Donnell, Stensland, & Lipchik, 2001), with evidence supporting that behavioral intervention itself can lead in some cases to headache improvement rivaling results obtained by using medication (Grazzi & Andrasik, 2010). Indeed, headache is one of the most common chronic pain disorders that can be managed effectively with behavioral approaches (Grazzi & Andrasik, 2010), especially when these approaches are utilized to prevent headaches as opposed solely to alleviate suffering once an episode becomes severe (Holroyd & Penzien, 1994). This chapter reviews the types of chronic headache conditions, headache medical etiologies as well as biopsychosocial contributing factors, and evidence-based interdisciplinary intervention approaches.

Headache Conditions

Accurately diagnosing and managing any headache syndrome initially requires differentiating between primary headaches and headaches secondary to other etiologies identified by history, laboratory, radiologic, or exam findings (Becker, 2017). Secondary headaches generally are sudden in onset and typically resolve once the identified cause has been treated. If left untreated, secondary headaches may become chronic in nature. "Red flags" for secondary headaches include age of onset over age 50, fever, and/or stiff neck. Underlying causes of secondary headaches vary in severity, and some can be life-threatening if left untreated (e.g., brain tumors, increased intracranial pressure, subarachnoid hemorrhage, meningitis, Lyme disease). Non-life-threatening secondary headaches may include post-concussive headaches, headaches that are medication side effects, headaches secondary to illnesses (such as sinusitis), and medication overuse headaches (MOH) or rebound headaches, a complication of poorly managed episodic headaches that become chronic secondary to analgesic overuse (Becker, 2017).

Primary headache syndromes are not associated with any demonstrable organic disease or structural neurologic abnormality. As such, laboratory and imaging tests generally are unremarkable (Clinch, 2015), with neurological and physical examinations generally normal. The pathophysiology of primary headache syndromes is not well-understood. The main focus of pharmacological treatment is to target neurologic dysfunction and involvement of the trigeminal nerve and cranial vessels. Subjective descriptions of pain and associated symptoms drive the diagnosis of primary headache syndromes. Positive indicators that the headaches are primary rather than secondary include a long duration of similar headaches, a family history of migraine, and a menstrual exacerbation in females (Lipton & Silberstein, 2015). Chronic migraine, chronic tension-type headache, hemicrania continua (including chronic cluster headaches), and new daily persistent headaches (NDPH) are the most commonly diagnosed primary chronic headache syndromes (Robbins, Grosberg, Napchan, Crystal, & Lipton, 2010).

Migraine

The prevalence of migraine and likely migraine in the U.S. population is 16%; female to male ratio is approximately 3:1 (Clinch, 2015). Migraine is a condition associated with an episodic instability of the neurovascular system, with serotonin and other neurotransmitters playing critical roles in the dysfunction (IHS, 2013). Migraine attacks vary in intensity and pattern of associated symptoms (such as nausea/vomiting, sensory sensitivities, vertigo, and blurred vision).

The two major subtypes of migraine are migraine with aura and migraine without aura. Auras are disturbances characterized by visual symptoms (positive visual phenomena including colorful lines and shapes, spots of light, pupil dilation, blurred vision, or loss of vision), sensory changes (tingling or numbness), vertigo, confusion, or language anomalies. During a migraine headache, patients may have abnormal exam findings such as aphasia and/or unilateral weakness. The neurovascular activity causes unilateral pounding and severe headache pain, lasting up to hours or even days at a time. This neurobiological disorder is characterized by increased brain sensitivity, hypersensitivity, or hyperexcitability. Hyperactivity and excitability of the trigeminal nerve and cranial vessels cause the release of substances that promote perivascular inflammation and dilation.

Migraine headaches generally are worsened by activity. Dysfunction of other areas of the nervous system, brainstem, and hypothalamus contribute to associated symptoms such as nausea, vomiting, photophobia, and osmophobia. Patients with chronic migraine represent the most disabled subpopulation of headache patients (Becker, 2017). Chronic migraine is diagnosed when migraines occur for 15 days or more per month for at least three months in the absence of organic pathology (Westergaard, Glümer, Hansen, & Jensen, 2014). It is conceptualized as a condition in which the threshold for developing a migraine has been lowered, resulting in attacks that occur with increased frequency (May & Schulte, 2016). Although common, migraines often are under-recognized and undertreated. Research shows that a significant portion of people with migraines do not seek care (Weeks, 2013). Almost half of those who do seek treatment do not receive a diagnosis, and their headaches are treated sub-optimally.

Patients with episodic migraines transition to chronic migraines at a rate of 2.5% per year (Weeks, 2013). Psychiatric disorders, other pain conditions, respiratory illness, and diseases associated with cardiac risk tend to be comorbid with migraine (Buse, Manack, Serrano, Turkel, & Lipton, 2010). Furthermore, there appear to be clusters of patient variables associated with chronic migraine, variables that include female gender (related to hormonal fluctuations), middle age, and being in a household with the lowest annual income (Weeks, 2013). Reproductive-aged women are particularly vulnerable to migraine (Smitherman et al., 2013).

Tension-Type Headache

Patients describe tension-type headaches as a squeezing band stretching across the bilateral forehead (IHS, 2013). These recurrent headaches can last from 30 minutes to days. They are uncomfortable and disruptive but generally are not described as severe or disruptive to sleep. Tension-type headaches often are associated with nausea and/or light or sound sensitivity. Patients with tension-type headaches may exhibit tightness of cervical muscles, causing limited range of neck motion, scalp tenderness, or allodynia. Tension-type headaches (as well as migraines) can occur because of flexion or extension injury of the neck, poor posture, anxiety, and/or teeth clenching or grinding (Rota et al., 2016).

Clinicians cannot always easily distinguish migraine from tension-type headache. Some experts suggest that primary care providers should assume that a chronic disabling headache is always migrainous (Jackson, Mancuso, Nickoloff, Bernstein, & Kay, 2017). However, the pharmacologic treatment for tension-type headaches and migraines is very different, so it is important to see a neurologist when there is lack of clarity in the diagnosis.

Hemicrania Continua

Hemicrania continua is a chronic headache characterized by persistent, unilateral head pain that varies in severity and that is associated with at least one additional troublesome autonomic symptom (eye redness and/or tearing, nasal congestion and/or runny nose, ptosis, and miosis) (Piña-Garza, 2013). Hemicrania continua headaches generally are of moderate intensity with occasional short bursts of piercing head pain and persist for more than three months without shifting sides and/or without periods of pain freedom.

Chronic cluster headache is a subtype of hemicrania continua. Cluster headache is characterized by unilateral head pain that occurs with autonomic features such as ptosis, miosis, eye lacrimation, eye conjunctival injection or redness, or rhinorrhea. These autonomic symptoms and the typically shorter duration of cluster headaches help to differentiate them from migraine headaches. Pain distribution is located in the unilateral trigeminal region. Episodic cluster headaches occur daily, usually one to eight times per day, for a period of a week. If no remission or painless period occurs, headaches are then classified as chronic cluster headaches. There is a positive correlation between chronic cluster headaches and a history of head injuries, and cluster headaches occur in males more than females at a ratio of roughly 5:1 (Piña-Garza, 2013).

New Daily Persistent Headache (NDPH)

New daily persistent headache (NDPH) is another primary headache disorder that negatively impacts quality of life for patients and is particularly challenging for providers to manage (Robbins et al., 2010). The one-year population prevalence of NDPH has been reported at 0.03– 0.1%, and NDPH affects children more than adolescents and adolescents more than adults. Youth are more likely to experience NDPH than chronic tension-type headaches. NDPHs develop very quickly and are unrelenting. NDPH often is refractory to many medications and commonly becomes chronic (Tyagi, 2012). Headache pain can last for years, regardless of the best treatment options, but often stops as suddenly as it starts; most patients experience complete remission in two years (Robbins et al., 2010).

NDPHs have at least two of the following pain characteristics: bilateral location, pressing/tightening (non-pulsating) quality, mild or moderate pain intensity, and no pain intensification with physical activity. This headache pain can be associated with light or sound sensitivity, or mild nausea, but not more than one of these additional complaints (IHS, 2013). NDPH can mimic chronic migraine or chronic tension-type headache. A large portion of NDPH sufferers have migrainous features and should be managed with treatments used to treat migraines (Tyagi, 2012). Due to the sudden onset of NDPH and its unrelenting nature, secondary causes must be evaluated. Work-up may include neuroimaging, lumbar puncture to evaluate intracranial pressure, and serologic evaluation to rule out inflammation or infection.

Chronic Headache Assessment

Providers should not initiate treatment prior to obtaining a comprehensive patient history, including a thorough medication history (Weeks, 2013), and this assessment should highlight or elicit characteristics to help differentiate between the various headache disorders (WHO, 2006).

Conceptualizing Headaches From a Biopsychosocial Framework

Assessing headache histories and current contributing factors is best completed through the lens of the biopsychosocial model. As discussed elsewhere in this volume, biomedical models describing pain in terms of direct transmission of impulses from the periphery to structures within the central nervous system have been replaced by biopsychosocial pain models capturing the complex interactions between biological and psychosocial factors. Psychosocial factors in these models often divide into behavioral, affective, and cognitive influences (Andrasik, Flor, & Turk, 2005). Biopsychosocial models assert that just as biological aspects of headache can be assessed and treated, especially as many chronic headache disorders like migraine likely have biological bases (WHO, 2006), psychological and social factors also must be assessed and treated. Due to the numerous identified comorbidities that may play parts in the development of these chronic pain conditions, proper history taking and symptom description become key to patient management and treatment success.

The risk of progression from episodic to chronic headaches is affected by both modifiable and non-modifiable biological factors. Non-modifiable risk factors include older age at onset of headache, female gender, Caucasian ethnicity, low education level, low socioeconomic status, and family history of headaches (Smitherman et al., 2013). Modifiable risk factors that can be optimized by medical management include obesity, medication overuse and/or poor medication compliance, stressful life events, caffeine overuse, poor sleep (including snoring and sleep apnea), neck injury, depression, asthma, and allergic rhinitis (Lipton & Silberstein, 2015; Bigal & Lipton, 2006). Understanding risk factors is an important step toward developing evidence-based treatments for preventing progression of worsening headache.

Concurrently with assessing the medical aspects of the patient's headache condition, assessing psychosocial factors also is important to inform treatment planning. Recommended components of psychosocial history include habit histories (e.g., nicotine, caffeine, alcohol, other substance use, sleep difficulties, eating), psychiatric history, social history (including family members' reactions to the headaches), areas of family conflict (especially when the headache sufferer is a child), impact of headaches on work and/or school functioning and performance including absences, and evidence of secondary gain (Weeks, 2013). Please see Appendix 1 for an example of a semi-structured headache history outline.

Various psychological conditions can contribute to and exacerbate headache conditions, and treatment for those conditions should be managed prior to or concurrently with treatment for headaches (Andrasik, 2003). Complicating conditions include mood and anxiety disorders, thought disorders, and personality disorders. There is a bidirectional relationship between psychiatric and migraine conditions, whereby one increases vulnerability for the other. For example, when a person experiences more frequent chronic headaches, psychological distress increases; additionally, a person with anxiety and depression is more likely to experience migraine disability and the migraine experience is more likely to be intractable. Depression, in particular, is predictive of episodic migraines becoming chronic (Andrasik, 2003).

Finally, patients with certain personality disorders experience a higher incidence of headaches than otherwise would be expected (Andrasik, 2003). Abbass,

Lovas, and Purdy (2008) connect this bidirectional relationship to some patients' proclivity toward somatization of emotions. Specifically, they discuss the fact that headache sufferers with alexithymia (difficulty identifying and experiencing emotions) or poor emotional insight are less likely to detect and then seek treatment for psychological distress, contributing to increased headaches. This dynamic is particularly impactful for headache sufferers who have difficulty regulating anger. Nicholson, Grambling, Ong, and Buenevar (2003) show, in a matched study, that a lead predictor of chronic headaches is anger turned inward.

Assessment Tools

Patient self-monitoring through utilization of a headache log is an essential component of assessment. The WHO (2006) recommends that patients keep a headache log for at least a few weeks. Headache logs also are used during treatment as a means of providing relatively reliable, objective information to efficiently evaluate clinical changes and treatment efficacy (Weeks, 2013). Especially during the assessment phase of migraine management, it is recommended that patients utilize a headache log to track and monitor headache frequency, intensity, duration, and disability, as well as possible triggers. Medication use and behavioral health interventions, including effectiveness, also should be tracked (Anderson & Kinikar, 2017; Weeks, 2013). Female patients can chart menstrual cycles on the log.

When patients record their observations and experiences of behavioral antecedents and consequences, they increase self-awareness and sense of self-efficacy, and they also empower their providers to tailor individualized treatment plans (Lawrence, Wodarski, & Wodarski, 2002). Patients and providers can use this data to better define the headache experience, specify antecedents, quantify target behaviors, and specify and measure desired outcomes. See Appendix 2 for an example of a headache log. Multiple variations exist and can be selected based on individualized patient need. There are various publicly available logs available online on websites such as the National Headache Foundation (https://headaches.org).

The Midas Disability Assessment (MIDAS) Questionnaire (Stewart et al., 2000) is an easily administered, validated, organized way to evaluate chronic headache pain, headache-related disability, and medication efficacy (Anderson & Kinikar, 2017). Furthermore, a provider can tailor acute medication treatment to severity of headache using the MIDAS score (Anderson & Kinikar, 2017). The MIDAS also is used by neurologists to assess efficacy of Botox in the treatment and prevention of chronic migraine.

Effective treatment of headache disorders typically entails utilizing an integrated approach with both medical and behavioral medicine treatment components (Holroyd et al., 2001). Thus, it is advisable to include a "stage of change" discussion between assessment and intervention (Prochaska Norcross, & DiClemente, 1994; Lawrence et al., 2002). Stage of change discussions help a provider match intervention to the patient's current needs and capabilities to benefit from intervention (Prochaska et al., 1994). Utilizing motivational interviewing (MI) techniques at this phase of intervention might lead to better treatment outcomes, given their ability to help a patient develop and pursue intrinsically motivated goals (Andrasik & Grazzi, 2014). Prochaska's stage of change model has been well-studied and applied in behavioral health change paradigms, and MI has been applied successfully to many health and non-health-related conditions (Miller & Rollnick, 2012). However, to date, very little research has been conducted to examine the potential benefits of combining MI with behavioral health treatments for headache disorders specifically (Andrasik & Grazzi, 2014).

Treatment of Chronic Headache Disorders

WHO (2006) outlines "five essential steps" for successful prevention and management of headache disorders: 1) the headache sufferer must seek treatment; 2) the provider must make the correct diagnosis; 3) treatment indicated for that diagnosis must be offered; 4) the headache sufferer must adhere to treatment as directed; and 5) the provider should follow up with the patient to assess treatment outcome, adjusting as needed. These steps should lead to a decrease in frequency of episodic headache occurrences that might otherwise become a chronic headache pain syndrome. They should also lead to a decrease in the number of visits to urgent care centers and emergency departments for severe episodic headaches.

Medical Approaches

There are two main categories of pharmaceutical treatment for primary headaches: 1) as needed or abortive medications, which are used to relieve pain and associated symptoms of individual headache attacks and to halt the progression of symptoms; and 2) preventative or prophylactic medications, which are used to reduce attack frequency, severity, and duration with the primary goal of restoring function and relieving pain (Lipton & Silberstein, 2015). Potential indicators for utilizing preventative medications include chronicity of headaches (three or more episodes per week), duration of individual attacks (longer than 24 hours), headaches that cause major disruptions in the patient's lifestyle (e.g., contributing to episodes of disability lasting three or more days), abortive treatment failure or overuse, abortive medication contraindications, and migraine variants such as hemiplegic migraines.

Abortive Treatment

It is critical to treat a migraine as quickly as possible, usually within 30 minutes of onset, to prevent central sensitization and associated allodynia, or the experience of feeling pain from normally non-painful stimuli. Allodynia is correlated with not only the duration of migraine illness but also the frequency of attacks (Mathew, 2011). If migraines are treated within the initial 30 minutes after onset, pain most often resolves within two hours and is less likely to recur (Anderson & Kinikar, 2017).

Abortive treatment varies based upon headache type. Medications specific for acute treatment of migraine include triptans and ergots, with triptans generally considered first-line treatment (Becker, 2017). Triptans are 5-HT1b and 5-HT1d receptor agonists thought to work by causing vasoconstriction of the cerebral blood vessels and by decreasing the release of neuropeptides in the first and second order neurons of the trigeminal complex (Burnstein, Collins, & Jakubowski, 2004). Triptans theoretically can cause constriction of the coronary arteries as well, and for this reason should be avoided in patients with a history of stroke, coronary artery disease, or peripheral vascular disease. They also should be avoided generally with patients with hemiplegic or basilar migraines. Triptans also carry a risk of causing medication overuse headache when used too often, so their use must be regulated to two to three times per week at most.

Beyond treatment of acute migraine, triptans can be used for other primary headache disorders. Unlike tension-type headaches where triptan medications have no therapeutic benefit, approximately 33% of patients with NDPH experience at least some pain relief, even if the headaches lack migrainous features (Robbins et al., 2010). Many patients with NDPH will fail every class of abortive and preventative medications without any sign of pain relief (Tyagi, 2012).

Ergots stimulate α-adrenergic and 5HT receptors to help to break a migraine headache cycle. The two main ergots are ergotamine and dihydroergotamine (DHE). Ergots can cause significant nausea. As with triptans, ergots should not be used in patients with history of stroke, cardiovascular disease, or hemiplegic or basilar migraines. DHE has fewer side effects than ergotamine but due to its low bioavailability must be administered intranasally, via intramuscular injection, or intravenously, and it is often used in the setting of triptan failure. DHE and triptans must not be used concurrently, as there is risk of serious side effects when one is used within 24 hours of the other. DHE also is used as an acute treatment for severe, refractory migraine in the hospital setting.

Over-the-counter medications also may help interrupt acute headache pain. Nonsteroidal anti-inflammatory drugs (NSAIDs) are helpful if a headache is reported to be mild to moderate. For migraine treatment, if triptans alone are not sufficient, the addition of an NSAID may help treat severe headache pain. However, care must be taken to avoid medication overuse headache when NSAIDs are prescribed for abortive treatment of migraines; use should be limited to 1–2 times per week at most. Symptom management should include the addition of an antiemetic if nausea is part of the migraine. Treating nausea is a mainstay of acute migraine treatment, with anti-nausea medications used liberally both in the outpatient and inpatient setting. Insufficient treatment of nausea often leads to dehydration, which can prolong the migraine attack. Other formulations of intranasal or intramuscular migraine medications such as intranasal lidocaine also may be an option if a patient cannot tolerate oral formulations.

Hemicrania continua is treated with the nonsteroidal anti-inflammatory drug Indomethacin (Prakash & Patel, 2017). Indomethacin provides rapid relief of symptoms, but can cause gastrointestinal upset and therefore should be taken with an acid-suppression medication. It should not be taken on a daily basis, given that daily use can result in medication overuse headache, gastrointestinal ulcers, and renal problems. If headache pain persists after proper treatment, another diagnosis should be evaluated as cause, since successful resolution of symptoms after appropriate treatment with Indomethacin is a good diagnostic tool for hemicrania continua.

For many chronic headache patients, acute medications are not sufficient to control attacks without raising the risk of medication overuse (Becker, 2017). Medication overuse headache (MOH) or likely MOH account for approximately 1% of chronic headache occurrences in the population (Grazzi et al., 2006). Patients are advised to take medications as early as possible during a migraine, which contributes to the problem of medication overuse. Many patients eventually overuse their abortive medications. It is important to recognize when this happens because patients rarely respond to preventative medications while overusing acute medications. Given the risk of MOH development and the impact on quality of life of chronic headaches, helping patients find the right balance between effective use of abortive therapies without overusing medication is important yet complex.

Preventative/Prophylactic Treatment

Medications do not cure migraines; they treat symptoms (Anderson & Kinikar, 2017). As such, it is important to monitor patients treated with medication so as to evaluate clinical response and adverse effects. Shared expectations should entail better control of headaches rather than cure. Patient education should emphasize that preventative therapies are used daily even in the absence of headache, in the hopes of preventing a headache episode. Patients must understand that acute medications may be necessary for breakthrough headaches, but the goal is to decrease headache occurrence and abortive medication use (Skeikh & Mathew, 2012). The initiation of a preventative medication should start at a low dose in order to limit side effects. Education needs to include the expectation that at least two months of use are required to determine efficacy of a preventative medication. The most important part of preventative therapy is to ensure compliance (Skeikh & Mathew, 2012).

Antiepileptic medications generally are well tolerated but can cause side effects that may lead to non-compliance. Migraine headaches and seizures appear to have similar biologic characteristics, and medications that lower hyperexcitability are helpful in reduction of events (Rothrock, 2012). Topiramate can cause weight loss, renal calculi, word finding issues, and paresthesias in hands and feet, but also can offer significant effectiveness in preventing migraine headaches. Useful in patients as young as 12 years, it has been approved by the Federal Drug

Administration for prevention of migraine headaches (Huntington, 2005). It should be used with caution in menstruating women given risk of teratogenicity should a female patient on Topiramate become pregnant. Valproic acid often is highly effective in preventing migraines, but also should be used with caution with women of childbearing age due to potential teratogenicity in pregnancy. Valproic acid is a good mood stabilizer and can offer benefit for patients with comorbid mood disorders.

Amitriptyline and nortriptyline are tricyclic antidepressants (TCAs) often prescribed for management of chronic migraine, NDPH, and chronic tension-type headache. Depression is commonly comorbid with chronic pain, yet studies fail to show the relationship between depression and treatment outcome for chronic headaches (Jackson et al., 2017). TCAs effectively reduce the headache burden of patients with chronic tension-type headaches, lowering the number of headaches by five to six per month (Jackson et al., 2017). TCAs can be useful if a patient also suffers from insomnia. Side effects may include dry mouth, excessive sedation, and weight gain. These medications also should be avoided in elderly patients due to anticholinergic side effects that can cause confusion and falls.

Onabotulinum toxin A (BoNT-A, or Botox) is the only U.S. Food and Drug Administration-approved treatment for prevention of chronic migraine. The benefit of BoNT-A as a prophylactic treatment for chronic migraine headache likely is due to its ability to counteract peripheral and central nociceptive sensitization through reversible chemical denervation of pericranial sensitive afferents (Barbanti, & Ferroni, 2017). BoNT-A does not work in chronic tension-type headaches and has not shown strong evidence to be helpful against chronic daily headaches (Barbanti, & Ferroni, 2017).

Insurance coverage and cost can be limiting factors for choosing Botox as a treatment option. If effective, Botox injections are performed every three months for migraine prevention. It is important to inform patients that it can take up to three sessions of Botox for efficacy of the treatment in prevention of migraine. Accordingly, many neurologists use concomitant oral preventive therapy for six to nine months while waiting for Botox to become effective.

The utility of beta-blockers in treating chronic migraine is unclear (Becker, 2017). However, everal beta-blockers such as metoprolol and propranolol are recommended by the American Academy of Neurology Guidelines and are commonly used as first-line therapy in migraine prevention (American Headache Society, 2012). For patients with chronic migraine who have other chronic conditions such as hypertension or anxiety, beta-blockers may be an appropriate option, particularly when other medications (such as onabotulinum toxin A) are not feasible.

Although other pharmacologic therapies commonly are used in the prevention of migraines, varying levels of evidence support their efficacy. These include SNRIs (venlafaxine, duloxetine), SSRIs (fluoxetine, citalopram), other antiepileptic drugs (gabapentin, pregabalin), and calcium channel blockers (verapamil), among others.

Very recently, the FDA approved a new medication for the preventive treatment of migraine, Aimovig (erenumab-aooe) (U.S. Food & Drug Administration, 2018). The medication is given by monthly injections and has a novel mechanism of action whereby it blocks the activity of calcitonin gene-related peptide (CGRP), a molecule implicated in migraine attacks. Initial data from clinical trials is promising, but post-marketing data will be important in understanding this drug's efficacy and safety long term.

Neuromodulation

Through the use of neuromodulation, multiple brain areas can be modulated to alleviate pain, hence reducing the need for pharmaceuticals (Yuan & Silberstein, 2015). Vagus nerve stimulation (VNS), which has been studied for the treatment of epilepsy and depression, has been shown to be associated with headache relief in several case reports (e.g., Magis, Gerard, & Schoenen, 2013). VNS may be effective for both acute and prophylactic treatment of headache, but the mechanism of action for various types of headaches has not been studied in depth; more trials are underway (Yuan & Silberstein, 2015).

Secondary, Medication Overuse, Hormonal, and Musculoskeletal Headache

Theoretically, treating the underlying cause of medication overuse headache and secondary headaches resolves these conditions (WHO, 2006). When serious secondary headache is suggested, a time-sensitive referral to a specialist is indicated. Treatment for medication overuse is abrupt withdrawal of the suspected medication (Hering & Steiner, 1991). Patients should be warned that initially they will experience worsening headache and may also have worsening nausea, vomiting, and sleep disruption. Patients whose headaches are influenced by hormonal fluctuations can benefit from a pharmaceutical approach based upon hormonal regulation. For those who experience musculoskeletal symptoms with their frequent episodic or chronic tension-type headaches, physiotherapy is indicated (WHO, 2006). Complementary strategies such as acupuncture and massage therapy also can be helpful in treating chronic tension-type headaches.

Psychosocial Approaches

Because thoughts, feelings, and behaviors are central in a chronic headache sufferer's experience, complete care for these patients must include behavioral health treatment (Nicholson, 2010). Behavioral health principles pertinent to all patients' care include intervention with readiness to change, self-efficacy, locus of control, and other cognitive factors. More intensive behavioral health treatment may be necessary for some patients, including those who have psychiatric comorbidity, significant sleep or stress complications, medication overuse patterns, and history of abuse. As such, it is increasingly common to incorporate behavioral health principles and, when possible, providers in a comprehensive treatment plan for chronic headache patients.

Meta-analytic quantitative reviews and evidence-based reviews conducted by various organizations and task forces studying children and adults with chronic headaches have supported efficacy for behavioral health treatment for typical migraine and tension-type headache (Andrasik, 2003). Of the more than 100 empirical studies that had been conducted to examine efficacy of biobehavioral therapies for headache by the year 2000 (Campbell, Penzien, & Wall, 2000), the following treatment options were deemed effective for migraine: relaxation training (Sorbi & Tellegen, 1986), thermal biofeedback combined with relaxation training (Wittchen, 1983), EMG biofeedback (Sorbi & Tellegen, 1984), and cognitive-behavioral therapy (Barrios, 1980; Sorbi & Tellegen, 1986; Richardson & McGrath, 1989). In 2006, Lipnick, Smitherman, Penizen, and Holroyd declared that various muscle relaxation training techniques, thermal and electeomyographic (EMG) biofeedback training, and cognitive-behavioral therapy aimed at stress management continue to be the most extensively researched and utilized behavioral health therapies for headache disorders.

The American Academy of Neurology—U.S. Consortium reports that patients seek behavioral and non-pharmacological migraine treatment for a variety of reasons, including patient preference, poor tolerance and/or response to preventative medications, medical contraindications for medications, pregnancy or pregnancy-related concerns, history of overuse of abortive medications, and significant stress or inadequate stress or pain-coping skills (Campbell et al., 2000). The goals of non-pharmacological treatment typically include the following: reduce headache frequency and severity, reduce disability related to headache, reduce reliance on medication that is poorly tolerated or undesired, enhance personal control of pain, and reduce distress and psychological symptoms related to headache.

Behavioral health treatment for headache differs from pharmacological treatment in that the primary change agent is the patient rather than something external. A patient's personal responsibility is critical in this approach, and his or her active involvement in the treatment can lead to a heightened sense of confidence about personal ability to prevent and manage headaches (Andrasik, 2003). Furthermore, increased mastery in headache management can lead to decreased headache-related disability (French et al., 2000). Therefore, evaluating and intervening with cognitive factors such as readiness to change, self-efficacy, and locus of control are powerful intervention points for behavioral health providers to utilize (Nicholson, 2010).

Education-Based Intervention

The World Health Organization (2006) declared that education is the key to successful healthcare for chronic headache patients. Just because the disorder is common does not mean it is inconsequential, or to be minimized with regards to significance or treatment. It is important that headache sufferers actively participate in the treatment process in order to optimize treatment effectiveness (Weeks, 2013), which fits with the current model of pain management as a collaboration between provider and patient (Nicholson, 2010).

Patients should receive specific, tailored, and understandable information in order to buy in to an integrated treatment plan for headache management (Andrasik & Grazzi, 2014), and they should have their questions answered early in the treatment process (Weeks, 2013). Some of the most important concepts for patient education include the following: basic information about headache pathology, information about the typical course of chronic headache development, reassurance once secondary headache pathology is ruled out that the nature of headaches is benign, the nature and importance of medication compliance, the importance of patient involvement in treatment, and how to successfully apply behavioral techniques (Andrasik & Grazzi, 2014).

Awareness and Management of Lifestyle Factors

Behavioral healthcare providers can help chronic headache sufferers make lifestyle changes that contribute to better headache management (Nicholson, 2010), as well as help them improve their ability to recognize and manage triggers. Lifestyle practices aimed at headache reduction are extremely important in effective management of headaches, particularly adherence to consistent, healthy sleep patterns. Chronic sleep deprivation makes it difficult for a chronic headache sufferer to find relief, regardless of the type of treatment offered. Patients should be encouraged to have well-structured sleep/wake patterns and to avoid naps and over-sleeping (Gilman, Palermo, Kabbouche, Hershey, & Powers, 2007). Patients who snore, or who may have sleep apnea, should have this evaluated and treated as necessary. Other lifestyle changes also can help headache sufferers improve their well-being. For example, headache sufferers can benefit from eating healthy meals at regular intervals, and reducing caffeine, nicotine, and alcohol use. Patients can work toward increasing aerobic exercise, improving time management, and increasing participation in pleasurable activities. Posture improvement and utilization of good ergonomic practices also can help reduce headache frequency and intensity (Peper, Miceli, & Harvey, 2016).

As previously mentioned, headache logs provide the best tool to evaluate modifiable lifestyle factors and to identify triggers (Nicholson, 2010). Information collected in a headache log can help the patient become aware of, and subsequently modify, behavioral factors, thereby reducing headache frequency and severity (Weeks, 2013).

Awareness and Management of Headache Triggers

Behavioral health providers can help patients identify and modify behavioral triggers for migraine headaches, as well as acquire self-regulation skills that can help moderate migraine experience (Grazzi & Andrasik, 2010). Of note, migraines often occur in circumstances that are predictable or provoked by triggers, though triggers do not necessarily cause migraines (Anderson & Kinikar, 2017).

Triggers can be grouped into the following categories: diet, environmental factors, hormonal changes (e.g., menstruation and menopausal fluctuations), stress and anxiety, head and neck pain (from trauma or other causes), physical exertion (including exercise or sexual activity), chronobiological factors (e.g., lack of or abundance of sleep, or schedule changes), and caffeine (Anderson & Kinikar, 2017). Some migraine patients identify potential triggers as an abundance of caffeine or caffeine withdrawal, dehydration, and/or hunger incurred by skipping meals. Other dietary triggers can include alcohol, certain additives (such as MSG and food coloring), or certain foods such as chocolate, aged cheese, hot dogs, deli meats, citrus, yogurt and other dairy products, gluten, yeast, frozen foods, and canned foods. Potential environmental triggers include conditions contributing to eye strain, bright lights/glare, smells, temperature or weather changes, barometric pressure changes, and altitude (Anderson & Kinikar, 2017). Psychological triggers can include experiencing emotional stress or experiencing the aftermath of a stressful event.

Trigger avoidance may be a helpful treatment component for the motivated patient, as managing triggers may reduce the frequency of headaches. Triggers can further be grouped into three categories: avoidable; unavoidable and unmanageable; and unavoidable and manageable (Nicholson, 2010). A behavioral health provider can help patients understand under which conditions they can make choices about trigger exposure, such as with mostly avoidable triggers like alcohol, certain foods, bright light, and loud noises. Triggers that cannot be avoided or managed include hormones, weather changes, and certain travel modes (e.g., sitting on an airplane). In these cases, the behavioral health provider can help patients understand the importance of skillfully managing the things they can effectively manage so as to have more reserve for things they cannot control. In other words, the provider can employ a problem-solving and acceptance strategy. The behavioral health provider also can help the patient learn coping skills in order to moderate the impact of the unavoidable headache.

Finally, triggers that are unavoidable but manageable involve sleep, stress, and skipping meals. Behavioral health providers can educate the patient regarding the importance of purposeful regulation of these health factors, thereby minimizing the detrimental impact of their dysregulation. For those unavoidable and manageable triggers, behavioral health providers can offer more intensive therapeutic treatment when needed, including therapies such as CBT for coping (Lipchik, Smitherman, Penizien, & Holroyd, 2006) and CBT-I for insomnia (Perlis, Jungquist, Smith, & Posner, 2008).

On the other hand, work by Martin, Callan, Kaur, and Gregg (2015) challenges the well-established practice of avoiding headache triggers. This work suggests that purposeful, titrated exposure may help patients desensitize to triggers, whereas avoidance may lead to reduced tolerance or sensitization to triggers. Defining "significant change" as 50% decrease in ratings for visual disturbance, negative affect, and headache intensity, Martin (2000) showed that desensitization to headache triggers is possible in some cases.

The implications of Martin's work are notable. Perhaps headaches can be managed better via an approach strategy akin to exposure work utilized in anxiety treatment. Martin's work also supports the avoidance theory of how triggers acquire the ability to elicit headaches, suggesting that avoidance of triggers may sensitize headache suffers in such a way that presentations of triggers subsequent to avoidance behaviors lead to increased pain experienced. Results in those earlier studies were variable, took place in laboratory conditions, and were derived with low numbers of subjects (n = 6), thus results were not robust. However, this continues to be a fertile construct to investigate, and promising findings supporting the idea that trigger avoidance is not inherently necessary, or even ideal, continue to emerge (Martin et al., 2014).

Specifically, researchers have developed an alternate approach to trigger management that they call *Learning to Cope with Triggers* (LCT) (Martin et al., 2014). The method involves exposure to triggers such as heat, tiredness, and stress/anger, with the goal of desensitization or improved tolerance (Martin et al., 2015). The rationale is that there are so many possible headache triggers, some of which cannot be avoided, that the mere act of trying to avoid triggers can be stressful (and stress itself is a well-established headache trigger). Just as avoidance exacerbates anxiety conditions and exposure can be used effectively to treat them, so too can avoidance exacerbate headaches and exposure be used in treatment (Martin et al., 2014).

Furthermore, the WHO (2006) notes that there appears to be a cumulative effect with triggers, whereby at some point they jointly overflow a threshold and a headache occurs. Finally, asking the sufferer to avoid triggers can lead to externalizing locus of control for managing headaches (Martin et al., 2015), a problem in that self-efficacy for headache management is associated with improved outcomes (French et al., 2000). In a randomized controlled trial, LCT was delivered to individuals across eight 60-minute sessions. Participants completed baseline, post-treatment, and follow-up assessments, which indicated that these individuals experienced greater improvement with the LTC approach than participants in three other conditions, as indicated by measures of headaches and medication consumption (Martin et al., 2014).

These researchers admit that the strategy of avoiding triggers for chronic headache management is so intuitive for patients and so embedded in the medical literature that an approach using an opposite strategy will have to be well described and validated before most people will consider its implementation (Martin et al., 2015). Additionally, some triggers (e.g., toxic smells, hunger, dehydration, inadequate sleep) are altogether best avoided as they are incongruent with health.

Behavioral-Based Interventions

Behavioral interventions for chronic headache management include relaxation training and utilization of biofeedback methods (Weeks, 2013). Relaxation techniques target the entire body. These techniques include deep breathing exercises, progressive muscle relaxation (PMR), guided imagery, and relaxation to music (Lawrence et al., 2002; Smith, Amutio, Anderson, & Aria, 1996). These techniques help headache sufferers become more confident in their own physiological control as they develop greater body awareness and the ability to achieve an overall more relaxed state (Weeks, 2013). The most common problem in utilizing relaxation-based coping strategies is the mere fact that many people neglect to do them, especially in early stages of treatment (Lawrence et al., 2002).

Biofeedback is a relaxation technique that utilizes specialized equipment to help a patient monitor and control headache pain responses. Biofeedback essentially involves contingent reinforcement of certain neurophysiologically based responses (i.e., muscle tension or blood flow), and certain verbal responses with positive feedback (Sanders, 2006). The processes enable patients to lower overall arousal and promote bodily relaxation by using the data from the instrumentation to measure, amplify, and feed physiological information back to the patient (Grazzi & Andrasik, 2010). Using that data, the patient improves control over the target response by learning to regulate it in a way conducive to well-being.

Biofeedback entails monitoring and impacting physiological responses usually considered involuntary or modulated unconsciously. A meta-analysis of biofeedback interventions for tension-type headaches integrating data from over 400 patients supported the efficacy of this approach, which yielded average symptom improvements of one standard deviation lasting an average of 14 years (Nestoriuc, Rief, & Martin, 2008). These improvements include large reductions in headache frequency, intensity, and headache index; significant medium effect size in reduction of muscle tension within session; significant small effect size across sessions; and small to medium effect size in reducing duration of headache episodes.

Thermal biofeedback, or hand-warming, electromyographic (EMG) biofeedback, and electrodermal biofeedback are the most common forms of this treatment modality (Grazzi & Andrasik, 2010). Thermal biofeedback involves measuring skin temperature, typically in the distal parts of the body (Grazzi & Andrasik, 2010). This form of biofeedback helps people counteract stress buildup by utilizing vasoconstriction and vasodilation to activate the parasympathetic nervous system. Electromyographic (EMG) biofeedback helps a headache sufferer learn to control striated skeletal muscles, a method that is most helpful for psychophysiological stress disorders. Electrodermal biofeedback involves increasing awareness of emotions via measuring skin electrical activity directly and indirectly.

Although beyond the scope of this chapter, special considerations in treating headache pain need be given for youth and older adults, medically compromised patients, patients with comorbid pain conditions, and women who intend to become or who are pregnant. Biofeedback and behavioral interventions can treat chronic headache effectively, with minimal if any side effects or complications (Grazzi & Andrasik, 2010). As such, these approaches may be particularly good treatment options for young patients, older adults, and patients for whom medication treatment is contraindicated.

Operant techniques for chronic headache intervention involve using positive reinforcement and contingency management, as well as strategies involving punishment, extinction, and stimulus control. When headache pain becomes chronic, as a result of problematic environmental, social, and familial factors, a sufferer may start to experience external factors that are not conducive to the headache management process (Fordyce, 1976; Fowler, 1975). This can be related to contingencies associated with dynamics such as attentional reinforcement when the sufferer actively expresses feeling unwell, versus little or no attention for well behavior; dosing strategies for medication that can foster dependence, such as PRN versus time-based dosing; and negative reactions from members of support systems who may resent the sufferer's change in functionality in the family system (Andrasik, 2003). Peck and Love (1986) defined these problems as "chronic pain traps" and considered them the natural byproducts of living with pain. These patterns of behaviors become "traps" when they lead to self-perpetuating cycles that reinforce problematic behavior.

As such, operant techniques focus on adjusting and deconstructing those contingencies. Andrasik (2003) recommends that treatment providers probe for environmental and related conditions that maintain headache behavior and may contribute to the pain experience itself. He encourages the provider to establish the rapport necessary so that he/she can shift focus in encounters from headache pain symptoms to coping behaviors. For example, rather than asking the headache sufferer how intense his/her headache pain is that day, the provider can ask how the patient is trying to manage headache pain. The provider also can encourage patients to continue setting and working on daily goals, even on days when their pain level is higher. See Table 13.1 for a list of pain traps and subsequent treatment approaches as outlined by Andrasik (2003) and adapted from Peck and Love's model (1986).

Cognitive Approaches

Cognitive factors that play critical roles in pain experience include attention, coping styles, beliefs, expectations, and memories about pain (Andrasik, Wittrock, & Passchier, 2005). Headache sufferers, especially those fearful of the pain experience, may have an attentional bias to pain. This in turn can lead them to be hypersensitive and over-responsive to headache pain cues. High resolution functional magnetic resonance imaging (fMRI) studies demonstrate that focusing attention on headache pain leads to activation in the periaqueductal gray region. Conversely, decreased activation in several areas involved with pain regulation (thalamus, insula, and parts of the anterior cingulate) result when the headache sufferer employs distraction (Andrasik, Flor, & Turk, 2005).

Table 13.1 Chronic Pain Traps and Strategies to Overcome Them

Pain Trap	Outcome If Not Managed	Treatment Approaches
Chronic Treatment Trap	Leads to repeated doctor shopping and frustration on the part of the patient and provider	1. Encourage patient to accept and take responsibility for own rehabilitation 2. Contract to cease shopping and commit to specific procedures 3. Teach others to ignore pain behavior and reward well or pain-coping behavior
Chronic Medication Trap	Leads to ever increasing amounts and types of medication, dependence, and lowered self-esteem and regard by others	1. Withdraw patient from all offending medications 2. Administer needed medications (except for abortive) on a time-based and not a pain-based schedule
"Take It Easy" Trap	Results in the patient slipping into the invalid role, a loss of rewards from the environment, depression, and an increased focus on pain	1. Gradually increase the patient's tolerance for simple activities 2. Gradually engage in activities that were performed before the condition developed
Chronic Resentment Trap	Spouse of significant other becomes angry because of a decrease in coupling activities and a shift in household duties and a continued focus on pain, which leads patient to become grouchy and demanding and to feel misunderstood; significant relationship problems often result	1. Renegotiate roles and responsibilities 2. Gradually reestablish reciprocal relationship 3. Work on improving communication and positive behaviors

(in Andrasik, 2003, p. S84, adapted from Peck & Love, 1986)

Cognitive-Behavioral Therapy (CBT), Including Stress Management

A foundational concept in psychology is that affect and behavior are directly related to cognition. In other words, the way a person interprets experiences directly contributes to subsequent emotion and behavior; to mediate mood, one must attend to cognitions. Beliefs about headache pain can contribute significantly to the chronic pain experience.

Maladaptive beliefs about pain include catastrophizing, withdrawal, avoidance, and self-criticism (Andrasik, Flor, & Turk, 2005). A person's beliefs about headache pain can affect them directly and indirectly (Andrasik, Flor, & Turk, 2005). One way that beliefs can impact the pain experience indirectly is by influencing attempts to cope with headaches. For example, if a person believes that the pain will get worse, or that he/she is helpless to impact the pain experience, then he/she may be less likely to engage in behavioral health strategies that otherwise could mitigate pain or increase functioning with pain. Conversely, believing that one can engage in actions that can improve headache management, a concept known as self-efficacy, can result in positive outcomes (e.g., increases in positive coping actions, increases in efforts to manage and prevent pain, and increases in pain tolerance) (French et al., 2000).

Cognitive-behavioral therapy (CBT) has been adapted to treat several chronic pain conditions, including chronic headache (Campbell et al., 2000). The use of this treatment modality stems from the observation that how a headache sufferer copes with everyday stresses and headache episodes can worsen the pain experience and increase associated disability and distress (Holroyd & Penzien, 1994). CBT entails altering belief structures, attitudes, and thoughts. It helps patients identify stressful circumstances that aggravate headaches, learn effective coping strategies, and discern how to limit negative psychological consequences related to recurrent headache (Holroyd & Penzien, 1994). CBT for chronic headaches also involves shifting cognitive beliefs that impact the management of the condition. For example, through cognitive reframing approaches, patients are taught to challenge maladaptive thoughts (e.g., "this pain is out of control and unbearable") and replace them with more rational and helpful thoughts (e.g., "although this pain is uncomfortable, I can tolerate it, and it will pass").

Stress is the most commonly cited headache antecedent (Martin et al., 2015). Coping skills training helps patients develop and use strategies to cope with stressors that trigger, exacerbate, or prolong headaches. To manage stressful life events, patients are taught self-regulation techniques as well as cognitive and behavioral coping skills (Weeks, 2013). Coping skills are intended to help relieve both the sensory components, through relaxation techniques and biofeedback, and the reactive components, through addressing thoughts and feelings associated with the pain experience.

CBT generally involves weekly face-to-face sessions between the patient and a trained professional. Course of treatment depends upon factors such as the treatment goals; the severity of the condition; the patient's engagement in the process; the clinician's competence with the method; and the quality of the therapeutic relationship. Variations in the delivery of CBT include group therapy, home-based formats, internet modalities, and other technology-based options (such as applications for smartphones).

Some empirical support exists for using CBT group therapy for treatment of moderately to severely disabled headache sufferers (Nash, Park, Walker, Gordon, & Nicholson, 2004). This research indicates that group treatment can result in decreased headache activity, reduced medication use, and overall improvement in quality of life. To optimize issues related to cost and efficiency, home-based formats have been developed as well. These formats involve introducing skills in the clinic, after which patients primarily work at home on their treatment (guided by written and audio material) (Grazzi & Andrasik, 2010).

There also is some support for treatment efficacy of self-help programs delivered via the internet (Ström, Pettersson, & Andersson, 2000). Finally, according to a lay publication from 2017, headache sufferers are using a variety of popular smartphone applications to manage their conditions: Relax Melodies, Acupressure: Heal Yourself, Manage My Pain Pro, Brainwave Tuner, iHeadache, Migraine Buddy, Curelator Headache, Migraine Diary, Migraine Relief Hypnosis, Migraine eDiary, and Headache Log (Shaefer, 2017). Empirical research needs to investigate the efficacy of these applications.

Acceptance-Based Interventions

Acceptance involves the willingness to experience occurrences as they are, without trying to change them or avoid them, and without allowing them to influence behavior (Chiros & O'Brien, 2011). These occurrences can involve thoughts, feelings, and physical sensations, including pain. Research shows that when acceptance is utilized, pain suffers can experience lower levels of pain, avoidance, depression, and disability (Andrasik, Flor, & Turk, 2005). Acceptance has demonstrated benefits for chronic pain sufferers, benefits that include improvements in emotional, social, and physical functioning (Chiros & O'Brien, 2011). Working within an acceptance framework can lead to decreases in catastrophizing and relinquishing of the struggle to control pain in favor of more values-driven behavior (Chiros & O'Brien, 2011).

For example, Chiros and O'Brien (2011) explored the relationships among acceptance, control, catastrophizing, pain symptoms, and coping in migraine sufferers using a diary methodology. They found that regardless of how much a patient had catastrophizing thoughts related to their migraines, high levels of acceptance were related to diminished levels of belief in those thoughts, as well as diminished expression of pain. There was also a diminished functional relationship between catastrophic thoughts and avoidance behaviors. Furthermore, patients with higher levels of control appraisals (i.e., they believe they have the ability and resources to manage headache pain) more actively engaged in activities. Of note, this research clarified that the notion of control is consistent with the concept of acceptance in that patients are not attempting to control the pain experience itself, but instead are perceiving increased ability to control the influence the pain has over their lives. These patients feel they can continue pursuing life goals in the direction of their values notwithstanding the pain experience. This work also established that pain severity need not be a moderator of activating acceptance. Rather, acceptance can exert beneficial effects regardless of the pain level. Therefore, utilizing an acceptance-based framework such as acceptance and commitment therapy (ACT) helps patients perceive pain in such a way that the adverse impact of various maladaptive thinking styles decreases, and participation in daily life increases (Harris, 2009).

General Psychosocial Intervention for Emotional Concerns

Headache pain always is both a physical and an emotional experience. For example, people's moods can be impacted by their beliefs about how well or poorly they can deal with their headaches and consequences; their moods in turn can impact muscle tension and other biochemical processes (Andrasik, Wittrock, & Passchier, 2005). Dealing with chronic headaches takes an emotional toll on the sufferer. Many chronic headache sufferers experience constant concern, worry, and fear of developing their next headache, creating feelings of a loss of control and guilt. As patients experience increasingly frequent headaches, their functionality is increasingly impaired, impacting their lives and relationships and becoming a driving force in their lives (Nichols, Ellard, Griffiths, Kamal, Underwood, & Taylor, 2017). There are at least six possible ways affect and headache pain can interact that can impact an individual's treatment: affect as a correlate of pain, a predisposing factor, a precipitating factor, an exacerbating factor, a consequence, and a maintaining factor (Fernandez, 2002). Depending on which relationship exists, various treatment plans can be developed.

Depression, anxiety, and anger in particular can exacerbate headache pain experience (Nicholson et al., 2003). Depression, anxiety, and other indicators of poor emotional adjustment have been associated with increased headache frequency (Lawrence et al., 2002). Moreover, people suffering from chronic pain conditions (including headache) often experience anger (Burns, Johnson, Devine, Mahoney, & Pawl, 1998). Anger and resentment can then confound the treatment process. It is unclear how to best account for these comorbidities when developing a treatment plan for headache management, but often cognitive-behavioral strategies should be primary in the course of treatment (Nicholson et al., 2003). Furthermore, stress and negative life experiences are associated with some types of headaches as well. Life stressors often precede tension headaches, and stressful incidents can trigger a migraine up to four days before its onset (D'Souza, Lumley, Kraft, & Dooley, 2008). There is a positive relationship between migraines and experiencing certain hardships in childhood (e.g., divorce, family conflict, abuse) (D'Souza et al., 2008). Therefore, treatment to help a person learn and use depression, anxiety, anger, and stress-management skills may be necessary when developing a comprehensive treatment plan for managing headache disorders.

When addressing the affective component of headache experiences, the behavioral treatment utilized should be tailored to the particular affective experience. For example, relaxation skills are indicated when the sufferer has comorbid anxiety. Maintaining healthy social relationships, behavioral activation, and increasing pleasurable activities are important strategies for mitigating depressive episodes for which headache sufferers may be at risk. Anger management skills include improving communication skills and learning to recognize anger cues so

Table 13.2 Treatment Suggestions Based on Operative Affect Model (Andrasik, Flor, & Turk, 2005, p. S89)

Affect as	Treatment Approach
Predisposer	Characterological change
Precipitant	Short-term intervention for affective trigger itself
Exacerbator	Focused intervention to defuse the aggravator
Perpetuator	Alter environmental conditions maintaining the pain
Consequence	Provide minimal attention to affect
Correlate	Third superordinate factor may be responsible; look elsewhere
Reciprocal relationship	Target both

as to begin early de-escalation techniques (e.g., distraction or deep breathing). Additionally, a useful treatment planning strategy was outlined by (Andrasik, Flor, & Turk, 2005), as it indicated behavioral treatment approaches based upon how affect specifically interplays with the experiences of headache sufferers (see Table 13.2).

Written Emotional Disclosure (WED)

One theory of stress reduction involves the idea that rather than avoid painful emotions and their related physiological components (such as headaches), it can be healthy to access, experience, and express painful affect (D'Souza et al., 2008). The premise is that doing so may promote habituation, as well as help build insight into the behaviors that contribute to headache occurrences. It also can aid the person's assimilation of cognitions and emotions, as well as ultimately help the person resolve stressors that trigger headaches. A technique for engaging in this practice is the Written Emotional Disclosure (WED). This process involves patients writing for 20 minutes daily on consecutive days about a stressful experience. Some research suggests that WED might help improve headache management for certain patients (Kraft, Lumley, D'Souza, & Dooley, 2008). However, other research does not support those results, finding no treatment effect for headache patients using WED (D'Souza, Lumley, Kraft, & Dooley, 2008).

"Alternative" Treatment Considerations

Some alternative or complementary treatments for migraines have limited evidence to date to confirm their utility, but patients may get value and benefit from trying them nonetheless. Examples include acupuncture, massage, and mind–body techniques such as yoga and tai chi (Anderson & Kinikar, 2017). Although some clinical trials have shown acupuncture to be helpful for treating headache, the evidence is not sufficient as of yet to recommend it as a primary option (Anderson & Kinikar, 2017). Headache sufferers who have tight, sore muscles in the back of the head, neck, and shoulders may find that massage helps relieve headache pain, especially in the case of tension-type headaches. However, to date, limited research supports this intervention. Chiropractic treatment for tension-type headache or cervicogenic headache (neck strain-related headache) is a treatment option as well, although many neurologists recommend against manipulation due to the number of strokes they see as result of neck adjustments (Albuquerque et al., 2011). Finally, some research indicates hypnosis might be an effective treatment for chronic pain, including chronic headache (Lawrence et al., 2002).

Conclusions

Headache disorders, which are prevalent across the world, cause considerable suffering for patients. These disorders can transition relatively easily from an occasional to a chronic problem, depending upon how they are managed at the onset. Chronic headache is a complex, multifaceted disease that involves multiple types of pain for patients, thereby requiring refined intervention approaches. Despite their ubiquitous presence, however, they remain a complex cluster of disorders to treat. Treatment options include strategies that help patients manage their condition, as well as strategies that help them cope with their pain. Using both pharmacological and non-pharmacological treatments in combination has been shown to optimize headache management. Including behavioral health components adds an increasingly robust pool of resources to a comprehensive treatment plan. While some behavioral health options such as relaxation training, biofeedback, and CBT strategies have been discussed in the literature and used with variable success in practice for years, other concepts are still being explored (e.g., whether or not to avoid triggers, writing about emotions daily in an effort to mitigate headache pain). Future research likely will continue to confirm the benefit of including behavioral health providers as part of an interdisciplinary treatment team for chronic headache patients.

References

Abbass, A., Lovas, D., & Purdy, A. (2008). Direct diagnosis and management of emotional factors in chronic headache patients. *Cephalalgia, 28*, 1305–1314.

Albuquerque, F. C., Hu, Y. C., Dashti, S. R., Abia, A. A., Clark, J. C., Alkire, B., . . . McDougall, C. G. (2011). Craniocervical arterial dissections as sequelae of chiropractic manipulation: Patterns of injury and management. *Journal of Neurosurgery, 115*(6), 1197–1205.

American Headache Society. (2012). *AAN summary of evidence-based guidelines for clinicians. Update: Pharmacologic treatment for episodic migraine prevention in adults.* Retrieved from www.aan.com/Guidelines/home/GetGuidelineContent/545

Anderson, A., & Kinikar, S. (2017). *Migraines: Approach to the management of adult patient.* Retrieved from Clinical Library, Clinical Practice Resource, Kaiser Permanente Medical Group.

Andrasik, F. (2003). Behavioral treatment approaches to chronic headache. *Neurological Sciences, 24*, S80–S85.

Andrasik, F., Flor, H., & Turk, D. C. (2005). An expanded view of psychological aspects in head pain: The biopsychosocial model. *Neurological Sciences, 26*, S87–S91.

Andrasik, F., & Grazzi, L. (2014). Biofeedback and behavioral treatments: Filling some gaps. *Neurological Sciences, 35*(1), S121–S127. Andrasik, F., Wittrock, D. A., & Passchier, J. (2005). Psychological mechanisms of tension-type headache. In J. Olsen, P. Goadsby, N. Ramadan, P. Tfelt-Hansen, & K. M. A. Welch (Eds.), *The headaches* (3rd Ed.), Philadelphia, PA: Lippincott Williams & Wilkins.

Andrasik, F., Wittrock, D. A., & Passchier, J. (2005). Psychological mechanisms of tension-type headache. *The headaches*, 3rd ed. Olsen J., Goadsby P., Ramadan N., Tfelt-Hansen P., & Welch K. M. A. (Eds.). Philadelphia, PA: Lippincott Williams & Wilkins.

Barbanti, P., & Ferroni, P. (2017). Onabotulinum toxin A in the treatment of chronic migraine: Patient selection and special considerations. *Journal of Rain Research, 10*, 2319–2329.

Barrios, F. X. (1980). Social skills training and psychosomatic disorders. In D. P. Rathjen & J. P. Foreyt (Eds.), *Social competence: Interventions for children and adults* (pp. 271–301). New York, NY: Pergamon.

Becker, W. J. (2017). The diagnosis and management of chronic migraine in primary care. *Headache: The Journal of Head and Face Pain, 57*(9), 1471–1481.

Bigal, M. E., & Lipton, R. B. (2006). Modifiable risk factors for migraine progression. *Headache, 46*, 1334–1343.

Burns, J. W., Johnson, B. J., Devine, J., Mahoney, N., & Pawl, R. (1998). Anger management style and the prediction of treatment outcomes among male and female chronic pain patients. *Behavioral Research and Therapy, 36*, 1051–1062.

Burnstein, R., Collins, B., & Jakubowski, M. (2004). Defeating migraines pain with triptans: A race against the development of cutaneous allodynia. *Annals of Neurology, 55*(1), 19–26.

Buse, D. C., Manack, A., Serrano, D., Turkel, C., & Lipton, R. B. (2010). Sociodemographic and comorbidity profiles of chronic migraine and episodic migraine sufferers. *Journal of Neurology, Neurology, Neurosurgery, and Psychiatry, 81*, 428–432.

Campbell, J. K., Penzien, D. B., & Wall, E. M. (2000). Evidence-based guidelines for migraine headache: Behavioral and physical treatments. *US Headache Consortium*. Retrieved from http://tools.aan.com/professionals/practice/pdfs/gl0089.pdf

Chiros, C., & O'Brien, W. H. (2011). Acceptance, appraisals, and coping in relation to migraine headache: An evaluation of interrelationships using daily diary methods. *Journal of Behavioral Medicine, 34*, 307–320.

Clinch, C. R. (2015). Evaluation & management of headache. In J. E. South-Paul, S. C. Matheny, & E. L. Lewis (Eds.), *Current diagnosis & treatment* (pp. 293–297). Chicago, IL: McGraw Hill Education.

D'Souza, P. J., Lumley, M. A., Kraft, C. A., & Dooley, J. A. (2008). Relaxation training and written emotional disclosure for tension or migraine headaches: A randomized, controlled trial. *Annals of Behavioral Medicine, 36*, 21–32.

Fernandez, E. (2002). *Anxiety, depression, and anger in pain: Research findings and clinical options.* Dallas, TX: Advanced Psychological Resource.

Flor, H., & Turk, D. C. (2005). Cognitive and learning aspects. In S. McMahon & M. Koltzenburg (Eds.), *Wall and Melzack's textbook of pain* (5th ed.). London: Churchill Livingstone.

Fordyce, W. E. (1976). *Behavioral methods for chronic pain and illness.* St. Louis, MO: Mosby.

Fowler, R. S. (1975). Operant therapy for headaches. *Headache, 15*, 1–6.

French, D. J., Holroyd, K. A., Pinnell, C., Malinoski, P. T., O'Donnell, F., & Hill, K. R. (2000). Perceived self-efficacy and headache-related disability. *Headache: The Journal of Head and Face Pain, 40*, 647–656.

GBD 2016 Disease and Injury Incidence and Prevalence Collaborators. (2017). Global, regional and national incidence, prevalence and years lived with disability for 328 disease and injuries for 195 countries, 1990–2016. *Lancet*, *390*, 1211–1259.

Gilman, D. K., Palermo, T. M., Kabbouche, M. A., Hershey, A. D., & Powers, S. W. (2007). Primary headache and sleep disturbance in adolescents. *Headache*, *47*, 1178–1194.

Grazzi, L., & Andrasik, F. (2010). Non-pharmacological approaches to migraine prophylaxis: Behavioral medicine. *Neurological Sciences*, *31*(1), S133–S135.

Grazzi, L., Usai, S., & Bussone, G. (2006). Chronic headaches: Pharmacological and non-pharmacological treatment. *Neurological Sciences*, *27*, S174–S178.

Harris, R. (2009). *ACT made simple: An easy-to-read primer on acceptance and commitment therapy*. Oakland, CA: New Harbinger.

Headache classification committee of the International Headache Society (IHS), (2013). The International classification of headache disorders, 3rd edition (beta version). *Cephalagia*, *33*(9), 629–808.

Hering, R., & Steiner, T. J. (1991). Abrupt outpatient withdrawal of medication in analgesic-abusing migraineurs. *Lancet*, *337*, 1442–1443.

Holroyd, K. A., O'Donnell, F. J., Stensland, M., & Lipchik, G. L. (2001). Management of chronic tension-type headache with tricyclic antidepressant medication, stress-management therapy, and their combination: A randomized control trial. *JAMA*, *285*, 2208–2215.

Holroyd, K. A., & Penzien, D. B. (1994). Psychosocial interventions in the management of recurrent headache disorders 1: Overview and effectiveness. *Behavioral Medicine*, *20*(2), 53–63.

Huntington, J., & Yaun, C. L. (2005). Topiramate (Topamax) for migraine prevention. *American Family Physician*, *72*(8), 1563–1564.

Jackson, J. L., Mancuso, J. M., Nickoloff, S., Bernstein, R., & Kay, C. (2017). Tricyclic and tetracyclic antidepressants for the prevention of frequent episodic or chronic tension tension-type headache in adults: A systematic review and meta-analysis. *Journal of General Internal Medicine*, *32*(12), 1351–1358.

Kraft, C. A., Lumley, M. A., D'Souza, P. J., & Dooley, J. A. (2008). Emotional approach coping and self-efficacy moderate the effects of written emotional disclosure and relaxation training for people with migraine headache. *British Journal of Health Psychology*, *13*(1), 67–71.

Lawrence, S. A., Wodarski, L. A., & Wodarski, J. (2002). Behavioral medicine paradigm: Behavioral interventions for chronic pain and headache. *Journal of Human Behavior in the Social Environment*, *5*(2), 1–14.

Lipchik, G. L., Smitherman, T. A., Penizien, D. B., & Holroyd, K. A. (2006). Basic principles and techniques of cognitive-behavioral therapies for comorbid psychiatric symptoms among headache patents. *Headache*, *46*(3), S119–S132.

Lipton, R. B., & Silberstein, S. D. (2015). Episodic and chronic migraine headache: Breaking down barriers to optimal treatment and prevention. *Headache: The Journal of Head and Face Pain*, *55*(Suppl 2), 103–122.

Lipton, R. B., Silberstein, S. D., Saper, J. R., Bigal, M. E., & Goadsby, P. J. (2003). Why headache treatment fails. *Neurology*, *60*(7), 1069–1070.

Magis, D., Gerard, P., & Schoenen, J. (2013). Transcutaneous Vagus Nerve Stimulation (TVNS) for headache prophylaxis: Initial experience. *Journal of Headache Pain*, *14*(1), 198.

Martin, P. R. (2000). Headache triggers: To avoid or not to avoid, that is the question. *Psychology and Health*, *15*, 801–809.

Martin, P. R., Callan, M., Kaur, A., & Gregg, K. (2015). Behavioral management of headache triggers: Three case examples illustrating a new effective approach (Learning to cope with triggers). *Behavior Change*, *32*(3), 202–208.

Martin, P. R., Reece, J., Callan, M., MacLeod, C., Kaur, A., Gregg, K., & Goadsby, P. J. (2014). Behavioral management of the triggers of recurrent headache: A randomized controlled trial. *Behavioral Research and Therapy, 61*, 1–11.

Mathew, N. T. (2011). Pathophysiology of chronic migraine and mode of action of preventive medications. *Headache, 51*(2), 84–92.

May, A., & Schulte, L. H. (2016). Chronic migraine: Risk factors, mechanisms and treatment. *Nature Reviews. Neurology, 12*(8), 455–464.

Miller, W. R., & Rollnick, S. (2012). *Motivational interviewing: Helping people for change* (3rd ed.). New York, NY: The Guilford Press.

Nash, J. M., Park, E. R., Walker, B. B., Gordon, N., & Nicholson, R. A. (2004). Cognitive-behavioral group treatment for disabling headache. *Pain Medicine, 5*(2), 178–186.

Nestoriuc, Y., Rief, W., & Martin, A. (2008). Meta-analysis of biofeedback for tension-type headache: Efficacy, specificity, and treatment moderators. *Journal of Consulting and Clinical Psychology, 76*(3), 379–396.

Nichols, V. P., Ellard, D. R., Griffiths, F. E., Kamal, A., Underwood, M., Taylor, S. J. C. (2017). The lived experience of chronic headache: A systematic review and synthesis of the qualitative literature. *BMJ Open, 7*, 1–11.

Nicholson, R. A. (2010). Chronic headache: The role of the psychologist. *Current Pain and Headache Reports, 14*(1), 47–54.

Nicholson, R. A., Grambling, S. E., Ong, J. C., & Buenevar, L. (2003). Differences in anger expression between individuals with and without headache after controlling for depression and anxiety. *Headache, 43*, 651–663.

Peck, C., & Love, A. (1986). Chronic pain. In N. J. King & A. Remenyi (Eds.), *Health care: A behavioral approach* (pp. 133–144). Sydney, Australia: Grune Stratton.

Peper, E., Miceli, B., & Harvey, R. (2016). Educational model for self-healing: Eliminating a chronic migraine with electromyography, autogenic training, posture, and mindfulness. *Biofeedback, 44*(3), 130–137.

Perlis, M. L., Jungquist, C., Smith, M. T., & Posner, D. (2008). *Cognitive behavioral treatment of insomnia: A session by session guide.* New York, NY: Springer.

Pina-Garza, J. E. (Ed.). (2013). *Fenichel's clinical pediatric neurology* (7th ed.). St. Louis, MO: Elsevier.

Prakash, S., & Patel, P. (2017). Hemicrania continua: Clinical review, diagnosis and management. *Journal of Pain Research, 10*, 1493–1509.

Prochaska, J. O., Norcross, J. C., & DiClemente. (1994). *Changing for good: A revolutionary six stage program for overcoming bad habits and moving your life positively forward.* New York, NY: Avon Books.

Richardson, G. M., & McGrath, P. J. (1989). Cognitive-behavioral therapy for migraine headaches: A minimal-therapist-contact approach versus a clinic-based approach. *Headache, 29*(6), 352–357.

Robbins, M. S., Grosberg, B. M., Napchan, U., Crystal, S. C., & Lipton, R. B. (2010). Clinical and prognostic subforms of new daily-persistent headache. *Neology, 74*, 1358–1364.

Rota, E., Evangelista, A., Ceccarelli, M., Ferrero, L., Milani, C., Ugolini, A., & Mongini, F. (2016). Efficacy of a workplace relaxation exercise program on muscle tenderness in a working community with headache and neck pain: A longitudinal, controlled study. *European Journal of Physical and Rehabilitation Medicine, 52*(4), 457–465.

Rothrock, J. F. (2012). Topiramate for migraine prevention: An update. *Headache, The Journal of Head and Face Pain, 52*(5), 859–860.

Sanders, S. H. (2006). Behavioral conceptualization and treatment for chronic pain. *The Behavior Analyst Today, 7*(2), 253–261.

Shaefer, A. (2017, June 2). *The best migraine apps of the year.* Retrieved from www.healthline.com/health/migraine/top-iphone-android-apps#modal-close

Skeikh, H. U., & Mathew, P. G. (2012). Acute and preventive treatment of migraine headache. *Techniques in Regional Anesthesia and Pain Management, 16*(1), 19–24.

Smith, J. C., Amutio, A., Anderson, J. P., & Aria, L. A. (1996). Relaxation: Mapping an uncharted world. *Biofeedback and Self-regulation, 21*(1), 63–90.

Smitherman, T. A., Burch, R., Sheikh, H., & Loder, E. (2013). The Prevalence, impact and treatment of migraine and severe headaches in the United States: A review of statistics from the national surveillance studies. *Headache: The Journal of Head and Face Pain. 53*(3), 427–436.

Sorbi, M., & Tellegen, B. (1984). Multimodal migraine treatment: Does thermal feedback add to the outcome? *Headache, 24,* 249–255.

Sorbi, M., & Tellegen, B. (1986). Differential effects of training in relaxation and stress-coping in patients with migraine. *Headache, 26*(9), 473–481.

Stewart, W. F., Lipton, R. B., Kolodner, K. B., Sawyer, J., Lee, C., & Liberman, J. N. (2000). Validity of the Migraine Disability Assessment (MIDAS) score in comparison to a diary-based measure in a population sample of migraine sufferers. *Pain, 88*(1), 41–52.

Ström, L., Pettersson, R., & Andersson, G. (2000). A controlled trial of self-help treatment of recurrent headache conducted via the internet. *Journal of Counseling and Clinical Psychology, 68*(4), 722–727.

Tyagi, A. (2012). New daily persistent headache. *Annals of Indian Academy of Neurology, 15*(1), S62–S65.

U.S. Food & Drug Administration. (2018). *FDA news release: FDA approves novel preventive treatment for migraine.* Retrieved from www.fda.gov/NewsEvents/Newsroom/Press Announcements/ucm608120.htm

Weeks, R. E. (2013). Application of behavioral therapies in adult and adolescent patients with chronic migraine. *Neurological Sciences, 34*(1), S11–S17.

Westergaard, M. L., Glümer, C., Hansen, E. H., & Jensen, R. H. (2014). Prevalence of chronic headache with and without medication overuse: Associations with socioeconomic position and physical and mental health status. *International Association for the Study of Pain, 155,* 2005–2013.

Wittchen, H. A. (1983). Biobehavioral treatment program (SEP) for chronic migraine patients. In K. A. Holroyd, B. Schlote, & B. Zenz (Eds.), *Perspectives in research on headache.* Toronto, Canada: Hogrefe.

World Health Organization. (2006). *Neurological disorders: Public health challenges.* Retrieved from www.who.int/mental_health/neurology/neurological_disorders_report_web.pdf

Yuan, H., & Silberstein, S. D. (2015). Vagus nerve stimulation and Headache. *Headache: The Journal and Head and Face Pain, 57,* 29–33.

Appendix 1

Sample Interview to Obtain History in a Headache Patient

Chief complaint: Headaches

History of Present Illness:

Mr./Ms. ******* is a _____ year old man/woman presenting today for evaluation of headaches.

Onset of headaches (age, # of years ago, any inciting head injury)

Description of headache

- Location in head:
- Type of pain (sharp, throbbing, stabbing, icepick, achy, dull):
- Severity of pain on scale of 1–10 (on average):
- Duration of headache (# minutes, hours, days):
- Presence of aura (yes/no, and description):

Associated symptoms

- Photophobia/phonophobia/osmophobia
- Nausea/Vomiting
- Lacrimation
- Rhinorrhea
- Facial flushing
- Loss of vision or blurring of vision

- Diplopia
- Tinnitus or pulsating tinnitus
- Other neurological symptoms (dysarthria, aphasia, numbness, weakness, confusion, vertigo)

Headache frequency: # times/week or month

Lifestyle Practices

Sleeping patterns:

- Any difficulty falling or staying asleep?
- Snoring?
- Average number of hours of sleep per night:

  Caffeine intake (coffee, tea, soda):
  Alcohol intake:
  Exercise routine (type and # of workouts per week):
  Stress (type and how significant):
  History of or current anxiety or depression:
  Use of over the counter analgesics (type and frequency of use per week):
  Known triggers for headaches:
  Family history of any headache disorder (migraines, cluster headaches, etc.):
  Prior prescription medications for headache (name, dose, efficacy, adverse effects):
  Current prescription medications for headache (name, dose, efficacy, adverse effects):

Appendix 2

Headache Log

Date	Attack Duration: Start/End	Pain Level at High Point, 1–10 (10 Is Worst Pain Possible)	Related Symptoms (Preceding and During Attack)	Location and Type of Pain (Throbbing, Stabbing, etc.)	Possible Triggers	Medication(s), Dosages, Time(s) Administered	Coping Skills Used (LTC Approach, De-catastrophized Thoughts, Dark Room, Cold Pack, etc.)	Pain Level at Low Point, 1–10 (10 Is Worst Pain Possible)	What May Have Made It Better? Worse?	Other Notes

14

Rheumatoid Arthritic Pain

Natasha S. DePesa, Chelsea Wiener,
and Jeffrey E. Cassisi

Rheumatoid Arthritis: Background

Arthritis is one of the leading causes of disability among Americans and has significant impacts on both physical and mental health (Theis, Roblin, Helmick, & Luo, 2018). Rheumatoid arthritis (RA), one of the more common forms of arthritis, is a chronic, progressive, inflammatory disease affecting approximately 1.3 million U.S. adults (Schiller, Lucas, Ward, & Peregoy, 2012). Women are diagnosed with RA at approximately two to three times the rate of men (CDC, 2018). The likelihood of RA onset increases with age and is highest among individuals in their sixties. Other risk factors include, but are not limited to, a history of smoking, obesity, and genetics (CDC, 2018).

Overall, direct medical costs for patients with RA in the United States may exceed $8 billion each year, including costs related to medical visits and prescriptions. Additionally, it is estimated that there are over $10 billion in additional annual indirect costs (e.g., loss of work, caregiving). For example, patients with RA miss an average of 2–30 days of work per year as a consequence of their disease (Cooper, 2000). These figures do not capture the premature mortality and impaired quality of life that can be associated with RA (Birnbaum et al., 2010).

Unlike the more common osteoarthritis (OA), which involves mechanical "wear and tear" of joint cartilage, RA is an autoimmune disorder. During the course of RA, immune cells attack the synovial membranes, or the flexible capsules surrounding joints, resulting in chronic inflammation, pain, stiffness, and eventual damage to cartilage and bone (Aletaha et al., 2010). Clinical synovitis ("swelling") of joints is necessary for diagnosis, with greater small joint involvement being characteristic of RA. Diagnosis can be made by clinical examination, and determination that swelling is not better accounted for by another etiology.

Diagnosis also is aided by anti-citrullinated protein antibody (ACPA) and rheumatoid factor (RF) serology tests and other blood tests of acute phase reactants such as C-reactive protein and erythrocyte sedimentation rate (Aletaha et al., 2010).

A number of commonly co-occurring physical and mental health conditions may impact both the experience of the disease process and patient care. Patients with RA are at greater risk for developing other chronic pain conditions. For example, approximately 15–20% of patients with RA have a comorbid diagnosis of fibromyalgia syndrome (FMS), as compared to 2–8% prevalence estimates in the general population (Dolan, Tung, & Raizada, 2016). Factors such as severe disease activity, psychosocial distress, and obesity increase the likelihood that patients with RA will develop FMS, which is characterized by more widespread pain, hyperalgesia, somatic symptoms such as fatigue and sleep disturbance, and cognitive symptoms such as difficulty concentrating (Wolfe et al., 2010; Wolfe, Häuser, Hassett, Katz, & Walitt, 2011). Other joint concerns, such as OA, can exacerbate symptoms and/or make it difficult for patients to distinguish between different types of pain. Due to the impact of the disease on the cardiovascular system, patients with RA are also at increased risk of cardiovascular events such as myocardial infarction and stroke (8% combined), and chronic obstructive pulmonary disease (8%; Dougados et al., 2014). Depression is highly prevalent in this population, with approximately 17% of individuals with RA also experiencing major depression (Matcham, Rayner, Steer, & Hotopf, 2013). Newly diagnosed patients especially may be at risk for mental health concerns (Bacconnier et al., 2015; Benka et al., 2014).

Characteristics of RA Pain

Overall, patients with RA experience many types of pain, and it may be very challenging for individuals to identify different pain signals and respond appropriately. Most patients with RA experience persistent intermittent joint pain, swelling, and stiffness as a normal part of the disease process (Aletaha et al., 2010; Smolen et al., 2010). This most commonly presents in the small joints, such as the wrists, hands, ankles, feet, and elbows, leading to related functional impairments such as difficulties walking, standing, gripping, completing personal care and hygiene, using a computer, and driving, among others. RA pain may be transient or longer lasting (e.g., minutes versus months) depending upon the severity of the disease, presence of inflammation, and patient responsiveness to medication. Additionally, both level and type of daily activity impact pain; inactivity can result in muscle atrophy and increased joint stiffness and pain, while vigorous or extended physical activity may trigger joint inflammation and pain (Metsios et al., 2008; Stenström & Minor, 2003).

Unfortunately for many individuals, RA pain may be chronic even when inflammation and disease activity are well controlled (Wolfe et al., 2014). Research suggests that chronic pain from RA may correspond with neurological changes (e.g., central sensitization) that increase the likelihood of developing other types of pain problems such as fibromyalgia syndrome (Lee, Nassikas, & Clauw, 2011; Wolfe et al., 2011). Chronic pain also may result from compensating for pain and related overuse of other areas (e.g., walking consistently with a limp to protect a painful ankle may lead to development of pain in a hip, knee, or back).

Patients with RA commonly experience flare-ups, often within the context of chronic pain. "Flares" are characterized by acute episodes of joint inflammation and pain and occur when there is a burst of disease activity that may attack joints for a few hours or even weeks at a time (e.g., see Bingham et al., 2009). Flares often are accompanied by fatigue and flu-like symptoms (Hewlett et al., 2012). The pain and functional limitations associated with flares tend to be more severe and disruptive than those experienced on an ongoing basis; patients often experience notable distress during these times (Hewlett et al., 2012). Helping patients develop a variety of healthy coping skills for managing both the chronic and acute pain components of RA is an essential aspect of treatment for the condition.

Biopsychosocial Considerations

An individual's pain experience may be influenced by a variety of biological, psychological, and social factors. Psychosocial factors at times contribute to the overall pain experience, while in turn being impacted by RA pain in a bidirectional relationship. For example, the experience of pain itself often negatively impacts a person's mood, anxiety, stress level, motivation, and sleep. However, difficulties with these same factors also potentiate and worsen the experience of pain (Gatchel, Peng, Peters, Fuchs, & Turk, 2007). Understanding RA within the context of the biopsychosocial model is critical to informing interdisciplinary treatment approaches.

Biological Factors

Biological factors such as disease severity and medication efficacy may influence pain experiences among patients with RA. Perhaps not surprisingly, those with greater disease severity (i.e., more inflammation and joint degeneration) often report higher levels of pain. Medication is currently the first line of treatment for patients with RA, and the availability and effectiveness of medications for RA has improved greatly over the last decade (Singh et al., 2012). Currently, the most common forms of pharmacological treatment are disease-modifying antirheumatic drugs (DMARDs such as methotrexate), usually taken in pill form; biologic agents, commonly a self-administered injection (e.g., adalimumab, etanercept); and combination therapy using both a DMARD and a biologic agent. These medications can help slow the general progression of RA, while corticosteroids (via pill or intraarticular injection) can help manage acute disease flares (Gøtzsche & Johnansen, 2009; Singh et al., 2012).

RA treatments are well tolerated generally, though not without common side effects. For example, methotrexate can be associated with increased risk of diarrhea, fatigue, malaise, and hair loss, while biologic treatments have immunosuppressant effects that, while effective in slowing the RA disease process, result in increased likelihood of common illness (Curtis et al., 2016; Keyser, 2011). Negative injection experiences (e.g., pain, burning, discomfort) and dislike or fear of injection are often additional barriers to biologic treatment (Bolge, Goren, & Tandon, 2015).

Physicians managing RA patients routinely perform exams, monitor blood inflammatory markers (e.g., C-reactive protein and erythrocyte sedimentation rate), and review imaging tests of affected joints in order to monitor the progression of the disease and the effectiveness of the medication regimen (Smolen et al., 2010). Although medication adherence is critical in effective disease management, adherence rates among RA patients are low (estimates range from 30% to 80%) and are impacted by patient perceptions of risks and benefits of treatment (Van den Bemt, Zwikker, & Van den Ende, 2012). Thus, addressing patient beliefs about RA and treatment may help facilitate adherence in this population and lead to more accurate measures of treatment effectiveness (Van den Bemt et al., 2012). It is important to note that some patients, such as pregnant women, patients in liver or kidney failure, or patients who have had prior adverse reactions, may not be able to safely be prescribed standard RA medications that otherwise could manage chronic RA pain and disease flares.

Obesity and physical activity also can significantly impact disease process and progression in a cyclical, bidirectional pattern. Specifically, patients with RA are less physically active in general than their healthy counterparts (Iversen, Brawerman, & Iversen, 2012). A sedentary lifestyle in turn often is associated with greater joint stiffness and muscle deconditioning, making movement and exercise more difficult and painful, as well as with obesity, placing further strain on joints. RA patients who are obese exhibit higher levels of disease activity, inflammation, and pain secondary to additional joint strain, as well as lower rates of remission (Liu et al., 2016). Of note, *overactivity* also can trigger inflammation, which increases pain and often necessitates an increased recovery period with limited activity. Inactivity or inconsistent activity over time tends to result in chronic physical dysfunction, increasing the likelihood of pain and related complications (Nielson, Jensen, Karsdorp, & Vlaeyen, 2013).

Given the poorer outcomes associated with obesity and limited physical activity, in addition to the heightened risk of cardiovascular disease among patients with RA, interventions focused on increasing and maintaining consistent physical activity are recommended (Iversen, Brawerman, & Iversen, 2012). Such interventions vary with the needs of the patient and may consist of engagement in a structured exercise program, exercise facilitated by a physical therapist, or interventions targeting psychosocial factors impacting exercise (e.g., anxiety about the risk of pain with increased movement, or depression contributing to low motivation). These interventions are associated with improvements in pain, strength, aerobic capacity, and perceived health (Iversen, Brawerman, & Iversen, 2012). Activity pacing may be a useful strategy to incorporate when helping RA patients gradually and safely build to the recommended 30 minutes of moderate physical activity five days per week (Haskell et al., 2007; Iversen, Brawerman, & Iversen, 2012).

While pain may interfere with sleep and contribute to feelings of fatigue among patients with RA, poor sleep and fatigue also may impact the experience of pain (Lee et al., 2013). Increased fatigue and sleep disturbances are common particularly among those with a comorbid diagnosis of FMS (Wolfe et al., 2010). Sleep interventions (e.g., cognitive-behavioral therapy for insomnia [CBT-I]) may be indicated, depending on symptom severity, to address these difficulties. While there is a paucity of research conducted with RA patients specifically, studies suggest that CBT-I can be effective in improving sleep for patients with other pain conditions such as osteoarthritis (Vitiello, Rybarczyk, Von Korff, & Stepanski, 2009) and spinal pain (Jungguist et al., 2010). Maladaptive cognitions contributing to poor sleep (e.g., "I've been hurting all day so I'll never be able to fall asleep") also can be targeted in treatment to improve sleep and fatigue symptoms.

Psychological Factors

Mental health concerns are common among patients with RA. For example, the prevalence of major depressive disorder is estimated to be around 17%, with nearly 40% of RA patients experiencing depressive symptoms more broadly (Matcham et al., 2013). Chronic comorbid depression is associated with greater disease severity; it also has been shown to result in higher rates of mortality and worse physical functioning even when controlling for disease severity and duration (Dougados et al., 2014; Morris, Yelin, Panopalis, Julian, & Katz, 2011). Additionally, persistent mental health concerns such as depression and anxiety increase the likelihood of developing comorbid FMS (Wolfe et al., 2011). Patients with comorbid FMS in turn experience greater depressive and anxiety symptoms, and often perceive their health to be poorer compared to those with RA alone (Dolan et al., 2016; Wolfe et al., 2014).

Beyond general mental health concerns, patients may experience acute psychological distress during flares and/or anxiety about triggering flares; this distress may result in avoidance of activity and subsequent deconditioning (Birkholtz, Aylwin, & Harman, 2004; Hewlett et al., 2012). Targeting psychological factors is an important part of RA treatment in terms of both physical and mental health outcomes.

Maladaptive thought patterns more generally may also impact the experience of RA symptoms and disease management. Catastrophizing thoughts regarding pain in particular may be associated with activity intolerance and avoidance (Sullivan et al., 2002). Additionally, in RA patients catastrophic thinking regarding the chronicity or severity of pain (e.g., "the pain will never end") and perceived uncontrollability of pain may further compound psychological distress (Hewlett et al., 2012). Lack of education regarding the disease and pain processes can lead to inaccurate beliefs (e.g., "I must push myself through this flare!" "If I don't move, my pain will go away"), further compounding catastrophic thinking tendencies. Providing psychoeducation regarding pain management and activity pacing, in addition to introducing cognitive-behavioral psychological approaches, may help address these maladaptive thought patterns and resulting ineffective coping patterns.

Substance use may impact both medication efficacy and disease outcomes among some patients with RA. Individuals with seropositive RA (those with particular antibodies associated with RA) who smoke cigarettes, for example, have reported more difficulty on composite measures of daily behavior that may be affected by RA (e.g., dressing, walking, grip) compared with those who never smoke (Bing et al., 2014). Additionally, smoking is associated with higher levels of pro-inflammatory cytokines and, in some studies, disease activity as indicated by a composite score of joint swelling, tenderness, blood tests, and subjective assessment of health for those with seropositive RA (Sokolove et al., 2016). By contrast, several studies have not found a significant relationship between cigarette smoking and disease activity among those with seronegative RA (Bing et al., 2014; Sokolove et al., 2016).

Increased amounts of alcohol are associated with increased risk of liver damage when consumed in conjunction with methotrexate (Humphreys et al., 2017). Humphreys and colleagues (2017) found that, in particular, consumption of over 168 grams of alcohol per week (approximately 12 standard U.S. drinks; NIAAA, n.d.) may increase risk of hepatotoxicity. Another study found that consumption of over 15 alcoholic beverages per *month* was associated with disease progression (Davis et al., 2013). Monitoring substance use may help prevent toxicity and other poor health outcomes and identify if substances are being used as maladaptive coping strategies among those with RA.

Social Factors

Pain, fatigue, and medications often contribute to weight gain, sleep difficulties, depression, low motivation, and associated distress (Irwin et al., 2012). Any combination of these factors may impact engagement in social activities and/or family dynamics (e.g., perceived failure to fulfill parental duties). The regular experience of pain often leads to reduced engagement with others, whether to avoid pain or to avoid feeling misunderstood regarding the disease and its impact. Indeed, unsatisfying interactions regarding RA, such as receiving unhelpful suggestions or perceptions of feeling misunderstood, are related to increased depressive symptoms; these, in turn, are related to worsening physical functioning and increased risk of mortality (Matcham, Rayner, Steer, & Hotopf, 2013; Morris, Yelin, Panopalis, Julian, & Katz, 2011; Revenson, Schiaffino, Majerovitz, & Gibofsky, 1991). In this way, feelings of being misunderstood and invalidated by others (e.g., "It's just arthritis") and associated difficulties accepting changes in functioning (e.g., "I've always taken care of myself AND everyone else") may increase depressive symptomatology, which may in turn exacerbate physical and social difficulties. By contrast, emotional support from others can help protect against depressed feelings (Benka et al., 2014; Revenson et al., 1991).

Social roles within the workplace also can be heavily impacted. Work productivity may be affected for those with RA due to pain, especially during flares, and associated loss of functioning. One review found that individuals with RA missed an average of 2.7 to 30 work days per year because of RA (Cooper, 2000), and many patients ultimately seek disability due to the impact of RA on livelihood. Specifically, work-related disability claim rates among those with RA are approximately 42–44%, compared to 22% among matched controls (Albers et al., 1999; Birnbaum et al., 2000). While RA clearly can have a profound impact on an individual's ability to perform job duties, such effects are not limited to financial repercussions. Seeking disability may impact an individual's view of identity (e.g., "I am disabled"), and ultimately may lead to maladaptive cognitions that perpetuate RA pain (e.g., "I am disabled and therefore I can't exercise").

Assessment of RA Pain

General pain assessment strategies are useful when assessing RA pain (see Chapter 2), although several additional considerations may help inform both conceptualization and treatment. For example, qualifying and quantifying pain location, course, and intensity are necessary, but it is important also to have a good understanding of 1) general RA symptoms, 2) frequency and intensity of flares, and 3) presence of other pain conditions, such as FMS, that may cloud the clinical picture. Patients frequently lack insight into the subtleties of pain and its overlap with other conditions that may, in and of themselves, be treatment targets.

It may be helpful throughout the assessment process to provide education and definitions as needed in order to increase patient health literacy and to help patients distinguish RA pain from other types. For example, not all patients will know what the term "flare" means. This can be an opportunity to gauge patient understanding and to identify misconceptions and/or unhelpful beliefs (such as "all pain is the same"). Clinicians also should be aware of how long patients have been diagnosed with RA, as patients with "early RA" (diagnosed within the past two years) are less likely to have good disease control, are more likely to experience frequent flares, have higher reported levels of distress, and have a higher likelihood of depression (Bacconnier et al., 2015; Benka et al., 2014). This information is helpful for conceptualizing the patient's pain experience and identifying intervention targets.

Assessment should focus not only on pain but also on functional impairments related to pain, which may manifest physically and emotionally. For example, a patient with severe RA in the hands who is a seamstress by trade may experience both physical and emotional impairment due to the impact of RA on her livelihood. The RA Pain Assessment Table (Table 14.1), created by this chapter's authors, displays sample questions that can be used to assess general pain characteristics

Table 14.1 RA Pain Assessment Table (Interview Guide)

Assessment Domain		Sample Questions
RA Pain Characteristics	Location(s)	• Where in your body do you notice that RA impacts you the most?
		• Where do you experience the most pain from RA?
	Onset/Duration/Course	• When were you diagnosed with RA? Were you experiencing this type of pain before then?
		• Has your pain been consistent since it began? Were there periods when it was worse?
		• How often have you experienced flare-ups over the past year?
	Quality	• How would you describe the pain you experience (aching, throbbing, sharp, dull, etc.)?
		• Does the pain feel different during a flare up?
	Intensity	• How intense has your pain been over the last week (0–10)?
		• Worst/Highest pain?
		• Lowest pain?
		• Average pain?
		• Current pain?
	Pain Interference	• How much has pain interfered with your daily activities over the past week? Which activities?
		• In what ways does pain impact your (quality of) life?
	Exacerbating Factors	• Have you noticed anything that tends to make the pain worse?
		• How does physical activity impact your pain?
		• How does stress (poor sleep, etc.) impact your pain?
	Mitigating Factors	• What medications do you use to manage RA? Is the disease well-managed?
		• What medications do you use to alleviate pain? How much do they help?
		• What other things help you alleviate pain?
		• What do you do to manage flare-ups?
	Coping Skills	• How do you cope with chronic pain/flares?

Other Pain Conditions	Evaluate other pain conditions as above	• Do you have any other conditions that lead to current pain? • Do you have any current pain related to past injuries? • Have you ever been diagnosed with another pain condition, such as fibromyalgia?
Daily Functioning/Lifestyle	Living Arrangements	• Do you live with others? With whom do you live? • What are things like within the home?
	Work/Daily Schedule	• Are you currently working? (If not, are you receiving disability?) • What does a typical day look like? Is it different on the weekends?
	Physical Activity	• What type of physical activity do you engage in regularly? (How often? For how long?)
	Sleep Quality	• How much sleep are you currently getting? Do you wake feeling rested? • Do you have difficulties falling or staying asleep? • Does pain impact your sleep?
	Energy	• How would you describe your energy throughout the day? • Do you ever nap/rest during the day?
	Alcohol/Tobacco Use	• How often do you have drinks containing alcohol? • Are you a former/current smoker?
Psychosocial Functioning	Perceived Well-Being	• How would you describe your overall health/well-being?
	Mood	• How would you describe your mood lately?
	Anxiety/Stress	• Do you ever have concerns with feeling sad or depressed? Irritability? • Have you had difficulties with feeling anxious, nervous, or on edge lately? Difficulties with worry? • What do you consider to be your major sources of stress at present?
	Social Support	• Who in your life is supportive of you? • Do you ever talk with others about RA/pain?
	Coping Skills	• How do you manage your day-to-day stress? • What do you do to help cope with pain (mood, etc.)?

and related impairments within a biopsychosocial framework. Questions relate to biological, psychological, and social characteristics and consequences of the pain, yielding a comprehensive picture of how RA impacts a patient's life. We recommend supplementing this interview-style assessment with standardized and normed self-report questionnaires to screen for depression, anxiety, and other related relevant psychosocial domains.

Of note, it may be helpful during assessment to distinguish between modifiable (such as a sedentary lifestyle) and non-modifiable (such as certain disease characteristics) factors affecting pain. Differentiating these factors can be helpful to both clinicians and patients in terms of informing effective treatment planning. Patients can improve self-management and self-efficacy by addressing modifiable factors through behavior change, and non-modifiable factors through building acceptance and coping skills. Case examples help illustrate the biopsychosocial assessment of RA patients.

Case Example #1: Shayna—Early RA

Assessment and Conceptualization

"Shayna" is a 35-year-old African American female living with her husband and two small children. Her primary complaints are related to difficulties managing pain during flares that seem to "come out of nowhere." She relates during the interview,

> I feel useless when I have a flare. I can't go to work; I can't even comb my daughter's hair. But, hey, I've got kids and I gotta keep up with them. I just try to take advantage of good days and push through the pain until I can't go any further. Then my husband jumps in and takes over until the flare is gone. He's my rock.

RA/Pain Characteristics

Shayna was diagnosed with RA a year and a half ago and has experienced "intense aching" in her hands and feet intermittently over the past two years. She experienced many RA flares during the first year and tried several different RA medications before settling on her current regimen. Though the pain has improved some over time, she still reports a few flares over past six months. She described her current day-to-day pain as tolerable (2–4/10 on average), but during flares pain is more intense (8/10), making walking and many daily activities very challenging.

Daily Functioning/Lifestyle

Shayna works part-time in an office environment in the morning and takes care of her kids in the afternoon and evening. On weekends, she and her family go on regular outings to the park. She is a lifetime non-smoker and drinks an "occasional glass of wine." Though she does not engage in structured exercise, she states, "I'm always on the go between chasing my kids and taking care of the house."

Psychosocial Functioning

Shayna describes general stress related to pain flares, taking time off work, financial strain, and raising children. However, during interview and on self-report measures, she denies depressed mood, anxiety, or any other mental health concerns. Her self-report on a measure of self-efficacy in managing chronic pain was low, indicating that she does not feel confident in her ability to manage her pain.

Conceptualization/Treatment Targets

Shayna is a generally well-adjusted individual who appears to be struggling with balancing RA/pain management and her roles within her family. She would likely benefit from brief intervention targeting her understanding of the relationship between activity and pain, including her current dysfunctional pattern of activity (i.e., overactivity followed by extended periods of recovery), any unhelpful beliefs that she has surrounding pain, physical activity, and social roles, and communication with her husband to facilitate seeking help before flares occur.

Case Example #2: Marie—RA with Comorbid FMS

Assessment and Conceptualization

"Marie" is a 57-year-old Caucasian female living with her husband of 36 years. She is seeking help to manage depression related to her chronic pain. She is tearful during the interview and describes having a poor quality of life.

> I just want to be a fun grandma and enjoy my grandkids, but I can't because of the pain. I know my husband cares about me, but he just doesn't understand what I'm going through. I'm not the same person I was when we married. All I do is just rest and pray to God that the pain will end. There's nothing else I can do.

RA/Pain Characteristics

Marie was diagnosed with RA six years ago, though she has experienced pain for longer. She provides a 9/10 average pain rating and describes intense "aching all over—my joints, my back, sometimes even my skin hurts!" She was diagnosed with comorbid FMS three years ago and attributes all of her pain to this diagnosis. She does not appear to be knowledgeable about how RA is likely contributing to her pain, despite observable deviations in her hands indicating severe disease activity. She dislikes injecting herself with medication weekly and admits to skipping doses because "it doesn't stop the pain."

Daily Functioning/Lifestyle

Marie is a former bank teller and has been unemployed for the past seven years; she states, "I'm disabled; I haven't been able to work for a while." She generally describes a sedentary lifestyle with very few structured or recreational activities. She is a non-smoker but reports drinking "a few martinis" when feeling down.

Psychosocial Functioning

During the interview and on psychological measures, Marie endorses moderately depressive symptoms that began around the time she stopped working due to her pain and related symptoms. She is very distressed about her current situation but denies any suicidal ideation and hopes that things can change, though she is not sure how. Her score on a measure of pain acceptance was low, suggesting that she likely focuses on controlling or eradicating pain and that her behavior is likely contingent upon her pain.

Conceptualization/Treatment Targets

Marie is struggling to manage her disease, pain, and mood, resulting in maladaptive patterns that have significantly impacted her quality of life. It is important for both the provider and Marie to understand that the pain she is experiencing is due to poorly controlled RA in addition to FMS. Thus, gaining better disease control will likely help her pain as well as her overall long-term health outcomes. In addition to ongoing education and symptom tracking to aid in the understanding of her pain experience, there are multiple potential treatment targets for the provider and Marie to consider: examining relationships between activity and pain, medication adherence, depressed mood, current dysfunctional pattern of underactivity, unhelpful thoughts and beliefs surrounding pain and disability, passive/limited coping, alcohol misuse, and communication with her husband, family, and healthcare providers. A team-based, patient-centered approach is ideal in this case. Collaboration with Marie's medical providers would facilitate addressing disease education and medication adherence issues in addition to increasing access to potential conjunctive treatment options such as psychiatric medications and physical therapy.

Evidence-Based Psychosocial Interventions for Patients With RA: An Overview

Anchored in the biopsychosocial model, evidenced-based psychosocial interventions for patients with RA may target a variety of pain- and disease-related outcomes. Intervention components aim to modify behaviors that may directly impact pain, enhance disease management, improve functioning, and/or increase coping skills for living well with chronic RA pain. Two well-studied psychological approaches, cognitive-behavioral therapy (CBT) and acceptance and commitment therapy (ACT), offer comprehensive theoretical frameworks to guide treatment of patients with RA from a multidimensional perspective.

Cognitive-Behavioral Therapy (CBT)

CBT is considered the gold standard among psychological interventions for a variety of chronic pain conditions, including arthritis (Csaszar, Bagdi, Stoll, & Szoke, 2014; Ehde, Dillworth, & Turner, 2014; Turner, Holtzman, & Mancl, 2007). CBT in patients with arthritis has resulted in medium to large treatment effects in improved coping and small, but significant, effects for depression, disability, and joint inflammation (Dixon, Keefe, Scipio, Perri, & Abernethy, 2007; Knittle, Maes, & De Gucht, 2010). This treatment approach generally targets reducing maladaptive cognitive patterns (e.g., pain catastrophizing, unhelpful thoughts and beliefs about pain and RA) and increasing adaptive and coping behaviors (e.g., appropriate physical activity, self-management). This broad framework allows therapists to work flexibly with the patient to identify specific cognitive and behavioral patterns that appear to impact functioning and quality of life, and to develop a treatment plan accordingly. An in-depth review of CBT as applied to chronic pain patients is found in Chapter 4 of this handbook.

Acceptance and Commitment Therapy (ACT)

Mindfulness and acceptance-based therapeutic approaches, such as ACT, increasingly are utilized in treating chronic pain and have been found to have treatment effects similar to other forms of CBT (Veehof, Oskam, Schreurs, & Bohlmeijer, 2011). Specifically, ACT interventions are associated with reduced depression and anxiety among chronic pain patients, moderate decreases in pain-related disabilities and small decreases in reported pain, and fewer numbers of subsequent pain-related medical visits (Vowles, McCracken, & O'Brien, 2011). The overall goal of ACT is to increase psychological flexibility via six core processes: mindfulness, acceptance, cognitive defusion, self-as-context, values, and committed action (see Hayes et al., 2006 for a detailed background of ACT). Two primary therapeutic processes, acceptance and values-based action, account for much of the observed improvements attributed to ACT in pain intervention research (Vowles, McCracken, & Eccleston, 2007; Vowles, McCracken, & O'Brien, 2011).

In the context of treating pain, ACT interventions aim to facilitate acceptance of chronic pain and subsequent disengagement from the struggle to deny or control it, while increasing appropriate engagement in personally valued activities (Veehof et al., 2011). A major benefit of an ACT approach is that it offers a flexible and inherently patient-centered framework aimed at reducing suffering and improving quality of life. Please see Chapter 5 for additional information on ACT as applied to chronic pain patients.

CBT Versus ACT for Patients With RA

Of note, although CBT and ACT interventions both result in similar overall improvements in RA patients, certain approaches may offer greater benefit to some patient subpopulations (Csaszar, Bagdi, Stoll, & Szoke, 2014; Turner, Holtzman, & Mancl, 2007; Veehof, Oskam, Schreurs, & Bohlmeijer, 2011; Zautra et al., 2008). For example, one randomized controlled trial comparing a CBT and mindfulness-based intervention in patients with RA found similar overall improvements; however, patients with recurring depression appeared to benefit most from the mindfulness-based approach, showing larger improvements in coping and pain catastrophizing (Zautra et al., 2008). These researchers suggested that patients with recurring depression may benefit particularly from the emotion regulation aspects of mindfulness-based approaches such as ACT, while a streamlined CBT approach may be adequate for patients without affective concerns.

Evidence-Based Psychosocial Interventions for Patients With RA: Key Components

CBT and ACT approaches each offer a comprehensive framework for approaching treatment of pain among patients with RA. While there are limited treatment protocols available for RA pain specifically, clinicians may easily adapt existing chronic pain protocols to meet the needs of patients with RA. Given the variety of biopsychosocial factors that impact RA and pain, successful treatment likely will involve a tailored combination of the following key intervention components (Ehde, Dillworth, & Turner, 2014).

Activity Pacing

Activity pacing, a common component of chronic pain interventions, easily can be incorporated into a treatment plan using a CBT or an ACT approach (Ehde, Dillworth, & Turner, 2014; McCracken & Samuel, 2007). In general, activity pacing for chronic pain focuses on improving and preserving physical functioning by striking a balance between over- and underactivity, and is associated with improvements in both pain severity and emotional distress (Nielson, Jensen, Karsdorp, & Vlaeyen, 2013). Activity pacing often begins with psychoeducation on relationships between physical activity and pain (Iversen, Brawerman, & Iversen, 2012). Patients often over-engage in activities when feeling relatively pain-free or on "good pain days," risking a resulting pain exacerbation and/or disease flare that necessitate extended periods of recovery. Conversely, other patients generally may avoid activity, making subsequent activity more fatiguing and/or painful. Activity pacing broadly entails monitoring activity levels, identifying an appropriate baseline level of activity, then engaging in consistent, daily activity balanced with pre-planned periods of rest (Iversen, Brawerman, & Iversen, 2012; Nielson, Jensen, Karsdorp, & Vlaeyen, 2013). The goal is to maintain or slowly increase activity over time. For patients with RA, additional titration of activity is needed in response to flares (Iversen, Brawerman, & Iversen, 2012). For example, a patient may develop a very light activity plan to maintain during flares, with a plan to increase activity gradually after recovery. Thus, activity pacing easily may be integrated into CBT and ACT protocols, both of which emphasize increases in valued and adaptive behaviors.

Nielson, Jensen, Karsdorp, and Vlaeyen (2013) provide a detailed review of the variety of activity pacing strategies. One commonly used approach involves using time- or goal-contingent activity goals, meaning patients engage in a healthy predetermined amount of activity (e.g., 15 minutes of walking or walking once around the neighborhood) regardless of pain. The general idea is that activity becomes contingent upon these goals, rather than upon pain. To establish an appropriate baseline level of activity, patients may record how much activity they are able to tolerate and then use the average amount as their initial activity goal. Subsequently, using principles of successive approximation and mastery, the daily activity goal (e.g., five minutes of walking) might gradually increase (e.g., to 7, 10, then 15 minutes of walking) until the patient reaches their general activity goal (e.g., 30 minutes of walking). See Appendix 1 for an example of an activity pacing worksheet using time-contingent goal setting.

Behavioral Activation (BA)

BA involves reengaging patients in enjoyable and valued activities and is associated with increased positive and decreased negative affect, suggesting that this strategy particularly may be helpful for patients with depressed mood or anhedonia (Lejuez, Hopko, Acierno, Daughters, & Pagoto, 2011). BA may be viewed as one of the main components of a CBT or ACT treatment plan, or as a brief, stand-alone treatment (Lejuez, Hopko, Acierno, Daughters, & Pagoto, 2011). Pain, or fear of pain, prevents many RA patients from engaging in previously enjoyable social or leisure activities. Values clarification is a vital component of BA (as well as ACT) that leads to (re-)engagement in meaningful activities, and that may facilitate development of new, possibly modified hobbies while generally increasing patient engagement to improve physical and psychological functioning (Lejuez, Hopko, Acierno, Daughters, & Pagoto, 2011).

Relaxation Training and Stress Reduction

A variety of relaxation training techniques, such as diaphragmatic breathing, progressive muscle relaxation, and guided imagery, often are used in multi-component interventions for chronic pain (Ehde, Dillworth, & Turner, 2014). Mindfulness-based stress reduction, a therapy aimed at using mindfulness as a means of reducing physiological and subjective stress, also has been shown to result in improved physical and mental health outcomes (Veehof, Oskam, Schreurs, & Bohlmeijer, 2011). Teaching patients relaxation strategies increases positive coping behaviors and is associated with decreased maladaptive pain beliefs (Ehde, Dillworth, & Turner, 2014). Biofeedback, an intervention aimed at improving parasympathetic control, has been associated with improved chronic pain outcomes, both as a stand-alone treatment and in conjunction with CBT (Ehde, Dillworth, & Turner, 2014). These strategies and therapeutic approaches share a theme of self-regulation, which has been found to result in improvements (particularly in depressive and anxiety symptoms) among patients with RA (Knittle, Maes, & De Gucht, 2010).

Cognitive Techniques

As previously discussed, maladaptive cognitions are an important intervention target for treating chronic pain as they may lead to psychological distress and poor disease management (e.g., someone thinks "the pain will never get better, no matter what I do!" and therefore does not implement pain management strategies). Pain catastrophizing, in particular, has been heavily researched and is associated with pain-related outcomes in RA, such as patient-reported outcomes of pain levels, perceived functional ability, perceived impact of disease, and composite measures of disease activity (Hammer, Uhlig, Kvien, & Lampa, 2017).

CBT approaches may address pain catastrophizing and other maladaptive thought patterns via a process known as cognitive restructuring (Ehde, Dillworth, & Turner, 2014), through which patients learn to identify and challenge unhelpful thought patterns in order to develop a more balanced perspective regarding the impact of their disease. For example, a patient struggling to play catch with her children due to pain may think initially, "I can't do anything fun with my kids anymore because of my pain!" However, after examining the "evidence against" this belief, the patient subsequently may conclude, "I love reading to my children, and I typically am able to do that pain-free." Thus, the patient may revise her belief to: "Pain from my RA interferes with a lot of my activities, but I still can do some things that I love."

ACT-based cognitive techniques also may be used to address catastrophizing and other unhelpful thoughts (Vowles, McCracken, & Eccleston, 2007; Zautra et al., 2008). Cognitive defusion, or the process of observing thoughts, may be used to enhance acceptance of chronic pain and disease, a process associated with improvements in pain-related outcomes (Vowles, McCracken, & Eccleston, 2007). Rather than focusing on the *content* of the thoughts (such as what is done in cognitive restructuring), cognitive defusion approaches help patients to change their *relationship* with their thoughts.

Rather than engaging in whether or not the thought is accurate, patients learn to move in valued directions notwithstanding painful thoughts (Hayes et al., 2006). Returning to the example above ("I can't do anything fun with my kids anymore because of my pain!"), a therapist using an ACT approach may encourage the patient to label this as "merely a thought." Rather than focusing on this thought or trying to change it, the therapist can prompt the patient to explore alternate valued activities (such as reading to her children). Such an approach may be helpful in many respects, as patient actions and goals become guided by personally held values rather than difficult thoughts and emotions.

Motivational Interviewing/Enhancement

Motivational interviewing/enhancement is a clinical approach that aims to help individuals resolve ambivalence toward making health-positive changes; see Miller and Rollnick (2012) for a detailed overview. For many patients, making behavioral changes can be very challenging, whether the changes might be to take medications as prescribed, increase physical activity, stop smoking, or ask for and accept help from others. By approaching patients in an open, accepting, and nonjudgmental manner and eliciting their personal reasons for and barriers to change, providers can help patients navigate the behavior change process more successfully. This approach also is useful in identifying which behavioral targets a patient is willing and ready to change, especially when multiple potential targets exist. While there is little research regarding motivational interviewing for RA patients specifically, evidence suggests that motivational interviewing can be helpful in targeting many domains that are relevant for patients with RA (e.g., increasing physical activity, improving medication adherence, weight management) (Georgopoulou, Prothero, Lempp, Galloway, & Sturt, 2016).

Collaboration With Other Disciplines

Effective treatment of RA pain and impairment often is improved by collaboration among healthcare professionals sharing a biopsychosocial framework

(Ehde, Dillworth, & Turner, 2014). For example, medical education and medication adherence issues may require additional consultation with the patient's healthcare team. Collaboration with physical therapy may help address difficulties with activity pacing, improving independence in activities of daily living, and identifying specific physical and functional barriers that may be targeted in treatment. Shared medical appointments (i.e., group healthcare visits with multiple providers, such as physicians, nurses, pharmacists, physical therapists, and behavioral health providers) afford opportunities for both patients and providers to identify and address complex treatment issues within a single visit (Shojania & Ratzlaff, 2010). The presence of other patients with similar issues also may offer the benefit of peer support and validation of the challenges of living with RA.

Measuring Patient Progress

Given the complex biopsychosocial presentation of RA, treatment may focus on a number of targets depending on the needs and preferences of the patient, such as pain intensity/characteristics, functional impairment, RA disease activity, psychological functioning (including depression, mood, anxiety, and quality of life), pain- and disease-related beliefs, pain catastrophizing, pain acceptance, and self-efficacy in managing chronic pain/disease.

Many assessment measures targeting these domains have been designed for clinical practice and/or research and are freely available. For example, the Multidimensional Health Assessment Questionnaire is a common clinical assessment measure that can be used for patients with RA (Pincus, Yazici, & Bergman, 2005; Pincus, 2007). This self-report measure, recommended by the American College of Rheumatology for tracking disease activity and patient functioning, elicits information from patients about functioning over the past week and provides three subscale scores: functional impairment, pain intensity, and global well-being (Anderson et al., 2012; Pincus, Yazici, & Bergman, 2007). While the total score can be used as one measure of disease symptom severity, it is important to note that scores are heavily influenced by the patient's perceptions and coping.

While formal and/or standardized measures are useful during initial assessments and evaluation of treatment outcomes (e.g., capturing overall reductions in depressive symptoms and improvements in self-efficacy), ongoing functional assessment and patient monitoring may be more helpful in guiding session-to-session intervention progress (e.g., examining functional relationships between pain, activity, and mood; identifying activity pacing goals). An example of a self-monitoring form and a brief, weekly functional assessment measure can be found in Appendices 2 and 3. Use of online and mobile technology increasingly is researched and integrated into clinical practice (Ehde, Dillworth, & Turner, 2014). The availability of mobile applications and wearable fitness trackers may facilitate monitoring and ecological momentary assessment of key variables (such as physical activity and pain) using a platform that is accessible and desirable to patients.

We will follow the previous case examples through intervention.

Case Example #1: Shayna—Early RA

CBT With Activity Pacing

Education and Monitoring

"Shayna" was provided with education about RA, acute versus chronic pain, and physical activity and was asked to keep a pain diary. In the following session, she noticed that her pain was significantly worse in the afternoons and evenings, and that she continued to be very busy until the pain became too intense to continue.

Treatment Focus

After discussing patterns observed in her diary and introducing principles of activity pacing, Shayna set the goal to take a 10–15-minute break every two hours to help prevent exacerbations in pain.

Addressing Barriers to Treatment

Shayna noticed that she could do more during the days she took breaks, but had challenges doing so consistently. In examining her cognitive patterns, she identified the belief that she was letting her family down by taking such frequent breaks, and this belief led to subsequent feelings of guilt. She challenged this belief in session and concluded that self-care helps her to be a better caregiver to her family. She was hesitant to ask her husband for help at first ("he does so much already"), but realized that she would rather ask for help before having to rely on him for help during a flare.

Final Session

Shayna's pre-/post-assessment measures showed significant improvement in self-efficacy in managing chronic pain. Shayna stated,

> I guess I had to realize that taking care of my family means taking care of myself. I hate that I have this disease and that I have to take so many breaks, but I also hate having flares. I'm still adjusting to all this, but I'm glad that I talked with my husband and that he supports me. I don't have to do everything all on my own.

Case Example #2: Marie—RA with Comorbid FMS

Team-Based Care, ACT

Education and Collaboration With Physician

It was important for "Marie" to receive education from both her mental health provider and her rheumatologist to develop a good understanding of her disease and the different types of pain she experienced. A motivational interviewing approach helped her to weigh the benefits and risks of RA medications, after which she began complying with her prescriptions. Marie's rheumatologist also prescribed duloxetine to help with both pain and mood management.

Treatment Focus

Marie was asked to keep a mood/activity/pain diary and noticed that her mood improved somewhat when she was around family, and worsened when she stayed in bed and focused on her pain. She explored her values in session and identified family as very important to her. She expressed a desire to be loving and present, and to do fun things with her grandchildren. She identified values-based activities that she could do with her grandchildren, even with pain, and set the initial goal to go to a movie with them. She also set a goal of walking around her block once per day to help improve stamina.

Addressing Barriers to Treatment

Marie felt unsteady when attempting to walk around her block and was afraid to continue. She agreed to a physical therapy referral to further assess the problem and to help her develop a safe home exercise plan. Marie had a difficult time meeting her values-based goals as well. It was important to address her belief that she can't do anything until her pain is gone, and to work toward accepting that her pain is chronic. Through cognitive defusion and mindfulness exercises, she began to practice living in the present moment (with pain) rather than delaying valued living indefinitely with the hope of total resolution of her pain. When she reached her goal of taking her grandchildren to a movie, she felt proud of herself and confident that she could find things to do with them despite her pain.

Final Session

Marie's pre-/post-assessment measures showed significant improvement in depressive symptoms (now falling in the mild range) and modest improvement in pain acceptance. Marie stated,

I still struggle with pain and depression at times, but I do think that I'm better overall. Even if I'm not happy, I am doing more things with my grandchildren and that means the world to me. It's hard to accept that the pain is here to stay. Sometimes I can't accept it. But I know that I'm working hard to get my life back and that pain doesn't have to control me.

Conclusions

RA is a multifaceted disease associated with complex patterns of pain, increased likelihood of mental health concerns, and reduced quality of life. Given the widespread impact of the disease and related pain, a biopsychosocial approach to assessment and treatment is likely to best meet the varied needs of patients with RA. Both CBT and ACT have been shown to be effective in treating chronic pain and associated emotional symptoms in this population. These therapeutic approaches offer flexible frameworks, facilitating patient-centered care and affording opportunity for the integration of a variety of evidence-based techniques to help patients improve management of their disease, pain, emotional distress, and quality of life.

Traditionally, psychosocial interventions for patients with RA have occurred within specialty mental health or pain settings; however, many patients never enter these settings, leaving significant unmet need. Behavioral health interventions for patients with RA recently are becoming more prominent in primary care and rheumatology settings (e.g., McCracken, Sato, Wainwright, House, & Taylor, 2014; Shojania & Ratzlaff, 2010). Collaborative care approaches provide the benefit of a unified treatment team to comprehensively address patient needs and improve disease and pain self-management. Integrated healthcare for patients with chronic pain is cost-effective and associated with improved short- and long-term clinical outcomes (Gatchel, McGeary, McGeary, & Lippe, 2014; Gatchel & Okifuji, 2006; Turk & Swanson, 2007). Patients with recurrent depressive episodes, who express greater distress, who have shorter disease duration, and/or who are at higher risk for chronic impairment appear to receive the greatest benefit from these types of interventions (Knittle, Maes, & De Gucht, 2010; van Koulil et al., 2007; Zautra et al., 2008).

References

Albers, J. M., Kuper, H. H., Van Riel, P. L., Prevoo, M. L., Van't Hof, M. A., Van Gestel, A. M., & Severens, J. L. (1999). Socio-economic consequences of rheumatoid arthritis in the first years of the disease. *Rheumatology*, *38*(5), 423–430.

Aletaha, D., Neogi, T., Silman, A. J., Funovits, J., Felson, D. T., Bingham, C. O., . . . Hawker, G. (2010). 2010 rheumatoid arthritis classification criteria: An American College of Rheumatology/European League Against Rheumatism collaborative initiative. *Arthritis & Rheumatism*, *62*(9), 2569–2581.

Anderson, J., Caplan, L., Yazdany, J., Robbins, M. L., Neogi, T., Michaud, K., . . . Kazi, S. (2012). Rheumatoid arthritis disease activity measures: American college of rheumatology recommendations for use in clinical practice. *Arthritis Care & Research, 64*(5), 640–647.

Bacconnier, L., Rincheval, N., Flipo, R-M., Goupille, P., Daures, J-P., Boulenger, J-P., & Combe, B. (2015). Psychological distress over time in early rheumatoid arthritis: Results from a longitudinal study in an early arthritis cohort. *Rheumatology, 54*(3), 520–527.

Benka, J., Nagyova, I., Rosenberger, J., Calfova, A., Macejova, Z., Lazurova, I., . . . Groothoff, J. W. (2014). Social support as a moderator of functional disability's effect on depressive feelings in early rheumatoid arthritis: A four-year prospective study. *Rehabilitation Psychology, 59*(1), 19.

Bing, L., Rho, Y. H., Cui, J., Iannaccone, C. K., Frits, M. L., Karison, E. W., & Shadick, N. A. (2014). Associations of smoking and alcohol consumption with disease activity and functional status in rheumatoid arthritis. *The Journal of Rheumatology, 41*(1), 24–30.

Bingham, C. O., Pohl, C., Woodworth, T. G., Hewlett, S. E., May, J. E., Rahman, M. U., . . . Alten, R. E. (2009). Developing a standardized definition for disease "flare" in rheumatoid arthritis (OMERACT 9 Special Interest Group). *The Journal of Rheumatology, 36*(10), 2335–2341.

Birkholtz, M., Aylwin, L., & Harman, R. M. (2004). Activity pacing in chronic pain management: One aim, but which method? Part one: Introduction and literature review. *British Journal of Occupational Therapy, 67*(10), 447–452.

Birnbaum, H., Barton, M., Greenberg, P. E., Sisitsky, T., Auerbach, R., Wanke, L. A., & Buatti, M. C. (2000). Direct and indirect costs of rheumatoid arthritis to an employer. *Journal of Occupational and Environmental Medicine, 42*(6), 588–596.

Birnbaum, H., Pike, C., Kaufman, R., Maynchenko, M., Kidolezi, Y., & Cifaldi, M. (2010). Societal cost of rheumatoid arthritis patients in the US. *Current Medical Research and Opinion, 26*(1), 77–90.

Bolge, S. C., Goren, A., & Tandon, N. (2015). Reasons for discontinuation of subcutaneous biologic therapy in the treatment of rheumatoid arthritis: A patient perspective. *Patient Preference and Adherence, 9*, 121–131.

Centers for Disease Control and Prevention (Page last updated April 3, 2018). *Rheumatoid arthritis*. Retrieved April, 7, 2018, from www.cdc.gov/arthritis/basics/rheumatoid-arthritis.html

Cooper, N. J. (2000). Economic burden of rheumatoid arthritis: A systematic review. *Rheumatology, 39*(1), 28–33.

Csaszar, N., Bagdi, P., Stoll, D. P., & Szoke, H. (2014). Pain and psychotherapy, in the light of evidence of psychological treatment methods of chronic pain based on evidence. *Journal of Psychology & Psychotherapy, 4*(3), 1.

Curtis, J. R., Xie, F., Mackey, D., Gerber, N., Bharat, A., Beukelman, T., . . . Ginsberg, S. (2016). Patients' experience with subcutaneous and oral methotrexate for the treatment of rheumatoid arthritis. *BMC Musculoskeletal Disorders, 17*, 405.

Davis, M. L. R., Michaud, K., Sayles, H., Conn, D. L., Moreland, L. W., Bridges, S. L. Jr, & Mikuls, T. R. (2013). Associations of alcohol use with radiographic disease progression in African Americans with recent onset rheumatoid arthritis. *The Journal of Rheumatology, 40*(9), 1498–1504.

Dixon, K. E., Keefe, F. J., Scipio, C. D., Perri, L. M., & Abernethy, A. P. (2007). Psychological interventions for arthritis pain management in adults: A meta-analysis. *Health Psychology, 26*(3), 241.

Dolan, L., Tung, L. L. D., & Raizada, S. R. (2016). Fibromyalgia in the context of rheumatoid arthritis: A review. *Fibromyalgia: Open Access, 1*(103), 2.

Dougados, M., Soubrier, M., Antunez, A., Balint, P., Balsa, A., Buch, M. H., . . . Hajjaj-Hassouni, N. (2014). Prevalence of comorbidities in rheumatoid arthritis and evaluation of their monitoring: Results of an international, cross-sectional study (COMORA). *Annals of the Rheumatic Diseases*, *73*(1), 62–68.

Ehde, D. M., Dillworth, T. M., & Turner, J. A. (2014). Cognitive-behavioral therapy for individuals with chronic pain: Efficacy, innovations, and directions for research. *American Psychologist*, *69*(2), 153.

Gatchel, R. J., McGeary, D. D., McGeary, C. A., & Lippe, B. (2014). Interdisciplinary chronic pain management: Past, present, and future. *American Psychologist*, *69*(2), 119.

Gatchel, R. J., & Okifuji, A. (2006). Evidence-based scientific data documenting the treatment and cost-effectiveness of comprehensive pain programs for chronic nonmalignant pain. *The Journal of Pain*, *7*(11), 779–793.

Gatchel, R. J., Peng, Y. B., Peters, M. L., Fuchs, P. N., & Turk, D. C. (2007). The biopsychosocial approach to chronic pain: Scientific advances and future directions. *Psychological Bulletin*, *133*(4), 581.

Georgopoulou, S., Prothero, L., Lempp, H., Galloway, J., & Sturt, J. (2016). Motivational interviewing: Relevance in the treatment of rheumatoid arthritis? *Rheumatology*, *55*(8), 1348–1356.

Gøtzsche, P. C., & Johnansen, H. K. (2009). Short-term low-dose corticosteroids vs. placebo and nonsteroidal anti-inflammatory drugs in rheumatoid arthritis (Review). *Cochrane Database of Systematic Reviews*, *1*. Art. No.: CD000189. doi:10.01002/14651858. CD000189.pub2

Hammer, H. B., Uhlig, T., Kvien, T. K., & Lampa, J. (2017). Pain catastrophizing is strongly associated with subjective outcomes, but not with inflammatory assessments in rheumatoid arthritis patients. *Arthritis Care & Research*, *13*. doi:10.1002/acr.23339

Haskell, W. L., Lee, I. M., Pate, R. R., Powell, K. E., Blair, S. N., Franklin, B. A., . . . Bauman, A. (2007). Physical activity and public health: Updated recommendation for adults from the American college of sports medicine and the American heart association. *Circulation*, *116*(9), 1081.

Hayes, S. C., Luoma, J. B., Bond, F. W., Masuda, A., & Lillis, J. (2006). Acceptance and commitment therapy: Model, processes and outcomes. *Behaviour Research and Therapy*, *44*(1), 1–25.

Hewlett, S., Sanderson, T., May, J., Alten, R., Bingham, C. O., Cross, M., . . . Bartlett, S. J. (2012). 'I'm hurting, I want to kill myself': Rheumatoid arthritis flare is more than a high joint count—an international patient perspective on flare where medical help is sought. *Rheumatology*, *51*(1), 69–76.

Humphreys, J. H., Warner, A., Costello, R., Lunt, M., Verstappen, S. M. M., & Dixon, W. G. (2017). Quantifying the hepatotoxic risk of alcohol consumption in patients with rheumatoid arthritis taking methotrexate. *Annals of the Rheumatic Disease*, *76*, 1509–1514.

Irwin, M. R., Olmstead, R., Carrillo, C., Sadeghi, N., FitzGerald, J. D., Ranganath, V. K., & Nicassio, P. M. (2012). Sleep loss exacerbates fatigue, depression, and pain in rheumatoid arthritis. *Sleep*, *35*(4), 537.

Iversen, M. D., Brawerman, M., & Iversen, C. N. (2012). Recommendations and the state of the evidence for physical activity interventions for adults with rheumatoid arthritis: 2007 to present. *International Journal of Clinical Rheumatology*, *7*(5), 489.

Jungguist, C. R., O'Brien, C., Matteson-Rusby, S., Smith, M. T., Pigeon, W. R., Xia, Y., . . . Perlis, M. L. (2010). The efficacy of cognitive behavioral therapy for insomnia in patients with chronic pain. *Sleep Medicine*, *11*(3), 302–309.

Keyser, F. D. (2011). Choice of biologic therapy for patients with rheumatoid arthritis: The infection perspective. *Curr Rheumatology Reviews*, *7*(1), 77–87.

Knittle, K., Maes, S., & De Gucht, V. (2010). Psychological interventions for rheumatoid arthritis: Examining the role of self-regulation with a systematic review and meta-analysis of randomized controlled trials. *Arthritis Care & Research*, *62*(10), 1460–1472.

Lee, Y. C., Lu, B., Edwards, R. R., Wasan, A. D., Nassikas, N. J., Clauw, D. J., Solomon, D. H., & Karlson, E. W. (2013). The role of sleep problems in central pain processing in rheumatoid arthritis. *Arthritis & Rheumatism*, *65*(1), 59–68.

Lee, Y. C., Nassikas, N. J., & Clauw, D. J. (2011). The role of the central nervous system in the generation and maintenance of chronic pain in rheumatoid arthritis, osteoarthritis and fibromyalgia. *Arthritis Research & Therapy*, *13*(2), 211.

Lejuez, C. W., Hopko, D. R., Acierno, R., Daughters, S. B., & Pagoto, S. L. (2011). Ten year revision of the brief behavioral activation treatment for depression: Revised treatment manual. *Behavior Modification*, *35*(2), 111–161.

Liu, Y., Hazlewood, G. S., Kaplan, G. G., Eksteen, B., & Barnabe, C. (2016). Impact of obesity on remission and disease activity in rheumatoid arthritis: A systematic review and meta-analysis. *Arthritis Care & Research*, *69*(2), 157–165.

Matcham, F., Rayner, L., Steer, S., & Hotopf, M. (2013). The prevalence of depression in rheumatoid arthritis: A systematic review and meta-analysis. *Rheumatology*, *52*(12), 2136–2148.

McCracken, L. M., & Samuel, V. M. (2007). The role of avoidance, pacing, and other activity patterns in chronic pain. *Pain*, *130*(1–2), 119–125.

McCracken, L. M., Sato, A., Wainwright, D., House, W., & Taylor, G. J. (2014). A feasibility study of brief group-based acceptance and commitment therapy for chronic pain in general practice: Recruitment, attendance, and patient views. *Primary Health Care Research & Development*, *15*(3), 312–323.

Metsios, G. S., Stavropoulos-Kalinoglou, A., van Zanten, J. V., Treharne, G. J., Panoulas, V. F., Douglas, K. M., . . . Kitas, G. D. (2008). Rheumatoid arthritis, cardiovascular disease and physical exercise: A systematic review. *Rheumatology*, *47*(3), 239–248.

Miller, W. R., & Rollnick, S. (2012). *Motivational interviewing: Helping people change* (3rd ed.). New York, NY: The Guilford Press.

Morris, A., Yelin, E. H., Panopalis, P., Julian, L., & Katz, P. P. (2011). Long-term patterns of depression and associations with health and function in a panel study of rheumatoid arthritis. *Journal of Health Psychology*. doi:10.1177/1359105310386635.

National Institute on Alcohol Abuse and Alcoholism. (n.d.). *What is a standard drink?* Retrieved March 18, 2018, from www.niaaa.nih.gov/alcohol-health/overview-alcohol-consumption/what-standard-drink

Nielson, W. R., Jensen, M. P., Karsdorp, P. A., & Vlaeyen, J. W. (2013). Activity pacing in chronic pain: Concepts, evidence, and future directions. *The Clinical Journal of Pain*, *29*(5), 461–468.

Pincus, T., Yazici, Y., & Bergman, M. (2005). Development of a Multi-Dimensional Health Assessment Questionnaire (MDHAQ) for the infrastructure of standard clinical care. *Clinical and Experimental Rheumatology*, *23* (Suppl), S19–28.

Pincus, T., Yazici, Y., & Bergman, M. (2007). A practical guide to scoring a Multi-Dimensional Health Assessment Questionnaire (MDHAQ) and Routine Assessment of Patient Index Data (RAPID) scores in 10–20 seconds for use in standard clinical care, without rulers, calculators, websites or computers. *Best Practice & Research Clinical Rheumatology*, *21*(4), 755–787.

Revenson, T. A., Schiaffino, K. M., Majerovitz, S. D., & Gibofsky, A. (1991). Social support as a double-edged sword: The relation of positive and problematic support to depression among rheumatoid arthritis patients. *Social Science & Medicine*, *33*(7), 807–813.

Schiller, J. S., Lucas, J. W., Ward, B. W., & Peregoy, J. A. (2012). Summary health statistics for US Adults: National health interview survey, 2010. *Vital and Health Statistics. Series 10, Data from The National Health Survey*, *252*, 1–207.

Shojania, K., & Ratzlaff, M. (2010). Group visits for rheumatoid arthritis patients: A pilot study. *Clinical Rheumatology*, *29*(6), 625–628.

Singh, J. A., Furst, D. E., Bharat, A., Curtis, J. R., Kavanaugh, A. F., Kremer, J. M., . . . Saag, K. G. (2012). 2012 Update of the 2008 American College of Rheumatology recommendations for the use of disease-modifying antirheumatic drugs and biologic agents in the treatment of rheumatoid arthritis. *Arthritis Care & Research, 64*(5), 625–639.

Smolen, J. S., Aletaha, D., Bijlsma, J. W., Breedveld, F. C., Boumpas, D., Burmester, G., . . . van der Heijde, D. (2010). Treating rheumatoid arthritis to target: Recommendations of an international task force. *Annals of the Rheumatic Diseases, 69*(4), 631–637.

Sokolove, J., Wagner, C. A., Lahey, L. J., Sayles, H., Duryee, M. J., Reimold, A. M., . . . Mikuls, T. T. R. (2016). Increased inflammation and disease activity among current cigarette smokers with rheumatoid arthritis: A cross-sectional analysis of US veterans. *Rheumatology, 55*(11), 1969–1977.

Stenström, C. H., & Minor, M. A. (2003). Evidence for the benefit of aerobic and strengthening exercise in rheumatoid arthritis. *Arthritis Care & Research, 49*(3), 428–434.

Sullivan, M. J. L., Rodgers, W. M., Wilson, P. M., Bell, G. J., Murray, T. C., & Fraser, S. N. (2002). An experimental investigation of the relation between catastrophizing and activity intolerance. *Pain, 100*, 47–53.

Theis, K. A., Roblin, D. W., Helmick, C. G., & Luo, R. (2018). Prevalence and causes of work disability among working-age U.S. adults, 2011–2013, NHIS. *Disability and Health Journal, 11*(1), 108–115.

Turk, D. C., & Swanson, K. (2007). Efficacy and cost-effectiveness treatment of chronic pain: An analysis and evidence-based synthesis. In M. E. Schatman & A. Campbell (Eds.), *Chronic pain management: Guidelines for multidisciplinary program development* (pp. 15–38). New York, NY: Informa Healthcare.

Turner, J. A., Holtzman, S., & Mancl, L. (2007). Mediators, moderators, and predictors of therapeutic change in cognitive—behavioral therapy for chronic pain. *Pain, 127*(3), 276–286.

Van den Bemt, B. J. F., Zwikker, H. E., & van den Ende, C. H. M. (2012). Medication adherence in patients with rheumatoid arthritis: A critical appraisal of the existing literature. *Expert Review of Clinical Immunology, 8*(4), 337–351.

van Koulil, S., Effting, M., Kraaimaat, F. W., Van Lankveld, W., Van Helmond, T., Cats, H., . . . Evers, A. W. M. (2007). Cognitive—behavioural therapies and exercise programmes for patients with fibromyalgia: State of the art and future directions. *Annals of the Rheumatic Diseases, 66*(5), 571–581.

Veehof, M. M., Oskam, M. J., Schreurs, K. M., & Bohlmeijer, E. T. (2011). Acceptance-based interventions for the treatment of chronic pain: A systematic review and meta-analysis. *Pain, 152*(3), 533–542.

Vitiello, M. V., Rybarczyk, B., Von Korff, M., & Stepanski, E. J. (2009). Cognitive behavioral therapy for insomnia improves sleep and decreases pain in older adults with co-morbid insomnia and osteoarthritis. *Journal of Clinical Sleep Medicine, 15*(4), 355–362.

Vowles, K. E., McCracken, L. M., & Eccleston, C. (2007). Processes of change in treatment for chronic pain: The contributions of pain, acceptance, and catastrophizing. *European Journal of Pain, 11*(7), 779–787.

Vowles, K. E., McCracken, L. M., & O'Brien, J. Z. (2011). Acceptance and values-based action in chronic pain: A three-year follow-up analysis of treatment effectiveness and process. *Behaviour Research and Therapy, 49*(11), 748–755.

Wolfe, F., Clauw, D. J., Fitzcharles, M. A., Goldenberg, D. L., Katz, R. S., Mease, P., . . . Yunus, M. B. (2010). The American college of rheumatology preliminary diagnostic criteria for fibromyalgia and measurement of symptom severity. *Arthritis Care & Research, 62*(5), 600–610.

Wolfe, F., Häuser, W., Hassett, A. L., Katz, R. S., & Walitt, B. T. (2011). The development of fibromyalgia—I: Examination of rates and predictors in patients with rheumatoid arthritis (RA). *Pain, 152*(2), 291–299.

Wolfe, F., Michaud, K., Busch, R. E., Katz, R. S., Rasker, J. J., Shahouri, S. H., . . . Haeuser, W. (2014). Polysymptomatic distress in patients with rheumatoid arthritis: Understanding disproportionate response and its spectrum. *Arthritis Care & Research, 66*(10), 1465–1471.

Zautra, A. J., Davis, M. C., Reich, J. W., Nicassario, P., Tennen, H., Finan, P., . . . Irwin, M. R. (2008). Comparison of cognitive behavioral and mindfulness meditation interventions on adaptation to rheumatoid arthritis for patients with and without history of recurrent depression. *Journal of Consulting and Clinical Psychology, 76*(3), 408.

Appendix 1
Activity Pacing Worksheet

Long-term goal: _____
(e.g., walk on treadmill for 30 minutes)

Step 1: Find your baseline. Record how long you can engage in your goal activity each day without triggering a pain flare.

Day	1	2	3	4	5	6	7	Average
Time								
Example	7 mins	5 mins	6 mins	7 mins	3 mins	4 mins	4 mins	**5.14 mins**

Step 2: Set your first pacing goal. Stick with your goal, even on the tough days! Remember, consistency is key. Record your progress.

Day	8	9	10	11	12	13	14
Goal							
Actual Time							
Example Goal	5 mins	5 mins	5 mins	5 mins	5 mins	5 mins	5 mins
Example Actual Time	5 mins	4 mins	5 mins	4 mins	5 mins	5 mins	5 mins

Step 3: Gradually increase your pacing goal. Remember, some increase in pain is normal, but you shouldn't be experiencing pain flares. Work with your providers to monitor your progress and help decide when to increase your pacing goals.

Day	15	16	17	18	19	20	21
Goal							
Actual Time							
Example Goal	7 mins	7 mins	7 mins	7 mins	7 mins	10 mins	10 mins
Example Actual Time	7 mins	6 mins	7 mins	7 mins	7 mins	9 mins	10 mins
Day	22	23	24	25	26	27	28
Goal							
Actual Time							

Appendix 2
Activity and Pain Diary

Pain Diary	Monday	Tuesday	Wednesday	Thursday	Friday	Saturday	Sunday
					0 (No Pain at All) to 10 (Worst Pain Possible)		
Morning							
	Avg Pain: ___	Avg Pain: ___	Avg Pain: ___	Avg Pain: ___	Avg Pain: ___	Avg Pain: ___	Avg Pain: ___
Afternoon							
	Avg Pain: ___	Avg Pain: ___	Avg Pain: ___	Avg Pain: ___	Avg Pain: ___	Avg Pain: ___	Avg Pain: ___
Evening							
	Avg Pain: ___	Avg Pain: ___	Avg Pain: ___	Avg Pain: ___	Avg Pain: ___	Avg Pain: ___	Avg Pain: ___

Weekly Goals:

Appendix 3
Weekly Functional Assessment Measure

1. Please rate your pain over the past week [0 (none)–10 (worst imaginable)]:

   Highest pain: _____
   Lowest pain: _____
   Average pain: _____
   Pain right now: _____

2. How much has pain interfered with the following over the past week [0 (not at all)–10 (completely)]?

   Daily activity: _____
   Mood: _____
   Quality of life: _____

3. Please describe your sleep over the past week:

   Average hours/night: _____
   Average quality [0 (not at all rested)—10 (completely rested)]: _____
   Difficulties (check those that apply):
   __ Falling asleep
   __ Staying asleep
   __ Waking up several times

4. How would you describe your mood over the past week?

   __ Poor
   __ Fair/Average
   __ Good

My mood was:
__ Worse than the week before
__ The same as the week before
__ Better than the week before

5. Please describe any exercise over the past week:

   Type of exercise: _____
   Duration of exercise: _____ minutes
   Number of days: _____

6. Did you achieve the goals that you set during the previous session? If no, what got in the way?

   _____

   _____

15

Urological Chronic Pelvic Pain Syndromes

Dean A. Tripp, Valentina Mihajlovic,
and J. Curtis Nickel

Introduction

Chronic pelvic pain is a common and debilitating set of disorders that affects both men and women. In women, chronic pelvic pain has a widespread etiology, as the reproductive tract, gastrointestinal system, urological organs, musculoskeletal system, and neurological system may all be involved (Howard, 2003). In men, however, chronic pelvic pain mainly manifests as prostatitis and may be due to bacterial infections of the urinary tract, detrusor-sphincter dysfunction, immunological dysfunction, interstitial cystitis, and/or neuropathic pain (Wagenlehner, Naber, Bschleipfer, Brähler, & Weidner, 2009). Considering the wide array of conditions and etiologies, this chapter focuses on a subset of chronic pelvic pain conditions known as urological chronic pelvic pain syndromes. However, we believe that much of the information and subsequent clinical implications/intervention suggestions would be relevant to other chronic pelvic pain conditions as well.

Urological chronic pelvic pain syndromes (UCPPS) present a significant healthcare challenge and are associated with a host of intra- and interpersonal difficulties, such as relationship challenges, disability, and overall decreased quality of life (QoL) primarily driven by pain. Two prominent urologic chronic pelvic pain conditions are chronic prostatitis/chronic pelvic pain syndrome (CP/CPPS) in males and interstitial cystitis/bladder pain syndrome (IC/BPS) diagnosed primarily in females. UCPPS has been notoriously difficult to diagnose and categorize (Nickel, 2002) but generally manifests as chronic pelvic/genital pain, along with variable urinary disturbances and sexual dysfunction (Krieger, Nyberg, & Nickel, 1999). Both CP/CPPS and IC/BPS can involve inflammatory and/or neurogenic findings in the bladder and/or prostate. However, no pathognomonic, histological, or radiological findings exist as a basis for diagnosis. As such, UCPPS are symptom complexes and diagnoses of exclusion, rather than specific disease entities (Mold-win, 2002).

The hallmark symptom of UCPPS is pain, which is often described in terms of its sensory components (e.g., burning, throbbing). However, as documented previously in the pain literature, the expression and impact of pain vary considerably within the context of differing psychosocial, interpersonal, behavioral, and biological traits of the individual patient and his/her environment (Sullivan et al., 2001). Cognitive-behavioral pain models commonly are used to guide interventions for chronic pain. These models and subsequent interventions emphasize the role of coping styles and skills in contributing to the individual's subjective experience of pain. Patient self-regulation is a key process in any type of chronic pain management. Indeed, the patient's self-awareness and problem-solving abilities mold his/her pain interpretations along with pain management strategies (Schaeffer et al., 2002; Tripp et al., 2006). For example, when patients believe they are unable to self-manage a situation or physical sensation and that the environment is not supportive, varying degrees of anxiety and appraisals of helplessness may arise, exacerbating pain.

Confirming and extending the initial work of Tripp et al. (2012) and Nickel and Tripp (2015), the Multidisciplinary Approach to the Study of Chronic Pelvic Pain (MAPP) Research Network recently conducted a study that characterized the location and spatial distribution of whole-body pain in UCPPS patients using a body map (Lai et al., 2017). Patients completed a battery of baseline measures, which included a body map describing the location of pain during the last week. Twenty-five percent of patients reported pelvic pain only, and of the 75% who reported pain beyond the pelvis, 38% reported widespread pain. Importantly, widespread pain was associated with greater non-pelvic pain severity and poorer psychosocial health; patients with a greater number of pain locations had greater non-pelvic pain severity, sleep disturbance, depression, anxiety, psychological stress, negative affect scores, and worse quality of life. As it relates to clinical practice, this research suggests that a body pain map (Figure 15.1) might aid in screening for patients with a high psychosocial burden and, based upon the patient's discrete clinical characteristics (i.e., localized versus systemic pain), inform personalized treatment.

Due to significant psychological comorbidities in patients with UCPPS, this chapter focuses on several empirically supported pain-associated psychosocial risk factors for UCPPS. Anchored in a biopsychosocial framework, we recognize and appreciate how psychological and environmental deficits reported by UCPPS patients are associated with fluctuations in pain and urinary symptoms that result in patient disability and ultimately a lower QoL. With no confirmed cure in sight, symptom and pain management for patient adjustment is strongly recommended; physicians need to recognize the psychosocial factors of UCPPS and strategize management options for the patient. As such, this chapter also highlights several clinical interventions that can be used to manage symptoms, including an

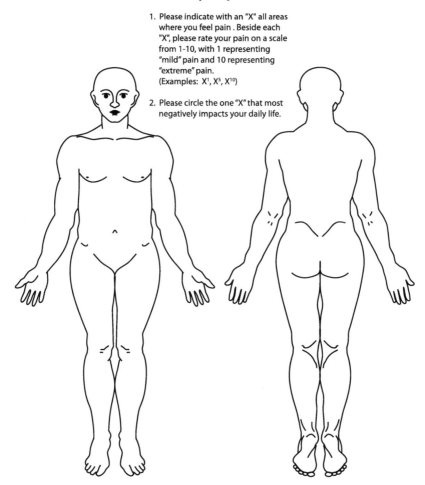

Where is your pain?

1. Please indicate with an "X" all areas where you feel pain . Beside each "X", please rate your pain on a scale from 1-10, with 1 representing "mild" pain and 10 representing "extreme" pain.
   (Examples: X^1, X^5, X^{10})

2. Please circle the one "X" that most negatively impacts your daily life.

Figure 15.1   Body Map to Indicate the Location of Pain

extensive outline of an empirically based therapeutic cognitive-behavioral model of symptom management.

Chronic Prostatitis/Chronic Pelvic Pain Syndrome (CP/CPPS)

The National Institutes of Health (NIH) define CP/CPPS as pelvic pain present for at least three of the previous six months, with or without voiding symptoms, and with no evidence of uropathogenic bacterial infection (Nickel, 2009). The hallmark symptom of CP/CPPS is persistent pain in the perineum, pelvic area, and/or genitalia (Krieger et al., 1999; Schaeffer et al., 2002). Prostatitis can be either bacterial or abacterial. Acute and chronic bacterial prostatitis (i.e., Category 1 and Category 2, respectively) are the best understood but least common of the prostatitis syndromes. CP/CPPS, with or without inflammation, is the third and most common category of prostatitis syndrome (Nickel, Downey, Hunter, & Clark, 2001). The fourth category is asymptomatic inflammatory prostatitis, in which white blood cells are present in semen-expressed prostatic secretions (EPS) or post-prostate massage urine samples (VB3) but with no associated pain.

Prevalence estimates indicate that CP/CPPS is one of the most common urological conditions in men; prostatitis accounts for 8% of urology outpatient visits in the United States and 3% in Canada (Nickel, Downey, Nickel, & Clark, 2002). CP/CPPS symptoms become most prominent between 35 and 65 years of age (Schaeffer et al., 2002; Collins, Stafford, O'Leary, & Barry, 1999). Prostatitis is the most common urologic diagnosis in men under age 50 and follows only benign prostatic hyperplasia in men over 50 (McBryde & Redington, 2002; Collins et al., 1999). Symptoms range considerably across socioeconomic status, race, and age. For example, Schaeffer et al. (2002) found that patients who were younger, had lower education, lower income, and were unemployed experienced more chronic pelvic pain symptoms (Schaeffer et al., 2002). The North American prevalence of CP/CPPS symptoms varies between 2% and 16% (Krieger et al., 1999; Schaeffer et al., 2002). Similar prevalence rates are found internationally, with estimated rates of 5% in Japan, 8% in China, 14% in Italy, 8% in Australia, and 12% in Nigeria (Kunishima, Mori, Kitamura, Satoh, & Tsukamoto, 2006; Liang et al., 2009; Bartoletti et al., 2007; Ferris et al., 2009; Ejike & Ezeanyika, 2008). Managing CP/CPPS comes at significant medical costs, upwards of $4,000 annually per patient (Calhoun et al., 2004).

Interstitial Cystitis/Bladder Pain Syndrome (IC/BPS)

The NIH, International Society for the Study of Bladder Pain Syndrome (ESSIC), and World Health Organization committees define IC/BPS as consisting of significant symptoms of chronic pelvic pain perceived to be related to the bladder, usually accompanied by other urinary symptoms, such as daytime and nighttime urinary frequency and/or urgency (Hanno, 2008). Characteristically, pain increases with bladder filling and improves with bladder emptying. Prevalence rates of IC/BPS are approximately 0.83–2.71% in women and 0.25–1.22% in men, with a 5:1 to 10:1 female preponderance (Clemens et al., 2007). IC/BPS alone is responsible for over four million outpatient physician or clinic visits per year in the United States (Chung, Liu, Li, & Lin, 2014), with associated costs equal to or greater than those associated with back pain, fibromyalgia, rheumatoid arthritis, and peripheral neuropathy (Clemens, Markossian, & Calhoun, 2009). It is reported that 40–50% of IC/BPS patients report significant work-related disability, including less work participation and long-term earning (Beckett, Elliott, Clemens, Ewing, & Berry, 2014; Ratner, Slade, & Greene, 1994).

Epidemiological studies of IC/BPS face obstacles, as there is no international consensus on the diagnosis of IC/BPS. Due to variations in diagnostic criteria for IC/BPS, prevalence rates across the world differ, with an estimation of IC/BPS prevalence worldwide previously suggested at approximately 2% (Hanno, 2005). The prevalence of IC/PBS has been reported as high as 2.6% in a cross-sectional Boston study with inclusion criteria that included self-reported pain associated with bladder filling that was relieved by urination present for at least three months (Hall et al., 2008). In another USA study, the prevalence rates of self-reported IC/PBS, IC/PBS-like symptoms, and pelvic pain among 823 female controls in the community were 3.7%, 4.4%, and 17.3%, respectively (Ibrahim, Diokno, Killinger, Carrico, & Peters, 2007).

Many IC/BPS patients report multiple pain locations outside of the pelvis. In an effort to enrich the understanding of IC/BPS pain experiences, Tripp et al. (2012) was the first to compare pain in patients with IC/BPS and controls using a whole-body diagram of visible body areas. They examined the association between patient adjustment factors and increasing numbers of body pain areas, which they refer to as pain phenotypes, in 193 female IC/BPS patients and 115 age-matched controls. Results showed that, compared to controls, patients reported more body pain locations (60% of controls had some sort of pain; 100% of patients had pelvic pain and 73% reported pain outside of the pelvis as well), pain severity, urinary symptoms, depression, pain catastrophizing, and diminished QoL. Interestingly, as the number of body pain locations increased, patients reported poorer psychosocial adjustment and diminished physical QoL; however, catastrophizing and low scores for mental QoL were consistent across all patients.

Following this work, the researchers posited that two distinct clinical phenotypes could be used to describe patients with UCPPS: pelvic pain only and pelvic pain beyond—that is, pain in the pelvic site, and pain in at least one pelvic site and at least one site outside the pelvic area, respectively (Clemens, 2014). To test that applicability of this characterization in women with IC/BPS, Nickel and Tripp (2015) examined body pain location mapping, and associated medical and psychosocial variables, in 173 female IC/BPS patients. They found that patients with pelvic pain beyond reported increased sensory type pain, poorer physical QoL, and greater somatic depression and sleep disturbance than patients with pelvic pain only, though the pelvic pain only group had higher sexual pain scores. Taken together, Nickel and Tripp (2015) support the existence of clinically relevant and distinct patient phenotypes in IC/BPS, contributing evidence for the concept of distinct clinical phenotypes in UCPPS (Clemens, 2014).

Recent work by Lai et al. (2017) confirmed this earlier work and added that 38% of their sample reported widespread pain. This work confirmed that widespread pain was associated with greater severity and poorer psychosocial health and that patients with a greater number of pain locations had greater non-pelvic pain severity, depression, anxiety, and worse quality of life.

The Advantage of Biopsychosocial Models

Current conceptualizations of chronic pain and the nature of individual differences in pain perception have been shaped by centuries of theoretical writings and major shifts in both culture and science (for review, see Rey, 1993). The traditional biomedical model of pain, which focused exclusively on pathophysiological explanations for persistent pain and assumed a patient's report of pain directly correlated with physical pathology (Gatchel, 1999), has been criticized; chronic pelvic pain (like most other forms of chronic pain) no longer is perceived as solely a physical phenomenon, and purely medical interventions are limited in efficacy. As suggested by Nickel, Downey, Ardern, Clark, and Nickel (2004), urological practitioners recognize that managing patients diagnosed with CP/CPPS is extremely challenging and often unsuccessful, especially with data suggesting that treatment strategies based on sequential application of monotherapies for patients with a long history of severe CP/CPPS may be suboptimal.

Other reviews of the available literature also reveal a paucity of data from properly designed and implemented clinical trials on which to justify an evidence-based approach to the treatment of CP/CPPS (McNaughton-Collins, MacDonald, & Wilt, 2000). Effective treatment for CP/CPPS remains elusive, likely due to its multifactorial pathogenesis (Schaeffer, 2006; Magistro et al., 2016).

Magistro and colleagues (2016) conducted a comprehensive review of the published literature on the treatment of CP/CPPS and practical evidence-based recommendations for management of symptoms, in an effort to formulate a best practice guideline for the management of CP/CPPS. They examined randomized controlled trials that evaluated antibiotics, α-blockers, anti-inflammatory and immune-modulating substances, hormonal agents, phytotherapeutics, neuromodulatory drugs, agents that modify bladder function, and physical treatment options. These failed to reveal a clear therapeutic benefit. Due to the multifactorial pathophysiology and various clinical presentations of CP/CPPS, management demands an individualized approach centered on the clinical profile of each patient. In summary, the biomedical model to date has not been solely successful in advancing a cure for CP/CPPS.

Similarly, Giannantoni and colleagues (2012) looked at the management of IC/BPS in the current literature. After examining randomized and non-randomized controlled trials of IC/BPS symptom management, they found that cyclosporine A and amitriptyline showed the greatest effect on symptom reduction in randomized trials and that the most frequently adopted treatment in non-randomized trials was oral pentosan polysulfate, with botulinum A toxin intradetrusorial injections becoming increasingly popular. Taken together, the lack of understanding of the pathophysiology of UCPPS reveals an inability to propose definitive conclusions about a gold standard intervention. Nevertheless, efforts continue for optimizing care of UCPPS patients.

Indeed, the data suggest that the experience and perception of pain is complex and maintained by biomedical, psychosocial, and behavioral variables whose associations are likely to evolve over time within any one person. A biopsycho-social model outlines illness as a dynamic and reciprocal process and integrates alternative physiological, psychological, and social-contextual variables that may affect and/or perpetuate pain. This model provides advantages over the biomedi-cal model (especially when examining patient reactivity to pain) by considering multiple facets of the patient's experience, including physical function, demo-graphic information (e.g., age, race, socioeconomic status), cognitive-behavioral functioning, and the impact of the patient's environment, including aspects of social support.

Specifically, a biopsychosocial model of pain asserts that biological aspects of chronic illness (e.g., changes in muscles, joints, or nerves generating nociceptive input) affect both psychological factors (e.g., catastrophizing, fear, helplessness) and the individual's social context (e.g., social activity, activities of daily living, interpersonal relationships) (Turk & Okifuji, 2002). Following nociceptive inputs, the perception or interpretation of this pain occurs, making individual patient characteristics central components of adaptive and/or maladaptive responses. Individual patient responses to pain undoubtedly are influenced by long-held beliefs about one's ability or inability to manage pain. Beliefs that self-generated coping responses likely will not be beneficial to the goal of managing pain are suggested to develop over a lifetime of somatic and interpersonal experiences and are referred to as low self-efficacy (Bandura, 1997; Chong, Cogan, Ran-dolph, & Racz, 2001; Jackson, Iezzi, Gunderson, Nagasaka, & Fritch, 2002; Jensen, Turner, & Romano, 1991). Moreover, beliefs of poor ability in self-management are associated with negative pain appraisals, which in turn influence subsequent coping attempts (Sullivan et al., 2001). As such, treatment approaches informed by this model and that integrate psychosocial interventions likely will contribute to improved patient outcomes.

Psychosocial Factors in CP/CPPS

Case conceptualization and treatment from a biopsychosocial perspective focus on providing the individual with specific techniques designed to help increase feel-ings of control over persistent and problematic symptoms like pain and secondary functional impact across a variety of domains. Essential to biopsychosocial pain models is identifying the most relevant physical, psychological, and environmental factors of the population at risk that contribute to the pain experience. Targeting modification of sensory, cognitive, behavioral, and environmental variables helps the patient develop greater symptom self-management. Research has identified several of the variables particularly relevant to the UCPPS patient population.

Stress/Anxiety

Chronic pain and stress have a bidirectional relationship. Chronic pain is associ-ated with dysregulation of the stress response system, including the HPA axis and the sympathetic nervous system, which may be important mechanisms under-lying UCPPS symptoms. Anxiety and stress are highly comorbid with UCPPS symptoms (e.g., CP/CPPS specifically in Egan & Krieger, 1994). Patients with CP/CPPS report greater stress, depression, anxiety, somatization, and obsessive-compulsive behavior and have greater HPA axis dysregulation than controls as shown in awakening cortisol responses. For example, in one study, patients' scores were 1.5 and 4 times higher than the controls' scores on measures of stress and anxiety, respectively (Anderson, Orenberg, Chan, Morey, & Flores, 2008).

CP/CPPS also is associated with symptoms (like pain or psychological seque-lae) that contribute to altered HPA axis responses under acute stress (Anderson, Orenberg, Morey, Chavez, & Chan, 2009). Cortisol exerts an anti-inflammatory effect, and an abnormally low cortisol level also may contribute to medical comorbidities through a pro-inflammatory state (Nijm & Jonasson, 2009). In CP/CPPS, stress may be assessed directly through cytokine levels. One study found that the degree of spousal concern and support correlates with lower seminal plasma IL-6 and IL-10, suggesting a positive physiological correlate to lowered stress (Miller et al., 2002).

Patients with IC/BPS report high medical comorbidity associated with greater pain, poor physical QoL, depression, sexual dysfunction, and stress (Nickel et al., 2010a, 2010b). IC/BPS-associated stress and anxiety are important markers of initiating and worsening functional urinary symptoms (Macaulay, Stern, Hol-mes, & Stanton, 1987; Baldoni, Ercolani, Baldaro, & Trombini, 1995). More than 60% of patients with IC/BPS report symptom exacerbation with stress (Koziol, Clark, Gittes, & Tan, 1993), with acute stress increasing bladder pain and urgency (Lutgendorf, Kreder, & Rothrock, 2000). The association between stress and pain increases when the severity of other symptoms increases (Rothrock, Lutgendorf, Kreder, Ratliff, & Zimmerman, 2001).

Researchers have posited a potential genetic link between IC/BPS and anxiety: compared to controls, patients with IC/BPS have a four-fold higher incidence of panic disorder (Weissman et al., 2004). Animal models also suggest a stress/anxiety symptom connection, with protracted psychological stress boosting bladder pain responses in high anxiety rats (Robbins, DeBerry, & Ness, 2007). Furthermore, patients with IC/BPS exhibit increased defensive emotional responses to threat-ening abdominal pain. Specifically, they demonstrate heightened perception—in the form of an increased startle response—to threatening, anticipatory bladder signals (Twiss et al., 2009). Finally, stress and pain may be exacerbated in IC/BPS by dysfunctional cognitive filtering, or attentional bias to pain amplification, in the central nervous system (Kilpatrick et al., 2010). Taken together, this body of research suggests that stress, whether from physical symptoms or psychosocial fac-tors, interacts in tandem with IC/BPS pain.

Although the impact of stress/anxiety on CP/CPPS and IC/BPS often is studied separately, we believe that the relationship between stress and UCPPS is generalizable. Fortunately, stress and its cognitive-emotional subcomponents are treatable targets. Thus, urologists, physiotherapists, and psychologists have begun developing and testing cognitive-behavioral management interventions in UCPPS populations (e.g., Anderson, Wise, Sawyer, & Chan, 2005; Brünahl et al., 2018; Nickel, Mullins, & Tripp, 2008; Tripp, Nickel, & Katz, 2011). Indeed, as discussed later in this chapter, some of the UCPPS treatment models developed are optimized for empirically supported psychosocial risk factor reduction for CP/CPPS (Brünahl et al., 2018; Nickel, Mullins, et al., 2008; Tripp et al., 2011) and are being examined in ongoing randomized controlled trials in IC/BPS patients by our group (discussed in the clinical interventions section of the chapter).

Given that negative self-talk has a strong negative impact on how patients feel and behave, common to all of these programs are interventions promoting the identification and disputing of such patterns (Brünahl et al., 2018; Nickel, Mullins, et al., 2008; Tripp et al., 2011). Simply talking with and trying to understand patient interpretations of stressful events (and their reactions to such stressors) can help adjust their internal dialogue and direct more health-focused behavior. Patients who perceive their environment as a potential source of pain suffer diminished life satisfaction and emotional adaptation. However, activities like walking and social engagement are associated with improved illness severity and QoL (Webster & Brennan, 1998).

Depression

Depression has been a concern for decades in urological health. Depression and CP/CPPS are significantly comorbid, with CP/CPPS patients having higher rates of depression than controls (Alexander & Trissel, 1996; Berghuis, Heiman, Rothman, & Berger, 1996). The literature suggests that almost 80% of patients with CP/CPPS report depression, with 5% reporting suicidal thinking (Alexander & Trissel, 1996). Another study found that 60% of patients with CP/CPPS went on to meet criteria for major depression, although none had received a diagnosis of or medication for depression (Egan & Krieger, 1994). Still others add that suicidal thinking is more common in patients with CP/CPPS than in healthy men (Mehik, Hellström, Sarpola, Lukkarinen, & Järvelin, 2001).

Pain and urinary symptoms also increase with depression, which is bidirectionally associated with early chronic prostatitis-like symptoms (Ku, Jeon, Kim, Lee, & Park, 2002). Women suffering from IC/BPS also are at risk for depression. Urinary frequency and urgency, depression scores, and lower education level were independent predictors of worse symptom severity in IC/BPS and CP/CPPS, with depression acting as one of the strongest predictors of symptom severity (Clemens, Brown, Kozloff, & Calhoun, 2006).

There is also some evidence that preexisting depression leads to worse outcomes in chronic pain. However, it is unclear whether baseline chronic pain affects outcomes in depression, and what variables mediate the relationship between pain and depression, especially in the CP/CPPS population (Williams & Shäfer, 2016). It also is unclear whether urinary-specific symptoms play a role in depression. Some studies have found that pain exclusively, not urinary symptoms, is associated with depression, and that pain and urinary symptoms in UCPPS should be assessed and interpreted separately (Griffith et al., 2015). However, in other samples, pain and urinary symptoms predict depression when combined into one construct (Katz et al., 2013). Questionnaires such as the NIH Chronic Prostatitis Symptom Index (Litwin et al., 1999), the O'Leary Sant Interstitial Cystitis Symptom and Problem Indices (O'Leary, Sant, Fowler, Whitmore, & Spolarich-Kroll, 1997), the McGill Pain Questionnaire (Melzack, 1975), and the Patient Health Questionnaire (Kroenke, Spitzer, & Williams, 2001) are examples of assessment tools available to evaluate the relationship between pain, urinary symptoms, and depression in both clinical practice and research.

The difficulties experienced by patients with chronic pelvic pain clearly are pervasive. One such difficulty is the co-occurrence of depression and anxiety. In a study comparing healthy controls to men and women with UCPPS, those with chronic pelvic pain experienced higher depression and anxiety, a decreased QoL, more difficulties with sleep and sexual functioning, higher levels of general stress, more childhood and adult trauma, worse coping with pain and illness, self-reported deficits in memory and concentration, and more widespread pain symptoms (Naliboff et al., 2015). Compared to men with UCPPS, women with UCPPS had more deficits in physical aspects of QoL, more childhood adversity and more non-urologic symptoms, including pain; this suggests that men and women experience UCPPS differently.

Treating depression is an important component of interdisciplinary management of chronic pelvic pain patients. Unfortunately, studies suggest that when compared to non-patients with anxiety and/or depression, patients with urological pain syndromes may experience less clinical benefit from medications for anxiety and depression (Clemens, Brown, & Calhoun, 2008). Pain and depression treatment outcome research suggests that referral for behavioral interventions, as discussed in the final section of this chapter, may be useful for UCCPS patients with clinical depression (Nickel et al., 2010b).

Caution must always to be exercised when managing depression. Patients with notable depression should be monitored appropriately by the clinic nurse or referred practitioner, particularly if the urologist suspects suicidal tendencies. Due to the strong comorbidity of depression and UCPPS, routine screening should be available for all incoming patients. It is concerning that many patients may be suffering from depressive symptoms without active treatment engagement for these symptoms. Further, a recent study highlighted that psychosocial risk factors are worrisome over and above both IC/BPS-specific symptoms and patient pain experience in predicting suicidal thinking in IC/BPS populations; depression was a predictor of patient distress in IC/BPS, with more than one in five patients reporting having had suicidal thoughts (Tripp et al., 2016).

Future research is needed to clarify the extent to which depression occurs and treatment is available for patients suffering from UCPPS. To our knowledge, no research has provided a clear message on the overall problem in the field with either the under-diagnosing or undertreatment of depressive symptoms. This research, which would have clear implications for clinical recommendations, may motivate universal psychosocial screening in this population.

Interpersonal Factors

Research provides some insights into how interpersonal responses and social support from romantic partners may impact patient functioning. Partner responses can be classified into three categories: *solicitous* (e.g., tries to get me to rest), *distracting* (e.g., tries to get me involved in some activity), and *negative* (e.g., gets angry with me) (Kerns, Turk, & Rudy, 1985). Among men with CP/CPPS, solicitous responses from partners were associated with worse patient adjustment and with higher levels of disability (Ginting, Tripp, & Nickel, 2011). However, interpreting clinical implications from this data may be challenging; it is possible that the partners responded solicitously in reaction to the patients' pain and levels of disability in situations where the patients physically were incapable of completing certain tasks and thus required their partners' help.

Studies with IC/BPS patients also have examined the influence of partner support and its association with pain, QoL, depression, and disability (Ginting, Tripp, Nickel, & Fitzgerald et al., 2011). Partner attempts at distraction (in response to patient pain behavior) diminished the impact of pain on mental QoL, but not physical QoL, depression, or disability. These results also indicated that at higher levels of distracting responses, the correlation between pain and mental QoL was not significant. By contrast, the correlation between pain and mental QoL was significant at moderate and lower levels of distracting partner responses.

Some results also highlight sexuality as a significant relationship concern for men with CP/CPPS. For example, reductions in frequency of sexual contacts have been reported by as many as 85% of men with CP/CPPS, and more than 50% report periodic or total impotence secondary to other symptoms like pain (Mehik et al., 2001). In comparison to control males, men with CP/CPPS report greater sexual dysfunction (i.e., lower libido, more erectile problems, impaired orgasm) and greater symptoms of depression (Smith, Pukall, Tripp, & Nickel, 2007). However, these men did not report significantly decreased sexual satisfaction or relationship functioning when compared to male controls. These results suggest that while men with CP/CPPS and their partners may experience sexual difficulties, CP/CPPS may not have a large negative impact on patients' intimate relationships.

Several studies have investigated sexual functioning in women with IC/BPS (Lui et al., 2014; Peters et al., 2007; Bogart, Suttorp, Elliott, Clemens, & Berry, 2011; Ottem, Carr, Perks, Lee, & Telchman, 2007; Simon, Landis, Erickson, & Nyberg, 1997; Whitmore, Siegel, & Kellogg-Spadt, 2007; Nickel et al., 2007). Taken together, the results suggest that IC/BPS symptoms have considerable influence on patients' sexual functioning. In comparison to controls, women with IC/BPS had significantly more sexual dysfunction and distress (Peters et al., 2007; Bogart et al., 2011; Ottem et al., 2007; Simon et al., 1997). Upwards of 90%

of women with IC/BPS reported varying degrees of lower abdominal, urethral, lower back, and vaginal pain (Whitmore et al., 2007). In addition to the physical impact on sexual functioning, IC/BPS sexual dysfunction symptoms have an emotional impact. Nickel et al. (2007) identified sexual functioning as a primary predictor of mental QoL in women with long-standing IC/BPS.

The UCPPS research on social support provides insights into intervention planning. For example, couples who were provided a motivational therapeutic assessment experienced significant decreases in pain, negative mood, and increases in martial satisfaction and positive mood from baseline to post-assessment when compared to a control group that received education about the gate control theory of pain (Miller, Cano, & Wurm, 2013). Motivational therapeutic assessment is based upon therapeutic models of assessment and motivational interviewing (collaborative conversations to strengthen a person's own motivation for and commitment to change). In this study, couples received feedback on their assessment in an empathic, nonjudgmental, and collaborative manner while using effective brief motivational interviewing strategies to encourage change talk (i.e., statements or nonverbal communications indicating the patient may be considering the possibility of changing his/her behavior). The motivational interviewing strategies included open-ended questioning, eliciting and affirming change talk, asking permission to share information, and summarizing responses (Miller et al., 2013). The principles applied in the motivational therapeutic assessment were selected from *Motivational Interviewing in Healthcare: Helping Patients Change Behavior* (Rollnick, Miller, & Butler, 2007) and *Building Motivational Interviewing Skills: A Practitioner Workbook* (Rosengren, 2009).

In another study, men with CP/CPPS who were distracted from their pain by their partner reportedly were more able to continue with their voluntary and obligatory activities of daily living, thereby diminishing the impact of their pain on their functional disability (Ginting et al., 2011). These researchers suggested that partners avoid solicitous responses, as men need to be more active in their lives in order to counter the high association between pain and disability. These clinical suggestions can be discussed within a general framework exploring how pain influences how patients "live their lives," probing for the types of social support they perceive and receive from their partners and others. Encouraging men to stay as active as possible despite the pain and symptoms is likely an important component of preventing disability. Indeed, exercise programs for CP/CPPS produced significant reductions in total chronic prostatitis symptoms, pain measures, and symptom QoL impact (Giubilei et al., 2007). Women with IC/BPS benefited from partner distraction from pain behavior, showing a diminished impact of pain on mental QoL (Ginting, Tripp, Nickel, & Fitzgerald et al., 2011).

Such findings have important clinical implications for couples impacted by UCPPS for whom adjunctive dyad-level psychosocial interventions, including psychoeducation for partners, should be considered. A behavioral counselor, an attending nurse, or a support group setting could deliver these psychoeducational interventions to partners about possible responses to expressions of patient pain.

Additionally, research focused on chronic musculoskeletal pain also lends itself to the importance of promoting functional autonomy as a buffer for the impact of pain intensity on pain-related disability (Matos, Bernardes, Goubert, & Beyers, 2017). This encompasses providing behavioral help and emotional/esteem support that aims to increase one's confidence to continue functioning and engaging in social and physical activities, despite pain. Though not yet examined in a chronic pelvic pain population, we believe that increasing individuals' knowledge and self-management skills to rely on others' support to improve functional autonomy is important in order to overcome functional obstacles posed by pain.

Quality of Life (QoL)

UCPPS symptoms severely impact patient QoL, a term used to broadly describe how well people function in life and their discernment of that well-being. There are many psychological factors contributing to the relationship between QoL and pain, including social support, pain-coping strategies, cognitive appraisals of pain, and other beliefs about pain. Overall, UCPPS patients report diminished QoL, partially resulting from the physician's frequent inability to offer biomedical treatments for these disabling syndromes (Kaye & Moldwin, 2009).

CP/CPPS symptoms are suggested to have a negative effect on QoL similar to having active Crohn's disease or a recent myocardial infarct (Collins, Stafford, O'Leary, & Barry, 1998; Weir, Browne, Roberts, Tunks, & Gafni, 1994; Wenninger, Heiman, Rothman, Berghuis, & Berger, 1996). Studies indicate that most men with CP/CPPS report significantly worse QoL than men without CP/CPPS (Ku, Kim, Lee, & Park, 2001; Turner et al., 2002). Wenninger et al. (1996) found that the most severe impact of CP/CPPS seemed to be on social interaction.

The primary symptom of CP/CPPS is persistent pain, which is also the optimum criterion in differentiating patients with CP, controls, and those with genitourinary problems like benign prostatic hyperplasia (McNaughton-Collins et al., 2001). Increased pain in men diagnosed with CP/CPPS is associated with worse QoL and greater overall symptom presentation (Ku et al., 2001; Litwin et al., 1999). McNaughton-Collins et al. (2002) reported that poorer mental and physical components of QoL were associated with worsening CP/CPPS symptom severity within the National Institutes of Health Chronic Prostatitis Cohort study. Studies also have found that those suffering IC/BPS experience poor QoL due to physical difficulties, emotion regulation issues, and decreased energy levels (Rothrock, Lutgendorf, Hoffman, & Kreder, 2002).

Although previous reports indicate that urinary scores and pain are associated with poorer QoL in patients with CP/CPPS in primary care and urology clinics (Turner et al., 2002), more recent CP/CPPS QoL data has shown that pain intensity acts as the strongest predictor of QoL, even after controlling for age, urinary scores, depressive symptoms, and partner status in adjusted regression models (Tripp, Nickel, Landis, Wang, Knauss, & the CPCRN Study Group, 2004). In particular, although pain and urinary symptoms both were associated with an increased likelihood of impaired QoL, pain contributed more than urinary symptoms. Other studies examining pain syndromes also have identified pain severity as the most influential factor for QoL (Ku et al., 2004). Further, Turner et al. (2002), examining men in primary care settings, reported that worse QoL was associated with greater pain and urinary symptoms, and that pain was associated more robustly with worse QoL than were urinary symptoms.

Catastrophizing

Pain-related catastrophizing is a negative, exaggerated cognitive schema that can emerge when a patient is in, or anticipates, pain (Sullivan, Bishop, & Pivik, 1995). Catastrophizing is assessed using the Pain Catastrophizing Scale (Sullivan et al., 1995) and captures three interrelated factors: rumination (inability to redirect thoughts away from the pain), magnification (expectancies for negative outcomes), and helplessness (perception that one is unable to do anything to reduce the pain's intensity). Rumination and magnification tend to be reactionary or proximal cognitive responses to pain, whereas helplessness may develop following persistent ruminative thoughts and/or protracted pain. There is little doubt that helplessness about one's pain and one's perceived ability to manage it are associated with feelings of despair.

Catastrophizing has long been known in the pain literature as a robust pain predictor in clinical and nonclinical samples (Sullivan et al., 1995). The first CP/CPPS catastrophizing study showed that it was associated with greater disability, depression, urinary symptoms, and pain (Tripp et al., 2006). Further, the helplessness factor was the strongest pain predictor, even when urinary symptoms and depression were controlled. Indeed, variables related to QoL, mood, catastrophizing, and the presence of widespread somatic symptoms showed the largest effect sizes when patients with UCPPS were compared to healthy controls (Naliboff et al., 2015).

Diminished mental QoL in men with CP/CPPS also has been predicted by greater helplessness and lower support from friends and family, even when demographics, medical status, and other psychosocial variables were controlled (Nickel et al., 2008). Helplessness, a predominant pain and QoL predictor in CP/CPPS, commonly is reported by patients with longer pain durations (four to seven years) (Sullivan, Stanish, Sullivan, & Tripp, 2002). The literature suggests that experiencing chronic symptoms, like pain, while also not receiving effective standard medical therapy may generate this helplessness in patients over time (Tripp & Nickel, 2011). However, cognitive-behavioral intervention programs have proven to be effective in reducing catastrophizing (Tripp et al., 2011).

In initial IC/BPS studies, patients reporting greater catastrophizing also reported greater depression, poorer mental health, social functioning, and vitality, and greater pain (Rothrock, Lutgendorf, & Kreder, 2003). A more recent cohort study of female patients with IC/BPS examined the unique and shared associations of patient QoL, IC/BPS symptoms, sexual functioning, pain, and

381

psychosocial factors (Tripp et al., 2009). Helplessness catastrophizing was the primary predictor of diminished mental QoL over the significant effects of factors such as older age. Catastrophizing is key in the relationships between pain and depression, and pain and disability, in IC/BPS patients (Crawford, 2017).

Consistent with the biopsychosocial model, research by Crawford (2017) demonstrates that a physical state (pain) can influence psychological processes (catastrophizing), which can influence physical and psychological outcomes (pain-related disability and depression). This highlights the importance of psychological factors, like catastrophizing, in a patient's experience of physical disability. Moreover, catastrophizing plays a role in the longitudinal relationship between depression and pain (Crawford, Tripp, et al., 2019). Specifically, depression at baseline led to catastrophizing six months later, which led to pain 12 months later, while controlling for pain, catastrophizing, and difficulties in emotion regulation at baseline (Crawford, Tripp, et al., 2019). These results speak to the stability of these variables over time and highlight the need for pain management strategies that target catastrophic thinking surrounding patients' pain experiences (as discussed later in the chapter).

The IC/BPS catastrophizing findings have directed current efforts in the areas of clinical assessment and management of psychosocial factors for improved patient adjustment. For patients diagnosed with IC/BPS who completed the clinically practical UPOINT (Urinary, Psychosocial, Organ Specific, Infection, Neurologic/Systemic, Tenderness of Skeletal Muscles) phenotyping classification system (Figure 15.2), the psychosocial domain (i.e., catastrophizing) identified those who also reported greater pain, urinary urgency, and frequency (Shoskes, Nickel, Rackley, & Pontari, 2009; Shoskes, Nickel, Dolinga, & Prots, 2009; Nickel, Shoskes, & Irvine-Bird, 2009). Although cause and effect relationships among pain, IC/BPS symptoms, and psychosocial parameters were not assessable in this study, it is likely that psychosocial factors (and catastrophizing in particular) significantly impact patient outcomes (Nickel et al., 2010a).

The Impact of Flares

The experience of UCPPS is widely believed to include symptom exacerbation (i.e., flares) and remissions; however, few studies have directly investigated this concept (Sutcliffe et al., 2014; Sutcliffe, Colditz et al., 2015). In a recent study by Sutcliffe, Bradley, et al. (2015), 57 female patients with IC/BPS from the MAPP Research Network participated in eight focus groups that explored the full spectrum of flares and their impact on patients' lives. The authors found that flare experiences were common and disruptive to patients' lives. The longer-term impact of flares included negative effects on sexual functioning and marital, family, and social relationships, as well as loss of employment or limited career and/or educational advancement. Given the negative impact of flares on patients' quality of life, it is critical to further research UCPPS flare etiology, treatment, and management. Currently, the flare literature suggests that providing patients with

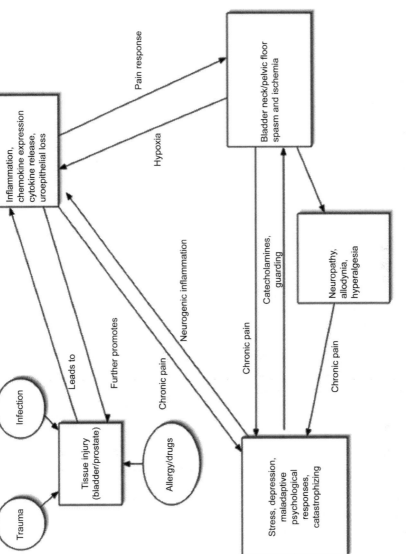

Figure 15.2 Multifactorial Etiology of UCPSS That Forms the Basis of the UPOINT Classification System

a sense of control over their symptoms and engaging them socially can improve outcomes (Sutcliffe, Colditz, et al., 2015).

Clinical Interventions

Several psychosocial interventions influence UCPPS outcomes. This section reviews behavioral coping strategies, relaxation techniques, mindfulness, and cognitive-behavioral approaches. All of these interventions are designed to target the psychosocial risk factors identified in previous research.

Behavioral Coping Strategies

Pain-contingent rest (i.e., avoiding activity due to pain) is a behavioral coping strategy significantly associated with disability. Pain-contingent rest was shown to be the strongest predictor of patient-reported disability in at least one study of a general primary care population (Spitzer, Kroenke, & Williams, 1999). Greater pain-contingent resting was the most robust predictor of poorer physical QoL functioning in a study sample of CP/CPPS patients (Nickel, Tripp, et al., 2008). Accordingly, interventions that aim to improve the overall QoL of patients by targeting increases in activity as a central goal may be beneficial to UCPPS populations (Sullivan et al., 2005). While prescribing physical exercise programs (Ginting, Tripp, Nickel, & Fitzgerald et al., 2011) or more general increases in activity is practical and helpful to many patients, caution must be taken due to patient variability in pain and physical comorbidities. Exercises that are prescribed to patients are intended for very specific muscles so that patients improve their posture and joint muscle balance and avoid exacerbating pelvic floor muscle overactivity and the recurrence of pain (Bradley, Rawlins, & Brinker, 2017).

Illness-focused coping (strategies discouraged in chronic pain treatment such as guarding and resting) is another important target in improving the mental and physical QoL of patients (Krsmanovic, Tripp, Nickel, Shoskes et al., 2014). As such, cognitive-behavioral self-management interventions for CP/CPPS that are designed to educate the patient about coping with distress, understanding cognitive patterns associated with greater pain, and practicing new methods of coping from an emotional and behavioral perspective may be a significant adjunctive treatment (Nickel, Mullins, et al., 2008). A shift away from illness-focused coping was included as a valuable part of the intervention suggested by Tripp et al. (2011) described below and is utilized in newer intervention models such as Brünahl et al.'s (2018).

Relaxation Techniques

Relaxation techniques are useful as an adaptive coping response to reduce distress associated with pain and to reduce pain sensations themselves. These strategies tend to focus on repetition of a single sensation or physical activity (such as deep, diaphragmatic breathing) in order to achieve the benefit of a calm physiological state (McCaffery & Pasero, 1999). Further, when utilizing physiotherapy and paradoxical relaxation training with CP/CPPS patients, Anderson and colleagues have shown significant improvements in pain, sexual dysfunction, and urinary symptoms at three months (Anderson, Wise, Sawyer, & Chan, 2006) and six months post-treatment (Anderson, Wise, Sawyer, Glowe, & Orenberg, 2011).

Mindfulness and Acceptance-Based Strategies

Acceptance and commitment therapy (ACT) is a psychological intervention that employs mindfulness and acceptance techniques. Mindfulness refers to purposeful observation of what is going on in oneself and the environment. Mindfulness techniques help patients redirect their attention away from streams of often unhelpful thought (i.e., catastrophizing thoughts) and toward the present moment (Harris, 2006; Kabat-Zinn, 1991). Mindful thinking interventions train the patient to examine his/her present experiences with a receptive and nonjudgmental mindset—that is, without automatically evaluating private experiences as good or bad, but simply experiencing them as they are. The aim is to reduce the impact and influence of unwanted thoughts, feelings, and sensations. Patients often are instructed in the use of guided home practice of mindful breathing and mindful eating, two basic techniques for inducing a calm mind.

ACT interventions also focus on developing "acceptance" of unwanted private experiences, as well as promoting commitment and action toward living a valued life (Harris, 2006). Acceptance-based strategies help patients identify deeply held values, set goals guided by these values, and take action to meet these goals. Patients identify important values in several life areas (e.g., intimate relationships, family, work, etc.) and set practical, obtainable goals for a few of these values. Patients then identify strategies to achieve these goals in order to become more aligned with these values. Veehof, Trompetter, Bohlmeijer, and Schreurs (2016) conducted a recent meta-analysis reviewing 25 randomized controlled trials that compared mindfulness and acceptance-based therapies for chronic pain with other interventions (e.g., education, medical treatment as usual, cognitive-behavioral therapy). They found moderate to large effect sizes for pain interference post-treatment and at follow-up. Fox, Flynn, and Allen (2011) conducted a pilot study examining the effect of mindfulness meditation on women with chronic pelvic pain. They found that mindfulness meditation resulted in significant improvement in daily pain, physical functioning, social functioning, and mental health. However, further research on the effects of ACT interventions in individuals with UCPPS is required.

A Cognitive-Behavioral Symptom Management Program for UCPPS

Cognitive-behavioral therapy (CBT) models suggest that cognitive factors are essential components of patient adjustment, but also include patient behaviors and patterns of observable responses. It is the interaction between thoughts and behavioral outcomes that is a point of explicit patient education and skill development. CBT models suggest that individuals are not passive in their interpretation of (and response to) the world around them. Indeed, individuals learn to respond to stressful and positive situations through learned experiences that help shape their individualized schema (i.e., organized internal cognitive representations of personal knowledge that act in a heuristic manner) (Beck, 1995). It is natural that individuals in pain occasionally may respond to stressors not as how an observer might interpret the event(s), but based on how they have constructed their own perception of the situation(s), which is in large part based on their internal schemata.

CBT programs commonly share several characteristics. CBT programs usually are problem-solving-oriented, extensively teach self-management skills with regard to monitoring and challenging dysfunctional and unsupported thinking, teach communication skills, make use of homework-based exercises, promote activity engagement, and prepare patients to anticipate setbacks in applying these new skills (Beck, 1995; Beck, Rush, Shaw, & Emery, 1979; Persons, Davidson, & Tompkins, 2001). These therapeutic tasks serve as guides to help patients identify and modify significant problem areas they may experience when adjusting to persistent symptoms, like chronic pain. The CBT framework, which is malleable, can be used in settings that range from individualized treatment to group settings (as is often found in multidisciplinary pain management programs).

The cognitive-behavioral symptom management program (CB-SMP; Tripp et al., 2011) was unique to UCPPS management because it is based on current empiric findings from UCPPS research and reviews. The use of current data to guide the targeting of particular variables associated with patient adjustment makes the CB-SMP "*specific*" to the pain-related fears and cognitions of the UCPPS population. What also makes the CB-SMP novel is that trained clinical urology nurses administer the program using a patient workbook, which increases quality assurance of program delivery. The workbook provides focused readings and session-by-session homework tasks over the course of the eight-week schedule. Each 60-minute session follows an agenda that the nurse leads interactively with a group of approximately six or seven patients.

Beginning with the initial meeting and continuing throughout the program, patients receive instruction regarding how to use a tool referred to as the "Reaction Record" (see Figure 15.3). The Reaction Record guides patients in identifying negative thoughts associated with pain, distress, and/or negative interpersonal appraisals. The Reaction Record is also the mechanism by which patients are guided in deliberating, recording, and engaging in positive coping choices. The use of the Reaction Record is necessary because many patients suffering chronic symptoms report difficulty in acknowledging or accepting their thoughts or feelings, many of which are associated with negative emotional states. Further, many people report that they are unaware that thinking that is said to occur automatically can have such significant associations with choices in behavior and the

Figure 15.3 Reaction Record

Instruction: *When you notice pain or mood getting worse ask yourself, "What is going through my mind at this moment?"*

Date/Time	Problem Situation:	Automatic Thoughts:	Emotion(s):	REACTION:	Adaptive Coping:
	What actual event led up to this event? (e.g., attempt to do some activity, movement you are afraid of, a verbal fight . . . etc.) What upsetting physical symptoms do you recall?	What are you saying to yourself about this problem situation? (e.g., this will never change, I can't do it, if I do it will make me worse, these symptoms are ruining my life) What were your thoughts or the picture in your mind at this time? How much did you believe each thought at that time? Rate each from 0–100%.	What emotion(s) did you feel at that time? (e.g., sad, angry, anxious, happy) How intense did you feel each of the emotions listed? Rate each from 0–100%.	What did you actually do following your thoughts and emotion(s)? How did you react? (e.g., resting, giving up attempt, argued, verbal confrontation, tried to ignore it, etc.)	Doing something different? Ask: "What is the evidence that the automatic thought is true or not true for me?" "If I keep reacting like this in the future, what benefit will I get from it?" "If I had a good friend _____ in this situation, what would I tell them to do?" Challenge Thought Column and Reaction Column! Then **go back** and **re-rate emotions** if you were to use these new thoughts to replace old ones you had.

subsequent reactions that follow. It is useful to have patients run through the chronology of automatic thinking and reactions to such thoughts because this is a key learning task of CBT models. It is particularly important that patients understand the connections between their automatic thoughts and their negative coping responses.

It is essential to have patients test out the relationships between their thinking, the emotions associated with that thinking, their behavioral responses, and the benefits they receive from such efforts. Perhaps a patient is managing quite well with his/her identified situation (e.g., pain flare-up, distressing urinary symptoms, or fight with spouse around issues of intimacy). In such cases, the Reaction Record is a useful tool to show approval and validation of such self-management. In contrast, if the patient reports elevated levels of catastrophic thinking, strong negative emotional response, and illness-focused coping behaviors, then the Reaction Record can be used as a tool to test novel methods of self-management.

The Reaction Record guides the patient through an examination of the evidence for the types of thinking he/she reports (e.g., catastrophic; "this situation will never get better"). It helps replace such thoughts with more realistic and helpful statements (e.g., "this may be difficult now, but these things have worked out before and I have always felt better in a day's time"). This process enables patients to examine new evidence-based ways of thinking and coping and to evaluate any proposed changes from the perspective of reducing the current negative emotional fallout.

Patients may find it difficult to report details of experiences with which they have current troubles. To alleviate such performance pressures during the CB-SMP program, patients use the Reaction Record to complete a weekly pain, mood, social support, and disability assessment; the goal is to help identify concurrent areas for discussion and intervention. These weekly assessments are essential so that session topics can be tailored to address the specific areas endorsed as problematic by the patients.

The workbook utilized by the urology nurse facilitator clearly defines the content of the CB-SMP sessions. The initial session introduces the program requirements, the program rationale, and the value of the CBT approach. During Sessions 2 and 3, patients receive instruction regarding the use of the Reaction Record as a tool to self-identify and modify catastrophic cognitions. The patients are taught how such thought patterns 1) are associated with greater negative affect; 2) often are unsupported by evidence in their environment; and 3) lead to poor choices in behavioral coping (e.g., becoming sedentary and discontinuing social activity that was once enjoyable).

During Sessions 4 through 6, patients identify and modify deficits in social support by practicing self-assertion communication exercises with their nurse, and then later with significant others in their lives. This type of communication is essential to establishing effective problem-solving in dyads, in families, and in other interpersonal contexts. The particular skills of using structured statements such as "*I feel. . .*" are reviewed, practiced, and then assigned for use with others as appropriate. Listening skills also are introduced, so that patients can learn to identify when their symptoms may be interfering with or biasing their interpretations of others' communication efforts.

Sessions 6 and 7 use the Reaction Record tool to identify and modify illness-focused behavioral coping strategies and to help the patient reengage in previously abandoned physical and social activities. In the eighth and final session, patients receive instruction regarding ongoing problem-solving and future self-management strategies following treatment. This type of maintenance concept is an essential ingredient of many self-management programs. In summary, the CB-SMP is the first comprehensive attempt to target specific empirically supported biopsychosocial variables (i.e., catastrophizing, social support) for symptom improvement in CP/CPPS.

The goals of the CB-SMP are similar to the goals of most CBT approaches: 1) initiate a *sense of hope* by helping patients establish the belief that the self-management of their symptoms can shift from a state of being devastating to manageable; 2) promote *self-efficacy* in symptom management through the acquisition of new thinking and new wellness-focused behavioral coping strategies. New strategies such as non-catastrophic thinking, positive self-coping statements, and mild–moderate exercise (e.g., walking program) are suggested and evaluated by patients. The new skills enable patients to stop being reactive in the face of their symptoms, providing a sense of mastery; 3) break established patterns of *schema-based automatic thinking*. The practice of self-management skills in the CB-SMP takes direct aim at breaking patterns of catastrophic thinking with the Reaction Record, which allows patients to build confidence that they can evoke change in the management of their condition; and 4) *facilitate long-term adjustment* by helping patients anticipate problems with their attempts at self-management. The closing session of the CB-SMP provides explicit education and discussion regarding self-management in the future. Patients are encouraged to practice their new skills on a regular basis, rather than just during times of perceived need.

Tripp et al. (2011) conducted this program with 11 men with CP/CPPS in order to examine the feasibility of this management program and its short-term effectiveness in reducing psychosocial risk factors and symptoms and in improving QoL. Results showed that the program was associated with significant reductions in pain severity, disability, and pain catastrophizing over the eight-week period. There was, however, no significant reduction in levels of depression or perceived social support. Though a pilot study, these results suggest that the CB-SMP's goal of targeting and ameliorating empirically identified psychosocial risk factors for poor patient outcomes in this population shows promise. Current research being conducted in Germany also should help establish new goals for program development (Brünahl et al., 2018).

The behavioral health provider plays an important role with this urological population (Shoskes et al., 2009), but the actual practice of utilizing an interdisciplinary approach in the treatment of UCPPS is at best rare, from what we can surmise. There are no data available detailing how many urological practices have psychosocial/interdisciplinary treatment models available to patients. The lack of interdisciplinary treatment may depend upon hospital or community resources, and not all psychologists and allied health professionals are trained in pain management.

With our ongoing clinical trial research on treatment programs for CP/CPPS and IC/BPS, we will continue to examine the positive life impact that such symptom-reduction methods can have for patients. This is an important endeavor because these studies will help demonstrate the benefit of behavioral health consultation and interventions. These manualized treatments are essential because they also allow a wider range of allied healthcare providers (e.g., trained nurses, social workers, behavioral counselors) to administer the interventions and assure treatment fidelity, making treatment more accessible and easily disseminated.

The latest ongoing IC/BPS treatment study by Krsmanovic et al. (2018) utilizes an online format to combat directly the staffing resource issues faced by hospitals and clinics. Adapted from the cognitive-behavioral symptom management program for chronic pelvic pain developed by Tripp and Nickel described above, which was tested with males diagnosed with CP/CPPS (Tripp et al., 2011), this online intervention is intended for women suffering from IC/BPS. It will consist of weekly modules containing text files, videos, and psychoeducational homework materials.

Through these sessions, patients will learn: 1) to understand their pain and how it affects QoL, and to accept ownership of their pain; 2) to practice pain relaxation and distraction techniques; 3) to identify and dispute idiosyncratic catastrophic thinking patterns around pain and other life events associated with symptoms; 4) to identify and reduce the idiosyncratic reliance on illness-focused behavioral coping; and 5) to prevent relapse, in the form of future problem-solving abilities from a health-focused thinking and behavior perspective (Krsmanovic et al., 2018). This study is a randomized controlled trial that targets IC/BPS patients in tertiary care clinics across North America. If established as effective, this new method of IC/BPS treatment delivery will allow women to access treatment modules in a convenient and private portal. Although such individual treatment models lose the social benefits of a group setting, they address delivery issues.

Concluding Comments

According to recent research, several psychosocial variables have negative relationships with the likelihood of UCPPS pain improvement, though these are not related specifically to urinary symptom outcome (Naliboff et al., 2017). The research reviewed and the suggestions proposed in this chapter highlight the important role that psychosocial variables play in patient responses to pain and standard biomedical treatment. The urologist must consider the influences of the patient's history with pain, his/her cognitive appraisals and behavioral coping responses (catastrophizing, resting), and the social milieu in which the pain occurs (social support). In many UCPPS cases, coping strategies and emotion regulation are important modifiers of the patient's quality of life. While this chapter in no way suggests that urologists become uro-psychologists, it does highlight patient risk factors that should be managed through appropriate discussions in the office, as well as referrals to allied healthcare professionals and the incorporation of inter-disciplinary care whenever possible.

References

Alexander, R. B., & Trissel, D. (1996). Chronic prostatitis: Results of an Internet survey. *Urology, 48*, 568–574.

Anderson, R. U., Orenberg, E. K., Chan, C. A., Morey, A., & Flores, V. (2008). Psychometric profiles and HPA axis function in men with chronic prostatitis/chronic pelvic pain syndrome (CP/CPPS). *The Journal of Urology, 179*, 956–960.

Anderson, R. U., Orenberg, E. K., Morey, A., Chavez, N., & Chan, C. A. (2009). Stress induced hypothalamus-pituitary-adrenal axis responses and disturbances in psychological profiles in men with chronic prostatitis/chronic pelvic pain syndrome. *The Journal of Urology, 182*, 2319–2324.

Anderson, R. U., Wise, D., Sawyer, T., & Chan, C. (2005). Integration of myofascial trigger point release and paradoxical relaxation training for treatment of chronic pelvic pain in men. *The Journal of Urology, 174*, 155–160.

Anderson, R. W., Wise, D., Sawyer, T., & Chan, C. A. (2006). Sexual dysfunction in men with chronic prostatitis/chronic pelvic pain syndrome: Improvement after trigger point release and paradoxical relaxation training. *The Journal of Urology, 176*, 1534–1539.

Anderson, R. W., Wise, D., Sawyer, T., Glowe, P., & Orenberg, E. K. (2011). 6-day intensive treatment protocol for refractory chronic prostatitis/chronic pelvic pain syndrome using myofascial release and paradoxical relaxation training. *The Journal of Urology, 185*, 1294–1299.

Baldoni, F., Ercolani, M., Baldaro, B., & Trombini, G. (1995). Stressful events and psychological symptoms in patients with functional urinary disorders. *Perceptual and Motor Skills, 80*, 605–606.

Bandura, A. (1997). *Self-efficacy: The exercise of control.* New York, NY: W.H. Freeman.

Bartoletti, R., Cai, T., Mondaini, N., Dinelli, N., Pinzi, N., Pavone, C., . . . Naber, K. G. (2007). Prevalence, incidence estimation, risk factors and characterization of chronic prostatitis/chronic pelvic pain syndrome in urological hospital outpatients in Italy: Results of a multicenter case-control observational study. *Journal of Urology, 178*, 2411–2415.

Beck, A., Rush, A. J., Shaw, B., & Emery, G. (1979). *Cognitive therapy for depression.* New York, NY: The Guildford Press.

Beck, J. S. (1995). *Cognitive therapy: Basics and beyond.* New York, NY: The Guildford Press.

Beckett, M. K., Elliott, M. N., Clemens, J. Q., Ewing, B., & Berry, S. H. (2014). Consequences of interstitial cystitis/bladder pain symptoms on women's work participation and income: Results from a national household sample. *The Journal of Urology, 191*, 83–88.

Berghuis, J. P., Heiman, J. R., Rothman, I., & Berger, R. E. (1996). Psychological and physical factors involved in chronic idiopathic prostatitis. *Journal of Psychosomatic Research, 41*, 313–325.

Bogart, L. M., Suttorp, M. J., Elliott, M. N., Clemens, J. Q., & Berry, S. H. (2011). Prevalence and correlates of sexual dysfunction among women with bladder pain syndrome/interstitial cystitis. *Urology, 77*, 576–580.

Bradley, M. H., Rawlins, A., & Brinker, C. A. (2017). Physical therapy for treatment of pelvic pain. *Physical Medicine & Rehabilitation Clinics, 28*, 589–601.

Brünahl, C. A., Klotz, S. G. R., Dybowski, C., Riegel, B., Gregorzik, S., Tripp, D. A., . . . Löwe, B. (2018). Combined cognitive-behavioural and physiotherapeutic therapy for patients with chronic pelvic pain syndrome (COMBI-CPPS): Study protocol for a controlled feasibility trial. *Trials*, *19*, 1–12. doi:10.1186/s13063-017-2387-4.

Calhoun, E. A., McNaughton-Collins, M., Pontari, M. A., O'Leary, M., Leiby, B. E., Landis, J. R., . . . Litwin, M. S. (2004). The economic impact of chronic prostatitis. *Archives of Internal Medicine*, *164*, 1231–1236.

Chong, G. S., Cogan, D., Randolph, P., & Racz, G. (2001). Chronic pain and self-efficacy: The effects of age, sex, and chronicity. *Pain Practice*, *1*, 338–343.

Chung, S. D., Liu, S. P., Li, H. C., & Lin, H. C. (2014). Health care service utilization among patients with bladder pain syndrome/interstitial cystitis in a single payer healthcare system. *PLoS One*, *9*, e87522.

Clemens, J. Q. *On behalf of the NIH MAPP Research Network: Update on the MAPP Project*. Presented at annual meeting of American Urological Association, Orlando, Florida, May 19, 2014. Retrieved December 23, 2017, from www.aua2014.org/webcasts/index.cfm?ID=6079,%203196&title=1&LanguageID=0

Clemens, J. Q., Brown, S. O., & Calhoun, E. A. (2008). Mental health diagnoses in patients with interstitial cystitis/painful bladder syndrome and chronic prostatitis/chronic pelvic pain syndrome: A case/control study. *The Journal of Urology*, *180*, 1378–1382.

Clemens, J. Q., Brown, S. O., Kozloff, L., & Calhoun, E. A. (2006). Predictors of symptom severity in patients with chronic prostatitis and interstitial cystitis. *The Journal of Urology*, *175*, 963–966.

Clemens, J. Q., Link, C. L., Eggers, P. W., Kusek, J. W., Nyberg, L. M., & McKinlay, J. B. (2007). Prevalence of painful bladder symptoms and effect on quality of life in black, Hispanic and white men and women. *The Journal of Urology*, *177*, 1390–1394.

Clemens, J. Q., Markossian, T., & Calhoun, E. A. (2009). Comparison of economic impact of chronic prostatitis/chronic pelvic pain syndrome and interstitial cystitis/painful bladder syndrome. *Urology*, *73*, 743–746.

Collins, M. M., Stafford, R. S., O'Leary, M. P., & Barry, M. J. (1998). How common is prostatitis? A national survey of physician visits. *The Journal of Urology*, *159*, 1224–1228.

Collins, M. M., Stafford, R. S., O'Leary, M. P., & Barry, M. J. (1999). Distinguishing chronic prostatitis and benign prostatic hyperplasia symptoms: Results of a national survey of physician visits. *Urology*, *53*, 921–925.

Crawford, A. (2017). *The role of emotion regulation in the relationship between pain, catastrophizing, depression, and disability in women with interstitial cystitis/bladder pain syndrome* (Master's thesis). Retrieved from ProQuest LLC. (Accession No. 10671787).

Crawford, A., Tripp, D. A., Nickel, J. C., Carr, L., Moldwin, R., Katz, L., & Muere, A. (2019). Depression and helplessness impact interstitial cystitis / bladder pain syndrome pain over time. *Canadian Urological Association Journal*, February 7; Epub ahead of print. http://dx.doi.org/10.5489/cuaj.5703.

Egan, J. K., & Krieger, J. N. (1994). Psychological problems in chronic prostatitis patients with pain. *The Clinical Journal of Pain*, *10*, 218–226.

Ejike, C. E., & Ezeanyika, L. U. (2008). Prevalence of chronic prostatitis symptoms in a randomly surveyed adult population of urban-community-dwelling Nigerian males. *International Journal of Urology*, *15*, 340–343.

Ferris, J. A., Pitts, M. K., Richters, J., Simpson, J. M., Shelley, J. M., & Smith, A. M. (2009). National prevalence or urogential pain and prostatitis-like symptoms in Australian men using the national institutes of health chronic prostatitis symptoms index. *BJU International*, *105*, 373–379.

Fox, S. D., Flynn, E., & Allen, R. H. (2011). Mindfulness meditation for women with chronic pelvic pain: A pilot study. *The Journal of Reproductive Medicine*, *56*, 158–162.

Gatchel, R. J. (1999). Perspectives on pain: A historical overview. In R. J. Gatchel & D. C. Turk (Eds.), *Psychosocial factors in pain: Critical perspectives* (pp. 3–17). New York, NY: The Guilford Press.

Giannantoni, A., Bini, V., Dmochowski, R., Hanno, P., Nickel, J. C., Proiettie, S., & Wyndaele, J. J. (2012). Contemporary management of the painful bladder: A systematic review. *European Urology, 61,* 29–53.

Ginting, J. V., Tripp, D. A., & Nickel, J. C. (2011). Self-reported spousal support modifies the negative impact of pain on disability in men with chronic prostatitis/chronic pelvic pain syndrome. *Urology, 78,* 1136–1141.

Ginting, J. V., Tripp, D. A., Nickel, J. C., Fitzgerald, M. P., & Mayer, R. (2011). Spousal support decreases the negative impact of pain on mental quality of life in women with interstitial cystitis/painful bladder syndrome. *BJU International, 108,* 713–717.

Giubilei, G., Mondaini, N., Minervini, A., Saieva, C., Lapini, A., Serni, S., . . . Carini, M. (2007). Physical activity of men with chronic prostatitis/chronic pelvic pain syndrome not satisfied with conventional treatments—could it represent a valid option? The physical activity and male pelvic pain trial: A double-blind, randomized study. *The Journal of Urology, 177,* 159–165.

Griffith, J. W., Stephens-Shields, A. J., Hou, X., Naliboff, B. D., Pontari, M., Edwards, T. C., . . . Landis, J. R. (2015). Pain and urinary symptoms should not be combined into a single score: Psychometric findings from the MAPP research network. *The Journal of Urology, 195,* 949–954.

Hall, S. A., Link, C. L., Pulliam, S. J., Hanno, P. M., Eggers, P. W., Kusek, J. W., & McKinlay, J. B. (2008). The relationship of common medical conditions and medication use with symptoms of Painful bladder syndrome: Results from the Boston area community health survey. *The Journal of Urolology, 180,* 593–598.

Hanno, P. M. (2005). International consultation on IC- Rome, September 2004/Forging an international consensus: Progress in painful bladder syndrome/interstitial cystitis. *International Urological Journal, 16,* S2–S34.

Hanno, P. M. (2008). Re-imaging interstitial cystitis. In J. C. Nickel (Eds.), *New developments in infection and inflammation in urology, urologic clinics of North America* (pp. 91–100). Philadelphia, PA: Elsevier.

Harris, R. (2006). Embracing your demons: An overview of acceptance and commitment therapy. *Psychotherapy in Australia, 12,* 2–8.

Howard, F. M. (2003). Chronic pelvic pain. *Obstetrics & Gynecology, 101,* 594–611.

Ibrahim, I. A., Diokno, A. C., Killinger, K. A., Carrico, D. J., & Peters, K. M. (2007). Prevalence of self-reported interstitial cystitis (IC) and interstitial cystitis-like symptoms among adult women in the community. *International Urology and Nephrology, 39,* 489–495.

Jackson, T., Iezzi, T., Gunderson, J., Nagasaka, T., & Fritch, A. (2002). Gender differences in pain perception: The mediating role of self-efficacy beliefs. *Sex Roles, 47,* 561–568.

Jensen, M. P., Turner, J. A., & Romano, J. M. (1991). Self-efficacy and outcome expectancies: Relationship to chronic pain coping strategies and adjustment. *Pain, 44,* 263–269.

Kabat-Zinn, J. (1991). *Full catastrophe living: Using the wisdom of your body and mind to face stress, pain, and illness.* New York, NY: Dell Pub.

Katz, L., Tripp, D. A., Nickel, J. C., Mayer, R., Reimann, M., & van Ophoven, A. (2013). Disability in women suffering from interstitial cystitis/bladder pain syndrome. *BJU International, 111,* 114–121.

Kaye, J., & Moldwin, R. (2009). Interstitial cystitis in men: Diagnosis, treatment and similarities to chronic prostatitis. In V. R. Preedy & R. S. Watson (Eds.), *Handbook of disease burdens and quality of life measures.* London: Springer.

Kerns, R. D., Turk, D. C., & Rudy, T. E. (1985). The West Haven-Yale Multidimensional Pain Inventory (WHYMPI). *Pain, 23,* 345–356.

Kilpatrick, L. A., Ornitz, E., Ibrahimovic, H., Hubbard, C. S., Rodriguez, L. V., Mayer, E. A., & Naliboff, B. D. (2010). Gating of sensory information differs in patients with interstitial cystitis/painful bladder syndrome. *The Journal of Urology, 184,* 958–963.

Koziol, J. A., Clark, D. C., Gittes, R. F., & Tan, E. M. (1993). The natural history of interstitial cystitis: A survey of 374 patients. *The Journal of Urology, 149,* 465–469.

Krieger, J. N., Nyberg, L., & Nickel, J. C. (1999). NIH consensus definition and classification of prostatitis. *JAMA, 282,* 236–237.

Kroenke, K., Spitzer, R. L., & Williams, J. B. (2001). The PHQ-9: Validity of a brief depression severity measure. *Journal of General Internal Medicine, 16,* 606–613.

Krsmanovic, A., Tripp, D. A., Nickel, J. C., Moldwin, R., Egerdie, R. B., Mayer, R., . . . Pontari, M. (2018). *Online self-management treatment program for women diagnosed with Interstitial Cystitis/Bladder Pain Syndrome (IC/BPS).* Manuscript in preparation.

Krsmanovic, A., Tripp, D. A., Nickel, J. C., Shoskes, D. A., Pontari, M., Litwin, M. S., & McNaughton-Collins, M. (2014). Psychosocial mechanisms of the pain and quality of life relationship for chronic prostatitis/chronic pelvic pain syndrome (CP/CPPS). *Canadian Urological Association Journal, 8,* 403–408.

Ku, J. H., Jeon, Y. S., Kim, M. E., Lee, N. K., & Park, Y. H. (2002). Psychological problems in young men with chronic prostatitis-like symptoms. *Scandinavian Journal of Urology and Nephrology, 36,* 296–301.

Ku, J. H., Kim, M. E., Lee, N. K., & Park, Y. H. (2001). Influence of environmental factors on chronic prostatitis-like symptoms in young men: Results of a community-based survey. *Urology, 58,* 853–858.

Ku, J. H., Kwak, C., Oh, S. J., Lee, E., Lee, S. E., & Paick, J. S. (2004). Influence of pain and urinary symptoms on quality of life in young men with chronic prostatitis-like symptoms. *International Journal of Urology: Official Journal of the Japanese Urological Association, 11,* 489–493.

Kunishima, Y., Mori, M., Kitamura, H., Satoh, H., & Tsukamoto, T. (2006). Prevalence of prostatitis-like symptoms in Japanese men: Population-based study in a town in Hokkaido. *International Journal of Urology, 13,* 1286–1289.

Lai, H. H., Jemielita, T., Sutcliffe, S., Bradley, C. S., Naliboff, B., Williams, D. A., . . . Landis, J. R. (2017). Characterization of whole body pain in urological chronic pelvic pain syndrome at baseline: A MAPP research network. *The Journal of Urology, 198,* 622–631.

Liang, C. Z., Li, H. J., Wang, Z. P., Xing, J. P., Hu, W. L., Zhang, T. F., . . . Tai, S. (2009). The prevalence of prostatitis-like symptoms in China. *Journal of Urology, 182,* 558–563.

Litwin, M. S., McNaughton-Collins, M., Fowler, F. J., Nickel, J. C., Calhoun, E. A., Pontari, M. A., . . . O'Leary, M. P. (1999). The national institutes of health chronic prostatitis symptom index: Development and validation of a new outcome measure. Chronic prostatitis collaborative research network. *The Journal of Urology, 162,* 369–375.

Lui, B., Su, M., Zhan, H., Yang, F., Li, W., & Zhou, X. (2014). Adding a sexual dysfunction domain to UPOINT system improves association with symptoms in women with interstitial cystitis and bladder pain syndrome. *Urology, 84,* 1308–1313.

Lutgendorf, S. K., Kreder, K. J., & Rothrock, N. E. (2000). Stress and symptomatology in patients with interstitial cystitis: A laboratory stress model. *The Journal of Urology, 164,* 1265–1269.

Macaulay, A. J., Stern, R. S., Holmes, D. M., & Stanton, S. L. (1987). Micturition and the mind: Psychological factors in the aetiology and treatment of urinary symptoms in women. *British Medical Journal (Clinical Research Ed.), 294,* 540–543.

Magistro, G., Wagenlehner, F. M. E., Grabe, M., Weidner, W., Stief, C. G., & Nickel, J. C. (2016). Contemporary management of chronic prostatitis/chronic pelvic pain syndrome. *European Urology, 69,* 286–297.

Matos, M., Bernardes, S. F., Goubert, L., & Beyers, W. (2017). Buffer or amplified? Longitudinal effects of social support for autonomy/dependence on older adults' chronic pain experiences. *Health Psychology, 36,* 1195–1206.

McBryde, C. F., & Redington, J. J. (2002). The prostatitis syndromes. *Primary Care Case Review*, *5*, 40–48.

McCaffery, M., & Pasero, C. (1999). Practical nondrug approaches to pain. In M. McCaffery & C. Pasero (Eds.), *Pain: Clinical manual* (pp. 399–427). St. Louis, MO: Mosby.

McNaughton Collins, M., MacDonald, R., & Wilt, T. J. (2000). Diagnosis and treatment of chronic abacterial prostatitis: A systematic review. *Annals of Internal Medicine*, *133*, 367–381.

McNaughton-Collins, M., Meigs, J. B., Barry, M. J., Walker, C. E., Giovannucci, E., & Kawachi, I. (2002). Prevalence and correlates of prostatitis in the health professionals follow-up study cohort. *The Journal of Urology*, *167*, 1363–1366.

McNaughton-Collins, M., Pontari, M. A., O'Leary, M. P., Calhoun, E. A., Santanna, J., Landis, J. R., . . . Litwin, M. S. (2001). Quality of life is impaired in men with chronic prostatitis: The chronic prostatitis collaborative research network. *Journal of General Internal Medicine*, *16*, 656–662.

Mehik, A., Hellström, P., Sarpola, A., Lukkarinen, O., & Järvelin, M. R. (2001). Fears, sexual disturbances and personality features in men with prostatitis: A population-based cross-sectional study in Finland. *BJU International*, *88*, 35–38.

Melzack, R. (1975). The McGill pain questionnaire: Major properties and scoring methods. *Pain*, *1*, 277–299.

Miller, L. J., Fischer, K. A., Goralnick, S. J., Litt, M., Burleson, J. A., Albertsen, P., & Kreutzer, D. L. (2002). Nerve growth factor and chronic prostatitis/chronic pelvic pain syndrome. *Urology*, *59*, 603–608.

Miller, L. R., Cano, A., & Wurm, L. H. (2013). A motivational therapeutic assessment improves pain, mood, and relationship satisfaction in couples with chronic pain. *Journal of Pain*, *14*, 525–537.

Moldwin, R. M. (2002). Similarities between interstitial cystitis and male chronic pelvic pain syndrome. *Current Urology Reports*, *3*, 313–318.

Naliboff, B. D., Stephens, A. J., Afari, N., Lai, H., Krieger, J. N., Hong, B., . . . Williams, D. (2015). Widespread psychosocial difficulties in men and women with urologic chronic pelvic pain syndromes: Case-control findings from the multidisciplinary approach to the study of chronic pelvic pain research network. *Urology*, *85*, 1319–1327.

Naliboff, B. D., Stephens, A. J., Lai, H. H., Griffith, J. W., Clemens, J. Q., Lutgendorf, S., . . . Landis, J. R. (2017). Clinical and psychosocial predictors of urological chronic pelvic pain symptom change in 1 year: A prospective study from the MAPP research network. *The Journal of Urology*, *198*, 848–857.

Nickel, J. C. (2002). Prostatitis and related conditions. In P. Walsh, M. F. Campbell & A. B. Retik. (Eds.), *Campbell's urology* (8th ed., pp. 603–630). Philadelphia, PA: W.B. Saunders Company.

Nickel, J. C. (2009). Words of wisdom. Re: Clinical phenotyping in chronic prostatitis/chronic pelvic pain syndrome and interstitial cystitis: A management strategy for urological chronic pelvic pain syndromes. *European Urology*, *56*, 881.

Nickel, J. C., Downey, J. A., Ardern, D., Clark, J., & Nickel, K. (2004). Failure of monotherapy strategy for the treatment of difficult chronic prostatitis/chronic pelvic pain syndrome patients. *The Journal of Urology*, *172*, 551–554.

Nickel, J. C., Downey, J. A., Hunter, D., & Clark, J. (2001). Prevalence of prostatitis-like symptoms in a population based study using the national institutes of health chronic prostatitis symptom index. *The Journal of Urology*, *165*, 842–845.

Nickel, J. C., Downey, J. A., Nickel, K. R., & Clark, J. M. (2002). Prostatitis-like symptoms: One year later. *BJU International*, *90*, 678–681.

Nickel, J. C., Mullins, C., & Tripp, D. A. (2008). Development of an evidence-based cognitive behavioral treatment program for men with chronic prostatitis/chronic pelvic pain syndrome. *World Journal of Urology*, *26*, 167–172.

Nickel, J. C., Shoskes, D. A., & Irvine-Bird, K. (2009). Clinical phenotyping of women with interstitial cystitis/painful bladder syndrome: A key to classification and potentially improved management. *The Journal of Urology, 182*, 155–160.

Nickel, J. C., & Tripp, D. A. (2015). Clinical and psychological parameters associated with pain pattern phenotypes in women with interstitial cystitis/bladder pain syndrome. *The Journal of Urology, 193*, 138–144.

Nickel, J. C., Tripp, D. A., Chuai, S., Litwin, M. S., McNaughton-Collins, M., Landis, J. R., . . . Kusek, J. (2008). Psychosocial variables affect the quality of life of men diagnosed with chronic prostatitis/chronic pelvic pain syndrome. *BJU International, 101*, 59–64.

Nickel, J. C., Tripp, D. A., Pontari, M., Moldwin, R., Mayer, R., Carr, L. K., . . . Nordling, J. (2010a). Psychosocial phenotyping of women with IC/BPS: A case control study. *The Journal of Urology, 183*, 167–172.

Nickel, J. C., Tripp, D. A., Pontari, M., Moldwin, R., Mayer, R., Carr, L. K., . . . Nordling, J. (2010b). Interstitial cystitis/painful bladder syndrome and associated medical conditions with an emphasis on irritable bowel syndrome, fibromyalgia and chronic fatigue syndrome. *The Journal of Urology, 184*, 1358–1363.

Nickel, J. C., Tripp, D. A., Teal, V., Propert, K. J., Burks, D., Foster, H. E., . . . Nyberg, L. M. (2007). Sexual function is a determinant of poor quality of life for women with treatment refractory interstitial cystitis. *The Journal of Urology, 177*, 1832–1836.

Nijm, J., & Jonasson, L. (2009). Inflammation and cortisol response in coronary artery disease. *Annals of Medicine, 41*, 224–233.

Rey, R. (1993). *History of pain.* Paris, FR: Editions la Découverte.

O'Leary, M. P., Sant, G. R., Fowler, F. J. J., Whitmore, K. E., & Spolarich-Kroll, H. J. (1997). The interstitial cystitis symptom index and problem index. *Urology, 49*, 58–63.

Ottem, D. P., Carr, L. K., Perks, A. E., Lee, P., & Telchman, J. M. H. (2007). Interstitial cystitis and female sexual dysfunction. *Urology, 69*, 608–610.

Persons, J., Davidson, J., & Tompkins, M. (2001). *Essential components of cognitive-behaviour therapy for depression.* Washington, DC: American Psychological Association.

Peters, K. M., Killinger, K. A., Carrico, D. J., Ibrahim, I. A., Diokno, A. C., & Graziottin, A. (2007). Sexual function and sexual distress in women with interstitial cystitis: A case-control study. *Urology, 70*, 543–547.

Ratner, V., Slade, D., & Greene, G. (1994). Interstitial cystitis. A patient's perspective. *The Urologic Clinics of North America, 21*, 1–5.

Robbins, M. T., DeBerry, J., & Ness, T. J. (2007). Chronic psychological stress enhances nociceptive processing in the urinary bladder in high-anxiety rats. *Physiology & Behaviour, 91*, 544–550.

Rollnick, S., Miller, W. R., & Butler, C. C. (2007). *Motivational interviewing in health care: Helping patients change behavior.* New York, NY: The Guildford Press.

Rosengren, D. B. (2009). *Building motivational interviewing skills: A practitioner workbook.* New York, NY: The Guildford Press.

Rothrock, N. E., Lutgendorf, S. K., Hoffman, A., & Kreder, K. J. (2002). Depressive symptoms and quality of life in patients with interstitial cystitis. *The Journal of Urology, 167*, 1763–1767.

Rothrock, N. E., Lutgendorf, S. K., & Kreder, K. J. (2003). Coping strategies in patients with interstitial cystitis: Relationships with quality of life and depression. *The Journal of Urology, 169*, 233–236.

Rothrock, N. E., Lutgendorf, S. K., Kreder, K. J., Ratliff, T. L., & Zimmerman, B. (2001). Stress and symptoms in patients with interstitial cystitis patients: A life stress model. *Urology, 57*, 422–427.

Schaeffer, A. J. (2006). Chronic prostatitis and chronic pelvic pain syndrome. *New England Journal of Medicine, 355*, 1690–1698.

Schaeffer, A. J., Landis, J. R., Knauss, J. S., Propert, K. J., Alexander, R. B., Litwin, M. J., . . . Nyberg, L. M. (2002). Demographic and clinical characteristics of men with chronic prostatitis: The national institute of health chronic prostatitis cohort study. *The Journal of Urology, 168,* 593–598.

Shoskes, D. A., Nickel, J. C., Dolinga, R., & Prots, D. (2009). Clinical phenotyping of patients with chronic prostatitis/chronic pelvic pain syndrome and correlation with symptom severity. *Urology, 73,* 538–543.

Shoskes, D. A., Nickel, J. C., Rackley, R. R., & Pontari, M. A. (2009). Clinical phenotyping in chronic prostatitis/chronic pelvic pain syndrome and interstitial cystitis: A management strategy for urologic chronic pelvic pain syndromes. *Prostate Cancer and Prostatic Diseases, 12,* 177–183.

Simon, L. J., Landis, J. R., Erickson, D. R., & Nyberg, L. M. (1997). The interstitial cystitis data base study: Concepts and preliminary baseline descriptive statistics. *Urology, 49,* 64–75.

Smith, K. B., Pukall, C. F., Tripp, D. A., & Nickel, J. C. (2007). Sexual and relationship functioning in men with chronic prostatitis/chronic pelvic pain syndrome and their partners. *Archives of Sexual Behavior, 36,* 301–311.

Spitzer, R. L., Kroenke, K., & Williams, J. B. (1999). Validation and utility of a self-report version of PRIME-MD: The PHQ primary care study. Primary care evaluation of mental disorders. Patient health questionnaire. *JAMA, 282,* 1737–1744.

Sullivan, M. J. L., Bishop, S. R., & Pivik, J. (1995). The pain catastrophizing scale: Development and validation. *Psychological Assessment, 7,* 524–532.

Sullivan, M. J., Stanish, W., Sullivan, M. E., & Tripp, D. A. (2002). Differential predictors of pain and disability in patients with whiplash injuries. *Pain Research & Management, 7,* 68–74.

Sullivan, M. J., Thorn, B., Haythornthwaite, J. A., Keefe, F., Martin, M., Bradley, L. A., & Lefebvre, J. C. (2001). Theoretical perspectives on the relation between catastrophizing and pain. *Clinical Journal of Pain, 17,* 52–64.

Sullivan, M. J., Ward, C. L., Tripp, D. A., French, D. J., Adams, H., & Stanish, W. D. (2005). Secondary prevention of work disability: Community-based psychosocial intervention for musculoskeletal disorders. *Journal of Occupational Rehabilitation, 15,* 377–392.

Sutcliffe, S., Bradley, C. S., Clemens, J. Q., James, A. S., Konkle, K. S., Kreder, K. J., . . . Berry, S. H. (2015). Urological chronic pelvic pain syndrome flares and their impact: Qualitative analysis in the MAPP network. *International Urogynecology Journal, 26,* 1047–1060.

Sutcliffe, S., Colditz, G. A., Goodman, M. S., Pakpahan, R., Vetter, J., Ness, T. J., . . . Lai, H. H. (2014). Urologic chronic pelvic pain syndrome symptom flares: Characterization of the full spectrum of flares at two sites of the MAPP research network. *BJU International, 114,* 916–925.

Sutcliffe, S., Colditz, G. A., Pakpahan, R., Bradely, C. S., Goodman, M. S., Andriole, G. L., & Lai, H. H. (2015). Changes in symptoms during urologic chronic pelvic pain syndrome symptom flares: Findings from one site of the MAPP research network. *Neurourology and Urodynamics, 34,* 188–195.

Tripp, D. A., & Nickel, J. C. (2011). The psychology of urological chronic pelvic pain: A primer for urologists who want to know how to better manage chronic prostatitis and interstitial cystitis. *American Urological Association, 30,* 386–395.

Tripp, D. A., Nickel, J. C., Fitzgerald, M. P., Mayer, R., Stechyson, N., & Hsieh, A. (2009). Sexual functioning, catastrophizing, depression and pain as predictors of quality of life in women suffering from interstitial cystitis/painful bladder syndrome. *Urology, 73,* 987–992.

Tripp, D. A., Nickel, J. C., & Katz, L. (2011). A feasibility trial of a cognitive-behavioural symptom management program for chronic pelvic pain for men with refractory chronic prostatitis/chronic pelvic pain syndrome. *Canadian Urological Association Journal*, *5*, 328–332.

Tripp, D. A., Nickel, J. C., Krsmanovic, A., Pontari, M., Moldwin, R., Mayer, R., . . . Nordling, J. (2016). Depression and catastrophizing predict suicidal ideation in tertiary care patients with interstitial cystitis/bladder pain syndrome. *Canadian Urological Association Journal*, *10*, 383–388.

Tripp, D. A., Nickel, J. C., Landis, J. R, Wang, Y. L., Knauss, J. S., & the CPCRN Study Group. (2004). Predictors of quality of life and pain in CP/CPPS: Findings from the NIH chronic prostatitis cohort study. *BJU International*, *94*, 1279–1282.

Tripp, D. A., Nickel, J. C., Wang, Y., Litwin, M. S., McNaughton-Collins, M., Landis, J. R., . . . Kusek, J. W. (2006). Catastrophizing and pain-contingent rest predict patient adjustment in men with chronic prostatitis/chronic pelvic pain syndrome. *Journal of Pain*, *7*, 697–708.

Tripp, D. A., Nickel, J. C., Wong, J., Pontari, M., Moldwin, R., Mayer, R., . . . Nordling, J. (2012). Mapping of pain phenotypes in female patients with bladder pain syndrome/interstitial cystitis and controls. *European Urology*, *62*, 1188–1194.

Turk, D. C., & Okifuji, A. (2002). Psychological factors in chronic pain: Evolution and revolution. *Journal of Consulting and Clinical Psychology*, *70*, 678–690.

Turner, J. A., Hauge, S., Von Korff, M., Saunders, K., Lowe, M., & Berger, R. (2002). Primary care and urology patients with male pelvic pain syndrome: Symptoms and quality of life. *The Journal of Urology*, *167*, 1768–1738.

Twiss, C., Kilpatrick, L., Craske, M., Buffington, C. A., Ornitz, E., Rodriguez, L. V., . . . Naliboff, B. D. (2009). Increased startle responses in interstitial cystitis: Evidence for central hyperresponsiveness to visceral related threat. *The Journal of Urology*, *181*, 2127–2133.

Veehof, M. M., Trompetter, H. R., Bohlmeijer, E. T., & Schreurs, K. M. (2016). Acceptance- and mindfulness-based interventions for the treatment of chronic pain: A meta-analytic review. *Cognitive Behavior Therapy*, *45*, 5–31.

Wagenlehner, F. M. E., Naber, K. G., Bschleipfer, T., Brähler, E., & Weidner, W. (2009). Prostatitis and male pelvic pain syndrome: Diagnosis and treatment. *Deutsches Ärzteblatt International*, *106*, 175–183.

Webster, D. C., & Brennan, T. (1998). Self-care effectiveness and health outcomes in women with interstitial cystitis: Implications for mental health clinicians. *Issues in Mental Health Nursing*, *19*, 495–519.

Weir, R., Browne, G., Roberts, J., Tunks, E., & Gafni, A. (1994). The meaning of illness questionnaire: Further evidence its reliability and validity. *Pain*, *58*, 377–386.

Weissman, M. M., Gross, R., Fryer, A., Heiman, G. A., Gameroff, M. J., Hodge, S. E., . . . Wickramaratne, P. J. (2004). Interstitial cystitis and panic disorder: A potential genetic syndrome. *Archives of General Psychiatry*, *61*, 273–279.

Wenninger, K., Heiman, J. R., Rothman, I., Berghuis, J. P., & Berger, R. E. (1996). Sickness impact of chronic nonbacterial prostatitis and its correlates. *The Journal of Urology*, *155*, 965–998.

Whitmore, K., Siegel, J. F., & Kellogg-Spadt, S. (2007). Interstitial cystitis/painful bladder syndrome as a cause of sexual pain in women: A diagnosis to consider. *The Journal of Sexual Medicine*, *4*, 720–727.

Williams, A. C., & Shäfer, G. (2016). How do we understand depression in people with persistent pain? *Journal of Contemporary Psychotherapy*, *46*, 149–157.

16

Orofacial Pain

John E. Schmidt and James M. Hawkins

The views expressed in this article reflect the results of research conducted by the authors and do not necessarily reflect the official policy or position of the Department of the Navy, Department of Defense, or the United States Government.

I am a military service member or federal/contracted employee of the United States Government. This work was prepared as part of my official duties. Title 17 U.S.C. 105 provides that "copyright protection under this title is not available for any work of the United States Government." Title 17 U.S.C. 101 defines a U.S. Government work as work prepared by a military service member or employee of the U.S. Government as part of that person's official duties.

Neither I nor any member of my family have any financial affiliations, conflict of interest, or commercial support with any corporate organization, any commercial product(s), or service(s) that may be mentioned in this publication.

Introduction

Orofacial pain (OFP) encompasses a wide range of conditions that may impact all aspects of a patient's life. The etiology of OFP is often multifactorial, making these conditions difficult to both diagnose and manage (Svensson & Kumar, 2016). Depending on the pain location (e.g., tooth, eye, ear, jaw, head, and/or face), patients often will present to either a dentist or a primary care physician for initial evaluation, many times followed by further evaluation from an oral surgeon, neurologist, and/or ENT provider. Based on the clinician's training and experience, the patient may receive a wide variety of treatment modalities. When improvement is minimal and pain persists, the patient may be best managed by an OFP specialist, typically a dentist who has completed a postgraduate university-based residency program in OFP. The residency training programs usually include two or three years of academic and clinical work, followed by a two-stage national board certification process via the American Academy of Orofacial Pain.

Psychosocial challenges may play a major role in the onset and maintenance of OFP conditions as they do for many other types of chronic pain, and evidence demonstrates that premorbid psychosocial factors such as depression, anxiety, and perceived stress may predict the onset and persistence of OFP conditions (Aggarwal, Macfarlane, Farragher, & McBeth, 2010; Ohrbach et al., 2013; Slade et al., 2013). Therefore, a whole person-centered care approach is pertinent to treatment success (Kress et al., 2015), and interventions that target psychosocial factors are paramount for effective long-term management of these chronic conditions. This has led many OFP providers to work closely with behavioral health colleagues in managing OFP patients and requires that the effective clinician clearly understand the importance of evidence-based psychological care for these patients.

Brief Overview of OFPs

"Orofacial pain" is defined as pain and dysfunction affecting motor and sensory transmission in the trigeminal nerve system and refers to pain associated with the hard and soft tissues of the head, face, and neck (de Leeuw & Klasser, 2013). Headache and tooth pain are the most common OFP conditions, while masticatory myalgia (chewing muscle pain), temporomandibular disorder (TMJ) pain, trigeminal neuropathy, and cervical myofascial pain referring to the head and face are other conditions frequently managed in an OFP clinic.

Conditions elsewhere in the body, such as cardiac referred pain or a lung neoplasm, also may cause OFP. The reason such a broad range of entities may contribute to OFP is based on the physiologic concept of trigeminal convergence, which describes the meeting of multiple cranial nerves (V, VII, IX, and X) and cervical nerves (C1–C5) conveying nociceptive and metaboreceptive information via a first order neuron onto an area of the brainstem referred to as the trigeminal subnucleus caudalis (aka trigeminocervical complex; see Figure 16.1). This area, similar to the dorsal horn in the spinal cord, is where this information may be processed and/or modulated prior to second order transmission to higher brain areas.

While there are other causes for OFP such as tumors or trauma, the majority of chronic OFP conditions have no easily identifiable etiology. For example, a patient may complain of intense jaw pain while chewing, whether or not there is actual tissue damage. This lack of a "cause" of the pain can be a significant stressor for the patient, as it may decrease hope for a "cure," and may lead to family, friends, and/or coworkers lacking understanding of and compassion for the patient. Additionally, pain occurring in the trigeminal system may have stronger meaning to the patient compared to pain in other parts of the body due to its proximity to areas vital for physical and social functioning. The aspects of functioning potentially impacted include the ability to breathe, eat and drink, speak,

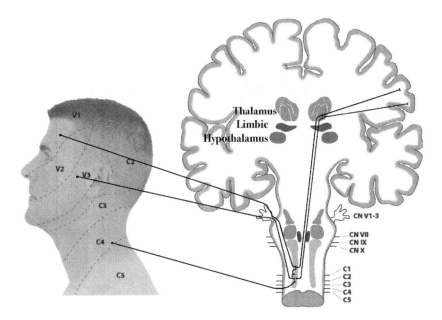

Figure 16.1   Trigeminal Convergence. Trigeminal and Cervical Nerves, As Well As Cranial Nerves VII, IX and X, Convey Metaboreceptive (Fatiguing) and Nociceptive (Painful) Information Synapse on a Small Area in the Brainstem, Referred to as the Trigeminal Subnucleus Caudalis.

CN = cranial nerve, C = cervical nerve, V = cranial nerve 5/trigeminal dermatome.

express intimacy, and express emotion (e.g., smile or frown). Therefore, pain and dysfunction in this area can contribute to a high perceived disability, possibly leading to absenteeism from work or school, withdrawal from normal social activities, and marital struggle.

The prevalence of OFP in the general population from epidemiological data varies depending upon the population sampled and mode of assessment. In a large survey study of more than 45,000 households, Lipton and colleagues (1993) found that over 20% of individuals experienced OFP within the past six months. Of these, about 80% experienced other pain sources beyond the trigeminal system (Lipton, Ship, & Larach-Robinson, 1993). This highlights the fact that OFP usually occurs as a result of multifaceted etiologies and may be accompanied by many comorbid conditions. These comorbid conditions typically include fibromyalgia, migraine and tension-type headaches, irritable bowel syndrome, PTSD, and more (Dahan, Shir, Velly, & Allison, 2015; Yunus, 2008).

Unfortunately, many patients do not readily disclose areas of concern outside of the typical scope of the provider's practice (e.g., a patient often will only tell a dentist about pain in the mouth and not other body pains), which can make providing a correct diagnosis and comprehensive effective care much more difficult (Hawkins et al., 2016). It therefore is imperative that clinicians be aware of this underreporting and specifically ask patients about the presence of other pain conditions and comorbidities during the clinical encounter, as optimal orofacial pain management may not be achieved without accounting for these in the treatment plan.

Brief Summary of Chapter Scope

This chapter focuses on the importance and efficacy of psychosocial interventions for the treatment and long-term management of OFP conditions. It begins with a brief discussion of conceptual issues related to psychosocial factors associated with OFP conditions such as affect, catastrophizing, and symptoms of posttraumatic stress disorder, and how these factors may influence treatment effectiveness and adherence. Next, it briefly reviews the research regarding the links between psychological factors and OFP conditions and examines the mechanisms that may be of particular interest to a clinician working with OFP patients.

Many interventions are available for OFP patients. These traverse a wide spectrum, from the biomechanical (e.g., splint therapy) to pharmacological (e.g., muscle relaxers) to more comprehensive interventions that address behavioral and psychosocial issues. We will focus on the content, benefits, and efficacy of psychosocial interventions, from brief techniques such as relaxation and habit reversal to more advanced treatment approaches, which include cognitive-behavioral therapy, biofeedback, and hypnosis. Many of these interventions have demonstrated efficacy in randomized controlled trials (RCTs), which will be discussed.

Relevance of Psychological Factors in OFP and Conceptual Frameworks

Understanding the importance of contributing psychosocial factors in the severity and chronicity of chronic pain conditions began soon after widespread adoption of Engel's biopsychosocial model (Borrell-Carrio, Suchman, & Epstein, 2004; Engel, 1977; Turk & Okifuji, 2002). There is a strong association between OFP conditions and psychosocial factors, as with other chronic pain and many chronic medical conditions (Turk & Okifuji, 2002; Zimmermann & Tansella, 1996) such as diabetes or lupus. Chronic OFP is associated with multisystem dysregulation, including disruption in both physiological systems (e.g., autonomic, inflammatory) (H. Chen, Nackley, Miller, Diatchenko, & Maixner, 2013; Schmidt & Carlson, 2009) and psychological systems (e.g., affect, catastrophizing) (Giannakopoulos, Keller, Rammelsberg, Kronmuller, & Schmitter, 2010; Turner, Brister, et al., 2005). These characteristics of OFP ensure that these conditions are challenging to manage and treat effectively.

Chronic OFP conditions often negatively impact many aspects of a patient's life. The condition and pain may interfere with daily activities and employment, reduce social interactions, and strain family relationships. As the OFP condition becomes chronic, the patient often will experience an increase in psychological distress. If the patient already struggles with symptoms of a psychiatric disorder such as an anxiety or depressive disorder, the presence of a chronic OFP is likely to exacerbate the mental health disorder (Carlson, 2008; Gatchel, Stowell, Wildenstein, Riggs, & Ellis, 2006).

The significance of identifying, evaluating, and addressing comorbid psychological factors in these patients has been highlighted in the Dual Axis Model developed by Dworkin (Dworkin, 2001) and Okeson (Okeson, 2014). In this model, Axis I includes the biological components, while Axis II includes the psychological responses or comorbidities. This model, which has demonstrated diagnostic utility in OFP practices, enables the clinician to have a broader understanding of the multifaceted nature of how the OFP condition impacts the patient from a more holistic perspective. Among OFP specialists, the application of the Dual Axis Model (Figure 16.2) highlights the complexity of OFP conditions, as

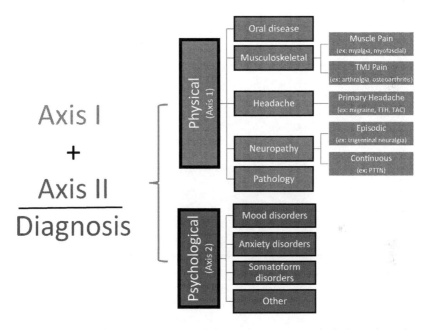

Figure 16.2 Simplified Dual Axis Model. Axis I Is Composed of Physical Orofacial Pain Sources, of which the Most Common Entities Are Listed Here. Axis II Is Composed of Psychologic Entities Which Can Impact the Patient's Orofacial Pain. The Combination of Axis I & II Lead to Diagnosis. An Exhaustive List of Physical and Psychologic Entities Is Beyond the Scope of This Chapter and Can Be Found in Dr. Okeson's Textbook Titled *Bell's Oral and Facial Pain*, 7th ed.

TMJ = temporomandibular joint, TTH = tension type headache, TAC = trigeminal autonomic cephalalgia, PTTN = painful traumatic trigeminal neuropathy

well as the importance of assessing and understanding psychosocial factors when developing effective treatment plans.

The biopsychosocial model (Engel, 1977) also serves as a helpful framework and guide when evaluating and treating chronic OFP conditions, as the experience and impact of chronic OFP are influenced strongly by the dynamic interactions among biological, psychological, and social factors. While the Dual Axis Model discussed above is useful for diagnostic evaluation, OFP conditions reflect an ongoing and dynamic interplay between biological processes and psychological functioning, while also impacting social aspects of a patient's life. The biopsychosocial model posited by Engel in 1977 initiated a long-overdue critical reassessment of the biomedical model of disease management.

Modern medical care, up to the time of Engel's alternative holistic approach, was focused primarily on treating the biological problem and managing physical symptoms. Engel offered a new paradigm that challenged the view that illness is a direct result of a biomedical change. Rather, he argued the following points: 1) the presentation of an illness is the result of interactive factors (biological, psychological, and social) and is not simply a biological problem; 2) the impact of a similar illness on each patient is unique; 3) psychological variables are major determinants of the presentation and course of an illness, as well as the efficacy of any treatment; 4) a biological problem may not be the sole reason for a patient adopting the "sick" role; and 5) the relationship between a patient and clinician may strongly influence treatment outcomes (Engel, 1977, 1980).

The biopsychosocial model has been used to improve diagnosis and treatment planning for OFP conditions.

Psychosocial Factors Associated With OFP

The associations among psychosocial factors and OFP conditions have been a focus of research for many years and are documented in numerous studies (Molin, Edman, & Schalling, 1973; Molin, Schalling, & Edman, 1973). In particular, pain severity, pain duration, and disability often are found to be strongly associated with psychological factors. In early studies (Carlson et al., 1993; Keefe & Dolan, 1986), these associations often were challenging to interpret due to small sample sizes yielding small effect size estimates. More recently, larger population-based longitudinal studies exploring the possible relationships among psychosocial factors and OFP conditions have resulted in stronger and more robust findings.

For example, Slade and colleagues (Slade et al., 2007) completed a prospective cohort study over a three-year period with the goal of determining whether significant psychological distress was predictive of a chronic OFP condition. Over the course of the study, approximately 9% of the 171 otherwise healthy females were diagnosed with a new onset OFP condition. Predictors of the OFP condition included depression, perceived stress, and overall mood. A more recent study by Kindler and colleagues followed a sample of over 3,000 participants for approximately nine years (Kindler et al., 2012). OFP conditions were diagnosed in 4.1% of the sample over the course of the study, with baseline affect (anxiety and depression) found to be significant predictors of OFP conditions.

The primary aim of these and other studies (Aggarwal et al., 2010; LeResche, 1997) was to determine, in long-term longitudinal cohort designs, potential predictors of the development of OFP conditions. Combined, the results of these studies strongly suggest the importance of understanding and treating psychosocial issues in chronic, as well as newly diagnosed, OFP patients.

Identifying predictors and risk factors that may contribute to an OFP condition became a major focus of the National Institutes of Dental and Craniofacial Research (NIDCR) with the funding and ongoing work of the Orofacial Pain: Prospective Evaluation and Risk Assessment (OPPERA) studies (Dworkin, 2011). The OPPERA studies, initiated in 2006, are a unique natural history approach to studying chronic pain conditions and have yielded helpful information about the associations among psychosocial factors and OFP conditions. The interested reader is referred to two issues of *The Journal of Pain* that were dedicated to papers based on OPPERA study data (2011, volume 12, number 11, supplement 3; and 2013, volume 14, number 12, supplement 2). Baseline data from the OPPERA studies comparing participants with and without OFP conditions found higher depression, anxiety, somatization, and perceived stress among the participants with OFP (Fillingim et al., 2011).

Part of the second phase of OPPERA included the longitudinal assessment of 2,737 participants who reported no OFP conditions at baseline. When assessed approximately three years later, 9% of the study sample reported new-onset OFP. Predictors of OFP onset included depression, somatization, and perceived stress (Fillingim et al., 2013). These and other data from the OPPERA studies highlight the importance of assessing patients in the psychosocial domains concurrent with assessing and treating the OFP from a biomedical perspective. Having an awareness of specific psychological factors, both psychiatric disorders and subclinical variations of psychological symptoms typically seen in OFP patients, is important for effective clinical assessment and management.

Depression

Associations between symptoms of depression and numerous chronic pain conditions (e.g., low back pain, knee pain, arthritis, fibromyalgia) have been studied for many years. Indeed, symptoms of depression are the most prevalent of all psychological issues in many chronic pain populations, including OFP patients (Kight, Gatchel, & Wesley, 1999). A clear understanding of the symptoms of depression, a working knowledge of the diagnostic criteria for major depressive disorder, and the ability to assess symptoms of depression in OFP patients are paramount to the efficacy of any psychosocial intervention. Readers are referred to the *Diagnostic and Statistical Manual of Mental Disorders V* (APA, 2013) for current diagnostic criteria.

Depressed affect correlates directly with increased pain severity (Romano & Turner, 1985; Sheng, Liu, Wang, Cui, & Zhang, 2017) and has been shown to exacerbate pain catastrophizing and cognitive distortions in patients with OFP conditions (Campbell et al., 2010; Velly et al., 2011). In addition, symptoms of depression may lead to negative social and interpersonal difficulties, contributing to a poor social support system for these patients. Particularly relevant to this patient population, symptoms of depression may result in lack of adequate oral hygiene and poor regular dental care, increasing the challenge of long-term care of the OFP patient (Humphrey, Lindroth, & Carlson, 2002).

A hallmark characteristic of a depressed individual is a lack of motivation to engage in self-care activities; thus, the patient with significant symptoms of depression may have difficulty adhering to any intervention (Bodner, 2006). This is concerning for OFP and other chronic pain patients particularly, given that interventions for chronic pain are highly dependent upon the patient adopting and integrating new pain management skills and changing long-standing patterns of behavior in order to improve daily functioning. Patients with symptoms of depression may experience suicidal ideation, which is a serious and potentially life-threatening condition. Referral to appropriate clinical providers for effective treatment is essential if a patient is experiencing suicidal ideation or intent.

Anxiety

Anxiety symptoms and disorders are more prevalent in OFP patients than in the general population and are associated with both the nociceptive component of pain as well as with anticipatory anxiety related to movements or activities that may exacerbate pain (Fillingim et al., 2011; Reiter, Emodi-Perlman, Goldsmith, Friedman-Rubin, & Winocur, 2015). Symptoms of anxiety and depression often co-occur, especially in chronic pain patients who commonly worry and catastrophize about pain-related functional limitations and pain triggers. Treating these issues concurrently can be challenging, especially given the differences in how they respond to an intervention.

Due to the high prevalence of anxiety symptoms among patients with major depressive disorder, an anxiety qualifier was added to the DSM-5 diagnostic criteria for major depression in order to capture patients with a depressive disorder concurrent with anxiety symptoms that may exacerbate negative affect (APA, 2013). The presence of significant symptoms of anxiety predicted the development of an OFP condition in several studies (Aggarwal et al., 2010; Fillingim et al., 2013). Anxiety symptoms often are directly targeted in multidisciplinary treatment for OFP conditions, typically concurrently with depressive symptoms.

In patients with a chronic OFP condition, the subjective experience of pain itself is often the source of anxiety. Anticipating an increase in pain will exacerbate fear and increase pain-related anxiety. Specifically, pain catastrophizing is a maladaptive cognitive processing style in which the individual magnifies the impact of a pain stimulus or potential pain stimulus, feels helpless in the context of ongoing pain severity, and has difficulty inhibiting pain-related thoughts before, during, and following an event that may have increased pain severity (Quartana, Campbell, & Edwards, 2009). This pattern of catastrophizing may result in avoiding activities that previously were normal day-to-day events for the patient.

Catastrophizing only recently has been explored in OFP conditions specifically and may be associated with the potential efficacy of treatment. In several studies, chronic OFP patients have reported higher levels of catastrophizing than patients with other chronic pain conditions (Gil-Martinez et al., 2016). In addition, a longitudinal study of 480 OFP patients found that higher levels of catastrophizing at baseline were associated with progression of clinically significant pain severity and disability at an 18-month follow-up (Velly et al., 2011). These data suggest that catastrophizing may contribute to the progression of an OFP condition over time. Further, higher levels of pain catastrophizing in OFP patients are associated with interference in activities of daily living and increase in healthcare utilization, as well as reduced mandibular range of motion and functioning (Davis, Stockstill, Stanley, & Wu, 2014; Turner, Brister, et al., 2005).

Symptoms of anxiety may result in parafunction, which is defined as movements or use of a body part that are considered outside of normal functioning. Parafunction may lead to abnormal wear and eventual breakdown of supportive tissues and structures (Glaros, Williams, & Lausten, 2005). In OFP conditions, parafunction often is identified as bruxism (grinding or clenching of the teeth by excessive overuse or bracing of the muscles of mastication, also termed non-functional tooth contact). Parafunction may be a result of the OFP condition where the patient maintains protective contraction of the muscles of mastication due to fear of re-injuring the site or of increasing pain due to normal use; parafunction also is associated with higher levels of perceived stress and anxiety (C. Y. Chen, Palla, Erni, Sieber, & Gallo, 2007). Conversely, parafunction may be an initial contributor to the OFP condition in that the patient may have engaged in teeth clenching/grinding for many years, which eventually led to the development of a painful OFP diagnosis and/or tooth wear (Giannakopoulos et al., 2010).

OFP patients often are diagnosed with either a generalized anxiety disorder (GAD) or posttraumatic stress disorder (PTSD) if the specific DSM-5 criteria are met (Okeson, 2014). Patients with GAD present with persistent, excessive, and often unrealistic worry that interferes with social and other activities of daily living. The worry can feel out of control and be focused on just about anything (e.g., health, finances, work, and family issues). The prevalence of GAD in OFP populations is significantly higher than in the general population (Yeung, Abou-Foul, Matcham, Poate, & Fan, 2017). For example, prevalence of significant anxiety and depressive symptoms in the international general population typically is around 10% and can range from 3.8 to nearly 25% depending on demographics and cultural factors (Remes, Brayne, van der Linde, & Lafortune, 2016). However, in patients with OFP conditions, significant anxiety and depression can range from 16 to 40% (Yeung et al., 2017).

Traumatic Stress and Posttraumatic Stress Disorder

The prevalence of symptoms of posttraumatic stress disorder (PTSD) among OFP patients is higher than in the general population, and exposure to traumatic stressors often is reported by this patient population. Lifetime prevalence estimates of PTSD in the general population range from 3 to 9.2% (APA, 2013; Atwoli, Stein, Koenen, & McLaughlin, 2015). In two studies exploring the associations among OFP and traumatic stressors/PTSD in large study samples (Ns = 1221 and 1478) by de Leeuw and colleagues, a significant number (50% to 52%) of study participants reported having experienced at least one traumatic stressor (de Leeuw, Bertoli, Schmidt, & Carlson, 2005a, 2005b). Pain severity, affective distress, sleep dysfunction, and disability were higher among the study participants reporting a traumatic stressor, and highest in those participants who met the criteria for a diagnosis of PTSD. The most frequently reported traumatic stressors included serious injury or death of a family member or close friend, severe motor vehicle accident, and sudden injury/accident.

Other studies also have found high prevalence of PTSD symptoms in OFP patients (Sherman, Carlson, Wilson, Okeson, & McCubbin, 2005). Furthermore, stressful life events and PTSD symptoms were found to be predictors of the development of temporomandibular joint (TMD) conditions in the OPPERA study (Fillingim et al., 2013), often occurring prior to the onset of an OFP condition.

The dynamic association between traumatic experiences and chronic OFP may be described as a mutual maintenance model (Sharp & Harvey, 2001), where certain aspects of PTSD exacerbate chronic pain and vice versa, such as avoidant coping, attentional bias, and trauma reminders. For example, anxiety is a primary characteristic of PTSD and may increase the subjective experience of pain severity while also decreasing pain tolerance and depleting cognitive coping resources in the patient with OFP. Depression and sleep dysfunction were found to influence pain severity significantly more in patients with PTSD than in those without PTSD in an analysis of this concept (Burris, Cyders, de Leeuw, Smith, & Carlson, 2009), suggesting mutual maintenance of the two conditions. Clinicians need to be aware of the symptoms of PTSD (APA, 2013) and how these symptoms manifest in OFP patients, given that PTSD symptoms are highly associated with pain severity and affective distress and thus may contribute to poor treatment adherence and effectiveness.

Somatic Symptoms

The DSM-5 included significant changes from the DSM-IV-TR in the area of somatic symptom disorders. These types of disorders now are known as somatic symptom and related disorders. The changes were made to better delineate these disorders for easier diagnosis and treatment planning (APA, 2013). Somatic symptom and related disorders are a group of disorders with predominant somatic presentation (e.g., pain, fatigue, neurological symptoms) that are highly distressing or are interfering in daily functioning. A cognitive component also is needed to fully meet criteria; specifically, the person experiences excessive thoughts (e.g., catastrophizing), feelings (e.g., health anxiety), or behaviors (e.g., excessive time and resources devoted to the symptoms) related to the somatic symptoms.

In addition to depressive and anxiety disorders, the DSM-5 diagnosis of somatic symptom disorder with predominant pain (previously pain disorder in the DSM-IV) also is given to OFP patients (Kroenke, 2007; Reiter et al., 2015). Somatic symptoms typically are assessed in studies of OFP, similar to studies of other chronic pain conditions. OFP patients report significantly higher somatic symptoms and behaviors compared to pain-free controls (McGregor et al., 1996; Schmidt & Carlson, 2009), with effect sizes in these two studies ranging from 0.71 to 0.98. In both of these studies, somatization was assessed using the somatic subscale of the System Check List-90 (SCL-90), which is a well-validated and comprehensive measure (Derogatis, 1994).

Psychological Assessment in OFP

The biopsychosocial model encourages a comprehensive assessment across multiple domains of functioning in order to fully understand how the dysfunction (e.g., OFP condition) is affecting the patient as a whole. As discussed above, OFP and other chronic pain conditions have affective, cognitive, social, and sensory aspects, all of which may impact OFP symptom severity and interfere in daily functioning. The general goal of psychological assessment is to identify symptoms that may exacerbate an OFP condition, make self-care more challenging, and serve as potential barriers to the efficacy of any intervention. Therefore, findings of significant psychological distress may necessitate referral for appropriate mental healthcare and support.

Assessment of Depressive Symptoms

Screening for depression in OFP patients is strongly encouraged, as these symptoms are the most prevalent in this chronic pain population. Several well-validated self-report screening tools may be used to assess for symptoms of depression. Currently, the most commonly used tool in many medical clinics is the Patient Health Questionnaire-9 (PHQ-9) (Kroenke, Spitzer, & Williams, 2001). The full version has nine items scored on a 4-point Likert scale. The items are based on the nine DSM criteria for diagnosing depressive disorders (APA, 2013). This measure has been validated in several large studies with a variety of patient populations (Kroenke & Spitzer, 2002; Lowe, Unutzer, Callahan, Perkins, & Kroenke, 2004). It is very easy to complete and takes about five minutes for the typical patient. Two short versions of the PHQ use two and four items (Kroenke, Spitzer, & Williams, 2003; Kroenke, Spitzer, Williams, & Lowe, 2010). The PHQ screener is free to download and use with no required permissions at this website: www. phqscreeners.com.

Other common depression screeners include the Hospital Anxiety and Depression Scale (HADS), the Center for Epidemiological Studies Depression scale (CES-D), and the Beck Depression Inventory-II (BDI-II). The HADS (Zigmund & Snaith, 1983) is a 14-item measure that includes seven items for depression and seven items for anxiety. The HADS, which measures anxiety and depression symptoms over the previous week, was developed for use with medical patients. This is a widely used, easy to administer, and publicly available measure with good psychometric properties (Luciano, Barrada, Aguado, Osma, & Garcia-Campayo, 2014).

The CES-D (Radloff, 1977) is a 20-item measure that clusters symptoms into somatic complaints, affect, and interpersonal constraints. This measure has demonstrated good psychometric properties in primary care settings (McQuaid, Stein, McCahill, Laffaye, & Ramel, 2000) and compares favorably to other self-report measures of depression (Shafer, 2006). However, the CES-D has more items than the other measures, so it takes longer for patients to complete.

Clinicians also may consider using the BDI-II, a well-known measure of depression (Beck, Steer, Ball, & Ranieri, 1996; Beck, Ward, Mendelson, Mock, & Erbaugh, 1961). This measure contains 21 items and has been tested extensively for validity and reliability (Harris & D'Eon, 2008; Titov et al., 2011). The content of the items was established through consensus among clinicians regarding depressive symptoms displayed by psychiatric patients. The BDI-II is copyrighted and users pay a fee to use this measure.

Screening for Anxiety Symptoms

The most commonly used measures for anxiety screening in OFP clinics are the Generalized Anxiety Disorder screener (GAD-7), the Hospital Anxiety and Depression Scale (HADS), and the Beck Anxiety Inventory (BAI). The GAD-7 is a 7-item measure and was developed for brief screening of symptoms of generalized anxiety (Spitzer, Kroenke, Williams, & Lowe, 2006). The items mirror some, but not all, of the DSM-5 criteria for generalized anxiety. This measure was validated initially with a large (n = 2740) sample of primary care patients and was found to have good psychometric properties (Kroenke, Spitzer, Williams, Monahan, & Lowe, 2007; Spitzer et al., 2006). The GAD-7 is short, requires no permission to use, and is available at this website: www.phqscreeners.com.

The HADS (Zigmund & Snaith, 1983), which is composed of seven items for depression and seven items for anxiety, is discussed in the depression screening section. The BAI (Beck, Epstein, Brown, & Steer, 1988) is a 21-item measure of anxiety, and each item is descriptive of subjective, somatic, or panic-related symptoms of anxiety. The BAI has demonstrated good psychometric properties in multiple patient populations (Arnold et al., 2004; Kabacoff, Segal, Hersen, & Van Hasselt, 1997). The BAI is copyrighted and users pay a fee to use this measure.

Other areas of function that may be clinically valuable to include in a more comprehensive psychological assessment are sleep functioning, fatigue, catastrophizing, and symptoms of posttraumatic stress.

Personality Factors and Disorders

The research on personality factors and disorders among OFP patients is limited but informative. The paucity of research in this area likely is due the unique resources and expertise required for a valid and thorough personality assessment. These resources typically are not found at an orofacial pain clinic. However, the clinician should be aware of the potential impact that personality characteristics may have on the utility and efficacy of interventions. Furthermore, an OFP patient with a diagnosable personality disorder may respond in unpredictable ways when attempting to integrate behavior change strategies into a set daily routine.

While there are several different ways to assess normal personality functioning, the Five-Factor Model (FFM) developed by Costa and McCrae (Costa, 1991; McCrae & Costa, 1985) is probably the most widely used and understood. The assessments and ease of interpretation made this approach more mainstream and useful in many clinical settings. The FFM assesses normal personality functioning along the following five characteristics: 1) neuroticism, 2) extraversion, 3) openness, 4) agreeableness, and 5) conscientiousness. The use of the FFM with chronic pain patients is surprisingly limited. Wade and colleagues, in a study of 205 chronic pain patients, found both extraversion and neuroticism to be strongly associated with perceptions of pain suffering, cognitive processing of pain, and illness behaviors (Wade, Dougherty, Hart, Rafii, & Price, 1992). Other studies using the neuroticism and extraversion subscales from the FFM inventory found both of these characteristics to be associated with pain coping and pain behaviors (Asghari & Nicholas, 2006; Pallegama, Ranasinghe, Weerasinghe, & Sitheeque, 2005; Raselli & Broderick, 2007). These results suggest that personality characteristics may influence cognitive processing of the impact and meaning of chronic pain and thus may have a moderating effect on successful pain coping and pain behaviors.

Based on the outcomes of these studies, there may be clinical utility in assessing normal personality structure during multidisciplinary evaluation and thereafter utilizing this information to help inform treatment planning and intervention. In the OPPERA study, neuroticism was associated with the development of an OFP condition; however, extraversion was not in this longitudinal cohort study (Fillingim et al., 2013). In a study of OFP patients using the short-form version of the FFM assessment (the NEO-Five Factor Inventory; Costa & McCrae, 1992), Schmidt and colleagues found that higher pain severity was associated with lower openness, while higher psychological distress was associated with higher neuroticism, lower extraversion, and lower openness (Schmidt, Hooten, & Carlson, 2011). Clarifying the relationships between personality traits and chronic OFP conditions may lead to pain management interventions that are individually modified based on personality characteristics.

The presence of a personality disorder presents a challenge for effective long-term OFP management. Personality disorder criteria are based on how a person relates to others and the nature of those interactions and represent a stable pattern of inner experiences and behavior that deviate markedly from the expectations of the individual's culture and societal norms. Personality disorders are pervasive and often inflexible, causing ongoing distress and impairment in daily functioning.

Research exploring the relationships among personality disorders and OFP conditions is very limited. In studies focused on other chronic pain conditions, personality disorders have demonstrated high comorbidity (Conrad et al., 2007; Tragesser, Bruns, & Disorbio, 2010; Vendrig, Derksen, & de Mey, 2000). Patients who present with personality disorders can be challenging to treat regardless of the severity and chronicity of the pain complaint. Non-adaptive coping styles and pervasive abnormalities in personality may interfere with treatment planning and adherence to any intervention that includes self-regulation or change in daily behavior patterns (e.g., exercise, CBT techniques).

Psychological Interventions

As with any treatment approach for a chronic problem, the primary goal is to help the patient return to normal daily functioning, or as close to it as possible. OFP conditions are complex problems that require careful management and treatment in a systematic fashion utilizing multiple strategies. As described previously, treatment planning should encapsulate the biopsychosocial approach as much as possible in order to achieve significant and lasting symptom relief and improvement in overall functioning.

Throughout treatment, standardized assessments should be used to determine ongoing treatment effectiveness. These assessments may include monitoring pain severity (e.g., pain Visual Analog Scale or the McGill Pain Inventory), symptoms of depression (e.g., Patient Health Questionnaire-9), symptoms of anxiety (e.g., Generalized Anxiety Disorder questionnaire-7), or severity of pain catastrophizing (e.g., Pain Catastrophizing Scale). In the developmental trials of the psychosocial interventions for OFP described below, standardized self-report assessments are used to determine treatment efficacy.

Habit Reversal

In the context of OFP conditions, habit reversal refers to controlling and changing behavior patterns that may exacerbate jaw muscle tension and increase pain. Habit reversal as a behavioral intervention was developed in the 1970s to target a variety of issues, including nervous tics and nail biting (Azrin & Nunn, 1973), and has demonstrated treatment effectiveness (Azrin, Nunn, & Frantz-Renshaw, 1982; Bate, Malouff, Thorsteinsson, & Bhullar, 2011). Many OFP patients engage in oral parafunctional habits such as clenching the jaw muscles, bruxism (clenching and grinding teeth together), and fingernail biting. The goal of habit reversal is to identify oral parafunction and to introduce and practice a competing behavior pattern.

For example, a patient may clench and maintain unnecessary tooth contact throughout a typical day, often unaware of this parafunctional activity. This patient can be instructed to complete a brief check and correct jaw position (tooth contact) and masseter muscle tension every couple of hours for a short amount of time (e.g., 15 seconds), letting the masseter muscles relax and stopping any ongoing tooth contact. This simple monitoring and relaxing of the masseter muscles may result in a decrease in OFP as well as a better awareness and control of the parafunctional behavior pattern over time.

In a study where OFP patients were randomized to either a standard splint therapy or a habit reversal group, Glaros and colleagues (Glaros, Kim-Weroha, Lausten, & Franklin, 2007) found the same benefit in pain reduction for both groups at one-month and one-year follow-ups. The patients in the habit reversal group were paged every two hours during the day as a reminder to check and correct tooth position and muscle tension.

Self-Regulation Strategies

Physical self-regulation strategies are designed to reduce the autonomic dysregulation present in chronic pain conditions. Autonomic dysregulation and chronic autonomic arousal may be significant contributors to the constellation of symptoms that many chronic OFP patients experience (Schmidt & Carlson, 2009). In a physical self-regulation program developed by Carlson and Bertrand, patients are taught a set of skills designed to reduce physiological activation (Carlson, Bertrand, Ehrlich, Maxwell, & Burton, 2001). This program includes proprioceptive awareness training (recognition and control of non-functional tooth contact, awareness and reduction of mandibular clenching and grinding), postural relaxation training, diaphragmatic breathing, sleep hygiene, and fluid, nutrition, and exercise management. The intervention is presented in two sessions typically spaced out by three to four weeks to allow the patient time to practice and identify barriers to skills utilization and to foster self-efficacy. In a controlled trial, patients were randomized to the physical self-regulation or standard splint therapy. Patients in both groups showed comparable improvement in pain severity, range of motion, and affective distress post-treatment. However, improvements were maintained in the PSR group, but not in the control group, at a 26-week follow-up assessment (Carlson et al., 2001).

Biofeedback

In the application of biofeedback, technology is used to capture and display a biomarker (e.g., skin temperature, muscle activity) for the patient. The patient learns, through different techniques such as diaphragmatic breathing, muscle activation, or relaxation, to exert volitional control over the biomarker with the goals of reducing pain and restoring normal function.

413

Biofeedback began to emerge as a useful therapeutic tool in the late 1950s with the development of surface electromyography (sEMG) systems for measuring muscle activity using surface sensors adhesively attached to the skin. One of the first published biofeedback articles described the effectiveness of a slow muscle stretching technique for muscle pain using sEMG and galvanic skin response (GSR) biofeedback (Toomin & Toomin, 1975). Early practitioners viewed biofeedback as a form of instrumental conditioning of psychophysiological systems (Schwartz, 1995). Many of the initial biofeedback studies focused on patients going through neuromuscular rehabilitation after experiencing a major stroke (Andrews, 1964; Brudny, 1982).

Modern biofeedback devices and technology can be used to display information on multiple biological signals, including skin temperature, skin conductance, respiration rate, muscle activity, and cardiovascular function, including heart-rate variability. The biofeedback modality most commonly used with OFP patients is sEMG for muscle control and retraining. Many OFP patients engage in daily parafunction such as clenching/grinding the teeth, bruxism, and unnecessary tooth contact, which contributes to the severity and chronicity of the OFP condition (Gameiro, da Silva Andrade, Nouer, & Ferraz de Arruda Veiga, 2006). However, OFP patients often are unaware of this pattern of abnormal muscle activity and its impact on pain severity. During sEMG biofeedback, surface electrodes are placed on the muscle (typically the masseter and/or temporalis muscles) and the muscle activity signal is shown on a computer screen for visual feedback to the patient. The patient learns to control the muscle activity using contractions and relaxations, while observing the visually presented data.

Biofeedback using sEMG for reducing masseter and temporalis muscle activity has been used clinically since the mid-1970s (Carlsson, Gale, & Ohman, 1975; Gessel, 1975). The use of sEMG biofeedback was endorsed as a scientifically supported intervention for muscle-related temporomandibular joint disorders by the American Dental Association in 1982 and again in 1990 (Mohl, Lund, Widmer, & McCall, 1990). Please see Crider and Glaros (1999) for a review of sEMG biofeedback in temporomandibular disorders.

A more recent review included 14 studies that used biofeedback-based treatments for OFP conditions (Crider, Glaros, & Gevirtz, 2005). These studies were grouped into three treatment types: 1) sEMG training using masseter muscle placement; 2) sEMG combined with cognitive-behavioral therapy (CBT); and 3) biofeedback-assisted relaxation training (BART). Overall, sEMG biofeedback training for OFP was determined to be efficacious according to the guidelines established by the Association for Applied Psychophysiology and Biofeedback (Association for Applied & Biofeedback, 2002). The strongest effect sizes were found in the two studies that tested sEMG biofeedback with CBT (Crockett, Foreman, Alden, & Blasberg, 1986; Turk, Zaki, & Rudy, 1993). In both randomized trials, the biofeedback condition was more effective in reducing pain intensity and duration than the other study conditions.

In a recent RCT, Mora and colleagues compared a weekly eight-session biofeedback-based CBT program to occlusal splint therapy worn for eight weeks (Mora, Weber, Neff, & Rief, 2013). While both treatments resulted in a significant reduction in pain and jaw-use limitations, patients in the biofeedback group reported a significant increase in pain-coping skills. All improvements were stable at a six-month follow-up in both groups, with greater improvements in the biofeedback group.

In biofeedback-assisted relaxation training (BART), the primary treatment target of biofeedback is not retraining muscles to reduce muscle activity, but instead maximizing effective systemic relaxation in the patient. BART approaches are used frequently in stress-related disorders such as OFP and other chronic medical conditions (e.g., chronic pain, asthma, headaches) (McGrady et al., 2003; Neblett, Mayer, Brede, & Gatchel, 2010; Nestoriuc, Martin, Rief, & Andrasik, 2008). In this context, the clinician displays biomarkers to the patient for monitoring his/her depth of relaxation during relaxation training. The clinician may utilize different biomarkers (e.g., masseter muscle activity, skin temperature, heart-rate variability). The efficacy of BART in OFP was assessed in two RCTs, with both studies finding a significant improvement in pain intensity compared to the other study conditions post-treatment and at one-year follow-up (Brooke & Stenn, 1983; Mishra, Gatchel, & Gardea, 2000).

Relaxation

Patients with OFP appear to over-respond to environmental stimuli with increased sympathetic activation, as evidenced by more rapid and shallow breathing and lower heart-rate variability (Curran, Carlson, & Okeson, 1996; Schmidt & Carlson, 2009). Relaxation techniques are useful yet easy to learn and can help alleviate sympathetic activation. Relaxation strategies range from simply resting the body in a relaxed position several times a day to more intensive techniques, such as progressive muscle relaxation. Some patients only require a brief introduction, education, and practice session before incorporating brief relaxation breaks into their daily routines. However, many OFP patients struggle with fostering postural relaxation; in these cases, more extensive training may be necessary, such as using BART as described above. Techniques that trigger the relaxation response as described by Benson (1975) include passive and progressive muscle relaxation, mindfulness meditation, and diaphragmatic breathing paired with postural relaxation.

Hypnosis

Hypnosis is a technique in which the clinician (or hypnotist) interacts with the patient and offers suggestions for imaginative experiences that result in alterations in perception, memory, and voluntary actions (Kihlstrom, 2008). Hypnosis has been used to treat many chronic pain populations, often with effective results

(Jensen & Patterson, 2014). However, responses may be highly variable and largely based on the hypnotizability of patients (Patterson & Jensen, 2003).

There only have been a few controlled trials assessing the efficacy of hypnosis in OFP patients. In a randomized study using a hypnotically induced relaxation condition, 40 chronic OFP patients were assigned to three different treatment modalities. The treatment groups included hypnosis, oral appliance, and education. Both the hypnosis and education conditions took place over five treatment sessions. The hypnosis and appliance conditions both were more effective than the education condition in reducing facial muscular sensitivity to palpation. Further, patients in the hypnosis condition reported significantly less perceived pain on post-treatment pain VAS (Winocur, Gavish, Emodi-Perlman, Halachmi, & Eli, 2002).

In another study, 41 chronic OFP patients were randomized to a hypnosis condition or a simple relaxation condition for five sessions (Abrahamsen, Baad-Hansen, & Svensson, 2008). The hypnosis condition included progressive relaxation, guided imagery, and hypnotic suggestions for changing pain perceptions. Patients were given CDs of the induction to practice outside of the sessions. Patients in the hypnosis group reported greater reduction on pain VAS post-treatment, as well as reduced use of pain medications. Interestingly, within the hypnosis group, the more hypnotically suggestive patients reported significantly larger decreases in pain severity than the less hypnotically suggestive patients.

Cognitive-Behavioral Therapy

In multidisciplinary pain treatment based on the biopsychosocial model, cognitive-behavioral therapy (CBT) has become a commonly used and effective approach for treating many types of chronic pain (Ehde, Dillworth, & Turner, 2014). CBT focuses on building awareness of the connections among emotional triggers, automatic thoughts, and behavioral responses. When tailored to a chronic pain population, CBT targets identifying and fostering change in negative and maladaptive automatic thought processes related to the pain experience (e.g., "My pain will never get better" or "My pain is in control, not me") and self-limiting behavior patterns (e.g., "I'd love to go to that family event, but it will make my pain worse and I will be miserable company" or "I know that exercise is good for me, but I am afraid that any exercise activity will make my pain worse"). These maladaptive thought processes and subsequent behaviors often result in the avoidance of social and pleasurable activities, physical deconditioning, and affective distress. By challenging these patterns with a trained therapist, the patient learns to identify distorted automatic thoughts and cognitions, to increase positive emotional experiences, and to reduce sedentary behavior.

The many forms of CBT available for chronic pain patients include different therapeutic components such as relaxation training, expressive writing, communication skills, and stress-management skills training. For example, Beverly Thorn developed an evidence-based manualized cognitive therapy program for chronic pain that is now widely used; it combines several pain management techniques within a CBT framework (Thorn, 2017).

There have been numerous studies with OFP patients comparing CBT to other treatment modalities or usual care. For example, Dworkin et al. (2002) randomized 117 OFP patients to usual care or to a comprehensive care condition, which consisted of usual care and a six-session CBT program tailored for OFP patients. The CBT program included education on self-care, training on identifying and modifying maladaptive thought patterns related to pain, relaxation training, pain-coping skills, and relapse prevention. The patients in the comprehensive care condition reported significantly lower pain intensity, significantly higher ability to control pain, and less pain interference in daily activities than the patients in the usual care group.

In a study that integrated daily electronic interviews and daily diaries, 158 patients were assigned randomly to CBT for pain management or to an education control condition focusing on self-care (Turner, Mancl, & Aaron, 2005). The treatments were completed over four individual sessions. While there were no significant differences in perceived pain between the two groups post-treatment, patients in the CBT group consistently showed greater improvements on the daily electronic interview items that focused on pain-related coping, catastrophizing, and maladaptive cognitions related to pain such as perceptions of disability. When the study participants were assessed at 3, 6, and 12 months post-treatment, patients in the CBT group reported significant improvements in perceived ability to manage pain, reduced catastrophizing, decreased pain intensity, decreased depression, and increased jaw function.

A similar study by Litt and colleagues (2009) that integrated ecological momentary assessment used a manualized six-session CBT program with 54 OFP patients randomized to CBT or usual care. Patients completed baseline and post-treatment assessments of affect, pain, and coping processes four times per day via cell phone during the week prior to the start of treatment, and for two weeks post-treatment. While the general retrospective assessment post-treatment did not suggest significant differences between treatment groups on pain, affect, or pain-related interference, the momentary assessment data suggested that the patients in the CBT condition experienced significantly less pain, less pain-related interference in daily activities, and improved cognitive coping with pain. These surprising disparities between the retrospective results and the momentary results on pain intensity have been found in other studies (Stone et al., 2003) and are considered to be due to the influence of other factors when patients are asked to recall pain intensity, such as worst pain experienced during the recall period (Stone, Schwartz, Broderick, & Shiffman, 2005).

CBT also has demonstrated efficacy in reducing the chronicity of an acutely reported OFP condition. Gatchel and colleagues randomly assigned 101 patients with acute jaw pain deemed to be at high risk for developing chronic OFP to an early intervention or non-intervention condition. The early intervention consisted of six one-hour sessions of combined CBT and biofeedback. At a one-year post-treatment follow-up, patients who received the intervention reported significantly lower pain and symptoms of depression and were less likely to have pursued subsequent treatment for jaw-related pain (Gatchel et al., 2006). Furthermore, patients in the non-intervention group were much more likely to have an affective disorder related to their pain (e.g., somatoform disorder) at the one-year follow-up.

In studies that have followed patients for long-term follow-up (typically one year), symptoms and functioning continue to improve for those patients who present with improvement immediately post-treatment (Dworkin, Huggins et al., 2002; Gardea, Gatchel, & Mishra, 2001; Gatchel et al., 2006; Turner, Mancl, & Aaron, 2006). This suggests that CBT approaches yield significant and lasting behavioral change and integrated coping skills. Overall, CBT appears to be an effective treatment approach for reducing pain and increasing emotional function, and the long-term effects are encouraging. However, the skills, techniques, and therapeutic stance necessary for successful CBT require a significant amount of training and experience. Further, CBT requires a significant commitment from the clinic and the patient in both time and adherence to treatment.

Summary

There has been considerable progress over the last 20 years in understanding the importance of approaching OFP conditions through the framework of the biopsychosocial model. Furthermore, research has identified several premorbid psychological factors that are predictive of an acute OFP problem becoming a chronic and life changing pain condition. The research presented in this chapter demonstrates the importance of considering psychosocial factors in OFP conditions, in terms of the etiology of OFP and the ongoing chronicity of these conditions. A diverse group of psychological interventions has demonstrated efficacy in reducing pain severity and increasing pain coping and psychological well-being in OFP patients. These outcomes emphasize the need for more widespread dissemination and integration of psychological interventions into the regular care and treatment planning of OFP patients.

References

Abrahamsen, R., Baad-Hansen, L., & Svensson, P. (2008). Hypnosis in the management of persistent idiopathic orofacial pain—clinical and psychosocial findings. *Pain, 136*(1–2), 44–52. doi:10.1016/j.pain.2007.06.013

Aggarwal, V. R., Macfarlane, G. J., Farragher, T. M., & McBeth, J. (2010). Risk factors for onset of chronic oro-facial pain—results of the North Cheshire oro-facial pain prospective population study. *Pain, 149*(2), 354–359. doi:10.1016/j.pain.2010.02.040

Andrews, J. M. (1964). Neuromuscular re-education of the hemiplegic with aid of electromyograph. *Arch Phys Med Rehabil, 45*, 530–532.

APA. (2013). *Diagnostic and statistical manual of mental disorders* (5th ed.). Arlington, VA: American Psychiatric Association.

Arnold, L. M., Lu, Y., Crofford, L. J., Wohlreich, M., Detke, M. J., Iyengar, S., & Goldstein, D. J. (2004). A double-blind, multicenter trial comparing duloxetine with placebo in the treatment of fibromyalgia patients with or without major depressive disorder. *Arthritis Rheum, 50*(9), 2974–2984. doi:10.1002/art.20485

Asghari, A., & Nicholas, M. K. (2006). Personality and pain-related beliefs/coping strategies: A prospective study. *Clinical Journal of Pain, 22*, 10–18.

Association for Applied, P., & Biofeedback. (2002). Template for developing guidelines for the evaluation of the clinical efficacy of psychophysiological interventions. *Appl Psychophysiol Biofeedback, 27*(4), 273–281.

Atwoli, L., Stein, D. J., Koenen, K. C., & McLaughlin, K. A. (2015). Epidemiology of posttraumatic stress disorder: Prevalence, correlates and consequences. *Current Opinions in Psychiatry, 28*(4), 307–311.

Azrin, N. H., & Nunn, R. G. (1973). Habit-reversal: A method of eliminating nervous habits and tics. *Behav Res Ther, 11*(4), 619–628.

Azrin, N. H., Nunn, R. G., & Frantz-Renshaw, S. E. (1982). Habit reversal vs negative practice treatment of self-destructive oral habits (biting, chewing or licking of the lips, cheeks, tongue or palate). *J Behav Ther Exp Psychiatry, 13*(1), 49–54.

Bate, K. S., Malouff, J. M., Thorsteinsson, E. T., & Bhullar, N. (2011). The efficacy of habit reversal therapy for tics, habit disorders, and stuttering: A meta-analytic review. *Clin Psychol Rev, 31*(5), 865–871. doi:10.1016/j.cpr.2011.03.013

Beck, A. T., Epstein, N., Brown, G., & Steer, R. A. (1988). An inventory for measuring clinical anxiety: Psychometric properties. *J Consult Clin Psychol, 56*(6), 893–897.

Beck, A. T., Steer, R. A., Ball, R., & Ranieri, W. (1996). Comparison of beck depression inventories -IA and -II in psychiatric outpatients. *J Pers Assess, 67*(3), 588–597. doi:10.1207/s15327752jpa6703_13

Beck, A. T., Ward, C. H., Mendelson, M., Mock, J., & Erbaugh, J. (1961). An inventory for measuring depression. *Arch Gen Psychiatry, 4*, 561–571.

Benson, H. (1975). *The relaxation response*. New York, NY: Avon Books.

Bodner, S. (2006). Psychologic considerations in the management of oral surgical patients. *Oral Maxillofac Surg Clin North Am, 18*(1), 59–72, vi. doi:10.1016/j.coms.2005.09.003

Borrell-Carrio, F., Suchman, A. L., & Epstein, R. M. (2004). The biopsychosocial model 25 years later: Principles, practice, and scientific inquiry. *Ann Fam Med, 2*(6), 576–582. doi:10.1370/afm.245

Brooke, R. I., & Stenn, P. G. (1983). Myofascial pain dysfunction syndrome-how effective is biofeedback-assisted relaxation training? In J. J. Bonica, U. Lindbloom, & A. Iggo (Eds.), *Advances in pain research and therapy* (Vol. 5, pp. 809–812). New York, NY: The Raven Press.

Brudny, J. (1982). Biofeedback in chronic neurological cases: Therapeutic electromyography. In L. White & B. Tursky (Eds.), *Clinical biofeedback: Efficacy and mechanisms*. New York, NY: Plenum Press.

Burris, J. L., Cyders, M. A., de Leeuw, R., Smith, G. T., & Carlson, C. R. (2009). Posttraumatic stress disorder symptoms and chronic orofacial pain: An empirical examination of the mutual maintenance model. *J Orofac Pain, 23*(3), 243–252.

Campbell, C. M., Kronfli, T., Buenaver, L. F., Smith, M. T., Berna, C., Haythornthwaite, J. A., & Edwards, R. R. (2010). Situational versus dispositional measurement of catastrophizing: Associations with pain responses in multiple samples. *J Pain, 11*(5), 443–453, e442. doi:10.1016/j.jpain.2009.08.009

Carlson, C. R. (2008). Psychological considerations for chronic orofacial pain. *Oral Maxillofac Surg Clin North Am, 20*(2), 185–195, vi. doi:10.1016/j.coms.2007.12.002

Carlson, C. R., Bertrand, P. M., Ehrlich, A. D., Maxwell, A. W., & Burton, R. G. (2001). Physical self-regulation training for the management of temporomandibular disorders. *J Orofac Pain, 15*(1), 47–55.

Carlson, C. R., Okeson, J. P., Falace, D. A., Nitz, A. J., Curran, S. L., & Anderson, D. (1993). Comparison of psychologic and physiologic functioning between patients with masticatory muscle pain and matched controls. *J Orofac Pain, 7*(1), 15–22.

Carlsson, S. G., Gale, E. N., & Ohman, A. (1975). Treatment of temporomandibular joint syndrome with biofeedback training. *J Am Dent Assoc, 91*(3), 602–605.

Chen, C. Y., Palla, S., Erni, S., Sieber, M., & Gallo, L. M. (2007). Nonfunctional tooth contact in healthy controls and patients with myogenous facial pain. *J Orofac Pain, 21*(3), 185–193.

Chen, H., Nackley, A., Miller, V., Diatchenko, L., & Maixner, W. (2013). Multisystem dysregulation in painful temporomandibular disorders. *J Pain, 14*(9), 983–996. doi:10.1016/j.jpain.2013.03.011

Conrad, R., Schilling, G., Bausch, C., Nadstawek, J., Wartenberg, H. C., Wegener, I., . . . Liedtke, R. (2007). Temperament and character personality profiles and personality disorders in chronic pain patients. *Pain, 133*(1–3), 197–209. doi:10.1016/j.pain.2007.07.024

Costa, P. T. (1991). Clinical use of the five-factor model: An introduction. *J Pers Assess, 57*(3), 393–398. doi:10.1207/s15327752jpa5703_1

Costa, P. T., & McCrae, R. R. (1992). *Revised NEO personality inventory (NEO-PI-R) and NEO five-factor inventory (NEO-FFI) manual.* Odessa, FL: Psychological Assessment Resources.

Crider, A. B., & Glaros, A. G. (1999). A meta-analysis of EMG biofeedback treatment of temporomandibular disorders. *Journal of Orofacial Pain, 13*(1), 29–37.

Crider, A. B., Glaros, A. G., & Gevirtz, R. N. (2005). Efficacy of biofeedback-based treatments for temporomandibular disorders. *Appl Psychophysiol Biofeedback, 30*(4), 333–345. doi:10.1007/s10484-005-8420-5

Crockett, D. J., Foreman, M. E., Alden, L., & Blasberg, B. (1986). A comparison of treatment modes in the management of myofascial pain dysfunction syndrome. *Biofeedback Self Regul, 11*(4), 279–291.

Curran, S. L., Carlson, C. R., & Okeson, J. P. (1996). Emotional and physiologic responses to laboratory challenges: Patients with temporomandibular disorders versus matched control subjects. *J Orofac Pain, 10*(2), 141–150.

Dahan, H., Shir, Y., Velly, A., & Allison, P. (2015). Specific and number of comorbidities are associated with increased levels of temporomandibular pain intensity and duration. *J Headache Pain, 16*, 528. doi:10.1186/s10194-015-0528-2

Davis, C. E., Stockstill, J. W., Stanley, W. D., & Wu, Q. (2014). Pain-related worry in patients with chronic orofacial pain. *J Am Dent Assoc, 145*(7), 722–730. doi:10.14219/jada.2014.37

de Leeuw, R., Bertoli, E., Schmidt, J. E., & Carlson, C. R. (2005a). Prevalence of posttraumatic stress disorder symptoms in orofacial pain patients. *Oral Surg Oral Med Oral Pathol Oral Radiol Endod, 99*(5), 558–568. doi:10.1016/j.tripleo.2004.05.016

de Leeuw, R., Bertoli, E., Schmidt, J. E., & Carlson, C. R. (2005b). Prevalence of traumatic stressors in patients with temporomandibular disorders. *Journal of Oral and Maxillofacial Surgery, 63*, 42–50.

de Leeuw, R., & Klasser, G. D. (Eds.). (2013). *Orofacial pain: Guidelines for assessment, diagnosis, and management* (5th ed.). Hanover Park, IL: Quintessence.

Derogatis, L. R. (1994). *Symptom checklist-90-R.* Minneapolis, MN: National Computer Symptoms.

Dworkin, S. F. (2001). Psychosocial issues. In J. P. Lund, R. Dubnerr, & B. Sessle (Eds.), *Orofacial pain: From basic science to clinical management* (pp. 115–127). Chicago, IL: Quintessence.

Dworkin, S. F. (2011). The OPPERA study: Act one. *J Pain, 12*(11 Suppl), T1–T3. doi:10.1016/j.jpain.2011.08.004

Dworkin, S. F., Huggins, K. H., Wilson, L., Mancl, L., Turner, J., Massoth, D., . . . Truelove, E. (2002). A randomized clinical trial using research diagnostic criteria for temporomandibular disorders-axis II to target clinic cases for a tailored self-care TMD treatment program. *J Orofac Pain, 16*(1), 48–63.

Dworkin, S. F., Turner, J. A., Mancl, L., Wilson, L., Massoth, D., Huggins, K. H., . . . Truelove, E. (2002). A randomized clinical trial of a tailored comprehensive care treatment program for temporomandibular disorders. *J Orofac Pain, 16*(4), 259–276.

Ehde, D. M., Dillworth, T. M., & Turner, J. A. (2014). Cognitive-behavioral therapy for individuals with chronic pain: Efficacy, innovations, and directions for research. *Am Psychol, 69*(2), 153–166. doi:10.1037/a0035747

Engel, G. L. (1977). The need for a new medical model: A challenge for biomedicine. *Science, 196*(4286), 129–136.

Engel, G. L. (1980). The clinical application of the biopsychosocial model. *Am J Psychiatry, 137*(5), 535–544. doi:10.1176/ajp.137.5.535

Fillingim, R. B., Ohrbach, R., Greenspan, J. D., Knott, C., Diatchenko, L., Dubner, R., . . . Maixner, W. (2013). Psychological factors associated with development of TMD: The OPPERA prospective cohort study. *J Pain, 14*(12 Suppl), T75–T90. doi:10.1016/j.jpain.2013.06.009

Fillingim, R. B., Ohrbach, R., Greenspan, J. D., Knott, C., Dubner, R., Bair, E., . . . Maixner, W. (2011). Potential psychosocial risk factors for chronic TMD: Descriptive data and empirically identified domains from the OPPERA case-control study. *J Pain, 12*(11 Suppl), T46–T60. doi:10.1016/j.jpain.2011.08.007

Gameiro, G. H., da Silva Andrade, A., Nouer, D. F., & Ferraz de Arruda Veiga, M. C. (2006). How may stressful experiences contribute to the development of temporomandibular disorders? *Clin Oral Investig, 10*(4), 261–268. doi:10.1007/s00784-006-0064-1

Gardea, M. A., Gatchel, R. J., & Mishra, K. D. (2001). Long-term efficacy of biobehavioral treatment of temporomandibular disorders. *J Behav Med, 24*(4), 341–359.

Gatchel, R. J., Stowell, A. W., Wildenstein, L., Riggs, R., & Ellis III, E. (2006). Efficacy of an early intervention for patients with acute temporomandibular disorder-related pain: A one-year outcome study. *J Am Dent Assoc, 137*(3), 339–347.

Gessel, A. H. (1975). Electromygraphic biofeedback and tricyclic antidepressants in myofascial pain-dysfunction syndrome: Psychological predictors of outcome. *J Am Dent Assoc, 91*(5), 1048–1052.

Giannakopoulos, N. N., Keller, L., Rammelsberg, P., Kronmuller, K. T., & Schmitter, M. (2010). Anxiety and depression in patients with chronic temporomandibular pain and in controls. *J Dent, 38*(5), 369–376. doi:10.1016/j.jdent.2010.01.003

Gil-Martinez, A., Grande-Alonso, M., La Touche, R., Lara-Lara, M., Lopez-Lopez, A., & Fernandez-Carnero, J. (2016). Psychosocial and somatosensory factors in women with chronic migraine and painful temporomandibular disorders. *Pain Res Manag, 3945673*. doi:10.1155/2016/3945673

Glaros, A. G., Kim-Weroha, N., Lausten, L., & Franklin, K. L. (2007). Comparison of habit reversal and a behaviorally-modified dental treatment for temporomandibular disorders: A pilot investigation. *Appl Psychophysiol Biofeedback, 32*(3–4), 149–154. doi:10.1007/s10484-007-9039-5

Glaros, A. G., Williams, K., & Lausten, L. (2005). The role of parafunctions, emotions and stress in predicting facial pain. *J Am Dent Assoc, 136*(4), 451–458.

Harris, C. A., & D'Eon, J. L. (2008). Psychometric properties of the Beck Depression Inventory—second edition (BDI-II) in individuals with chronic pain. *Pain, 137*(3), 609–622. doi:10.1016/j.pain.2007.10.022

Hawkins, J. M., Schmidt, J. E., Hargitai, I. A., Johnson, J. F., Howard, R. S., & Bertrand, P. M. (2016). Multimodal assessment of body pain in orofacial pain patients. *Pain Medicine, 17*, 961–969. doi:10.1093/pm/pnv093

Humphrey, S. P., Lindroth, J. E., & Carlson, C. R. (2002). Routine dental care in patients with temporomandibular disorders. *J Orofac Pain, 16*(2), 129–134.

Jensen, M. P., & Patterson, D. R. (2014). Hypnotic approaches for chronic pain management: Clinical implications of recent research findings. *Am Psychol, 69*(2), 167–177. doi:10.1037/a0035644

Kabacoff, R. I., Segal, D. L., Hersen, M., & Van Hasselt, V. B. (1997). Psychometric properties and diagnostic utility of the Beck Anxiety Inventory and the State-Trait Anxiety Inventory with older adult psychiatric outpatients. *J Anxiety Disord, 11*(1), 33–47.

Keefe, F. J., & Dolan, E. (1986). Pain behavior and pain coping strategies in low back pain and myofascial pain dysfunction syndrome patients. *Pain, 24*(1), 49–56.

Kight, M., Gatchel, R. J., & Wesley, L. (1999). Temporomandibular disorders: Evidence for significant overlap with psychopathology. *Health Psychol, 18*(2), 177–182.

Kihlstrom, J. F. (2008). The domain of hypnosis, Revisited. In M. R. Nash & A. J. Barnier (Eds.), *The Oxford handbook of hypnosis: Theory, research and practice* (pp. 21–52). New York, NY: Oxford University Press.

Kindler, S., Samietz, S., Houshmand, M., Grabe, H. J., Bernhardt, O., Biffar, R., . . . Schwahn, C. (2012). Depressive and anxiety symptoms as risk factors for temporomandibular joint pain: A prospective cohort study in the general population. *J Pain, 13*(12), 1188–1197. doi:10.1016/j.jpain.2012.09.004

Kress, H. G., Aldington, D., Alon, E., Coaccioli, S., Collett, B., Coluzzi, F., . . . Sichere, P. (2015). A holistic approach to chronic pain management that involves all stakeholders: Change is needed. *Curr Med Res Opin, 31*(9), 1743–1754. doi:10.1185/03007995.201 5.1072088

Kroenke, K. (2007). Somatoform disorders and recent diagnostic controversies. *Psychiatr Clin North Am, 30*(4), 593–619. doi:10.1016/j.psc.2007.08.002

Kroenke, K., & Spitzer, R. L. (2002). The PHQ-9: A new depression diagnostic and severity measure. *Psychiatric Annals, 32*(9), 509–515.

Kroenke, K., Spitzer, R. L., & Williams, J. B. (2001). The PHQ-9: Validity of a brief depression severity measure. *J Gen Intern Med, 16*(9), 606–613.

Kroenke, K., Spitzer, R. L., & Williams, J. B. (2003). The patient health questionnaire-2: Validity of a two-item depression screener. *Med Care, 41*(11), 1284–1292. doi:10.1097/01. MLR.0000093487.78664.3C

Kroenke, K., Spitzer, R. L., Williams, J. B., & Lowe, B. (2010). The patient health questionnaire somatic, anxiety, and depressive symptom scales: A systematic review. *Gen Hosp Psychiatry, 32*(4), 345–359. doi:10.1016/j.genhosppsych.2010.03.006

Kroenke, K., Spitzer, R. L., Williams, J. B., Monahan, P. O., & Lowe, B. (2007). Anxiety disorders in primary care: Prevalence, impairment, comorbidity, and detection. *Ann Intern Med, 146*(5), 317–325.

LeResche, L. (1997). Epidemiology of temporomandibular disorders: Implications for the investigation of etiologic factors. *Crit Rev Oral Biol Med, 8*(3), 291–305.

Lipton, J. A., Ship, J. A., & Larach-Robinson, D. (1993). Estimated prevalence and distribution of reported orofacial pain in the United States. *J Am Dent Assoc, 124*(10), 115–121.

Litt, M. D., Shafer, D. M., Ibanez, C. R., Kreutzer, D. L., & Tawfik-Yonkers, Z. (2009). Momentary pain and coping in temporomandibular disorder pain: Exploring mechanisms of cognitive behavioral treatment for chronic pain. *Pain, 145*(1–2), 160–168. doi:10.1016/j.pain.2009.06.003

Lowe, B., Unutzer, J., Callahan, C. M., Perkins, A. J., & Kroenke, K. (2004). Monitoring depression treatment outcomes with the patient health questionnaire-9. *Med Care, 42*(12), 1194–1201.

Luciano, J. V., Barrada, J. R., Aguado, J., Osma, J., & Garcia-Campayo, J. (2014). Bifactor analysis and construct validity of the HADS: A cross-sectional and longitudinal study in fibromyalgia patients. *Psychol Assess, 26*(2), 395–406. doi:10.1037/a0035284

McCrae, R. R., & Costa, P. T. (1985). Updating Norman's "Adequate Taxonomy": Intelligence and personality dimensions in natural language and in questionnaires. *J Pers Soc Psychol, 49*(3), 710–721.

McGrady, A. V., Kern-Buell, C., Bush, E., Devonshire, R., Claggett, A. L., & Grubb, B. P. (2003). Biofeedback-assisted relaxation therapy in neurocardiogenic syncope: A pilot study. *Appl Psychophysiol Biofeedback, 28*(3), 183–192.

McGregor, N. R., Butt, H. L., Zerbes, M., Klineberg, I. J., Dunstan, R. H., & Roberts, T. K. (1996). Assessment of pain (distribution and onset), Symptoms, SCL-90-R Inventory responses, and the association with infectious events in patients with chronic orofacial pain. *J Orofac Pain, 10*(4), 339–350.

McQuaid, J. R., Stein, M. B., McCahill, M., Laffaye, C., & Ramel, W. (2000). Use of brief psychiatric screening measures in a primary care sample. *Depress Anxiety, 12*(1), 21–29. doi:10.1002/1520–6394(2000)12:1 < 21::AID-DA3 > 3.0.CO;2-U

Mishra, K. D., Gatchel, R. J., & Gardea, M. A. (2000). The relative efficacy of three cognitive-behavioral treatment approaches to temporomandibular disorders. *J Behav Med, 23*(3), 293–309.

Mohl, N. D., Lund, J. P., Widmer, C. G., & McCall, W. D., Jr. (1990). Devices for the diagnosis and treatment of temporomandibular disorders. Part II: Electromyography and sonography. *J Prosthet Dent, 63*(3), 332–336.

Molin, C., Edman, G., & Schalling, D. (1973). Psychological studies of patients with mandibular pain dysfunction syndrome. 2. Tolerance for experimentally induced pain. *Sven Tandlak Tidskr, 66*(1), 15–23.

Molin, C., Schalling, D., & Edman, G. (1973). Psychological studies of patients with mandibular pain dysfunction syndrome. 1. Personality traits in patients and controls. *Sven Tandlak Tidskr, 66*(1), 1–13.

Mora, M. C. S., Weber, D., Neff, A., & Rief, W. (2013). Biofeedback-based cognitive-behavioral treatment compared with occlusal splint for temporomandibular disorder. *Clinical Journal of Pain, 29*(12), 1057–1065.

Neblett, R., Mayer, T. G., Brede, E., & Gatchel, R. J. (2010). Correcting abnormal flexion-relaxation in chronic lumbar pain: Responsiveness to a new biofeedback training protocol. *Clin J Pain, 26*(5), 403–409. doi:10.1097/AJP.0b013e3181d2bd8c

Nestoriuc, Y., Martin, A., Rief, W., & Andrasik, F. (2008). Biofeedback treatment for headache disorders: A comprehensive efficacy review. *Appl Psychophysiol Biofeedback, 33*(3), 125–140. doi:10.1007/s10484-008-9060-3

Ohrbach, R., Bair, E., Fillingim, R. B., Gonzalez, Y., Gordon, S. M., Lim, P. F., . . . Slade, G. D. (2013). Clinical orofacial characteristics associated with risk of first-onset TMD: The OPPERA prospective cohort study. *J Pain, 14*(12 Suppl), T33–T50. doi:10.1016/j.jpain.2013.07.018

Okeson, J. P. (2014). Bell's Oral and Facial Pain, Seventh Edition. In *Bell's oral and facial pain* (7th ed., pp. 1–546). Hanover Park, IL: Quintessence Publishing Co, Inc.

Pallegama, R. W., Ranasinghe, A. W., Weerasinghe, V. S., & Sitheeque, M. A. (2005). Anxiety and personality traits in patients with muscle related temporomandibular disorders. *J Oral Rehabil, 32*(10), 701–707. doi:10.1111/j.1365-2842.2005.01503.x

Patterson, D. R., & Jensen, M. P. (2003). Hypnosis and clinical pain. *Psychol Bull, 129*(4), 495–521.

Quartana, P. J., Campbell, C. M., & Edwards, R. R. (2009). Pain catastrophizing: A critical review. *Expert Rev Neurother, 9*(5), 745–758. doi:10.1586/ern.09.34

Radloff, L. (1977). The CES-D scale: A self-report depression scale for research in the general population. *Applied Psychological Measurement, 1,* 385–401.

Raselli, C., & Broderick, J. E. (2007). The association of depression and neuroticism with pain reports: A comparison of momentary and recalled pain assessments. *J Psychosom Res, 62,* 313–320.

Reiter, S., Emodi-Perlman, A., Goldsmith, C., Friedman-Rubin, P., & Winocur, E. (2015). Comorbidity between depression and anxiety in patients with temporomandibular disorders according to the research diagnostic criteria for temporomandibular disorders. *J Oral Facial Pain Headache, 29*(2), 135–143. doi:10.11607/ofph.1297

Remes, O., Brayne, C., van der Linde, R., & Lafortune, L. (2016). A systematic review of reviews on the prevalence of anxiety disorders in adult populations. *Brain Behav*, *6*(7), e00497. doi:10.1002/brb3.497

Romano, J. M., & Turner, J. A. (1985). Chronic pain and depression: Does the evidence support a relationship? *Psychol Bull*, *97*(1), 18–34.

Schmidt, J. E., & Carlson, C. R. (2009). A controlled comparison of emotional reactivity and physiological response in masticatory muscle pain patients. *J Orofac Pain*, *23*(3), 230–242.

Schmidt, J. E., Hooten, W. M., & Carlson, C. R. (2011). Utility of the NEO-FFI in multi-dimensional assessment of orofacial pain conditions. *J Behav Med*, *34*(3), 170–181. doi:10.1007/s10865-010-9298-0

Schwartz, M. S. (1995). *Biofeedback: A practitioner's guide* (2nd ed.). New York, NY: The Guilford Press.

Shafer, A. B. (2006). Meta-analysis of the factor structures of four depression questionnaires: Beck, CES-D, Hamilton, and Zung. *J Clin Psychol*, *62*(1), 123–146. doi:10.1002/jclp.20213

Sharp, T. J., & Harvey, A. G. (2001). Chronic pain and posttraumatic stress disorder: Mutual maintenance. *Clin Psychol Rev*, *21*, 857–877.

Sheng, J., Liu, S., Wang, Y., Cui, R., & Zhang, X. (2017). The link between depression and chronic pain: Neural mechanisms in the brain. *Neural Plast*, *2017*, 9724371. doi:10.1155/2017/9724371

Sherman, J. J., Carlson, C. R., Wilson, J. F., Okeson, J. P., & McCubbin, J. A. (2005). Posttraumatic stress disorder among patients with orofacial pain. *J Orofac Pain*, *19*(4), 309–317.

Slade, G. D., Bair, E., Greenspan, J. D., Dubner, R., Fillingim, R. B., Diatchenko, L., . . . Ohrbach, R. (2013). Signs and symptoms of first-onset TMD and sociodemographic predictors of its development: The OPPERA prospective cohort study. *J Pain*, *14*(12 Suppl), T20–T32, e21–23. doi:10.1016/j.jpain.2013.07.014

Slade, G. D., Diatchenko, L., Bhalang, K., Sigurdsson, A., Fillingim, R. B., Belfer, I., . . . Maixner, W. (2007). Influence of psychological factors on risk of temporomandibular disorders. *J Dent Res*, *86*(11), 1120–1125.

Spitzer, R. L., Kroenke, K., Williams, J. B., & Lowe, B. (2006). A brief measure for assessing generalized anxiety disorder: The GAD-7. *Arch Intern Med*, *166*(10), 1092–1097. doi:10.1001/archinte.166.10.1092

Stone, A. A., Broderick, J. E., Schwartz, J. E., Shiffman, S., Litcher-Kelly, L., & Calvanese, P. (2003). Intensive momentary reporting of pain with an electronic diary: Reactivity, compliance, and patient satisfaction. *Pain*, *104*(1–2), 343–351.

Stone, A. A., Schwartz, J. E., Broderick, J. E., & Shiffman, S. S. (2005). Variability of momentary pain predicts recall of weekly pain: A consequence of the peak (or salience) memory heuristic. *Pers Soc Psychol Bull*, *31*(10), 1340–1346. doi:10.1177/0146167205275615

Svensson, P., & Kumar, A. (2016). Assessment of risk factors for oro-facial pain and recent developments in classification: Implications for management. *J Oral Rehabil*, *43*(12), 977–989. doi:10.1111/joor.12447

Thorn, B. E. (2017). *Cognitive therapy for chronic pain* (2nd ed.). New York, NY: The Guilford Press.

Titov, N., Dear, B. F., McMillan, D., Anderson, T., Zou, J., & Sunderland, M. (2011). Psychometric comparison of the PHQ-9 and BDI-II for measuring response during treatment of depression. *Cogn Behav Ther*, *40*(2), 126–136. doi:10.1080/16506073.2010.550059

Toomin, M. K., & Toomin, H. (1975). GSR Biofeedback in psychotherapy: Some clinical observations. *Psychotherapy*, *12*(1), 33–38.

Tragesser, S. L., Bruns, D., & Disorbio, J. M. (2010). Borderline personality disorder features and pain: The mediating role of negative affect in a pain patient sample. *Clin J Pain*, *26*(4), 348–353. doi:10.1097/AJP.0b013e3181cd1710

Turk, D. C., & Okifuji, A. (2002). Psychological factors in chronic pain: Evolution and revolution. *J Consult Clin Psychol, 70*(3), 678–690.

Turk, D. C., Zaki, H. S., & Rudy, T. E. (1993). Effects of intraoral appliance and biofeedback/stress management alone and in combination in treating pain and depression in patients with temporomandibular disorders. *J Prosthet Dent, 70*(2), 158–164.

Turner, J. A., Brister, H., Huggins, K., Mancl, L., Aaron, L. A., & Truelove, E. L. (2005). Catastrophizing is associated with clinical examination findings, activity interference, and health care use among patients with temporomandibular disorders. *J Orofac Pain, 19*(4), 291–300.

Turner, J. A., Mancl, L., & Aaron, L. A. (2005). Brief cognitive-behavioral therapy for temporomandibular disorder pain: Effects on daily electronic outcome and process measures. *Pain, 117*(3), 377–387. doi:10.1016/j.pain.2005.06.025

Turner, J. A., Mancl, L., & Aaron, L. A. (2006). Short- and long-term efficacy of brief cognitive-behavioral therapy for patients with chronic temporomandibular disorder pain: A randomized, controlled trial. *Pain, 121*(3), 181–194. doi:10.1016/j.pain.2005.11.017

Velly, A. M., Look, J. O., Carlson, C., Lenton, P. A., Kang, W., Holcroft, C. A., & Fricton, J. R. (2011). The effect of catastrophizing and depression on chronic pain—a prospective cohort study of temporomandibular muscle and joint pain disorders. *Pain, 152*(10), 2377–2383. doi:10.1016/j.pain.2011.07.004

Vendrig, A. A., Derksen, J. J., & de Mey, H. R. (2000). MMPI-2 Personality Psychopathology Five (PSY-5) and prediction of treatment outcome for patients with chronic back pain. *J Pers Assess, 74*(3), 423–438. doi:10.1207/S15327752JPA7403_6

Wade, J. B., Dougherty, L. M., Hart, R. P., Rafii, A., & Price, D. D. (1992). A canonical correlation analysis of the influence of neuroticism and extraversion on chronic pain, suffering, and pain behavior. *Pain, 51*(1), 67–73.

Winocur, E., Gavish, A., Emodi-Perlman, A., Halachmi, M., & Eli, I. (2002). Hypnorelaxation as treatment for myofascial pain disorder: A comparative study. *Oral Surg Oral Med Oral Pathol Oral Radiol Endod, 93*(4), 429–434.

Yeung, E., Abou-Foul, A., Matcham, F., Poate, T., & Fan, K. (2017). Integration of mental health screening in the management of patients with temporomandibular disorders. *Br J Oral Maxillofac Surg, 55*(6), 594–599. doi:10.1016/j.bjoms.2017.03.014

Yunus, M. B. (2008). Central sensitivity syndromes: A new paradigm and group nosology for fibromyalgia and overlapping conditions, and the related issue of disease versus illness. *Semin Arthritis Rheum, 37*(6), 339–352. doi:10.1016/j.semarthrit.2007.09.003

Zigmund, A. S., & Snaith, R. P. (1983). The hospital anxiety and depression scale. *Acta Psychiatrica Scandinavica, 67*, 361–370.

Zimmermann, C., & Tansella, M. (1996). Psychosocial factors and physical illness in primary care: Promoting the biopsychosocial model in medical practice. *J Psychosom Res, 40*(4), 351–358.

17

Treating Chronic Pain in Personality-Disordered Patients

Jessica Ketterer

The role of personality factors in both the experience and treatment of chronic pain has become an increasingly important focus within behavioral medicine. Personality traits may influence the development and continuance of, and overall psychological and physical adjustment to, enduring pain conditions. There has been considerable research into the connection between pain and personality (e.g., Gustin, Burke, Peck, Murray, & Henderson, 2016). Indeed, even a search for determinants of a "pain-prone personality" has been undertaken; however, to date a singular depiction of this proposed personality type is not empirically supported (e.g., Naylor, Boag, & Gustin, 2017).

Personality traits should be viewed as factors that *modify* pain-related treatments and outcomes, rather than exclusive precipitants of chronic pain disorders (Kalira, Treisman, & Clark, 2013; Penfold, St Denis, & Mazhar, 2016). Although personality traits generally are seen as pervasive and enduring, the destabilizing effects of long-standing pain, as well as commonly comorbid psychiatric symptomatology, may reshape a patient's personality attributes over time (Gustin et al., 2016). Accordingly, caution must be taken when diagnosing personality disorders within this population (Kalira et al., 2013) and when drawing conclusions about directionality of pain–personality relationships.

This chapter investigates the intersection of personality factors and pain, as well as the features that may account for the unique perceptions and experiences of pain among personality-disordered individuals. A multimodality approach to psychological treatment of this population will draw from several therapeutic techniques. Special consideration will be given to the therapeutic relationship in these often complex, challenging cases. Suggestions for macro-interventions within the patient's immediate environment, as well as in the multidisciplinary medical team at large, also will be reviewed.

Prevalent Personality Characteristics of Chronic Pain Patients

Investigation of both state- and trait-dependent personality factors is essential to the comprehensive psychosocial understanding and treatment of chronic pain. Emotionally laden traits (e.g., high hypochondriasis, hysteria, and depression as measured by the Minnesota Multiphasic Personality Inventory-2) have been generally associated with persistent pain conditions. This profile, however, is confounded by items assessing somatic concerns (Naylor, Boag, & Gustin, 2017). The higher-order personality trait of neuroticism, thought to represent a susceptibility for negative emotionality and lowered distress tolerance, has been implicated in chronic pain conditions through the mechanism of pain catastrophizing and associated anxiety (Kadimpati, Zale, Hooten, Ditre, & Warner, 2015).

Perhaps the most substantiated association exists between enduring pain and the profile of elevated harm avoidance and lowered self-directedness, as measured by the Temperament and Character Inventory (Cloninger, Przybeck, & Svrakic, 1994; Conrad, Wegener, Geiser, & Kleiman, 2013). Patients with high harm avoidance are overly cautious, pessimistic, and prone to fear and reassurance-seeking. The attribute of diminished self-directedness typically is exemplified by identity disturbance, low self-esteem/efficacy, an external locus of control, amotivation, and impaired goal setting (Gustin et al., 2016; Malmgren-Olsson & Bergdahl, 2006). Furthermore, this personality profile has been implicated consistently in the diagnosis of personality-disordered pathology (Conrad et al., 2007). Correspondingly, a high rate of diagnosable personality disorders (12–18%) is found within the chronic pain population. This is higher than the prevalence rate of personality disorders within the population at large, which is approximately 10% (Fischer-Kern et al., 2011).

Diagnosable personality disorders are exemplified by inflexible and pervasive cognitive, affective, interpersonal, and/or behavioral patterns considered deviant to cultural expectations and that have endured (at least) since adolescence or early adulthood. These patterns are associated with significant distress and impairment in several functional domains (American Psychiatric Association, 2013). Personality disorders are overrepresented in a number of chronic pain conditions, including headache/migraine, spinal pain, fibromyalgia, temporomandibular jaw and related facial pain, and lower back pain. The most commonly identified personality disorders among chronic pain patients include histrionic, dependent, obsessive compulsive, and borderline personality types (Dixon-Gordon, Whalen, Layden, & Chapman, 2015).

Borderline Personality Disorder

The prevalence of borderline personality disorder (BPD) within the general population is estimated to range from 1.6% to 5.9% (American Psychiatric Association, 2013). BPD is overrepresented in the primary care setting (6–26%), likely due to this population's tendency toward high healthcare utilization (American Psychiatric Association, 2013; Bender et al., 2001; Gross et al., 2002). BPD is especially overrepresented within the chronic pain population, with the incidence rate estimated as 30% (Sansone & Sansone, 2015). In one study of patients with diagnosed BPD, 65% held a lifetime DSM-IV diagnosis of pain disorder, 89% endorsed current pain symptomatology, and 21.5% experienced daily medical-related issues (Heath, Paris, Laporte, & Gill, 2017). Specifically, patients with BPD exhibit significantly more pain disorders (particularly chronic fatigue syndrome, fibromyalgia, temporomandibular disorders, osteoarthritis, low back pain, and carpal tunnel syndrome) than patients diagnosed with other personality disorders (Biskin, Frankenburg, Fitzmaurice, & Zanarini, 2014).

The remainder of this chapter focuses on BPD, the most prevalent and widely researched personality diagnosis of patients with enduring pain conditions. For information regarding other personality disorders among people with chronic pain, see Kayhan (2016) for histrionic personality disorder; Zampieri, Tognola, and Galego (2014) for dependent personality disorder; and Fischer-Kern et al. (2011) and Proctor et al. (2013) for obsessive-compulsive personality disorder.

Patients diagnosed with BPD demonstrate impaired tolerance of physical, emotional, and environmental challenges. They are commonly critical and rejecting of self and/or others. Paradoxically, BPD patients possess an intense fear of abandonment, and as a result often experience interpersonal discord (Robins & Rosenthal, 2011). Mentalization abilities, which allow reflection on our own and others' potential mental states and allow us to make sense of our personal and social worlds, are impaired in patients with BPD (Bateman & Fonagy, 2010). Pervasive negative emotionality, patterns of alternating between inhibition and overexpression of emotions, phobic-like reactivity to physical and emotional pain and loss, transitory paranoia culminating in crisis-level or dissociative states, and recurrent self-mutilating or suicidal behaviors or ideation also predominate the clinical portrait of BPD (American Psychiatric Association, 2013; McMain, Korman, & Dimeff, 2001).

The BPD patient's various maladaptive cognitive and behavioral strategies to avoid experiencing strong emotions predict overall symptom severity above and beyond patterns of emotional dysregulation or general intolerance of distress (Morton, Snowdon, Gopold, & Guymer, 2012). Other common manifestations of BPD include high emotional sensitivity and reactivity coupled with a slow return to baseline, impulsivity, depressive symptomatology, lowered distress tolerance, emotional numbing and thought suppression, trauma, and strain related to sustained interpersonal discord. These manifestations and characteristics in toto help explain the link between borderline symptoms and chronic pain (Biskin et al., 2014; Dixon-Gordon, Berghoff, & McDermott, 2017; Linehan, 1993; Mun, Karoly, Ruehlman, & Kim, 2016; Tragesser, Bruns, & Disorbio, 2010; You & Meagher, 2017). See the *Diagnostic and Statistical Manual of Mental Disorders*, Fifth

Edition, pp. 663–666 for full diagnostic criteria (American Psychiatric Association, 2013).

BPD and Chronic Pain

The above-mentioned chronic stressors, coupled with behavioral and environmental factors (e.g., health risk behaviors such as non-compliance and self-harm, insufficient medical care related to stigma), are thought to increase allostatic load and overall chronic physical tension. The resulting heightened inflammatory response leads to immune system dysregulation, cardiovascular and metabolic disturbance, and inefficient pain control/pain hypersensitivity (Dixon-Gordon et al., 2017; You & Meagher, 2017). Moreover, the reciprocal psychological downward spiral ensuing from somatic preoccupation, occupational difficulties, sleep disturbance, conscious or unconscious exploitation of the "sick role," disability, the common co-occurrence of substance abuse, lowered trust within patients' support systems, and the grief response associated with diminished quality of life, all of which are directly related to the pain condition itself, commonly overwhelm the BPD sufferer's inefficient, often maladaptive coping mechanisms (Campbell, Bruno, Darke, & Degenhardt, 2015; Carpenter, Wood, & Trull, 2016; Ducasse, Courtet, & Olie, 2014; Linehan, 1993; Sagula & Rice, 2004; Randy, Sansone, Tahir, Buckner, & Wiederman, 2008).

Catastrophizing is one such mechanism common to patients with BPD and/or chronic pain. Pain catastrophizing is a set of negatively skewed cognitions associated with rumination, magnification, and helplessness about actual or anticipated pain (Campbell et al., 2015; Kalira et al., 2013; Sansone, Watts, & Wiederman, 2014). The resulting emotional and behavioral responses (most commonly fear and avoidance) directly predict depression, disability, and pain severity itself (Mun et al., 2016; Schutze, Rees, Preece, & Schutze, 2010). Correspondingly, individuals with BPD report greater pain intensity, use more pain medications, and evidence more disability than chronic pain sufferers without a BPD diagnosis (Sansone & Sansone, 2012) or with a baseline diagnosis of another personality disorder (Biskin et al., 2014). Please see Figure 17.1 for a visual representation of a proposed cycle of chronic pain development and/or perpetuation in BPD patients.

Special Consideration: Suicidality

While chronic pain is not directly life-threatening, the often high level of symptom burden and reductions in quality of life can lead to psychopathology and increased suicide risk (Hassett, Aquino, & Ilgen, 2014). Recent estimates indicate that completed suicide accounts for 1.4% of deaths worldwide (World Health Organization, 2017). Concerningly, the risk of completed suicide in chronic pain patients is 2%. Furthermore, among chronic pain patients the rate of lifetime suicidal ideation is 23%, lifetime suicidal plan is 9%, and lifetime

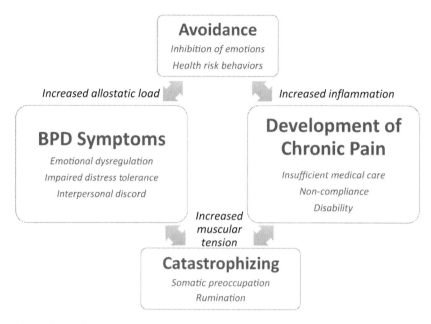

Figure 17.1 Proposed Cycle of Chronic Pain Development and/or Perpetuation in BPD Patients

suicide attempts is 15% among chronic pain patients (Calati, Artero, Courtet, & Lopez-Castroman, 2016).

Eight specific risk factors for suicidality emerged from Tang and Crane's meta-analysis (2006): family history of completed suicide; previous suicide attempt; clinical diagnosis of comorbid depression; female gender; sleep-onset insomnia; and pain qualities such as type, intensity, and duration of symptoms. The authors also emphasized that several ancillary psychological factors contribute to suicidality: helplessness and hopelessness regarding perceived ability to cope with pain or to achieve pain relief; pain catastrophizing; physical and psychological avoidance; a desire to escape from pain; and problem-solving deficits (Tang & Crane, 2006). It was also observed that chronic pain sufferers develop a sense of fearlessness about death related to chronic habituation to hyperalgesia. Finally, from an interpersonal perspective, "thwarted belongingness" and perceived burdensomeness often are associated with suicidal ideation, commonly related to guilt about needing to depend upon others due to pain and associated functional limitations (Hooley, Franklin, & Nock, 2014).

Self-injurious and suicidal behaviors, gestures, or attempts are a common part of BPD symptomatology occurring to counteract dissociation and/or feelings of emptiness, to regulate distress, or to punish oneself (Cardenas-Morales et al., 2011; Ducasse et al., 2014). It is estimated that nearly 75% of those with BPD attempt suicide (Black, Blum, Pfohl, & Hale, 2004), while 8–10% complete suicide (American Psychiatric Association, 2013).

Paradoxically, despite the observed propensity for BPD patients to develop chronic pain conditions, this population commonly demonstrates decreased acute pain sensitivity as brought about by self-injurious behaviors (Sansone & Sansone, 2007). Research into this "pain paradox" has implicated dissociative states, aversive arousal, enhanced anti-nociception brought about from repeated self-inflicted injuries, attentional shift, lowered body awareness, and associated neuroanatomical abnormalities associated with BPD in the reduced experience of acute pain (Carpenter & Trull, 2015; Ducasse et al., 2014; Ginzburg, Biran, Aryeh, Tsur, & Defrin, 2017; Koenig, Thayer, & Kaess, 2016; Magerl, Burkart, Fernandez, Schmidt, & Treede, 2012).

In general, assessing for risk for suicidality and self-injurious behaviors, as well as commonly co-occurring substance abuse, is especially important in comprehensive assessment and treatment of patients with co-occurring BPD and chronic pain.

Perceptions as "Difficult Patients"

Treating patients with co-occurring BPD and chronic pain (who are often diagnosed with other medical and psychiatric comorbidities as well) can be challenging. Many treatment providers consider these patients to be "difficult," given their (typically) intense emotionality, common non-adaptive and high-risk behaviors, and high utilization of the healthcare system (Kalira et al., 2013). Interpersonal instability and intense fear of abandonment can lead these patients to be perceived as "clingy," demanding, controlling, intimidating, overly exaggerative, uncooperative, and/or manipulative (Bland & Rossen, 2005; Hay & Passik, 2000; Sansone & Sansone, 2015).

BPD patients with chronic pain are also at high risk for "splitting" staff members and quickly shifting "alliances," discord and division among treating staff members, violation of professional boundaries, and overall demoralization of their treatment teams (Livesley, Dimaggio, & Clarkin, 2015). In turn, staff members may experience a great degree of countertransference, often either withdrawing or retaliating to protect themselves and/or colleagues and other patients. Levels of burnout are particularly high. Professional caregivers often report less empathy toward these patients, doubt or minimize patient symptoms or reports, and are more pessimistic about patients' treatment outcomes. These experiences and behaviors often create a significant amount of dissonance within providers, who generally perceive themselves to be both compassionate and competent (Bodner, Cohen-Fridel, & Iancu, 2011; Hay & Passik, 2000; Knaak, Szeto, Fitch, Modgill, & Patten, 2015; Livesley et al., 2015). As a result of this reactivity, these patients' behavioral patterns may persist, their suffering may continue as treatment is compromised, and providers may lose the opportunity to help and develop further skillsets (Kalira et al., 2013). This perpetuates a "cycle of stigmatization," to which both patient and provider contribute (Figure 17.2).

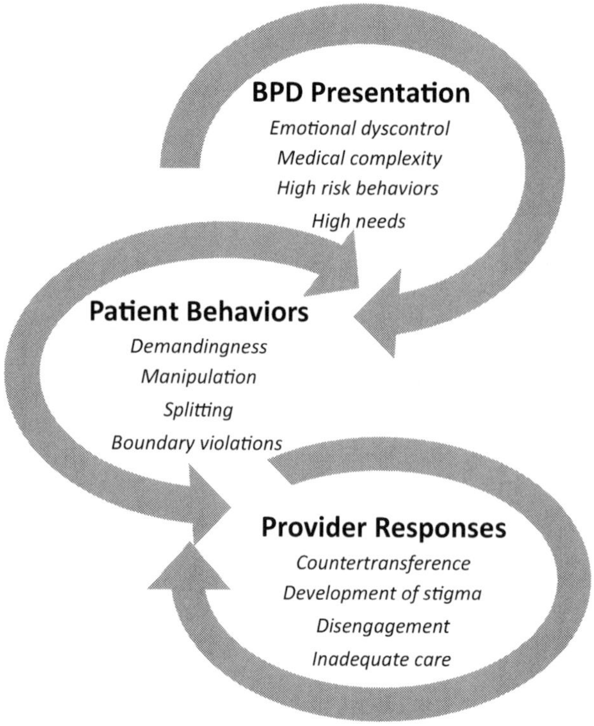

Figure 17.2 Considerations Leading to Potential Negative Treatment Outcomes in Those With BPD and Chronic Pain

Providers often interpret these patients' intense and difficult behaviors as deliberate and manipulative, rather than as a symptom of the personality disorder itself (Aviram, Brodsky, & Stanley, 2006). Additionally, just as it is widely recognized that chronic pain persists despite lack of clear tissue pathology, chronic pain also is often widely stigmatized. An estimated 38% of chronic pain sufferers endorse the experience of internalized stigma from members of their medical, occupational, and social environments. Often these patients perceive that their pain is not taken seriously, that their credibility is questioned, and that they are dismissed by their providers (De Ruddere & Craig, 2016). This internalized stigma has been compounded unintentionally by the current "opioid crisis," as providers and society at large become wary and scrutinize more closely the pharmacological treatment of chronic pain (Buchman, Ho, & Illes, 2016). The resultant inadequate pain control and evaluation/treatment, coupled with senses of isolation, demoralization, marginalization, and shame, reduced self-efficacy, and increased anxiety, anger, and depression, greatly impact these patients' quality of life (Carr, 2016; Waugh, Byrne, & Nicholas, 2014).

Intervention

As highlighted, both personality pathology and chronic pain are complex present-ing problems that span psychological and physical symptoms; impaired cognitive, emotional, and behavioral control; maladaptive coping strategies; metacognitive deficits; interpersonal discord; and the environmental concerns that promulgate these difficulties (e.g., Livesley et al., 2015). Effective, comprehensive treatment requires an eclectic and interdisciplinary approach toward conceptualization and intervention. The treatment should be geared toward both the individual and his/her environment and tailored to the individual's unique presentation and psycho-social context (Beatson & Rao, 2014).

This section of this chapter reviews interventions at the level of patient, treatment team, and caregivers. These interventions share overarching common factors and recommendations, regardless of the multimodal theoretical and treat-ment approach. First, psychologists should promote a highly structured treat-ment framework and environment. Second, they should undertake an active role while emphasizing a collaborative, supportive patient–therapist relationship. They should focus on in-session affect and dynamics, while addressing any treatment-interfering behaviors. Third, interventions should centralize on a combination of acceptance-based and active, change-oriented strategies. Finally, therapists should consider their support and accessible consultations to be paramount (Beatson & Rao, 2014).

Experts recommend constructing a treatment contract that outlines the ration-ale behind approaches, therapeutic interventions, expected course and duration of treatment, confidentiality, behavioral expectations, and general office policies. Such a document, in conjunction with associated collaborative discussions, will promote structure and consistency while containing treatment-interfering behav-iors. The contract should enhance the patient's sense of safety, while also keep-ing emotional reactivity in check throughout treatment. (See Appendix 1 for an example.) Despite its importance, consistency of approach is often challenged by the very factors it aims to control (Beatson & Rao, 2014; Linehan, 1993; Livesley et al., 2015).

Regarding therapeutic relationships, Linehan (1993) recognizes the impor-tance of validation and affirmation of the patient's experiences in enhancing his/her engagement and motivation for treatment. Validation especially is important to members of this often-stigmatized and marginalized group. Validation conveys a nonjudgmental understanding of the BPD/chronic pain patient's emotionality and reactive behaviors (even if ultimately maladaptive) given the patient's life situ-ation and current experiences. It allows patients the likely corrective experience of being understood by a treatment provider (Linehan, 1993; Livesley et al., 2015).

Therapists convey validation by not rushing the patient as he/she expresses emotions and by articulating and interpreting the patient's complex and often-overwhelming experiences (McMain et al., 2001; Robins & Rosenthal, 2011). However, validation is necessary but not sufficient. To the contrary, validation

433

without an active problem-solving approach becomes invalidating in itself. Further, the therapist should not excessively corroborate a patient's maladaptive beliefs (Linehan, 1993; McMain et al., 2001). By gently challenging the patient, the therapist conveys that the patient is not overly fragile and thereby increases the patient's sense of self-efficacy (Robins & Rosenthal, 2011).

Interventions With Patients

Effective coping with chronic pain requires that the patient actively participate in and commit to treatment regimens and recommendations. It is important that practitioners accurately convey the importance of physical conditioning, the practice of mind–body strategies, activity management training, and medical and medicinal compliance in chronic pain management (Blackledge & Hayes, 2001; Linton & Fruzzetti, 2014). Elucidation of the sick role and related maladaptive illness behaviors is necessary while promoting the practice of active coping strategies (Kalira et al., 2013). Furthermore, it is important to establish therapeutic objectives of decreasing life-threatening behaviors, as well as therapy and/or medical treatment-interfering behaviors (McMain et al., 2001). Clarifying personal values can help the patient commit to treatment goals. However, competing thoughts, feelings, and self-destructive deportment common to this population may interfere with valued action, highlighting the need for active psychotherapeutic strategies as previously addressed (Blackledge & Hayes, 2001; Kalira et al., 2013; Vowles & McCracken, 2010).

Several related but distinct treatment approaches have been validated for use within this unique population (Table 17.1). No singular approach contains the entire spectrum of interventions needed to address these patients' complex presentations. Although the literature deems all of these approaches to be effective (and not differing substantially in terms of outcome), dialectical behavioral therapy offers advantages for treating suicidal and self-injurious patients (Beatson & Rao, 2014; Livesley et al., 2015).

The practice of mindfulness has received a significant amount of attention as a vehicle for change for both borderline personality and chronic pain disorders.

Table 17.1 Empirically Validated Treatments for BPD and Chronic Pain in Adults

Borderline Personality Disorder	Chronic Pain
Cognitive Behavioral Therapy (CBT)	Acceptance and Commitment Therapy (ACT)
Dialectical Behavior Therapy (DBT)	Biofeedback
Mentalization-Based Treatment (MBT)	Cognitive Behavioral Therapy (CBT)
Psychiatric Management	Medication Management
Schema-Focused Therapy (SFT)	Mindfulness-Based Stress Reduction (MBSR)
Systems Training for Emotional Predictability and Problem Solving (STEPPS)	Behavioral Therapy (BT)
	Physical Therapy
Transference-Focused Therapy (TFP)	

Adapted from Beatson & Rao (2014) and Sturgeon (2014).

Mindfulness is employed as a technique within, or adjunctive to, several psycho-therapeutic approaches (e.g., Bawa et al., 2015; Beatson & Rao, 2014; Kalira et al., 2013; McCracken & Vowles, 2014; Rizvi, Steffel, & Carson-Wong, 2013; Sturgeon, 2014; Veehof, Trompetter, Bohlmeijer, & Schreurs, 2016).

Mindfulness is described as nonjudgmental contact with a person's current internal state, enacted with a sense of openness and curiosity, with no attempt to modify what is observed. Sustained attention is focused on sensory information. Important insights into the patient's emotions, sensations, thoughts, and behavioral urges result, along with the recognition that these internal and external states are transitory, while the self-as-observer remains present. The practitioner gains the ability to turn his/her attention intentionally to a new focus as desired (Blackledge & Hayes, 2001; Livesley et al., 2015; Robins & Rosenthal, 2011). Various techniques guide the patient who practices mindfulness to experience reality without distortion; to accept his/her current states; to release attachments that lead to personal suffering; to act with intention rather than through automatic processes or because of emotional extremes; and to utilize the patient's inherent capacity for wisdom (Linehan, 1987; Linehan, 1993; Robins & Rosenthal, 2011).

Individual Treatment Targets

Reduction of Avoidance Behaviors

Experiential avoidance, which stands in opposition to mindfulness, ultimately propagates suffering. Chronic distress and pain teach individuals that these states are harmful, even dangerous, and must be avoided. Cognitive and behavioral strategies then are employed to avoid contact with these aversive internal and external states (Livesley et al., 2015). From an acceptance and commitment therapy (ACT) perspective, however, these states and resulting intense emotions are not the main source of suffering; rather, the mechanisms of avoidance that obstruct valued living become the treatment targets (Blackledge & Hayes, 2001). Indeed, thought suppression and other avoidance behaviors actually can increase contact with whatever the person is trying to avoid (e.g., attempting to suppress pain sensations results in less pain tolerance; attempting to suppress emotions results in increased frequency and intensity of emotions) (Blackledge & Hayes, 2001; McCracken, Carson, Eccleston, & Keefe, 2004). Furthermore, other harmful behavioral avoidance attempts (e.g., substance abuse, interpersonal attacks, violence, social isolation and withdrawal) also are significant concerns (Blackledge & Hayes, 2001).

Mindfulness skills are the antithesis of these behaviors. By gradually exposing the patient to his/her emotional and physical states, the practice of mindfulness provides a vehicle for extinguishing avoidance conducts (Linehan, 1993). Thereafter, the patient can incorporate positive coping skills, as well as behavioral techniques and regimens. ACT-based experiential exercises and metaphors can alter the patient's view of the (theretofore) avoided emotions and sensations, which in turn can reduce the patient's aversion to them (Blackledge & Hayes, 2001).

Promotion of Acceptance

Although symptoms of both BPD and chronic pain ultimately can be managed effectively, both conditions are enduring in nature with relapsing/remitting patterns. Therefore, tension between acceptance and change often exists within this patient population. Paradoxically, change may only occur after a patient accepts certain aspects of his/her experiences. (McCracken et al., 2004; Veehof et al., 2016). Through a dialectical process, Linehan (1993) advocated flexible movement between acceptance and change polarities through problem-solving and acceptance strategies—namely, mindfulness and values-based exercises. Both collections of strategies are vital when addressing ongoing chronic concerns (Linehan, 1993; McMain et al., 2001; Robins & Rosenthal, 2011). Efforts may then move away from behaviors that keep the person "stuck," to meaningful and valued behaviors (McCracken et al., 2004).

Emotion Regulation

Strong emotionality is both a cause and effect of the BPD/chronic pain patient's multifaceted concerns. Fundamental to emotion regulation is understanding the nature of emotions and the person's experience of them, an understanding brought about by accurate observation, description, and labeling practices (Linehan, 1993). Education regarding cognitive distortions can clarify both the antecedents and consequences of emotions, thereby enhancing the patient's general awareness (Robins & Rosenthal, 2011). Direct cognitive restructuring exercises, as well as ACT-based cognitive defusion techniques (e.g., paradox, confusion, meditation), can provide relief and promote psychological flexibility (Blackledge & Hayes, 2001; Linton & Fruzzetti, 2014). Through mindfulness, patients may recognize the temporary nature of emotionally laden thoughts and states, which can distort perceptions of reality. Mindfulness can aid a person in choosing flexible, valued action rather than reacting by automatic response. This practice also can counteract distraction and dissociative-like states that impede cognitive and behavioral functioning in the face of strong emotions.

Moreover, as an inherently self-compassionate practice, mindfulness can serve as a conduit for reducing self-judgment for emotional experiences (Blackledge & Hayes, 2001; Luoma & Platt, 2015; McCracken & Vowles, 2014; Robins & Rosenthal, 2011). Finally, practitioners can encourage patients to develop regulatory health behaviors (e.g., maintaining healthy diet and exercise, improving sleep hygiene, avoiding unhealthy substances) and to increase pleasurable activities in order to reduce their vulnerability to strong emotions (McMain et al., 2001).

Distress Tolerance

Interventions to enhance the ability of a BPD/chronic pain patient to tolerate physical or emotional distress are essential to effective individual and interpersonal management. Patients learn to shift attention away from strong emotions and their precipitants and to act in a manner opposite to the emotions (e.g., deep breathing) (McMain et al., 2001). Self-soothing techniques (e.g., engaging all of one's senses by taking a bath, listening to music, immersing in nature) aid in regulating emotional states and pain crises. Mindful engagement in pleasurable, immersive activities can distract the patient from aversive states (Robins & Rosenthal, 2011).

It is recommended that patients compose a list of such activities to which they can refer when distressed. Patients also can prevent escalation of crises through grounding practices (e.g., abdominal breathing, brief mindfulness techniques focused upon aspects of their surroundings, planting their feet on the floor, focusing on the textures of a mindfulness object) (Livesley et al., 2015). Furthermore, psychotherapists can focus on the observation of shifting affect, the use of defusion techniques, and the practice of soothing behaviors in session, thereby giving the patient a model for managing these states (Beatson & Rao, 2014).

Reduction of Catastrophizing

As emphasized previously, catastrophizing is a cognitive distortion common to both BPD and the experience of chronic pain. Catastrophizing amplifies the experience of pain sensations as well as negative emotionality. It often leads to fear-based experiential avoidance behaviors that promote chronicity of symptoms (Hollander et al., 2010). From a cognitive-behavioral perspective, automatic, overly anxious cognitions related to physical and emotional pain-related stimuli and events promote this cycle (Burns, Day, & Thorn, 2012). Relatedly, intervention through CBT cognitive restructuring methods (as part of a comprehensive treatment) also reduces catastrophizing, increases self-efficacy, and ultimately enhances the patient's sense of control over pain (Turner, Holtzman, & Mancl, 2007).

Ruminative catastrophic thought, which involves selective attention and automatic interpretations and judgments, serves to magnify threats. These thought patterns are at odds with the flexible, intentional, "detached" attention promoted by mindful awareness (Schutze et al., 2010). Thus, acceptance and mindfulness practices can increase measured awareness of such thoughts without immersion into the suffering that the thoughts promote or the interference that the thoughts create regarding desired action (Vowles, McCracken, & Eccleston, 2008).

Pain catastrophizing is reduced by psychoeducation regarding the biological underpinnings of acute versus chronic pain; the amplifying impact of cognitions and affect on pain experience; and the important distinction between pain and tissue damage. Other important educational targets include the biopsychosocial model of pain, the fear–avoidance–disability cycle, the impact of pain-related behaviors on the chronicity of pain, and the rationale and efficacy surrounding behavioral treatment strategies. All of this education content reduces catastrophic thought content (Burns et al., 2012; Hollander et al., 2010; Linton & Fruzzetti, 2014).

Coping With Medical Treatment

Considering the known associations between trauma history and the development of BPD and chronic pain conditions, as well as trauma history and lower emotional and physical distress tolerance (American Psychiatric Association, 2013), this patient group is uniquely sensitive to the impact of painful or anxiety-provoking procedures or appointments. In turn, this greatly impacts compliance. Specific interventions such as relaxation training, hypnosis, exposure therapy, and cognitive rehearsal aid the patient in complying and coping with the necessary aspects of treatment. Patients also benefit from psychotherapy appointments scheduled around medical encounters. It is helpful if psychologists working within an integrative, rather than co-located, model be present to "coach" patients through potentially stressful procedures and/or engage in co-visits with medical providers whenever feasible. The present therapist also can aid the patient when communicating with medical providers, as well as assist the patient with comprehension when he/she is in a state of high distress (Hay & Passik, 2000).

Interpersonal Effectiveness

The ability to interact productively with professional and familial caregivers is crucial to the BPD/chronic pain patient's successful treatment. Insight-oriented, perspective-taking, and mentalization exercises are important vehicles for interpersonal effectiveness (Beatson & Rao, 2014). Communication and assertiveness strategies, such as the "DEAR MAN" module from DBT, also are impactful (Beatson & Rao, 2014).

"DEAR MAN" Skills for Interpersonal Effectiveness	
D	escribe the situation
E	xpress how you feel about it
A	ssert what you want
R	einforce the other person
M	indfully
A	ppearing confident
N	egotiate

The therapist can help the patient prepare for encounters with the medical team by helping clarify goals and overall agenda; by clarifying and/or practicing questions (or requests) of providers; by helping to distinguish between current emotional as opposed to physical needs; and by rehearsing for the medical encounters. The clinician can also help to disentangle patients' valid concerns within conflict, if present, and help the patient effectively communicate positions (Hay & Passik, 2000).

Interventions With the Medical Team

Education and Coordination

Interventions with the patient's treatment team initially should focus on education regarding the BPD/chronic pain patient's multifaceted presentation. This enhances the patient's understanding, management skillset, and sense of efficacy (Hay & Passik, 2000). Clinicians must emphasize the patient's unique need for a sense of control, strong abandonment fears, and impaired interpersonal functioning. Furthermore, elucidation of treatment-interfering behaviors is essential. Education about patient presentations can reduce over-identification with behaviors and associated countertransference and related negative emotionality, as well as promote maintenance of consistent care (Feely, Havyer, Lapid, & Swetz, 2013; Peteet, Meyer, & Miovic, 2011). By providing education and insight into the occurrence and ramifications of stigma, psychologists promote their medical colleagues' objectivity and enhance the patient–provider relationship.

Trainings, routine consultations and collaborations, and staff coordination can improve the provider's communication and management skills. Staff coordination is critical in promoting clinician cohesion, establishing consistent protocols, and reducing overall risk (Livesley et al., 2015). Staff must be educated on the polarity of splitting behaviors. Providers can aid each other in monitoring for boundary issues, commonly indicated by deviation in protocol and the development of team member discord (Hay & Passik, 2000).

Enhancing Patient's Sense of Safety

The treatment team plays an important role in enhancing the patient's sense of safety and control. Patients with BPD often respond best when functioning within a predictable environment. Whenever possible, minimize the number of caregivers involved in the patient's direct care. It is imperative that the patient's team members remain consistent. Finally, enhance patient boundaries if possible (e.g., ensure privacy, knock before entering the room, inform the patient of necessary procedures, ask permission before enacting them) (Feely et al., 2013).

Maximizing Effectiveness of Provider Demeanor

The provider's demeanor and approach significantly influences the working relationship between provider and patient (a particularly important relationship for this patient population). The provider should adopt an air of curiosity into the patient's condition, coupled with genuine receptiveness and respect. Address problems and concerns from the patient's perspective; this approach will enhance a sense of collaboration (Hay & Passik, 2000). Conveying a sense of legitimacy regarding the patient's concerns and experiences will enable the provider to engage with the patient notwithstanding prior invalidating responses.

439

The provider also should communicate a sense of commitment to the patient and the treatment, thereby lessening the patient's fears of abandonment. The provider also should convey a sense of optimism regarding effective treatment, while at the same time highlighting realistic expectations (Kalira et al., 2013).

The provider's tone should be calm, controlled, and neutral (Feely et al., 2013). Passik, Byers, and Kirsh (2007) suggest several mindful self-awareness exercises to use prior to *and* during patient interactions. Before interaction, the authors recommend identifying the patient's cognitions, emotions, and physiological responses that arise when anticipating the upcoming encounter. If these responses are likely to interfere with treatment, it is advised that providers address and cope with reactivity effectively. Providers should then reflect upon treatment choice and progress. While interacting with the patient, providers are encouraged to again take the patient's point of view in observing and experiencing the encounter's proceedings, adjusting the interaction as needed (Passik et al., 2007).

Promoting Structure

Scheduling regular visits, involving the family (whenever possible) to aid in compliance, and encouraging the patient to actively participate in his/her care provides essential structure (Wasan, Wootton, & Jamison, 2005). Providers and patient should settle upon the components of treatment and goals at the onset, possibly codifying the agreements in a written contract. The patient's roles and responsibilities, along with those of the provider, should be spelled out explicitly. Expectations, procedures, length of office visits, medication monitoring, emergency options both in and outside regular business hours, and repercussions for non-compliance should be addressed in the contract (Kalira et al., 2013; Passik et al., 2007). In addition, a collaborative discussion regarding the framework of treatment is recommended. Providers should communicate the rationale underlying all aspects of the regimen. Communication, collaboration, and integration with other services and providers involved in the patient's care can help promote a united "holding environment" (Beatson & Rao, 2014). Delineate and clarify the role and scope of practice of each provider and each service(Beatson & Rao, 2014; Passik et al., 2007).

Addressing Behaviors

Early containment of potentially dangerous or disruptive behaviors is crucial. Rules and consequences should be clearly stated to patients and caregivers and (equally important) must be employed consistently. However, take care to avoid making the patient feel overly criticized or punished when addressing behaviors. Positive reinforcement of compliance enhances the patient's functioning; applaud the patient's successes (Feely et al., 2013; Hay & Passik, 2000; Kalira et al., 2013). However, do not intermittently reinforce the patient's problematic behaviors. For example, by eventually "giving in" to the patient, the provider actually can strengthen the problematic behaviors. Meet inappropriate behaviors with the least attention possible, while at the same time enforcing and enacting behavioral contingencies. Punishment and arguments are ineffective with this population (and actually may also serve to enhance discord) regardless of the provider's frustrations (Nordgren, 2007).

Increasing Awareness of Risk of Prescribing Opioids

People with BPD are significantly more likely to use opioids than the general patient population (use in past year: OR = 1.39, 95% CI = 1.12–1.72; lifetime use: OR = 1.47, 95% CI = 1.25–1.72) (Saha et al., 2016). BPD patients are twice as likely to be prescribed opioids as patients with other personality disorders. This is concerning, given the common associations with BPD and substance use disorders, depression, and suicide (Frankenburg, Fitzmaurice, & Zanarini, 2014).

Correspondingly, patients with BPD are nearly twice as likely to meet criteria for opioid use disorder (OR = 1.68, CI = 1.21–2.32) (Saha et al., 2016). Researchers attribute this greater likelihood to the proposed dysregulation of the endogenous opioid system underlying BPD development, and associated impulsivity and self-harm behaviors (Tragesser et al., 2013). As such, medication monitoring is especially important with this patient population, particularly through the implementation of opioid use contracts. Finally, given the emotional dysregulation inherent to the disorder, it is essential to monitor *how* the medication is utilized (e.g., during times of stress versus pain) (Frankenburg et al., 2014; Tragesser, Jones, Robinson, Stutler, & Stewart, 2013).

Supporting the Team

The treatment team's emotional health is paramount. Regular debriefing sessions enable providers to verbalize and process emotions, receive support from other team members, obtain perspective and recommendations regarding behavioral management strategies, and provide a united front (Feely et al., 2013; Peteet et al., 2011).

Interventions With Caregivers

BPD and chronic pain can have a profound impact on, and in turn be impacted by, familial functioning. Thus, special consideration and interventions with caregivers are vital (American Psychiatric Association, 2013; Edlund, Carlsson, Linton, Fruzzetti, & Tillfors, 2015; McMain et al., 2001). Family members' involvement in treatment has been associated with favorable outcomes for individual patients. Indeed, family members have been referred to as "collateral providers" (Hoffman, Buteau, Hooley, Fruzetto, & Bruce, 2003). Including family members in treatment can shift contingent and reinforced behaviors within the patient's immediate environment (e.g., selective responsivity to escalated emotions and outbursts, overly solicitous responses to pain behaviors); allow for modeling of desired behaviors; enhance in vivo practice of skills (e.g., distress tolerance skills); alter communication patterns; and, overall, improve functioning of patients and their caregivers (Uliaszek, Wilson, Mayberry, Cox, & Maslar, 2014).

Providing caregivers with psychoeducation regarding chronic pain and personality disorders and symptoms, as well as providing insight into the patient's unique presentation, can enhance predictability, clarity, and self-efficacy within the family members' interactions as well as caregiving roles. However, the clinician must avoid (intentional or unintentional) perpetuation of stigma and caregiver-related helplessness associated with these complex presentations (Hoffman et al., 2003). Correspondingly, training caregivers in enhanced validation and conveyance of acceptance toward the patient, as well as in reinforcing well behaviors, is impactful (Edlund et al., 2015). The patient's involvement (to his/her comfort level and abilities) in social activities and responsibilities can enhance his/her sense of mastery, belongingness, and contribution (Cowan, 2013). Family members also can enhance the patient's compliance with treatment parameters, including monitoring of opioid therapy where applicable (Brady, McCauley, & Back, 2016). Finally, it is essential that caregivers be provided with support as they help patients navigate their complicated conditions (Cowan, 2013).

Conclusion

Personality disorders are associated with dysregulated perceptual, emotional, behavioral, and interpersonal attributes that account for unique perceptions and experiences of chronic pain. A multimodality, highly structured approach to both the psychological and medical treatment of chronic pain in this population is necessary and must draw from several validated, individual, and macro-interventions. Acceptance and mindfulness techniques are particularly effective in ameliorating core issues such as avoidance behaviors, catastrophic thought patterns, emotional dysregulation, distress tolerance, and the pain experience itself. Interpersonal concerns, which are paramount, can be addressed by individual interventions as well as emotionally corrective interactions with informal and professional caregivers. Although this highly marginalized population's concerns are undoubtedly complex, optimism regarding effective treatment is both reasonable and highly encouraged.

References

American Psychiatric Association. (2013). *Diagnostic and statistical manual of mental disorders (DSM-5)*. Arlington, VA, American Psychiatric Publications.

Aviram, R. B., Brodsky, B. S., & Stanley, B. (2006). Borderline personality disorder, stigma, and treatment implications. *Harvard Review of Psychiatry*, 14(5), 249–256. doi:10.1080/10673220600975121

Bateman, A., & Fonagy, P. (2010). Mentalization based treatment for borderline personality disorder. *World Psychiatry*, 9(1), 11–15. doi:10.1093/med:psych/9780198527664.003.0003

Bawa, F. L. M., Mercer, S. W., Atherton, R. J., Clague, F., Keen, A., Scott, N. W., & Bond, C. M. (2015). Does mindfulness improve outcomes in patients with chronic pain?

Systematic review and meta-analysis. *British Journal of General Practice, 65*(635), e387–e400. doi:10.3399/bjgp15X685297

Beatson, J., & Rao, S. (2014). Psychotherapy for borderline personality disorder. *Australas Psychiatry, 22*(6), 529–532. doi:10.1177/1039856214555531

Bender, D. S., Dolan, R. T., Skodol, A. E., Sanislow, C. A., Dyck, I. R., McGlashan, T. H., ... Gunderson, J. G. (2001). Treatment utilization by patients with personality disorders. *American Journal of Psychiatry, 158*(2), 295–302. doi:10.1176/appi.ajp.158.2.295

Biskin, R. S., Frankenburg, F. R., Fitzmaurice, G. M., & Zanarini, M. C. (2014). Pain in patients with borderline personality disorder. *Personality and Mental Health, 8*(3), 218–227. doi:10.1002/pmh.1265

Black, D. W., Blum, N., Pfohl, B., & Hale, N. (2004). Suicidal behavior in borderline personality disorder: Prevalence, risk factors, prediction, and prevention. *Journal of Personality Disorders, 18*(3), 226–239. doi:10.1521/pedi.18.3.226.35445

Blackledge, J. T., & Hayes, S. C. (2001). Emotion regulation in acceptance and commitment therapy. *Journal of Clinical Psychology, 57*(2), 243–255. doi:10.1002/1097-4679(200102)57:2 < 243::aid-jclp9 > 3.3.co;2-o

Bland, A. R., & Rossen, E. (2005). Clinical supervision of nurses working with patients with borderline personality disorder. *Issues in Mental Health Nursing, 26*(5), 507–517. doi: 10.1080/01612840590931957

Bodner, E., Cohen-Fridel, S., & Iancu, I. (2011). Staff attitudes toward patients with borderline personality disorder. *Comprehensive Psychiatry, 52*(5), 548–555. doi:10.1016/j.comppsych.2010.10.004

Brady, K. T., McCauley, J. L., & Back, S. E. (2016). Prescription opioid misuse, abuse, and treatment in the United States: An update. *American Journal of Psychiatry, 173*(1), 18–26. doi:10.1176/appi.ajp.2015.15020262

Buchman, D. Z., Ho, A., & Illes, J. (2016). You present like a drug addict: Patient and clinician perspectives on trust and trustworthiness in chronic pain management. *Pain Medicine, 17*(8), 1394–1406. doi:10.1093/pm/pnv083

Burns, J. W., Day, M. A., & Thorn, B. E. (2012). Is reduction in pain catastrophizing a therapeutic mechanism specific to cognitive-behavioral therapy for chronic pain? *Translational Behavioral Medicine, 2*(1), 22–29. doi:10.1007/s13142-011-0086-3

Calati, R., Artero, S., Courtet, P., & Lopez-Castroman, J. (2016). Framing the impact of physical pain on suicide attempts: A reply to Stubbs. *Journal of Psychiatric Research, 72*, 102–103. doi:10.1016/j.jpsychires.2015.10.018

Campbell, G., Bruno, R., Darke, S., & Degenhardt, L. (2015). Associations of borderline personality with pain, problems with medications and suicidality in a community sample of chronic non-cancer pain patients prescribed opioids for pain. *General Hospital Psychiatry, 37*(5), 434–440. doi:10.1016/j.genhosppsych.2015.05.004

Cardenas-Morales, L., Fladung, A. K., Kammer, T., Schmahl, C., Plener, P. L., Connemann, B. J., & Schonfeldt-Lecuona, C. (2011). Exploring the affective component of pain perception during aversive stimulation in borderline personality disorder. *Psychiatry Research, 186*(2–3), 458–460. doi:10.1016/j.psychres.2010.07.050

Carpenter, R. W., Wood, P. K., & Trull, T. J. (2016). Comorbidity of borderline personality disorder and lifetime substance use disorders in a nationally representative sample. *Journal of Personality Disorders, 30*(3), 336–350. doi:10.1521/pedi_2015_29_197

Carpenter, R. W., & Trull, T. J. (2015). The pain paradox: Borderline personality disorder features, self-harm history, and the experience of pain. *Personality Disorders: Theory, Research, and Treatment, 6*(2), 141. doi: 10.1037/per0000112

Carr, D. B. (2016). Patients with pain need less stigma, not more. *Pain Medicine, 17*(8), 1391–1393. doi:10.1093/pm/pnw158

Cloninger, C. R., Przybeck, T. R., & Svrakic, D. M. (1994). *The Temperament and Character Inventory (TCI): A guide to its development and use*. St. Louis, MO: Center for Psychobiology of Personality, Washington University.

Conrad, R., Schilling, G., Bausch, C., Nadstawek, J., Wartenberg, H. C., Wegener, I., . . . Liedtke, R. (2007). Temperament and character personality profiles and personality disorders in chronic pain patients. *Pain, 133*(1–3), 197–209. doi:10.1016/j.pain.2007.07.024

Conrad, R., Wegener, I., Geiser, F., & Kleiman, A. (2013). Temperament, character, and personality disorders in chronic pain. *Current Pain and Headache Reports, 17*(3), 318. doi:10.1007/s11916-012-0318-3

Cowan, P. (2013). *ACPA family manual*. Monroeville, PA: American Chronic Pain Association.

De Ruddere, L., & Craig, K. D. (2016). Understanding stigma and chronic pain: A state-of-the-art review. *Pain, 157*(8), 1607–1610. doi:10.1097/j.pain.0000000000000512

Dixon-Gordon, K. L., Berghoff, C. R., & McDermott, M. J. (2017). Borderline personality disorder symptoms and pain in college students: The role of emotional suppression. *Journal of Personality Disorders*, 1–12. doi:10.1521/pedi_2017_31_300

Dixon-Gordon, K. L., Whalen, D. J., Layden, B. K., & Chapman, A. L. (2015). A systematic review of personality disorders and health outcomes. *Canadian Psychology, 56*(2), 168–190. doi:10.1037/cap0000024

Ducasse, D., Courtet, P., & Olie, E. (2014). Physical and social pains in borderline disorder and neuroanatomical correlates: A systematic review. *Current Psychiatry Reports, 16*(5), 443. doi:10.1007/s11920-014-0443-2

Edlund, S. M., Carlsson, M. L., Linton, S. J., Fruzzetti, A. E., & Tillfors, M. (2015). I see you're in pain—The effects of partner validation on emotions in people with chronic pain. *Scandinavian Journal of Pain, 6*, 16–21.

Feely, M. A., Havyer, R. D., Lapid, M. I., & Swetz, K. M. (2013). Management of end-of-life care and of difficult behaviors associated with borderline personality disorder. *Journal of Pain Symptom Management, 45*(5), 934–938. doi:10.1016/j.jpainsymman.2012.04.004

Fischer-Kern, M., Kapusta, N. D., Doering, S., Horz, S., Mikutta, C., & Aigner, M. (2011). The relationship between personality organization and psychiatric classification in chronic pain patients. *Psychopathology, 44*(1), 21–26. doi:10.1159/000317271

Frankenburg, F. R., Fitzmaurice, G. M., & Zanarini, M. C. (2014). The use of prescription opioid medication by patients with borderline personality disorder and axis ii comparison subjects: A 10-year follow-up study. *The Journal of Clinical Psychiatry, 75*(4), 357–361. http://doi.org/10.4088/JCP.13m08557

Ginzburg, K., Biran, I., Aryeh, I. G., Tsur, N., & Defrin, R. (2018). Pain perception and body awareness among individuals with borderline personality disorder. *Journal of Personality Disorders, 32*(5), 618–635. doi: 10.1521/pedi_2017_31_316

Gross, R., Olfson, M., Gameroff, M., Shea, S., Feder, A., Fuentes, M., . . . Weissman, M., M. (2002). Borderline personality disorder in primary care. *Archives of Internal Medicine, 162*(1), 53–60. doi:10.1001/archinte.162.1.53

Gustin, S. M., Burke, L. A., Peck, C. C., Murray, G. M., & Henderson, L. A. (2016). Pain and personality: Do individuals with different forms of chronic pain exhibit a mutual personality? *Pain Practice, 16*(4), 486–494. doi:10.1111/papr.12297

Hassett, A. L., Aquino, J. K., & Ilgen, M. A. (2014). The risk of suicide mortality in chronic pain patients. *Current Pain and Headache Report, 18*(8), 436. doi:10.1007/s11916-014-0436-1

Hay, J. L., & Passik, S. D. (2000). The cancer patient with borderline personality disorder: Suggestions for symptom-focused management in the medical setting. *Psychooncology, 9*(2), 91–100. doi:10.1002/(SICI)1099-1611(200003/04)9:2 < 91::AID-PON437 > 3.0.CO;2-8

Heath, L. M., Paris, J., Laporte, L., & Gill, K. J. (2017). High prevalence of physical pain among treatment-seeking individuals with borderline personality disorder. *Journal of Personality Disorders*, 1–7. doi:10.1521/pedi_2017_31_302

Hoffman, P. D., Buteau, E., Hooley, J. M., Fruzetto, A. E., & Bruce, M. L. (2003). Family members' knowledge about borderline personality disorder: Correspondence with their levels of depression, burden, distress, and expressed emotion. *Family Process, 42*(4), 469–478. doi:10.1111/j.1545-5300.2003.00469.x

Hollander, M. D., De Jong, J. R., Volders, S., Goossens, M. E., Smeets, R. J., & Vlaeyen, J. W. (2010). Fear reduction in patients with chronic pain: A learning theory perspective. *Expert Review of Neurotherapeutics, 10*(11), 1733–1745. doi:10.1586/ern.10.115

Hooley, J. M., Franklin, J. C., & Nock, M. K. (2014). Chronic pain and suicide: Understanding the association. *Current Pain and Headache Report, 18*(8), 435. doi:10.1007/s11916-014-0435-2

Kadimpati, S., Zale, E. L., Hooten, M. W., Ditre, J. W., & Warner, D. O. (2015). Associations between neuroticism and depression in relation to catastrophizing and pain-related anxiety in chronic pain patients. *PLoS One, 10*(4), e0126351. doi:10.1371/journal.pone.0126351

Kalira, V., Treisman, G. J., & Clark, M. R. (2013). Borderline personality disorder and chronic pain: A practical approach to evaluation and treatment. *Current Pain and Headache Report, 17*(8), 350. doi:10.1007/s11916–013–0350-y

Kayhan, F., Küçük, A., Satan, Y., İlgün, E., Arslan, Ş., & İlik, F. (2016). Sexual dysfunction, mood, anxiety, and personality disorders in female patients with fibromyalgia. *Neuropsychiatric Disease and Treatment, 12*, 349. doi:10.2147/NDT.S99160

Knaak, S., Szeto, A. C., Fitch, K., Modgill, G., & Patten, S. (2015). Stigma towards borderline personality disorder: Effectiveness and generalizability of an anti-stigma program for healthcare providers using a pre-post randomized design. *Borderline Personality Disorder and Emotion Dysregulation, 2*(1), 9. doi:10.1186/s40479-015-0030-0

Koenig, J., Thayer, J. F., & Kaess, M. (2016). A meta-analysis on pain sensitivity in self- injury. *Psychological Medicine, 46*(8), 1597–1612. doi: 10.1017/S0033291716000301

Linehan, M. (1987). Dialectical behavioral therapy: A cognitive behavioral approach to parasuicide. *Journal of Personality Disorders, 1*(4), 328–333. doi: 10.1521/pedi.1987.1.4.328

Linehan, M. (1993). *Cognitive-behavioral treatment of borderline personality disorder.* New York, NY: The Guilford Press.

Linton, S. J., & Fruzzetti, A. E. (2014). A hybrid emotion-focused exposure treatment for chronic pain: A feasibility study. *Scandinavian Journal of Pain, 5*(3), 151–158. doi:10.1016/j.sjpain.2014.05.008

Livesley, W. J., Dimaggio, G., & Clarkin, J. F. (2015). *Integrated treatment for personality disorder: A modular approach.* New York, NY: The Guilford Press.

Luoma, J. B., & Platt, M. G. (2015). Shame, self-criticism, self-stigma, and compassion in acceptance and commitment therapy. *Current Opinion in Psychology, 2*, 97–101.

Magerl, W., Burkart, D., Fernandez, A., Schmidt, L. G., & Treede, R-D. (2012). Persistent antinociception through repeated self-injury in patients with borderline personality disorder. *Pain, 153*(3), 575–584. doi:10.1016/j.pain.2011.11.021

Malmgren-Olsson, E. B., & Bergdahl, J. (2006). Temperament and character personality dimensions in patients with nonspecific musculoskeletal disorders. *Clinical Journal of Pain, 22*(7), 625–631. doi:10.1097/01.ajp.0000210907.65170.a3

McCracken, L. M., Carson, J. W., Eccleston, C., & Keefe, F. J. (2004). Acceptance and change in the context of chronic pain. *Pain, 109*(1–2), 4–7. doi:10.1016/j.pain.2004.02.006

McCracken, L. M., & Vowles, K. E. (2014). Acceptance and commitment therapy and mindfulness for chronic pain: Model, process, and progress. *American Psychologist, 69*(2), 178–187. doi:10.1037/a0035623

McMain, S., Korman, L. M., & Dimeff, L. (2001). Dialectical behavior therapy and the treatment of emotion dysregulation. *Journal of Clinical Psychology, 57*(2), 183–196. doi:10.1002/1097–4679(200102)57:2 < 183::AID-JCLP5 > 3.0.CO;2-Y

Morton, J., Snowdon, S., Gopold, M., & Guymer, E. (2012). Acceptance and commitment therapy group treatment for symptoms of borderline personality disorder: A public sector pilot study. *Cognitive and Behavioral Practice, 19*(4), 527–544. doi:10.1016/j.cbpra.2012.03.005

Mun, C. J., Karoly, P., Ruehlman, L., & Kim, H. (2016). Borderline personality features and pain severity: Exploring the mediational role of depression and catastrophizing. *Journal of Social and Clinical Psychology, 35*(5), 386–400. doi:10.1521/jscp.2016.35.5.386

Naylor, B., Boag, S., & Gustin, S. M. (2017). New evidence for a pain personality? A critical review of the last 120 years of pain and personality. *Scandinavian Journal of Pain, 17*, 58–67. doi:10.1016/j.sjpain.2017.07.011

Nordgren, J. C. (2007). Observations on managing medical patients with borderline personality. *Journal of Pharmacy Practice, 20*(5), 377–384. doi:10.1177/0897190007304983

Passik, S. D., Byers, K., & Kirsh, K. L. (2007). Empathy and the failure to treat pain. *Palliative and Supportive Care, 5*(2), 167–172. doi:10.1017/S1478951507070241

Penfold, S., St Denis, E., & Mazhar, M. N. (2016). The association between borderline personality disorder, fibromyalgia and chronic fatigue syndrome: Systematic review. *British Journal of Psychiatry Open, 2*(4), 275–279. doi:10.1192/bjpo.bp.115.002808

Peteet, J. R., Meyer, F. L., & Miovic, M. K. (2011). Possibly impossible patients: Management of difficult behavior in oncology outpatients. *Journal of Oncology Practice, 7*(4), 242–246. doi:10.1200/JOP.2010.000122

Proctor, S. L., Estroff, T. W., Empting, L. D., Shearer-Williams, S., & Hoffmann, N. G. (2013). Prevalence of substance use and psychiatric disorders in a highly select chronic pain population. *Journal of Addiction Medicine, 7*(1), 17–24. doi:10.1097/ADM.0b013e3182738655

Rizvi, S. L., Steffel, L. M., & Carson-Wong, A. (2013). An overview of dialectical behavior therapy for professional psychologists. *Professional Psychology: Research and Practice, 44*(2), 73.

Robins, C. J., & Rosenthal, M. Z. (2011). Dialectical behavior therapy. *Acceptance and Mindfulness in Cognitive Behavior Therapy: Understanding and Applying the New Therapies*, 164–192.

Sagula, D., & Rice, K. G. (2004). The effectiveness of mindfulness training on the grieving process and emotional well-being of chronic pain patients. *Journal of Clinical Psychology in Medical Settings, 11*(4), 333–342. doi:10.1023/B:JOCS.0000045353.78755.51

Saha, T. D., Kerridge, B. T., Goldstein, R. B., Chou, S. P., Zhang, H., Jung, J., . . . Grant, B. F. (2016). Nonmedical prescription opioid use and DSM-5 nonmedical prescription opioid use disorder in the United States. *The Journal of Clinical Psychiatry, 77*(6), 772–780. doi:10.4088/JCP.15m10386

Sansone, R. A., & Sansone, L. A. (2007). Borderline personality and the pain paradox. *Psychiatry (Edgmont), 4*(4), 40–46.

Sansone, R. A., & Sansone, L. A. (2012). Chronic pain syndromes and borderline personality. *Innovations in Clinical Neuroscience, 9*(1), 10–14.

Sansone, R. A., & Sansone, L. A. (2015). Borderline personality in the medical setting. *The Primary Care Companion for CNS Disorders, 17*(3).

Sansone, R. A., Tahir, N. A., Buckner, V. R., & Wiederman, M. W. (2008). The relationship between borderline personality symptomatology and somatic preoccupation among internal medicine outpatients. *Primary Care Companion to the Journal of Clinical Psychiatry, 10*(4), 286–290.

Sansone, R. A., Watts, D. A., & Wiederman, M. W. (2014). Pain, pain catastrophizing, and past mental healthcare utilization. *Journal of Psychosomatic Research, 76*(2), 169–171. doi:10.1016/j.jpsychores.2013.11.013

Schutze, R., Rees, C., Preece, M., & Schutze, M. (2010). Low mindfulness predicts pain catastrophizing in a fear-avoidance model of chronic pain. *Pain, 148*(1), 120–127. doi:10.1016/j.pain.2009.10.030

Sturgeon, J. A. (2014). Psychological therapies for the management of chronic pain. *Psychology Research and Behavior Management, 7*, 115–124. doi:10.2147/PRBM.S44762

Tang, N. K., & Crane, C. (2006). Suicidality in chronic pain: A review of the prevalence, risk factors and psychological links. *Psychological Medicine, 36*(5), 575–586. doi:10.1017/S0033291705006859

Tragesser, S. L., Bruns, D., & Disorbio, J. M. (2010). Borderline personality disorder features and pain: The mediating role of negative affect in a pain patient sample. *Clinical Journal of Pain, 26*(4), 348–353. doi:10.1097/AJP.0b013e3181cd1710

Tragesser, S. L., Jones, R. E., Robinson, R. J., Stutler, A., & Stewart, A. (2013). Borderline personality disorder and risk for prescription opioid use disorder. *Journal of Personality Disorders, 27*(4):427–441. doi:10.1521/pedi_2013_27_094

Turner, J. A., Holtzman, S., & Mancl, L. (2007). Mediators, moderators, and predictors of therapeutic change in cognitive-behavioral therapy for chronic pain. *Pain, 127*(3), 276–286. doi:10.1016/j.pain.2006.09.005

Uliaszek, A. A., Wilson, S., Mayberry, M., Cox, K., & Maslar, M. (2014). A pilot intervention of multifamily dialectical behavior group therapy in a treatment-seeking adolescent population: Effects on teens and their family members. *The Family Journal, 22*(2), 206–215. doi:10.1177/1066480713513554

Veehof, M., Trompetter, H., Bohlmeijer, E. T., & Schreurs, K. M. G. (2016). Acceptance- and mindfulness-based interventions for the treatment of chronic pain: A meta-analytic review. *Cognitive Behaviour Therapy, 45*(1), 5–31. doi:10.1080/16506073.2015.1098724

Vowles, K. E., & McCracken, L. M. (2010). Comparing the role of psychological flexibility and traditional pain management coping strategies in chronic pain treatment outcomes. *Behaviour Research and Therapy, 48*(2), 141–146. doi:10.1016/j.brat.2009.09.011

Vowles, K. E., McCracken, L. M., & Eccleston, C. (2008). Patient functioning and catastrophizing in chronic pain: The mediating effects of acceptance. *Health Psychology, 27*(2S), S136–S143. doi:10.1037/0278–6133.27.2(Suppl.).S136

Wasan, A. D., Wootton, J., & Jamison, R. N. (2005). Dealing with difficult patients in your pain practice. *Regional Anesthesia and Pain Medicine, 30*(2), 184–192. doi:10.1016/j.rapm.2004.11.005

Waugh, O. C., Byrne, D. G., & Nicholas, M. K. (2014). Internalized stigma in people living with chronic pain. *The Journal of Pain, 15*(5), 550.e1–550.e10. doi:10.1016/j.jpain.2014.02.001

World Health Organization. (2017). *Preventing suicide: A resource for media professionals: Update 2017*. Retrieved from www.who.int/mental_health/suicide-prevention/resource_booklet_2017/en/

You, D. S., & Meagher, M. W. (2017). Association between borderline personality features and temporal summation of second pain: A cross-sectional study. *Behavioral Medicine, 43*(3), 208–217. doi:10.1080/08964289.2017.1322935

Zampieri, M. A. J., Tognola, W. A., & Galego, J. C. B. (2014). Patients with chronic headache tend to have more psychological symptoms than those with sporadic episodes of pain. *Arquivos de neuro-psiquiatria, 72*(8), 598–602. doi:10.1590/0004-282X20140084

Appendix 1

Sample Pain-Based Psychotherapy Treatment Contract

Pain Management Psychotherapy Contract

Patient's Agreement

The goal of therapy is to help you feel more in control of your pain condition and to help you live your best life possible regardless of your pain. Although unable to get rid of the source of your pain directly, therapy will teach you strategies to help you cope with the pain itself, as well as the thoughts, feelings, and behaviors that often go with it, reduce your level of disability, and ultimately help you to more effectively manage your pain yourself.

Components of Therapy

Mindfulness

Mindfulness is the ability to bring about awareness and acceptance. Mindfulness practitioners learn to focus their mind and observe what they are feeling and thinking without judging their experience. These skills can help your reaction to painful thoughts, emotions, and sensations.

Distress Tolerance

Distress tolerance skills teach you how to distract and soothe yourself in a healthy manner while experiencing physical or emotional distress.

Emotion Management

Emotion management skills address emotional sensitivity, mood swings, and long-lasting depression, anxiety, or anger. Examples of skills include learning to identify and label emotions, increasing positive moods, and decreasing vulnerability to negative moods.

Interpersonal Effectiveness

Interpersonal effectiveness skills allow you to improve relationships within your treatment teams or social environments. These skills include effective communication, taking others' perspectives, letting people know what you need in a respectful way, and asking for help when needed.

Relaxation Training

Through practices such as deep breathing, muscle relaxation, visualization, and imagery exercises, you can reduce the effect of physical and mental stress—which often can make pain seem worse.

Activation/Reduction of Fear of Pain

Many people with chronic pain have drastically reduced their activity levels. You will be able to gradually and safely increase activity levels, in terms of both time and intensity, to improve functioning. We can also work together with physical therapists to meet these goals.

Changing Thinking Styles

Often people in pain develop overly negative or anxious thinking styles that actually make pain and its experience worse. You will learn how to identify these "unhelpful" thoughts and replace them with more balanced, flexible, and adaptive ones.

Acceptance and Commitment

Those in pain often feel that their condition "runs" their life. We will help you to better identify your values and goals and outline a path to work toward them. You will learn ways, when the physical source of pain is unchangeable, to move forward and live a meaningful and fulfilling life despite pain.

Target Behaviors Agreement

Harm to Self or Others

If suicidal, self-harm, or outwardly violent behaviors are a problem for you, reducing these behaviors will be a primary treatment goal. We will construct a clear safety plan that specifies steps needed to make sure you stay safe. It is required that clients sign a contract to reduce suicidal, self-injurious, or violent behaviors.

Therapy-Interfering Behaviors

You agree to work on any other problems that interfere with the progress of therapy, such as arriving late for sessions/cancelling multiple times, not paying fees, disrespecting your therapist, other clients, providers, or office staff, passive and/or aggressive behaviors, misusing any pain medications if prescribed, non-compliance with treatment recommendations, attending therapy under the influence of drugs or alcohol, or providing information to the treatment team that is inaccurate, misleading, or inconsistent, etc. If such behaviors continue after discussion with your therapist and coaching on how to change the behaviors, you may be discharged from the practice.

Opioid Use

If prescribed opioid medication, and if recommended by your prescribing provider, you agree to the monitoring of opioid use as outlined by that provider. This may include pill-counting, distribution of medication by a trusted person involved in your therapy, intervention within any treatment-interfering behaviors (e.g., repeated attempts to obtain medications in between agreed-upon appointment times, ingesting medications inappropriately, etc.), random urine drug screenings, etc.

Involving Others in Treatment

To help address all aspects of the pain experience, we regularly consult, and potentially co-treat, with physicians, psychiatrists, pharmacists, and physical and occupational therapists. It is often also helpful to involve friends and family members in your treatment to support your goals and at-home recovery.

Confidentiality

In general, the privacy of all communications between a patient and a psychologist is protected by law, and I can only release information about our work to others with your written permission (Confidentiality Agreement enclosed). But there are a few exceptions.

In most legal proceedings, you have the right to prevent me from providing any information about your treatment. In some proceedings in which your emotional condition is an important issue, a judge may order my testimony. I am also legally required to take action to protect others from harm, such as in the case of abuse (e.g., children, elderly, the disabled). If I believe that you are threatening serious bodily harm to another, I am required to take protective actions. ***Furthermore, if you threaten to harm yourself, I may be required to seek hospitalization for you or to contact family members or others who can help provide protection.***

In consultation with another professional, I make every effort to avoid revealing the identity of my patients. The other professional is also legally bound to keep the information confidential. If you don't object, I will not tell you about these consultations unless I feel that it is important to our work together.

Therapy Course

The initial consultation is scheduled for ___ hour. Treatment will last for ___ weeks, at a frequency of ___ times per week, for a duration of ____ minutes per session. More or less frequent sessions are sometimes scheduled, depending on your needs.

Cancellation Policy

Sessions must be cancelled a minimum of ___ hours in advance, or a cancellation fee of ____ will be charged (except in cases of emergency). In the interest of progress in therapy, if you no-show __ times you **will be discharged from the practice**.

Payment Policy

All associated fees and co-payments will be collected immediately prior to each session.

> ***I agree to the terms set above in this therapy agreement.***
>
> *Client Signature:* _____
>
> *Date:*_____
>
> *Therapist Signature:* _____
>
> *Date:*_____

18

Co-occurring Depression, Anxiety, and Chronic Pain

Jennifer M. Caspari

Overview

Chronic pain, defined as pain that persists for three months or more (Merskey & Bogduk, 1994), is a widespread public health problem throughout the world. Approximately 20% of the global population experiences chronic pain (Goldberg & McGee, 2011), including 30–50 million adults in the United States (Joranson & Lietman, 1994). Over the last few decades, pain theories have moved away from a biomedical model, which assumes that an individual's pain results from specific physical damage that can be confirmed by objective test data, with subsequent medical interventions directed toward repairing physical pathology, to the widely accepted biopsychosocial model, according to which tissue damage, psychological, and sociocultural factors all interact to determine an individual's unique pain experience (Turk, 2002a).

The International Association for the Study of Pain presently defines pain as "an unpleasant sensory and emotional experience associated with actual or potential tissue damage, or described in terms of such damage" (Merskey & Bogduk, 1994, p. 210). In 2016, pain researchers proposed a revised definition in order to better capture the current multidimensional understanding of pain: "a distressing experience associated with actual or potential tissue damage with sensory, emotional, cognitive, and social components" (Williams & Craig, 2016, p. 2420). This revised definition further underscores the role of psychosocial factors in pain perception.

Pain is a subjective experience involving a complex interaction between physical, psychological, and environmental variables (Flor & Herman, 2004; Nicholas, 2008). Chronic pain, by definition, persists over a lengthy time period. Medical treatments for chronic pain cannot eliminate all pain in all people. Though statistics vary widely depending upon the chronic pain condition, studies demonstrate that pain medications in general only reduce chronic pain by 30–40% (Turk, 2002b). Research also has demonstrated that even when statistically significant reductions in pain are reported, these improvements are not necessarily accompanied by increased physical and/or emotional functioning (Turk, 2002b).

Numerous studies have found that chronic pain and psychiatric disorders frequently co-occur (Dersh, Polatin, & Gatchel, 2002). Much of this research focuses on depression and anxiety, which are regarded as important contributors to the experience of pain (Woo, 2010). A recent meta-analytic review (Burke, Mathias, & Denson, 2015) found that chronic pain patients (when compared to healthy controls) consistently report experiencing more problems in a range of psychological domains, are more depressed, and are more anxious both in general and in response to pain. Further, they experience the greatest psychological difficulty in areas that are directly tied to the physical experience of pain, such as pain anxiety and somatization. A large study conducted by the World Health Organization that assessed 5,438 patients from 15 primary care sites and 14 countries found that among the 22% of patients who reported consistent pain for more than six months, there was a four-fold increase in associated depressive and anxiety disorders (Gureje, Simon, & Von Korff, 2001). These relationships were consistent across cultures. Overall, data indicate that chronic pain is associated with comparable rates of anxiety and depression, with an average psychiatric comorbidity rate of around 35% (Von Korff et al., 2005).

A bidirectional relationship exists between psychiatric symptoms and chronic pain such that patients with depression and anxiety are more likely to experience greater levels of pain when chronic pain conditions are present, and having a chronic pain condition contributes to an increase in depression and anxiety. Anxiety and depression can lower pain tolerance thresholds while increasing pain intensity, sense of disability, and perception of distressing physical symptoms. This, in turn, can perpetuate pain-related dysfunction (Banks & Kerns, 1996; Dersh et al., 2002; Turk & Okifuji, 2002). It has been well-established in the pain literature that emotional distress is associated with higher anticipation and reports of pain and higher reactivity to pain (Sullivan & Katon, 1993; Kirmayer, Robbins, & Paris, 1994; Rhudy & Meagher, 2000; Turk & Okifuji, 2002).

Depression and anxiety can contribute to distorted automatic thought patterns, such as making unrealistic predictions about the future, or overly focusing on and exaggerating the negative aspects of an experience (Beck, 1979). When individuals with premorbid depression and anxiety develop chronic pain, their automatic thought patterns negatively alter their perceptions and appraisals of pain in ways that intensify the pain experience (Dersh et al., 2002; Thorn, 2017). For example, individuals with anxiety attend more to their pain and perceive pain as more threatening, while being less able to ignore pain-related information (which magnifies pain perception) (Crombez, Vervaet, Lysens, Baeyens, & Eelen, 1998).

Although these bidirectional relationships are well-accepted, research supports the conclusion that depression and anxiety are more commonly a consequence rather than a cause of chronic pain (Gamsa, 1990; Banks & Kerns, 1996; Korff & Simon, 1996; Fishbain, Cutler, Rosomoff, & Rosomoff, 1997; Asmundson & Katz, 2009; Miller & Cano, 2009; Poole, White, Blake, Murphy, & Bramwell, 2009; Burke et al., 2015). The range of possible pain experiences is wide and varied. An individual's response to chronic pain may reflect a variety of factors, including characteristics of the pain, thoughts, feelings, and behaviors, and interpersonal and sociocultural factors (e.g., social support). The daily challenges associated with chronic pain can be numerous and include decreased enjoyment of regular activities, loss of physical function, role changes, and relationship difficulties (Levenson, 2005). For many, the taxing nature of chronic pain is difficult to manage and may lead to the emergence of depression and/or anxiety.

Pain is uniquely both a sensory and an emotional experience (Banks & Kerns, 1996), and the subjective experience of chronic pain is not related solely to physiological stimulation. Melzack and Wall's (1965) gate control theory proposed that physiological perception of pain is influenced by emotions and cognition. An individual's emotional reactions to pain sensation and cognitive appraisals of both the pain signal and the emotional reactions to this signal contribute to the subjective experience of chronic pain.

It has been proposed that chronic pain is more likely than other chronic medical conditions to lead to depression and anxiety due to the uniquely challenging nature of stressors associated with chronic pain, including the aversive physical sensations, fear associated with pain sensations, physical impairment and disability, secondary losses such as inability to maintain daily roles, financial strain, relationship challenges, and possibly perceiving invalidating responses from the medical system. Further, the fears commonly associated with chronic pain are multifaceted: fear that pain will last indefinitely, fear that pain will interfere with meaningful activities, fear of progressive impairment and disability, and fear of underlying yet undetected disease (Banks & Kerns, 1996).

Data indicate that having multiple pain conditions, pain of increased duration, increased severity of pain, pain that is reported to more greatly interfere with activities of daily living, frequent pain episodes, diffuse pain, and pain that seems refractory to treatment are associated with a greater risk of psychological distress (Krause, Wiener, & Tait, 1994; Kroenke et al., 1994; Bair, Robinson, Katon, & Kroenke, 2003; Brox, Storheim, Holm, Friis, & Reikeras, 2005; Odegard, Finset, Mowinckel, Kvien, & Uhlig, 2007; Gureje et al., 2008). Further, lack of perceived self-control over pain has been associated with the emergence of depression and anxiety (Turk, Okifuji, & Scharff, 1995; Banks & Kerns, 1996). In contrast, research also indicates that chronic pain patients are less likely to become depressed when they believe they can continue to function even with pain, and that they can maintain control in their lives (Turk et al. 1995). As noted above, thought patterns play a key role in depression and anxiety, as well as in how one thinks about his/her pain experience (e.g., how he/she assesses pain severity, chronicity, controllability, predictability, endurability, and interference in life). This, in turn, influences the emergence of depression and anxiety. In other words, research indicates that people with chronic pain may experience distorted thought patterns, from which depression and anxiety follow (Banks & Kerns, 1996). The manner in which an individual with chronic pain behaves (e.g., restricting range of activities) and the reactions of others (e.g., family and friends reinforcing low levels of activity and withdrawn behavior via increased attention and reduction in responsibilities) also contribute to the emergence of depression and anxiety (Banks & Kerns, 1996; Turk, 2002a).

Aspects of Chronic Pain That Increase Risk of Depression and Anxiety

- Having multiple pain conditions
- Pain of increased duration
- Increased severity of pain
- Pain that more greatly interferes with daily activities
- Frequent pain episodes
- Diffuse pain
- Pain that seems refractory to treatment
- Lack of perceived control over pain
- Distorted thought patterns about pain (including how one assesses pain severity, chronicity, and controllability)
- Unhelpful pain-related behaviors (e.g., restricting activities, withdrawing socially)
- Responses from others that reinforce unhelpful pain behaviors

---

Unrecognized and untreated depression and anxiety can interfere significantly with pain treatment, and the patient's ability to live a personally satisfying life with chronic pain (Dersh et al., 2002). Depression and anxiety impair work, social, and physical functioning and create an added financial burden on society. Depression and anxiety in chronic pain patients are associated with poorer health-related quality of life, and with greater pain intensity ratings, disability, and pain interference with daily activities (Dersh et al., 2002; Poole et al., 2009; Holmes, Christelis, & Arnold, 2012). Perhaps not surprisingly, co-occurring depression and anxiety impact chronic pain patients more than either depression or anxiety alone. In one study, for example, individuals with depression, anxiety, and chronic pain reported experiencing 42.6 disability days (defined as the number of days that pain kept the individual from usual activities) in the prior three months. In comparison, "pain only" patients experienced 18.1 disability days; "pain and anxiety" patients experienced 32.2 disability days; and "pain and depression" patients experienced 38.0 disability days in the prior three months (Bair, Wu, Damush, Sutherland, & Kroenke, 2008).

Depression, Anxiety, Chronic Pain, and Suicide Risk

Risk factors for suicide in the general population include the following: mental health disorders, physical illness, recent or impending loss (e.g., work, family, social role), alcohol and substance abuse, impulsive behavior, isolation, availability of lethal means, sense of hopelessness, previous suicide attempts, and family history of suicide (Mann et al., 2005; Centers for Disease Control and Prevention, 2010). Many of these risk factors are present in those with chronic pain, and chronic pain has been associated with elevated rates of suicide-related behaviors and completed suicides (Edwards, Smith, Kudel, et al., 2006). A 2006 literature review found that rates of suicidal ideation (SI) and suicide attempts are two to three times higher among people with chronic pain when compared to the general population (Tang & Crane, 2006). The review highlighted pain-specific risk factors of suicide, including helplessness and hopelessness about pain, the desire to escape from pain, decreased problem-solving abilities, long pain duration, and the presence of comorbid insomnia with pain. Further, pain-related catastrophizing, which is associated with anxiety and depression, has been found to be a risk factor for SI in individuals with depression, with highest SI scores found among those with high levels of both depression and pain-related catastrophizing (Edwards, Smith, Kudel, et al., 2006).

It has been postulated that catastrophizing is a strong risk factor for SI because it reduces the use and effectiveness of adaptive coping skills, limits the effectiveness of treatment, increases feelings of hopelessness, and has a negative impact on one's social support system while increasing isolation (Edwards, Smith, Kudel, et al., 2006). Several pain-specific risk factors for suicide may be exacerbated when an individual experiences depression and anxiety with chronic pain. For example, depression increases a sense of hopelessness (Beck, Steer, Beck, & Newman, 1993), and anxiety increases avoidance and a desire to escape pain (Crombez et al., 1998). Consequently, lower levels of depression and anxiety are associated with lower SI (Edwards, Smith, Kudel, et al., 2006).

Overview of General and Pain-Specific Suicide Risk Factors

General Risk Factors

- Mental health disorders
- Physical illness
- Recent or impending loss (e.g., work, family, social roles)

- Alcohol/substance abuse
- Impulsive behavior
- Isolation
- Availability of lethal means (e.g., firearms, excess medications)
- Sense of hopelessness
- Previous suicide attempts
- Family history of suicide

Pain-Specific Risk Factors

- Comorbid depression and anxiety (increased risk with increased severity)
- Pain-related catastrophizing
- Helplessness and hopelessness about pain
- Desire to escape from pain
- Decreased problem-solving abilities (can also be a general risk factor)
- Long pain duration
- Availability of opiates
- Comorbid insomnia with pain
- Greater acute pain severity at pain onset

Most suicide attempts occur within one year of the onset of suicidal ideation (Kessler, Borges, & Walters, 1999), which highlights the importance of early identification of pain specific and general factors that may increase suicide risk. The research examining pain onset and SI is limited. Edwards et al. (2007) investigated SI in hospitalized burn injury patients, and found that pain severity at hospital discharge was the most robust discharge risk factor for SI. There are several possible mechanisms by which acute pain severity is linked to SI. Greater acute pain severity is associated with the likelihood of developing chronic pain (Edwards, 2005), which in turn is associated with the development of depression (McBeth, Macfarlane, & Silman, 2002; Harris, Cook, Victor, DeWilde, & Beighton, 2005). Moreover, greater acute pain severity may also be associated with poorer coping responses, pain-related catastrophizing (Edwards et al., 2007), and a larger detrimental effect on an individual's social environment leading to decreased interpersonal support, which increases risk for SI and suicidal behavior (Berkman, Glass, Brissette, & Seeman, 2000).

Edwards et al. (2007) postulated that pain severity may be associated most robustly with SI in the early stages following pain onset, whereas other factors assume more prominent roles over long durations of persistent pain. For example, a study examining over 1,500 chronic pain patients with a mean pain duration of over three years, who were seeking treatment at a university hospital pain management center, found that pain severity was not associated with SI. The

457

magnitude of depressive symptoms and the degree of pain-related catastrophizing were the two most consistent predictors of SI (Edwards, Smith, Kudel, et al., 2006).

Inasmuch as pain-specific risk factors for SI may change over time, it is important to assess mood symptoms and suicidal ideation at multiple times points. Clinicians may not have the opportunity to know an individual during his/her acute pain experience. Thus, the clinician should gather information about the patient's entire pain experience, including onset of pain, acute pain experience, and transition from acute to chronic pain. This information will enable the clinician to more accurately understand and assess suicide risk.

Even absent several risk factors, people with chronic pain are potentially vulnerable to suicide, as the presence of any pain condition has been associated with SI, plan, and attempt (Braden & Sullivan, 2008). Basic suicide assessment in chronic pain patients should include asking about predisposing vulnerabilities (e.g., depression, anxiety, substance use, previous history of suicidal behavior, previous psychiatric treatment); precipitating factors (e.g., conflict, break-up of relationship, change in pain); current mental status and mental health symptoms; current suicidal thinking (active/passive); access to lethal means; planning (including lethality of plan); intent/attitude toward current plan; and protective factors/contraindications (e.g., coping skills, hopeful attitude toward the future, strong social support) (Fowler, 2012).

Drug overdose constitutes the most commonly reported plan and method of attempt among people with chronic pain (Smith, Edwards, Robinson, & Dworkin, 2004). Therefore, clinicians must assess access to pain medication and other lethal means, as well as work with the individual, his/her support system, and medical providers to limit access for patients at risk of suicide. Examples include having loved ones manage and dispense medications and having medical providers prescribe pain medication in small quantities. Appendix 1 (Clinician Handout) provides an overview of suicide assessment in individuals with chronic pain.

In addition to the factors that can reduce suicide risk noted above, another protective factor is a positive and supportive therapeutic relationship. It is helpful for clinicians to adopt a calm, caring, concerned, and curious stance when assessing suicide (Fowler, 2012), utilizing therapeutic rapport to aid the effectiveness of interventions for co-occurring depression and anxiety. This in turn reduces SI. Interventions designed to decrease pain catastrophizing may not only positively impact symptoms of depression and anxiety but also lessen the risk of suicide (Edwards, Smith, Kudel, et al., 2006).

Transition From Acute to Chronic Pain and Associated Psychological Distress

The stress of chronic pain relates in part to its referential meaning. Pain signifies danger, and the instinct to interpret pain as danger leads to anxiety and fear. Acute pain serves the useful function of signaling that damage or harm has occurred.

The natural response to pain is to engage in some form of self-protective behavior, for instance, trying to escape the danger, reducing activity, or resting until the pain resolves. Chronic pain, however, differs qualitatively from acute pain. Pain that evolves from acute to chronic loses its adaptive qualities and no longer provides a reliable indicator of ongoing damage or harm.

Gatchel (1991) developed a three-stage conceptual model of the transition from acute pain to chronic pain disability and associated psychosocial distress. As pain becomes chronic, Gatchel suggested, individuals undergo psychological changes that create behavioral and psychological problems in addition to the original pain experience. Stage one of Gatchel's model is associated with typical emotional reactions to acute pain (e.g., fear, anxiety, worry). A person enters the second stage if pain persists beyond the accepted timeframe for acute pain. Stage two encompasses a variety of behavioral and psychological reactions and problems, such as learned helplessness, distress, anger, and somatization. These reactions result from a sense of suffering with the chronic nature of the pain. Gatchel suggested that how psychological and behavioral problems manifest depends upon the individual's preexisting personality and psychological characteristics, as well as current socioeconomic factors and environmental circumstances. Stage two of the model utilizes a diathesis-stress framework, in which the stress of coping with chronic pain exacerbates an individual's preexisting characteristics or diatheses. Gatchel further hypothesized that as these reactions and problems persist, the individual's life begins to revolve completely around the pain. The individual then enters stage three, which can be viewed as acceptance of some aspects of a "sick role." The sick role excuses the person from his/her normal responsibilities and social obligations which, for some, may become a powerful reinforcer for not working to regain functioning (Dersh, 2002). Adopting the sick role is also shaped by responses from significant others that may either promote an active response to chronic pain or the sick role (Turk & Okifuji, 2002).

More general models may help explain increases in psychological distress when transitioning from acute to chronic pain. Chronic pain by definition is associated with longer-lasting aversive stimulation than acute pain and, thus, can be more physically stressful. In addition, chronic pain typically is more psychologically stressful; chronic exposure to pain can drain cognitive, behavioral, and emotional resources due to the demands placed upon the person to tolerate the pain emotionally while also devising and implementing coping strategies.

Biologic explanations of the relationship between depression, anxiety, and chronic pain suggest that these conditions share neurobiology and neuroanatomical pathways. Research indicates that monoamines (i.e., serotonin and norepinephrine), gamma-aminobutyric acid (GABA), glutamate, adenosine, cannabinoids, and other neuropeptides are relevant to the development of depression, anxiety, and pain (Symreng & Fishman, 2004). Neuroimaging studies using functional MRI of individuals with chronic pain and depression and/or anxiety reveal common areas of brain activation (e.g., prefrontal cortex, amygdala, anterior cingulate cortex), suggesting pertinent pathways between these conditions

(Charney, 2003; Porro, 2003; Neugebauer, Li, Bird, & Han, 2004; Robinson et al., 2009). Activation of the sympathetic nervous system, involvement of the hypothalamic–pituitary axis, and a decrease in the number of benzodiazepine receptors in the frontal cortex are additional mechanisms that may help explain the association between depression, anxiety, and chronic pain (Symreng & Fishman, 2004).

Comorbidity of Depression, Anxiety, and Chronic Pain Within a Diathesis-Stress Framework

Diathesis broadly refers to any biological or psychological characteristic of a person that increases his or her chance of developing a disorder. Stress refers to an environmental or life circumstance perceived by the individual as threatening to his or her physical or psychological well-being and exceeding his or her ability to cope (Lazarus & Folkman, 1984). The diathesis-stress model suggests that for a disorder to develop, both diathesis and stress must interact. Thus, an individual with a diathesis for a disorder develops that disorder only if challenged by a stressor (Banks & Kerns, 1996). The comorbidity of depression, anxiety, and chronic pain can be conceptualized within a diathesis-stress framework. Research has established a shared genetic diathesis for depression and anxiety (Mineka, Watson, & Clark, 1998; Middeldorp, Cath, Van Dyck, & Boomsma, 2005). Therefore, an individual may have a genetic diathesis that makes him/her more likely to develop depression and anxiety with chronic pain.

Several potential psychological diatheses for depression and anxiety exist among people with chronic pain. For example, Beck's (1967, 1979) cognitive distortion model suggests that the diathesis may take the form of negative core beliefs, which manifest as negative thoughts about the self, the world, and the future. Abramson, Seligman, and Teasdale's (1978) learned helplessness model suggests that the diathesis may take the form of making internal, stable, and global attributions when confronted with a highly aversive situation. Fordyce's (1976) behavioral model suggests that the diathesis may emerge as deficits in instrumental skills.

The diathesis-stress framework indicates the importance of identifying vulnerability and stress factors that may contribute to and maintain depression and anxiety. Vulnerabilities refer to the individual's characteristic and potentially maladaptive style of processing information and responding to chronic pain. The diathesis-stress framework also highlights the importance of identifying in each individual with chronic pain the uniquely challenging or stressful aspects of his or her chronic pain experience. Areas to assess include, but are not limited to, the individual's beliefs about pain, perceived ability to control pain, degree of emotional distress and tolerance for such emotion, experiences with healthcare providers and responses to such experiences, beliefs regarding limitations, impact of pain on life activities, and other stressful events in one's life (Banks & Kerns, 1996).

Beliefs About Chronic Pain

Individuals respond to chronic illness in part based upon their beliefs about the illness and its symptoms. Emotions and behaviors are influenced by the person's interpretations of events rather than exclusively by objective facts. Beliefs about the meaning of chronic pain, the ability to control pain, its impact on one's life, and concerns about the future are key aspects of both a person's expectations about pain and his/her motivation for behavior, either adaptive or maladaptive. For example, maladaptive behaviors may result from beliefs that one has a serious and disabling condition, that disability is a required aspect of pain, that physical activity is dangerous, or that pain provides a constant reason for ignoring responsibilities (Turk, 2003). The maladaptive behaviors may include avoiding physical movement and activity, stopping activity at the first sign of discomfort, withdrawing from family and friends, and utilizing other passive coping strategies that stem from a sense of helplessness over pain.

Bidirectional relationships exist between thoughts, depression, and anxiety such that maladaptive thoughts can lead to the development of depression and anxiety, and symptoms of depression and anxiety impact thoughts. Research demonstrates that beliefs and their associated thoughts regarding chronic pain can influence the development of depression and anxiety, physical functioning, behavioral responses and coping efforts, and response to treatment (Turk & Okifuji, 2002). Depression and anxiety also represent components of a broader construct of negative affectivity, which can lead to changes in a person's thinking patterns (Mitchell & Campbell, 1988; Watson et al., 1995). For example, when depressed, people with chronic pain may engage in negative rumination and a perseverative cognitive style, defined as persistent thinking about negative events in the past or future (Brosschot, Pieper, & Thayer, 2005). Pincus and Williams (1999) proposed that depression within the context of chronic pain differs from depression among other populations, such that people with chronic pain tend to focus on suffering, dependency, and invalidity. Consistent worrying, a common component of anxiety, involves a focus on future potential threat, imagined catastrophes, and uncertainties (Segerstrom, Stanton, Alden, & Shortridge, 2003). As noted above, chronic pain patients commonly worry about how pain will impact their futures, as well as think that the perceived threat of the pain will last indefinitely.

Research demonstrates that cognitive errors, defined as negatively distorted beliefs about oneself or one's situation, consistently are linked to mood symptoms (such as depression and anxiety) as well as self-reported pain severity (Dufton, 1990; Gil, Williams, Keefe, & Beckham, 1990). Cognitive errors significantly influence a person's pain experience. Catastrophizing, and other forms of cognitive distortions, reinforce and exacerbate negative emotions and often result in a negative outlook which, in turn, contributes to depression and/or anxiety (Beck & Alford, 2009). Anxiety and depression increase the likelihood of making cognitive errors, which can result in avoidance of activity, leading to a greater sense of disability. Thus, emotional responses affect biological and behavioral responses, which lead to further increased emotional distress, producing a vicious cycle (Truchon, 2001).

Pain-related catastrophic thinking, defined by Quartana, Campbell, and Edwards (2009, p. 2) as "the tendency to magnify the threat value of pain stimulus and to feel helpless in the context of pain, and by a relative inability to inhibit pain-related thoughts in anticipation of, during or following a painful encounter," powerfully influences pain and a person's sense of disability. Individuals who cata-strophize expect the worst from their pain, ruminate about pain sensations, and feel helpless about controlling their pain. Thus, catastrophizing can increase depression and anxiety, and research indicates that people who catastrophize do not adjust to pain as well as people without catastrophic beliefs (Thorn, Boothby, & Sullivan, 2002). Burton, Tillotson, Main, & Hollis (1995) found that catastrophizing was the most significant predictor of back pain chronicity—almost seven times more powerful than the rest of the variables studied. Flor, Behle, and Birbaumer (1993) discovered that catastrophizing is related to higher levels of self-reported pain, and individuals who improved after pain treatment had a reduction in catastrophizing, while those who did not improve had no reduction in their levels of catastrophic thinking. Catastrophizing leads to hypervigilance about pain and decreased ability to focus on non-pain stimuli, and is believed to be associated with poorer treat-ment outcomes by blocking one's ability to use adaptive coping strategies such as relaxation exercises and imagery (Thorn et al., 2002).

Fear and Avoidance of Activity

Fear is a natural reaction to pain. People in acute pain reasonably may seek to avoid fear-provoking activities. However, fear and anxiety may serve as barriers to treatment and recovery of people with chronic pain. Research indicates that pain-related anxiety and fear may amplify the pain experience of chronic pain patients (Crombez, Vlaeyen, Heuts, & Lysens, 1999). Anxiety causes sympathetic nervous system arousal and associated physical sensations (e.g., increased heart rate, short-ness of breath, sweating, and muscle tension). Pain-related anxiety leads to an increased focus on and preoccupation with the body and pain. This increased focus, in turn, increases the likelihood that the patient misinterprets or mislabels physiological symptoms of anxiety as pain, overemphasizes symptoms of pain, and/or perceives oneself as disabled (McCracken et al., 1998; Turk, 2003).

People with chronic pain often mistakenly perceive physical hurt as harm. Fearful patients (i.e., those who believe they are being harmed) attend more to signals of threat. These patients are less able to ignore pain-related information, further exacerbating their perceptions of harm and increasing their fear (Crombez, Vervaet, Lysens, Baeyens, & Eelen, 1998). It has also been proposed that people with pain conditions may use worry as a strategy for reducing somatic arousal associated with pain, and subsequently may become prone to developing general-ized anxiety disorder (McWilliams, Goodwin, & Cox, 2004).

Individuals with higher levels of pain-related anxiety tend to anticipate higher levels of pain than people with low anxiety. Anticipation of pain often results in more passive coping. For example, people with high pain-related anxiety typically avoid pain-related activities (such as movement/exercise) due to anticipation and fear of pain (McCracken & Gross, 1993; Turk & Okifuji, 2002; Vlaeyen & Linton, 2000). Researchers postulate that behavioral performance of individuals with chronic pain may not depend upon the actual pain but rather on their anticipation of pain based upon previous experiences. If a previous behavior resulted in increased pain, and the pain decreased once the activity stopped, then similar activities will be avoided in the future in order to reduce the likelihood of the pain reoccurring. In other words, the rationale for avoiding a given activity may not be related to the pain at that moment but rather to the anticipation of pain and associated physical arousal that may amplify pain. Avoiding activity, and subsequently experiencing increased pain during movement due to physical deconditioning and anxiety, reinforces one's beliefs about the disabling nature of chronic pain (Vlaeyen, Kole-Snijders, Boeren, & Van Eek, 1995).

Once beliefs and pain expectations are formed, they are typically stable, as people tend to act in accord with their established beliefs. People also tend to avoid experiences that challenge or invalidate those beliefs. A person's negative perceptions regarding his/her ability to perform a given activity contribute to a maladaptive cycle—the failure to perform the activity reinforces his/her perception of helplessness, incapacity, sense of disability, and the pervasiveness of chronic pain. From a behavioral learning perspective, chronic pain can result in reduced positive reinforcement; activities that previously were pleasant now become accompanied or followed by pain (and thus become punishing). Further, as a person increasingly restricts his/her activities, muscles become more deconditioned. As a result, less activity is needed to cause pain (Banks & Kerns, 1996). People with chronic pain who avoid activity out of fear of pain or injury do not experience exposure to feared activities without negative consequences or corrective feedback. Therefore, they do not have the opportunity to experience rewards and/or to establish the belief that they can successfully confront a feared activity without the anticipated negative consequences (Turk & Okifuji, 2002). Thus, patients can become trapped in a cycle of reduced reinforcement, reduced activity, pain, depression, and anxiety. Moreover, their pain and emotional distress behaviors over time may come to be reinforced by how the people around them respond. For example, positive reinforcement (e.g., receiving sympathetic attention from others) and negative reinforcement (e.g., avoiding annoying household tasks) may contribute over time to the maintenance of pain behaviors.

Learned Helplessness and Self-Efficacy

Seligman's (1975) learned helplessness model of depression proposed that, following exposure to uncontrollable outcomes, an individual develops helplessness, or the expectation of being unable to control future outcomes through personal actions, even though they may be controllable. The interpretation of uncontrollable events is important; individuals who make internal, stable, or global attributions (i.e., have a depressive attributional style) are at risk for depression following an uncontrollable negative event (Abramson et al., 1978). Thus, individuals who make internal ("It's my fault I have chronic pain"), stable ("My pain worsens every time I try to exercise"), and global ("I can't control my pain because nothing in my life is controllable") attributions of their pain are more likely to experience depression and anxiety.

People often perceive chronic pain as an uncontrollable negative event, as it is an aversive experience that is often inescapable and difficult to ease. Over time, the chronic nature of pain may lead an individual to believe that there is nothing he or she can do to control the pain. Research has demonstrated that increases in pain severity predict decreases in perceived self-control and increases in life interference due to pain, which together predict increases in depression (Rudy, Kerns, & Turk, 1988). Smith, Peck, and Ward (1990) found that a sense of helplessness mediated the relationship between disease severity and depression among rheumatoid arthritis patients. Further, Turk and colleagues (Turk et al., 1995) found that individuals do not experience depressive symptoms if they believe they can continue to function and if they believe that they have some control over the pain. These findings suggest that it is not necessarily chronic pain itself that leads to depressive symptoms, but rather how an individual appraises his/her ability to manage the pain. Therefore, helping individuals restore a sense of control can alleviate symptoms of depression and anxiety.

Learned helplessness and the sense of lack of control are related to self-efficacy. Self-efficacy is the belief that one can successfully engage in a behavior to produce a desired outcome. Bandura (1977) proposed that given sufficient motivation to engage in a behavior, a person's self-efficacy beliefs determine whether the behavior will be initiated, how much effort the person will expend, and how long he/she will sustain that effort in the face of obstacles/aversive experiences. Self-efficacy beliefs are also related to mood. Research indicates a negative relationship between self-efficacy, depression and anxiety, such that individuals with lower self-efficacy levels tend both to give up in the face of difficulties and to experience higher levels of depression and anxiety (Albal & Kutlu, 2010; Tahmassian & Jalali Moghadam, 2011). From a self-efficacy perspective, coping behaviors are mediated by a person's efficacy beliefs that situational demands do not exceed his/her ability to cope.

For example, research demonstrates that self-efficacy is predictive of level of performance of physical tasks in people with back pain (Council, Ahern, Follick, & Kline, 1988), and self-efficacy expectations paralleled actual exercise levels during pain treatment (Dolce, Crocker, Moletteire, & Doleys, 1986). It has been proposed that individuals with low self-efficacy beliefs are less likely to use coping responses or persist in the presence of aversive experiences than people with high efficacy expectations (Turk & Okifuji, 2002), and it is important to consider that depression and anxiety are factors that tend to lower self-efficacy.

There is a bidirectional relationship between emotional distress and self-efficacy such that emotional distress exacerbates low self-efficacy, and low self-efficacy (and associated limited use of coping skills) increases distress. More specifically, if an individual believes that he/she can do little to manage pain symptoms, then he/she likely will put forth minimal effort in trying to use coping skills. This in turn may lead to increased emotional distress and amplified pain symptoms.

Anxiety, in the form of anticipation of pain, during and following physical tasks interacts with self-efficacy to determine level of physical performance (Turk & Okifuji, 2002). Furthermore, increases in perceived control and self-efficacy are associated with improvement in pain and sense of disability, lower levels of state anxiety, and greater use of adaptive coping skills (Keefe et al., 1997; Scharloo & Kaptein, 1997; Smarr et al., 1997). Cioffi (1991) suggested the relationship between self-efficacy and behavioral activation in people with chronic pain may be influenced by self-efficacy's impact on anxiety, such that perceived self-efficacy decreases anxiety and associated physical arousal, and therefore an individual approaches tasks in less physical distress. Further, Cioffi asserted that an efficacious individual may be better able to divert attention away from potentially distressing sensations and to persist in tasks despite distress.

Treatment Considerations

Depression and anxiety may be precipitated or exacerbated by numerous losses and stressors that accompany chronic pain and associated physical impairment. Difficulty maintaining activities of daily life such as work, recreational activities, and sexual function may interfere with an individual's ability to maintain relationships. Financial strain caused by medical bills, missed time at work, and/or job loss may further increase stress. Chronic pain can increase social isolation, sense of meaninglessness and purposelessness in life. Uncertainty about the future may occur as the result of life roles changing. All of this, in turn, can result in feelings of sadness, grief, and anger (Holmes et al., 2012), as well as anxiety and depressive symptoms.

Patients may also experience loss related to body image, sense of vitality, self-concept, and self-esteem. Chronic pain often leads to the loss of sleep, which can further amplify mood symptoms (Banks & Kerns, 1996). Due to the numerous potential sources of widespread loss and stress associated with living with chronic pain, it is imperative that psychosocial treatment is integrated, whole person-centered, and anchored in a biopsychosocial framework.

Common Themes of Psychosocial Treatment

Effective treatment of patients experiencing comorbid depression, anxiety and chronic pain can be difficult. It is generally agreed in the literature that utilizing an integrated treatment approach typically is most effective, particularly when related to behavioral outcomes such as returning to work (Hoffman, Papas, Chatkoff, &

Kerns, 2007). Integrated and multidisciplinary treatment may include interventions such as physical and/or occupational therapy, psychosocial intervention, and pharmacological treatment. While evidence-based psychosocial interventions for chronic pain differ in conceptualization and specific skills taught, there are common themes. These include striving to empower chronic pain patients to live lives they find meaningful and instilling the belief that pain does not need to dictate behavior. There is an assumption across psychosocial interventions that treatment is not aimed at eliminating pain per se, although the intensity and frequency of chronic pain may diminish. Rather, intervention seeks to help chronic pain patients live effective and satisfying lives despite persistent pain.

In general, psychosocial interventions for chronic pain focus upon restoring function rather than eliminating pain (Turk, 2003). Use of active coping strategies is associated with reduced pain severity, lower levels of depression and less functional impairment, while the reverse applies to use of passive coping strategies (Brown & Nicassio, 1987). There is a common aim across interventions to enhance active coping strategies such as exercise, task persistence, seeking social support, and using cognitive strategies such as modifying distorted thoughts or cognitive defusion, while decreasing passive strategies that are aimed at relinquishing control and dependency upon others such as avoidance of activity, pain-contingent rest, and wishful thinking.

It has been proposed that the stress associated with chronic pain typically exacerbates symptoms of depression and anxiety. At the same time, depression and anxiety intensify the pain experience. Over time, the dynamic and reinforcing relationships between chronic pain, depression and anxiety may become so interrelated that it may not be possible to treat the conditions independently (Dersh, 2002). Psychosocial interventions for depression, anxiety, and chronic pain share many common elements. For example, treatments for depression and chronic pain, as well as treatments for anxiety and chronic pain, focus on increasing activity levels (e.g., engaging in physical exercise may serve the triple purpose of increasing muscle strength, increasing behavioral activation, and exposing an individual to specific pain-related activities that have been avoided out of fear). Further, treatments for anxiety and pain both include strategies for reducing arousal, such as relaxation exercises (McWilliams et al., 2004). Thus, while depression and anxiety are distinct conditions, and it is possible to experience one without the other, depression and anxiety frequently exist concurrently. Therefore, the presence of one should prompt assessment of the other (Woo, 2010).

Motivation and Readiness to Change

Psychosocial intervention for chronic pain, regardless of the specific theory or intervention used, primarily involves teaching patients to use self-management skills to reduce pain's control on their lives and enhance functioning and quality of life. Initiating and maintaining behavior change is often quite difficult. Learning and practicing self-management skills will likely not occur if the chronic pain patient does not have a strong motivation for change (Jensen, Nielson, & Kerns, 2003). An individual's beliefs and expectations about how pain should be treated impacts his/her motivation for behavior change. This in turn influences the outcome of the treatment.

Individuals who do not agree with a self-management approach to chronic pain report greater pain, less satisfaction with treatment, and limited ability to control pain, as well as endorse beliefs that they are disabled, beliefs that emotions do not influence pain, and beliefs in a medical cure to pain (Shutty et al., 1990; Jensen, Nielson, Romano, Hill, & Turner, 2000). Further, Williams and Keefe (1991) found that individuals who are most adaptive in their coping style have strong internal loci of control, strong beliefs in others such as health professionals, and weak beliefs in chance (i.e., beliefs that pain outcomes are related to fate or luck). Individuals with depression and anxiety are less likely to have these characteristics. For example, depression and anxiety are associated with greater external locus of control, lower internal locus of control, greater belief in being disabled by pain, greater catastrophizing, and greater belief in chance (Benassi, Sweeney, & Dufour, 1988; Chorpita & Barlow, 1998; Crisson & Keefe, 1988; Jensen, Turner, & Romano, 2007). Thus, depression and anxiety decrease a person's sense of control, and if people with chronic pain believe they are not in control of their condition, they are less likely to adhere to a self-management treatment program.

Kerns, Rosenberg, Jamison, Caudill, and Haythornthwaite (1997) proposed that individuals with chronic pain vary in their readiness to accept and adopt a self-management approach to pain. The readiness-to-change model asserts that people who believe strongly that their pain is solely of medical origin requiring physical treatment are not likely to accept or utilize self-management skills (as these strategies are not perceived as important or beneficial). Individuals who acknowledge that medical intervention is limited, believe their current pain behaviors pose risk, believe self-management strategies have potential benefits, and believe they are capable of taking action may be more willing to accept and adopt a self-management approach (Kerns et al., 1997; Schwarzer, Lippke, & Luszczynska, 2011). The presence of depression and anxiety symptoms, along with low self-efficacy, decreased motivation to be active, lack of social support, and fear that activity will increase pain, leads to less engagement in self-management strategies (Bair et al., 2009) and less opportunity to receive positive reinforcement for self-management. Consequently, self-management behaviors are perceived as unimportant, which further decreases the utilization of these behaviors (Jensen et al., 2003).

Identifying pre-treatment beliefs that may interfere with treatment is important, as modifying unhelpful beliefs prior to formal treatment may increase acceptance of intervention, facilitate remaining in treatment throughout the treatment course, and increase the likelihood of the patient adhering to self-management exercises (Turk & Okifuji, 2002). For example, clinicians might match preparatory information regarding treatment to the patient's readiness to adopt a self-management approach. Clinicians also might provide intervention aimed at strengthening an individual's readiness to adopt greater responsibility for pain management prior to initiating a more formal treatment protocol.

Intervention may utilize motivational interviewing (MI) techniques to explore and resolve patient ambivalence regarding behavioral change (Miller & Rollnick, 2012). According to the MI approach, there are three critical components of motivation: importance, confidence, and readiness. It has been proposed that motivation to stop unhelpful pain behaviors and to engage in helpful self-management behaviors increases if patients with chronic pain are aware of the negative consequences of unhelpful coping in their lives and believe that adaptive coping will help them reach valued goals. MI emphasizes a collaborative approach in which confidence, importance, and readiness are elicited from the individual with chronic pain, and the individual's autonomy is strengthened.

An MI approach involves the clinician expressing empathy to help establish an environment for change. The clinician asks questions as opposed to solely providing information (e.g., "What are your thoughts on the effect of inactivity versus gentle exercise on your muscles?"), eliciting statements about discrepancies between current behaviors and personal goals, and encouraging statements that self-management behaviors will decrease this discrepancy. Further, the clinician strives to "roll with resistance" by avoiding arguing, criticizing, hurrying, or labeling the individual with pain and supports self-efficacy by asking questions that elicit statements that reflect helpful self-efficacy beliefs (e.g., "What do you think it will take to increase your confidence that you will be able to be more active despite pain?"). The clinician then reflects back these statements to the patient in order to encourage more self-efficacy talk (Miller & Rollnick, 2012).

Self-efficacy and a sense of control are imperative both for the initial behavior change and for maintenance. There is an assumption in the literature that long-term maintenance of helpful changes occurs only if the individual attributes success to his/her own efforts. When assessing an individual's readiness for change and motivation for treatment, the clinician must remember that (as described above) symptoms of depression and anxiety impact an individual's self-efficacy beliefs. Those beliefs in turn impact the patient's perceived ability to take responsibility for pain management and his/her overall response to treatment.

Baseline depressive symptoms and poor functional status are predictive of depressive symptoms over time (Wells, Burnam, Rogers, Hays, & Camp, 1992). Therefore, treating depression and anxiety prior to more specific chronic pain treatment may decrease the risk of continued symptoms and the negative impact of symptoms on chronic pain. Research indicates that the presence of depression is also predictive of future episodes of pain (Leino & Magni, 1993; Croft et al., 1995). Accordingly, initially treating depression may decrease pain over time. Even when premorbid depression and anxiety are not present, the bidirectional relationship between depression, anxiety, and chronic pain indicates that living with chronic pain can lead to the development of anxiety and depression. Therefore, providing adaptive coping skills early in treatment may reduce the risk of chronic pain causing depression and anxiety.

Many studies support the finding that individuals with comorbid depression and pain respond poorly to treatment when compared to pain patients who are not depressed (Bair et al., 2003). A multinational study that was part of the World Mental Health Surveys initiative investigated the relationship between depression, anxiety, and a range of physical conditions (Scott et al., 2007). Results indicated that having comorbid depression and anxiety increases the risk of several physical conditions reoccurring; heart disease and chronic pain had the strongest associations with depression and anxiety disorders.

A 2002 literature review by McCracken and Turk, which examined the outcome of CBT and behavioral treatment for chronic pain, identified predictors of treatment outcome. The review indicated that individuals experiencing better treatment outcomes have stronger beliefs in control over pain, engage in less catastrophic and negative thinking about pain, and experience less depression and anxiety. People with high emotional distress may not function as well as less distressed individuals and may not participate as well in treatment that requires effort and concentration. High emotional distress can also be a marker for other factors that hinder treatment. These factors include poor emotional self-management, poor problem-solving skills, use of additional non-adaptive coping skills, poor social support, and/or financial stress. Thus, the combination of high emotional distress, poor coping abilities, and other psychosocial factors may hinder treatment outcomes (McCracken & Turk, 2002).

Methods to Increase Self-Efficacy and Utilization of Self-Management Skills

As noted above, depression, anxiety, and living with chronic pain can lower self-efficacy. Clinicians can help enhance an individual's self-efficacy in utilizing self-management skills by encouraging the individual to use skills, helping the individual explore personal reasons for learning and practicing new skills, helping the person to identify and incorporate positive reinforcers for using self-management skills, providing opportunities to observe others with chronic pain using self-management skills, and discussing (and developing a plan to address) any barriers to using adaptive coping skills.

Further, individuals will typically not stop using maladaptive skills and begin utilizing adaptive ones until they believe that maladaptive strategies will result in negative outcomes and adaptive strategies will result in positive outcomes. Thus, clinicians should facilitate discussions around outcome expectancies and the individual's own beliefs about the benefits of self-management strategies. It may be useful to encourage the patient to start using self-management strategies and to monitor the resultant benefits over time even if he/she remains skeptical of possible benefits. This strategy relates to Bandura's (1977) belief that the most effective way to build self-efficacy is through experience. Clinicians can enhance a patient's awareness of the importance of utilizing adaptive skills, and encourage ongoing use of those skills, by discussing both the observed benefits of the newly acquired skills and the negative impact of depression, anxiety, and chronic pain on function (Jensen et al., 2003).

While certain strategies may be maladaptive relative to maintaining depression, anxiety, and chronic pain, notably those same strategies may be adaptive at eliciting strong reinforcement. If self-management strategies are being punished (e.g., if exercise is consistently followed by increases in pain, if family members discourage use of self-management and do not give the patient as much attention when he/she uses adaptive skills, or if self-management strategies interfere with other valued activities), and maladaptive strategies are being reinforced, then maintaining use of adaptive skills during or after treatment may be quite challenging. Thus, incorporating strategies to strengthen reinforcement of adaptive coping skills throughout treatment should be considered. For example, the clinician can help the patient devise a method whereby the patient rewards him/herself for using adaptive skills. Or the clinician may meet with family members in order to discuss the utility of providing positive reinforcement of self-management skills (Jensen et al., 2003).

Treatment Matching

Self-reported pain intensity, response to pain, and response to treatment for chronic pain may be influenced by a range of factors, including meaning given to the pain, attentional focus, mood, prior learning history, cultural background, environmental contingencies, social supports, and financial resources, among others (Turk, 2002a). Research supports the notion that there is often much variability in response to psychosocial interventions for chronic pain (Turk & Okifuji, 1998; Gatchel & Epker, 1999). It is helpful to remember that diagnostic categories are typically quite broad; at the same time, two patients with the same medical diagnosis may have significant biopsychosocial differences. Indeed, the biopsychosocial perspective assumes that the provider(s) will offer a patient with chronic pain an intervention that takes into account the physical, psychological, and social characteristics unique to that individual.

Studies demonstrate that people with chronic pain who are classified into different groups based upon behavioral and psychosocial characteristics respond differently to the same treatment (e.g., Turk & Okifuji, 2002). For example, individuals classified as "adaptive copers," "dysfunctional," or "interpersonally distressed" on the West-Haven-Yale Multidimensional Pain Inventory (WHYMPI; Kerns, Turk, & Rudy, 1985) have been found to respond differently to treatment (Gatchel, 2004). Research indicates that adaptive copers tend to report high levels of social support, relatively low levels of pain, and low pain interference in their lives, while responding well to intervention. People with a dysfunctional profile perceive their pain severity as high, report much pain interference in their lives, and report a high degree of psychological distress because of their pain with associated low levels of activity. Finally, people who are interpersonally distressed are similar to people with a dysfunctional classification; they also perceive that significant others are not supportive (Gatchel, 2004). By understanding psychosocial differences, including level of reported psychological distress and social support, interventions can be modified to meet an individual's needs. For example, people who report they lack social support may benefit from interventions that focus on interpersonal and communication skills.

Acceptance-based and cognitive-behavioral interventions for depression, anxiety, and chronic pain share similar overall effects (Veehof, Oskam, Schreurs, & Bohlmeijer, 2011). Behavioral elements of both approaches encourage a person to engage in behavioral activities regardless of distressing thoughts or emotions (Forman et al., 2012). In general, cognitive-behavioral therapy (CBT) for chronic pain focuses on reducing pain and distress by modifying physical sensations, distorted thought patterns, and maladaptive behaviors. Acceptance and commitment therapy (ACT) for chronic pain focuses on improving functioning through awareness of experience, nonjudgmental acceptance of experience, identification of life values, values-based action, and increased psychological flexibility.

Both CBT and ACT are behaviorally based interventions that share the objective of decreasing the interference of pain in a person's life and improving functioning. However, there is a key difference: CBT emphasizes reappraisal of emotionally distressing stimuli and ACT emphasizes changing responses to emotionally distressing stimuli by discouraging emotional suppression (Hofman & Asmundson, 2008). CBT generally is considered to be a more control-oriented treatment focused on solving problems, whereas ACT is regarded as acceptance based (Hayes & Duckworth, 2006).

A common factor in psychological interventions for chronic pain is emphasis on the consequences that pain has on one's life (rather than on pain intensity) as a way of addressing adaptive behavioral change (Kerns, Sellinger, & Goodin, 2011). A randomized controlled trial conducted by Wetherell et al. (2011) comparing ACT and CBT for chronic pain found that both types of intervention improve pain interference, depression and pain-related anxiety in individuals with chronic pain. Notably, CBT and ACT are not clinically incompatible; some interventions share common processes, and interventions from both approaches can be utilized in treatment. For example, an individual must first be aware of, and observe, his/her thoughts before deciding whether to change them or mentally distance from them. Moreover, certain CBT techniques, such as cognitive reframing, may be viewed as a variant of the ACT technique of creating cognitive distance from thoughts and staying in the present moment (Heimberg & Ritter, 2008).

Research has demonstrated that a chronic pain patient's history of depression influences whether acceptance-based intervention or CBT will be most effective. More specifically, patients with a history of recurrent depression may benefit more from acceptance-based intervention than CBT (Zautra et al., 2008). Further, since acceptance-based interventions focus on decreasing experiential avoidance, increasing acceptance, exploring values, and values-based living (see below for more information), they may be more suitable than traditional CBT interventions for individuals who demonstrate high levels of avoidance and low levels of

Jennifer M. Caspari

Table 18.1 ACT Versus CBT: Points of Consideration

Patient Characteristic	Treatment Suggestion
Moderate to high symptoms of depression; recurrent depression with anxiety	ACT/mindfulness may be most effective
Low to moderate symptoms of depression with anxiety; no history of recurrent depression	ACT or CBT equally effective
Concrete thinking; preference for precise intervention	CBT may be most effective
High degree of avoidance; low levels of life meaning	ACT may be most effective
Low self-confidence and self-efficacy	CBT may be most effective
Low levels of acceptance and psychological flexibility	ACT may be most effective
High degree of catastrophic thinking	CBT (with targeted treatment for catastrophizing) may be most effective
High degree of ruminative thinking that is perceived as uncontrollable	ACT/mindfulness may be most effective

meaning in life. By specifically addressing an individual's psychosocial needs, the clinician may be able to enhance the clinical effectiveness of the intervention.

Table 18.1 provides points of consideration for utilization of CBT versus ACT.

Evidence-Based Treatment Approaches

Cognitive-Behavioral Therapy for Depression, Anxiety, and Chronic Pain

Cognitive-behavioral therapy (CBT) has been studied and utilized extensively for the treatment of depression, anxiety, and chronic pain (Hofmann & Smits, 2008; Morley et al., 1999; Sudak, 2012). Morley et al. (1999) conducted a systematic review and meta-analysis of 25 randomized controlled trials of CBT and behavioral therapy for chronic pain in adults and concluded that psychological treatment based on the principles of CBT is effective. CBT for chronic pain (CBT-CP) is based upon a strong therapeutic relationship that encourages patients with chronic pain to adopt an active, problem-solving approach in order to cope with the many challenges associated with living with chronic pain (Murphy et al., 2014).

There are several primary aims of CBT-CP that effectively reduce symptoms of anxiety and depression, as well as help restore function in people with chronic pain. These include: 1) helping individuals alter counterproductive beliefs that their problems are unmanageable, which in turn helps them become resourceful problem solvers and enables them to cope effectively with their pain, emotional distress, and psychosocial difficulties; 2) assisting individuals in learning to monitor their thoughts, emotions, and behaviors, while also identifying the relationships between these factors and environmental events, pain, emotional distress, and psychosocial difficulties; 3) teaching individuals to develop and maintain effective and adaptive ways of thinking and responding (e.g., problem-solving in daily activities, reducing catastrophizing following increases in pain after activity); and 4) teaching individuals to perform behaviors (e.g., relaxation exercises and exercise) in order to cope effectively with pain, emotional distress, and psychosocial difficulties (Adams, Poole, & Richardson, 2006).

Chapter 4 discusses in detail CBT applications in chronic pain populations. However, one component of CBT interventions bears special mention in this chapter devoted to comorbid depression and anxiety—engagement in pleasant activities. As noted above, people with chronic pain often avoid various activities, including enjoyable ones. They may avoid these activities due to fear of pain, the belief that they are physically incapable of engaging in the activity, or the desire to avoid interacting with others and having to possibly talk about their pain. Avoidance of pleasant activities can lead to decreased self-esteem, increased anxiety and depression, and decreased quality of life.

Increasing engagement in pleasant activities is a common component of CBT-CP (Murphy et al., 2014; Wetherell et al., 2011). The benefits of increased engagement in pleasant activities include shifting cognitive focus from activities that feel restricting or unpleasant to enjoyable activities; providing opportunities for healthy distraction from pain; increasing socialization; improving concentration; developing a sense of purposeful direction; and enhancing quality of life (Murphy et al., 2014). However, identifying pleasant activities when living with chronic pain can be challenging for several reasons. Depression and anxiety can lessen both one's ability to identify activities and motivation to engage in them. Psychosocial challenges (such as limited finances) may be a barrier. Chronic pain and resultant poor sleep may leave a person feeling too tired to participate in activities. Further, individuals may believe they cannot physically engage in the activities even if they want to. By explaining the benefits of engaging in pleasant activities and exploring creative and adaptive ways to participate in those activities despite pain, the clinician may help facilitate a patient's increased activity level (Murphy et al., 2014).

Acceptance-Based Therapy for Depression, Anxiety, and Chronic Pain

Research conducted over the past decade supports new developments in interventions for comorbid depression, anxiety, and chronic pain, including acceptance and commitment therapy (ACT). ACT focuses on enhancing positive and flexible behavior patterns rather than on eliminating symptoms (Hayes, 2004). This includes shifting attention away from coping strategies that emphasize control or resolution of the patient's distress or problem and toward processes such as psychological flexibility, acceptance, mindfulness, and values (Hayes, 2004; McCracken,Vowles, & Eccleston, 2005).

Various studies provide support for the role of enhancing psychological flexibility as an effective treatment intervention for anxiety, depression, and chronic pain (Kashdan, 2010; McCracken & Velleman, 2010; Masuda & Tully, 2011). Psychological flexibility is defined as "a process based in the interaction of cognition and direct environmental contingencies that allows a person's behavior to persist or change in line with their long term goals and values" (McCracken & Velleman, 2010, p. 141). The theory underlying the helpfulness of psychological flexibility posits that there are two sets of influences on behavior: those arising from direct contact with the environment, behavior, and associated consequences; and those arising from cognitively based processes, such as rules.

Individuals who hold rigid beliefs about pain tend to make behavioral decisions based on these beliefs. For example, an individual holding the belief "if I go for a walk, I will definitely feel more pain" is likely to make the decision to avoid walking as a result of this belief. This decision in turn limits opportunities for direct experience with walking and changing this belief if the experience is positive, further fueling inflexible thinking and restricted functioning (Hayes, Strosahl, & Wilson, 1999). Components of psychological flexibility can counteract this. These components include acceptance, contact with the present moment, mindfulness, and values-based action (Hayes, Luoma, Bond, Masuda, & Lillis, 2006).

Research demonstrates that acceptance-based interventions are effective for anxiety (Vollestad, Nielsen, & Nielsen, 2012), depression (Teasdale et al., 2002; Morgan, 2003), and living with chronic pain. A study by McCracken and Vowles (2008) demonstrated that in a sample of adults with chronic pain, total acceptance and values scores on self-reported measures of acceptance of pain and values (defined as importance of personal values such as relationships and health, and success at living according to values) negatively correlate with pain-related distress, pain-related anxiety, depression, depression-related interference with functioning, and physical and psychosocial disability.

Acceptance of pain involves reacting to pain-related experiences without trying to control or avoid the experience, particularly when doing so has a negative impact on one's quality of life, and engaging in valued activities and working to achieve personal goals regardless of pain (McCracken & Eccleston, 2005). A greater acceptance of pain is associated with lower pain intensity, less pain-related anxiety and avoidance, less depression, less physical and psychosocial disability, more daily uptime, and improved work status (McCracken, 1998).

These findings have been supported by other studies that have demonstrated associations between acceptance and mental well-being, less attention to pain, more engagement with daily activities, higher motivation to complete activities, higher efficacy in the performance of daily activities, and less disability/improved functional status (Esteve, Ramírez-Maestre, & López-Martínez, 2007; McCracken & Eccleston, 2003; Viane et al., 2003; Viane, Crombez, Eccleston,

Devulder, & De Corte, 2004). A 2011 meta-analytic review on the effects of acceptance-based therapies on mental and physical health in people with chronic pain found a medium effect size for pain intensity, depression, anxiety, physical well-being, and quality of life (Veehof et al., 2011).

Jacob, Kerns, Rosenberg, and Haythornthwaite (1993) proposed that adopting a more accepting stance toward pain may lead to a greater confidence in ability to cope with pain, less depression, and less observable pain behavior. When individuals do not accept that they have chronic pain, they often become caught up in a distressing, unending, and futile struggle to end the pain. This struggle may lead to constantly searching for a pain resolution that does not exist, persistently checking for any sign of pain so that it can be avoided, and subsequently missing out on the benefits that derive from engaging in life (McCracken, 1998). Acceptance involves disengaging from the struggle with pain; realistically approaching pain and pain-related circumstances; and engaging in beneficial daily activities. These, in turn, decrease depression and anxiety.

Review studies indicate that mindfulness interventions in general help reduce stress, anxiety, depression, and chronic pain (Hofmann, Sawyer, Witt, & Oh, 2010; Chiesa & Serretti, 2011). It has been proposed that mindfulness-based interventions are associated with a general reduction in stress because they encourage individuals to relate to physical symptoms in a more open and less judgmental way, so that when they occur they are less distressing. This is supported by a systematic review by Chiesa and Serretti (2011) on mindfulness-based interventions for chronic pain, which found that mindfulness interventions may increase pain acceptance and tolerance, decrease stress levels, decrease depressive symptoms, and enhance quality of life. Chapter 5 discusses in detail various mindfulness-based interventions for chronic pain.

Conclusion

Depression and anxiety are commonly comorbid with chronic pain, and there is a bidirectional relationship between these mental health conditions and chronic pain. Anxiety and depression can increase pain severity, thereby exacerbating a person's pain experience; living with chronic pain can lead to depression and anxiety. If unrecognized and untreated, depression and anxiety can negatively impact both an individual's ability to effectively engage in treatment and treatment outcomes. If an individual experiences high levels of depression and/or anxiety, outcomes may be improved by the individual engaging in psychosocial intervention to decrease symptoms of depression and anxiety prior to more specific chronic pain intervention. The individual's history of experiencing comorbid depression and anxiety may make certain psychosocial interventions more effective than others. For example, research supports the effectiveness of acceptance-based interventions over cognitive-behavioral interventions for individuals with high levels of depression and/or recurrent depression with anxiety. Many evidence-based psychosocial interventions for comorbid depression, anxiety, and chronic pain exist. Although experiencing these conditions can be overwhelming and demoralizing, psychosocial clinicians are well-equipped to assist individuals with comorbid depression, anxiety, and chronic pain in enhancing their sense of confidence and hope and improving their functioning and quality of life.

References

Abramson, L.Y., Seligman, M. E., & Teasdale, J. D. (1978). Learned helplessness in humans: Critique and reformulation. *Journal of Abnormal Psychology, 87*(1), 49-74.

Adams, N., Poole, H., & Richardson, C. (2006). Psychological approaches to chronic pain management: Part 1. *Journal of Clinical Nursing, 15*(3), 290–300.

Albal, E., & Kutlu, Y. (2010). The relationship between the depression coping self- efficacy level and perceived social support resources. *Journal of Psychiatric Nursing, 1*(3), 115–120.

Asmundson, G. J., & Katz, J. (2009). Understanding the co-occurrence of anxiety disorders and chronic pain: state-of-the-art. *Depression and Anxiety, 26*(10), 888–901.

Bair, M. J., Matthias, M. S., Nyland, K. A., Huffman, M. A., Stubbs, D. L., Kroenke, K., & Damush, T. M. (2009). Barriers and facilitators to chronic pain self-management: A qualitative study of primary care patients with comorbid musculoskeletal pain and depression. *Pain Medicine, 10*(7), 1280–1290.

Bair, M. J., Robinson, R. L., Katon, W., & Kroenke, K. (2003). Depression and pain comorbidity: A literature review. *Archives of Internal Medicine, 163*(20), 2433–2445.

Bair, M. J., Wu, J., Damush, T. M., Sutherland, J. M., & Kroenke, K. (2008). Association of depression and anxiety alone and in combination with chronic musculoskeletal pain in primary care patients. *Psychosomatic Medicine, 70*(8), 890–897.

Bandura, A. (1977). Self-efficacy: Toward a unifying theory of behavioral change. *Psychological Review, 84*(2), 191–215.

Banks, S. M., & Kerns, R. D. (1996). Explaining high rates of depression in chronic pain: A diathesis-stress framework. *Psychological Bulletin, 119*(1), 95–110.

Beck, A. T., & Alford, B. A. (2009). *Depression: Causes and treatment.* Philadelphia, PA: University of Pennsylvania Press.

Beck, A. T. (1967). *Depression: Clinical, experimental, and theoretical aspects.* Philadelphia, PA: University of Pennsylvania Press.

Beck, A. T. (1979). *Cognitive therapy and the emotional disorders.* New York, NY: International Universities Press.

Beck, A. T., Steer, R. A., Beck, J. S., & Newman, C. F. (1993). Hopelessness, depression, suicidal ideation, and clinical diagnosis of depression. *Suicide and Life-Threatening Behavior, 23*(2), 139–145.

Benassi, V. A., Sweeney, P. D., & Dufour, C. L. (1988). Is there a relation between locus of control orientation and depression? *Journal of Abnormal Psychology, 97*(3), 357–367.

Berkman, L. F., Glass, T., Brissette, I., & Seeman, T. E. (2000). From social integration to health: Durkheim in the new millennium. *Social Science & Medicine, 51*(6), 843–857.

Braden, J. B., & Sullivan, M. D. (2008). Suicidal thoughts and behavior among adults with self- reported pain conditions in the national comorbidity survey replication. *The Journal of Pain, 9*(12), 1106–1115.

Brosschot, J. F., Pieper, S., & Thayer, J. F. (2005). Expanding stress theory: Prolonged activation and perseverative cognition. *Psychoneuroendocrinology, 30*(10), 1043–1049.

Brown, G. K., & Nicassio, P. M. (1987). Development of a questionnaire for the assessment of active and passive coping strategies in chronic pain patients. *PAIN, 31*(1), 53–64.

Brox, J. I., Storheim, K., Holm, I., Friis, A., & Reikeras, O. (2005). Disability, pain, psychological factors and physical performance in healthy controls, patients with sub- acute and chronic low back pain: A case-control study. *Journal of Rehabilitation Medicine, 37*(2), 95–99.

Burke, A. L., Mathias, J. L., & Denson, L. A. (2015). Psychological functioning of people living with chronic pain: A meta-analytic review. *British Journal of Clinical Psychology, 54*(3), 345–360.

Burton, A. K., Tillotson, K. M., Main, C. J., & Hollis, S. (1995). Psychosocial predictors of outcome in acute and subchronic low back trouble. *Spine, 20*(6), 722–728.

Centers for Disease Control and Prevention. (CDC). National Center for Injury Prevention and Control. (2010). *Suicide: Risk and protective factors.* Retrieved September 2017, from www.cdc.gov/ViolencePrevention/suicide/riskprotectivefactors.html

Charney, D. S. (2003). Neuroanatomical circuits modulating fear and anxiety behaviors. *Acta Psychiatrica Scandinavica, 108*(s417), 38–50.

Chiesa, A., & Serretti, A. (2011). Mindfulness-based interventions for chronic pain: A systematic review of the evidence. *The Journal of Alternative and Complementary Medicine, 17*(1), 83–93.

Chorpita, B. F., & Barlow, D. H. (1998). The development of anxiety: The role of control in the early environment. *Psychological Bulletin, 124*(1), 3–21.

Cioffi, D. (1991). Beyond attentional strategies: A cognitive-perceptual model of somatic interpretation. *Psychological Bulletin, 109*(1), 25–41.

Council, J. R., Ahern, D. K., Follick, M. J., & Kline, C. L. (1988). Expectancies and functional impairment in chronic low back pain. *Pain, 33*(3), 323–331.

Crisson, J. E., & Keefe, F. J. (1988). The relationship of locus of control to pain coping strategies and psychological distress in chronic pain patients. *Pain, 35*(2), 147–154.

Croft, P. R., Papageorgiou, A. C., Ferry, S., Thomas, E., Jayson, M. I., & Silman, A. J. (1995). Psychologic distress and low back pain: Evidence from a prospective study in the general population. *Spine, 20*(24), 2731–2737.

Crombez, G., Vervaet, L., Lysens, R., Baeyens, F., & Eelen, P. (1998). Avoidance and confrontation of painful, back-straining movements in chronic back pain patients. *Behavior Modification, 22*(1), 62–77.

Crombez, G., Vlaeyen, J. W., Heuts, P. H., & Lysens, R. (1999). Pain-related fear is more disabling than pain itself: Evidence on the role of pain-related fear in chronic back pain disability. *Pain, 80*(1), 329–339.

Dersh, J., Polatin, P. B., & Gatchel, R. J. (2002). Chronic pain and psychopathology: Research findings and theoretical considerations. *Psychosomatic Medicine, 64*(5), 773–786.

Dolce, J. J., Crocker, M. F., Moletteire, C., & Doleys, D. M. (1986). Exercise quotas, anticipatory concern and self-efficacy expectancies in chronic pain: A preliminary report. *Pain, 24*(3), 365–372.

Dufton, B. D. (1990). Cognitive failure and chronic pain. *The International Journal of Psychiatry in Medicine, 19*(3), 291–297.

Edwards, R. R. (2005). Individual differences in endogenous pain modulation as a risk factor for chronic pain. *Neurology, 65*(3), 437–443.

Edwards, R. R., Bingham, C. O., Bathon, J., & Haythornthwaite, J. A. (2006). Catastrophizing and pain in arthritis, fibromyalgia, and other rheumatic diseases. *Arthritis Care & Research, 55*(2), 325–332.

Edwards, R. R., Magyar-Russell, G., Thombs, B., Smith, M. T., Holavanahalli, R. K., Patterson, D. R., . . . Fauerbach, J. A. (2007). Acute pain at discharge from hospitalization is a prospective predictor of long- term suicidal ideation after burn injury. *Archives of Physical Medicine and Rehabilitation, 88*(12), S36–S42.

Edwards, R. R., Smith, M. T., Kudel, I., & Haythornthwaite, J. (2006). Pain-related catastrophizing as a risk factor for suicidal ideation in chronic pain. *Pain, 126*(1), 272–279.

Esteve, R., Ramírez-Maestre, C., & López-Martínez, A. E. (2007). Adjustment to chronic pain: The role of pain acceptance, coping strategies, and pain-related cognitions. *Annals of Behavioral Medicine, 33*(2), 179–188.

Fishbain, D. A., Cutler, R., Rosomoff, H. L., & Rosomoff, R. S. (1997). Chronic pain-associated depression: Antecedent or consequence of chronic pain? A review. *The Clinical Journal of Pain, 13*(2), 116–137.

Flor, H., Behle, D. J., & Birbaumer, N. (1993). Assessment of pain-related cognitions in chronic pain patients. *Behavior Research and Therapy, 31*(1), 63–73.

Flor, H., & Hermann, C. (2004). Biopsychosocial models of pain. In R. H. Dworkin & W. S. Breitbart (Eds.), *Psychosocial aspects of pain: A handbook for health care providers. Progress in pain research and management* (Vol. 27, pp. 47–75). Seattle: IASP Press.

Fordyce, W. E. (1976). *Behavioral methods for chronic pain and illness*. St. Louis, MO: Mosby.

Forman, E. M., Chapman, J. E., Herbert, J. D., Goetter, E. M., Yuen, E. K., & Moitra, E. (2012). Using session-by-session measurement to compare mechanisms of action for acceptance and commitment therapy and cognitive therapy. *Behavior Therapy, 43*(2), 341–354.

Fowler, J. C. (2012). Suicide risk assessment in clinical practice: Pragmatic guidelines for imperfect assessments. *Psychotherapy, 49*(1), 81–90.

Gamsa, A. (1990). Is emotional disturbance a precipitator or a consequence of chronic pain? *Pain, 42*(2), 83–195.

Gatchel, R. J. (1991). Early development of physical and mental deconditioning in painful spinal disorders. *Contemporary Conservative Care for Painful Spinal Disorders*, 278–289.

Gatchel, R. J. (2004). Comorbidity of chronic pain and mental health disorders: The biopsychosocial perspective. *American Psychologist, 59*(8), 795–805.

Gatchel, R. J., & Epker, J. (1999). Psychosocial predictors of chronic pain and response to treatment. *Psychosocial Factors in Pain: Critical Perspectives*, 412–434.

Gureje, O., Simon, G. E., & Von Korff, M. (2001). A cross-national study of the course of persistent pain in primary care. *Pain, 92*(1), 195–200.

Gureje, O., Von Korff, M., Kola, L., Demyttenaere, K., He, Y., Posada-Villa, J., . . . Iwata, N. (2008). The relation between multiple pains and mental disorders: Results from the World Mental Health Surveys. *PAIN, 135*(1), 82–91.

Gil, K. M., Williams, D. A., Keefe, F. J., & Beckham, J. C. (1990). The relationship of negative thoughts to pain and psychological distress. *Behavior Therapy, 21*(3), 349–362.

Goldberg, D. S., & McGee, S. J. (2011). Pain as a global public health priority. *BMC Public Health, 11*(1), 770–775.

Harris, T., Cook, D. G., Victor, C., DeWilde, S., & Beighton, C. (2005). Onset and persistence of depression in older people—results from a 2-year community follow-up study. *Age and Ageing, 35*(1), 25–32.

Hayes, S. C. (2004). Acceptance and commitment therapy, relational frame theory, and the third wave of behavioral and cognitive therapies. *Behavior Therapy, 35*(4), 639–665.

Hayes, S. C., & Duckworth, M. P. (2006). Acceptance and commitment therapy and traditional cognitive behavior therapy approaches to pain. *Cognitive and Behavioral Practice, 13*(3), 185–187.

Hayes, S. C., Luoma, J. B., Bond, F. W., Masuda, A., & Lillis, J. (2006). Acceptance and commitment therapy: Model, processes and outcomes. *Behavior Research and Therapy, 44*(1), 1–25.

Hayes, S. C., Strosahl, K. D., & Wilson, K. G. (1999). *Acceptance and commitment therapy*. New York, NY: The Guilford Press.

Heimberg, R. G., & Ritter, M. R. (2008). Cognitive behavioral therapy and acceptance and commitment therapy for the anxiety disorders: Two approaches with much to offer. *Clinical Psychology: Science and Practice, 15*(4), 296–298.

Hoffman, B. M., Papas, R. K., Chatkoff, D. K., & Kerns, R. D. (2007). Meta-analysis of psychological interventions for chronic low back pain. Health Psychology, 26(1), 1–9.

Hofmann, S. G., Sawyer, A. T., Witt, A. A., & Oh, D. (2010). The effect of mindfulness- based therapy on anxiety and depression: A meta-analytic review. Journal of Consulting and Clinical Psychology, 78(2), 169–183.

Hofmann, S. G., & Smits, J. A. (2008). Cognitive-behavioral therapy for adult anxiety disorders: A meta-analysis of randomized placebo-controlled trials. The Journal of Clinical Psychiatry, 69(4), 621–632.

Holmes, A., Christelis, N., & Arnold, C. (2012). Depression and chronic pain. Medical Journal of Australia, 10, 17–20.

Jacob, M. C., Kerns, R. D., Rosenberg, R., & Haythornthwaite, J. (1993). Chronic pain: Intrusion and accommodation. Behavior Research and Therapy, 31(5), 519–527.

Jensen, M. P., Nielson, W. R., & Kerns, R. D. (2003). Toward the development of a motivational model of pain self-management. The Journal of Pain, 4(9), 477–492.

Jensen, M. P., Nielson, W. R., Romano, J. M., Hill, M. L., & Turner, J. A. (2000). Further evaluation of the pain stages of change questionnaire: Is the transtheoretical model of change useful for patients with chronic pain? Pain, 86(3), 255–264.

Jensen, M. P., Turner, J. A., & Romano, J. M. (2007). Changes after multidisciplinary pain treatment in patient pain beliefs and coping are associated with concurrent changes in patient functioning. Pain, 131(1–2), 38–47.

Joranson, D. E., & Lietman, R. (1994). The McNeil national pain survey. New York, NY: Louis Harris and Associates.

Kashdan, T. B. (2010). Psychological flexibility as a fundamental aspect of health. Clinical Psychology Review, 30(7), 865–878. http://doi.org/10.1016/j.cpr.2010.03.001

Keefe, F. J., Affleck, G., Lefebvre, J. C., Starr, K., Caldwell, D. S., & Tennen, H. (1997). Pain coping strategies and coping efficacy in rheumatoid arthritis: A daily process analysis. Pain, 69(1), 35–42.

Kerns, R. D., Rosenberg, R., Jamison, R. N., Caudill, M. A., & Haythornthwaite, J. (1997). Readiness to adopt a self-management approach to chronic pain: The Pain Stages of Change Questionnaire (PSOCQ). Pain, 72(1), 227–234.

Kerns, R. D., Sellinger, J., & Goodin, B. R. (2011). Psychological treatment of chronic pain. Annual Review of Clinical Psychology, 7, 411–434.

Kerns, R. D., Turk, D. C., & Rudy, T. E. (1985). The West Haven-Yale multidimensional pain inventory (WHYMPI). Pain, 23(4), 345–356.

Kessler, R. C., Borges, G., & Walters, E. E. (1999). Prevalence of and risk factors for lifetime suicide attempts in the National Comorbidity Survey. Archives of General Psychiatry, 56(7), 617–626.

Kirmayer, L. J., Robbins, J. M., & Paris, J. (1994). Somatoform disorders: Personality and the social matrix of somatic distress. Journal of Abnormal Psychology, 103(1), 125–136.

Krause, S. J., Wiener, R. L., & Tait, R. C. (1994). Depression and pain behavior in patients with chronic pain. The Clinical Journal of Pain, 10(2), 122–127.

Kroenke, K., Spitzer, R. L., Williams, J. B., Linzer, M., Hahn, S. R., deGruy III, F.V., & Brody, D. (1994). Physical symptoms in primary care: Predictors of psychiatric disorders and functional impairment. Archives of Family Medicine, 3(9), 774–779.

Lazarus, R. S., & Folkman, S. (1984). Coping and adaptation. The Handbook of Behavioral Medicine, 282–325.

Leino, P., & Magni, G. (1993). Depressive and distress symptoms as predictors of low back pain, neck-shoulder pain, and other musculoskeletal morbidity: A 10-year follow-up of metal industry employees. Pain, 53(1), 89–94.

Levenson, J. (Ed.). (2005). Textbook of psychosomatic medicine. Washington, DC: American Psychiatric Publishing.

Mann, J. J., Apter, A., Bertolote, J., Beautrais, A., Currier, D., Haas, A., . . . Mehlum, L. (2005). Suicide prevention strategies: A systematic review. *Jama*, *294*(16), 2064–2074.

Masuda, A., & Tully, E. C. (2011). The role of mindfulness and psychological flexibility in somatization, depression, anxiety, and general psychosocial distress in a nonclinical college sample. *Journal of Evidence-Based Complementary & Alternative Medicine*, *17*(1), 66–71.

McBeth, J., Macfarlane, G. J., & Silman, A. J. (2002). Does chronic pain predict future psychological distress? *Pain*, *96*(3), 239–245.

McCracken, L. M. (1998). Learning to live with the pain: Acceptance of pain predicts adjustment in persons with chronic pain. *Pain*, *74*(1), 21–27.

McCracken, L. M., & Eccleston, C. (2003). Coping or acceptance: what to do about chronic pain? *Pain*, *105*(1–2), 197–204.

McCracken, L. M., & Eccleston, C. (2005). A prospective study of acceptance of pain and patient functioning with chronic pain. *Pain*, *118*(1), 164–169.

McCracken, L. M., Faber, S. D., & Janeck, A. S. (1998). Pain-related anxiety predicts nonspecific physical complaints in persons with chronic pain. *Behavior Research and Therapy*, *36*(6), 621–630.

McCracken, L. M., & Gross, R. T. (1993). Does anxiety affect coping with chronic pain? *Clinical Journal of Pain*, *9*, 253–259.

McCracken, L. M., & Turk, D. C. (2002). Behavioral and cognitive—behavioral treatment for chronic pain: Outcome, predictors of outcome, and treatment process. *Spine*, *27*(22), 2564–2573.

McCracken, L. M., & Velleman, S. C. (2010). Psychological flexibility in adults with chronic pain: A study of acceptance, mindfulness, and values-based action in primary care. *Pain*, *148*(1), 141–147.

McCracken, L. M., Vowles, K. E., & Eccleston, C. (2005). Acceptance-based treatment for persons with complex, long standing chronic pain: A preliminary analysis of treatment outcome in comparison to a waiting phase. *Behaviour Research and Therapy*, *43*(10), 1335–1346.

McCracken, L. M., & Vowles, K. E. (2008). A prospective analysis of acceptance of pain and values-based action in patients with chronic pain. *Health Psychology*, *27*(2), 215–220.

McWilliams, L. A., Goodwin, R. D., & Cox, B. J. (2004). Depression and anxiety associated with three pain conditions: Results from a nationally representative sample. *Pain*, *111*(1), 77–83.

Melzack, R., & Wall, P. D. (1965). Pain mechanisms: A new theory. *Science*, *150*, 971–979.

Merskey, H., & Bogduk, N. (Eds.). (1994). *Classification of chronic pain: Descriptions of chronic pain syndromes and definitions of terms* (2nd ed.). Seattle: IASP Press.

Miller, L. R., & Cano, A. (2009). Comorbid chronic pain and depression: Who is at risk? *The Journal of Pain*, *10*(6), 619–627.

Miller, W. R., & Rollnick, S. (2012). *Motivational interviewing: Helping people change*. New York, NY: The Guilford Press.

Middeldorp, C. M., Cath, D. C., Van Dyck, R., & Boomsma, D. I. (2005). The co- morbidity of anxiety and depression in the perspective of genetic epidemiology: A review of twin and family studies. *Psychological Medicine*, *35*(5), 611–624.

Mineka, S., Watson, D., & Clark, L. A. (1998). Comorbidity of anxiety and unipolar mood disorders. *Annual Review of Psychology*, *49*(1), 377–412.

Mitchell, S., & Campbell, E. A. (1988). Cognitions associated with anxiety and depression. *Personality and Individual Differences*, *9*(4), 837–838.

Morgan, D. (2003). Mindfulness-based cognitive therapy for depression: A new approach to preventing relapse. *Psychotherapy Research*, *13*(1), 123–125.

Morley, S., Eccleston, C., & Williams, A. (1999). Systematic review and meta-analysis of randomized controlled trials of cognitive behaviour therapy and behaviour therapy for chronic pain in adults, excluding headache. *Pain*, *80*(1–2), 1–13.

Murphy, J. L., McKellar, J. D., Raffa, S. D., Clark, M. E., Kerns, R. D., & Karlin, B. E. (2014). *Cognitive behavioral therapy for chronic pain among veterans: Therapist manual.* Washington, DC: U.S. Department of Veterans Affairs.

Nicholas, M. K. (2008). Pain management in musculoskeletal conditions. *Best Practice and Research: Clinical Rheumatology, 22*, 451–470.

Neugebauer, V., Li, W., Bird, G. C., & Han, J. S. (2004). The amygdala and persistent pain. *The Neuroscientist, 10*(3), 221–234.

Odegard, S., Finset, A., Mowinckel, P., Kvien, T. K., & Uhlig, T. (2007). Pain and psychological health status over a 10-year period in patients with recent onset rheumatoid arthritis. *Annals of the Rheumatic Diseases, 66*(9), 1195–1201.

Pincus, T., & Williams, A. (1999). Models and measurements of depression in chronic pain. *Journal of Psychosomatic Research, 47*(3), 211–219.

Poole, H., White, S., Blake, C., Murphy, P., & Bramwell, R. (2009). Depression in chronic pain patients: Prevalence and measurement. *Pain Practice, 9*(3), 173–180.

Porro, C. A. (2003). Functional imaging and pain: Behavior, perception, and modulation. *The Neuroscientist, 9*(5), 354–369.

Quartana, P. J., Campbell, C. M., & Edwards, R. R. (2009). Pain catastrophizing: A critical review. *Expert Review of Neurotherapeutics, 9*(5), 745–758.

Rhudy, J. L., & Meagher, M. W. (2000). Fear and anxiety: Divergent effects on human pain thresholds. *Pain, 84*(1), 65–75.

Robinson, M. J., Edwards, S. E., Iyengar, S., Bymaster, F., Clark, M., & Katon, W. (2009). Depression and pain. *Frontiers in Bioscience, 14*(503), 5031–5051.

Rudy, T. E., Kerns, R. D., & Turk, D. C. (1988). Chronic pain and depression: Toward a cognitive-behavioral mediation model. *Pain, 35*(2), 129–140.

Scharloo, M., & Kaptein, A. A. (1997). Measurement of illness perceptions in patients with chronic somatic illness: A review. In K. J. Petrie & J. Weinman (Eds.), *Perceptions of health and illness: Current research applications.* London: Harwood.

Schwarzer, R., Lippke, S., & Luszczynska, A. (2011). Mechanisms of health behavior change in persons with chronic illness or disability: The Health Action Process Approach (HAPA). *Rehabilitation Psychology, 56*(3), 161–170.

Scott, K. M., Bruffaerts, R., Tsang, A., Ormel, J., Alonso, J., Angermeyer, M. C., . . . Gasquet, I. (2007). Depression—anxiety relationships with chronic physical conditions: Results from the World Mental Health Surveys. *Journal of Affective Disorders, 103*(1), 113–120.

Segerstrom, S. C., Stanton, A. L., Alden, L. E., & Shortridge, B. E. (2003). A multidimensional structure for repetitive thought: What's on your mind, and how, and how much? *Journal of Personality and Social Psychology, 85*(5), 909–921.

Seligman, M. E. (1975). *Helplessness: On depression, development, and death.* San Francisco, CA: Freeman.

Shutty, M. S. Jr., DeGood, D. E., & Tuttle, D. H. (1990). Chronic pain patients' beliefs about their pain and treatment outcomes. *Archives of Physical Medicine and Rehabilitation, 71*(2), 128–132.

Smarr, K. L., Parker, J. C., Wright, G. E., Stucky-Ropp, R. C., Buckelew, S. P., Hoffman, R. W., O'Sullivan, F. X., & Hewett, J. E. (1997). The importance of enhancing self-efficacy in rheumatoid arthritis. *Arthritis & Rheumatology, 10*(1), 18–26.

Smith, M. T., Edwards, R. R., Robinson, R. C., & Dworkin, R. H. (2004). Suicidal ideation, plans, and attempts in chronic pain patients: Factors associated with increased risk. *Pain, 111*(1), 201–208.

Smith, T. W., Peck, J. R., & Ward, J. R. (1990). Helplessness and depression in rheumatoid arthritis. *Health Psychology, 9*(4), 377–389.

Sudak, D. M. (2012). Cognitive behavioral therapy for depression. *Psychiatric Clinics, 35*(1), 99–110.

Sullivan, M., & Katon, W. (1993). Somatization: The path between distress and somatic symptoms. *APS Journal*, *2*(3), 141–149.

Symreng, I., & Fishman, S. M. (2004). Anxiety and pain. *Pain Clinical Updates*, *12*(7), 1–6.

Tahmassian, K., & Jalali Moghadam, N. (2011). Relationship between self-efficacy and symptoms of anxiety, depression, worry and social avoidance in a normal sample of students. *Iranian Journal of Psychiatry and Behavioral Sciences*, *5*(2), 91–98.

Tang, N. K., & Crane, C. (2006). Suicidality in chronic pain: A review of the prevalence, risk factors and psychological links. *Psychological Medicine*, *36*(5), 575–586.

Teasdale, J. D., Moore, R. G., Hayhurst, H., Pope, M., Williams, S., & Segal, Z. V. (2002). Metacognitive awareness and prevention of relapse in depression: Empirical evidence. *Journal of Consulting and Clinical Psychology*, *70*(2), 275–287.

Thorn, B. E. (2017). *Cognitive therapy for chronic pain: A step-by-step guide*. New York, NY: The Guilford Press.

Thorn, B. E., Boothby, J. L., & Sullivan, M. J. (2002). Targeted treatment of catastrophizing for the management of chronic pain. *Cognitive and Behavioral Practice*, *9*(2), 127–138.

Truchon, M. (2001). Determinants of chronic disability related to low back pain: Towards an integrative biopsychosocial model. *Disability and Rehabilitation*, *23*(17), 758–767.

Turk, D. C. (2002a). Biopsychosocial Perspective on Chronic Pain. In D. C. Turk & R. J. Gatchel (Eds.), *Psychological approaches to PAIN MANAGEMENT: A practitioner's handbook* (2nd ed.). New York, NY: The Guilford Press.

Turk, D. C. (2002b). Clinical effectiveness and cost effectiveness of treatment for chronic pain patients. *The Clinical Journal of Pain*, *18*, 355–365.

Turk, D. C. (2003). Cognitive-behavioral approach to the treatment of chronic pain patients. *Regional Anesthesia and Pain Medicine*, *28*(6), 573–579.

Turk, D. C., & Okifuji, A. (1998). Treatment of chronic pain patients: Clinical outcomes, cost- effectiveness, and cost-benefits of multidisciplinary pain centers. *Critical Reviews™ in Physical and Rehabilitation Medicine*, *10*(2), 181–208.

Turk, D. C., Okifuji, A., & Scharff, L. (1995). Chronic pain and depression: Role of perceived impact and perceived control in different age cohorts. *Pain*, *61*(1), 93–101.

Turk, D. C., & Okifuji, A. (2002). Psychological factors in chronic pain: Evolution and revolution. *Journal of Consulting and Clinical Psychology*, *70*(3), 678–690.

Veehof, M. M., Oskam, M. J., Schreurs, K. M., & Bohlmeijer, E. T. (2011). Acceptance-based interventions for the treatment of chronic pain: A systematic review and meta-analysis. *PAIN*, *152*(3), 533–542.

Viane, I., Crombez, G., Eccleston, C., Poppe, C., Devulder, J., Van Houdenhove, B., & De Corte, W. (2003). Acceptance of pain is an independent predictor of mental well-being in patients with chronic pain: Empirical evidence and reappraisal. *Pain*, *106*(1), 65–72.

Viane, I., Crombez, G., Eccleston, C., Devulder, J., & De Corte, W. (2004). Acceptance of the unpleasant reality of chronic pain: Effects upon attention to pain and engagement with daily activities. *Pain*, *112*(3), 282–288.

Vlaeyen, J. W., Kole-Snijders, A. M., Boeren, R. G., & Van Eek, H. (1995). Fear of movement/(re) injury in chronic low back pain and its relation to behavioral performance. *Pain*, *62*(3), 363–372.

Vlaeyen, J. W., & Linton, S. J. (2000). Fear-avoidance and its consequences in chronic musculoskeletal pain: A state of the art. *Pain*, *85*(3), 317–332.

Vollestad, J., Nielsen, M. B., & Nielsen, G. H. (2012). Mindfulnessand acceptance-based interventions for anxiety disorders: A systematic review and meta-analysis. *British Journal of Clinical Psychology*, *51*(3), 239–260.

Von Korff, M., & Simon, G. (1996). The relationship between pain and depression. *British Journal of Psychiatry*, *168*(30), 101–108.

Von Korff, M., Crane, P., Lane, M., Miglioretti, D. L., Simon, G., Saunders, K., . . . Kessler, R. (2005). Chronic spinal pain and physical-mental comorbidity in the United States: Results for the national comorbidity survey replication. *Pain*, *113*(3), 331–339.

Watson, D., Clark, L. A., Weber, K., Assenheimer, J. S., Strauss, M. E., & McCormick, R. A. (1995). Testing a tripartite model: II. Exploring the symptom structure of anxiety and depression in student, adult and patient samples. *Journal of Abnormal Psychology, 104,* 15–25.

Wells, K. B., Burnam, M. A., Rogers, W., Hays, R., & Camp, P. (1992). The course of depression in adult outpatients: Results from the Medical Outcomes Study. *Archives of General Psychiatry, 49*(10), 788–794.

Wetherell, J. L., Afari, N., Rutledge, T., Sorrell, J. T., Stoddard, J. A., Petkus, A. J., Solomon, B. C., Lehman, D. H., Liu, L., Lang, A. J., & Atkinson, J. H. (2011). A randomized, controlled trial of acceptance and commitment therapy and cognitive-behavioral therapy for chronic pain. *Pain, 152*(9), 2098–2107.

Williams, A. C., & Craig, K. D. (2016). Updating the definition of pain. *Pain. 157*(11), 2420–2423.

Williams, D. A., & Keefe, F. J. (1991). Pain beliefs and the use of cognitive-behavioral coping strategies. *Pain, 46*(2), 185–190.

Woo, A. (2010). Depression and anxiety in pain. *Reviews in Pain, 4*(1), 8–12.

Zautra, A. J., Davis, M. C., Reich, J. W., Nicassario, P., Tennen, H., Finan, P., Kratz, A., Parrish, B., & Irwin, M. R. (2008). Comparison of cognitive behavioral and mindfulness meditation interventions on adaptation to rheumatoid arthritis for patients with and without history of recurrent depression. *Journal of Consulting and Clinical Psychology, 76*(3), 408–421.

Appendix 1
Clinician Handout

Overview of Suicide Assessment in Individuals With Chronic Pain

Using a calm, caring, concerned, and curious stance, directly inquire about each of the topic areas below. Please note that this handout provides an overview of suicide assessment and does not include all possible areas of inquiry.

Predisposing Vulnerabilities

- History of depression
- History of anxiety
- History of other mental health disorders
- History of substance use
- History of suicidal thinking, self-harm, and/or suicidal behavior
- Previous psychiatric treatment including psychiatric hospitalizations

Precipitating Factors

- Change in pain
- Long pain duration
- Insomnia/sleep difficulties
- Recent/new loss or stressor
- Recent/new interpersonal conflict
- Decrease in social support (e.g., break-up of romantic relationship)

Current Mental Status/Mental Health Symptoms

- Current thought processes (e.g., illogical, irrational)
- Delusions and/or bizarre thinking
- Limited problem-solving abilities
- Current depression, anxiety, and/or additional mental health symptoms
- Current substance use

Suicidal Thinking and Thought Content

- Active suicidal ideation (i.e., desire to die accompanied by a plan for how to carry out death)
- Passive suicidal ideation (i.e., desire to die without having a plan for how carry out the death)
- Pain catastrophizing (i.e., tendency to describe pain experience in exaggerated terms, to ruminate on pain, and/or to feel more helpless/hopeless about pain)
- Desire to escape pain

Access to Lethal Means

- Access to pain medications and potentially lethal amounts and types of medications
- Access to firearms
- Access to other lethal means (may be related to specific suicidal plan)

Suicidal Planning and Intent/Attitude Toward Plan

- Current suicide plan
- Lethality of plan
- Current intent to act on plan

Protective Factors

- Hopeful attitude toward the future/future-oriented
- Strong perceived social support/sense of connectedness
- Adaptive coping skills and problem-solving skills
- Sense of responsibility toward others (e.g., children, partner)
- Religious beliefs/spirituality
- Engaged in therapy/therapeutic relationship

19
Co-occurring PTSD and Chronic Pain

John D. Otis and Christina Hardway

Introduction

Pain is a complex process of perception that not only includes the sensory experience attributable to the stimulation of nociceptors but is also influenced by psychological, behavioral, and social elements. Pain typically is considered an adaptive reaction that alerts a person to some type of injury. Most often the pain resolves on its own after a period of appropriate rest or conservative treatment, and the person returns to his/her prior level of functioning.

However, for some people the experience of pain persists beyond when it is considered an adaptive sensation, and its effects permeate into multiple functional domains. Chronic pain is defined as "an unpleasant sensory and emotional experience associated with actual or potential tissue damage, or described in terms of such damage." Pain that persists for longer than three months is considered chronic pain (IASP, 2012).

Although pain can be caused by normal degenerative changes that occur in the body over time, pain may also be secondary to injuries resulting from potentially traumatic events such as motor vehicle accidents, complications from medical interventions, violent domestic altercations, or military combat. As a result, it is not uncommon for people with chronic pain to endorse symptoms consistent with posttraumatic stress disorder (PTSD).

On their own, chronic pain and PTSD symptoms can each interfere with daily functioning (Breivik, Collett, Ventafridda, Cohen, & Gallacher, 2006; Westphal et al., 2011), but when they co-occur they are associated with even greater impairment, pain, and PTSD symptoms, increased use of healthcare resources, lower quality of life, greater use of opiates, and higher levels of emotional disorders (Noel et al., 2016; Outcalt, Ang, et al., 2014; Outcalt, Yu, Hoen, Pennington, &

Krebs, 2014). As a result, research investigating the underlying mechanisms that may account for the high rates of comorbidity, and studies examining ways to provide the most effective psychological treatments for individuals with pain and PTSD, has burgeoned since the turn of the century (Brennstuhl, Tarquinio, & Montel, 2015).

In this chapter, we will provide a review of the literature examining the comorbidity and interaction between chronic pain and PTSD. First, we provide a review of the prevalence of both chronic pain and PTSD and their impact on psychological and physical functioning. Next, we present theoretical models describing the potential mechanisms by which these two conditions may interact with one another. Lastly, we present recommendations for treating comorbid chronic pain and PTSD. The chapter concludes with implications for clinicians and future directions for research and treatment refinements.

Chronic Pain

Prevalence and Costs

Pain is a highly prevalent condition in the United States, with approximately 56% of individuals experiencing some degree of pain in the last three months (Nahin, 2015). Further, a substantial percentage of the population suffers from chronic pain, with estimates ranging from 11.2% to 15.6% (Nahin, 2015; Riskowski, 2014). Estimates of the national costs of pain in the United States range from $560 to $635 billion per year when considering annual healthcare costs and costs associated with lower productivity (Gaskin & Richard, 2012).

Pain prevalence varies by ethnicity and socioeconomic position, with non-Hispanic Caucasians and those in lower socioeconomic positions reporting chronic pain at higher prevalence rates (Riskowski, 2014). Veterans represent a subgroup particularly impacted by pain (Nahin, 2017). A recent study found that as many as 44% of soldiers returning from deployment endorsed chronic pain (Toblin, Quartana, Riviere, Walper, & Hoge, 2014). Pain prevalence rates also vary by country. For example, across 15 European countries and Israel, 19% of respondents indicated they had suffered from pain of moderate to severe intensity for at least six months, but these rates varied from 12% in Spain to 30% in Norway (Breivik et al., 2006).

Psychological and Functional Impact

Studies suggest that chronic pain often is associated with high rates of functional impairment and emotional disorders. For example, in a survey of individuals with chronic pain from 16 countries, approximately 50% indicated that pain interfered with a range of daily activities, including their ability to sleep, drive, exercise, walk, attend social functions, and work around the house (Breivik et al., 2006). Over 60% of respondents reported that they were less able to work outside of their homes, 19% reported having lost their jobs, and 13% indicated they had changed jobs as a result of pain.

Given the high rates of functional impairment associated with chronic pain, it is not surprising that patients with chronic pain often report symptoms of anxiety and depression. For example, the estimated rates of depression among people with chronic pain range from 30% to 54% (Banks & Kerns, 1996; Elliott, Renier, & Palcher, 2003; Bair, Robinson, Katon, & Kroenke, 2003). In turn, these negative emotions also can contribute to the overall experience of pain. One study found that for patients with lower back pain, anxiety accounted for 14% of pain severity and 32% of disability (Staerkle et al., 2004).

The Cognitive-Behavioral Fear-Avoidance Model of Pain may provide some insight into the interaction between anxiety and pain (Vlaeyen & Linton, 2000). According to this model, when some individuals experience a painful condition, they interpret it as overly threatening, a process called "catastrophizing." This interpretation contributes to an increased fear of pain, the avoidance of activities that have the potential to cause pain, guarding behaviors (e.g., bracing, walking slowly), and hypervigilance to painful sensations. All of these factors can contribute to increased anxiety and depressed mood (Flink, Boersma, & Linton, 2013; Racine et al., 2016; Ramirez-Maestre, Esteve, Ruiz-Parraga, Gomez-Perez, & Lopez-Martinez, 2017).

As negative emotions and avoidance increase, pain and the individual's perceptions of pain can increase. In contrast, in the absence of serious somatic pathology, when individuals employ more adaptive coping strategies in response to pain (e.g., cognitive coping and maintaining appropriate levels of activity), pain and individuals' perceptions of it can decrease. A biopsychosocial conceptualization of the relationship between the experience of pain and emotional disorders may help inform the development of non-pharmacological treatments for chronic pain and underscore the importance of an interdisciplinary pain management approach that includes behavioral medicine. Chapter 18 contains an in-depth review of the relationships between chronic pain, depression, and anxiety.

Posttraumatic Stress Disorder (PTSD)

Posttraumatic stress disorder (PTSD) may result when a person has directly or indirectly experienced a traumatic event such as combat, a natural disaster, serious injury, or sexual violence. Individuals suffering from PTSD may persistently re-experience the event in ways such as intrusive thoughts, nightmares, or flashbacks, the experience of emotional distress or physical reactivity after exposure to reminders of the event, the avoidance of trauma-related stimuli, the experience of a worsening of negative thoughts or feelings, and the exhibition of increased reactivity and arousal (e.g., irritability or hypervigilance). These symptoms cause distress or impairment and last for more than a month (American Psychiatric Association, 2013). Moreover, even if a person does not meet the diagnostic criteria for PTSD after experiencing a traumatic event, he/she can still experience PTSD-related symptoms that can be impairing and interfering.

Prevalence and Costs

Traumatic experiences in the United States are fairly common. Based on the responses of a national sample of adults in the U.S., the number of people who have been exposed to a traumatic event is very high (89.7%), and exposure to multiple traumatic events is typical (Kilpatrick et al., 2013). Kilpatrick and colleagues (2013) found that, according to DSM-5 criteria, the prevalence rates for a PTSD diagnosis were 8.3% for lifetime, 4.7% over the past 12 months, and 3.8% over the past six months. The prevalence rates of PTSD varied by gender, with 5.4% of males and 11% of women meeting criteria for PTSD. It is also possible that the rates of PTSD are generally under-represented. In a study of primary care patients, only 11% of those who met diagnostic criteria for PTSD had a documented PTSD diagnosis in their medical record (Liebschutz et al., 2007).

According to findings from the National Epidemiological Survey of Alcohol and Related Conditions, the prevalence of PTSD among different ethnic groups in the United States differs significantly. Compared with the lifetime prevalence among Caucasians (7.4%), African Americans experienced a significantly higher rate of PTSD (8.7%). The rate for Hispanics was similar (7.0%), and the rate for Asians (4.0%) was significantly lower than that for Caucasians (Roberts, Gilman, Breslau, Breslau, & Koenen, 2011).

The rates of PTSD vary across countries as well. According to the World Mental Health Survey (Koenen et al., 2017), higher income countries have a higher prevalence of PTSD. For example, in an Australian sample, lifetime prevalence of PTSD was 7.3% and in the United States it was 6.9%; however, the prevalence of PTSD was lower in countries like Colombia (1.8%) and the Ukraine (4.8%). Individuals with PTSD living in high-income countries sought treatment at about twice the rate of those living in low- or lower middle income countries (53.5% versus 22.8%; Koenen et al., 2017).

Some research indicates that having multiple exposures increases the risk of developing PTSD. MacDonald and colleagues examined data from the 4,023 participants in the National Survey of Adolescents. Of these participants, 1,868 (46.4%) reported exposure to a traumatic event (along with other psychopathological and demographic data). As the number of exposures increased, so too did the likelihood of developing PTSD and comorbid disorders (MacDonald, Danielson, Resnick, Saunders, & Kilpatrick, 2010).

Psychological and Functional Impact

Exposure to traumatic events and PTSD is associated with difficulties with emotion regulation, conflict with others, suicidality, lower quality of life, missed work, and increased disability (Ehring & Quack, 2010; Westphal et al., 2011; Seligowski, Lee, Bardeen, & Orcutt, 2015; Sareen et al., 2007; Seligowski, Rogers, & Orcutt, 2016). In addition, PTSD is associated with health issues that include cardiovascular, respiratory, and gastrointestinal disorders, and cancer (Sareen et al., 2007).

Although the experience of PTSD may promote poor healthcare behaviors, it has been suggested that PTSD may result in biochemical changes in the brain that can contribute to the expression of health-related vulnerabilities. Research indicates that following a traumatic event, the development of PTSD precedes the development of anxiety and depression; however, receiving all three psychiatric diagnoses is more likely than receiving a diagnosis of PTSD alone or either PTSD and comorbid depression or anxiety (Ginzburg, Ein-Dor, & Solomon, 2010). PTSD also negatively impacts the well-being of people with preexisting depression. Among a sample of veterans diagnosed with depression, individuals who also screened positive for signs of PTSD had more severe symptoms, including higher levels of suicidal ideation, a greater number of healthcare visits, and lower levels of social support (Campbell et al., 2007).

Pain and PTSD Comorbidity

There is broad consensus that significant comorbidity exists between PTSD symptomology and chronic pain (Brennstuhl et al., 2015; Jenewein et al., 2009; Scioli-Salter et al., 2015). Determining the comorbidity rates between these two disorders, however, presents challenges because the rates of comorbidity vary depending upon the sample population examined.

For example, PTSD can be assessed among chronic pain patients and, conversely, chronic pain can be assessed among patients with PTSD (Brennstuhl et al., 2015). Some estimates suggest that among those with PTSD, 50% to 75% also have chronic pain (Scioli-Salter et al., 2015). The high rate of pain is understandable given that the causes of PTSD often involve physical injury. In contrast, the average rate of PTSD among patients with chronic pain is estimated to be between 9% and 10%; however, rates of PTSD can range from less than 1% to 57% depending on the type of pain reported or the pain setting surveyed (Fishbain, Pulikal, Lewis, & Gao, 2017; Siqveland, Hussain, Lindstrøm, Ruud, & Hauff, 2017).

Findings from meta-analyses suggest that patients with back pain have lower rates of PTSD than patients with widespread pain or fibromyalgia. Among back pain patients, estimates of comorbid PTSD are less than 1% (Fishbain et al., 2017; Siqveland et al., 2017), but for patients with widespread chronic pain, estimates are 20.5% (Siqveland et al., 2017). The rates are particularly high (39.7%) for individuals who experience miscellaneous pain or fibromyalgia.

Among people who have pain secondary to motor vehicle accidents, the rate of PTSD is estimated to be 46.7% (Fishbain et al., 2017). Veterans with pain are a particularly vulnerable population, with a rate of PTSD as high as 50.1% (Fishbain et al., 2017). Comorbidity between pain and symptoms of PTSD also has been found among children and adolescents, with 32% of youth with chronic pain also showing symptoms of PTSD compared with 8% of youth without chronic pain (Noel et al., 2016).

Psychological and Functional Impact

When individuals experience both chronic pain and PTSD symptoms, they are likely to have more symptoms of PTSD, greater levels of pain, higher levels of negative emotions (including anxiety and depression), and greater disability than patients who have chronic pain or PTSD independently (Asmundson, Wright, & Stein, 2004; Jenewein et al., 2009; Outcalt, Ang, et al., 2014; Outcalt et al., 2015; Palyo & Beck, 2005; Sullivan et al., 2009). The severity of pain and PTSD symptoms also impacts psychosocial functioning (e.g., social interactions, communication, and emotion), which may be mediated by changes in perceived control over one's life (Palyo & Beck, 2005).

Research also suggests that there may be a reciprocal relationship among chronic pain, PTSD symptoms, and sleep (Powell, Corbo, Fonda, Otis, Milberg, & McGlinchey, 2015). The exacerbating effect of comorbid PTSD symptoms and chronic pain on negative emotions, intensity of pain, and interference in daily activities has been found across several populations, including veterans in general (Outcalt, Ang, et al., 2014; Outcalt et al., 2015), female veterans in particular (Asmundson et al., 2004), victims of motor vehicle accidents (Jenewein et al., 2009), and youth (Noel et al., 2016).

Patients with pain and PTSD are at higher risk of opioid prescription, abuse, and overdose (Cochran et al., 2016; Schwartz et al., 2006). Veterans are particularly vulnerable to addiction, as many veterans with chronic, painful health conditions face challenges reintegrating into society after serving in the military. Recent studies have found that compared with 6.5% of veterans without mental health disorders, 17.8% of veterans with PTSD and 11.7% with other mental health diagnoses but without PTSD received opioid prescriptions for pain diagnoses. Of those who were prescribed pain medication, veterans with PTSD were more likely than those without mental health disorders to receive higher-dose opioids, receive two or more opioids concurrently, receive sedative hypnotics concurrently, or obtain early opioid refills. Further, receiving prescription opioids was associated with an increased risk of adverse clinical outcomes such as self-inflicted injuries, overdoses, and violence-related injuries for all veterans, which was most pronounced in veterans with PTSD (Seal et al., 2012). In 2010, 60% of the drug overdose deaths in the U.S. were related to prescription medications, with veterans twice as likely to die from a drug overdose as non-veterans (Bohnert, Ilgen, Galea, McCarthy & Blow, 2011).

While comorbid chronic pain and PTSD predicts higher levels of depression and anxiety (Outcalt, Ang, et al., 2014), PTSD influences disability beyond the effects of mood disorders (Outcalt et al., 2015). Even after controlling for depression in a sample of patients with chronic pain, the presence of PTSD predicted lower quality of life, more disability, and worse physical functioning (Outcalt et al., 2015). Pain self-efficacy, pain catastrophizing, and the centrality of pain were worse among veterans with comorbid pain and PTSD than with veterans who had pain alone (Outcalt, Ang, et al., 2014). Comorbidity between chronic pain and PTSD also impacts the extent to which the disorders interfere with daily activities and physical well-being. Veterans who present with comorbid pain and PTSD symptoms utilize more healthcare resources than veterans who present with pain or PTSD alone (Outcalt, Yu, et al., 2014).

PTSD also is related to the number of disability days, even after controlling for depression (Outcalt et al., 2015). The heightened level of interference also appears among youth who experience comorbidity of pain and PTSD. A study found that youth with chronic pain and PTSD symptoms had lower health-related quality of life (as measured using the Pediatric Quality of Life Inventory, which assesses physical, emotional, school, and social functioning variables) (Noel et al., 2016).

Altered Pain Processing

Some research has sought to determine whether PTSD impacts how individuals process painful sensations. Defrin and colleagues (2008) compared the differences in how individuals with PTSD, anxiety, or a healthy control group perceived a variety of somatosensory and painful experimentally induced stimuli. The individuals with PTSD reported the highest levels of chronic pain and more regions of the body where they experienced pain. Interestingly, sensory testing indicated that participants with PTSD had higher pain thresholds; however, when they experienced suprathreshold mechanical and heat stimuli, the group with PTSD rated their experience as more intense than the other groups (Defrin et al., 2008).

There is, however, contradictory evidence about the ways in which individuals with PTSD process pain. While some studies have found that the pain thresholds of participants with PTSD are higher compared to non-PTSD participants, other studies have found they are lower, and still others found no differences (Moeller-Bertram, Keltner, & Strigo, 2012). There is clearly a need for continued studies in this area before definitive conclusions can be reached.

There is some evidence that individuals with PTSD (Jenewein et al., 2016) and pain-related conditions such as fibromyalgia (Jenewein et al., 2013) have deficits in their contingency learning abilities, as well as difficulty distinguishing between cues that consistently predict non-painful stimuli and those that sometimes predict painful and sometimes predict non-painful stimuli. In other words, individuals with PTSD may be more likely to experience a fearful response that generalizes beyond specific stimuli, and this may contribute to the link between PTSD and chronic pain. Using a painful unconditioned stimulus paradigm, Jenewein and colleagues (2016) examined whether patients with PTSD, compared with a group of matched healthy control participants, exhibited an impaired response to fear conditioning. In terms of their fear ratings, patients who had PTSD were less able to distinguish between a conditioned visual stimulus which was always followed by a non-painful unconditioned stimulus (i.e., a "safe" visual stimulus) compared with a conditioned visual stimulus that was followed by a painful unconditioned stimulus half of the time (i.e., an "unsafe" visual stimulus). The authors attribute this impairment to a "fear-learning deficit" among patients with PTSD and suggest that patients with PTSD might be more likely to overgeneralize their fear reactions; they may have deficiencies in their ability to inhibit fear; or they may be more vulnerable to conditioning within a context. The authors also suggest that, because of these fear-learning deficiencies, patients with PTSD may be more likely to generalize fear and experience greater levels of anxiety and sensitivity to pain (Jenewein et al., 2016).

Theoretical Models of Pain and PTSD Comorbidity

At the turn of the century, researchers began proposing theoretical models that might explain the considerable rates of concurrence between chronic pain and PTSD (Asmundson, Coons, Taylor, & Katz, 2002; Otis, Pincus, & Keane, 2006; Brennstuhl et al., 2015; Sharp & Harvey, 2001). Sharp and Harvey presented one of the first of these, the Mutual Maintenance Model, in 2001. Shortly thereafter, the Shared Vulnerability Model was proposed (Asmundson et al., 2002). In subsequent years, there has been growing discussion regarding whether the connection between chronic pain and PTSD may be maintained and mediated by other factors like negative emotions including anxiety and depression. The Triple Vulnerability Model, which was originally proposed as a model of the etiology of anxiety by Barlow (2002), was extended by Otis et al. (2006) to help explain the concurrence between chronic pain and PTSD. Additional research focuses on possibly complex and interweaving etiologies between trauma and pain (Brennstuhl et al., 2015). The various models of pain and PTSD are not mutually exclusive (Asmundson & Katz, 2009; Asmundson et al., 2002), and they continue to be explored through several research programs examining the onset and course of chronic pain and PTSD following potentially traumatic events (Brennstuhl et al., 2015; Jenewein et al., 2009; Stratton et al., 2014).

The following is a brief review of several models describing the potential interaction between chronic pain and PTSD.

Mutual Maintenance Model

The Mutual Maintenance Model was one of the first models to provide an explanatory account of the high degree of comorbidity between chronic pain and PTSD. Sharp and Harvey (2001) reviewed years of evidence and identified several potential mechanisms through which PTSD and chronic pain may mutually maintain one another. The first mechanism, attentional biases, disposes people with PTSD to attend disproportionately to stimuli that could be threatening, while chronic pain sufferers attend disproportionately to pain. Second, sensitivity to anxiety is a mechanism whereby both groups over-attend to anxiety cues, potentially misinterpreting them. This acute sensitivity also may be accompanied by catastrophic cognitions and a more intense, fearful response to anxiety cues. A third mechanism is that chronic pain may serve as an ongoing reminder of the trauma, precipitating arousal and avoidance. Fourth, persistent avoidance in coping exacerbates both conditions. For people with chronic pain, the avoidance of exertion leads to more physical vulnerability. For people with PTSD, the avoidance prevents them from activating the fear network and thus prevents possible resolution, serving to maintain arousal and the associated symptoms. Fifth, depression reduces healthy activity in both chronic pain and PTSD patients, decreasing physical activity for chronic pain sufferers and reducing the likelihood that PTSD sufferers will be exposed to stimuli related to the trauma that would help them engage in healthy processing. Sixth, anxiety intensifies the perception of pain, and because anxiety is present in PTSD, the perception of pain is increased, leading to more disability and restricted activity. Finally, both conditions are characterized by higher levels of maladaptive cognitive strategies, thereby reducing the resources that can be devoted to healthier and more adaptive cognitions.

Shared Vulnerability Model

According to the Shared Vulnerability Model, there is a subset of mutual maintenance factors that could render an individual vulnerable to developing both PTSD and chronic pain (Asmundson & Katz, 2009; Asmundson et al., 2002). Environmentally driven exposures (e.g., combat, motor vehicle accidents, sexual assault) in combination with vulnerabilities such as a predisposition to harm avoidance, the trait of negative affectivity, anxiety sensitivity (i.e., fear of the symptoms of anxiety), and a low alarm threshold (i.e., the physiological aspects of the fight or flight processes) may trigger an emotional response that contributes to the development of PTSD and chronic pain. In particular, anxiety sensitivity has emerged as a dispositional characteristic that may account for these high levels of comorbidity. Asmundson and colleagues proposed that the shared vulnerabilities may be influenced by genetic factors. In the presence of a traumatic event, dispositional characteristics like anxiety sensitivity may combine with other person-level characteristics, like lower thresholds for the perception of threat and a selective attention to threatening cues, to produce agitation, anxiety, and other emotional responses (Asmundson et al., 2002; Asmundson & Katz, 2009).

Triple Vulnerability Model

According to the Triple Vulnerability Model, three vulnerabilities must be present in order for an anxiety disorder to develop: a biological vulnerability, a generalized psychological vulnerability (e.g., experiences of low control over environment, over-controlling parents), and a specific psychological vulnerability (e.g., experiences that might focus anxiety on a specific situation or object such as social anxiety, panic, specific phobia) (Barlow, 2002). Otis and colleagues (2006) extended this model to explain the comorbidity of chronic pain and PTSD by suggesting that there may be related biological, psychological, and specialized psychological vulnerabilities that contribute to the development of both disorders, and that vulnerability to experience one of the disorders may actually contribute to the development of the other.

The first vulnerability is a generalized biological vulnerability in the form of a genetically inherited tendency to respond anxiously when faced with a threat, such as a painful injury or a traumatic event. Evidence is accumulating that supports a genetic predisposition in the development of PTSD (Cornelis, Nugent, Amstadter, & Koenen, 2010), and recent studies are examining the role of genetics in a number of chronic pain conditions (Jacobsen et al., 2013; James, 2017).

The second vulnerability is a general psychological vulnerability based upon childhood learning experiences that instill ideas such as "the world is not a safe place" and "people cannot be trusted," or that foster a sense that events are uncontrollable. These vulnerabilities can develop when parents either are overly restrictive or neglectful, and/or when children cannot develop the skills and self-confidence necessary to navigate or overcome obstacles. Thus, this vulnerability may set the stage for the use of ineffective coping responses later in life.

The third vulnerability is a specific psychological vulnerability in which people learn to focus their anxiety on specific situations. As found in the literature, exposure to a traumatic event (e.g., abuse, military combat, painful injury) is not sufficient in and of itself to cause one to develop chronic pain or PTSD. One must develop the sense that these events, including one's own emotional reactions to them, are proceeding in an unpredictable and uncontrollable manner. Thus, when negative emotions and a sense of uncontrollability arise, chronic pain or PTSD may emerge.

One particular specific psychological vulnerability that may influence the development of chronic pain and PTSD is catastrophizing. Catastrophizing is a key factor in the transition from acute to chronic pain (Vlaeyen & Linton, 2000) and has also been described as a vulnerability in the development of PTSD (Bryant & Guthrie, 2007). Research indicates that veterans with PTSD and pain report significantly less control over their pain, greater impact of emotions on their pain, and a greater use of catastrophizing than veterans who have chronic pain but no significant PTSD symptoms (Alschuler & Otis, 2012).

Importantly, while the Triple Vulnerability Model implies that biological and psychological vulnerabilities to develop chronic pain and PTSD may already exist, notably the model also acknowledges that these vulnerabilities can be moderated to some extent by variables such as the presence and use of adaptive coping skills and social support. This suggests that treatment interventions with the goals of increasing a person's sense of controllability over salient events and challenging catastrophic thinking may be well suited for pain and PTSD.

Psychological Treatment for Comorbid Chronic Pain and PTSD

Clinicians often describe challenges when attempting to provide effective clinical care for patients who have both chronic pain and PTSD. For example, some clinicians report that when providing therapy for patients with pain and PTSD, symptoms such as hypervigilance and avoidance can interfere with establishing pain treatment goals related to being more physically active or increasing social activities. Difficulties also can arise when treatment starts to focus on helping patients examine and challenge their own beliefs related to pain. Due to factors such as avoidance, these patients are at risk for dropping out of treatment prematurely or simply never returning to treatment. Similarly, clinicians providing care for patients with PTSD often describe how trauma-related treatment can increase the self-report of chronic pain and the observation of avoidance behaviors that can interfere with treatment progress. Clinicians report feeling frustrated that they lack the training and ability to address both of these related conditions. As a result of this interaction, patients may not receive an adequate dose of treatment for either pain or PTSD.

In an effort to develop a more seamless and effective system for treating patients with comorbid pain and PTSD, Plagge, Lu, Lovejoy, Karl, and Dobscha (2013) investigated the use of a collaborative care and behavioral activation approach to the treatment of pain and PTSD in a sample of 58 Iraq and Afghanistan veterans. Using a collaborative treatment approach involving a physiatrist, psychologist, and practitioners in primary care, the treatment team conducted a biopsychosocial assessment of the participants' needs and developed treatment recommendations for providers. The treatment consisted of eight sessions of a behavioral activation for PTSD treatment that included pain management skills such as relaxation training and anger management. Specialties such as occupational therapy, mental health, and physical therapy were included as needed. The results indicated significant improvements in PTSD, pain severity, and interference. In addition, participants reported being satisfied with the program.

Another approach to addressing the experience of chronic pain and PTSD has been to treat both conditions simultaneously. Using the Triple Vulnerability Model as a guide for determining the essential elements of treatment, Otis, Keane, Kerns, Monson, and Scioli (2009) developed and pilot tested an integrated treatment for veterans with chronic pain and PTSD. Using a multi-step approach that included meetings with research collaborators with specific expertise in chronic pain and PTSD treatment to decide on treatment elements, tailoring the treatment based on feedback from patients and therapists, and developing treatment manuals for standardization, a 12-session integrated treatment for chronic pain and PTSD was created. The treatment included several components from cognitive processing therapy (CPT) for PTSD (Monson et al., 2006) and CBT for chronic pain management (Otis, 2007).

Although study data supported the feasibility of this treatment approach, a number of limitations were identified over the course of the study (Otis et al., 2009). First, it was not uncommon for participants to arrive late or miss therapy sessions. Study therapists noted that missed appointments created gaps in the treatment that reduced retention of information between sessions and decreased the participants' ability to learn and effectively deploy skills as needed. Feedback from some participants suggested that they did not want to come to the VA Hospital for 12 sessions, as they were hoping for more immediate relief from their symptoms. Several participants asked whether a "quicker" form of therapy was available to help them regain their function and quality of life. This feedback precipitated interest in developing an integrated treatment that could be delivered in a more "intensive" manner.

Otis, Pincus, Scioli-Salter, Keane, and Comer (manuscript submitted for publication) developed and pilot tested the Pain and Trauma Intensive Outpatient Treatment (PATRIOT) Program, a brief, intensive (three-week, six-session) integrated chronic pain and PTSD treatment. The overall goal was to develop a program that was 1) effective and acceptable to veterans; 2) practical to use by therapists; and 3) transportable (so it could be used in any clinical setting). The substantial literature documenting the efficacy of intensively delivered treatment approaches for psychological disorders supported this approach to treatment (Craske, Maidenberg, & Bystritsky, 1995; Hazlet-Stevens & Craske, 2002; Morisette, Spiegel, & Heinrichs, 2005; Deacon & Abramowitz, 2006).

During treatment development, it was decided that several unique elements would be included. Specifically, study therapists from the initial 12-session program had reported that some of the cognitive elements (i.e., trust/safety, intimacy, and self-esteem) did not resonate with every veteran. For example, veterans who did not have issues with intimacy seemed less engaged when discussing material covering that topic. In order to address this concern, it was decided that although the PATRIOT Program would continue to have a strong cognitive component, the information presented would be tailored to each veteran's specific needs. Three modules were created to accomplish this goal: Module 1 = Anger Management, Module 2 = Power and Control, and Module 3 = Safety and Trust. This modification enabled the therapist to deliver content tailored to the needs of the individual patient. For instance, if the patient and the therapist collaboratively determined that the patient's maladaptive cognitions were predominately stuck on decisions made by powerful others or thoughts that he/she lacked the ability to make changes in his/her life, the therapy session would focus on content delivered in Module 2. However, all three modules were made available for the patient to review.

Research demonstrating a high prevalence of sleep problems in veterans with chronic pain and PTSD prompted the inclusion of a stronger sleep hygiene component and skills to address nightmares. In addition, a greater emphasis was placed on teaching ways of developing and maintaining social support.

A therapist manual and a patient workbook were created with key elements of treatment identified in each session. Eight veterans with pain and PTSD participated in the study. At post-treatment there were significant reductions in PTSD symptoms based upon the Clinician Administered Assessment of PTSD (CAPS). Reductions in depressive symptoms, pain, and catastrophic thinking also were observed from pre- to post-treatment. No veterans dropped out of the treatments. Participants and therapists jointly agreed that delivering treatment on a more intensive schedule allowed for the development of increased therapeutic momentum and patient–therapist connection.

With continued support and controlled evaluations, the PATRIOT Program may offer a brief, cost-effective, and more easily accessible treatment option for individuals who could benefit from learning skills to manage chronic pain and PTSD. Although this study was conducted with veterans, this approach might be particularly helpful in certain civilian clinical settings, i.e., where the patient cannot come repeatedly to a clinic for therapy sessions even though he/she has experienced chronic pain and varied traumas.

Clinical Implications for Assessment and Treatment and Future Directions

Given the high rates of comorbidity between chronic pain and PTSD, it is likely that many patients who seek care for chronic pain are also experiencing symptoms of PTSD. Considering the manner in which these two conditions may interact with one another, it is important that clinicians assess for PTSD when conducting chronic pain evaluations. Patients are often well aware of how their experience of pain and PTSD interact with one other.

While clinicians may anticipate that the onset of pain and PTSD are associated with the same event, this is not always the case. In a recent randomized controlled trial assessing chronic pain and PTSD in a VA Medical Center, approximately 50% of veterans reported that their first traumatic experience preceded their military service. There were often multiple traumatic experiences that occurred throughout life; when asked to rate which traumatic event was the most bothersome, many veterans reported that childhood traumatic experiences troubled them the most.

In addition to asking about trauma exposure over the course of a person's life in the clinical interview, the clinician can choose from a number of quick and easily administered self-report questionnaires to assess for PTSD symptoms. For example, the PTSD Checklist (PCL) is a brief, 17-item self-report questionnaire designed to assess PTSD symptomatology. Presented with a list of PTSD symptoms, patients indicate the extent to which they have been bothered by each symptom during the past month using a 5-point Likert-type scale (Weathers et al., 2013). Versions of the PCL exist for military personnel (PCL-M), civilians (PCL-C), and for specific identified stressors (PCL-S; Weathers et al., 2013).

Other key areas to explore during the chronic pain assessment include the use of maladaptive coping strategies such as catastrophizing and avoidance, both of which likely are to be involved in the maintenance of pain and PTSD. Exploring the relationship between pain and PTSD in the interview or through written homework assignments may be an effective way to educate patients about how pain and PTSD interact with one another, and to help them more effectively process the meaning of the traumatic event.

Understanding how PTSD has impacted a patient's life enables a therapist to deliver treatment in a more thoughtful and effective manner. The presence of a trauma history sometimes can cause unexpected reactions to interventions that might seem to have a low likelihood of causing harm or distress. Consider the following example:

> I was teaching a veteran with chronic knee pain some strategies for learning how to relax. That afternoon, the topic was diaphragm breathing and visual imagery. I was sitting in front of the patient in a chair and he had started practicing deep breathing. I had already collected information from him describing a relaxing place he wanted to visualize in his mind while he was practicing breathing. For him, the image was of a beautiful green hillside on a summer day, a clear blue sky, with a slight breeze. I looked at my notes for a moment and guided him through the practice with his description of the image I had written down on my notepad, but when I looked up from my notes there were tears running down his face. I stopped the practice and asked him what was happening. He responded, "I was there, I could see the hillside, and smell the fresh air . . . and then the shells just started coming down." Unknown to me, my patient had a trauma history of receiving incoming mortar fire in Vietnam and I had just unraveled his defenses.

This example highlights the importance of assessing and understanding all of the vulnerabilities that patients bring with them into treatment. While this specific example was military in nature, similar patient reactions can result from other types of trauma or loss.

Patients who have chronic pain and PTSD can present in a variety of ways. Some patients may hesitate to engage in activities that typically are part of CBT for chronic pain. For example, patients with PTSD may be less likely to engage in behavioral activation activities that involve increased socialization and seeking out of social support if there were violations related to trust associated with the traumatic event.

Similarly, when conducting cognitive exercises that involve developing alternate ways of thinking about pain, a patient with PTSD may adopt a "worst case scenario" approach to coping with life's challenges. He/she may resist suggestions by a therapist that his/her way of thinking is non-adaptive or somehow flawed. Providers also may encounter patients with pain and PTSD who have prior experience with addiction and are wary of taking any type of pain medication that might lead them down a path toward substance abuse. These individuals are highly motivated to find non-pharmacological methods to manage their symptoms.

A provider may experience heightened levels of apprehension about how to provide the best care once he/she realizes that the chronic pain patient also has PTSD. Providers should keep an open mind, assessing the patient's motivation to engage in interventions prior to developing and assigning goals, and explaining the rationale behind various approaches. A diagnosis of PTSD should never be used to exclude a person from CBT for pain; each person is unique and his/her individual experience should be used to guide clinical decision-making.

If an integrated approach to pain and PTSD treatment is not feasible, or if addressing symptoms of one condition is necessary for treatment to proceed (e.g., patient experiences difficulty trusting the provider, improper use of pain medication or substances, severe depression, active homicidal or suicidal ideation), then those areas should be addressed prior to implementing CBT in order to maximize treatment effectiveness. Consider involving a physician if there is concern about a pain medication plan, or if other comorbid psychiatric disorders need to be addressed. Given the importance of increased activity and strengthening to the management of chronic pain, rehabilitation therapists (i.e., occupational therapists and physical therapists) should be included whenever possible to assist in developing safe and achievable activity goals.

Future research is needed to refine and test theoretical models describing the interaction between chronic pain and PTSD. Potential mechanisms that may serve to maintain both conditions should be investigated, including both neurobiological mechanisms and underlying vulnerabilities. Research should prioritize developing and testing treatments that specifically target the mechanisms and vulnerabilities underlying both pain and PTSD. For example, a pilot study is currently underway at the Center for Anxiety and Related Disorders at Boston University to assess the feasibility, acceptability, and potential efficacy of utilizing the unified protocol for transdiagnostic treatment of emotional disorders (UP; Barlow et al., 2017) with patients who have chronic pain and comorbid emotional disorders (Otis, 2018). As evidence-based treatments for pain and PTSD are developed, it is important that we expand the "reach" of our evidence-based treatments for these disorders so that they can be made available for the widest possible number of patients in need of services.

Taken together, all of this research will help increase our understanding of these disorders and their efficacious treatment. Ultimately, this research should translate into improving treatments for patients suffering from pain and PTSD so that more people gain the skills necessary to return to healthy everyday functioning.

References

Alschuler, K., & Otis, J. D. (2012). Coping strategies and beliefs about pain in veterans with comorbid chronic pain and significant levels of posttraumatic stress disorder symptoms. *European Journal of Pain, 16*(2), 312–319. doi:10.1016/j.ejpain. 2011.06.010

American Psychiatric, Association, D. S. M. T. F. (2013). *Diagnostic and statistical manual of mental disorders: DSM-5*. Retrieved from http://dsm.psychiatryonline.org/book. aspx?bookid=556

Asmundson, G. J. G., Coons, M. J., Taylor, S., & Katz, J. (2002). PTSD and the experience of pain: Research and clinical implications of shared vulnerability and mutual maintenance models. *Canadian Journal of Psychiatry, 47*(10), 930–937. doi:10.1177/070674370204701004

Asmundson, G. J. G., & Katz, J. (2009). Understanding the co-occurrence of anxiety disorders and chronic pain: State-of-the-art. *Depression and Anxiety, 26*, 888–901. doi:10.1002/da.20600

Asmundson, G. J. G., Wright, K. D., & Stein, M. B. (2004). Pain and PTSD symptoms in female veterans. *European Journal of Pain, 8*(4), 345–350. doi:10.1016/j.ejpain.2003.10.008

Bair, M. J., Robinson, R. L., Katon, W., & Kroenke, K. (2003). Depression and pain comorbidity: A literature review. *Archives of Internal Medicine, 163*(20), 2433–2445. doi:10.1001/archinte.163.20.2433

Banks, S. M., & Kerns, R. D. (1996). Explaining high rates of depression in chronic pain: A diathesis-stress framework. *Psychological Bulletin, 119*(1), 95–110. doi:10.1037/0033-2909.119.1.95

Barlow, D. H. (2002). *Anxiety and its disorders* (2nd ed.). New York, NY: The Guilford Press.

Barlow, D. H., Farchione, T. J., Bullis, J. R., Gallagher, M. W., Murray-Latin, H., Sauer-Zavala, S., . . . Cassiello-Robbins, C. (2017). The unified protocol for transdiagnostic treatment of emotional disorders compared with diagnosis-specific protocols for anxiety disorders. *JAMA Psychiatry, 74*(9), 867–868. doi:10.1001/jamapsychiatry.2017.2164

Bohnert, A. S., Ilgen, M. A., Galea, S., McCarthy, J. F., & Blow, F. C. (2011). Accidental poisoning mortality among patients in the Department of Veterans Affairs Health System. *Med Care, 49*, 393–396. doi:10.1097/MLR.0b013e318202aa27

Breivik, H., Collett, B., Ventafridda, V., Cohen, R., & Gallacher, D. (2006). Survey of chronic pain in Europe: Prevalence, impact on daily life, and treatment. *European Journal of Pain, 10*(4), 287–333. doi:10.1016/j.ejpain.2005.06.009

Brennstuhl, M., Tarquinio, C., & Montel, S. (2015). Chronic pain and PTSD: Evolving views on their comorbidity. *Perspectives in Psychiatric Care, 51*(4), 295–304. doi:10.1111/ppc.12093

Bryant, R. A., & Guthrie, R. M. (2007). Maladaptive self-appraisals before trauma exposure predict posttraumatic stress disorder. *Journal of Consulting and Clinical Psychology, 75*(5), 812–815. doi:10.1037/0022-006X.75.5.812

Campbell, D. G., Felker, B. L., Liu, C. F., Yano, E. M., Kirchner, J. E., Chan, D., . . . Chaney, E. F. (2007). Prevalence of depression-PTSD comorbidity: Implications for clinical practice guidelines and primary care-based interventions. *Journal of General Internal Medicine, 22*(6), 711–718. doi:10.1007/s11606-006-0101-4

Cochran, G., Bacci, J. L., Ylioja, T., Hruschak, V., Miller, S., Seybert, A. L., & Tarter, R. (2016). Prescription opioid use: Patient characteristics and misuse in community pharmacy. *Journal of the American Pharmacists Association, 56*(3), 248–256. doi:10.1016/j.japh.2016.02.012

Cornelis, M. C., Nugent, N. R., Amstadter, A. B., & Koenen, K. C. (2010). Genetics of posttraumatic stress disorder: Review and recommendations for genome-wide association studies. *Current Psychiatry Reports, 12*(4), 313–326. doi:10.1007/s11920-010-0126-6

Craske, M. G., Maidenberg, E., & Bystritsky, A. (1995). Brief cognitive-behavioral versus nondirective therapy for panic disorder. *Journal of Behavior Therapy & Experimental Psychiatry, 26*, 113–120. doi:10.1016/0005-7916(95)00003-I

Deacon, B. J., & Abramowitz, J. S. (2006). A pilot study of two-day cognitive-behavioral therapy for panic disorder. *Behaviour Research and Therapy, 44*, 807–817. doi:10.1016/j.brat.2005.05.008

Defrin, R., Ginzburg, K., Solomon, Z., Polad, E., Bloch, M., Govezensky, M., & Schreiber, S. (2008). Quantitative testing of pain perception in subjects with PTSD—Implications for the mechanism of the coexistence between PTSD and chronic pain. *Pain, 138*(2), 450–459. doi:10.1016/j.pain.2008.05.006

Ehring, T., & Quack, D. (2010). Emotion regulation difficulties in trauma survivors: The role of trauma type and PTSD symptom severity. *Behavior Therapy, 41*(4), 587–598. doi:10.1016/j.beth.2010.04.004

Elliott, T. E., Renier, C. M., & Palcher, J. A. (2003). Chronic pain, depression, and quality of life: Correlations and predictive value of the SF-36. *Pain Medicine*, *4*(4), 331–339. doi:10.1111/j.1526-4637.2003.03040.x

Fishbain, D. A., Pulikal, A., Lewis, J. E., & Gao, J. (2017). Chronic pain types differ in their reported prevalence of Post -Traumatic Stress Disorder (PTSD) and there is consistent evidence that chronic pain is associated with ptsd: An evidence-based structured systematic review. *Pain Medicine*, *18*(4), 711–735. doi:10.1093/pm/pnw065

Flink, I. L., Boersma, K., & Linton, S. J. (2013). Pain Catastrophizing as repetitive negative thinking: A development of the conceptualization. *Cognitive Behaviour Therapy*, *42*(3), 215–223. doi:10.1080/16506073.2013.769621

Gaskin, D. J., & Richard, P. (2012). The economic costs of pain in the United States. *The Journal of Pain*, *13*(8), 715–724. doi:10.1016/j.jpain.2012.03.009

Ginzburg, K., Ein-Dor, T., & Solomon, Z. (2010). Comorbidity of posttraumatic stress disorder, anxiety and depression: A 20-year longitudinal study of war veterans. *Journal of Affective Disorders*, *123*(1–3), 249–257. doi:10.1016/j.jad.2009.08.006

Hazlet-Stevens, H., & Craske, M. G. (2002). Brief cognitive-behavioral therapy: Definition and scientific foundations. In F. W. Bond & W. Dryden (Eds.), *Handbook of brief cognitive behaviour therapy*. New York, NY: John Wiley & Sons.

International Association for the Study of Pain (IASP) Taxonomy. (2012). *Descriptions of chronic pain syndromes and definitions of pain terms* (2nd ed.). Seattle: IASP Press. Retrieved from: https://www.iasp-pain.org/Education/Content.aspx?ItemNumber=1698&navItemNumber=576

Jacobsen, L. M., Schistad, E. L., Storesund, A., Pedersen, L. M., Espeland, A., Rygh, L. J., & Gjerstad, J. (2013). The MMP1 rs1799750 2G allele is associated with increased low back pain, sciatica, and disability after lumbar disk herniation. *Clinical Journal of Pain*, *29*(11), 967–971. doi:10.1097/AJP.0b013e31827df7fd

James, S. K. (2017). Chronic postsurgical pain: Is there a possible genetic link? *British Journal of Pain*, *11*(4), 1178–185. doi:10.1177/2049463717723222

Jenewein, J., Erni, J., Moergeli, H., Grillon, C., Schumacher, S., Mueller-Pfeiffer, C., . . . Hasler, G. (2016). Altered pain perception and fear-learning deficits in subjects with posttraumatic stress disorder. *The Journal of Pain*, *17*(12), 1325–1333. doi:10.1016/j.jpain.2016.09.002

Jenewein, J., Moergeli, H., Sprott, H., Honegger, D., Brunner, L., Ettlin, D., . . . Hasler, G. (2013). Fear-learning deficits in subjects with fibromyalgia syndrome? *European Journal of Pain*, *17*(9), 1374–1384. doi:10.1002/j.1532-2149.2013.00300.x

Jenewein, J., Moergeli, H., Wittmann, L., Büchi, S., Kraemer, B., & Schnyder, U. (2009). Development of chronic pain following severe accidental injury: Results of a 3-year follow-up study. *Journal of Psychosomatic Research*, *66*(2), 119–126. doi:10.1016/j.jpsychores.2008.07.011

Kilpatrick, D. G., Resnick, H. S., Milanak, M. E., Miller, M. W., Keyes, K. M., & Friedman, M. J. (2013). National estimates of exposure to traumatic events and PTSD prevalence using DSM-IV and DSM-5 criteria. *Journal of Traumatic Stress*, *26*(5), 537–547. doi:10.1002/jts.21848

Koenen, K. C., Ratanatharathorn, A., Ng, L., McLaughlin, K. A., Bromet, E. J., Stein, D. J., & . . . Kessler, R. C. (2017). Posttraumatic stress disorder in the World Mental Health Surveys. *Psychological Medicine*, *47*(13), 2260–2274. doi:10.1017/S0033291717000708

Liebschutz, J., Saitz, R., Brower, V., Keane, T. M., Lloyd-Travaglini, C., Averbuch, T., & Samet, J. H. (2007). PTSD in urban primary care: High prevalence and low physician recognition. *Journal of General Internal Medicine*, *22*(6), 719–726. http://doi.org/10.1007/s11606-007-0161-0

Macdonald, A., Danielson, C. K., Resnick, H. S., Saunders, B. E., & Kilpatrick, D. G. (2010). PTSD and comorbid disorders in a representative sample of adolescents: The risk associated with multiple exposures to potentially traumatic events. *Child Abuse & Neglect, 34*(10), 773–783. doi:10.1016/j.chiabu.2010.03.006

Moeller-Bertram, T., Keltner, J., & Strigo, I. A. (2012). Pain and posttraumatic stress disorder—Review of clinical and experimental evidence. *Neuropharmacology, 62*(2), 586–597. doi:10.1016/j.neuropharm.2011.04.028

Monson, C. M., Schnurr, P. P., Resick, P. A., Friedman, M. J., Young-Xu, Y., & Stevens, S. P. (2006). Cognitive processing therapy for veterans with military-related posttraumatic stress disorder. *Journal of Consulting and Clinical Psychology, 74*(5), 898–907. doi:10.1037/0022–006x.74.5.898

Morisette, S. B., Spiegel, D. A., & Heinrichs, N. (2005). Sensation-focused intensive treatment for panic disorder with moderate to severe agoraphobia. *Cognitive and Behavioral Practice, 12*, 17–29. doi:10.1016/S1077-7229(05)80036-7

Nahin, R. L. (2015). Estimates of pain prevalence and severity in adults: United States, 2012. *The Journal of Pain, 16*(8), 769–780. doi:10.1016/j.jpain.2015.05.002

Nahin, R. L. (2017). Severe pain in veterans: The effect of age and sex, and comparisons with the general population. *The Journal of Pain, 18*(3), 247–254. doi:10.1016/j.jpain.2016.10.021

Noel, M., Wilson, A. C., Holley, A. L., Durkin, L., Patton, M., & Palermo, T. M. (2016). Posttraumatic stress disorder symptoms in youth with vs without chronic pain. *Pain, 157*(10), 2277–2284. doi:10.1097/j.pain.0000000000000642

Otis, J. D. (2007). *Managing chronic pain: A cognitive-behavioral therapy approach, therapist guide.* Treatments that Work Series. New York, NY: Oxford University Press.

Otis, J. D. (2018). The application of the unified protocol for transdiagnostic treatment of emotional disorders to chronic pain. *The Behavior Therapist, 41*, 248–252.

Otis, J. D., Keane, T., Kerns, R. D., Monson, C., & Scioli, E. (2009). The development of an integrated treatment for veterans with comorbid chronic pain and posttraumatic stress disorder. *Pain Medicine, 10*(7), 1300–1311. doi:10.1111/j.1526-4637.2009.00715.x

Otis, J. D., Pincus, D. P., Scioli-Salter, E., Keane, T., & Comer, J. S. Intensive treatment of chronic pain and PTSD: The PATRIOT program. Manuscript submitted for publication.

Otis, J. D., Pincus, D. B., & Keane, T. M. (2006). Comorbid chronic pain and posttraumatic stress disorder across the lifespan: A review of theoretical models. In G. Young, K. Nicholson, & A. W. Kane (Eds.), *Psychological knowledge in court: PTSD, pain, and TBI* (pp. 242–268). Boston, MA: Springer.

Outcalt, S. D. P., Ang, D. C. M. D., Wu, J. M. S., Sargent, C. B. A., Yu, Z. P., & Bair, M. J. M. D. M. S. (2014). Pain experience of Iraq and Afghanistan Veterans with comorbid chronic pain and posttraumatic stress. *Journal of Rehabilitation Research and Development, 51*(4), 559–570. doi:10.1682/JRRD.2013.06.0134

Outcalt, S. D. P., Kroenke, K., Krebs, E. E., Chumbler, N. R., Wu, J., Yu, Z., & Bair, M. J. (2015). Chronic pain and comorbid mental health conditions: Independent associations of posttraumatic stress disorder and depression with pain, disability, and quality of life. *Journal of Behavioral Medicine, 38*(3), 535–543. doi:10.1007/s10865-015-9628-3

Outcalt, S. D. P., Yu, Z., Hoen, H. M., Pennington, T. M., & Krebs, E. E. (2014). Health care utilization among veterans with pain and posttraumatic stress symptoms. *Pain Medicine, 15*(11), 1872–1879. doi:10.1111/pme.12045

Palyo, S. A., & Beck, J. G. (2005). Post-traumatic stress disorder symptoms, pain, and perceived life control: Associations with psychosocial and physical functioning. *Pain, 117*(1–2), 121–127. doi:10.1016/j.pain.2005.05.028

Plagge, P. M., Lu, M. W., Lovejoy, T. I., Karl, A. I., & Dobscha, S. K. (2013). Treatment of Comorbid Pain and PTSD in returning veterans: A collaborative approach utilizing. *Behavioral Activation, Pain Medicine, 14*(8), 1164–1172. doi:10.1111/pme.12155

Powell, M. A., Corbo, V., Fonda, J., Otis, J. D., Milberg, W., & McGlinchey, R. (2015). Sleep quality and re-experiencing symptoms of posttraumatic stress disorder predict reported physical pain in OEF/OIF veterans. *Journal of Traumatic Stress, 28,* 322–329.

Racine, M., Moulin, D. E., Nielson, W. R., Morley-Forster, P. K., Lynch, M., Clark, A. J., . . . Jensen, M. P. (2016). The reciprocal associations between catastrophizing and pain outcomes in patients being treated for neuropathic pain: A cross-lagged panel analysis study. *Pain, 157*(9), 1946–1953. doi:10.1097/j.pain.0000000000000594

Ramirez-Maestre, C., Esteve, R., Ruiz-Parraga, G., Gomez-Perez, L., & Lopez-Martinez, A. E. (2017). The key role of pain catastrophizing in the disability of patients with acute back pain. *International Journal of Behavioral Medicine, 24*(2), 239–248. doi:10.1007/s12529-016-9600-9

Riskowski, J. L. (2014). Associations of socioeconomic position and pain prevalence in the United States: Findings from the National Health and Nutrition Examination Survey. *Pain Medicine, 15*(9), 1508–1521. doi:10.1111/pme.12528

Roberts, A. L., Gilman, S. E., Breslau, J., Breslau, N., & Koenen, K. C. (2011). Race/ethnic differences in exposure to traumatic events, development of post-traumatic stress disorder, and treatment-seeking for post-traumatic stress disorder in the United States. *Psychological Medicine, 41*(1), 71–83. doi:10.1017/S0033291710000401

Sareen, J., Cox, B. J., Stein, M. B., Afifi, T. O., Fleet, C., & Asmundson, G. G. (2007). Physical and mental comorbidity, disability, and suicidal behavior associated with posttraumatic stress disorder in a large community sample. *Psychosomatic Medicine, 69*(3), 242–248. doi:10.1097/PSY.0b013e31803146d8

Schwartz, A. C., Bradley, R., Penza, K. M., Sexton, M., Jay, D., Haggard, P. J., Garlow, S. J., & Ressler, K. J. (2006). Pain medication use among patients with posttraumatic stress disorder. *Psychosomatics, 47,* 136–142. doi:10.1176/appi.psy.47.2.136

Scioli-Salter, E. R., Forman, D. E., Otis, J. D., Gregor, K., Valovski, I., & Rasmusson, A. M. (2015). The shared neuroanatomy and neurobiology of comorbid chronic pain and PTSD: Therapeutic implications. *The Clinical Journal of Pain, 31*(4), 363–374. doi:10.1097/AJP.0000000000000115

Seal, K. H., Shi, Y., Cohen, G., Cohen, B. E., Maguen, S., Krebs, E. E., & Neylan, T. C. (2012). Association of mental health disorders with prescription opioids and high-risk opioid use in US veterans of Iraq and Afghanistan. *Journal of the American Medical Association, 307*(9), 940–947. doi:10.1001/jama.2012.234

Seligowski, A. V., Lee, D. J., Bardeen, J. R., & Orcutt, H. K. (2015). Emotion regulation and posttraumatic stress symptoms: A meta-analysis. *Cognitive Behaviour Therapy, 44*(2), 87–102. doi:10.1080/16506073.2014.980753

Seligowski, A. V., Rogers, A. P., & Orcutt, H. K. (2016). Relations among emotion regulation and DSM-5 symptom clusters of PTSD. *Personality and Individual Differences, 92,* 104–108. doi:10.1016/j.paid.2015.12.032

Sharp, T. J., & Harvey, A. G. (2001). Chronic pain and posttraumatic stress disorder: Mutual maintenance? *Clinical Psychology Review, 21*(6), 857–877. doi:10.1016/S0272-7358(00)00071-4

Siqveland, J., Hussain, A., Lindstrøm, J. C., Ruud, T., & Hauff, E. (2017). Prevalence of posttraumatic stress disorder in persons with chronic pain: A meta-analysis. *Frontiers in Psychiatry, 8*(164), 1–8. doi:10.3389/fpsyt.2017.00164

Staerkle, R., Mannion, A. F., Elfering, A., Junge, A., Semmer, N. K., Jacobshagen, N., Grob, D., Dvorvak, J., & Boos, N. (2004). Longitudinal validation of the Fear-Avoidance Beliefs Questionnaire (FABQ) in a Swiss-German sample of low back pain patients. *European Spine Journal, 13*(4), 332–340. doi:10.1007/s00586-003-0663-3

Stratton, K. J., Clark, S. L., Hawn, S. E., Amstadter, A. B., Cifu, D. X., & Walker, W. C. (2014). Longitudinal interactions of pain and posttraumatic stress disorder symptoms in U.S. military service members following blast exposure. *The Journal of Pain*, *15*(10), 1023–1032. doi:10.1016/j.jpain.2014.07.002

Sullivan, M. J. L., Thibault, P., Simmonds, M. J., Milioto, M., Cantin, A. P., & Velly, A. M. (2009). Pain, perceived injustice and the persistence of post-traumatic stress symptoms during the course of rehabilitation for whiplash injuries. *Pain*, *145*(3), 325–331. doi:10.1016/j.pain.2009.06.031

Toblin, R. L., Quartana, P. J., Riviere, L. A., Walper, K. C., & Hoge, C. W. (2014). Chronic pain and opioid use in US soldiers after combat deployment. *JAMA Internal Medicine*, *174*(8), 1400–1401. doi:10.1001/jamainternmed.2014.2726

Vlaeyen, J. S., & Linton, S. J. (2000). Fear-avoidance and its consequences in chronic musculoskeletal pain: A state of the art. *Pain*, *85*(3), 317–332. doi:10.1016/S0304-3959(99)00242-0

Weathers, F. W., Litz, B. T., Keane, T. M., Palmieri, P. A., Marx, B. P., & Schnurr, P. P. (2013). *The PTSD checklist for DSM-5 (PCL-5)*. Scale available from the National Center for PTSD. Retrieved from www.ptsd.va.gov; www.ptsd.va.gov/professional/assessment/adult-sr/ptsd-checklist.asp

Westphal, M., Olfson, M., Gameroff, M. J., Wickramaratne, P., Pilowsky, D. J., Neugebauer, R., . . . Neria, Y. (2011). Functional impairment in adults with past posttraumatic stress disorder: Findings from primary care. *Depression and Anxiety*, *28*(8), 686–695. doi:10.1002/da.20842

20

Psychological Treatment of Chronic Pain in Pediatric Populations

Jody Thomas and Anya Griffin

Introduction

Pediatric chronic pain is a significant worldwide public health concern with potentially long-lasting complications that can persist into adulthood (Walker, Dengler-Crish, Rippel, & Bruehl, 2010). Estimated prevalence rates for chronic pain in youth under 18 years vary but generally range from 25% to 40% (King et al., 2011; Mahrer, Gold, Luu, & Herman, 2018; Tumin et al., 2018; Huguet & Miro, 2008; Stanford, Chambers, Biesanz, & Chen, 2008). The most common pediatric pain conditions, in order of frequency, are tension-type headaches, migraine headaches, abdominal pain, musculoskeletal pain, fibromyalgia, and complex regional pain syndrome (CRPS) (Palermo, 2012).

Chronic pain also is a very common problem that can arise secondary to chronic illnesses such as juvenile idiopathic arthritis, sickle cell disease, cystic fibrosis, cancer, limb amputation, and inflammatory bowel disease (Palermo, 2012). Chronic pain prevalence is higher in females than in males across nearly all diagnoses, although the mechanisms explaining these sex differences are unclear (Palermo, 2012; King et al., 2011). Incidence increases with age for nearly all pain conditions. A large-scale study of hospitalized pediatric chronic pain patients found an average age of 13.5 years, with females outnumbering males 2.41 to 1 (Coffelt, Bauer, & Carroll, 2013).

Pediatric chronic pain is associated with difficulties across multiple domains of functioning, which in turn can negatively influence overall quality of life. These difficulties include physical disability, psychological/emotional difficulties, sleep disturbances, and decreases in school attendance (Hechler et al., 2015; Gold, Mahrer, Yee, & Palermo, 2009; Mahrer et al., 2018). In a bidirectional relationship, these difficulties subsequently can further increase the pain experience. It follows that pediatric chronic pain intervention should involve an interdisciplinary mind–body approach (Mahrer et al., 2018), and that effective intervention will be anchored in a biopsychosocial framework and incorporate varied treatment targets (Geraghty & Buse, 2015; Masters, 2006).

Youth with chronic pain utilize specialty medical care at higher rates than youth without chronic pain; however, they utilize mental health resources at lower rates (Tumin et al., 2018), despite evidence that incorporating behavioral health interventions improves outcomes for chronic pain patients, as discussed throughout this chapter. A recent cost analysis found that interdisciplinary pediatric chronic pain treatment programs were associated with reduced inpatient and emergency visits, reduced hospitalization costs (approximately $36,228/patient annually), and increased insurance costs savings (approximately $11,482/patient annually) (Mahrer et al., 2018).

Although research of this nature is increasing, a general challenge when treating pediatric chronic pain is that a vast majority of pain research is conducted on adults. This is similar to research within numerous other areas of science and medicine. This insufficiency of pediatric-specific research, when paired with a pediatric chronic pain population with high needs, requires that the field adapt the adult scientific knowledge to pediatric populations when holes in research exist. Effectively treating a child's chronic pain requires compensating for the ways that biological, psychological, and social factors of the pediatric pain experience differ from those of the adult pain experience.

This chapter explores critical factors relevant to the effective treatment of pediatric chronic pain. After discussing the biopsychosocial model as applied to a pediatric population, it examines the process of assessment, specific targets of intervention, factors impacting treatment, treatment approaches, and treatment modalities.

Biopsychosocial Model Applied to Pediatric Populations

Although outdated and repeatedly disproven, the biomedical model is one of the most prevalent and persistent models still influencing the conceptualization of pain in the current medical system (Betsch, Gorodzinsky, Finley, Sangster, & Chorney, 2017; Bursch, Walco, & Zeltzer, 1998). This model views pain as a biological process that can be identified and corrected through medical intervention alone. It implies that pain correlates directly with tissue damage, and that correcting that damage is the primary solution for pain. For youth in chronic pain, this is a potentially damaging and treatment-inhibiting framework (Bursch et al., 1998) because in most cases, the chronic pain experience is no longer a product of tissue damage but results from disruptions in the pain signaling system itself. Often, there is no tissue damage to resolve as the initial injury (if there was one) already has been treated to the extent possible. Overemphasis on tissue damage or prolonged searches for a tissue damage etiology can not only be ineffective but also increase patient and family distress and resistance to effective treatments that take into account the entirety of the pain experience. Negative and ineffective treatment experiences often result.

In contrast, the biopsychosocial model posits that pain is influenced by biological, psychological, and social subsystems interacting at multiple levels. In children and adults, pain perception involves the integration and interpretation of sensory input. This sensory input is either dampened or enhanced by pain transmission and inhibitory systems and is modulated by biological processes, psychological/developmental factors, and social/cultural context (see Figure 20.1). The biopsychosocial model as applied to pediatric chronic pain moves away from differentiating between physical and psychological pain and toward incorporating a multidimensional view that includes the biological, psychological, social, and environmental components of the pain experience (Bursch et al., 2003; Bursch et al., 1998; Maynard, Amari, Wieczorek, Christensen, & Slifer, 2009; Zeltzer, Tsao, Bursch, & Myers, 2005).

Effectively treating pediatric chronic pain requires a shared provider–patient–family understanding of the biopsychosocial model (Geraghty & Buse, 2015; Masters, 2006), which facilitates individualized conceptualization of chronic pain specific to the youth's experience. An important implication of this model is that treating the psychological factors of the pain experience is essential to treating chronic pain (Coakley & Wihak, 2017; Bursch et al., 1998). As such, it becomes critical to normalize rather than pathologize psychological pain factors and their treatment (Bursch et al., 1998; Zeltzer et al., 2005).

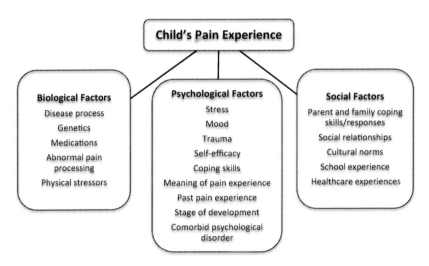

Figure 20.1 Biopsychosocial Model of Pain as Applied to Children and Adolescents

It can be helpful to explain to families that whether or not a child has chronic pain, psychological distress such as depression, anxiety, and daily stress impact the body's biological processes and the brain's modulation of pain signals. Because the pain signaling system itself has become disrupted and dysfunctional in a child with chronic pain, it is critical to address the psychological factors that are inherent in the system. A chronic pain cycle is exacerbated by the fact that experiencing pain often will generate a negative psychological state and, in turn, the negative psychological state will worsen the experience of pain.

It is especially important to engage children and their families by explaining and normalizing the psychology of pain inasmuch as many pain-related medical conditions are coupled with stigma; children incorrectly can be perceived as drug-seeking or exaggerating symptoms for some sort of secondary gain (Martin et al., 2018). This stigma can be exacerbated in conditions such as sickle cell anemia, where racial and cultural factors create the potential for even more bias (Wailoo, 2014). Stigma and fear of stigma may contribute to initial resistance toward psychological interventions, and this process is influenced by unique individual beliefs and cultural factors that warrant attention and consideration (Martin et al., 2018).

For example, cultural differences exist regarding how pain is perceived and the role that psychological factors may or may not play (see Chapter 23). On the individual family level, there may be critical differences in the perceived value of addressing psychosocial factors. For example, families that perceive the solution to depression as just needing to "buck up" or "get over it" can have challenges accepting the role of psychological factors in the pain experience. These factors can complicate insufficient understanding of the biopsychosocial model (Geraghty & Buse, 2015; Masters, 2006) and limit understanding of the potential benefits and role of psychological services in treating pediatric pain.

While under-recognizing psychosocial factors as effective treatment targets reduces overall outcomes for pediatric pain patients, so too can under-emphasizing biological factors and/or treatments. Pediatric pain can be undertreated and the child's experience invalidated when providers dismiss pain symptoms as "just psychological," rather than incorporating psychosocial information into a larger, more complex case conceptualization. In short, the identification and treatment of psychological factors does *not* preclude the need to offer biologically based treatments when appropriate. It is important that patients and families know and understand how all physiological factors are being concurrently and appropriately evaluated and addressed. Lingering questions of "did they miss something?" can haunt parents and youth alike; create unnecessary anxiety; damage provider–patient–family relationships; and reduce the family's engagement in the treatment process. A high level of coordination between interdisciplinary providers therefore is essential in order to devise, communicate, and administer an effective intervention approach addressing the entirety of the pain experience.

Treating pediatric chronic pain effectively requires understanding and compensating for biological, psychological, and social differences between the pediatric and adult pain experiences (Friedrichsdorf et al., 2016). Providers from all disciplines should take into consideration the developing brains and bodies of children and adolescents, which are very different from the mature physiology of adults.

Biological factors that are unique to youth influence which medical interventions are appropriate. The differences are complex and multifaceted and include immune functioning, metabolism, rate of growth, neurobiology, and neuroanatomy (Stanford et al., 2008). These pediatric biological factors influence aspects of intervention such as medication selection and dosing; providers must strongly consider long-term effects of medication and medical interventions given the amount of lifespan remaining. In some ways, these biological differences offer distinct advantages and an improved prognosis for children when compared to adults with the same pain conditions. Children and adolescents with chronic pain have greater rates of healing and, generally, much lower incidences of comorbid diseases than adult patients (Friedrichsdorf et al., 2016). In short, youth are still growing and developing and typically are healthier than adults. These factors impact children's tolerance of medical interventions and their bodies' capacity to heal.

Understanding the psychological components of the pediatric pain experience requires a solid grounding in developmental and social psychology. Children still are developing emotional and physiological self-regulation and are undergoing expected hormonal changes that influence mood. These typical developmental changes impact the pain experience as well as the child's tolerance of and response to treatment (Bursch et al., 2003). Although the chronic pain experience itself may elicit feelings of helplessness and lack of control in both child and adult patients, these feelings in youth may be amplified by their status as minors, age-appropriate limited independence, and the fact that they remain under the protection and guidance of caregivers (Bursch et al., 2003).

A pediatric patient's sense of control and power in the medical system (i.e., a system wherein adults often consent on his/her behalf to medical interventions) often is much less than that of an adult. Medical providers can exacerbate these natural developmental frustrations by failing to communicate with the child in age-appropriate language that he/she can understand or by failing to consider the child's opinions and perspectives about healthcare decisions. Thus, ensuring that provider–patient interactions provide the youth with a sense of control whenever possible can be very helpful (Palermo, 2012; Roth-Isigkeit, Thyen, Stoven, Schwarzenberger, & Schmucker, 2005; Yazdani & Zeltzer, 2013).

The social world of a child also is profoundly different from that of an adult. While workplace difficulties frequently challenge adult pain patients, school disruption is a major issue for youth, and school is where many limitations in functioning are most evident (Clementi, Kao, & Monico, 2017; Logan, Simons, & Kaczynski, 2009). Educational growth is dependent upon continuous learning and progression in acquired knowledge and skills over time. When children miss significant time from school due to pain or to focus on medical treatments, they often quickly fall behind their peers. Indeed, school and academics often are primary concerns of both patients and families (Vitulano, 2003; Logan et al.,

2009). Frequent school absences, decreased academic performance, school-related stress, and poor academic competence are common (Logan, Simons, Stein, & Chastain, 2008). Frequency and severity of academic issues can vary by diagnosis, ranging from challenges with attention and focus to complete inability to attend school (Logan et al., 2009).

A child's relationships with parents and siblings are the core of his or her daily experience and thus need to be addressed over the course of treatment (Lewandowski, Palermo, Stinson, Handley, & Chambers, 2010). Changes in family dynamics secondary and/or contributing to the child's pain experience need also be addressed (Logan & Scharff, 2005). Families often require support and guidance as they move toward returning to "normal" family functioning and routines within the context of the child's pain (Palermo, 2012). Additionally, adults often have friends who can understand and support a journey through a major health crisis. In contrast, children and adolescents often do not, as their same-age peers simply do not have the experience or capacity to do so. This lack of peer support and understanding can result in both physical and psychological isolation (Walker, Claar, & Garber, 2002). Given that the majority of pediatric chronic pain patients are over the age of 10 years (with most in adolescence; Zernikow et al., 2012), these social and peer disruptions can be especially challenging at a time of life when there is great emphasis on belonging, on being part of a group, and on not being seen as different. Pain and its functional impact can create significant barriers as identity and social ties develop (Eccleston, Crombez, Scotford, Clinch, & Connell, 2004).

Assessment

The first step in pediatric chronic pain intervention is a comprehensive individual child and family assessment in order to identify which biopsychosocial factors are impacting the child's chronic pain experience. A thorough assessment will identify targets of intervention and their order of importance, including patterns (physical, behavioral, social, and psychological) that may be contributing to the youth's pain experience and subsequent dysfunction. Once those patterns have been identified, goals can be formulated and prioritized. This critical first step, when conducted in collaboration with the child and family, increases personal motivation and adherence during the treatment process.

A cornerstone of assessment is a semi-structured or structured clinical interview to gather relevant background information, including information about biopsychosocial factors that may affect a child's pain experience (Bursch et al., 1998). The interview may be conducted in conjunction with an interdisciplinary treatment team involved in pain management clinics (e.g., medical providers, physical therapists, occupational therapists, psychologist). Pain is a subjective experience; allow the child to share his or her story *before* the parents share their perspective, as the child may be influenced by parental feedback and interpretations of his/her pain. This also communicates to the child that he/she is a partner in treatment planning, which helps build rapport and promotes future collaboration on treatment goals and adherence to pain management treatment. The child should explain how he/she came to be in the psychologist's office and what happened along that journey, with parents adding their perspectives and details afterwards.

It also is important to explore the family's perception of their interactions with the medical system thus far. To facilitate this discussion, patients and family members must feel understood, and their feelings about any previous negative experiences validated. Attempts to rationalize or defend previous negative experiences likely will impede the family's receptivity toward recommendations and adherence to treatment protocols.

Standardized child and parent self-report measures can be helpful during the assessment phase of intervention. Numerical rating scales help quantify the pain experience (Miró, Castarlenas, & Huguet, 2009). Child self-report and parent measures can help to assess various aspects of a child's pain patterns and daily behaviors, pain interference, emotional/social factors, and functional outcomes (Jacobson et al., 2015; McGrath et al., 2008; Varni et al., 2010; Cohen et al., 2007).

In particular, assessing emotional distress (e.g., anxiety, fears about pain, catastrophic thoughts about the pain experience) is critical to fully conceptualize the child's pain experience (Crombez et al., 2003; Fisher et al., 2014; Fisher, Heathcote, Eccleston, Simons, & Palermo, 2017; Tran et al., 2015; Simons, Sieberg, Carpino, Logan, & Berde, 2011). Providers often also utilize pain diaries to further detail the impact of pain on daily life (Cohen et al., 2007). Current technology allows for digital diaries of pain experiences and cueing of the patient's report via push notifications on smartphone and iPad apps. Please see Chapter 2 for a summary of some of the most common and evidence-based pediatric chronic pain assessment measures.

Targets of Intervention

Child and Family Understanding of the Pain Experience and Treatment

As discussed previously, critical components of intervention include explaining the biopsychosocial model and developing goals in multiple domains of the patient's life. The family's response to the biopsychosocial model can help guide the prioritization of treatment goals. For example, a child who cannot yet accept the role of psychological factors in the pain experience will require a different approach than a child who is ready to work on new ways to dissociate from the pain experience.

The desire for the "magic pill" often comes up to varying degrees during this process. As developmentally expected, the thoughts and beliefs of many children tend to focus exclusively on parents or providers fixing the problem and making the pain "go away." The clinician should expand the child's focus to include developing new coping strategies, increasing functioning, and reframing his/her thoughts about the pain experience. It is helpful for the clinician to normalize the desire for a simple, often purely biological answer for what is, in fact, a complex problem. Families may become confused or frustrated when the "answer" to the problem includes difficult work and sometimes more discomfort before significant symptom relief (Bursch et al., 1998; Bursch et al., 2003).

Children and families often find it challenging to accept the "up and down" nature of the treatment process. Recovery is not a direct linear process, but most often entails periods of physical and psychological progress and regression. Providing this context and framework from the outset can help prepare families for the process of intervention, manage expectations, and maintain motivation during periods of regression. Families also may struggle with the concept that, in many cases (depending on the pain condition), function will improve before significant pain relief (Friedrichsdorf et al., 2016).

Patient and Family Relationship With and Trust of the Medical Team and System

Intervention should begin with exploring the family's experiences with, beliefs about, and understanding of pain and pain treatment. Many youths with chronic pain have had negative past treatment experiences that need to be addressed, including previous negative interactions with medical providers. Patient and family resistance to psychosocial intervention often is rooted in defensiveness secondary to previous negative treatment experiences. These include encountering the stigma that can be associated with chronic pain, and direct or indirect implications by a previous provider that the youth's pain experience is intentionally exaggerated; is behavioral or psychological in origin; is not serious; or is invalid in some other way (Bursch et al., 2003; Bursch, 2006; Campo & Fritz, 2001). Previous providers' framing of pediatric pain in this way may even have altered treatment choices, thereby leading the family to believe that all providers think the child's pain is "all in his/her head" (Betsch et al., 2017; Cohen, Quintner, & Buchanan, 2011; Martin et al., 2018; Robbins et al., 2005).

In addition, parents may have the impression that providers believe the parents are causing or contributing to their child's pain in some way through their parenting; such impressions may be extremely stressful and erode trust in the medical community (Betsch et al., 2017; Cohen et al., 2011). Directly addressing these issues and experiences promotes therapeutic rapport and helps build a strong, trust-based working alliance between the patient and providers. Psychologists can help patients and families improve their relationships with medical providers by teaching families self-advocacy skills, teaching how to interact and collaborate effectively with medical providers, teaching how to differentiate between past and present experiences, and helping families understand the specific roles and perspectives of the various medical providers.

Sleep

Sleep disturbance is common in children and adolescents with chronic pain (Palermo & Kiska, 2005), with prevalence rates estimated at over 50% (Roth-Isigkeit et al., 2005; Long, Krishnamurthy, & Palermo, 2007; Palermo, Toliver-Sokol, Fonareva, & Koh, 2007). Typical issues include sleep-onset latency, poor sleep quality, short duration, and frequent night awakenings (Lewandowski, Palermo, De la Motte & Fu, 2010; Palermo et al., 2007). The relationship between pain and sleep is bidirectional in that pain symptoms are predictive of the quality of sleep, and the quality of sleep is predictive of next day pain experience (Valrie, Bromberg, Palermo, & Schanberg, 2013; Roth-Isigkeit et al., 2005). The sleep disruption–pain relationship is also moderated by mood, with positive mood weakening it and negative mood exacerbating it (Valrie et al., 2013). Addressing sleep disturbance often is one of the fundamental goals of pediatric pain intervention; failing to work on sleep makes it much more challenging to address other issues that also drive the pain experience, including neurological arousal and mood (Lewin & Dahl, 1999; Fales, Palermo, Law, & Wilson, 2015).

Although pain itself may negatively impact sleep, there also are relevant behavioral factors that lend themselves to intervention (Palermo, 2012; Lewandowski, Palermo, De la Motte, et al., 2010). Parents may become more lenient with household rules about sleep habits when the child experiences pain at night. They may allow the child to sleep with them in their bed, to remain up late at night due to pain symptoms, or to nap during the day. A proper sleep hygiene plan is critical to pain management; setting goals around improving sleep is important (Valrie et al., 2013; Lewin & Dahl, 1999).

Improving behavioral and psychological sleep patterns requires understanding the current maladaptive patterns and identifying targets for intervention. Historically, this has been accomplished via sleep diaries (Palermo, 2012), but modern technology allows for the use of devices like smartphones and fitness trackers in order to accurately and contemporaneously capture sleep patterns. Identifying the barriers to good sleep enables the practitioner to design appropriate interventions, which may include optimizing effective timing of sleep and pain medication; learning relaxation and self-regulation skills; making positive changes in the environment (e.g., darkness, temperature, noise); and changing behaviors (e.g., limiting naps, maintaining consistent bedtimes and bedtime routines, increasing exercise, limiting screen time) (Valrie et al., 2013).

Cognitive and Affective Patterns

Many cognitive and affective processes relevant to the pain process warrant addressing during the course of treatment. These include a patient's expectations, cognitive patterns, interpretations, attention, beliefs, meaning-making, mood and affect, anxiety, and fear, as well as appraisals of both pain and factors related to the pain experience (Coakley & Wihak, 2017; Bursch et al., 1998).

Research demonstrates that anxiety, fear, worries, and pain catastrophizing are the psychological factors most predictive of pediatric pain and subsequent disability (Palermo, 2012; Leeuw et al., 2007; Crombez et al., 2003; Kashikar-Zuck et al., 2013; Larsson & Sund, 2007). Pain catastrophizing refers to the child's mental ruminations about, magnification of, and feelings of helplessness about pain. A negative cognitive-affective response to anticipated or actual pain, it has been associated with a number of important pain-related outcomes (Quartana, Campbell, & Edwards, 2009).

Actively addressing and changing the patient's tendency toward pain catastrophizing significantly improves his/her pain experience (Friedrichsdorf et al., 2016). Thought stopping, cognitive restructuring, problem-solving, challenging negative thoughts, and positive self-talk often are the components of cognitive-behavioral therapy (CBT) interventions utilized with pediatric chronic pain patients to address these maladaptive cognitive patterns (Palermo, 2012; Levy et al., 2010; Connelly & Schanberg, 2006). *Cognitive Behavioral Therapy for Children and Adolescents* (Palermo, 2012) constitutes a useful resource for a more complete explanation of CBT interventions in the pediatric population.

Psychological Comorbidities

Youth with chronic pain have significantly higher rates of anxiety and depression than their healthy peers, though the exact rates are not clear in the existing research. de la Vega, Groenewald, Bromberg, Beals-Erickson and Palermo (2018) found that adolescents with chronic pain demonstrate more symptoms of depression and anxiety than peers without chronic pain. Similarly, studies that have looked at mental health cohorts have found higher rates of recurrent pain in children with anxiety and depression than those without (Egger, Costello, Erkanli & Angold, 1999). The mechanisms are complicated: while psychological distress is a possible contributing factor to the pain experience, pain and its impact on functioning both contribute to psychological distress. For the chronic pain patient in emotional distress, it is more important that the practitioner determines how to interrupt the cycle (in order to bring relief) rather than determining whether the distress or the pain came first.

Previous trauma is a significant risk factor for the development of pediatric chronic pain. Noel et al. (2016) found that 32% of youth with chronic pain reported significant PTSD symptoms, compared to 8% of a healthy comparison population. Furthermore, parents of youth with chronic pain frequently struggle with symptoms of PTSD, with 20% reporting significant symptoms compared to 1% of a comparison group of parents with healthy children (Noel et al., 2016). Noel et al. (2016) also found that among parents in the chronic pain group, higher PTSD symptoms were associated with higher child-reported pain intensity. One recent study found that 80% of youth with chronic pain endorsed adverse childhood experiences (ACEs), which were associated with a higher prevalence of anxiety, depression, and fear of pain (Nelson, Simons, & Logan, 2018). Most reported

ACEs that pre-dated the child's pain experience. Common ACEs included sexual and physical abuse, neglect, and significant losses such as the death of someone close.

Treatment of comorbid psychological conditions needs to happen concurrently with chronic pain treatment. Psychological distress can affect the severity of the pain experience and degree of functional impairment, as well as the prognosis for recovery (Kashikar-Zuck et al., 2001; Eccleston et al., 2004). Patients may state that they believe their anxiety or depression symptoms will improve "when the pain goes away." However, they may have difficulty accepting the fact that their pain likely will not resolve until their psychological distress is sufficiently addressed.

Coping Skills

Coping skills empower youth to disrupt the various physical, psychological, emotional, and cognitive patterns that contribute to the complexity of the pain experience. Notably, the skills and abilities that children need to learn in order to manage chronic pain often are far more advanced than what is developmentally typical, and well beyond what is expected of their healthy peers. It can be useful to provide this developmental context to parents and caregivers, whose worries and fears can manifest as anger and frustration whenever the child struggles to do something that is important in treatment but that is naturally challenging at his/her developmental stage. By providing the parents with this developmental context regarding coping skills, the practitioner enables the parents to understand the following: when a child faces challenges, the parents' helpful and supportive responses (as opposed to punishing or shaming responses) helps facilitate the child's emerging problem-solving skills.

Adhering to chronic pain treatment recommendations requires impulse control and executive functioning skills that may be challenging for children and adolescents whose frontal lobes still are actively developing (Duckworth & Steinberg, 2015). These skills need to be taught in developmentally appropriate ways, rather than assumed to exist at baseline. Correspondingly, self-regulation skills are of paramount importance for managing pain and subsequent distress; however, children typically exhibit inconsistent abilities to regulate their bodies and their emotions while proceeding through development (Vohs & Baumeister, 2016). General stress-management skills usually are more important for this population than for their typical peers, as the stress experienced by pain patients significantly affects their health and ability to function. Worries about school, stress about friends, and conflict with family affect all children and adolescents; however, the direct impact of these worries on the pain experience requires chronic pain patients to become extremely good at managing the stresses of normal life. The specific coping skills taught will vary according to the patient's age and developmental level. Once acquired, these skills can improve mood, interrupt some of the physiological processes of pain, and build the child's sense of self-efficacy about changing his/her own experience. Coping skills often are taught through behavioral health interventions that include diaphragmatic and related breathing techniques, mindfulness practices, meditation, self-hypnosis, and progressive muscle relaxation (Jastrowski Mano et al., 2013; Waelde et al., 2017). Successfully teaching these skills requires adapting to the child's individual needs and paying attention to the potential for uneven areas of development and developmental regressions that may occur with the stress of the illness process.

Current, rapidly changing technology options can be a powerful adjunct and support in this area. It can be helpful to discuss with patients and their parents how to incorporate technology into a treatment plan. For example, there are several meditation, relaxation, and CBT apps designed for children, including Headspace, Dreamy Kid, Smiling Mind, Meditations for Kids, and Breathe, Think, Do. Notably, however, studies establishing the efficacy of these apps do not currently exist.

Adherence to Treatment Plans

It is developmentally typical for children in many stages of childhood to lack a sense of responsibility. This can inhibit the patient's ability to develop the high level of discipline necessary to adhere to the often demanding and difficult protocols of physical therapy and occupational therapy, while keeping up with social and academic responsibilities and engaging in necessary health behaviors. Parents, medical providers, and other caregivers often express frustration at youth compliance challenges, without contextualizing these struggles as developmentally expected.

Unfortunately, the consequences (e.g., pain flairs, medical setbacks) of poor follow through for children in chronic pain are significantly greater than the consequences for healthy children (e.g., missed homework assignments, incomplete chores). Parents and caregivers who intentionally or unintentionally invoke shame and/or punish the child for these natural challenges often contribute ultimately to decreased motivation and increased stress (Palermo, 2012). Given the importance of youth being motivated for treatment, and the negative role of stress in the pain process, this particular dynamic is highly unproductive. More productive are behavior plans that pair desired behaviors with reinforcement and rewards (customized to a child's particular interests), behavioral exposure to increases in productive activity that do not result in worsened symptoms, activity pacing, and scheduling of pleasant activities (Palermo, 2012).

The treatment of chronic pain often requires intentionally putting the patient in significantly painful situations on a daily basis in order to gain the long-term benefits of pain relief and increased functioning. Maintaining this focus on long-term benefits requires significant abilities to delay gratification and maintain mature self-discipline. This is particularly challenging for normally developing children who typically lack appreciation for long-term consequences and for whom the short-term consequences of any choice or action are much more relevant and influential in their decision-making (Duckworth & Steinberg, 2015). Practitioners can teach strategies to families and patients that break down larger goals into a step-by-step process, which allows for setting short-term goals that are intentionally and concretely linked to the overall goal of pain relief. The parallel example of math homework can help parents understand this concept. Rarely do children do math homework because of an overwhelming desire to understand math or to enrich their academic lives; they do it because the assignment is due tomorrow and they want a good grade and their teacher's approval.

Social Skills

Social skills, which significantly influence the chronic pain experience, are important to target in treatment (Forgeron et al., 2010). Social skills development is a normal process of childhood, and the demand for these skills on the chronic pain patient is very high. Patients have to display a high degree of finesse and ability to self-advocate, to explain their experiences, and to elicit what they need from medical providers, family, peers, and other significant adults (e.g., teachers) in their world (Palermo, Valrie, & Karlson, 2014). This can be challenging under the best of circumstances; it certainly is more difficult when experiencing significant physical and/or emotional distress.

It does not help that pain often is an invisible and misunderstood illness that leaves patients with the extra burden of "proving" their distress to others. This has particular implications for navigating peer relationships in that experiencing and attempting to effectively manage chronic pain (including managing social expectations) is often at odds with the child's desire to fit in among a peer population that typically has little experience with or understanding of major health issues (Palermo, 2012). Teaching these specific social skills through techniques like role play can help when the child's normal development has not yet caught up to the demands of the disease and the treatment processes.

Pain Management Skills

Psychotherapy for pediatric chronic pain often focuses on distress management because of the often grueling and painful nature of physical and occupational therapy, the process of desensitization, and/or medical procedures. The mindsets and coping skills of both the child and the members of his or her family regarding the treatment process are key to the efficacy of treatment, and to preventing the treatment itself from causing traumatic stress (Palermo et al., 2014). These essential skills can include cognitive reframing, positive self-talk, controlled dissociation, exposures, and self-regulation skills. Adults with chronic pain likely have developed the cognitive skills necessary to understand that pain from treatment actually may be productive. However, youth with chronic pain may not fully comprehend this challenging concept. They need support to understand that treatment is an opportunity for mastering skills and building self-efficacy by overcoming major challenges, as opposed to yet another perceived victimization experience (Palermo, 2012).

As part of the treatment process, children typically are expected to learn to function through pain, and to no longer treat the simple presence of pain as a reason to limit function. Families often are told that improved function will come before pain reduction, and further that improved function helps facilitate pain reduction (Friedrichsdorf et al., 2016). This process entails overriding one of the most primal human instincts: attend to pain and avoid whatever causes pain. Clearly, this instinct serves people well most of the time. However, that same instinct does not serve the chronic pain patient without a process for modification; to the contrary, it can keep him/her very impaired.

Eliminating pain often is not possible in the short term, and attempts to universally avoid it nearly always hinder recovery (Palermo, 2012). Thus, one of the most important pain management skills that patients need to acquire is the ability to *discriminate* between "good" or "productive" pain and "unhelpful" or "unproductive" pain. Productive pain serves the purpose of moving treatment forward toward the eventual goal of symptom relief. For example, pain from physical therapy exercises can further the process of desensitization and long-term pain relief. In contrast, unproductive pain does not serve any larger purpose. It simply hurts and does not facilitate recovery.

Distinguishing productive pain from unproductive pain is extremely important when the simple rule of pain avoidance is no longer a useful way to guide behavior. As such, youth with chronic pain must learn what is often a very new and important skill: how to determine when to push and function through the pain, and when pushing through could actually lead to more damage or hinder recovery. Psychologists can help the child make this determination, often in collaboration with physical therapists, occupational therapists, and physicians (to whom the specific determination often falls). Psychologists can play an essential role in teaching coping and pain management skills to function through the pain when appropriate (see below). By discussing the importance of these differentiation skills with the patient, the psychologist also can help directly with adherence by providing a context for intervention components that exacerbate pain in the short term, as well as helping with motivation by connecting productive pain with larger recovery goals.

Parents and caregivers also must develop the ability to differentiate between their child's productive and unproductive pain and (relatedly) when to attend to their child's pain and when to redirect the child toward coping skills. Attending to and preventing pain in one's children are among the most primal human parental instincts, because pain is designed to warn of potential danger and threats to health. As such, helping both children and parents conceptualize why and how productive pain signals are different (and unhelpful) is necessary to allow them to give themselves permission to ignore or dissociate from the signals (Palermo et al., 2014; Palermo, 2012).

519

Once a child and his/her family members can differentiate between types of pain, they can learn how to use dissociation skills to cope with productive pain. These skills include distraction, self-hypnosis, biofeedback, and/or CBT skills (Ehde, Dillworth, & Turner, 2014; Eccleston et al., 2014; Palermo, Eccleston, Lewandowski, Williams, & Morley, 2010). Children nearly always and instinctively use distraction to cope with pain (e.g., using videos or games), but they may not have conceptualized this in terms of self-efficacy and control to alter their pain experience. Helping children frame distraction in this way opens up the opportunity for them to utilize it with more intention and therapeutic purpose.

Becoming more skilled regarding when and how to attend to pain also informs the very important skill of activity pacing, another task of discrimination. How does one decide when to function and when to rest? What factors does one attend to in order to make that decision? Pain patients at times can exhibit rigid thinking and an "all or nothing" mentality (Vervoort, Goubert, Eccleston, Bijttebier, & Crombez, 2005; Eccleston et al., 2004). Learning flexible and critical thinking skills enables patients to make the necessary judgment calls regarding when and how to push themselves. Coordination with other treatment providers is critical as patients work to acquire these skills. As school is one of the primary environments for a child, pacing also is important in that setting. The specifics on how to pace and what accommodations should be made are based upon the child's specific needs, which are often included in a formal school plan (Logan et al., 2008; Palermo, 2012). More detail on how to effectively interact with schools is discussed later in this chapter.

Family and Social Dynamics

Though there is abundant evidence that family dynamics impact symptom presentation and treatment course of youth with chronic pain (Logan & Scharff, 2005; Logan et al., 2012; Huestis et al., 2017), the precise mechanisms and mediating factors are not yet completely delineated. Family interaction patterns inevitably change in order to accommodate the new stressor of the child's pain, and parents need support replacing any maladaptive patterns that have developed or preexisted with more functional ones. Families benefit from support as they learn how to balance their natural desires to nurture and care for a sick child with the need to set firm boundaries; to provide significant structure; to maintain a sense of routine and normalcy despite increased stress; and to push their child to function through productive pain and interventions that significantly (even if temporarily) increase pain.

The impact of pediatric pain also extends to parents experiencing their own significant levels of distress (Palermo & Eccleston, 2009). Tolerating their child's distress, and enduring the ambiguity and delayed positive rewards of the long process of pain treatment, can be the most challenging aspects of the parental experience. Parents often need significant support in order to maintain their engagement in the treatment process. Levels of disability in youth with chronic pain increase as parental distress increases, particularly when paired with maladaptive parenting approaches (Cohen, Vowles, & Eccleston, 2010; Eccleston et al., 2004; Langer, Romano, Mancl & Levy, 2014; Palermo & Chambers, 2005).

Parental responses to their child's pain are among the more frequent family factors examined in the literature. Parents may exhibit "solicitous responses," which include frequently attending to and asking about a child's pain, or allowing the child to avoid regular activities or responsibilities (Miró, Vegas, Gertz, Jensen, & Engel, 2017). From a behavioral perspective, a solicitous response style inadvertently reinforces pain behaviors. A considerable amount of research demonstrates how "sick role" behaviors and functional disability are associated with solicitous parenting (Cohen et al., 2010; Eccleston et al., 2004; Langer et al., 2014; Miró et al., 2017). These findings provide a foundation for family system contingency-based interventions for chronic pain. Helping parents learn to minimize catastrophic responses that reinforce focus on the pain experience and distress has become an important therapeutic goal (Coakley & Wihak, 2017; Eccleston, Palermo, Fisher, & Law, 2012; Huestis et al., 2017; Sieberg et al., 2017). This includes teaching parents a variety of alternative skills, such as learning to shift focus away from pain behaviors.

Taken together, the extant literature supports family level intervention as a way to enhance optimal functioning in children with chronic pain (Peterson & Palermo, 2004; Sieberg et al., 2017). Parents often need concrete guidance on when and how to raise their expectations of the child's behavior and functioning, how to effectively help the child develop necessary coping skills, and how to cope with their own complicated feelings and emotions about the child's pain.

The impact of pediatric chronic pain on siblings has not been well-studied, but is often evident through clinical interviews and parental reports. Siblings of youth with chronic pain identify changes in family dynamics and relationships (Gorodzinsky et al., 2013). Siblings may develop resentment and frustration about the proportion of parental attention and resources devoted to the child in pain, resentment and frustration that may manifest in internalizing or externalizing symptoms. Family therapy can help the family unit process and cope with these dynamics and feelings. Additionally, discovering and altering the patterns that influence the child's pain experience in order to improve outcomes naturally involves the essential roles of siblings and peers. Intervention, therefore, needs to extend beyond the parents to include the entire family and social support system.

School and Academic Issues

Chronic pain has negative effects on academic performance and school attendance, which may result in emotional distress and school avoidance (Clementi et al., 2017; Logan et al., 2009). Specifically, pain as well as pain medications may reduce executive functioning, reduce concentration and the ability to sustain attention, and hamper the ability to engage in an academic environment (Weiss et al., 2017). Fatigue associated with chronic pain also can make it challenging to get to school on time, physically and cognitively endure the full school day, and complete homework at night (Palermo, 2012; Logan et al., 2009).

A child's stress level is influenced by how well his/her dynamics with teachers, school administrators, and peers are managed (Logan et al., 2009). Many pain symptoms are invisible, which may further complicate relationships as patients can be perceived as "faking it," or their attention, mood, and pain symptoms framed as behavioral issues rather than medical symptoms. These dynamics can contribute to children developing a number of fears about the school environment (e.g., fear of the environment itself triggering pain, uncertainty about his/her ability to perform academically, anxiety about catching up on academic work, social anxiety about how to deal with peers and teachers who aren't understanding).

Families benefit from receiving consultation and often direct support around negotiating concrete short- and long-term plans with the school, including any necessary accommodations. These plans often come in the form of a 504 plan or Individualized Education Plan (IEP) (Logan et al., 2009; Bursch et al., 2003; Palermo, 2012). As part of this process, it can be helpful to educate school personnel about the nature of the child's pain condition and how it may impact school attendance and academic performance. This communication should include multidisciplinary recommendations covering biological, psychological, and social factors.

Insufficient attention to school-related issues over the course of treatment raises the risk of symptom regression once the patient attempts to return to the school environment with all the stress it creates and coping skills it demands. Common school accommodations for students with chronic pain include:

- Extended time for tests and assignments
- Modified work assignments to reduce "busy work"
- Identified child advocate within the school setting to help navigate the appropriate accommodations
- Modified schedule (shorter school day) for students with endurance issues secondary to their pain condition
- Combination of classes attended at school and classes taken at home (online, home hospital, or independent study)
- An identified school location for rest, recovery, and use of pain-coping skills (with the goal of facilitating the child's ability to stay at school longer)
- Plan for navigating hallways when they are less busy in order to avoid pain exacerbations from being touched/moved by normal hallway action. This may include permission to leave class late or early
- Extra set of books to avoid potential pain exacerbations or increased fatigue due carrying books between class and home
- Physical accommodations to minimize pain triggers (e.g., permission to take elevators, avoid stairs, well-placed locker)
- Permission to leave class if student needs to rest/recover
- Any relevant accommodations for anxiety or depression, if applicable

Other Factors Impacting Course of Treatment

Coordination of Treatment Providers

Pediatric chronic pain cannot be treated efficiently or effectively in silos, and coordination among interdisciplinary providers is essential (Simons, Logan, Chastain, & Cerullo, 2010; Simons, Sieberg, Pielech, Conroy, & Logan, 2012). It is challenging and time-consuming to manage the logistics of such coordination, but failure to do so inherently limits the effectiveness of any one provider and contributes to the possibility of wasting limited resources. It is critical that providers explain and ensure understanding of treatment recommendations, including the benefits of a multidisciplinary pain management team (Mahrer et al., 2018). The specific methods of collaboration depend upon the setting; however, the common overarching focus is supporting and coordinating each discipline's specific treatment goals. For inpatient and intensive outpatient programs, frequent (several times per week or even daily) interdisciplinary rounding is common. Outpatient treatment will benefit from frequent communication via conversations, confidential e-mails, and the sharing of notes.

Mental health providers need to understand the nature of the treatment being offered by other providers so that the psychotherapeutic work supports all other aspects of treatment.

This includes being able to identify the coping and pain management skills needed for patients to successfully engage with other providers and their treatment recommendations (including occupational and physical therapy, and painful procedures such as nerve blocks or other types of injections). Psychologists can play a key role in preparing children for these procedures by treating previous medical traumas that could interfere with outcomes and by supporting the child through the procedure(s). However, in order to perform these functions appropriately (with adequate lead time for preparation and intervention), the psychologist must know which procedures are being considered and when they might take place. Thus, once again, multidisciplinary coordination and communication serve as cornerstones of the treatment process.

Underlying Pathophysiology of the Pain and Degree of Functional Disability

The biological components of the pain experience and the underlying pathophysiology of pain impact the treatment course, the provider choice of intervention, and the targets of interventions. The treatment of some conditions may be more potentially distressing and difficult to tolerate than others. Conditions such as complex regional pain syndrome (CRPS) may be seen as particularly unfair, and enduring treatment particularly difficult. At present, standard treatment for CRPS includes a process of desensitization, requiring the child to intentionally and repeatedly put himself/herself in painful situations in order to help reset the dysfunctional pain signaling system, to regain strength, and to learn to overcome the strong basic instinct to avoid painful stimuli (Hechler et al., 2015). Without the proper support, this process can seem like another victimization experience rather than an opportunity for growth and healing. CRPS and its treatment can seem more abstract and difficult to grasp for families than conditions like chronic migraine headaches or abdominal pain, which can fall more easily into a typical conceptualization of the pain experience.

The degree of functional disability impacts the course of treatment as well. A child who has been symptomatic for only weeks or a few months typically will have a less complicated course than a child who has been very impaired for a long period of time. Because of challenges of misdiagnosis and lack of knowledge of pediatric pain syndromes in the general medical community, it is not unusual for chronic pain patients to have been dealing with some level of pain and subsequent disability for months or years. Patterns of thoughts, behaviors, and emotions become more engrained and difficult to treat with time, as a "new normal" develops.

In addition, the more debilitating the symptoms, the more challenging it can be to create opportunities for good coping. For instance, the social connection needed to combat symptoms of depression and anxiety can be more challenging if the child is extremely isolated and not attending school or playing with friends. The parents' stress level is often higher and the family dynamic more impacted if the severity of the child's symptoms makes it difficult or impossible for a parent to work. Even attending outpatient treatment can be extremely difficult and stressful for families if the child struggles to get out of bed or ride in a car. These practical issues deeply influence the treatment course. Helping the family to problem-solve (and to develop their own problem-solving skills) is often an essential investment of time and treatment resources.

Stages of Development

A child's stage of development also influences the treatment process. Development is often uneven across domains, and there are wide ranges in developmental capacities at any particular age. Therefore, the consideration of individual differences and the whole child is essential.

A child's cognitive developmental stage, including factors such as capacity for abstract as opposed to concrete thought, influences his/her ability to understand pain and utilize coping skills (Lynch, Kashikar-Zuck, Goldschneider, & Jones, 2007). Consider the child's cognitive style, tendency toward obsessive thinking, and flexibility/rigidity when selecting interventions. This can be particularly relevant when comorbid diagnoses such as autism spectrum disorder are present.

Emotional development also is important to consider. As children get older, they are better able to understand and control their own emotions, and to understand and respond to the emotions of others. These abilities can influence the pain experience, and the pain experience can influence this area of development

(Lynch et al., 2007). One may see a regression in emotional development as a result of pain, or a stunting of emotional growth because of it (Palermo, 2012). Emotional development also encompasses the development of behavioral competence, and the increasing ability to control one's own behavior, direct one's own activity, and, particularly notable in the case of pain, intentionally override natural instincts and control reactivity.

Social developmental stage also is important in pain treatment. Understanding his/her impact on others, and correctly interpreting and responding to the social cues of others, influences a child's ability to interact effectively with medical providers, family, and peers. The ability to successfully and functionally elicit appropriate support from others and to navigate peer relationships can be challenging for youth with pain; however, these skills are essential components of successful functioning with pain (Palermo, 2012; Bursch et al., 2003).

Social development is tied closely to language development. Children who do not yet have good language skills may struggle to explain their pain to others, and sometimes even to themselves. This presents challenges to being able to adequately cope with that pain experience, and to elicit appropriate responses from those around them, including friends, family, and healthcare providers.

Treatment Approaches

A variety of treatment approaches are used in psychosocial intervention for children with chronic pain. The research of psychological therapies often does not delineate clearly between techniques. The landmark Cochrane review on psychological therapy and chronic pain in children (Eccleston et al., 2014) reviewed the use of relaxation, hypnosis, coping skills training, biofeedback, and cognitive-behavioral therapy. The review found that psychological interventions are effective in reducing the intensity of pain for chronic headache, recurrent abdominal pain, fibromyalgia, and sickle cell disease.

Cognitive-behavioral therapy (CBT), which enjoys the greatest empirical support, has become the primary mode of psychosocial intervention for this population (Palermo, 2012). Multiple randomized controlled trials demonstrate improvement in pain and pain-related problems across a wide spectrum of chronic pain syndromes (Ehde et al., 2014; Eccleston et al., 2014). CBT targets the maladaptive cognitive, behavioral, and psychological patterns that often emerge as a result of the pain experience and/or contribute to it (Palermo et al., 2010). CBT often includes a significant amount of psychoeducation, as a child's and family's understanding of pain and the biopsychosocial model is essential to successful treatment.

There are many mind–body therapy interventions that have been utilized frequently in pediatric chronic pain treatment. Acceptance and commitment therapy (ACT) mindfulness-based approaches are establishing themselves as methods of treatment for chronic pain (Veehof, Trompetter, Bohlmeijer, & Schreurs, 2016; Pielech, Vowles, & Wicksell, 2017). One of the goals of ACT is to help patients recognize the ways in which their attempts to suppress, manage, and control emotional experiences impact their symptom presentation. Therapists and clients work to increase psychological flexibility through core ACT processes: acceptance, the opposite of experiential avoidance; cognitive defusion, in which negative thoughts are observed mindfully instead of avoided or reasoned away; chosen values; and committed action. While more research is needed regarding efficacy, mediating factors, and optimized delivery of ACT to children and adolescents, the initial work in this area shows promise for improved functioning and physical performance (Gauntlett-Gilbert, Connell, Clinch, & McCracken, 2012; Wicksell & Greco, 2008; Wicksell, Olssen, & Hayes, 2011).

Mindfulness, which has been utilized increasingly with children in school settings to combat psychological distress, has been demonstrated effective in adults with chronic pain (Britton et al., 2014). Moreover, there is promising data on the effective use of mindfulness to treat pediatric chronic pain (Jastrowski Mano et al., 2013; Waelde et al., 2017). Yoga, a component of many mindfulness interventions, is an important biophysical pain management tool utilized in the treatment of pediatric chronic pain (Evans, Tsao, Sternlieb, & Zeltzer, 2009; Kraag, Zeegers, Kok, Hosman & Abu-Saad, 2006).

Hypnosis enjoys good empirical support in the treatment of chronic pain (Eccleston et al., 2014; Vlieger et al., 2007; Tomé-Pires & Miró, 2012; Kohen, 2010) and can be extremely useful on many levels within the pediatric chronic pain population. It facilitates effective dissociation from pain and efficient self-regulation; hypnosis also combines well with CBT and provides a context for disrupting maladaptive patterns and creating more adaptive responses (Yapko, 2012). The goal in pediatric populations often is to instruct the patient on the self-hypnotic technique as an empowerment tool to use for symptom management and shifting perceptions of pain (Brown Rojas, and Gouda, 2017), which builds self-efficacy.

Technology-based interventions are helpful for youth with chronic pain, promoting mind–body integration through methods such as biofeedback and virtual reality (VR). Biofeedback is a technology-based training tool that measures biophysical information and physiological responses of a person's autonomic arousal (Coakley & Wihak, 2017). Biofeedback enables youth with chronic pain to assess, monitor, and shift physiological and psychological responses to pain. This tool offers a concrete "gaming" quality, which offers visual feedback of physiological responses on a computer screen as the child engages in specific types of breathing exercises to manipulate heart-rate variability, as well as uses with other CBT and muscle relaxation techniques (Coakley & Wihak, 2017).

Treatment Delivery Modalities

Pediatric chronic pain intervention is delivered in many modalities, with the combination of medical and non-pharmacological treatments often the most effective (Yazdani & Zeltzer, 2013). Typically, the primary method of psychological service for youth with chronic pain is individual therapy (Eccleston et al., 2014). This modality allows providers to meet specific needs and tailor treatment goals, pace, and interventions for each individual. The amount of individual work, family work, and parenting work depends upon the child's chronological age and developmental level (e.g., older children typically work more independently), as well as the specific barriers to progress and targets of intervention as identified during the assessment process. For example, dysfunctional family dynamics might be the most significant factor in symptom presentation for some patients, while for others the lack of self-regulation skills might be primary.

There has been a recent increase in research regarding the use of group therapy interventions for pediatric chronic pain (Coakley, Wihak, Kossowsky, Iversen, & Donado, 2017; Huestis et al., 2017; Palermo et al., 2010). Group-based formats for adolescents and their parents have yielded improvements in pain catastrophizing, acceptance, and protective parenting (Asen & Scholz, 2010; Coakley et al., 2017; Huestis et al., 2017). Additionally, these same studies found similar positive effects on functional disability, pain interference, fatigue, anxiety, and depression. In general, girls respond well to group pain treatment formats, which demonstrates a broader need to provide this type of intervention because the pediatric chronic pain population is largely female (Boerner, Eccleston, Chambers, & Keogh, 2017). Group treatment delivery also can help address the challenges of high demand and limited resources.

Family therapy and parenting work are important intervention modalities, given the central role that parents play in a child's world and subsequently in his/her pain treatment (Sieberg et al., 2017; Van Slyke & Walker, 2006). One meta-analysis found that including parents in psychological therapies reduces pain levels in children (Eccleston et al., 2012). The review found that CBT significantly improves child symptoms, and problem-solving therapy significantly improves parent behavior and parent mental health immediately post-treatment.

Although treatment often is provided to individual families, treatment also can be conducted within a multifamily group setting. For example, the Comfort Ability course developed at Boston Children's Hospital by Dr. Rachel Coakley and her team (Coakley et al., 2017) offers a day-long chronic pain intervention for youth and their parents and incorporates cognitive-behavioral psychoeducation, relaxation and coping skills development, and parent training for pain management. Multifamily group interventions have been demonstrating significant improvements and may be an excellent method of treatment delivery (Coakley et al., 2017; Huestis et al., 2017).

Inpatient treatment may be necessary for patients unable to function in daily life or in an outpatient setting, and who thus require a higher level of structure and support. Perhaps the most notable challenge of this approach is that the success of inpatient intervention requires intense coordination of the multidisciplinary team (e.g., pain specialists, nursing staff, occupational therapists, physical therapists, psychologists, psychiatrists). However, these resources may be limited in some settings; the capacity for structured coordination is not always feasible or available.

When utilizing pharmacological interventions inpatient, a team approach is critical in order to optimize improvements in mobility, to manage daily functioning goals, to reduce catastrophic thoughts about pain, and to develop effective coping skills.

Additionally, given the primacy of goals such as increasing functioning and returning to normal activities, the inpatient setting presents challenges inasmuch as it is far removed from the typical environment in which children function. As such, while at times inpatient settings are used for stabilization, typically the transition to an outpatient setting is accomplished as soon as possible. However, if done well, there is evidence for the efficacy of intensive inpatient work, and evidence that improvements can be maintained at follow-up (Hechler et al., 2014; Hirschfeld et al., 2012).

Given the contradictory nature of the goal to function independently and the experience at an inpatient setting, intensive outpatient programs (IOPs) are becoming more popular for the treatment of children and adolescents coping with severe disability and uncontrolled pain. The number of IOPs in the United States is limited, but institutions that have them include Lucile Packard Children's Hospital at Stanford, Boston Children's Hospital, Cleveland Clinic Children's, and Seattle Children's Hospital. The programs typically last three to eight weeks, require multiple hours of intervention each day, and commonly include daily coordination with physical therapy, occupational therapy, psychology, and other medical providers (Logan et al., 2012). Family and parenting work also are included, and many programs have a school component as well.

These programs are not without their practical challenges for the family, given that they require intense participation and may require relocation away from home for long periods of time. Often this involves a tremendous commitment of financial resources, separation from other family members, and time off from work. Given these sacrifices, it is useful to know that the research strongly supports the efficacy of these programs. Positive impacts on pain intensity, functional disability, mood symptoms, and readiness to change have all been identified (Hechler et al., 2011; Simons et al., 2012; Logan et al., 2012). Benefits can be profound for patients with high levels of pain-related disability and distress (e.g., patients with conditions such as CRPS), including patients who struggled to progress in the less structured, typical outpatient setting. IOPs can produce rapid and dramatic improvements in physical and emotional functioning, and decreases in disability (Simons et al., 2012; Logan et al., 2012).

The need for more cost-effective and accessible services has prompted the increasing use of technology interventions for the treatment of pediatric chronic pain. Given the scarcity of qualified pediatric pain management providers and the abundance of patients in need, telehealth and internet-based interventions hold out the possibility of better meeting the ever-growing demands for care. This is particularly relevant for patients who live in rural or remote areas without good access to appropriate pediatric chronic pain healthcare resources.

The research on internet-based intervention is promising (Fisher, Law, Palermo, & Eccleston, 2015; Law et al., 2017; Palermo et al., 2016; Palermo et al., 2018), but there is much to be clarified about the necessary components, legal and ethical issues, and effective methods of delivery. There is promising evidence that internet-based peer support programs can lead to improvements in pain intensity, activity limitations, health distress, and self-efficacy, and some limited evidence of pain reduction (Bender, Radhakrishnan, Diorio, Englesakis, & Jadad, 2011; Law et al., 2017). Internet-delivered CBT intervention shows promise for impacting both child and parent experiences of pain, including reductions in children's activity limitations and improvements in parent behavioral and mood responses to pain (Palermo et al., 2016; Palermo et al., 2018). A 2015 meta-analysis found psychological therapies delivered remotely demonstrate at least some efficacy in reducing the intensity or severity of pain after treatment across conditions (Fisher et al., 2015). It was noted that all these therapies were behavioral and cognitive-behavioral in nature, and that more research is needed to further understand the efficacy and the process.

Future Directions

The need for more research is a persistent theme in pediatric chronic pain. As is often the case for pediatric populations, more needs to be done to continue to clarify the most effective treatments and to improve the ability to deliver those treatments efficiently. Currently, demand firmly outpaces available resources. As a field, pain medicine continues to embrace the utility of the biopsychosocial model, to acknowledge that children are not simply small adults, to take advantage of medical advances, and to explore the use of technology in order to increase efficiency and to reach a broader audience.

References

Asen, E., & Scholz, M. (2010). *Multi-family therapy: Concepts and techniques.* New York, NY: Routledge.

Bender, J. L., Radhakrishnan, A., Diorio, C., Englesakis, M., & Jadad, A. R. (2011). Can pain be managed through the Internet? A systematic review of randomized controlled trials. *PAIN, 152*(8), 1740–1750.

Betsch, T. A., Gorodzinsky, A. Y., Finley, G. A., Sangster, M., & Chorney, J. (2017). What's in a name? health care providers' perceptions of pediatric pain patients based on diagnostic labels. *The Clinical Journal of Pain, 33*(8), 694–698.

Boerner, K. E., Eccleston, C., Chambers, C. T., & Keogh, E. (2017). Sex differences in the efficacy of psychological therapies for the management of chronic and recurrent pain in children and adolescents: A systematic review and meta-analysis. *Pain, 158*(4), 569–582.

Britton, W. B., Lepp, N. E., Niles, H. F., Rocha, T., Fisher, N. E., & Gold, J. S. (2014). A randomized controlled pilot trial of classroom-based mindfulness meditation compared to an active control condition in sixth-grade children. *Journal of School Psychology, 52,* 263–278.

Brown, M. L., Rojas, E., & Gouda, S. (2017). A mind—body approach to pediatric pain management. *Children, 4*(6), 50.

Bursch, B. (2006). Somatization disorders. In M. Hersen & J. C. Thomas (Eds.), Robert T. Ammerman (Volume Ed.), *Comprehensive handbook of personality and psychopathology, volume III: Child psychopathology*. New York, NY: John Wiley & Sons.

Bursch, B., Joseph, M. H., Zeltzer, L. K., Schechter, N. L., Berde, C. B., & Yaster, M. (2003). Pain-associated disability syndrome. In N. L. Schechter, C. B. Berde, & M. Yaster (Eds.), *Pain in infants, children, and adolescents* (pp. 841–848). Philadelphia, PA: Lippincott, Williams, & Williams.

Bursch, B., Walco, G. A., & Zeltzer, L. (1998). Clinical assessment and management of chronic pain and pain-associated disability syndrome. *Journal of Developmental and Behavioral Pediatrics, 19*(1), 45–53.

Campo, J. V., & Fritz, G. (2001). A management model for pediatric somatization. *Psychosomatics, 42*(6), 467–476.

Clementi, M. A., Kao, G. S., & Monico, E. (2017). Pain acceptance as a predictor of medical utilization and school absenteeism in adolescents with chronic pain. *Journal of Pediatric Psychology, 43*(3), 294–302.

Coakley, R., & Wihak, T. (2017). Evidence-based psychological interventions for the management of pediatric chronic pain: New directions in research and clinical practice. *Children, 4*(2), 9.

Coakley, R., Wihak, T., Kossowsky, J., Iversen, C., & Donado, C. (2017). The comfort ability pain management workshop: A preliminary, nonrandomized investigation of a brief, cognitive, biobehavioral, and parent training intervention for pediatric chronic pain. *Journal of Pediatric Psychology*.

Coffelt, T. A., Bauer, B. D., & Carroll, A. E. (2013). Inpatient characteristics of the child admitted with chronic pain. *Pediatrics, 132*(2), e422–e429.

Cohen, L. L., Lemanek, K., Blount, R. L., Dahlquist, L. M., Lim, C. S., Palermo, T. M., . . . Weiss, K. E. (2007). Evidence-based assessment of pediatric pain. *Journal of Pediatric Psychology, 33*(9), 939–955.

Cohen, M., Quintner, J., & Buchanan, D. (2011). Stigmatization of patients with chronic pain: The extinction of empathy. *Pain Medicine, 12*, 1637–1643.

Cohen, L. L., Vowles, K. E., & Eccleston, C. (2010). Parenting an adolescent with chronic pain: An investigation of how a taxonomy of adolescent functioning relates to parent distress. *Journal of Pediatric Psychology, 35*, 748–757.

Connelly, M., & Schanberg, L. (2006). Latest developments in the assessment and management of chronic musculoskeletal pain syndromes in children. *Current Opinion in Rheumatology, 18*(5), 496–502.

Crombez, G., Bijttebier, P., Eccleston, C., Mascagni, T., Mertens, G., Goubert, L., & Verstraeten, K. (2003). The child version of the pain catastrophizing scale (PCS-C): A preliminary validation. *Pain, 104*(3), 639–646.

de la Vega, R., Groenewald, C., Bromberg, M. H., Beals-Erickson, S. E., & Palermo, T. M. (2018). Chronic pain prevalence and associated factors in adolescents with and without physical disabilities. *Developmental Medicine & Child Neurology, 60*(6), 596–601.

Duckworth, A. L., & Steinberg, L. (2015). Unpacking self-control. *Child Development Perspectives, 9*(1), 32–37.

Eccleston, C., Crombez, G., Scotford, A., Clinch, J., & Connell, H. (2004). Adolescent chronic pain: Patterns and predictors of emotional distress in adolescents with chronic pain and their parents. *Pain, 108*, 221–229.

Eccleston, C., Palermo, T. M., Fisher, E., & Law, E. (2012). Psychological interventions for parents of children and adolescents with chronic illness. *Cochrane Database of Systematic Reviews, 8*(8).

Eccleston, C., Palermo, T. M., Williams, A. C. D. C., Lewandowski Holley, A., Morley, S., Fisher, E., & Law, E. (2014). Psychological therapies for the management of chronic and recurrent pain in children and adolescents. *The Cochrane Library*, *5*.

Egger, H. L., Costello, E. J., Erkanli, A., & Angold, A. (1999). Somatic complaints and psychopathology in children and adolescents: Stomach aches, musculoskeletal pains, and headaches. *Journal of the American Academy of Child & Adolescent Psychiatry*, *38*(7), 852–860.

Ehde, D. M., Dillworth, T. M., & Turner, J. A. (2014). Cognitive-behavioral therapy for individuals with chronic pain: Efficacy, innovations, and directions for research. *American Psychologist*, *69*(2), 153.

Evans, S., Tsao, J. C., Sternlieb, B., & Zeltzer, L. K. (2009). Using the biopsychosocial model to understand the health benefits of yoga. *Journal of Complementary and Integrative Medicine*, *6*(1).

Fales, J., Palermo, T. M., Law, E. F., & Wilson, A. C. (2015). Sleep outcomes in youth with chronic pain participating in a randomized controlled trial of online cognitive-behavioral therapy for pain management. *Behavioral Sleep Medicine*, *13*(2), 107–123.

Fisher, E., Heathcote, L. C., Eccleston, C., Simons, L. E., & Palermo, T. M. (2017). Assessment of pain anxiety, pain catastrophizing, and fear of pain in children and adolescents with chronic pain: A systematic review and meta-analysis. *Journal of Pediatric Psychology*, *43*(3), 314–325.

Fisher, E., Heathcote, L., Palermo, T. M., de C Williams, A. C., Lau, J., & Eccleston, C. (2014). Systematic review and meta-analysis of psychological therapies for children with chronic pain. *Journal of Pediatric Psychology*, *39*(8), 763–782.

Fisher, E., Law, E., Palermo, T. M., & Eccleston, C. (2015). Psychological therapies (remotely delivered) for the management of chronic and recurrent pain in children and adolescents. *Cochrane Database of Systematic Reviews (Online)*, *3*, CD011118.

Forgeron, P. A., King, S., Stinson, J. N., McGrath, P. J., MacDonald, A. J., & Chambers, C. T. (2010). Social functioning and peer relationships in children and adolescents with chronic pain: A systematic review. *Pain Research and Management*, *15*(1), 27–41.

Friedrichsdorf, S. J., Giordano, J., Desai Dakoji, K., Warmuth, A., Daughtry, C., & Schulz, C. A. (2016). Chronic pain in children and adolescents: Diagnosis and treatment of primary pain disorders in head, abdomen, muscles and joints. *Children*, *3*(4), 42.

Gauntlett-Gilbert, J., Connell, H., Clinch, J., & McCracken, L. M. (2012). Acceptance and values-based treatment of adolescents with chronic pain: Outcomes and their relationship to acceptance. *Journal of Pediatric Psychology*, *38*(1), 72–81.

Geraghty, M. E., & Buse, D. C. (2015). The biopsychosocialspiritual impact of chronic pain, chronic illness, and physical disabilities in adolescence. *Current Pain Headache Rep*, *19*, 51.

Gold, J. I., Mahrer, N. E., Yee, J., & Palermo, T. M. (2009). Pain, fatigue and health-related quality of life in children and adolescents with chronic pain. *Clinical Journal of Pain*, *25*, 407–441.

Gorodzinsky, A. Y., Davies, W. H., Tran, S. T., Medrano, G. R., Bernacki, J. M., Burks, L. M., ... Weisman, S. J. (2013). Adolescents' perceptions of family dynamics when a sibling has chronic pain. *Child Health Care*, *42*(4), 333–352.

Hechler, T., Kanstrup, M., Holley, A. L., Simons, L. E., Wicksell, R., Hirschfeld, G., & Zernikow, B. (2015). Systematic review on intensive interdisciplinary pain treatment of children with chronic pain. *Pediatrics*, *136*, 115–127.

Hechler, T., Martinl, A., Blankenburgl, M., Schroederl, S., Kosfelderl, J., Hölscherl, L., ... Zernikowl, B. (2011). Specialized multimodal outpatient treatment for children with chronic pain: Treatment pathways and long-term outcome. *European Journal of Pain*, *15*(9), 976–984.

Hechler, T., Ruhe, A. K., Schmidt, P., Hirsch, J., Wager, J., Dobe, M., . . . Zernikow, B. (2014). Inpatient-based intensive interdisciplinary pain treatment for highly impaired children with severe chronic pain: Randomized controlled trial of efficacy and economic effects. *PAIN, 155*(1), 118–128.

Hirschfeld, G., Hechler, T., Dobe, M., Wager, J., von Lützau, P., Blankenburg, M., . . . Zernikow, B. (2012). Maintaining lasting improvements: One-year follow-up of children with severe chronic pain undergoing multimodal inpatient treatment. *Journal of Pediatric Psychology, 38*(2), 224–236.

Huguet, A., & Miró, J. (2008). The severity of chronic pediatric pain: An epidemiological study. *The Journal of Pain, 9*(3), 226–236.

Huestis, S. E., Kao, G., Dunn, A., Hilliard, A. T., Yoon, I. A., Golianu, B., & Bhandari, R. P. (2017). Multi-family pediatric pain group therapy: Capturing acceptance and cultivating change. *Children, 4*(12), 106.

Jacobson, C. J. Jr, Kashikar-Zuck, S., Farrell, J., Barnett, K., Goldschneider, K., Dampier, C., . . . DeWitt, E. M. (2015). Qualitative evaluation of pediatric pain behavior, quality, and intensity item candidates and the PROMIS pain domain framework in children with chronic pain. *The Journal of Pain, 16*(12), 1243–1255.

Jastrowski Mano, K. E., Salamon, K. S., Hainsworth, K. R., Anderson Khan, K. J., Ladwig, R. J., Davies, W. H., & Weisman, S. J. (2013). A randomized, controlled pilot study of mindfulness-based stress reduction for pediatric chronic pain. *Alternative Therapy Health Medicine, 19*, 8–14.

Kashikar-Zuck, S., Goldschneider, K. R., Powers, S. W., Vaught, M. H., & Hershey, A. D. (2001). Depression and functional disability in chronic pediatric pain. *The Clinical Journal of Pain, 17*(4), 341–349.

Kashikar-Zuck, S., Sil, S., Lynch-Jordan, A. M., Ting, T. V., Peugh, J., Schikler, K. N., . . . Powers, S. W. (2013). Changes in pain coping, catastrophizing, and coping efficacy after cognitive-behavioral therapy in children and adolescents with juvenile fibromyalgia. *The Journal of Pain, 14*(5), 492–501.

King, S., Chambers, C. T., Huguet, A., MacNevin, R. C., McGrath, P. J., & MacDonald, A. J. (2011). The epidemiology of chronic pain in children and adolescents revisited: A systemic review. *Pain, 152*, 2729–2738.

Kohen, D. P. (2010). Long-term follow-up of self-hypnosis training for recurrent headaches: What the children say. *International Journal of Clinical and Experimental Hypnosis, 58*(4), 417–432.

Kraag, G., Zeegers, M. P., Kok, G., Hosman, C., Abu-Saad, H. H. (2006). School programs targeting stress management in children and adolescents: A meta-analysis. *Journal of School Psychology, 44*, 449–472.

Langer, S. L., Romano, J. M., Mancl, L., & Levy, R. L. (2014). Parental catastrophizing partially mediates the association between parent-reported child pain behavior and parental protective responses. *Pain Research Treatment, 751097.*

Larsson, B., & Sund, A. M. (2007). Emotional/behavioural, social correlates and one-year predictors of frequent pains among early adolescents: Influences of pain characteristics. *European Journal of Pain, 11*(1), 57–57.

Law, E. F., Fisher, E., Howard, W. J., Levy, R., Ritterband, L., & Palermo, T. M. (2017). Longitudinal change in parent and child functioning after internet-delivered cognitive-behavioral therapy for chronic pain. *Pain, 158*(10), 1992–2000.

Leeuw, M., Goossens, M. E., Linton, S. J., Crombez, G., Boersma, K., & Vlaeyen, J. W. (2007). The fear-avoidance model of musculoskeletal pain: Current state of scientific evidence. *Journal of Behavioral Medicine, 30*(1), 77–94.

Levy, R. L., Langer, S. L., Walker, L. S., Romano, J. M., Christie, D. L., Youssef, N., . . . Jeffery, R. W. (2010). Cognitive-behavioral therapy for children with functional abdominal pain and their parents decreases pain and other symptoms. *The American Journal of Gastroenterology*, *105*(4), 946.

Lewandowski, A. S., Palermo, T. M., De la Motte, S., & Fu, R. (2010). Temporal daily associations between pain and sleep in adolescents with chronic pain versus healthy adolescents. *Pain*, *151*(1), 220–225.

Lewandowski, A. S., Palermo, T. M., Stinson, J., Handley, S., & Chambers, C. T. (2010). Systematic review of family functioning in families of children and adolescents with chronic pain. *The Journal of Pain*, *11*(11), 1027–1038.

Lewin, D. S., & Dahl, R. E. (1999). Importance of sleep in the management of pediatric pain. *Journal of Developmental and Behavioral Pediatrics*, *20*(4), 244–252.

Logan, D. E., Carpino, E. A., Chiang, G., Condon, M., Firn, E., & Gaughan, V. J. (2012). A day-hospital approach to treatment of pediatric complex regional pain syndrome: Initial functional outcomes. *The Clinical Journal of Pain*, *28*(9).

Logan, D. E., & Scharff, L. (2005). Relationships between family and parent characteristics and functional abilities in children with recurrent pain syndromes: An investigation of moderating effects on the pathway from pain to disability. *Journal of Pediatric Psychology*, *30*(8), 698–707.

Logan, D. E., Simons, L. E., & Kaczynski, K. J. (2009). School functioning in adolescents with chronic pain: The role of depressive symptoms in school impairment. *Journal of Pediatric Psychology*, *34*(8), 882–892.

Logan, D. E., Simons, L. E., Stein, M. J., & Chastain, L. (2008). School impairment in adolescents with chronic pain. *The Journal of Pain*, *9*(5), 407–416.

Long, A. C., Krishnamurthy, V., & Palermo, T. M. (2007). Sleep disturbances in school-age children with chronic pain. *Journal of Pediatric Psychology*, *33*(3), 258–268.

Lynch, A. M., Kashikar-Zuck, S., Goldschneider, K. R., & Jones, B. A. (2007). Sex and age differences in coping styles among children with chronic pain. *Journal of Pain and Symptom Management*, *33*(2), 208–216.

Mahrer, N. E., Gold, J. I., Luu, M., & Herman, P. M. (2018). A cost-analysis of an interdisciplinary pediatric chronic pain clinic. *Journal of Pain*, *19*(2), 158–165.

Martin, S. R., Cohen, L. L., Mougianis, I., Griffin, A., Sil, S., & Dampier, C. (2018). Stigma and pain in adolescents hospitalized for sickle cell vasoocclusive pain episodes. *The Clinical Journal of Pain*, *34*(5), 438–444.

Masters, K. S. (2006). Recurrent abdominal pain, medical interventions, and biofeedback: What happened to the biopsychosocial model? *Applied Psychophysiology and Biofeedback*, *31*, 155–165.

Maynard, C. S., Amari, A., Wieczorek, B., Christensen, J. R., & Slifer, K. J. (2009). Interdisciplinary behavioral rehabilitation of pediatric pain-associated disability: Retrospective review of an inpatient treatment protocol. *Journal of Pediatric Psychology*, *35*(2), 128–137.

McGrath, P. J., Walco, G. A., Turk, D. C., Dworkin, R. H., Brown, M. T., Davidson, K., . . . Zeltzer, L. (2008). Core outcome domains and measures for pediatric acute and chronic/recurrent pain clinical trials: PedIMMPACT recommendations. *The Journal of Pain*, *9*(9), 771–783.

Miró, J., Castarlenas, E., & Huguet, A. (2009). Evidence for the use of a numerical rating scale to assess the intensity of pediatric pain. *European Journal of Pain*, *13*(10), 1089–1095.

Miró, J., de la Vega, R., Gertz, K. J., Jensen, M. P., & Engel, J. M. (2017). The role of perceived family social support and parental solicitous responses in adjustment to bothersome pain in young people with physical disabilities. *Disability and Rehabilitation*, 1–8.

Nelson, S., Simons, L. E., & Logan, D. (2018). The incidence of adverse childhood experiences (ACEs) and their association with pain-related and psychosocial impairment in youth with chronic pain. *The Clinical Journal of Pain*, *34*(5), 402–408.

Noel, M., Wilson, A. C., Holley, A. L., Durkin, L., Patton, M., & Palermo, T. M. (2016). Posttraumatic stress disorder symptoms in youth with vs without chronic pain. *Pain*, *157*(10), 2277–2284.

Palermo, T. M. (2012). *Cognitive-behavioral therapy for chronic pain in children and adolescents.* Oxford: Oxford University Press.

Palermo, T. M., & Kiska, R. (2005). Subjective sleep disturbances in adolescents with chronic pain: Relationship to daily functioning and quality of life. *The Journal of Pain*, *6*(3), 201–207.

Palermo, T. M., & Chambers, C. T. (2005). Parent and family factors in pediatric chronic pain and disability: An integrative approach. *Pain*, 119, 1–4.

Palermo, T. M., Dudeney, J., Santanelli, J. P., Carletti, A., & Zempsky, W. T. (2018). Feasibility and acceptability of internet-delivered cognitive behavioral therapy for chronic pain in adolescents with sickle cell disease and their parents. *Journal of Pediatric Hematology/Oncology*, *40*(2), 122–127.

Palermo, T. M., & Eccleston, C. (2009). Parents of children and adolescents with chronic pain. *Pain*, *146*, 15–17.

Palermo, T. M., Eccleston, C., Lewandowski, A., Williams, A., & Morley, S. (2010). Randomized controlled trials of psychological therapies for management of chronic pain in children and adolescents: An updated meta-analysis review. *Pain*, *148*(3), 387–397.

Palermo, T. M., Law, E. F., Fales, J., Bromberg, M. H., Jessen-Fiddick, T., & Tai, G. (2016). Internet-delivered cognitive-behavioral treatment for adolescents with chronic pain and their parents: A randomized controlled multicenter trial. *Pain*, *157*(1), 174.

Palermo, T. M., Toliver-Sokol, M., Fonareva, I., & Koh, J. L. (2007). Objective and subjective assessment of sleep in adolescents with chronic pain compared to healthy adolescents. *The Clinical Journal of Pain*, *23*(9), 812.

Palermo, T. M., Valrie, C. R., & Karlson, C. W. (2014). Family and parent influences on pediatric chronic pain: A developmental perspective. *American Psychologist*, *69*(2), 142.

Peterson, C. C., & Palermo, T. M. (2004). Parental reinforcement of recurrent pain: The moderating impact of child depression and anxiety on functional disability. *Journal of Pediatric Psychology*, *29*(5), 331–341.

Pielech, M., Vowles, K. E., & Wicksell, R. (2017). Acceptance and commitment therapy for pediatric chronic pain: Theory and application. *Children*, *4*(2), 10.

Quartana, P. J., Campbell, C. M., & Edwards, R. R. (2009). Pain catastrophizing: A critical review. *Expert Review of Neurotherapeutics*, *9*(5), 745–758.

Roth-Isigkeit, A., Thyen, U., Stöven, H., Schwarzenberger, J., & Schmucker, P. (2005). Pain among children and adolescents: Restrictions in daily living and triggering factors. *Pediatrics*, *115*(2), e152–e162.

Robbins, P. M., Smith, S. M., Glutting, J. J., & Bishop, C. T. (2005). A randomized controlled trial of a cognitive-behavioral family intervention for pediatric recurrent abdominal pain. *Journal of Pediatric Psychology*, *30*, 397–408.

Sieberg, C. B., Smith, A., White, M., Manganella, J., Sethna, N., & Logan, D. E. (2017). Changes in maternal and paternal pain-related attitudes, behaviors, and perceptions across pediatric pain rehabilitation treatment: A multilevel modeling approach. *Journal of Pediatric Psychology*, *42*(1), 52–64.

Simons, L. E., Logan, D. E., Chastain, L., & Cerullo, M. (2010). Engagement in multidisciplinary interventions for pediatric chronic pain: Parental expectations, barriers, and child outcomes. *The Clinical Journal of Pain*, *26*(4), 291–299.

Simons, L. E., Sieberg, C. B., Carpino, E., Logan, D., & Berde, C. (2011). The Fear of Pain Questionnaire (FOPQ): Assessment of pain-related fear among children and adolescents with chronic pain. *The Journal of Pain*, *12*(6), 677–686.

Simons, L. E., Sieberg, C. B., Pielech, M., Conroy, C., & Logan, D. E. (2012). What does it take? Comparing intensive rehabilitation to outpatient treatment for children with significant pain-related disability. *Journal of Pediatric Psychology*, *38*(2), 213–223.

Stanford, E. A., Chambers, C. T., Biesanz, J. C., & Chen, E. (2008). The frequency, trajectories and predictors of adolescent recurrent pain: A population-based approach. *Pain*, *138*(1), 11–21.

Tomé-Pires, C., & Miró, J. (2012). Hypnosis for the management of chronic and cancer procedure-related pain in children. *International Journal of Clinical and Experimental Hypnosis*, *60*(4), 432–457.

Tran, S. T., Jastrowski Mano, K. E., Hainsworth, K. R., Medrano, G. R., Anderson Khan, K., Weisman, S. J., & Davies, W. H. (2015). Distinct influences of anxiety and pain catastrophizing on functional outcomes in children and adolescents with chronic pain. *Journal of Pediatric Psychology*, *40*, 744–755. doi:10.1093/jpepsy/jsv029

Tumin, D., Drees, D., Miller, R., Wrona, S., Hayes, D. Jr, Tobias, J. D., & Bhalla, T. (2018). Health care utilization and costs associated with pediatric chronic pain. *The Journal of Pain*, *19*(9), 973–982.

Valrie, C. R., Bromberg, M. H., Palermo, T., & Schanberg, L. E. (2013). A systematic review of sleep in pediatric pain populations. *Journal of Developmental and Behavioral Pediatrics: JDBP*, *34*(2), 120.

Van Slyke, D. A., Walker, L. S. (2006). Mothers' responses to children's pain. *Clinical Journal of Pain*, *22*(4), 387–391.

Varni, J. W., Stucky, B. D., Thissen, D., DeWitt, E. M., Irwin, D. E., Lai, J. S., . . . DeWalt, D. A. (2010). PROMIS pediatric pain interference scale: An item response theory analysis of the pediatric pain item bank. *The Journal of Pain*, *11*(11), 1109–1119.

Veehof, M. M., Trompetter, H. R., Bohlmeijer, E. T., & Schreurs, K. M. G. (2016). Acceptance- and mindfulness-based interventions for the treatment of chronic pain: A meta-analytic review. *Cognitive Behaviour Therapy*, *45*(1), 5–31.

Vervoort, T., Goubert, L., Eccleston, C., Bijttebier, P., & Crombez, G. (2005). Catastrophic thinking about pain is independently associated with pain severity, disability, and somatic complaints in school children and children with chronic pain. *Journal of Pediatric Psychology*, *31*(7), 674–683.

Vitulano, L. A. (2003). Psychosocial issues for children and adolescents with chronic illness: Self-esteem, school functioning and sports participation. *Child Adolescent Psychiatric Clinics of North America*, *12*, 585–592.

Vlieger, A. M., Menko-Frankenhuis, C., Wolfkamp, S. C., Tromp, E., & Benninga, M. A. (2007). Hypnotherapy for children with functional abdominal pain or irritable bowel syndrome: A randomized controlled trial. *Gastroenterology*, *133*(5), 1430–1436.

Vohs, K. D., & Baumeister, R. F. (Eds.). (2016). *Handbook of self-regulation: Research, theory, and applications*. New York, NY: The Guilford Press.

Waelde, L. C., Feinstein, A. B., Bhandari, R., Griffin, A., Yoon, I. A., & Golianu, B. (2017). A Pilot study of mindfulness meditation for pediatric chronic pain. *Children*, *4*(5), 32.

Wailoo, K. (2014). *Dying in the city of the blues: Sickle cell anemia and the politics of race and health*. Chapel Hill, NC: UNC Press Books.

Walker, L. S., Claar, R. L., & Garber, J. (2002). Social consequences of children's pain: When do they encourage symptom maintenance? *Journal of Pediatric Psychology*, *27*(8), 689–698.

Walker, L. S., Dengler-Crish, C. M., Rippel, S., & Bruehl, S. (2010). Functional abdominal pain in childhood and adolescence increases risk for chronic pain in adulthood. *Pain*, *150*, 568–572.

Weiss, K. E., Harbeck-Weber, C., Zaccariello, M. J., Kimondo, J. N., Harrison, T. E., & Bruce, B. K. (2017). Executive functioning in pediatric chronic pain: Do deficits exist? *Pain Medicine*, *19*(1), 60–67.

Wicksell, R. K., & Greco, L. A. (2008). Acceptance and commitment therapy for pediatric chronic pain. In L. A. Greco & S. C. Hayes (Eds.), *Acceptance and mindfulness treatments for children and adolescents: A practitioner's guide* (pp. 89–113). Oakland, CA: New Harbinger Publications.

Wicksell, R. K., Olsson, G. L., & Hayes, S. C. (2011). Mediators of change in acceptance and commitment therapy for pediatric chronic pain. *Pain, 152*(12), 2792–2801.

Yapko, M. D. (2012). *Trancework: An introduction to the practice of clinical hypnosis.* Abingdon: Routledge.

Yazdani, S., & Zeltzer, L. (2013). Treatment of chronic pain in children and adolescents. *Pain Management, 3*(4), 303–314.

Zeltzer, L. K., Tsao, J. C., Bursch, B., & Myers, C. D. (2005). Introduction to the special issue on pain: From pain to pain-associated disability syndrome. *Journal of Pediatric Psychology, 31*(7), 661–666.

Zernikow, B., Wager, J., Hechler, T., Hasan, C., Rohr, U., Dobe, M., . . . Blankenburg, M. (2012). Characteristics of highly impaired children with severe chronic pain: A 5-year retrospective study on 2249 pediatric pain patients. *BMC Pediatrics, 12*(1), 54.

21

Psychiatric Treatment Approaches for Pediatric Pain

Ian Kodish

Introduction

The neurophysiologic complexity of chronic pain disorders in youth calls for coordinated interdisciplinary approaches anchored in a biopsychosocial model of care that regards emotional health as an essential component. Pain amplifies developmental challenges in children, heightening risk of subsequent anxiety and depressive disorders. However, psychiatric care often is neglected due to limited provider access and challenges of integrating treatments across specialties. The multifactorial nature of pediatric pain disorders increasingly is understood to be highly impacted by experiential and parental factors, including parental trauma and psychopathology (Neville, Soltani, Pavlova, & Noel, 2018). Thus, addressing the socioemotional needs of youth with chronic pain requires a broad approach that addresses individual functioning while simultaneously optimizing patients' environments, working within family contexts to best facilitate adaptive coping. Effective psychiatric intervention can play a crucial role in restoring neurophysiologic and emotional functioning, enabling youth with chronic pain to reengage in activities critical to their recovery.

Nurturing social, cognitive, and emotional development is a foundational initiative in child and adolescent psychiatry. The tremendous burden of pain disorders can hinder a child's development across all of these domains. Additional indirect effects of chronic pain (e.g., missed schooling, exasperated parents, restricted social opportunities) further deprive children of experiences and settings that drive adaptive learning. The neurophysiologic impact of chronic pain in children also is thought to directly impair cognitive functioning, as reflected by an overall achievement lag in both reading and math, and a direct association between greater numbers of pain sites and poorer reading scores (Kosola et al., 2017).

Remarkably, studies reveal that approximately 25% of youth experience chronic pain, defined as pain persisting over three months (King et al., 2011), and recent decades have seen the increasing prevalence of chronic pain in both children and adolescents. Rates also tend to increase across development, with chronic pain disorders most commonly emerging in early adolescence. This is also when higher prevalence rates begin to arise among females, and findings suggest that adolescent girls tend to have less favorable treatment outcomes compared to boys (Zernikow et al., 2012). Even in youth, chronic pain symptoms are highly distressing, costly, and debilitating, with 8% reporting their pain to be severe and disabling (Huguet & Miró, 2008). While the prognosis of chronic pain disorders in youth tends to be much more favorable compared to that of adults, particularly for musculoskeletal pain disorders (Sherry, Wallace, Kelley, Kidder, & Sapp, 1999), without comprehensive treatment, symptoms are likely to persist into adulthood (Walker, Dengler-Crish, Rippel, & Bruehl, 2010).

Rehabilitative efforts are thus focused on addressing impairments early and utilizing interdisciplinary approaches designed to build resilience through engagement and support. Despite heterogeneity in approaches, intensive rehabilitative treatments for chronic pain also have revealed positive effects on relieving disability as well as comorbid psychiatric symptoms (Hechler et al., 2015). While providing reassurance and expressing an expectation of recovery enhances engagement, children and their families also should be aware that the treatment course can be variable and protracted and that recurrence is common, particularly within the first several months after symptom resolution.

Neurodevelopmental Context of Chronic Pain

Complex neurocognitive processes, such as emotion regulation and executive functioning, are known to mature into early adulthood, parallel to extensive synaptic refinements in highly integrative brain regions such as prefrontal and superior temporal cortices that subsequently regulate these functions (Gogtay & Thompson, 2010). Through developmental plasticity, these regions become specialized to integrate widely distributed inputs across multiple primary sensory modalities, including pain sensation. When severe, pain signals can be so salient that they command attentional, cognitive, and emotional resources away from these dynamic integrative networks. These demands increasingly impact developmental refinements of circuits that underlie higher cognitive processing, creating alterations in cortical sensitivity and compromising the ability to modulate this input.

Youth with chronic pain are particularly vulnerable due to the high intensity and unpredictable chronicity of the pain stimulus. Even brief emotionally demanding situations (stressful living conditions or very poor sleep) contribute to significant alterations in pain processing, which induces heightened nociceptive and affective reactivity to experiences that might be considered benign under more favorable conditions (Cheatle et al., 2016). These associative networks continually become integrated and refined, so that chronic pain signals may become highly linked to emotional reactivity, more directly conveying a sense of emotional distress.

Reducing the emotional impact of these pain signals by utilizing our understanding of neurodevelopment and learning-induced changes in brain function thus can be critical to advancing treatment effectiveness. In the context of maladaptive brain signaling, child and adolescent psychiatrists strive to reestablish emotional and behavioral functioning in youth, including those with chronic pain, by stimulating neuroplasticity through medications and experiences designed to restore more adaptive brain functioning.

One aspect of brain functioning that increasingly is understood to improve neuroplasticity is restorative sleep. Known to be highly influential in neuroanatomical plasticity, memory consolidation, and mood regulation, restorative sleep has become appreciated for influencing pain sensitivity (Cheatle et al., 2016). Enabling the nervous system to adapt and refine requires intensive reorganization of synaptic connections, thought to be highly dependent on REM and slow-wave sleep rhythms, both of which increasingly emerge in longer sleep times (Landmann et al., 2014).

Developmental shifts in neuroplasticity also are thought to impact the timing of onset of neuropathic pain. Chronic pain signals affect stress hormones and other developmentally programed neuroendocrine signals that drive neuroplasticity within emotional processing regions of the brain, including the amygdala (Nelson, Lau, & Jarcho, 2014). These regions are known to adaptively attune to specific environmental expectancies that shift across development, so alterations in neuroendocrine signaling may misalign these opportunities for maturation of emotional networks.

Neuroinflammatory processes also are increasingly understood to underlie certain pain disorders, contributing to cortical hyperexcitability in nociceptive processing pathways among children with migraine and recurrent abdominal pain (Pas et al., 2018). In treatment studies of adults with pain disorders, neuroinflammatory markers also have been associated with less improvement in pain intensity (Lasselin et al., 2016). Interestingly, the lower prevalence of neuropathic pain observed in younger children may be driven by poorly differentiated neuroimmune responses to pain. In early development, the immune response to injury is thought to be more restricted, with nociceptive input becoming more salient only after maturation and specialization of immune reactivity, prompting specific cytokine responses that heighten nociceptive sensitivity (Fitzgerald & McKelvey, 2016). It may therefore be possible for functional and somatic symptoms to blossom later in development as manifestations of previous injuries or traumas that shaped emerging pain or motor processing networks, only to be expressed after a prolonged dormant period until developmental refinements enable network specialization.

Conceptualizing Chronic Pain

Appropriate psychiatric management of pediatric chronic pain begins with a thorough assessment, including a broad focus on socioemotional functioning and screening for psychiatric comorbidities. Younger children lack a firm cognitive appreciation for the quality, intensity, or specific pattern of their pain, so using adapted scales (such as pictures of emotional faces) can be helpful for measuring pain severity with some consistency (Rabin, Brown, & Alexander, 2017; Hauer & Houtrow, 2017). Enhancing the ability of youth to describe their pain experience also fosters the development of emotion identification and communication skills critical for emotional regulation more broadly.

Evaluating pain utilizing a biopsychosocial model further requires additional input from people in the children's environment (family, caregivers, teachers, coaches). This enables the development of a detailed profile examining how physical and socioemotional functioning may be impacted. It also allows for closer inspection of specific factors that may contribute to (or maintain) pain responses and offers opportunities to shape these factors and enhance functioning more globally.

Chronic pain disorders are conceptualized using a variety of pathophysiological classifications (nociceptive, neuropathic, or idiopathic) of abnormal pain sensitivity relating to findings of nerve damage, inflammation, body distribution, and medical comorbidities. These symptom constellations carry significant overlap and often fluctuate with varying symptoms and degrees of clinical severity (Gmuca & Sherry, 2017). This is even truer in children, often eliciting anxiety and frustration in families eager to identify a stable diagnosis with predictable and effective treatment approaches. These diagnostic challenges further hamper research efforts examining the pharmacologic management of these pain syndromes, with data dominated by findings from adult or animal populations, and off-label use of medicine often is required for comprehensive approaches to care (Sobin, Heinrich, & Drossman, 2017).

Although clearly it is important to thoughtfully evaluate chronic pain, symptoms often lack organic etiology (Wallis & Fiks, 2015). Treatments tend to focus on behavioral and emotional recovery in spite of pain, highlighting the importance of addressing functional symptoms. Functional disorders may be conceptualized (and therefore treated) quite differently based upon which specialty is managing the care. Youth with chronic pain most commonly struggle with headaches, generalized pain, or abdominal discomfort (Zernikow et al., 2012). The initial presentation often dictates which specialty is engaged, with headaches most often managed by neurologists, abdominal pain by pediatric gastroenterology (GI) specialists, and musculoskeletal pain by general practitioners and pain specialists.

In defining musculoskeletal pain disorders, "amplified musculoskeletal pain" is a broad clinical term that encompasses localized and diffuse amplified pain conditions, chronic regional pain syndrome (CRPS), and fibromyalgia. CRPS is described as both a neuropathic pain syndrome and an amplified musculoskeletal pain syndrome. Mean presentation is at age 13 years, while CPRS is much less commonly seen in young children (Rabin et al., 2017). Juvenile fibromyalgia syndrome (JFMS) is a chronic musculoskeletal pain condition specifically diagnosed in youth who present with noninflammatory pain symptoms in multiple sites, with additional minor somatic complaints, including anxiety, fatigue, headaches, poor sleep, numbness, and soft-tissue swelling (Yunus & Masi, 1985). While research in children is limited, psychological factors are thought to contribute to symptom severity in adults, including greater pain sites, greater spread of pain beyond the site of an injury, and a resulting increase in benzodiazepine and opioid use (Streltzer, Eliashof, Kline, & Goebert, 2000).

Within psychiatric domains, pain disorders recently have been reconceptualized to fall within the broader domain of somatic symptom disorders (American Psychiatric Association, 2013). Somatization is understood as a physical manifestation of various symptoms (including pain) without clear organic etiology. While this process is common in mild forms to all healthy individuals, expressing distress through physical symptoms is particularly common in younger children. When severe, symptoms can cause significant impairment and warrant clinical attention.

Some youth with chronic pain present without any identifiable medical etiology, and their impairments are conceptualized primarily by the distress associated with pain. Instead of the previous "pain disorder" diagnosis, the excessive thoughts, feelings, and behaviors related to pain symptoms that lack medical etiology are now conceptualized as a somatic symptom disorder, with the specifier "with predominant pain." The chronicity and severity of symptoms also are specified (with persistent defined as lasting over six months), while pain is the only specific symptom descriptor.

Other somatization diagnoses include functional neurological symptom disorders (FNSD). These are characterized by impaired neurologic symptoms thought to be functional in nature, such as severe unexplained weakness or non-epileptic seizures. Common psychiatric comorbidities of somatization include anxiety disorders (often with symptoms of separation anxiety or social anxiety), which also are known to impact neurophysiologic sensitivity and reactivity, and which further complicate assessment and management of somatic symptoms (Vinall, Pavlova, Asmundson, Rasic, & Noel, 2016).

While imaging and laboratory studies may be useful to establish a fuller clinical picture and rule out other pathologic processes, they lack significant predictive value for diagnosing pain syndromes in children (Rabin et al., 2017). Clinical examination is still the gold standard for diagnosis. Due to the high comorbidity of chronic pain with psychiatric symptoms in youth, clinical approaches increasingly are utilizing emotional and behavioral health perspectives to enhance treatment interventions.

Providers also must be sensitive to the notion that pain symptoms are very impactful to youth and their families, whose reactions commonly are described in clinical settings as being "out of proportion" to history and physical exam. Children and their families often perceive their providers as implying that the symptoms are not real. Even inadvertent use of stigmatizing language can lead quickly to a sense of invalidation, distrust, and frustration in patients and families. This also is commonly amplified by differing opinions on clinical management, such as provider preference to focus on psychological and coping factors in lieu of further medical work-up.

Therefore, youth and their caregivers should be offered extensive psychoeducation regarding evidence-based approaches to optimizing chronic pain management in an effort to reduce the anxiety and uncertainty of the condition. Once formulated, it is important to disseminate the case conceptualization and treatment approach among the broader care provider team in an effort to maintain fidelity to treatment strategies. This alignment can be essential for carrying through on treatment strategies that can be emotionally challenging to follow for all parties involved (and may actually result in brief escalation of symptoms), allowing youth to stay on a path toward recovery and avoid unnecessary and potentially harmful interventions.

Psychiatric and Behavioral Comorbidities in Chronic Pain

Anxiety is significantly more common in youth with chronic pain, with some estimates up to 60–80% (Vinall et al., 2016). Most common anxiety symptoms in this population include school phobia, separation anxiety, PTSD, and social anxiety, often further complicating approaches to pain management (Vinall et al., 2016). In addition, increasing evidence highlights the influence of trauma on subsequent pain symptomatology, including both cognitive appraisals and behavioral avoidance (Neville et al., 2018). This pattern can intensify social and functional impairments. Avoidant youth may feel easily overwhelmed and avoid even normative challenges, instead increasingly relying on parents or trusted adults for emotional support and a sense of protection. This process of fear avoidance contributing to escalating anxiety sensitivity parallels the development and sensitivity to chronic pain; findings suggest a strong association between the patient's anxiety with both the presentation and fluctuation of pain, as well as the response to treatment (Cunningham et al., 2016).

Catastrophic thinking also is thought to contribute to the intensity of chronic pain symptoms due to the amplification of threat appraisals that fuel behavioral avoidance. Avoidance of this threat subsequently becomes highly reinforcing. These maladaptive behavioral and cognitive responses further diminish normative experiences critical for developing adaptive responses and improving clinical and functional outcomes. Beyond preventing engagement in rehabilitative physical therapies, avoidance of activities further results in deconditioning and atrophy, and exacerbates muscular reactivity and guarded movement (Asmundson, Norton, & Norton, 1999). These findings suggest that avoidance urges may be a risk factor for (as well as a consequence of) pain sensitivity, and that this vulnerable population requires active management strategies.

Indeed, while pain-related cognitions such as catastrophizing, angry thoughts, and fear-avoidance beliefs are common, they also are predictive of poor adjustment to chronic pain (Cunningham et al., 2016). Conversely, enhancing optimism and behavioral activation is widely known to be an effective treatment strategy in youth for specific management of depression and anxiety disorders and is increasingly utilized in rehabilitative approaches for chronic pain disorders (Cousins, Cohen, & Venable, 2015). In trying to bolster optimism, motivation, and activation, treatment approaches require sensitivity to balance each priority. Initially this may call for increase in support and temporary reduction in overall task demands, while immediately engaging in opportunities to face normative challenges. Success during these times will be defined according to participation rather than performance.

In addition to behavioral activation, increased willingness to self-manage pain has been associated with decreased functional disability, reduced depression symptoms, less fear of pain, and improved use of adaptive coping strategies (Logan, Conroy, Sieberg, & Simons, 2012). Many U.S. states require adolescents as young as 13 years to consent to care for psychiatric medicines, so including the patients in treatment decisions is not only therapeutic but also may be mandated. Intensive treatment programs have emphasized approaches to enhance this willingness, eliciting the perspectives of youth to incorporate their preferences and enabling children to become stronger agents in their care.

The emotional toll of chronically painful experiences may lead to significant disturbances in conduct, anxiety, or mood, warranting a comorbid diagnosis of an adjustment disorder. When chronic or severe, or associated with comorbid trauma, symptoms may meet criteria for posttraumatic stress disorder (PTSD), thought to result in chronically heightened vigilance to signals of pain and stress. This affects cognitive and behavioral functioning to trigger intense avoidance urges or dissociative cognitive responses, even occasionally triggering internally driven re-experiencing symptoms.

The prevalence of PTSD in cross-sectional studies of youth with chronic pain is estimated to be 32% as opposed to 8% in the general population (Noel et al., 2016). Not surprisingly, among youth with chronic pain, higher levels of PTSD symptoms are related to higher pain intensity and pain interference (Noel et al., 2016). Parent comorbidity of PTSD also is much greater among youth with chronic pain (8% compared to 1%) (Vinall et al., 2016), and heightened pain intensity in children is directly associated with higher levels of PTSD symptoms in parents (Neville et al., 2018). Parental trauma history may increase the likelihood of a parent referencing pain signals in his/her child as threatening or triggering, shaping their evaluative nature. This speaks to the importance of supporting parental functioning as a means of enhancing the child's emotional regulation skills and self-efficacy, particularly in the context of parents witnessing repeated and distressing pain in their loved one.

More broadly, mothers of youth with chronic abdominal pain reported more anxiety symptoms than mothers of children in a healthy control group (Garber,

Zeman, & Walker, 1990). Large population studies reveal a high association of parental pain history with risk of chronic pain in their children, a risk that is further amplified when both parents have a history of pain impairments (Hoftun, Romundstad, & Rygg, 2012). Higher rates in children also are seen among families with lower parental education levels (Fryer, Cleary, Wickham, Barr, & Taylor-Robinson, 2017). Conversely, stronger treatment responses were seen when both parents were present and participated in rehabilitative therapy programs, shifting their responses to pain signals in their child (Sieberg et al., 2017). As somatic impairments may signal emotional distress in youth, it is important to remain vigilant to the familial or environmental risks for neglect, abuse, or other forms of trauma and to address these safety concerns through comprehensive approaches to care.

Similar to findings in the general population, studies of psychiatric comorbidity in youth with chronic headaches reveal that girls tend to exhibit heightened symptoms of anxiety and depression, while boys show heightened risk for externalizing problems (Egger, Angold, & Costello, 1998). Other findings reveal a much stronger association with anxiety among girls, with both genders at equal risk for depression (Egger, Costello, Erkanli, & Angold, 1999). When compared to youth without chronic pain, youth with chronic abdominal pain also were found to be at greater risk of subsequently developing depressive and anxiety disorders in adulthood (Vinall et al., 2016), regardless of whether the pain persisted (Hotopf, Carr, Mayou, Wadsworth, & Wessely, 1998).

Neurodevelopmental disorders (such as genetic syndromes) and broader clinical diagnoses (such as ASD) often contribute to sensory alterations that impact pain regulation (Riquelme, Hatem, & Montoya, 2018). Signals that typically might be interpreted as mild or irrelevant can be highly distressing to youth with neuroanatomical vulnerabilities in pain processing networks. Thermoregulation and sensory modulation may be impaired such that small changes in temperature or pressure might be overwhelmingly aversive. Pain signaling itself can be highly amplified in neurodevelopmental conditions, yet can also be concealed by communication impairments, so staying vigilant to the potential impact of pain on emotional and behavioral dysregulation is imperative.

Psychiatric disorders may further result in repetitive behaviors that create high vulnerability to pain sensitivity, such as restrictive eating disorders or chronic high exposure to marijuana use (Camilleri, 2018; Yamamotova, Bulant, Bocek, & Papezova, 2017). Both nutritional restriction and excessive cannabinoid exposure are thought to gradually impair neurologic signaling in gastrointestinal pathways resulting in visceral discomfort, nausea, and pain sensitivity (Caes, Orchard, & Christie, 2017). These signals then drive further maladaptive food avoidance behaviors, intensifying medical risks from extensive weight loss (including neurophysiologic impairments that even further compromise pain regulation) (Norris et al., 2014).

Given the escalating prevalence of depressive disorders in youth, it is unsurprising that youth with chronic pain are at higher risk. A retrospective study of children who were very impaired by chronic pain revealed even higher association with depressive disorders (24%) than anxiety disorders (19%) (Zernikow et al., 2012). Pain-related impairments also were greater with comorbid depression. Therefore, addressing impairments in both anxiety and depression is critical for improving functioning in youth with chronic pain and for interrupting the progression of disability. Delays in treatment can contribute to increasing impact of chronic pain on developmental processes. This can lead to stasis or even regression in some functions over time, often clinically manifesting as increased reliance on parents to support more and more basic functions of daily living.

Treatment Strategies

Treating youth with chronic pain requires thoughtful approaches tailored to the specific needs of the child and his or her family, as well as consistency and alignment among providers. This is particularly challenging in disorders that fluctuate so dynamically, and that are not easily remedied by traditional treatments. Yet successful treatment additionally demands an unhurried approach, as fully elucidating the impairments and concerns of the child and caregivers is critical to instilling an expectation of recovery. Furthermore, behavioral recommendations often hinge on ignoring distressing pain signals and pushing through in spite of avoidance urges. In the context of these challenges, pharmacologic approaches often are seen as critical for comforting patients with severe chronic pain sensitivity who also struggle with significant behavioral avoidance or other psychiatric comorbidities (Hauer & Houtrow, 2017).

Yet for youth who struggle with chronic pain syndromes in the absence of significant psychiatric comorbidity, research is very limited on the utility of psychiatric medicines. Studies of pain management tend to examine relatively short treatment intervals, with few head to head comparisons to guide medication choices in youth. Studies also routinely exclude psychiatric comorbidity or adjunctive use of medicines, thereby limiting their generalizability to broader clinical populations. Furthermore, identifying significant treatment responses in RCTs examining pharmacotherapy for chronic pain is limited by the relatively high placebo responses often observed in the control groups, particularly among children. This further emphasizes the importance of psychoeducation and treatment alliance with families whose motivation and beliefs in the potential for success may be more impactful to improvement. Beyond pain relief, increasing emphasis is placed on restoring function and satisfaction rather than on directly impacting nociception, with some suggestion that these approaches also may carry indirect benefits of necessitating fewer opiates, surgeries, or hospitalizations (Tseng, Weiss, Harrison, Hansen, & Bruce, 2014).

Therefore, reviews of the efficacy of pharmacotherapy in youth with chronic pain generally tend to highlight the lack of convincing clinical evidence regarding the use of antidepressants to treat chronic non-cancer pain in children or adolescents (Cooper et al., 2017a). Many clinical pain experts similarly recommend against prescribing medicines as the primary approach to manage chronic non-organic musculoskeletal or abdominal pain, and instead endorse an array of behavioral and psychological approaches that have similar efficacy (Abbott et al., 2018; Hauer & Houtrow, 2017). See Chapter 20 of this volume for a discussion of these approaches. Yet pharmacotherapy with psychotropic agents is generally considered clinically indicated (in conjunction with psychotherapeutic, behavioral, and rehabilitative approaches) when the severity of depression and anxiety are highly impairing or prevent engagement in the therapeutic activities required to stimulate recovery. This type of stepped-care model, tailoring the intensity of treatment to the individual patient and family's needs, has been demonstrated to improve access and outcomes (Peterson, Anderson, Bourne, Mackey, & Helfand, 2018).

Fortunately, psychoeducation is known to be a powerful tool in treating functional disorders, with improvements noted in a substantial portion of patients simply based on the patient's acquisition of a better understanding of their disorder and of ways to conceptualize impairments within a biopsychosocial model (Hall-Patch et al., 2010). This enables families to approach symptoms with less rigid distinctions between mind and body, and between the voluntary or involuntary nature of symptoms (Caes, Orchard, & Christie, 2017). These insights further allow parents to continue supporting treatments that may be against their current instincts by informing a nonjudgmental behavioral framework for responding effectively to their child's pain symptoms.

Additionally, even though there is a role for using pharmacologic agents in treating youth with chronic pain, it is important to recognize that all forms of recovery in chronic pain work to engage and modify neural pathways responsible for modulating and integrating motor processing, emotional function, and pain processing (Becerra et al., 2014). Therefore, an emphasis on enhancing activities (including participation in occupational and physical therapy) can function as a rehabilitative motor therapy and as a broader neurophysiologic intervention, priming the brain toward learning and adaptation just as medications might. Psychiatrists can serve a valuable role in steering families away from a narrow focus on pharmacotherapy and shift treatment priorities toward psychoeducational and behavioral therapies that have demonstrated effectiveness in the management of chronic pain in addition to childhood anxiety and depressive disorders.

Nevertheless, when indicated, psychiatric medicines are thought to play a valuable role in the management of emotional and behavioral impairments seen in youth with chronic pain. Clinical research findings, while limited, can inform treatment approaches when using psychotropics in youth with chronic pain syndromes. The following is a list of pharmacologic categories commonly used by child and adolescent psychiatrists to address symptoms common in this population.

Antidepressants (SSRIs, SNRIs, Tricyclics)

Pharmacokinetic effects of *SSRIs* include a blockade of synaptic reuptake and an increase in serotonergic tone, thought to drive neuroplasticity and gradually lead to alterations in synaptic responsivity within brain networks that modulate anxiety and depression. Instead of peripheral nerve changes in pain intensity (nociception), antidepressant effects are thought to be driven by modulation of cognitive and affective pain responses. These changes are believed to alter the responsivity of broader networks that integrate and regulate emotional reactivity and mood states, impacting cortical networks that govern pain responses. Clinical use of antidepressants in youth is discussed in detail elsewhere in the literature (e.g., Kodish, Rockhill, Ryan, & Varley, 2011). In general, clinical practice calls for using lower doses when starting psychotropics in youth, including SSRIs. Additionally, anxious children tend to be more sensitive to side effects of this class of medications and may benefit from even more conservative initial dosing with regular monitoring and gradual titration.

The analgesic effects of antidepressants are thought to be driven additionally by the combined blockade of serotonin and norepinephrine from synaptic reuptake (Khouzam, 2016). The noradrenergic properties of *SNRIs* and tricyclic antidepressants (*TCAs*) are thought to contribute to their enhanced clinical efficacy in adults with chronic neuropathic pain, with lower rates of relapse compared to SSRIs (Cohen & Mao, 2014; Rosenzweig-Lipson et al., 2007). This noradrenergic tone also is thought to enrich the activation of descending inhibitory neurons in the dorsal horn of the spinal cord involved in modulating pain processing pathways.

Choices of specific psychiatric medications to target depression and anxiety symptoms in patients with chronic pain therefore increasingly shifted toward utilizing TCAs, particularly among GI and neurology providers (Gmuca & Sherry, 2017). Even more recently, SNRI agents (including duloxetine, venlafaxine, or milnacipran) have been used as first-line agents in patients with chronic pain, particularly when comorbid anxiety or depression is a concern.

The practice of prescribing antidepressants to youth has been impacted significantly by findings of reports of heightened suicidal thinking (but not completed suicides) in youth treated with SSRIs. Treatment practices now call for warning youth and their families about the risks of activation and suicidal thinking when prescribing any antidepressant, as well as implementing a safety and monitoring plan before initiating treatment (Gmuca & Sherry, 2017). This requirement has diminished the comfort of non-psychiatrists to prescribe this medication class, in spite of many agents proving to have very good tolerability.

There currently are only two RCTs evaluating the effectiveness of antidepressants in youth with chronic pain, and both revealed limited benefits: one study evaluated the use of amitriptyline (a TCA) and the second study was an open-label trial of citalopram (an SSRI). Amitriptyline treatment was associated with mild improvement on measures of quality of life, yet pain frequency and intensity were unaffected, and study design was considered suboptimal (Bahar, Collins, Steinmetz, & Ament, 2008). The other study of amitriptyline in youth with chronic pain failed to reveal differences in ratings of pain relief or satisfaction with treatment (Saps et al., 2009). Due to adverse effects including hypotension, drowsiness, and constipation, as well as potentially lethal arrhythmia in overdose, TCAs should be used carefully in youth.

While milnacipran is approved for the treatment of adults with major depression in Europe, its approved use in the U.S. is limited to treatment of adult fibromyalgia. A small study of milnacipran for JFMS did find mild clinical improvements without significant side effects, but was an uncontrolled open trial (Arnold, Bateman, Palmer, & Lin, 2015).

In contrast to adults, positive findings of SNRIs for chronic pain in youth are very limited. While still not as commonly used as SSRIs for anxiety, duloxetine also has shown clinical evidence robust enough to warrant FDA approval for treatment of youth with generalized anxiety disorder (GAD) (Strawn et al., 2015). In contrast, the clinical evidence of SSRIs for the treatment of anxiety in youth is based primarily on studies of OCD, and none are specifically approved for GAD. The most common side effects reported with duloxetine include nausea, dry mouth, insomnia, drowsiness, fatigue, and dizziness. Duloxetine does tend to be less constipating than TCAs and can be titrated more quickly.

Venlafaxine also may be considered to treat acute and chronic neuropathic pain. It is thought to possess weaker binding to serotonin and norepinephrine transporters compared to other SNRIs. Also unlike duloxetine, at very low doses venlafaxine acts primarily as an SSRI, while its properties as an SNRI prevail only as the dose is increased. Cardiac conduction abnormalities have been reported in a small number of patients, and blood pressure increases can occur (Combes, Peytavin, & Théron, 2001); therefore, venlafaxine should be prescribed with caution in patients with cardiac disease.

Limited support for the use of SSRIs for recurrent abdominal pain comes from a prospective open-label trial revealing significant benefit of citalopram on response rate, with good tolerance (Campo et al., 2004). Yet a much larger study examining citalopram for youth with functional abdominal pain did not reveal any benefits, with mild increase in side effects among the treatment group (Roohafza, Pourmoghaddas, Saneian, & Gholamrezaei, 2014). A very small open trial of fluoxetine used in youth with JFMS similarly showed heightened sensitivity to side effects with only mild benefit on measures of both pain and impact of illness after 12 weeks of treatment (Mariutto, Stanford, Kashikar-Zuck, Welge, & Arnold, 2012).

Interestingly, though, a recent retrospective review of youth with functional abdominal pain managed by gastroenterologists revealed a greater response to SSRIs than to TCAs, even after controlling for psychiatric factors (Zar-Kessler, Belkind-Gerson, Bender, & Kuo, 2017). Discontinuation rates were similar, with diarrhea more common in the SSRI group and constipation among those treated with TCAs. Treatment providers described hesitancy in using SSRIs due to warnings around escalated suicidality, yet only 6% of the SSRI treatment group reported mood disturbance compared to 14% treated with TCAs. Despite being based on retrospective findings, these results may suggest that youth with functional abdominal pain are more responsive to the benefits of SSRIs than adults, even at relatively low doses.

Sleep Medicines (Mirtazapine, Trazodone, Melatonin, α-agonists)

Although there are no FDA-approved medications for the treatment of insomnia in youth, several agents with sedating properties have revealed symptomatic benefits and are frequently used in clinical practice. Furthermore, due to the high comorbidity of sleep disorders in youth with chronic pain and the therapeutic benefits of sleep improvement on pain symptoms, prescribing psychotropics to address sleep difficulties is increasingly common. The prevalence of sleep disturbances in youth with chronic pain is estimated to range between 50% and 80%, highlighting the bidirectional relationship and importance of addressing sleep when optimizing pain management (Cheatle et al., 2016). SSRIs and SNRIs do not tend to improve sleep, and some have been associated with sleep fragmentation, calling for use of alternate agents. Similar to other psychotropics, sleep aids are specifically chosen based on the side effect profile in addition to the potential to target adjunctive symptoms. As many agents can be used for multiple clinical indications (including several psychiatric conditions), clinicians generally tailor treatment approaches to best address the constellation of symptoms the patient is experiencing.

Mirtazapine is a relatively unique antidepressant agent that has antagonistic effects on serotonin and norepinephrine receptors, as well as α-2 antagonism. Most commonly prescribed for depression (MDD), anxiety (GAD), and PTSD, its actions boost serotonergic and noradrenergic activity. Yet it is commonly used to treat sleep impairments due to its sedating properties, thought to be driven by type 1 histaminergic blockade, which is more prominent at lower doses. Its use has been associated with reduced sleep latency and improved total sleep time and sleep efficiency (Mayers & Baldwin, 2005).

Studies of mirtazapine in adults have revealed limited benefits for pain in patients with cancer and those with recurrent headache (Bendtsen & Jensen, 2004). Clinical benefits for management of nausea and improving appetite also have been demonstrated, often facilitating weight gain (Kim et al., 2008). As such, use of mirtazapine may be beneficial to target sleep, appetite, and nausea symptoms common among youth with chronic abdominal pain. The sedating response that improves sleep tends to be relatively rapid, yet increased dosages typically are not helpful for induction of appetite or sleep onset. Safety and efficacy have not been established in children and adolescents, and treatment may result in anticholinergic effects. Yet in clinical practice, the medicine tends to be well-tolerated and carries less potential for interactions than many other psychotropic agents.

Trazodone is approved in adults for treatment of depression and is also commonly used for the treatment of insomnia. It primarily blocks 5HT2 receptors and serotonin reuptake. Onset tends to be rapid, yet the dose is often titrated for response if ineffective, while excess dosages may lead to "hangover" effects the following morning or other anticholinergic effects. If effective, treatment is often well tolerated and so can be continued for extended periods of time, although other studies have shown benefit more restricted to the early stages of treatment (James et al., 1998).

In addition to addressing sleep impairment, trazodone has shown efficacy in improving functional chest pain (Clouse, Lustman, Eckert, Ferney, & Griffith, 1987), as well as pain and sleep quality in adults with fibromyalgia and diabetic neuropathy (Morillas-Arques, Rodriguez-Lopez, Molina-Barea, Rico-Villademoros, & Calandre, 2010). Furthermore, it has shown good efficacy in the management of pediatric headaches, while other commonly used agents lack effectiveness compared to placebos (El-Chammas et al., 2013), highlighting its potential utility in this population. Trazodone also may improve the effectiveness of other agents used to treat depression, and is often prescribed in combination with SSRIs, while monitoring for risk of serotonin syndrome at high doses. Youth with sleep impairments often respond to lower doses than used to treat depression, yet may also be more sensitive to side effects, including priapism in boys.

Melatonin has been shown to facilitate sleep induction by stimulating the suprachiasmatic nucleus that regulates diurnal cycles in the hypothalamus. While not FDA-approved, it is commonly used to address sleep problems, including in children and adolescents. In adults, melatonin has demonstrated effectiveness in reducing sleep latency. Findings further suggest it may confer some analgesic benefit in patients with fibromyalgia, IBS, and migraine headaches, yet benefits were not found in functional dyspepsia (Danilov & Kurganova, 2016).

Clonidine, an α-2 adrenergic agonist, commonly is used for several psychiatric symptoms in addition to pain management. Several findings show benefits for neuropathic pain, benefits thought to be based on alterations in the responsiveness of descending pain circuits that modulate peripheral processing and sensory input (Manelli et al., 2017). Clonidine and other central α-2 agonists are thought to target these projections and impact the hyperalgesia associated with neuropathic pain and other pain disorders. Intrathecal administration occasionally is used to target severe chronic pain.

In child and adolescent psychiatry, clonidine most commonly is prescribed for sleep induction and behavioral management, particularly in children with neurodevelopmental disorders. Approved for use in ADHD, clonidine also is thought to be helpful for hyper-arousal symptoms associated with PTSD and impulse control deficits in youth, including in ASD (Belkin & Schwartz, 2015). Interestingly, studies also have revealed associated improvements in certain IBS symptoms, including reducing postprandial gastric volume, enhancing colonic compliance, and alleviating abdominal pain (Chen, Ilham, & Feng, 2017). Yet its side effect profile and short half-life limits long-term use and may not optimize sleep impairments.

Due to its physiologic effects, clonidine tends to be short-lived and cause a rapid drop in blood pressure. While this is helpful for hypertension in adults, it often results in excessive sedation or dizziness in youth, particularly at higher dosages. Furthermore, rapid discontinuation may result in reactive hypertension, and some overdoses in children have resulted in fatality (Ming, Mulvey, Mohanty, & Patel, 2011). Therefore, clinical practice calls for a cardiovascular evaluation before starting a child on clonidine, including collecting familial history. While routine screening with an EKG is not necessary, blood pressure and pulse should be assessed regularly. Longer acting forms are more recently available and may be used if its clinical benefit is too short-lived.

Guanfacine, another central α-2 agonist, is used increasingly in the management of externalizing behaviors in youth, and carries less risk of hypotension and sedation. Guanfacine is approved for ADHD and is longer acting than clonidine with a more modest effect on lowering blood pressure. Although its half-life approaches 20 hours, it also comes in a slightly longer acting formulation, which may be less sedating. Similar to clonidine, it also is helpful for addressing neurophysiologic reactivity in patients with sensory sensitivities or tic disorders. Although clinical studies are lacking, studies have revealed potential benefits of guanfacine on animal models of neuropathic pain (Sabetkasaie, Vala, Khansefid, Hosseini, & Sadat Ladgevardi, 2004).

Anticonvulsants (Carbamazepine, Gabapentin, Pregabalin)

Anticonvulsants inhibit the release of glutamate by antagonizing voltage-sensitive sodium channels, increasing the threshold for seizure activity. Anticonvulsants have a long history as pharmacologic agents used to target chronic pain. Several agents also have shown effectiveness in the management of acute mania in adults with bipolar disorder. Common side effects include sweating, headache, nausea, and abdominal pain, with more serious effects including motor impairments and liver inflammation. The most widely used agents, gabapentin, pregabalin, and carbamazepine, are approved by the FDA for the treatment of neuropathic pain in adults. While recent review found no evidence to support or refute the use of antiepileptic drugs to treat chronic non-cancer pain in children and adolescents (Cooper et al., 2017b), this medication class commonly is used in pediatric patients with chronic pain.

In addition to its use for pain from neuralgia, *carbamazapine* also is FDA-approved for the treatment of acute mania in adult patients with bipolar disorder. Open-label trials also support its potential use in treating pediatric mania (Liu et al., 2011), with one study highlighting its potential utility in management of PTSD in youth (Stamatakos & Campo, 2010). Carbamazepine also is considered first-line treatment for trigeminal neuralgia in adults (Deli, Bosnyak, Pusch, Komoly, & Feher, 2013). Its mild anticholinergic properties may contribute to sedation or blurred vision, and benign leukopenia is common. More concerning, agranulocytosis and aplastic anemia are rare but dangerous side effects, as well as is the potential for rash associated with Stevens-Johnson syndrome. Hyponatremia also is possible and calls for regular blood monitoring. Its pharmacokinetics result in induction of liver enzymes that metabolize a host of medicines (including carbamazepine itself), resulting in the need for upward dose adjustments and monitoring for changes in plasma levels.

Gabapentin is the best-studied anticonvulsant used in management of adult chronic pain, revealing benefits for central and peripheral neuropathic pain, visceral hyperalgesia, autonomic dysfunction, and spasticity (Fornasari, 2017). Its mechanism of action primarily targets voltage-gated calcium channels to diminish excessive neuronal activity and excitatory neurotransmitter release. Occasionally used to target anxiety symptoms in youth, gabapentin is much more commonly used clinically in the management of chronic pain and partial seizures. Several case reports also have described benefits in children with reduction in pain behavior and improvement in sleep, but placebo-controlled trials are lacking (Correia, Soares, Azurara, & Palaré, 2017; Robinson & Malow, 2013). One recent RCT examined the efficacy of gabapentin compared to amitriptyline for CPRS and neuropathic pain in children (Brown et al., 2016). The medicines proved similar in efficacy for pain and sleep disruption, with no differences in adverse side effects.

Treatment usually is initiated in youth at low doses spread across the day and then is gradually titrated upwards for clinical effect. Patients often are observed within two weeks, yet an adequate trial can require two months or more. Its pharmacokinetic effects are thought to diminish at higher doses with more limited bioavailability. In children younger than 5, higher relative doses may be required due to enhanced metabolism. Although generally well-tolerated, sedation and ataxia are somewhat common and dose dependent. Nighttime doses are thought to facilitate sleep onset and improve slow-wave sleep. In children under 12, gabapentin use has been associated with increased emotional reactivity and hyperactivity, warranting monitoring for these activating side effects in young patients. Drug–drug interactions are not thought to be problematic, and gabapentin often is used as adjunctive treatment for patients not optimally responding to other agents. Unlike other anticonvulsants, gabapentin is not thought to be an effective treatment for acute mania.

Pregabalin is thought to have a similar mechanism of action as gabapentin, designed as a leucine analog to facilitate diffusion across the blood–brain barrier, without direct effects on GABA receptors. This may contribute to pregabalin providing analgesic effects more quickly than gabapentin. Pregabalin is FDA-approved for treatment of adult fibromyalgia and often seen as first-line treatment for neuropathic pain and comorbid anxiety. However, there are no approved medicines for JFMS.

Recently, the safety and efficacy of pregabalin in adolescents with fibromyalgia was evaluated in a randomized, double-blind, placebo-controlled trial with a six-month open-label extension (Arnold et al., 2016). While secondary measures of pain intensity were reduced significantly when measured at various intervals across treatment, no significant improvements were seen at the endpoint of treatment. Furthermore, a higher incidence of adverse events was seen compared to adults, including dizziness and nausea, raising the need for careful monitoring in pediatric populations.

Atypical Antipsychotics (Risperidone, Olanzapine, Quetiapine)

Used in youth primarily to manage acute agitation, antipsychotics may have a limited role in pain management when symptoms are severe and unresponsive to traditional treatments. Published studies evaluating the utility of antipsychotics for chronic pain have been uncontrolled (Khouzam, 2016), and due to long-term concerns for metabolic side effects, use in children should be limited. Antipsychotic agents may have relevance for severe behaviors such as obsessional thinking, severe agitation, or destructive self-harm behaviors, often exacerbated by severe chronic pain in youth.

Atypical antipsychotic agents have broader receptor profiles than traditional antipsychotics (which primarily act through D2 blockade), including blockade of serotonin 2A receptors. This is thought to enhance dopamine release in specific brain regions, possibly mitigating against some motor and cognitive side effects. Children may be more sensitive to the side effects of antipsychotics, and use of these medications in children should be monitored even more closely than in adults.

Risperidone is the most commonly used antipsychotic agent in children and adolescents, approved for use in teens with schizophrenia and other psychotic disorders, for acute mania in children over 10, and for agitation and irritability in children with ASD over 5. Risperidone can be used at very low dosages and administered in various formulations (liquid, pill, dissolvable tablet), but cannot be compelled intramuscularly or intravenously, limiting its use for acute agitation in an uncooperative patient. It is commonly associated with sedation and weight gain and carries greater risk of hyperprolactinemia and extrapyramidal motor impairments as compared to other atypical antipsychotics.

Risperidone has shown limited benefits in small studies of adults with fibromyalgia and other chronic pain conditions, with mild reductions in pain severity and improvements in measures of psychosocial functioning (Davis, Chen, & Glick, 2003). However, its limited evidence base and association with problematic long-term side effects limits its use for youth with chronic pain in the absence of other severe psychopathology.

Quetiapine is an atypical antipsychotic also approved for schizophrenia and bipolar mania in adolescents, as well as for depression in adults. This benefit, unique among antipsychotics, may come from partial agonism at 5HT1A receptors, particularly at higher dosages. At low doses (commonly used in youth), quetiapine primarily exhibits antihistaminergic properties, contributing to sedation and increases in appetite. Therefore, quetiapine often is used to address sleep problems in patients with severe depression or PTSD to reduce hypervigilance and cognitive perseveration and to normalize sleep architecture. It has shown adjunctive benefit when combined with SSRIs for several indications, including depression, PTSD, and severe anxiety disorders.

In terms of addressing pain symptoms, quetiapine has revealed some benefits for adults with fibromyalgia and migraine disorders (Calandre & Rico-Villademoros, 2012), including improvements on measures of depressed mood. Yet most randomized trials have revealed negative results (Jimenez, Sundararajan, & Covington, 2018). Recent review suggested that quetiapine use may be considered for short-term approaches to reduce pain in fibromyalgia patients with comorbid depression while monitoring for problematic side effects, including weight gain (Walitt, Klose, Üçeyler, Phillips, & Häuser, 2016). Dry mouth and orthostatic hypotension also are common, with dizziness potentially limiting tolerance. Cardiac conduction abnormalities have been noted, particularly in patients with polypharmacy. Yet quetiapine is associated with a low rate of extrapyramidal motor effects and hyperprolactinemia.

Olanzapine similarly is approved for use in schizophrenia and bipolar mania, as well as for treatment-resistant depression in adults when used in combination with fluoxetine. Thought to possess strong efficacy in the management of adults with schizophrenia and agitation, it also is associated with the greatest weight gain and risk of metabolic side effects, including diabetes. As such, body mass index should be tracked closely, along with fasting lipids and glucose within the first three months of treatment. Sedation is also common, thought to be due to blockade of histamine 1 receptors.

Olanzapine also possesses the strongest evidence among antipsychotics for treating complex chronic pain conditions in adults (Jimenez et al., 2018). Its use is associated with decreased severity of pain associated with fibromyalgia (Rico-Villademoros, Hidalgo, Dominguez, García-Leiva, & Calandre, 2005) and with improved management of chronic headaches (Silberstein et al., 2002). Olanzapine also was found to suppress morphine-induced emesis and alleviate sleep dysregulation associated with neuropathic pain (Davis et al., 2003). Studies for pediatric pain are lacking, and concerns around heightened sensitivity to side effects among pediatric populations (as well as among adult populations with pain disorders) have limited its use in pediatric patients with chronic pain to those with severe distress after other more traditional agents have been ineffective.

Newer Pharmacologic Considerations (Ketamine, Cannabis)

Ketamine, an NMDA receptor antagonist with diverse clinical properties, is known to be integral for learning-induced neuroplasticity. Ketamine has shown recent promise in initial studies as an agent capable of yielding remarkable and rapid improvement in depressive symptoms, through inducing neuroplasticity (Liu, Liu, Wang, Zhang, & Li, 2017). Use of ketamine as anesthesia for minor procedures also is common in the pediatric population, as youth do not exhibit the untoward cognitive effects common in adults, effects that are thought to result only after maturational changes in NMDA receptor profiles. However, evidence for its effectiveness to manage chronic pain is still limited.

Sub-anesthetic doses have been shown to offer potential for significant pain relief in some studies of patients with CPRS (Sheehy et al., 2015). Studies of anxiety disorders in youth also suggest that targeting NMDA receptors can induce neuroplasticity that drives recovery, even potentiating the clinical benefit of exposure-based therapies (Klass, Glaubitz, Tegenthoff, & Lissek, 2017). Utilizing this medication class in pediatric patients with pain, particularly those with psychiatric comorbidity, may offer valuable new treatment opportunities.

Despite some preliminary data supporting the utility of *cannabinoid* treatment in managing neuropathic pain in adults (Romero-Sandoval, Fincham, Kolano, Sharpe, & Alvarado-Vázquez, 2018), research is lacking in children. Although commonly used in the management of chronic pain and nausea associated with advanced pediatric cancers, associated risks (including greater risk of developing psychosis and depression later in development) of cannabinoid use in youth limit their broader appeal (Starzer, Nordentoft, & Hjorthoj, 2018). As such, the American Academy of Pediatrics recommends against the use of medical marijuana outside of rare populations with debilitating disease (Ammerman, Ryan, & Adelman, 2015).

Adolescent use of marijuana is thought to have escalated recently in the context of legalization for recreational adult use in several states. Youth with chronic abdominal pain may be particularly susceptible to self-medicating, as some describe significant short-term relief with marijuana, enabling food intake. However, heavy chronic use gradually induces neurological susceptibility to rebound hyperemesis and persistent abdominal discomfort at baseline (Sorensen, DeSanto, Borgelt, Phillips, & Monte, 2017). Yet cannabinoids generally possess a more favorable side effect profile compared to many other clinically used medications, and their potential therapeutic benefits may offer promise in alleviating pain disorders while indirectly minimizing the risks of using alternate agents.

Conclusions and Future Directions

Youth with chronic pain require comprehensive treatment approaches that bridge the traditional mind–body duality in medicine and address the importance of emotional health on physical functioning. Psychiatrists can support recovery through interventions aimed at bolstering learning and neuroplasticity through both experiential and pharmacologic effects. Addressing psychiatric comorbidity can be critical to reduce the emotional impact on the intensity and persistence of pain symptoms. Psychotropic medication should be reserved for significant comorbidity or treatment resistance and employed at lower doses with more careful monitoring for any exacerbation of symptoms. The analgesic effect of antidepressants tends to appear more rapidly and at lower doses than the antidepressant effect, and other psychiatric medication classes have shown some promise in their potential to alleviate the burden of chronic pain disorders in children and adolescents. Continuing to advance our understanding of the clinical benefits of these medications in populations of youth with chronic pain is important, as is the development of insights into the specific neurophysiologic signatures of various pain disorders and how they may be impacted by coordinated treatment strategies.

References

Abbott, R. A., Martin, A. E., Newlove-Delgado, T.V., Bethel, A., Whear, R. S., Coon, J. T., & Logan, S. (2018). Recurrent abdominal pain in children: Summary evidence from 3 systematic reviews of treatment effectiveness. *Journal of Pediatric Gastroenterology & Nutrition, 67*(1), 23–33.

American Psychiatric Association. (2013). *Diagnostic and statistical manual of mental disorders* (5th ed.). Arlington, VA: American Psychiatric Publishing.

Ammerman, S., Ryan, S., & Adelman, W. P., Committee on Substance Abuse, Committee on Adolescence. (2015). The impact of marijuana policies on youth: Clinical, research, and legal update. *Pediatrics, 135*(3), e769–785.

Arnold, L. M., Bateman, L., Palmer, R. H., & Lin, Y. (2015). Preliminary experience using milnacipran in patients with juvenile fibromyalgia: Lessons from a clinical trial program. *Pediatric Rheumatology Online Journal, 13*(27). doi:10.1186/s12969-015-0025-9

Arnold, L. M., Schikler, K. N., Bateman, L., Khan, T., Pauer, L., Bhadra-Brown, P., Clair, A., Chew, M. L., & Scavone, J. (2016). Safety and efficacy of pregabalin in adolescents with fibromyalgia: A randomized, double-blind, placebo-controlled trial and a 6-month open-label extension study. *Pediatric Rheumatology Online Journal, 14*(1), 46. doi:10.1186/s12969-016-0106-4

Asmundson, G. J., Norton, P. J., & Norton, G. R. (1999). Beyond pain: The role of fear and avoidance in chronicity. *Clinical Psychology Review, 19*(1), 97–119.

Bahar, R. J., Collins, B. S., Steinmetz, B., & Ament, M. E. (2008). Double-blind placebo-controlled trial of amitriptyline for the treatment of irritable bowel syndrome in adolescents. *Journal of Pediatrics, 152*(5), 685–689.

Becerra, L., Sava, S., Simons, L. E., Drosos, A. M., Sethna, N., Berde, C., Lebel, A. A., & Borsook, D. (2014). Intrinsic brain networks normalize with treatment in pediatric complex regional pain syndrome. *Neuroimage: Clinical, 10*(6), 347–369.

Belkin, M. R., & Schwartz, T. L. (2015). Alpha-2 receptor agonists for the treatment of post-traumatic stress disorder. *Drugs in Context, 4*, 212286. doi:10.7573/dic.212286

Bendtsen, L., & Jensen, R. (2004). Mirtazapine is effective in the prophylactic treatment of chronic tension-type headache. *Neurology, 62*(10), 1706–1711.

Brown, S., Johnston, B., Amaria, K., Watkins, J., Campbell, F., Pehora, C., & McGrath, P. (2016). A randomized controlled trial of amitriptyline versus gabapentin for complex regional pain syndrome type I and neuropathic pain in children. *Scandinavian Journal of Pain, 13*, 156–163.

Caes, L., Orchard, A., & Christie, D. (2017). Connecting the mind–body split: Understanding the relationship between symptoms and emotional well-being in chronic pain and functional gastrointestinal disorders. *Healthcare (Basel), 5*(4). doi:10.3390/healthcare5040093.

Calandre, E. P., & Rico-Villademoros, F. (2012). The role of antipsychotics in the management of fibromyalgia. *CNS Drugs, 26*(2), 135–153.

Camilleri, M. (2018). Cannabinoids and gastrointestinal motility: Pharmacology, clinical effects, and potential therapeutics in humans. *Neurogastroenterology & Motility, 10*, e13370. doi:10.1111/nmo.13370

Campo, J.V., Perel, J., Lucas, A., Bridge, J., Ehmann, M., Kalas, C., . . . Brent, D. A. (2004). Citalopram treatment of pediatric recurrent abdominal pain and comorbid internalizing disorders: An exploratory study. *Journal of the American Academy of Child & Adolescent Psychiatry, 43*(10), 1234–1242.

Cheatle, M. D., Foster, S., Pinkett, A., Lesneski, M., Qu, D., & Dhingra, L. (2016). Assessing and managing sleep disturbance in patients with chronic pain. *Anesthesiology Clinics, 34*(2), 379–393.

Chen, L., Ilham, S. J., & Feng, B. (2017). Pharmacological approach for managing pain in irritable bowel syndrome: A review article. *Anesthesia & Pain Medicine, 7*(2), e42747. doi:10.5812/aapm.42747

Clouse, R. E., Lustman, P. J., Eckert, T. C., Ferney, D. M., & Griffith, L. S. (1987). Low-dose trazodone for symptomatic patients with esophageal contraction abnormalities. A double-blind, placebo-controlled trial. *Gastroenterology, 92*(4), 1027–1036.

Cohen, S. P., & Mao, J. (2014). Neuropathic pain: Mechanisms and their clinical implications. *British Medical Journal, 5*(348), f7656.

Combes, A., Peytavin, G., & Théron, D. (2001). Conduction disturbances associated with venlafaxine. *Annals of Internal Medicine, 134*(2), 166–167.

Cooper, T. E., Heathcote, L. C., Clinch, J., Gold, J. I., Howard, R., Lord, S. M., . . . Wiffen, P. J. (2017a). Antidepressants for chronic non-cancer pain in children and adolescents. *The Cochrane Database of Systematic Reviews, 8*, CD012535. doi:10.1002/14651858. CD012535.pub2

Cooper, T. E., Wiffen, P. J., Heathcote, L. C., Clinch, J., Howard, R., Krane, E., . . . Wood, C. (2017b). Antiepileptic drugs for chronic non-cancer pain in children and adolescents. *The Cochrane Database of Systematic Reviews, 8*, CD012536. doi:10.1002/14651858. CD012536.pub2

Correia, C. R., Soares, A. T., Azurara, L., & Palaré, M. J. (2017). Use of gabapentin in the treatment of chronic pain in an adolescent with sickle cell disease. *BMJ Case Reports, 21.* doi:10.1136/bcr-2016-218614

Cousins, L. A., Cohen, L. L., & Venable, C. (2015). Risk and resilience in pediatric chronic pain: Exploring the protective role of optimism. *Journal of Pediatric Psychology, 40*(9), 934–942.

Cunningham, N. R., Jagpal, A., Tran, S. T., Kashikar-Zuck, S., Goldschneider, K. R., Coghill, R. C., & Lynch-Jordan, A. M. (2016). Anxiety adversely impacts response to cognitive behavioral therapy in children with chronic pain. *Journal of Pediatrics, 171*, 227–233.

Danilov, A., & Kurganova, J. (2016). Melatonin in chronic pain syndromes. *Pain & Therapy, 5*(1), 1–17.

Davis, J. M., Chen, N., & Glick, I. D. (2003). A meta-analysis of the efficacy of second-generation antipsychotics. *Archives of General Psychiatry, 60*(6), 553–564.

Deli, G., Bosnyak, E., Pusch, G., Komoly, S., & Feher, G. (2013). Diabetic neuropathies: Diagnosis and management. *Neuroendocrinology, 98*(4), 267–280.

Egger, H. L., Angold, A., & Costello, E. J. (1998). Headaches and psychopathology in children and adolescents. *Journal of the American Academy of Child & Adolescent Psychiatry, 37*(9), 951–958.

Egger, H. L., Costello, E. J., Erkanli, A., & Angold, A. (1999). Somatic complaints and psychopathology in children and adolescents: Stomach aches, musculoskeletal pains, and headaches. *Journal of the American Academy of Child & Adolescent Psychiatry, 38*(7), 852–860.

El-Chammas, K., Keyes, J., Thompson, N., Vijayakumar, J., Becher, D., & Jackson, J. L. (2013). Pharmacologic treatment of pediatric headaches: A meta-analysis. *JAMA Pediatrics, 167*(3), 250–258.

Fitzgerald, M., & McKelvey, R. (2016). Nerve injury and neuropathic pain—A question of age. *Experimental Neurology, 275*(2), 296–302.

Fornasari, D. (2017). Pharmacotherapy for neuropathic pain: A review. *Pain & Therapy, 6* (Suppl 1), 25–33.

Fryer, B. A., Cleary, G., Wickham, S. L., Barr, B. R., & Taylor-Robinson, D. C. (2017). Effect of socioeconomic conditions on frequent complaints of pain in children: Findings from the UK millennium cohort study. *BMJ Paediatrics Open, 1*(1), e000093. doi:10.1136/bmjpo-2017-000093

Garber, J., Zeman, J., & Walker, L. S. (1990). Recurrent abdominal pain in children: Psychiatric diagnoses and parental psychopathology. *Journal of the American Academy of Child & Adolescent Psychiatry, 29*(4), 648–656.

Gmuca, S., & Sherry, D. D. (2017). Fibromyalgia: Treating pain in the juvenile patient. *Paediatric Drugs, 19*(4), 325–338.

Gogtay, N., & Thompson, P. M. (2010). Mapping gray matter development: Implications for typical development and vulnerability to psychopathology. *Brain & Cognition, 72*(1), 6–15.

Hall-Patch, L., Brown, R., House, A., Howlett, S., Kemp, S., Lawton, G., . . . NEST collaborators. (2010). Acceptability and effectiveness of a strategy for the communication of the diagnosis of psychogenic nonepileptic seizures. *Epilepsia, 51*(1), 70–78.

Hauer, J., & Houtrow, A. J. (2017). Pain assessment and treatment in children with significant impairment of the central nervous system. *Pediatrics, 139*(6). doi:10.1542/peds.2017-1002

Hechler, T., Kanstrup, M., Holley, A. L., Simons, L. E., Wicksell, R., Hirschfeld, G., & Zernikow, B. (2015). Systematic review on intensive interdisciplinary pain treatment of children with chronic pain. *Pediatrics, 136*(1), 115–127. doi:10.1542/peds.2014-3319

Hoftun, G. B., Romundstad, P. R., & Rygg, M. (2012). Factors associated with adolescent chronic non-specific pain, chronic multisite pain, and chronic pain with high disability: The young-HUNT study 2008. *Journal of Pain, 13*(9), 874–883.

Hotopf, M., Carr, S., Mayou, R., Wadsworth, M., & Wessely, S. (1998). Why do children have chronic abdominal pain, and what happens to them when they grow up? Population based cohort study. *British Medical Journal, 316*(7139), 1196–200.

Huguet, A., & Miró, J. (2008). The severity of chronic pediatric pain: An epidemiological study. *Journal of Pain, 9*(3), 226–236.

James, K., Walsh, J. K., Erman, M., Erwin, C. W., Jamieson, A., Mahowald, M., . . . Catesby Ware, J. (1998). Subjective hypnotic efficacy of trazodone and zolpidem in DSMIII—R primary insomnia. *Human Psychopharmacology, 13*(3), 191–198.

Jimenez, X. F., Sundararajan, T., & Covington, E. C. (2018). A systematic review of atypical antipsychotics in chronic pain management: Olanzapine demonstrates potential in central sensitization, fibromyalgia, and headache/migraine. *Clinical Journal of Pain, 34*(6), 585–591.

Kim, S. W., Shin, I. S., Kim, J. M., Kim, Y. C., Kim, K. S., Kim, K. M., Yang, S. J., & Yoon, J. S. (2008). Effectiveness of mirtazapine for nausea and insomnia in cancer patients with depression. *Psychiatry & Clinical Neurosciences, 62*(1), 75–83.

King, S., Chambers, C. T., Huguet, A., MacNevin, R. C., McGrath, P. J., Parker, L., & MacDonald, A. J. (2011). The epidemiology of chronic pain in children and adolescents revisited: A systematic review. *Pain, 152*(12), 2729–2738.

Kodish, I., Rockhill, C., Ryan, S., & Varley, C. (2011). Pharmacotherapy for anxiety disorders in children and adolescents. *Pediatric Clinics of North America, 58*(1), 55–72.

Kosola, S., Mundy, L. K., Sawyer, S. M., Canterford, L., van der Windt, D. A., Dunn, K. M., & Patton, G. C. (2017). Pain and learning in primary school: A population-based study. *Pain, 158*(9), 1825–1830.

Khouzam, H. R. (2016). Psychopharmacology of chronic pain: A focus on antidepressants and atypical antipsychotics. *Postgraduate Medicine, 128*(3), 323–330.

Klass, A., Glaubitz, B., Tegenthoff, M., & Lissek, S. (2017). d-Cycloserine facilitates extinction learning and enhances extinction-related brain activation. *Neurobiology of Learning & Memory, 144*, 235–247. doi:10.1016/j.nlm.2017.08.003

Landmann, N., Kuhn, M., Piosczyk, H., Feige, B., Baglioni, C., Spiegelhalder, K., . . . Nissen, C. (2014). The reorganisation of memory during sleep. *Sleep Medicine Reviews, 18*(6), 531–541.

Lasselin, J., Kemani, M. K., Kanstrup, M., Olsson, G. L., Axelsson, J., Andreasson, A., . . . Wicksell, R. K. (2016). Low-grade inflammation may moderate the effect of behavioral treatment for chronic pain in adults. *Journal of Behavioral Medicine, 39*(5), 916–924.

Liu, B., Liu, J., Wang, M., Zhang, Y., & Li, L. (2017). From serotonin to neuroplasticity: Evolvement of theories for major depressive disorder. *Frontiers in Cellular Neuroscience, 11*(305). doi:10.3389/fncel.2017.00305

Liu, H.Y., Potter, M. P., Woodworth, K.Y., Yorks, D. M., Petty, C. R., Wozniak, J. R., Biederman, J. (2011). Pharmacologic treatments for pediatric bipolar disorder: A review and meta-analysis. *Journal of the American Academy of Child & Adolescent Psychiatry, 50*(8), 749–762.

Logan, D. E., Conroy, C., Sieberg, C. B., & Simons, L. E. (2012). Changes in willingness to self- manage pain among children and adolescents and their parents enrolled in an intensive interdisciplinary pediatric pain treatment program. *Pain, 153*(9), 1863–1870.

Manelli, L. D., Micheli, L., Crocetti, L., Giovannoni, M. P., Vergelli, C., & Ghelardini, C. (2017). α2 Adrenoceptor: A target for neuropathic pain treatment. *Mini-Reviews in Medicinal Chemistry, 17*, 95–107.

Mariutto, E. N., Stanford, S. B., Kashikar-Zuck, S., Welge, J. A., & Arnold, L. M. (2012). An exploratory, open trial of fluoxetine treatment of juvenile fibromyalgia. *Journal of Clinical Psychopharmacology, 32*(2), 293–295.

Mayers, A. G., & Baldwin, D. S. (2005). Antidepressants and their effect on sleep. *Human Psychopharmacology, 20*(8), 533–559.

Ming, X., Mulvey, M., Mohanty, S., & Patel, V. (2011). Safety and efficacy of clonidine and clonidine extended-release in the treatment of children and adolescents with attention deficit and hyperactivity disorders. *Adolescent Health, Medicine & Therapeutics, 2*, 105–112.

Morillas-Arques, P., Rodriguez-Lopez, C. M., Molina-Barea, R., Rico-Villademoros, F., & Calandre, E. P. (2010). Trazodone for the treatment of fibromyalgia: An open-label, 12-week study. *BMC Musculoskeletal Disorders, 11*(204). doi:10.1186/1471-2474-11-204

Nelson, E. E., Lau, J.Y., & Jarcho, J. M. (2014). Growing pains and pleasures: How emotional learning guides development. *Trends in Cognitive Science, 18*(2), 99–108.

Neville, A., Soltani, S., Pavlova, M., & Noel, M. (2018). Unravelling the relationship between parent and child PTSD and pediatric chronic pain: The mediating role of pain catastrophizing. *Journal of Pain, 19*(2), 196–206.

Nguyen, M., Tharani, S., Rahmani, M., & Shapiro, M. (2014). A review of the use of clonidine as a sleep aid in the child and adolescent population. *Clinical Pediatrics, 53*(3), 211–216.

Noel, M., Wilson, A. C., Holley, A. L., Durkin, L., Patton, M., & Palermo, T. M. (2016). Posttraumatic stress disorder symptoms in youth with vs without chronic pain. *Pain, 157*(10), 2277–2284.

Norris, M. L., Robinson, A., Obeid, N., Harrison, M., Spettigue, W., & Henderson, K. (2014). Exploring avoidant/restrictive food intake disorder in eating disordered patients: A descriptive study. *International Journal of Eating Disorders, 47*(5), 495–499.

Pas, R., Ickmans, K., Van Oosterwijck, S., Van der Cruyssen, K., Foubert, A., Leysen, L., . . . Meeus, M. (2018). Hyperexcitability of the central nervous system in children with chronic pain: A systematic review. *Pain Medicine, 19*(12), 2504–2514. doi:10.1093/pm/pnx320

Peterson, K., Anderson, J., Bourne, D., Mackey, K., & Helfand, M. (2018). Effectiveness of models used to deliver multimodal care for chronic musculoskeletal pain: A rapid evidence review. *Journal of General Internal Medicine, 33*(Suppl 1), 71–81.

Rabin, J., Brown, M., & Alexander, S. (2017). Update in the treatment of chronic pain within pediatric patients. *Current Problems in Pediatric & Adolescent Health Care, 47*(7), 167–172.

Rico-Villademoros, F., Hidalgo, J., Dominguez, I., García-Leiva, J. M., & Calandre, E. P. (2005). Atypical antipsychotics in the treatment of fibromyalgia: A case series with olanzapine. *Progress in Neuro-Psychopharmacology & Biological Psychiatry, 29*(1), 161–164.

Riquelme, I., Hatem, S. M., & Montoya, P. (2018). Reduction of pain sensitivity after somatosensory therapy in children with autism spectrum disorders. *Journal of Abnormal Child Psychology, 46*(8), 1731–1740. doi:10.1007/s10802-017-0390-6

Robinson, A. A., & Malow, B. A. (2013). Gabapentin shows promise in treating refractory insomnia in children. *Journal of Child Neurology, 28*(12), 1618–1621.

Romero-Sandoval, E. A., Fincham, J. E., Kolano, A. L., Sharpe, B. N., & Alvarado-Vázquez, P. A. (2018). Cannabis for chronic pain: Challenges and considerations. *Pharmacotherapy, 38*(6), 651–662.

Roohafza, H., Pourmoghaddas, Z., Saneian, H., & Gholamrezaei, A. (2014). Citalopram for pediatric functional abdominal pain: A randomized, placebo-controlled trial. *Neurogastroenterology & Motility, 26*(11), 1642–1650.

Rosenzweig-Lipson, S., Beyer, C. E., Hughes, Z. A., Khawaja, X., Rajarao, S. J., Malberg, J. E., . . . Schechter, L. E. (2007). Differentiating antidepressants of the future: Efficacy and safety. *Pharmacology & Therapeutics, 113*(1), 134–153.

Sabetkasaie, M., Vala, S., Khansefid, N., Hosseini, A. R., & Sadat Ladgevardi, M. A. (2004). Clonidine and guanfacine-induced antinociception in visceral pain: Possible role of alpha 2/I2 binding sites. *European Journal of Pharmacology, 501*(1–3), 95–101.

Saps, M., Youssef, N., Miranda, A., Nurko, S., Hyman, P., Cocjin, J., & Di Lorenzo, C. (2009). Multicenter, randomized, placebo-controlled trial of amitriptyline in children with functional gastrointestinal disorders. *Gastroenterology, 137*(4), 1261–1269.

Sherry, D. D., Wallace, C. A., Kelley, C., Kidder, M., & Sapp, L. (1999). Short-and long-term outcomes of children with complex regional pain syndrome type I treated with exercise therapy. *Clinical Journal of Pain, 15*(3), 218–223.

Sheehy, K. A., Muller, E. A., Lippold, C., Nouraie, M., Finkel, J. C., & Quezado, Z. M. (2015). Subanesthetic ketamine infusions for the treatment of children and adolescents with chronic pain: A longitudinal study. *BMC Pediatrics, 15*(198). doi:10.1186/s12887-015-0515-4

Sieberg, C. B., Smith, A., White, M., Manganella, J., Sethna, N., & Logan, D. E. (2017). Changes in maternal and paternal pain-related attitudes, behaviors, and perceptions across pediatric pain rehabilitation treatment: A multilevel modeling approach. *Journal of Pediatric Psychology, 42*(1), 52–64.

Silberstein, S. D., Peres, M. F., Hopkins, M. M., Shechter, A. L., Young, W. B., & Rozen, T. D. (2002). Olanzapine in the treatment of refractory migraine and chronic daily headache. *Headache, 42*(6), 515–518.

Sobin, W. H., Heinrich, T. W., & Drossman, D. A. (2017). Central neuromodulators for treating functional GI disorders: A primer. *American Journal of Gastroenterology, 112*(5), 693–702.

Sorensen, C. J., DeSanto, K., Borgelt, L., Phillips, K. T., Monte, A. A. (2017). Cannabinoid hyperemesis syndrome: Diagnosis, pathophysiology, and treatment-a systematic review. *Journal of Medical Toxicology, 13*(1), 71–87.

Stamatakos, M., & Campo, J. V. (2010). Psychopharmacologic treatment of traumatized youth. *Current Opinion in Pediatrics, 22*(5), 599–604.

Starzer, M. S. K., Nordentoft, M., & Hjorthøj, C. (2018). Rates and predictors of conversion to schizophrenia or bipolar disorder following substance-induced psychosis. *American Journal of Psychiatry, 175*(4), 343–350.

Strawn, J. R., Prakash, A., Zhang, Q., Pangallo, B. A., Stroud, C. E., Cai, N., & Findling, R. L. (2015). A randomized, placebo-controlled study of duloxetine for the treatment of children and adolescents with generalized anxiety disorder. *Journal of the American Academy of Child & Adolescent Psychiatry, 54*(4), 283–293.

Streltzer, J., Eliashof, B. A., Kline, A. E., & Goebert, D. (2000). Chronic pain disorder following physical injury. *Psychosomatics, 41*(3), 227–234.

Tseng, A. S., Weiss, K., Harrison, T., Hansen, D., & Bruce, B. (2014). Pain relief as a primary treatment goal: At what point does functioning and well-being become more important? A case study of an adolescent with debilitating chronic pain. *Pain Research & Management, 19*(4), 219–223.

Vinall, J., Pavlova, M., Asmundson, G. J., Rasic, N., & Noel, M. (2016). Mental health comorbidities in pediatric chronic pain: A narrative review of epidemiology, models, neurobiological mechanisms and treatment. *Children (Basel), 3*(40). doi:10.3390/children3040040

Walitt, B., Klose, P., Üçeyler, N., Phillips, T., & Häuser, W. (2016). Antipsychotics for fibromyalgia in adults. *The Cochrane Database of Systematic Reviews, 6*, CD011804. doi:10.1002/14651858.CD011804.pub2

Walker, L. S., Dengler-Crish, C. M., Rippel, S., & Bruehl, S. (2010). Functional abdominal pain in childhood and adolescence increases risk for chronic pain in adulthood. *Pain, 150*(3), 568–572.

Wallis, E. M., & Fiks, A. G. (2015). Nonspecific abdominal pain in pediatric primary care: Evaluation and outcomes. *Academic Pediatrics, 15*(3), 333–339.

Yamamotova, A., Bulant, J., Bocek, V., & Papezova, H. (2017). Dissatisfaction with own body makes patients with eating disorders more sensitive to pain. *Journal of Pain Research, 10*, 1667–1675.

Yunus, M. B., & Masi, A. T. (1985). Juvenile primary fibromyalgia syndrome. A clinical study of thirty-three patients and matched normal controls. *Arthritis & Rheumatology, 28*(2), 138–145.

Zar-Kessler, C. A. M., Belkind-Gerson, J., Bender, S., & Kuo, B. M. (2017). Treatment of functional abdominal pain with antidepressants: Benefits, adverse effects, and the gastroenterologist's role. *Journal of Pediatric Gastroenterology & Nutrition, 65*(1), 16–21.

Zernikow, B., Wager, J., Hechler, T., Hasan, C., Rohr, U., Dobe, M., . . . Blankenburg, M. (2012). Characteristics of highly impaired children with severe chronic pain: A 5-year retrospective study on 2249 pediatric pain patients. *BMC Pediatrics, 12*(54). doi:10.1186/1471-2431-12-54

22

Psychological and Psychiatric Treatment of Chronic Pain in Geriatric Populations

Luis Richter, Shruti Shah, and Stephanie Wheeler

We live in the midst of a longevity revolution. A 2010 United Nations report predicts 188%, 351%, and 1004% increases in the populations over ages 65, 85, and 100 years respectively over the next four decades. In 2017, the United Nations estimated that individuals older than 60 years represented 13% of the world population (UN Department of Economic and Social Affairs, 2017). The U.S. Census Bureau (2011) estimates that by 2030, adults over the age of 65 will represent 20% of the population. The elderly constitute a vulnerable population who experience not only more pain but also a higher prevalence of undertreatment for pain (Baumbauer et al., 2016; Daoust et al., 2014).

The contributions of physiological (e.g., degenerative conditions, changes in body composition) and psychological (e.g., adjusting to physical disability, depression) factors must be discussed not within a vacuum but rather as a network of converging currents. Treatment considerations subsequently must come from a variety of interdisciplinary modalities. Chronic pain science no longer supports exclusively using monotherapy with traditional analgesic agents, particularly as increased age is accompanied by metabolic and pharmacokinetic changes that increase vulnerability to medication side effects and fatalities (Unutzer, Ferrell., Lin, & Marmon, 2004).

Within the literature, the terms "older adults," "geriatric adults," and "elderly adults" have been commonly used interchangeably to describe adults over the age of 65 years. The prevalence of chronic pain in this population has been estimated at between 25% and 76% for community-dwelling and between 83% and 93% for residential-dwelling adults (Abdullah et al., 2013). Arthritis, tissue injury, bone and joint problems, visceral pain (e.g., pain associated with constipation), peripheral neuropathy, myofascial pain, or a mixture of these processes can cause persistent pain in older adults. The three most common sites of pain in the elderly are back, leg/knee, and hip. However, there may be gender differences, as musculoskeletal problems have been found to be more prevalent in older women, whereas neuropathic pain may be more prevalent in older men (Mailis-Ganon et al., 2008).

Compared to their younger counterparts, geriatric patients may present with more complex health profiles, along with generation-specific beliefs surrounding the expression of pain and its management, which may impact the pain assessment process and thus contribute to possible under-detection and/or undertreatment of pain (Herr & Garand, 2001). Undertreated pain can result in multiple adverse consequences, including increased agitation and psychiatric symptoms (e.g., depression, social isolation, sleep disturbance, and amplified dementia-related behavioral disturbances) (Malara et al., 2016; Sampson et al., 2015); reductions in perceived quality of life and engagement in activities (Reyes-Gibby, Aday, & Cleeland, 2002); mobility issues (Cavalieri, 2002); and increased risk for falls (Stubbs et al., 2014). Effective treatment of pain can help mitigate or reverse these consequences. For example, Husebo et al. (2014) demonstrated that long-term care patients with dementia and behavioral disturbances experienced reductions in agitated behaviors after receiving an eight-week individualized pain treatment regimen. To help minimize complications of under-detected or undertreated pain, we recommend that clinicians recognize the unique aspects of working with geriatric patients and then make necessary modifications to standard comprehensive pain evaluation and treatment approaches to accommodate for these unique needs.

Assessment

A thorough assessment of a patient's medical problems and of the impact of pain on daily activities (i.e., "functional impact" of pain) allows the patient and physician to collaboratively discuss factors that will influence long-term pain management. Depressed mood, avoidance of activities due to fear of triggering pain or injury, and beliefs about the causes and consequences of pain are important features of the patient's subjective pain experience that will impact treatment and outcomes (Von Korff, 2013).

Although older adults (> age 65) amass more medical conditions that can lead to a higher frequency of pain complaints, their reported levels of pain intensity tend to be lower than those of middle-aged adults (ages 45–65) (Langley, 2011). There has been an observed tendency in older adults toward stoicism, or the endurance of pain or hardship without a display of feelings and without complaint (Helme & Gibson, 2001). While this trait may encompass an element of resilience toward adjusting to illness (Cook & Chastain, 2001), the tendency to endure pain without outward expression can also pose a challenge to accurate pain assessment and measurement of response to intervention. Stoicism becomes an even more complex factor when it co-exists with other variables common in older adults such as cognitive impairment, sensory impairments, and polypharmacy (Arnold, 2008; Segal, Scogin, & Floyd, 2012).

Assessment of geriatric pain shares similar elements to evaluation of adult pain and may include the following components: type of pain (nociceptive, neuropathic, mixed), location of pain, pain intensity, subjective description of pain, and history of pain (onset, frequency, triggers, patterns, periods of relief, pain medication history). Additionally, it is recommended that the geriatric pain assessment approach include flexibility to accommodate for potential communication barriers (e.g., hearing, vision, cognitive impairments), which can lead to misinterpretation of important information (Herr & Garand, 2001). If sensory deficits exist, steps should be taken to ensure the patient has access to assistive devices (e.g., eyeglasses, large-print visual aids, hearing aids, voice amplifiers) prior to the start of the assessment. Sensory deficits also may require modifying the environment in which the assessment is taking place, such as relocating to a quieter location, dimming or brightening lights, or minimizing environmental distractions. Use of a brief cognitive screen, such as the St Louis University Mental Status Exam (SLUMS; Tariq, Tumosa, Chibnall, Perry, & Morley, 2006) or the Montreal Cognitive Assessment (MOCA; Nasreddine et al., 2005), to quickly clarify a patient's level of global cognitive functioning is recommended as part of a comprehensive geriatric pain evaluation; presence of cognitive impairment can impact the patient's ability to provide an accurate self-report, understand treatment options, and adhere to treatment recommendations. If moderate–severe cognitive impairments exist, reliance on behavioral indicators of pain, collateral report, and/or results from multiple, incidental assessments that track patterns of pain behaviors, potential triggers, and response to treatment, may be necessary.

It also recommended that clinicians evaluating geriatric pain remain mindful about the potential impact of race/ethnic and generational differences on the expression and reporting of pain, and on reception to treatment within a geriatric population. For example, some older adults may accept pain, in addition to other health conditions, as a normal component of the aging process (Sarkisian, Hays, & Mangione, 2002). This normative view of the pain experience may lead to minimizing one's subjective pain experiences, inadvertently putting the patient at risk for undertreatment.

Accounting for racial differences in which pain may be experienced and subjectively described are also important aspects to consider when assessing for pain in geriatric patients. Green, Baker, Smith, and Sato (2003) found that, compared to their White counterparts, older African Americans enrolled in their study endorsed higher pain levels, more suffering, and less control of their pain levels. They also generally endorsed higher levels of depressive and posttraumatic symptoms when reporting pain levels. Though these authors did not specify if co-occurring depressive symptoms and trauma were secondary to pain or preexisting, these results also may have implications for how pain impacts quality of life differently in these two populations. Therefore, it is recommended that clinicians consider the influence of diversity factors, in addition to generational influences, when conceptualizing how pain is subjectively experienced and reported during a comprehensive pain assessment.

Use of self-report assessment tools can augment the pain evaluation process by improving the accuracy of information gathered and allowing for repeat measurement to gauge changes in pain across time and in response to treatment. Though research is still underway regarding the psychometric properties of several available pain intensity self-report measures, especially when assessing those with cognitive impairment (Wynne, Ling, & Remsburg, 2000), these tools can assist the patient in articulating his/her subjective pain experience while the clinician attempts to gather objective data useful for treatment planning.

As discussed in Herr and Garand (2001), one of the most commonly used approaches in comprehensive pain assessment involves using numeric rating scales (NRS), such as the Brief Pain Inventory (Cleeland & Ryan, 1994), which prompts patients to rate the intensity of their pain experience using a numeric scale of increasing pain intensity (e.g., 0 = no pain, 10 = extreme, unbearable pain). Verbal descriptor scales (VDS) are similar to the numerical rating scales but require the patient to select a verbal description of pain intensity (e.g., "no pain," "mild pain," "moderate pain," "severe pain," "extreme pain," "pain as bad as could be"). Some versions of verbal descriptor scales also provide a visual illustration of a thermometer (Herr & Mobily, 1993), and patients are prompted to rate their pain intensity, with higher "temperatures" on the thermometer representing increased pain intensity levels.

Patients with low health literacy, difficulties with abstract reasoning, or dyslexia may respond better to a pictorial pain scale, such as the Faces Pain Scale—Revised (FPS-R), which was originally developed for use in children (FPS; Bieri, Reeve, Champion, Addicoat, & Ziegler, 1990). This measure requires respondents to point to a facial expression that matches or represents their pain intensity; facial expressions range from content to progressively more distressed. In a study comparing the usability of various types of pain scales, older adults preferred to complete a verbal descriptor scale, independent of demographic status (e.g., level of education, race, sex) and cognitive status (Herr, Spratt, Mobily, & Richardson, 2004). However, as discussed below, supplemental assessment via observational pain instruments is recommended when assessing pain in cognitively impaired older adults.

For those with cognitive impairment, or those who are unable to communicate their pain experience reliably or utilize self-report measures, tools based on direct observation may yield valuable information regarding the pain experience that may otherwise be overlooked or misinterpreted. The Pain Assessment In Advanced Dementia (PAINAD; Warden, Hurely, & Volicer, 2003) is a commonly used tool, especially in care settings, for helping providers assess pain based on data gathered during three- to five-minute observational periods. This measure requires caregivers to observe the older adult when he/she is engaged in an activity and to note changes in body language, facial expressions, degree to which the patient can be consoled, breathing, and negative vocal expressions. Observations indicative of higher pain levels, such as labored breathing, loud moaning/groaning, facial grimacing, agitated body language, and difficulty being consoled, yield higher scores on the PAINAD. If administered over the course of several observational periods, changes in the PAINAD total score may be indicative of increased or decreased pain levels relative to some type of intervention.

While several pain assessment tools currently available in the public domain (e.g., PAINAID, NRS, VDS) are referenced frequently in the pain literature, there are ongoing efforts to improve the psychometric properties of these tools, especially for use with cognitively impaired patients (Lichtner et al., 2014). These tools also do not shed light on the source of pain. Therefore, clinicians should avoid relying on these tools as their main method of information gathering and instead integrate them within a larger, more comprehensive assessment approach (Herr et al., 2004; Qi & Kay, 2012).

Brief Overview of Pharmacological Considerations

Medications commonly are used to treat pain in the elderly. Ongoing assessment of medication risks and benefits is essential, balancing the risks of untreated pain with the risks of adverse effects of medications.

Acetaminophen is the drug of choice for mild to moderate pain (AGS, 2009). It is prudent to limit the dose to 3 grams in 24 hours, or 2 grams in 24 hours for those over age 80 years and those who drink alcohol regularly (AGS, 2009). The American Geriatrics Society Guidelines (2002, 2009) recommend that nonsteroidal anti-inflammatories (NSAIDs) be used with caution because older patients have more frequent side effects and adverse drug reactions. In addition to elevated risks of gastrointestinal bleeding and renal failure, NSAIDs are associated with worsening blood pressure control and heart failure exacerbations. If NSAIDs are prescribed, treatment should be of short duration. Serotonin norepinephrine reuptake inhibitors or selective serotonin reuptake inhibitors may be indicated in patients with both depression and chronic pain (Makris et al., 2014). When available, non-pharmacologic interventions (e.g., mindfulness, cognitive-behavioral therapy, physical therapy, acupuncture) should be integrated into the treatment plan as opposed to relying on pharmacological interventions alone (see Table 22.1).

Opioid medications are recommended by the American Geriatrics Society for severe pain. On balance, opioids have a better safety profile than NSAIDs. Nonetheless, a careful risk assessment for misuse or abuse should be performed to determine safety prior to prescribing opioids (Dowell, Haegerich, & Chou, 2016). Although abuse and misuse trends are lower in older adults, there is a higher mortality risk for older adults when opioids are being misused (Kuehn, 2010; West, Severtson, Green, & Dart, 2015). This increased mortality risk is attributed to both comorbid physical vulnerabilities and an increased risk of opioid overdose when there is suicidal intent. Opioids also can cause constipation, increase the risk of falls, and may cause or worsen cognitive problems in elderly patients. A stimulant

Table 22.1 Evidence-Based Non-pharmacologic Treatments for Persistent Pain the Elderly

Treatment	Level of Evidence	Comments
Acupuncture	Meta-analysis of RCT	Consider use as adjunctive therapy
Mindfulness/meditation	RCT	
Massage	RCT	Consider use as adjunctive therapy
Self-management education programs	Meta-analysis of RCT	
Exercise	RCT	Program should include strengthening, flexibility, balance training, and cardiovascular fitness

Sources for this table include Abdullah et al. (2013); AGS (2002); and AGS (2009).

RCT = randomized controlled trial

laxative should be prescribed with any opioid, due to the inevitable constipation that occurs with opioid medications.

The CDC updated guidelines for prescribing opioids for chronic pain in 2016. That report noted that opioid-related overdose risk was dose dependent and that overdose deaths and injuries were positively associated with older age (Dowell, Haegerich, & Chou, 2016). Elderly patients with chronic pain who have taken opioids for many years may find that their dose of opioids is reduced or eliminated by their prescriber as a result of this report. It is recommended that providers be sensitive to the confusion and distress that are common reactions in response to these changes and consider setting more time aside to provide education and even consider employing motivational strategies for opioid adherence in older adults (Chang, Compton, Almeter, & Fox, 2014). The optimal weaning strategy is not known, but reducing opioid doses by 10% per week is widely accepted (Dowell, Haegerich, & Chou, 2016). Some patients may do better with decreasing dosage by 10% per month. It is important to provide non-opioid pharmacotherapy and non-pharmacologic therapies, as appropriate, to provide pain relief.

Prescribers must monitor a patient's response to medications and adjust accordingly (AGS, 2009). It is important to know if the patient is taking the medication as prescribed, with careful assessment for overmedication, abuse, or undermedication. This can often be verified by obtaining information from the patient and family or caregivers, if possible.

For elderly patients, it is particularly important to "start low and go slow," starting with a low dose of medication and titrating the dose up slowly (AGS, 2002, 2009; Dowell, Haegerich, & Chou, 2016). Elderly patients are more likely to experience adverse side effects from medications due to decreased metabolism of drugs and decreased adaptive physiology. For instance, elderly patients are 2–4 times more likely to experience gastrointestinal bleeding from NSAIDs compared with younger patients (Li, Geraghty, Mehta, & Rothwell, 2017), and renal clearance of medications decreases by about 10% per decade beginning at age 30 (Malec & Shega, 2015). Older patients often have multiple comorbidities and may be taking multiple medications, which increases the risk of medication interactions.

Patients and their families should be informed of the expected outcome and time course of any diagnosed serious illness. It is important to elicit the patient's values and beliefs around such illnesses and to gain an understanding of the patient's goals of care. Despite recent efforts to promote completion of advance care directives for end-of-life care, the proportion of adults who have completed these remains low (36.7%), even among adults with chronic illnesses (38.2%) (Yadav et al., 2017). For adults with advanced dementia, it may be too late to have these discussions when considering decision-making capacity (Vries & Drury-Ruddlesden, 2018). With dementia patients, there could be fluctuating levels of cognitive ability and lucidity, posing significant challenges in determining capacity (Trachsel, Hermann, and Biller-Adorno, 2014). If at least one of the four commonly used legal standards of decision-making capacity (choice, understanding, appreciation, or reasoning) is impaired, then the individual is judged to lack medical decision-making capacity (Kolva, Rosenfield, & Saracino, 2017).

With terminally ill cancer patients, understanding (44.2%) and appreciation (49%) are the most commonly impaired components of capacity. In these cases, the discussions should be made with the medical power of attorney or legal guardian, which is often a family member acting as the surrogate decision maker. If comfort and quality of life are the primary goals of care, palliative care should be initiated, ideally provided by an interdisciplinary team, with pain management a primary goal. In the setting of end-of-life palliative or hospice care, the intent is to relieve suffering. Therefore, it is possible that the amount of medication needed to sufficiently relieve pain will have an unintended consequence of hastening death, but this is supported by contemporary views on medical ethics (LiPuma & DeMarco, 2015).

Non-pharmacological Interventions

Several behavioral interventions for pain have been vetted effectively with an older population, albeit with a need for larger studies to confirm and elaborate on particular modifications (Mcguire, Nicholas, Asghari, Wood, & Main, 2014; Ehde, Dillworth, & Turner, 2014; Park & Hughes, 2012). In 2014, the American Psychological Association (APA) published guidelines for psychologist practice with older adults in *The American Psychologist*, guidelines that included considerations for modifying existing treatments for this population (APA, 2014). These general recommendations can be applied to pain interventions for this population as well, including considering adjusting the pace of treatment; accommodating for sensory limitations; adapting treatment for the setting (e.g., clinic, home, hospital, or long-term care facility); enlisting family, caregivers, and institutional systems in the care plan; and using a multimodal approach with attention to grief/loss, cognitive decline, and stressful practical problems that may not be as common in younger adults (e.g., access to transportation, navigating a changing medical system, affording medical care).

There is empirical support for utilizing CBT interventions for pain management with older adults (Nicholas et al., 2017), with a likely additive effect when combined with behavioral interventions for sleep disorders (Vitiello et al., 2014). There also is some preliminary, but promising, support for using mindfulness-based interventions (Morone, Greco, & Weiner, 2008), biofeedback (Middaugh & Pawlick, 2002), exercise/balancing interventions (Rhayun, Eun-Ok, Paul, & Sang-Cheol, 2003), group educational programs (Rybarczyk, DeMarco, DeLaCruz, Lapidos, & Fortner, 2001), and encouraging the use of assistive devices (Mann, Ottenbacher, Fraas, Tomita, & Granger, 1999).

Depression Interventions and Pain

Treating depression as a component of a comprehensive pain management plan in geriatric populations is important. The relationship between pain and depression is bidirectional and complex, with recent research exploring possible links in genetic and brain neurochemical underpinnings (Boakye et al., 2016). Persistent pain consistently has been identified as a strong predictor of depression (Gleicher, Croxford, Hochman, & Hawker, 2011) and even suicidal ideation in older adults (Tektonidou, Dasgupta, & Ward, 2011). In turn, some evidence indicates that depression may worsen disability and pain (Creamer, Lethbridge-Cejku, Hochberg, 2000; Lamb et al., 2000; Kroenke, Katon, Robinson, & Blair, 2003).

Lin et al. (2003) conducted a randomized controlled trial with a large sample of older adults (1,801 adults greater than 60 years of age). These patients either were assigned to a comprehensive depression primary care program that consisted of educational interventions, behavioral activation, problem-solving therapy, close monitoring of response to antidepressant medication, and collaboration between psychology, nursing, and primary care physicians, or to a usual care group that consisted of routine antidepressant options and referrals to specialty care. The patients assigned to the comprehensive integrated depression care program showed significant reductions in pain, improved quality of life, and improvements on functional measures.

It is important to screen for suicide whenever there is significant chronic pain in older adults, as chronic pain represents a significant suicide risk factor (even when controlling for other risk factors such as mood and age) (Illegen, Kleingberg, & Ignacio, 2013). However, certain types of pain have been found to have a stronger relationship with suicide risk than others, including lower back pain, neuropathic pain, and psychogenic pain.

Cognitive-Behavioral Therapy

Attitudinal and cognitive constructs that often are targeted by cognitive-behavioral interventions appear to be as relevant in older adults as in their younger counterparts. Both lower self-efficacy and higher fear-avoidance constructs have been linked to higher reports of pain intensity in older adults (Turner, Ersek, & Kemp, 2005; Basler, Luckmann, Wolf, & Quint, 2008). Although some evidence indicates that older adults are less likely to elevate a fear-avoidance measure, they report higher levels of pain when they do endorse these beliefs and behaviors (Cook, Brawer, & Vowles, 2006). Nicholas et al. (2017) were able to employ a brief cognitive-behavioral-based pain management intervention with community-dwelling older adults (mean age 73.9). The CBT-based intervention group significantly outperformed an exercise-attention control group. The significant decrease in self-reported pain was evident and mostly maintained, with lower pain scores noted up to one-year post-treatment.

Many older adults also rely on family and paid caregivers for care and support, and there is some evidence that caregivers' beliefs may affect patients' level of coping with chronic pain (Cano, Miller, Loree, 2009; Oliver et al., 2013; Ferriera & Sharman, 2007). Matos, Bernardes, Goubert, and Beyers (2017) described the complex relationship between social support, functional abilities, and chronic pain in a sample of 173 older adults using structural equation modeling. Whether or not social support was perceived as promoting and enhancing autonomy significantly moderated the relationship between pain intensity and pain-related disability. However, this relationship was entirely mediated by the effect the social support had on the older adult's internal sense of self-efficacy. In other words, the benefits of social support are cancelled out if the internal sense of self-efficacy is unchanged by the support offered. However, social support can be a powerful buffer against pain-related disability when it enhances the internal sense of self-efficacy. This model suggests that interventions could be designed to enlist caregivers in order to reduce the effect of pain intensity on pain-related disability.

Sleep Interventions and Pain

The association between higher pain levels and disturbed sleep has been particularly observed in older adults (Chen, Hayman, Shmerling, Bean, & Leveille, 2011). There is strong evidence that sleep problems worsen pain (Haack, Lee, Cohen, Mullington, 2009; Lautenbacher, Kundermann, & Krieg, 2006; Tiede et al., 2010). Although it is often a bidirectional relationship, evidence suggests that the effect of poor sleep on pain is stronger than the effect of pain on disrupting sleep (Koffel et al., 2016). For example, poor sleep has been conceptualized as a direct contributing factor to increased pain in older adults suffering from osteoarthritis (Smith, Quartana, Okonkwo, & Nasir, 2009).

Successfully treating insomnia in older adults has been shown to affect a wide array of health-related quality of life symptoms (Dixon, Morgan, Mathers,

Thompson, & Tomey, 2006). Even short-term sleep interventions have the potential to reduce pain catastrophizing beliefs (Lerman, Finan, Smith, & Haythornthwaite, 2017). When older adults report higher levels of insomnia, cognitive-behavioral treatments for pain that also include behavioral interventions for insomnia (CBT-PI) have been found to outperform cognitive-behavioral interventions for pain alone (CBT-P) (McCurry et al., 2014; Vitiello et al., 2013). Even when controlling for levels of depression, clear and sustained improvements in sleep can yield long-term benefits (up to 18 months) toward reducing pain in an older adult population (Vitiello et al., 2014).

A major challenge in treating sleep problems in older adults is that healthcare professionals often fail to assess for sleep quality in this population, possibly due to an assumption often shared by both the patient and the healthcare professional that sleep problems are simply a part of "normal aging" (Liu & Ancoli-Israel, 2006). Sleep problems are common in older adults (with some estimates as high as 50%) but are not an inevitable part of aging (Crowley, 2011; Voyer, Verreault, Mengue, & Morin, 2006). Older adults tend to report more secondary sleep problems related to medical and psychiatric diagnoses, side effects of medications, and circadian rhythm disruption than younger and middle-age adults. Therefore, treatment of sleep problems in older adults must include careful consideration of contributing factors that may be less common in a younger population. However, there is strong evidence across multiple studies that the same traditional behavioral treatments for insomnia, including cognitive-behavioral, behavioral-only (e.g., sleep restriction), and relaxation-based strategies, that help younger adults significantly improve sleep in older adults (Irwin, Cole, & Nicassio, 2006; Ancoli-Israel & Avalon, 2006). Even when the cause of insomnia is presumed to be secondary to medical conditions, older adults still benefit significantly from behavioral interventions (Rybarczyk et al., 2005).

Mindfulness-Based Interventions for Pain

Although there are not many large clinical trials, mindfulness-based interventions to treat chronic pain in older adults represent a burgeoning area of study (Morone & Greco, 2007). For example, Morone et al. (2008) applied an eight-week mindfulness-based behavioral pain intervention with community-dwelling adults over the age of 65 suffering from chronic low back pain and demonstrated improvements in both chronic pain acceptance and activity engagement. There is also evidence that a daily mindfulness-based meditation intervention for six weeks could help reduce pain associated with postherpetic neuralgia in older adults (Lerman et al., 2017).

Biofeedback and Imagery

A small amount of evidence suggests that biofeedback and relaxation-based interventions can help older adults with chronic pain. Middaugh and Pawlick (2002)

571

found that older adults were just as likely as their younger peers to develop the necessary self-regulation skills associated with biofeedback and to benefit from these skills as verified by lower post-treatment pain scores. There was also a published pilot study finding that guided imagery can shorten hospital stays and decrease pain (Antall & Kresevic, 2004). However, these studies were conducted with higher-functioning older adults, without confirming whether these interventions could be effectively adapted for a cognitively impaired population or for older adults living in long-term care facilities.

Group Multicomponent Educational Interventions

Chronic pain also has been treated in an underserved older population as part of a more general group multicomponent wellness intervention (GMW) (Rybarczyk et al., 2001). GMW interventions have been found to be both cost-saving (Caudill, Schnabel, Zuttermeister, Benson, & Friedman, 1991; Lorig et al., 1999) and effective in improving pain management (Von Korff et al., 1998). Rybarczyk et al.'s study designed an educational intervention consisting of eight two-hour classes for older adults (with a mean age of 67.6 years, 66% African American), taught by a clinical psychologist and primary care physician, that covered a wide array of behavioral medicine interventions including relaxation training, exercise and nutrition education, mindfulness meditation, problem-solving and effective communication skills, and cognitive interventions. Their treatment group reported significant decreases in pain symptoms when compared with a control group. Improvement in pain management was attributed at least partially to an increased health locus of control, a factor that has been significantly linked with improvement in functioning and chronic pain (Keedy, Keffala, Altmaier, & Chen, 2014), as well as with maintenance of healthy behaviors including improved sleep and exercise. Although the lower self-reported pain symptoms were not maintained after a year, the positive attitudinal changes in self-efficacy appeared to be more enduring.

Exercise-Based Interventions

Although many of the conditions associated with chronic pain in the elderly are degenerative in nature, there is still value to preventative and rehabilitation-based interventions (Park & Hughes, 2012). Most notably, fall prevention should be considered as a paramount component of any comprehensive treatment plan for older adults. Chronic pain has been identified as a significant contributing factor to increasing the risk of falls (Stubbs et al., 2014; Patel et al., 2014). In the elderly, opioids also are associated with a higher risk of falls (Daoust et al., 2018). In turn, falls can aggravate the physical conditions associated with pain, result in more pronounced levels of disability, and even precipitate an untimely death for an older adult (Stevens, Mack, Paulozzi, & Ballesteros, 2008).

Exercise-based interventions that improve balance and strength have been found to be effective in reducing the prevalence of falls in older adults. Tai chi has been explored as one of these interventions for older adults. Tai chi has been found to reduce multiple fall risk by about 47.6% (Wolf et al., 1996). The significant effects of tai chi on reducing falls (including injurious falls) have been observed at six months post-treatment even when using a control group consisting of basic stretching-based exercises (Li et al., 2005). There is also some evidence that a 12-week tai chi intervention may not only lead to improved physical functioning but may also significantly reduce pain in an older population with osteoarthritis (Rhayun et al., 2003).

Assistive Devices

There is a surprisingly paltry amount of literature examining the effects of assistive devices (e.g., walkers, scooters, wheelchairs); however, when used correctly, they can prevent falls and improve functioning and independence (Abdullah et al., 2013). Mann, Hurren, and Tomita (1995) found that older adults with moderate to severe levels of osteoarthritis reported high levels of satisfaction with assistive devices, particularly since these devices helped them improve their level of engagement in activities. However, this same study also found that most older adults tend to have inadequate information regarding how to use the devices appropriately and how to identify additional devices to improve functioning, highlighting a need for a higher level of occupational therapy involvement.

There also is a lack of research aimed at understanding the factors that influence a decision to adopt or reject a recommended assistive device, with a certain subset of older adults refusing to use them despite medical recommendations and recurring falls (Aminzadeh & Edwards, 1998; McCreadie & Tinker, 2005). Mann et al. (1999) conducted a randomized controlled trial that assigned participants to either an assistive device interventions group or to a standard control group. They found that participants in the assistive device group not only showed improvements in functional independence and incurred fewer healthcare costs but also had significantly lower pain scores at 18 months.

Complementary/Alternative Medicine (CAM)

The American Geriatrics Society (AGS) (2002) identified transcutaneous electrical nerve stimulation (TENS) as a notable consideration for managing pain effectively in older adults. Age does not appear to be a significant contraindication toward tolerating or benefiting from the intervention, although older adults may need a higher amplitude adjustment on the TENS (Simon, Riley, Fillingim, Bishop, & George, 2015). Weiner et al. (2003) conducted a randomized controlled trial that found support for the use of percutaneous electric nerve stimulation (PENS), which is similar to TENS, with an older adult population. In this study, older adults assigned to the PENS treatment group experienced significantly lower pain scores after a six-week intervention when compared to a sham-PENS and physical therapy group. The effects of the intervention also were maintained at a three-month follow-up.

Several randomized controlled trials have found that acupuncture can reduce pain significantly, even when compared to a credible sham acupuncture control (Miller et al., 2011; Ezzo, Hadhazy, Birch, Lao, Kaplan, & Hochenberg, 2001). Recent meta-analytic reviews have found moderate effect sizes for acupuncture relieving pain (Yuan et al., 2016; Vickers et al., 2012; Chiu, Hsieh, & Tsai, 2017), establishing acupuncture as a reasonable referral for pain management. There is even some evidence with an older adult population that acupuncture may outperform TENS treatment in reducing pain (Grant, Bishop-Miller, Winchester, Anderson, & Faulkner, 1999), and that acupuncture and TENS can be combined effectively as complementary treatments for pain (Itoh, Itoh, Katsumi, & Kitakoji, 2009).

A few studies have explored the effects of physical touch and massage on reducing pain in the elderly. One study found that slow-stroke back massages from nursing staff for ten minutes for seven consecutive evenings significantly reduced pain and anxiety in hospitalized older adults recovering from a recent stroke (Mok & Woo, 2004). Another study found that a particular type of gentle massage therapy called "Tender Touch" adapted for elderly adults with dementia in a long-term care facility led to diminished pain and anxiety scores, as well as improvements in the connections between often agitated patients and their assigned nurses (Sansone & Schmitt, 2012). However, a more recent study did not find significant results when comparing pain measures of a massage intervention group and a control group for older adults with dementia in a long-term care facility (Kapoor & Orr, 2017).

Closing Remarks and Recommendations for Further Research

There are several medical and behavioral treatment options for effectively managing pain in older adults, and this continues to be an area of significant research and innovation. However, systemic challenges in effectively delivering these treatments remain prominent (Molton & Terril, 2014). Older adults often face more practical barriers (e.g., lack of transportation, financial limitations, reliance on family assistance) and have to navigate an increasingly complex medical system with less face-to-face provider time (Putnam, 2007; Bentley, 2003; Goins, Williams, Carter, Spencer, & Solovieva, 2005). Traditional care also often fails to consider factors with circular causality associated with pain in older adults, including depression, sleep, and functional limitations (Szcerbinska, Hirdes, Zyckowska, 2012; Liu & Ancoli-Israel, 2006).

The construct of older adults or elderly is not homogenous, with evidence that the oldest of the old (> age 85), African American and ethnic minorities, and those struggling with cognitive impairment are more likely to have undertreated pain (Malec & Shega, 2015). Although behavioral and exercise-based interventions for pain are presumed to be effective across ethnically diverse groups, there is a lack of research examining possible disparities or barriers for treatment in ethnically diverse older adults. There is some evidence of differences in preferred pain management and coping strategies among older adults, with African Americans tending to more often prefer the use of prayer as part of their coping repertoire for chronic pain (Park, Lavin, & Couturier, 2014). As diversity factors often have been linked to health disparities, future research with older adults needs to consider these variables particularly within the context of life course (e.g., migration experiences, socioeconomic fluctuations, family backgrounds, discriminatory histories) (Hummer, Benjamins, & Rogers, 2004).

Although the number of research articles on pain management in older adults has increased, the construct of what constitutes older adults remains notably variegated. Understanding the "within group differences" in older adults that may influence treatment considerations largely remains understudied. These include considering differences in age, particularly between the oldest (ages 90 and above) and the youngest within this grouping (e.g., 65–75), setting differences (residential care versus community-dwelling), diversity factors (ethnicity, gender, sexual orientation), and differences in levels of physical and cognitive functioning. However, there is enough evidence in the literature that with thoughtful modifications, systemic changes, and an integrated biopsychosocial approach, chronic pain in the older adults can be managed effectively.

References

Abdullah, A., Adams, N., Bone, M., Elliott, A., Gaffin, J., Jones, D., . . . Schofield, P. (2013). Guidance of management of pain in older adults. *Age and Ageing, 42*, i1–i57. doi:10.1093/ageing/afs200.

AGS Panel on Persistent Pain in Older Persons. (2002). The management of persistent pain in older adults. *Journal of American Geriatrics Society, 50*, 205–224.

AGS Panel on Pharmacological Management of Persistent Pain in Older Persons. (2009). Pharmacological management of persistent pain in older persons. *Journal of American Geriatrics Society, 57*(8), 1331–1346.

The American Psychological Association. (2014). Guidelines for psychological practice with older adults. *American Psychologist, 69*(1), 34–65.

Aminzadeh, F., & Edwards, N. (1998). Exploring seniors' views on the use of assistive devices in fall reduction. *Public Health Nursing, 15*(4), 297–304. doi:10.1111/j.1525-1446.1998.tb00353.x

Ancoli-Israel, S., & Ayalon, L. (2006). Diagnosis and treatment of sleep disorders in older adults. *American Journal of Geriatric Psychiatry, 14*, 95–103.

Antall, G. F., & Kresevic, D. (2004). The use of guided imagery to manage pain in an elderly orthopaedic population. *Orthopaedic Nursing, 23*, 335–340.

Arnold, M. (2008). Polypharmacy and older adults: A role for psychology and psychologists. *Professional Psychology: Research and Practice, 39*(3), 283–289. doi:10.1037/0735-7028.39.3.283.

Basler, H., Luckmann, J., Wolf, U., & Quint, S. (2008). The fear-avoidance beliefs, physical activity, and disability in elderly individuals with chronic low back pain and health controls. *Clinical Journal of Pain, 24*, 604–610.

Baumbauer, K. M., Young, E. E., Starkweather, A. R., Guite, J. W., Russell, B. S., & Manworren, R. C. (2016). Managing chronic pain in special populations with emphasis on pediatric, geriatric and drug abuse populations. *The Medical Clinics of North America*, *100*(1), 183–197.

Bentley, J. M. (2003). Barriers to accessing health care: The perspective of elderly people within a village community. *International Journal of Nursing Studies*, *40*(1), 9–21.

Bieri, D., Reeve, R. A., Champion, G. D., Addicoat, L., & Ziegler, J. B. (1990). The faces pain scale for the self-assessment of the severity of pain experienced by children: Initial validation and preliminary investigation for ratio scale properties. *Pain*, *41*, 139–150.

Boakye, P., Olechowski, C., Rashiq, S., Verrier, M., Kerr, B., ... Dick, B. D. (2016). A critical review of neurobiological factors involved in the interactions between chronic pain, depression, and sleep disruption. *Clinical Journal of Pain*, *32*(4), 327–336. doi:10.1097/AjP0000000000000260

Cano, A., Miller, L. R., Loree, A. (2009). Spouse beliefs about partner chronic pain. *Journal of Pain*, *10*, 486–492.

Caudill, M., Schnabel, R., Zuttermeister, P., Benson, H., & Friedman, R. (1991). Decreased clinic use by chronic pain patients: Response to behavioral medicine intervention. *Clinical Journal of Pain*, *7*, 305–310.

Cavalieri, T. A. (2002). Pain management in the elderly. *Journal of the American Osteopathic Association*, *102*, 481–485.

Chang, P., Compton, P., Almeter, P., & Fox, C. H. (2014). The effect of motivational interviewing on prescription opioid adherence among older adults with chronic pain. *Perspective in Psychiatric Care*, *51*(3), 211–219.

Chen, Q., Hayman, L. L., Shmerling, R. H., Bean, J. F., & Leveille, S. G. (2011). Characteristics of chronic pain associated with sleep difficulty in older adults: The Maintenance of balance, independent Living, intellect, and zest in the elderly (MOBILIZE) Boston study. *Journal of the American Geriatrics Society*, *59*, 1385–1392.

Chiu, H.Y., Hsieh, Y. J., & Tsai, P. S. (2017). Systematic review and meta-analysis of acupuncture to reduce cancer-related pain. *European Journal of Cancer Care*, *26*(2). doi:10.1111/ecc.12457

Cleeland, C. S., & Ryan, K. M. (1994). Pain assessment: Global use of the brief pain inventory. *Annals of Academy of Medicine Signapore*, *23*(2), 129–138.

Cook, A. J., Brawer, P. A., & Vowles, K. E. (2006). The fear-avoidance model of chronic pain: Validation and age analysis using structural equation modelling. *Pain*, *121*, 195–206.

Cook, A. J., & Chastain, D. C. (2001). The classification of patients with persistent pain: Age and sex differences. *Pain Research & Management*, *6*, 142–151.

Creamer, P., Lethbridge-Cejku, M., & Hochberg, M. C. (2000). Factors associated with functional impairment in symptomatic knee osteoarthritis. *Rheumatoloy*, *39*, 490–496.

Crowley, K. (2011). Sleep and sleep disorders in older adults. *Neuropsychology Review*, *21*(1), 41053.

Daoust, R., Paquet, J., Lavigne, G., Sanogo, K., & Chauny, J. M. (2014). Senior patients with moderate to severe pain wait longer for analgesic medication in EDs. *American Journal Emergency Medicine*, *32*(4), 315–319.

Daoust, R., Paquet, J., Moore, L, Emond, M., Gosseline, S., Lavigne, G., ... Chauny, J. M. (2018). Recent opioid use and fall-related injury among older patients with trauma. *CMAJ*, *190*(14), E500–E506. doi:https://doi.org/10/1503/cmaj.171286

Dixon, S., Morgan, K., Mathers, N., Thompson, J., & Tomey, M. (2006). Impact of cognitive behavior therapy on health-related quality of life among hypnotic users with chronic insomnia. *Behavioral Sleep Medicine*, *4*(2), 71–84.

Dowell, D., Haegerich, T. M., & Chou, R. (2016). CDC guideline for prescribing opioids for chronic pain—United States, 2016. *JAMA*, *315*(15). doi:10.1001/jama.2016.1464

Ehde, D. M., Dillworth, T. M., & Turner, J. A. (2014). Cognitive-behavioral therapy for individuals with chronic pain: Efficacy, innovations, and directions for research. *American Psychologist, 69*(2), 153–166.

Ezzo, J., Hadhazy, V., Birch, S., Lao, L., Kaplan, G., & Hochenberg, M. (2001). Acupuncture for osteoarthritis of the knee: A systematic review. *Arthritis & Rheumatology, 44*, 815–825. doi:10.1002/1529-0131

Ferriera, V. M., & Sharman, A. M. (2007). The relationship of optimism, pain, and social support to well-being in older adults with osteoarthritis. *Aging and Human Development, 62*, 255–274. doi:10.2190/0KMV-RU7X-CAQM-0RRA

Gleicher, Y., Croxford, R., Hochman, J., & Hawker, G. (2011). A prospective study of mental health care for comorbid depressed mood in older adults with painful osteoarthritis. *BMC Psychiatry, 11*, 147–157. doi:10.1186/1471-244X-11-147

Goins, R. T., Williams, K. A, Carter, M. W., Spencer, M., & Solovieva, T. (2005). Perceived barriers to health care access among rural older adults: A qualitative study. *The Journal of Rural Health, 21*(3), 206–213. doi:10.1111/j.1748-0361.2005.tb00084.x

Grant, D. J., Bishop-Miller, J., Winchester, D. M., Anderson, M., & Faulkner, S. (1999). A randomized comparative trial of acupuncture versus transcutaneous electrical nerve stimulation for chronic back pain in the elderly. *Pain, 82*, 9–13.

Green, C. R., Baker, T. A., Smith, E. M., & Sato, Y. (2003). The effect of race in older adults presenting for chronic pain management: A comparative study of black and white Americans. *The Journal of Pain, 4*(2), 82–90.

Haack, M., Lee, E., Cohen, D. A, Mullington, J. M. (2009). Activation of the prostaglandin system in response to sleep loss in healthy humans: Potential mediator of increased spontaneous pain. *Pain, 145*, 136–141.

Helme, R. D., & Gibson, S. J. (2001). The epidemiology of pain in elderly people. *Clinics in Geriatric Medicine, 17*, 417–431.

Herr, K. A., & Garand, L. (2001). Assessment and measurement of pain in older adults. *Clinics in Geriatric Medicine, 17*(3), 457–478.

Herr, K. A., & Mobily, P. (1993). Comparison of selected pain assessment tools for use with the elderly. *Applied Nursing Research, 6*(1), 39–46.

Herr, K. A., Spratt, K., Mobily, P., & Richardson, G. (2004). Pain intensity assessment in older adults: Use of experimental pain to compare psychometric properties and usability of selected pain scales with younger adults. *The Clinical Journal of Pain, 20*(4), 207–219.

Hummer, R., Benjamins, M. R., & Rogers, R. G. (2004). Racial and ethnic disparities in health and mortality among the U.S. elderly population. In N. B. Anderson, R. A. Bulatao, & B. Cohen (Eds.), *Critical perspectives on racial and ethnic differences in health in late life*. Washington, DC: National Academies Press. Retrieved from www.ncbi.nlm. nih.gov/books/NBK25532/doi:10.17226/11086

Husebo, B. S., Ballard, C., Cohen-Mansfield, J., Seifert, R., & Aarsland, D. (2014). The response of agitated behavior to pain management in persons with dementia. *The American Journal of Geriatric Psychiatry, 22*(7), 708–717.

Illegen, M. A., Kleingberg, F., & Ignacio, R. V. (2013). Non-cancer pain conditions and suicide risk. *Jama Psychiatry, 70*(7), 692–697. doi:10.1001/jamapsychiatry.2013.908

Irwin, M. R., Cole, J. C., & Nicassio, P. M. (2006). Comparative meta-analysis of behavioural interventions for insomnia and their efficacy in middle-aged adults and in older adults 55+ years of age. *Health Psychology, 25*, 3–14.

Itoh, K., Itoh, S., Katsumi, Y., & Kitakoji, H. (2009). A pilot study on using acupuncture and transcutaneous electrical nerve stimulation to treat chronic pain non-specific low back pain. *Complementary Therapies in Clinical Practice, 15*(1), 22–25. doi:10.1016/j. ctcp.2008.09.003

Kapoor, Y., & Orr, R. (2017). Effect of therapeutic massage on pain in patients with dementia. *Dementia, 16*(1), 119–125.

Keedy, N. H., Keffala, V. J., Altmaier, E. M., & Chen, J. J. (2014). Health locus of control and self-efficacy predict back pain rehabilitation outcomes. *The Iowa Orthopaedic Journal, 34,* 158–165.

Koffel, E., Kroenke, K., Bair, M. J., Leverty, D., Polusny, M. A., & Krebs, E. E. (2016). The bidirectional relationship between sleep complaints and pain: Analysis of data from a randomized trial. *Health Psychology, 35*(1), 41–49.

Kolva, E., Rosenfield, B., & Sarcino, R. (2018). Assessing decision-making capacity of terminally ill patients with cancer. *American Journal of Geriatric Psychiatry, 26(5),* 523–531.

Kroenke, K., Katon, W., Robinson, R., & Blair, M. (2003). Depression and pain comorbidity: A literature review. *Archives of Internal Medicine, 163*(20), 2433–2445. doi:10.1001/archinte.163.20.2433

Kuehn, B. M. (2010). FDA promotes safer use of analgesics in older adults with chronic pain. *JAMA, 304*(17), 1883–1884.

Lamb, S., Guralnik, J., Buchner, D., Ferruci, M., Hochberg, Simonsick, E., & Fried, L. (2000). Factors that modify the association between knee pain and mobility limitation in older women: The women's health and aging study. *Annals of the Rheumetic Diseases, 59*(5), 331–337. doi:10.1136/ard.59.5.331

Langley, P. C. (2011). The prevalence, correlates, and treatment of pain in the European Union. *Current Medical Research and Opinion, 27,* 463–480. doi:10.1185/03007995.2010.542136

Lautenbacher, S., Kundermann, B., Krieg, J. C. (2006). Sleep deprivation and pain perception. *Sleep Med Reviews, 10,* 357–369.

Lerman, S. F, Finan, P. H., Smith, M. T., & Haythornthwaite, J. A. (2017). Psychology interventions that target sleep reduce pain catastrophizing in knee osteoarthritis. *Pain, 158*(11), 2189–2195. doi:10.1097/j.pain.0000000000001023

Li, L., Geraghty, O. C., Mehta, Z., & Rothwell, P. M. (2017). Age-specific risks, severity, time course, and outcome of bleeding on long-term antiplatelet treatment after vascular events: A population-based cohort study. *Lancet, 390,* 490–499. doi:10.1016/S0140-6736(17)30770-5

Li, F., Harmer, P., Fisher, J., McAulet, E., Chaumeton, N., Eckstrom, E., Wilson, N. (2005). Tai Chi and fall reductions in older adults: A randomized controlled trial. *The Journals of Gerontology, 60*(2), 187–194.

Lichtner, V., Dowding, D., Esterhuizen, P., Closs, S. J., Long, A. F., Corbett, A., & Brings, M. (2014). Pain assessment for people with dementia: A systematic review of systematic reviews of pain assessment tools. *BMC Geriatrics, 14,* 138.

Lin, E. H. B., Katon, W., Von Korff, M., Tang, L., Williams, J. W., Kroenke, K., . . . Unutzer, J. (2003, November 12). Effect of improving depression care on pain and functional outcomes among older adults with arthritis. *JAMA, 290*(18). Retrieved from www.jamanetwork.com

LiPuma & DeMarco. (2015). Expanding the use of continuous sedation until death: Moving beyond the last resort for the terminally Ill. *The Journal of Clinical Ethics, 26*(2), 121–132.

Liu, L., & Ancoli-Israel, S. (2006). Insomnia in the older adult. *Sleep Medicine Clinics, 1,* 409–421.

Lorig., K. R., Sobel, D. S., Stewart, A. L., Brown, B. W., Bandura, A., Ritter, P., . . . Holman, H. R. (1999). Evidence suggesting that a chronic disease self-management program can improve health status while reducing hospitalization: A randomized trial. *Medical Care, 37*(1), 5–14.

Mailis-Ganon, A., Nicholson, K., Yegneswraan, B., & Zurokowski, M. (2008). Pain Characteristics of adults 65 years of age and older referred to a tertiary care pain clinic. *Pain Research & Management, 13,* 389–394.

Makris, U. E., Abrams, R. C., Gurland, B., & Reid, M. C. (2014). Management of persistent pain in the older patient. A clinical review. *JAMA*, *312*(8), 825–836.

Malara, A., Debiase, G. A., Bettarini, F., Ceravolo, F., Di Cello, S., Gara, M., . . . Rispoli, V. (2016). Pain assessment in elderly with behavioral and psychological symptoms of dementia. *Journal of Alzheimer's Disease*, *50*(4), 1217–1225. doi:10.3233/JAD-150808

Malec, M., & Shega, J. W. (2015). Pain management in the elderly. *The Medical Clinics of North America*, *99*(2), 337–350.

Mann, W. C., Hurren, D., & Tomita, M. (1995). Assistive devices used by home-based elderly persons with arthritis. *American Journal of Occupational Therapy*, *49*, 810–820.

Mann, W. C, Ottenbacher, K. J., Fraas, L., Tomita, M., & Granger, C. V. (1999). Effectiveness of assistive technology and environmental interventions in maintaining independence and reducing home care costs for the frail elderly. *Archives of Family Medicine*, *8*, 210–217.

Matos, M., Bernardes, S. F., Goubert, L., & Beyers., L. (2017). Buffer or amplifier? Longitudinal effects of social support for functional autonomy/dependence on older adults' chronic pain experience. *Health Psychology*, *36*(12), 1195–1206.

McCreadie, C., & Tinker, A. (2005). The acceptability of assistive technology to older people. *Ageing & Society*, *25*(1), 91–110.

McCurry, S. M, Shortreed, S. M, Von Korff, M., Balderson, B. H., Baker, L. D., Rybarczyk, B. D., & Vitiello, M. V. (2014). Who benefits from CBT for insomnia in primary care? Important patient selection and trial design lessons from longitudinal results of the lifestyles trial. *Sleep*, *37*(20), 299–308. doi:10.5665/sleep.3402

McGuire, B. E, Nicholas, M. K., Asghari, A., Wood, B. M., & Main, C. J. (2014). The effectiveness of psychological treatments for chronic pain in older adults: Cautious optimism and an agenda for research. *Current Opinion in Psychiatry*, *27*(5), 380–384.

Middaugh, S. J., & Pawlick, K. (2002). Biofeedback and behavioural treatment of persistent pain in the older adult: A review and a study. *Applied Psychophysiology and Biofeedback*, *27*, 185–202.

Miller, E., Maimon, Y., Rosenblatt, Y., Mendler, A., Hasner, A., Barad, A., . . . Lev-ari, S. (2011). Delayed effect of acupuncture treatment in OA of the knee: A blinded, randomized, controlled trial. *Evidence-based Complementary and Alternative Medicine, 2011*. doi:10.1093/ecam/nen080. Retrieved from https://www.hindawi.com/journals/ecam/2011/792975/cta/

Mok, E., & Woo, C. P. (2004). The effects of slow-stroke massage on anxiety shoulder pain in elderly stroke patients. *Complementary Therapies in Nursing & Midwifery*, *10*, 209–216.

Molton, I. R., & Terrill, A. L. (2014). Overview of persistent pain in older adults. *American Psychologist*, *69*(2), 197–207. doi:10.1037/a0035794

Morone, N. E., & Greco, C. M. (2007). Mind—body interventions for chronic pain in older adults: A structured review. *Pain Medicine*, *8*(4), 359–374.

Morone, N. E., Greco, C. M., & Weiner, D. K. (2008). Mindfulness meditation for the treatment of chronic low back pain in older adults: A randomized controlled pilot study. *Pain*, *134*(3), 310–319.

Nasreddine, Z. S., Phillips, N. A., Bedirian, V., Charbonneau, S., Collins, I., Cummings, J. L., & Chertkow, H. (2005). The Montreal cognitive assessment, MoCA., A brief screening tool for mild cognitive impairment. *Journal of the American Geriatrics Society*, *53*(4), 695–699.

Nicholas, M. K., Asghari, A., Blyth, F. M, Wood, B. M., Murray, R., McCabe, R., . . . Overton, S. (2017). Long-term outcomes from training in self-management of chronic pain in an elderly population: A randomized controlled trial. *Pain*, *158*(1), 86–95.

Oliver, D. P., Wittenber-Lyles, E., Washington, K., Kruse, R. L., Albright, D. L., Baldwin, P. K., . . . Demiris, G. (2013, May 31). Hospice caregivers' experiences with pain management: "I'm not a doctor, and I don't know if I helped her go faster or slower". *Journal of Pain Symptom Management*, *46*(6). doi:10.1016/j.jpainsymman.2013.02.011

Park, J., & Hughes, A. K. (2012). Nonpharmacological approaches to the management of chronic pain in community-dwelling older adults: A review of empirical evidence. *Progress in Geriatrics*, *60*(3), 555–568.

Park, J., Lavin, R., & Couturier, B. (2014, December 11). Choice of nonpharmacological pain therapies by ethnically diverse older adults. *Pain Management*, *4*(6). https://doi.org/10.2217/pmt.14.43

Patel, K.V., Phelan, E.A., Leveille, S. G., Lamb, S. E., Missikpode, C., Wallace, R. B., . . . Turk, D. C. (2014). High prevalence of falls, fear of falling, and impaired balance in older Adults with pain in the United States: Findings from the 2011 national health and aging trends study. *Journal of American Geriatrics Society*, *62*, 1844–1852.

Putnam, M. (2007). *Ageing and disability: Crossing network lines*. New York, NY: Springer Publishing Company.

Qi, S., & Kay, D. (2012). The psychometric properties, feasibility, and utility of behavioural-observation methods in pain assessment of cognitively impaired elderly people in acute and long-term care: A systematic review. *JBI Library of Systematic Reviews*, *10*(17), 977–1085.

Reyes-Gibby, C. C., Aday, L., & Cleeland, C. (2002). Impact of pain on self-rated health in the community-dwelling older adults. *Pain*, *95*(1–2), 75–82.

Rhayun, S., Eun-Ok, L., Paul, L., & Sang-Cheol, B. (2003). Effects of tai chi exercise on pain, balance, muscle strength, and perceived difficulties in physical functioning in older women with osteoarthritis: A randomized clinical trial. *The Journal of Rheumatology*, *30*(9), 2039–2044.

Rybarczyk, B., DeMarco, G., DeLaCruz, M., Lapidos, S., & Fortner, B. (2001). A classroom mind/body wellness intervention for older adults with chronic illness: Comparing immediate and 1-year benefits. *Behavioral Medicine*, *27*, 15–27.

Rybarczyk, B., Stepanski, E., Fogg, L., Lopez, M., Barry, P., & Davis, A. (2005). A placebo-controlled test of cognitive-behavioral therapy for comorbid insomnia in older adults. *Journal of Consulting and Clinical Psychology*, *73*, 1164–1174.

Sampson, E. L., White, N., Lord, K., Leurent, B., Vickerstaff, V., Scott, S., & Jones, L. (2015). Pain, agitation, and behavioural problems in people with dementia admitted to general hospital wards: A longitudinal cohort study. *Pain*, *156*(4), 675–683. http://doi.org/10.1097/j.pain.0000000000000095

Sansone, P., & Schmitt, L. (2012). Providing tender touch massage to elderly nursing home residents: A demonstration project. *Geriatric Nursing*, *21*(6), 303–307. https://doi.org/10.1067/mgn.2000.108261

Sarkisian, C. A., Hays, R. D., & Mangione, C. M. (2002). Do older adults expect to age successfully? The association between expectations regarding aging and beliefs regarding healthcare seeking among older adults. *Journal of the American Geriatrics Society*, *50*, 1837–1843. doi:10.1046/j.1532-5415.2002.50513.x

Segal, D. L., Scogin, F., & Floyd, M. (2012). Evidence-based psychological treatments for geriatric depression. In F. Scogin & A. Shah (Eds.), *Making evidence-based psychological treatments work with older adults* (pp. 87–130). Washington, DC: American Psychological Association.

Simon, C. B., Riley, J. L, Fillingim, R. B., Bishop, M. D., & George, S. Z. (2015). Age group comparisons of TENS response among individuals with chronic axial low back pain. *The Journal of Pain*, *16*(12), 1268–1279. https://doi.org/10.1016/j.jpain.2015.08.009

Smith, M. T., Quartana, P. J., Okonkwo, R. M., & Nasir, A. (2009). Mechanisms by which sleep disturbance contributes to osteoarthritis pain: A conceptual model. *Current Pain Headache Reports*, *13*(6), 447–454.

Stevens, J. A, Mack, K. A., Paulozzi, L. J., & Ballesteros, M. F. (2008). Self-reported falls and fall-Related injuries among persons aged ≥ 65 years—United States, 2006. *Journal of Safety Research*, *39*(3), 345–349.

Stubbs, B., Binnekade, T., Eggermont, L., Sepehry, A. A., Partchay, S., & Schofield, P. (2014). Pain and the risk for falls in community-dwelling older adults: Systematic review and meta-analysis. *Archives of Physical Medicine and Rehabilitation, 95*(1), 175–187.

Szcerbinska, K. K., Hirdes, J. P., & Zyckowska, J. J. (2012). Good news and bad news: Depressive symptoms decline and undertreatment increased with age in home care and institutional settings. *The American Journal of Geriatric Psychiatry, 20*, 1045–1056. doi:10.1097/JGP.0b013d3182331702

Tariq, S. H., Tumosa, N., Chibnall, J. T., Perry, H. M., & Morley, J. E. (2006). The St. Louis University Mental Status Examination (SLUMS) for detecting mild cognitive impairment and dementia is more sensitive than the Mini Status Exam (MMSE)—a pilot study. *American Journal of Geriatric Psychiatry, 14*, 900–910.

Tektonidou, M. G., Dasgupta, A., & Ward, M. M. (2011). Suicidal ideation among adults with arthritis: Prevalence and subgroups at highest risk. Data from the 2007–2008 national health and nutrition examination survey. *Arthritis Cara & Research, 63*, 1322–1333. doi:10/1002/acr.20516

Tiede, W., Magerl, W., Baumgärtner, U., Durrer, B., Ehlert, U., Treede, R. D. (2010). Sleep restriction attenuates amplitudes and attentional modulation of pain-related evoked potentials, but augments pain ratings in healthy volunteers. *Pain, 148*, 36–42.

Trachsel, M., Hermann, H., & Biller-Adorno, N. (2014). Cognitive fluctuations as a challenge for the assessment of decision-making capacity in patients with dementia. *American Journal of Alzheimer's Disease & Other Dementias, 30*(4), 360–363.

Turner, J. A., Ersek, M., & Kemp, C. (2005). Self-efficacy for managing pain is associated with disability, depression and pain coping among retirement community residents with chronic pain. *Journal of Pain, 6*, 471–479.

UN Department of Economic and Social Affairs. (2017). *World population prospects: The 2017 revision.* Published online Retrieved from https://esa.un.org/unpd/wpp/Publications/Files/WPP2017_KeyFindings.pdf

Unutzer, J., Ferrell., B., Lin, E. H., & Marmon, T. (2004). Pharmacotherapy of pain in depressed older adults. Journal of the American Geriatrics Society, 52, 1916–1922. doi:10.1111/j.1532-5415.2004.52519.x

U.S. Census Bureau. (2011). *The older population: 2010.* Retrieved from www.census.gov/prod/cen2010/briefs/c2010br-09.pdf

Vickers, A. J., Cronin, A. M., Maschino, B. S., Lewith, G., MacPherson, H., Victor, N., ...Linde, K. (2013). Acupuncture for chronic pain: Individual patient data meta-analysis. *Archives of Internal Medicine, 172*(19), 1444–1453. doi:10.1001/archinternmed.2012.3654

Vitiello, M. V., McCurry, S. M., Shortreed, S. M., Balderson, B. H., Baker, L. D., Keefe, F. J., ...Von Korff, M. (2013, May 27). Cognitive-behavioral treatment for comorbid insomnia and osteoarthritis pain in primary care: The lifestyles randomized controlled trial. *Journal of American Geriatrics Society, 61*(6), 947–956. doi:10.1111/jgs.12275

Vitiello, M. V., McCurry, S. M. Shortreed, S. M., Balderson, B. H., Baker, L. D., Keefe, F. J., ...Von Korff, M. (2014, May 12). Short-term improvement in insomnia symptoms predicts long-term improvements in sleep, pain, and fatigue in older adults with comorbid osteoarthritis and Insomnia. *Journal of American Geriatrics Society, 61*(6), 947–956. doi:10.1016/j.pain.2014.04.032

Von Korff, M. C. (2013). Tailoring chronic pain care by brief assessment of impact and prognosis. *JAMA Internal Medicine, 173*(12), 1126–1127.

Von Korff, M. C., Cherkin, D. E., Saunders, K. M., Rutter, C., Moore, J., Lorig, K., ... Comite, F. (1998). A randomized trial of a lay person-led self-management group intervention for back pain patients in primary care. *Spine, 23*(23), 2608–2615.

Voyer, P., Verreault, R., Mengue, P. N., & Morin, C. M. (2006). Prevalence of insomnia and its associated factors in elderly long-term care residents. *Archives of Gerontology and Geriatrics, 42*, 1–20.

Vries, K. D., & Drury-Ruddlesden, J. (2018). Advance care planning for people with dementia: Ordinary everyday conversation. *Dementia*. doi:10.1177/1471301218764169.

Warden, V., Hurely, A. C., & Volicer, L. (2003). Development and psychometric evaluation of the pain assessment in advanced dementia (PAINAD) scale. *Journal of American Medical Directors Association*, *4*(1), 9–15.

Weiner, D. K., Rudy, T. E., Glick, R. M., Boston, J. R., Lieber, S. J., Morrow, L. A., & Taylor, S. (2003). Efficacy of percutaneous electrical nerve stimulation for the treatment of chronic low back pain in older adults. *Journal of the American Geriatrics Society*, *51*, 599–608.

West, N., Severtson, S., Green, J. L., & Dart, R. C. (2015). Trends in abuse and misuse of prescribed opioids among older adults. *Drug & Alcohol Dependence*, *149*, 117–121.

Wolf, S. L., Barnhart, H. X., Kutner, N. G., McNeely, E., Coogler, C., Xu, T., & Atlanta FICSIT Group. (1996). Reducing frailty and falls in older persons: An investigation of Tai Chi and computerized balance training. *Journal of the American Geriatrics Society*, *44*, 489–497.

Wynne, C., Ling, S. M., & Remsburg., R. (2000). Comparison of pain assessment instruments in cognitively intact and cognitively impaired nursing home residents. *Geriatric Nursing*, *21*(1), 20–23. doi:10.1067/mgn.2000.105793

Yadav, R. N, Gabler, N. B., Cooner, E., Kent, S., Kim, J., Herbst, N., . . . Courtright, K. R. (2017). Approximately one in three adults completes any type of advance directive for end-of-life care. *Health Affairs*, *36*(7), 1244–1251. doi:10.1377/hlthaff.2017.0175

Yuan, Q. L., Wang, P., Liang, L., Sun, F., Yong-song, C., Wen-tao, W., . . . Zhang, Y. G. (2016). Acupuncture for musculoskeletal pain: A meta-analysis and meta-regression of sham-controlled randomized clinical trials. *Scientific Reports*, *6*. doi:10.1038/srep30675

23

Pain and Culture

Differences in Experience and Treatment, Challenges of Measurement and Some Recommendations

Nuwan Jayawickreme and Eva Pugliese

Background

The physical experience of pain is universal and is the most common reason why people around the world seek medical attention (Todd & Incayawar, 2014). In general terms, pain receptors in the human body respond to damaging or potentially damaging stimuli by sending threat signals through the spinal cord to the brain. The brain creates the sensation of pain in order to direct conscious attention and physiological responses such as inflammation to the part(s) of the body in need of attention. In this way, the basic physiological underpinnings of the pain experience are universal to all humans independent of culture, geographical location, ethnicity, gender, or age. Although the physical experience of pain is universal, the threshold (i.e., the point at which someone perceives a stimulation to be painful), tolerance of, and response to pain and pain treatments varies from person to person, depending in part on how the individual's cultural background impacts the meaning he/she makes of that experience (Bates, 1987). Thus, it is vital that medical and psychosocial providers working with chronic pain patients understand the role of culture in the experience of pain in order to inform effective assessment and intervention approaches.

Zborowski (1952, 1969) was the first to propose the notion that the culturally determined meaning ascribed to pain has an impact on how that pain is experienced. Zborowski believed that "pain, like so many other physiological phenomena, acquires specific social and cultural significance" (Zborowski, 1952,

p. 17). An anthropologist, Zborowski conducted a qualitative study of veterans of Jewish, Italian, Irish, or Caucasian Protestant backgrounds at a veterans' hospital in Bronx, NY and found that each ethnic group had attitudes and responses to pain unique to that group.

For example, Zborowski found that while Jewish-Americans and Italian-Americans had a lower pain threshold and lower pain tolerance than the other groups studied, they also assigned different meaning to their pain experience. Specifically, Jewish-Americans had what Zborowski called "a future oriented anxiety" in that they were more concerned by whether their pain indicated an underlying serious medical health condition and how this would impact their families. Italian-Americans, on the other hand, had a "present-oriented apprehension" in that they were more concerned with gaining relief from their pain as soon as possible. Zborowski's analysis at times verged on negative stereotyping, veering from data to broad ethnic caricatures (e.g., "the Jewish culture allows the patient to be demanding and complaining," Zborowski, 1952, p. 23). Nevertheless, his work stands out as the first modern analysis of how culture impacts the meaning assigned to pain.

Around the same time as Zborowski's qualitative study, Beecher (1956) also examined the degree to which the meaning ascribed to pain by the patient impacts how that pain is experienced. Beecher (1956) studied injured veterans of World War II and hypothesized that their beliefs about the benefits of leaving the battlefield resulted in their experiencing little or no pain at all despite their significant physical injuries. Though Beecher did not look specifically at cultural attitudes, his findings highlighted the degree to which the pain experience is determined by the meaning assigned by the patient to that pain.

However, researchers have failed to meaningfully build on this early work regarding the impact that culture has on the pain experience. In its 2011 report, "Relieving Pain in America," the Institute of Medicine notes that "the pain literature has not explored the experiences of diverse populations, much less subpopulations of racial groups, with respect to acute, chronic, or cancer pain" (p. 67). Furthermore, many of the studies that do address the impact of culture on pain unfortunately have substantive methodological limitations, with little direct assessment of specific cultural variables and with small or convenience samples or use of chart data (Green et al., 2003; Lasch, 2000; Rahim-Williams, Riley, Williams, & Fillingim, 2012).

This chapter summarizes existing empirical findings on the impact of culture on pain and provides some recommendations for both researchers and practitioners on how to conceptualize the relationship between cultural factors and the pain experience. It reviews the extant literature on pain and culture with the goals of 1) identifying reliable research findings that describe the impact of sociocultural variables on the pain experience; 2) providing some future research directions to guide researchers, with a focus on culturally valid assessment of pain; and 3) recommending best practices when working with chronic pain patients from different cultural backgrounds.

Culture

Cohen (2009) noted in a review of definitions of culture provided by anthropologists and psychologists that, while there are indeed many definitions of culture in the research literature, there now exists an emerging consensus on what culture is. Specifically, culture can be defined as information shared across generations that reflects the successful adaptation of humans to their environments. This information exists both in the social world in the form of norms (e.g., stoicism in the presence of pain), contingencies (e.g., if one behaves in a stoic manner, then she will be respected more by her community), and in the individual's mind in the form of attitudes (e.g., stoicism is the appropriate way to deal with pain) and behavioral tendencies (e.g., not discussing one's pain with others).

Thus, individuals engage in "acts of meaning" (Bruner, 1990) that are seen by those around them as meaningful. These acts are governed by cultural scripts (Ryder, Ban, & Chentsova-Dutton, 2011): heuristics learned from one's sociocultural environment that determine meaning-making and behavior. What is considered successful adaptation varies from geographic location to geographic location, and thus one can see different cultural scripts that stem from specific systems of meaning, which in turn stem from specific environmental realities. Such systems of meaning and cultural scripts influence attitudes toward, as well as the attention given to, pain, and as a result influence pain perception and expression as well as responses to pain (Bates & Edwards, 1992).

To illustrate this process, whereby specific environmental realities lead to specific systems of meaning and cultural scripts, let's consider the largest indigenous nation in South America, the Quichua people of the Andes. Incayawar and Maldonado-Bouchard (2013) found that the Quichua tend to actively cope with their pain rather than verbalize it. This particular behavioral cultural script is a product of the Quichua belief that complaining is pointless, as it will not lead to any assistance that might ameliorate the pain. This stoic attitude stems in all likelihood from a system of meaning reflecting the economic reality that the Quichua nation is especially impoverished, with the poverty rate being 85% (Incayawar & Maldonado, 2013).

Cohen (2009) argues for an expansive view of culture that includes not only psychological variables, such as the widely studied independent sense of self (i.e., the self is seen as unique and distinct from others) versus interdependent sense of self (i.e., the self is subsumed by group affiliation; Markus & Kitayama, 1991), but also sociodemographic variables such as religion, socioeconomic status (SES) and country region. This chapter adopts this more expansive definition of culture. Specifically, it focuses on cultural variables that have been examined in the pain literature, namely ethnicity, perceived racial discrimination, stoicism, and locus of control.

Ethnicity

While the majority of studies examining pain in diverse communities have used ethnic group as a proxy measure of culture, ethnic group is not the same as cultural affiliation (Lasch, 2000). Many different cultures can exist within a particular ethnic group. For example, within individuals of the same ethnicity, those of low SES are culturally distinct from those of high SES (Stephens, Markus, & Phillips, 2014). For this reason, interpreting any ethnic differences in the experience of pain as evidence of cultural differences should be done with caution.

A number of studies have examined ethnic differences in the experience of pain, focusing on pain created in healthy individuals in laboratory settings. Both Zborowski (1952, 1969) and Beecher (1956) were of the opinion that such studies were limited in their ability to identify differences in the meaning ascribed to pain. That said, while temporary pain experienced in the context of a research study obviously is not the same as the chronic pain experienced by those seeking treatment, reactions to pain experienced in a research context have been shown to predict reactions to subsequent clinical pain (see Palit et al., 2013 for a discussion). As such, these laboratory studies do provide insight into ethnic differences in the experience of chronic pain.

Rahim-Williams et al. (2012) reviewed the research on ethnic differences in the experience of experimental pain, focusing on differences between African Americans and non-Hispanic Whites, and differences between non-Hispanic Whites and other ethnic groups. These analyses indicated that African Americans overall had lower pain tolerance (i.e., they perceived lower levels of stimulation as painful) than non-Hispanic Whites and also perceived greater pain intensity and pain unpleasantness. Furthermore, Hispanics had lower pain tolerance than non-Hispanic Whites.

A number of individual research studies compared other ethnic groups (e.g., Indians, Eskimos and non-Hispanic Whites [Meehan, Stoll, & Hardy, 1954], non-Hispanic Whites and Indians living in India [Nayak, Shiflett, Eshun, & Levine, 2000], Danish Whites and Indians [Gazerani & Arendt-Nielsen, 2005], "Occidentals" of European descent and Nepalese porters in Nepal [Clark & Clark, 1980]). One should be cautious about interpreting broad ethnic differences on the basis of a single study; nevertheless, in reviewing the pattern of findings, Rahim-Williams et al. (2012) noted a pattern where ethnic minority group differences seen in the United States and in Europe were smaller or in the opposite direction when members of those ethnic groups were tested in their country of origin. In other words, ethnic minority status in a particular country, rather than membership in that particular ethnic group per se, may be what is associated with lower pain tolerance and greater pain intensity.

Perceived Discrimination as an Explanation of the Relationship Between Ethnic Minority Status and Pain

One possible explanation for the relationship between ethnic minority status and pain is that members of ethnic minority groups are more likely to experience discrimination based on membership in that ethnic group. A large body of research exists that documents the negative impact of perceived discrimination on physical and mental health in ethnic minorities (see Pascoe & Smart-Richman, 2009, for a review). Recent studies have examined specifically the impact of discrimination on pain in ethnic minority groups. Edwards (2008) found that perceived lifelong discrimination was one of the strongest predictors of back pain in African Americans, but not in non-Hispanic Whites. Burgess et al. (2009) found that even after controlling for SES and other health-related variables, there was a significant relationship between bodily pain and perceived discrimination. Lastly, Goodin et al. (2013) found that racial discrimination was associated with lower pain tolerance in African Americans but not in non-Hispanic Whites.

It remains unclear what mechanism underlies the relationship between perceived discrimination and pain in individuals with ethnic minority status. However, Goodin et al. (2013) propose two mechanisms that have promise. First, ethnic minority individuals are, as a consequence of the discrimination they have experienced, more hypervigilant—i.e., their sensory systems become more sensitive to indicators of threat in the environment. This hypervigilance may lead to a greater focus on and amplification of pain, which results in reduced pain tolerance. Second, the chronic stress caused by constant discrimination leads to changes in the neuroendocrine, autonomic, and immune systems, which in turn leads to greater pain sensitivity. Notably, both of these proposed mechanisms demonstrate how sociocultural variables (e.g., perceived racial discrimination) influence neurobiological changes, which in turn leads to greater pain. Hopefully researchers will continue to test hypotheses that involve the interaction between sociocultural variables and neurobiological and other physiological processes.

Stoicism

People from cultures that value stoicism (i.e., the repression of pain expression) respond differently to their pain than people from cultures that value expressivity. For example, overall Asian Americans have a lower pain prevalence rate than other ethnic groups in the United States, in part due to their stoicism and reluctance to express pain (Institute of Medicine, 2011). Stoic individuals tend to avoid showing emotional responses to pain, as they do not want to be perceived as "weak." In addition, they may deny even having pain so as to avoid admitting weakness or burdening others. Such individuals may avoid seeking care altogether because they have learned to deal with their pain independently. In contrast, people from cultures that value expressivity learn that it is appropriate and culturally acceptable to respond vocally to pain. In this way, they are encouraged to seek attention to help manage their pain and to help those in pain.

Bates, Edwards, and Anderson (1993) examined ethnic and cultural differences in chronic pain. They found that Polish Americans and what they termed "Old Americans" (predominately Protestant Americans who had been in the United States for at least three generations and did not identify themselves as belonging to a particular ethnic group) were less expressive of pain than Italian-Americans and Hispanic Americans. Bates et al. (1993) argued that if one lives in a sociocultural setting where outward emotional expressions of pain are discouraged, one develops cultural scripts regarding the expression of pain that privileges a stoic response. These cultural scripts may lead not only to less reporting of pain but also to a reduced experience of pain. This is because these cultural scripts impact not only psychological and behavioral responses to pain but also the neurobiological processing of sensory information.

Recent research studies have focused on how stoicism and neurobiological processes interact to influence the pain experience. Palit et al. (2013) examined the mechanisms underlying stoicism in Native Americans, a population where this behavioral tendency is common (Barkwell, 2005; Haozous, Knobf, & Brant, 2011; Kramer, Harker, & Wong, 2002). Palit et al. (2013) note that Native Americans, along with Hispanic Americans and African Americans, are at the greatest risk for chronic pain in the United States. However, whereas Hispanic Americans and African Americans have higher pain sensitivity (as noted above), Native Americans tend to minimize the expression of pain. In an experimental pain study, they examined differences in pain processing and found that Native Americans experience less pain and engage in less pain signaling than non-Hispanic Whites. Furthermore, Native Americans had reduced scores on a physiological measure of spinal sensitization, temporal summation of the nociceptive flexion reflex threshold, indicating that pain signals are minimized in the spinal cord prior to those signals being relayed to the brain.

Palit et al. (2013) suggest that this minimizing of pain signaling is the result of group differences in descending (i.e., brain-to-spinal cord) pain inhibitory mechanisms. Specifically, Native Americans have overacting descending inhibitory mechanisms that lead to reduced sensitization of the spinal cord and consequently less immediate pain. However, Palit et al. (2013) hypothesize that such habitual dampening of pain actually increases the likelihood of future pain. Specifically, individuals with overactive descending inhibitory mechanisms will, over the long term, exhaust their capacity to inhibit pain, leading to greater pain sensitivity. The authors note that this process explains why, of all American ethnic groups, Native Americans experience the greatest age-related increase in lower back pain. This finding provides further evidence that sociocultural variables interact with neurobiological processes to influence the experience of pain.

Locus of Control

The degree to which one perceives oneself to be in control versus not in control of one's life and surroundings (i.e., whether one has an internal versus external locus of control) varies across cultures. Collectivistic cultures (i.e., most non-Western countries), for example, tend to promote an external locus of control, whereas in the United States, individuals tend to have a more internal locus of control (e.g., Norenzayan, Choi, & Nisbett, 2002). There is some evidence that locus of control is related to pain intensity. Bates et al. (1993) found that people with an external locus of control experienced significantly higher pain intensity than people with an internal locus of control. A regression analysis found that locus of control remained a significant predictor of pain intensity in a model that also included ethnicity and age. Bates et al. (1993) acknowledge that their cross-sectional data does not allow them to establish a causal relationship between locus of control and pain intensity, and that greater pain intensity could lead one to develop more of an external locus of control or vice versa.

More research clearly is needed in this regard. For instance, a body of evidence suggests that while internal locus of control is related to a reduced risk for anxiety and depression in the United States, it is related to an increased risk for these mental illnesses in collective cultures (see Cheng, Cheung, Chio, & Chan, 2013 for a discussion). This cultural variation in the impact of locus of control possibly can be seen in the experience of pain. Furthermore, it is unclear whether certain ethnic minority groups in the United States (such as Asian Americans) that report lower levels of pain have an internal or external locus of control.

Summary of Cultural Variables Related to Pain and Future Directions for Research

Despite the relative paucity of research examining the impact of culture on the experience of pain, there are now a number of empirically grounded relationships identified between sociocultural variables and neurobiological processes associated with pain. Specifically, both racial discrimination and stoicism have been found to interact with neurobiological processes to influence the pain experience. Numerous other sociocultural variables—in particular patient-level variables such as culturally specific attitudes and behavioral tendencies—conceivably could impact the experience of pain. To date this topic has been under-researched (Green et al., 2003). Hopefully future research will uncover these relationships. We also hope that researchers replicate the findings discussed above with larger and more culturally varied samples.

Researchers also should examine the intersection between gender/sex and culture in the pain experience, an issue that to date has received scant attention in the literature. A few studies have examined how gender/sex interacts with ethnicity to determine the pain experience. These findings suggest that White women are more likely to report lower pain tolerance and more frequent pain than White men, but that this gender difference is not seen in other ethnic groups (Riley & Gilbert, 2002; Walsh, Schoenfeld, Ramamurthy, & Hoffman, 1989). More research is needed on how gender/sex interacts with cultural variables beyond ethnicity. Such studies would need large sample sizes in order to be sufficiently powered to identify such interaction effects (Goodin, Sibille, & Fillingim, 2013).

Another topic that should be studied further is the relationship between pain and religion. A few studies have examined this relationship with mixed results. Some indicate that chronic pain patients who look to a higher power for strength and support have better physical and mental health (e.g., Bush et al., 1999). Others suggest that private religious practice is related to poor physical health and is unrelated to pain intensity and functional impairment due to pain in pain patients (Rippentrop, Altmaier, Chen, Found, & Keffala, 2005). Again, significantly more research is needed in this domain.

Cross-Cultural Use of Pain Measures—A Lack of Valid Instruments

As researchers continue to examine the impact of culture on pain experiences, it is vital that they address a key problem in the pain literature: a lack of culturally valid measures of pain. The Institute of Medicine (2011) cites "a lack of valid and objective pain assessment measures" (pg. 8) as a main reason for the failure of so many Americans to receive adequate care for their pain.

In most medical settings across the world, pain is assessed using self-report pain measures. Indeed, a number of self-report pain measures have been developed and validated for specific non-English speaking populations outside of the United States, such as the Chinese Cancer Pain Assessment Tool (Chung, Wong, & Yang, 2001) and the Italian Pain Questionnaire (De Benedittis, Massei, Nobili, & Pieri, 1988). However, there remains a dearth of pain measures that have been validated for use across the numerous ethnic and cultural groups in the United States (Booker & Herr, 2015; Green et al. 2003).

One particular issue regarding the cross-cultural use of measures of pain that has yet to be addressed adequately in the literature is whether a particular measure meets *measurement equivalence* in the specific population of interest. In other words, the measure must assess pain in the same manner across different populations (Chen, 2008; Millsap, 2011). Measurement equivalence is met by establishing four increasingly restraining criteria (Millsap, 2011; Fischer & Fontaine, 2011):

1. *Functional Equivalence*: the construct being measured is observed across different populations
2. *Structural Equivalence*: the factor structure of the measure is the same across different populations
3. *Metric Equivalence*: individual items on the measure load onto the same factors with the same strength across different populations
4. *Scalar Equivalence*: the same total score on a measure refers to the same level of the underlying latent variable across different populations; in other words, if two individuals from different cultures have the same score on a pain measure, both of those individuals are actually experiencing the same level of pain

Obviously, the construct of pain is present worldwide, thus meeting the criterion of functional equivalence. A few studies have examined the factor structure of various pain measures in order to establish structural equivalence. For example, the Pain Beliefs and Perceptions Inventory (Goli, Yanchuk, & Torkaman, 2015) was indeed shown to have structural equivalence. However, as far as we know, no study of pain measures has examined metric and scalar equivalence.

The potential lack of scalar equivalence in the most commonly used measures of pain should concern both researchers and practitioners who use total scores when interpreting self-report measures of pain, as one can only compare total scores of a particular measure across different populations when scalar equivalence has been established. In particular, if a measure does not have scalar equivalence, cutoff scores for clinically significant pain as developed for one population cannot be used for another population. In other words, cutoff scores used to identify individuals with clinically significant pain in a particular cultural group may not be used to identify clinically significant pain in a different cultural group. If researchers and practitioners rely blindly on total scores, they may miss true differences in pain intensity between culturally distinct groups.

As Chen (2008) notes, the failure to establish metric and scalar equivalence can lead not only to the failure to identify real cultural group differences but also to the identification of false differences between cultural groups. For example, in Bates et al.'s (1993) study (described above) of the relationship between pain intensity, locus of control, and ethnicity in an American sample, pain intensity was measured by the widely used McGill Pain Questionnaire (Melzack, 1975). Given the lack of evidence that this questionnaire has metric and scalar equivalence in the diverse populations studied by these researchers, interpreting the reported differences in pain intensity across ethnic groups must be done cautiously.

In another example of how using pain measures in culturally diverse populations without established metric and scalar equivalence can lead to findings that are hard to interpret, Calvillo and Flaskerud (1993) found that although Mexican and Caucasian patients self-reported identical levels of pain using the McGill Pain Questionnaire, the nurses perceived more pain in the Caucasian patients. This finding could be explained in two ways. On the one hand, the nurses may have been less sensitive toward the Mexican patients' pain, discriminating (explicitly or implicitly) against them. Alternatively, the McGill Pain Questionnaire's lack of metric and scalar equivalence could result in what appears to be similar pain scores across the two groups, when in fact an accurate assessment would establish a difference between the two groups. There is some evidence that Hispanic populations tend to use the extreme ends of the scale when answering self-report questionnaires (e.g., Weech-Maldonado, Elliot, Oluwole, Schiller, & Hays, 2008; Hui & Triandis, 1989). As a result, Hispanic individuals may make the cutoff for clinical pain when in reality they have subclinical pain. In other words, the nurses' perception that the Caucasian patients experienced more intense pain indeed may be accurate.

This lack of measurement equivalence is seen in not only pain measures but also many medical and psychological measures that are widely used around the world (see, for example, Jayawickreme, Verkuilen, Jayawickreme, Acosta, & Foa, 2017; Rasmussen, Verkuilen, Ho, & Fan, 2015). This lack of valid measures should concern medical researchers and practitioners working with diverse populations in the United States. Without measures with established measurement equivalence and valid cutoff scores, we will continue to misunderstand cultural differences in the experience of many medical and psychological constructs, including pain.

Rather than relying exclusively upon total scores of self-report pain questionnaires, we suggest that practitioners pay more attention to patients' responses to individual items and ask follow-up questions about items the patients endorse. Practitioners should augment their use of self-report measures with open-ended interviews that allow the patients to fully describe their pain experiences. Narayan (2010) suggests using an explanatory model interview, where the interviewer asks a series of open-ended questions designed to get a sense of how the patient experiences and makes sense of his/her pain, as well as his/her goals for treatment. Examples of questions on Narayan's (2010, p. 43) explanatory model interview include the following:

"What do you think is causing your pain?"
"Why do you think [your pain] started when it did?"
"Who helps you when you have pain? How do they help?"

Treatment Recommendations for Practitioners Working With Diverse Populations

The dearth of research examining how culture impacts pain makes the task of identifying empirically based treatment recommendations a challenge. Furthermore, even if there was a substantial body of research looking at the impact of a particular culture on pain, the clinical utility of the information would be limited by the fact that significant within-culture variation exists in the pain experience (Lasch, 2000). For example, just because Native Americans tend to react to pain in a stoic manner does not mean that a particular Native American patient seeking treatment for pain will have such a stoic attitude. Morris, Chiu, and Liu (2015) argue that within-culture variability exists because an individual's behavior is determined not by a single, monolithic culture but rather by the interaction of different cultures such as ethnicity, gender, and SES. That said, as Bates et al. (1993, p. 111) note, "to ignore cultural attitudes, meanings, norms and standards of behavior is to miss very important clues that would allow enhanced assessment and treatment."

We propose that practitioners adopt an ideographic approach whereby each patient is seen as a unique individual influenced by multiple cultures as opposed to a single culture. Narayan (2010) provides a number of useful best practices that enable practitioners to gather the information needed to determine the pain experience from the patient's perspective. First, she argues that rather than relying on cultural stereotypes, understand the patient as a unique individual. Second, rather than assuming the patient's pain experience based upon what you know about how individuals from that particular cultural group *typically* experience pain, assess the patient's own personal pain experience. Of course, one does not want to fully discount the utility of knowledge of how individuals from a particular culture tend to experience pain. Such knowledge will enable practitioners to anticipate what cultural differences to expect and perceive as normal for that patient, especially if the differences do not match the clinician's own cultural framework and beliefs about pain. Narayan (2010) additionally notes that practitioners should be aware of their own ethnocentrism; they should not assume that all individuals have the same beliefs about and experiences of pain. By learning about the different ways in which individuals from different cultural groups experience pain, practitioners can move beyond their own sense of the "right" way to experience and deal with pain.

Finally, include the patient in the decision-making process. Providers should assess whether the patient's needs and expectations align with the plan for care (Martin & Barkley, 2016). For example, patients from non-Western cultures that value collectivism (i.e., a focus on the common good rather on the individual) prefer to make health decisions as a family, in contrast to patients from Western cultures who value independence and autonomy (Xue, Wheeler & Avernethy, 2011). Other reviews have found that many Mexican Americans and Black Americans prefer to make healthcare decisions as a family (Thomas, Wilson, Justice, Birch, & Sheps, 2008).

Furthermore, decisions about pain management usually include discussions about the possible use of pain medications. While pain medications are widely used in the Western world, some non-Western patients prefer not to use opioids or other pain medications. These patients, who may be reluctant to use opioid pain medications because of cultural taboos and fears, may prefer instead to use remedies more familiar to their culture such as herbs or energy-based therapies (Lovering, 2006). In addition, many patients refuse opioids due to fear of addiction. Shavers, Bakos, and Sheppard (2010) found that Black American and Hispanic American patients expressed more fear of addiction to opioids than White Americans.

The clinician's role includes providing information regarding both the potential benefits of the medications and the risks of addiction, all the while respecting alternative medicines and the patient's treatment preferences. Narayan (2010) recommends using the LEARN model—Listen, Explain, Acknowledge, Recommend, Negotiate—to educate and encourage patients regarding treatment that may be unfamiliar or uncomfortable to them but that has been shown empirically to benefit their health. This model is a useful tool for practitioners to understand the patient's perspective while also encouraging cultural practices that the patient perceives as beneficial (e.g., religious rituals) as long as there is no empirical evidence indicating that alternative treatment is harmful.

Conclusion

Practitioners in the United States are treating ever more diverse populations. For this reason, researchers need to better understand the degree to which the pain experience is influenced by culture. There now exists a small body of research indicating that cultural variables, such as racial discrimination and stoicism, interact with neurobiological processes to influence the pain experience. Hopefully the research in this area will continue. In addition, the measurement equivalence of self-report measures of pain needs to be established before such measures can be interpreted with confidence across different cultural groups. In the meantime, practitioners should focus less on the total scores of such measures and more on responses to individual items, and they should also augment their use of self-report measures with an open-ended interview that encourages the patient to describe his or her pain experience. Practitioners should familiarize themselves with the literature reviewed in this chapter and adopt an ideographic approach to pain assessment and pain management, especially with patients whose cultural backgrounds differ from that of the clinician. Finally, medical and psychology training programs should ensure that their graduates have a proper understanding of the mechanisms by which culture impacts the experience of pain and how to incorporate that knowledge into their clinical practice.

References

Barkwell, D. (2005). Cancer pain: Voices of the Ojibway people. *Journal of Pain and Symptom Management, 30,* 454–464.

Bates, M. S. (1987). Ethnicity and pain: A biocultural model. *Social Science and Medicine, 24,* 47–50.

Bates, M. S., & Edwards, W. T. (1992). Ethnic variations in the chronic pain experience. *Ethnicity and Disease, 2,* 63–83.

Bates, M. S., Edwards, W. T., & Anderson, K. O. (1993). Ethnocultural influences on variation in chronic pain perception. *Pain, 52,* 101–112.

Beecher, H. (1956). Relationship of the significance of wound to the pain experience. *JAMA, 161,* 1604–1613.

Booker, S., & Herr, K. (2015). The state-of-"cultural validity" of self-report pain assessment tools in diverse older adults. *Pain Medicine, 16,* 232–239.

Bruner, J. (1990). *Acts of meaning.* Cambridge, MA: Harvard University Press.

Burgess, D. J., Grill, J., Noorbaloochi, S., Griffin, J. M., Ricards, J., van Ryn, M., & Partin, M. R. (2009). The effect of perceived racial discrimination on bodily pain among older African American men. *Pain Medicine, 10,* 1341–1352.

Bush, E. G., Rye, M. S., Brant, C. R., Emery, E., Pargament, K. I., & Riessinger, C. A. (1999). Religious coping with chronic pain. *Applied Psychophysiology and Biofeedback, 24,* 249–260.

Calvillo, E. R., & Flaskerud, J. H. (1993). Evaluation of the pain response by Mexican American and Anglo American women and their nurses. *Journal of Advanced Nursing Practice, 18,* 451–459.

Chen, F. F. (2008). What happens if we compare chopsticks with forks? The impact of making inappropriate comparisons in cross-cultural research. *Journal of Personality and Social Psychology, 95,* 1005–1018.

Cheng, C., Cheung, S., Chio, J. H., & Chan, M. S. (2013). Cultural meaning of perceived control: A meta-analysis of locus of control and psychological symptoms across 18 cultural regions. *Psychological Bulletin, 139,* 152–188.

Chung, J. W., Wong, T. K., & Yang, J. C. (2001). A preliminary report on the Chinese Cancer Pain Assessment Tool (CCPAT): Reliability and validity. *Acta Anaesthesiol Sin, 39,* 33–40.

Clark, W. C., & Clark, S. B. (1980). Pain responses in Nepalese porters. *Science, 229,* 410–412.

Cohen, A. (2009). Many forms of culture. *American Psychologist, 64*, 194–204.

De Benedittis, G., Massei, R., Nobili, R., & Pieri, A. (1988). The Italian pain questionnaire. *Pain, 33*, 53–62.

Edwards, R. R. (2008). The association of perceived discrimination with low back pain. *Journal of Behavioral Medicine, 31*, 379–389.

Fischer, R., & Fontaine, J. R. J. (2011). Methods for investigating structural equivalence. In D. Matsumoto & F. J. R. Van de Vijver (Eds.), *Cross-cultural research methods in psychology* (pp. 179–215). New York, NY: Cambridge University Press.

Gazerani, P., & Arendt-Nielsen, L. (2005). The impact of ethnic differences in response to capsaicin-induced trigeminal sensitization. *Pain, 117*, 223–229.

Goli, Z., Yanchuk, V., & Torkaman, Z. (2015). Cross-cultural adaptation and validation of the Russian version of the Pain Beliefs and Perceptions Inventory (R-PBPI) in patients with chronic pain. *Current Psychology, 34*, 772–780.

Goodin, B. R., Glover, T. L., King, C. D., Sibille, K. T., Cruz-Almeida, Y. C., Staud, R., . . . Fillingim, R. B. (2013). Perceived racial discrimination, but not mistrust of medical researchers, predicts the heat pain tolerance of African Americans with symptomatic knee osteoarthritis. *Health Psychology, 32*, 1117–1126.

Goodin, B. R., Sibille, K., & Fillingim, R. B. (2013). Gender and ethnic differences in responses to pain and its treatment. In M. Incayawar & K. H. Todd (Eds.), *Culture, brain, and analgesia: Understanding and managing pain in diverse populations* (pp. 240–257). New York, NY: Oxford University Press.

Green, C. R., Anderson, K. O., Baker, T. A., Campbell, L. C., Decker, S., Fillingim, R. B., . . . Vallerand, A. H. (2003). The unequal burden of pain: Confronting racial and ethnic disparities in pain. *Pain Medicine, 4*, 277–294.

Haozous, E. A., Knobf, M. T., & Brant, J. M. (2011). Understanding the cancer pain experience in American Indians of the Northern Plains. *Psycho-Oncology, 20*, 404–410.

Hui, H. C., & Triandis, H. C. (1989). Effects of culture and response format on extreme response style. *Journal of Cross-Cultural Psychology, 20*, 296–309.

Incayawar, M., & Maldonado-Bouchard, S. (2013). We feel pain too: Asserting the pain experience of the Quichua people. In M. Incayawar & K. H. Todd (Eds.), *Culture, brain, and analgesia: Understanding and managing pain in diverse populations* (pp. 61–74). New York, NY: Oxford University Press.

Institute of Medicine of the National Academies. (2011). *Relieving pain in America: A blueprint for transforming prevention, care, education, and research.* Washington, DC: National Academies Press.

Jayawickreme, N., Verkuilen, J., Jayawickreme, E., Acosta, K., & Foa, E. B. (2017). Measuring depression in a non-Western war-affected displaced population: Measurement equivalence of the beck depression inventory. *Frontiers in Psychology, 8*, 1670. doi:10.3389/fpsyg.2017.01670

Kramer, B. J., Harker, J. O., & Wong, A. L. (2002). Arthritis beliefs and self-care in an urban American Indian population. *Arthritis and Rheumatism, 47*, 588–594.

Lasch, K. E. (2000). Culture, pain, and culturally sensitive pain care. *Pain Management Nursing, 1*(Suppl 1), 16–22.

Lovering, S. (2006). Cultural attitudes and beliefs about pain. *Journal of Transcultural Nursing, 17*, 389–395.

Markus, H. R., & Kitayama, S. (1991). Culture and the self: Implications for cognition, emotion, and motivation. *Psychological Review, 98*, 224–253.

Martin, E. M., & Barkley, T. W. (2016). Improving cultural competence in end-of-life pain management. *Nursing, 46*, 41–42.

Meehan, J. P., Stoll, A. M., & Hardy, J. D. (1954). Cutaneous pain threshold in the Native Alaskan Indian and Eskimo. *Journal of Applied Physiology, 6*, 397–400.

Melzack, R. (1975). The McGill pain questionnaire: Major properties and scoring methods. *Pain*, *1*, 277–299.

Millsap, R. E. (2011). *Statistical approaches to measurement invariance*. New York, NY: Routledge.

Morris, M. W., Chiu, C., & liu, Z. (2015). Polycultural psychology. *Annual Review of Psychology*, *66*, 631–659.

Narayan, M. C. (2010). Culture's effects on pain assessment and management. *The American Journal of Nursing*, *110*, 38–49.

Nayak, S., Shiflett, S. C., Eshun, S., & Levine, F. M. (2000). Culture and gender effects in pain beliefs and the prediction of pain tolerance. *Cross-Cultural Research*, *34*, 135–151.

Norenzayan, A., Choi, I., & Nisbett, R. E. (2002). Cultural similarities and differences in social inference: Evidence from behavioral predictions and lay theories of behavior. *Personality and Social Psychology Bulletin*, *28*, 109–120.

Palit, S., Kerr, K. L., Kuhn, B. L., Terry, E. L., DelVentura, J. L., Bartley, E. J., . . . Rhudy, J. L. (2013). Exploring pain processing differences in native Americans. *Health Psychology*, *32*, 1127–1136.

Pascoe, E. A., & Smart-Richman, L. (2009). Perceived discrimination and health: A meta-analytic review. *Psychological Bulletin*, *135*, 531–554.

Rahim-Williams, B., Riley, J. L., Williams, A. K., & Fillingim, R. B. (2012). A quantitative review of ethnic group differences in experimental pain response: Do biology, psychology, and culture matter? *Pain Medicine*, *13*, 522–540.

Rasmussen, A., Verkuilen, J., Ho, E., & Fan, Y. (2015). Posttraumatic stress disorder among refugees: Measurement invariance of Harvard Trauma Questionnaire scores across global regions and response patterns. *Psychological Assessment*, *27*, 1160–1170.

Riley, J. L., & Gilbert, G. H. (2002). Racial differences in orofacial pain. *Journal of Pain*, *3*, 284–291.

Rippentrop, A. E., Altmaier, E. M., Chen, J. J., Found, E. M., & Keffala, V. J. (2005). The relationship between religion/spirituality and physical health, mental health, and pain in a chronic pain population. *Pain*, *116*, 311–321.

Ryder, A. G., Ban, L. M., & Chentsova-Dutton, Y. E. (2011). Towards a cultural-clinical psychology. *Social and Personality Psychology Compass*, *5*, 960–975.

Shavers, V. L., Bakos, A., & Sheppard, V. B. (2010). Race, ethnicity, and pain among the U.S. adult population. *Journal of Health Care for the Poor and Underserved*, *21*, 177–220.

Stephens, N. M., Markus, H. R., & Phillips, L. T. (2014). Social class culture cycles: How three gateway contexts shape selves and fuel inequality. *Annual Review of Psychology*, *65*, 611–634.

Thomas, R., Wilson, D. M., Justice, C., Birch, S., & Sheps, S. (2008). A literature review of preferences for end of-life care in developed countries by individuals with different cultural affiliations and ethnicity. *Journal of Hospice and Palliative Nursing*, *10*, 162–163.

Todd, K. H., & Incayawar, M. (2014). Relevance of pain and analgesia in multicultural societies. In M. Incayawar & K. H. Todd (Eds.), *Culture, brain, and analgesia: Understanding and managing pain in diverse populations* (pp. 1–5). New York, NY: Oxford University Press.

Walsh, N. E., Schoenfeld, L., Ramamurthy, S., & Hoffman, J. (1989). Normative model for cold pressor test. *American Journal of Physical Medicine and Rehabilitation*, *68*, 6–11.

Weech-Maldonado, R., Elliott, M. N., Oluwole, A., Schiller, K. C., & Hays, R. D. (2008). Survey response style and differential use of CAHPS rating scales by Hispanics. *Medical Care*, *46*, 963–968.

Xue, D., Wheeler, J. L., & Avernethy, A. P. (2011). Cultural differences in truth-telling to cancer patients: Chinese and American approaches to the disclosure of "bad news." *Progress in Palliative Care*, *19*, 125–131.

Zborowski, M. (1969). *People in pain*. San Francisco, CA; Jossey-Bass.

Zborowski, M. (1952). Cultural components in response to pain. *Journal of Social Issues*, *8*, 16–30.

Index

Note: Page numbers in *italics* indicate figures and in **bold** indicate tables on the corresponding pages.

Made in the USA
Coppell, TX
28 June 2020